Lecture Notes in Computer Science 11590

Commenced Publication in 1973
Founding and Former Series Editors:
Gerhard Goos, Juris Hartmanis, and Jan van Leeuwen

More information about this series at http://www.springer.com/series/7409

Panayiotis Zaphiris · Andri Ioannou (Eds.)

Learning and Collaboration Technologies

Designing Learning Experiences

6th International Conference, LCT 2019
Held as Part of the 21st HCI International Conference, HCII 2019
Orlando, FL, USA, July 26–31, 2019
Proceedings, Part I

 Springer

Editors
Panayiotis Zaphiris
Cyprus University of Technology
Limassol, Cyprus

Andri Ioannou
Cyprus University of Technology
Limassol, Cyprus

ISSN 0302-9743   ISSN 1611-3349   (electronic)
Lecture Notes in Computer Science
ISBN 978-3-030-21813-3   ISBN 978-3-030-21814-0   (eBook)
https://doi.org/10.1007/978-3-030-21814-0

LNCS Sublibrary: SL3 – Information Systems and Applications, incl. Internet/Web, and HCI

This Springer imprint is published by the registered company Springer Nature Switzerland AG
The registered company address is: Gewerbestrasse 11, 6330 Cham, Switzerland

Foreword

The 21st International Conference on Human-Computer Interaction, HCI International 2019, was held in Orlando, FL, USA, during July 26–31, 2019. The event incorporated the 18 thematic areas and affiliated conferences listed on the following page.

A total of 5,029 individuals from academia, research institutes, industry, and governmental agencies from 73 countries submitted contributions, and 1,274 papers and 209 posters were included in the pre-conference proceedings. These contributions address the latest research and development efforts and highlight the human aspects of design and use of computing systems. The contributions thoroughly cover the entire field of human-computer interaction, addressing major advances in knowledge and effective use of computers in a variety of application areas. The volumes constituting the full set of the pre-conference proceedings are listed in the following pages.

This year the HCI International (HCII) conference introduced the new option of "late-breaking work." This applies both for papers and posters and the corresponding volume(s) of the proceedings will be published just after the conference. Full papers will be included in the *HCII 2019 Late-Breaking Work Papers Proceedings* volume of the proceedings to be published in the Springer LNCS series, while poster extended abstracts will be included as short papers in the HCII 2019 *Late-Breaking Work Poster Extended Abstracts* volume to be published in the Springer CCIS series.

I would like to thank the program board chairs and the members of the program boards of all thematic areas and affiliated conferences for their contribution to the highest scientific quality and the overall success of the HCI International 2019 conference.

This conference would not have been possible without the continuous and unwavering support and advice of the founder, Conference General Chair Emeritus and Conference Scientific Advisor Prof. Gavriel Salvendy. For his outstanding efforts, I would like to express my appreciation to the communications chair and editor of *HCI International News,* Dr. Abbas Moallem.

July 2019   Constantine Stephanidis

HCI International 2019 Thematic Areas
and Affiliated Conferences

Thematic areas:

- HCI 2019: Human-Computer Interaction
- HIMI 2019: Human Interface and the Management of Information

Affiliated conferences:

- EPCE 2019: 16th International Conference on Engineering Psychology and Cognitive Ergonomics
- UAHCI 2019: 13th International Conference on Universal Access in Human-Computer Interaction
- VAMR 2019: 11th International Conference on Virtual, Augmented and Mixed Reality
- CCD 2019: 11th International Conference on Cross-Cultural Design
- SCSM 2019: 11th International Conference on Social Computing and Social Media
- AC 2019: 13th International Conference on Augmented Cognition
- DHM 2019: 10th International Conference on Digital Human Modeling and Applications in Health, Safety, Ergonomics and Risk Management
- DUXU 2019: 8th International Conference on Design, User Experience, and Usability
- DAPI 2019: 7th International Conference on Distributed, Ambient and Pervasive Interactions
- HCIBGO 2019: 6th International Conference on HCI in Business, Government and Organizations
- LCT 2019: 6th International Conference on Learning and Collaboration Technologies
- ITAP 2019: 5th International Conference on Human Aspects of IT for the Aged Population
- HCI-CPT 2019: First International Conference on HCI for Cybersecurity, Privacy and Trust
- HCI-Games 2019: First International Conference on HCI in Games
- MobiTAS 2019: First International Conference on HCI in Mobility, Transport, and Automotive Systems
- AIS 2019: First International Conference on Adaptive Instructional Systems

Pre-conference Proceedings Volumes Full List

1. LNCS 11566, Human-Computer Interaction: Perspectives on Design (Part I), edited by Masaaki Kurosu
2. LNCS 11567, Human-Computer Interaction: Recognition and Interaction Technologies (Part II), edited by Masaaki Kurosu
3. LNCS 11568, Human-Computer Interaction: Design Practice in Contemporary Societies (Part III), edited by Masaaki Kurosu
4. LNCS 11569, Human Interface and the Management of Information: Visual Information and Knowledge Management (Part I), edited by Sakae Yamamoto and Hirohiko Mori
5. LNCS 11570, Human Interface and the Management of Information: Information in Intelligent Systems (Part II), edited by Sakae Yamamoto and Hirohiko Mori
6. LNAI 11571, Engineering Psychology and Cognitive Ergonomics, edited by Don Harris
7. LNCS 11572, Universal Access in Human-Computer Interaction: Theory, Methods and Tools (Part I), edited by Margherita Antona and Constantine Stephanidis
8. LNCS 11573, Universal Access in Human-Computer Interaction: Multimodality and Assistive Environments (Part II), edited by Margherita Antona and Constantine Stephanidis
9. LNCS 11574, Virtual, Augmented and Mixed Reality: Multimodal Interaction (Part I), edited by Jessie Y. C. Chen and Gino Fragomeni
10. LNCS 11575, Virtual, Augmented and Mixed Reality: Applications and Case Studies (Part II), edited by Jessie Y. C. Chen and Gino Fragomeni
11. LNCS 11576, Cross-Cultural Design: Methods, Tools and User Experience (Part I), edited by P. L. Patrick Rau
12. LNCS 11577, Cross-Cultural Design: Culture and Society (Part II), edited by P. L. Patrick Rau
13. LNCS 11578, Social Computing and Social Media: Design, Human Behavior and Analytics (Part I), edited by Gabriele Meiselwitz
14. LNCS 11579, Social Computing and Social Media: Communication and Social Communities (Part II), edited by Gabriele Meiselwitz
15. LNAI 11580, Augmented Cognition, edited by Dylan D. Schmorrow and Cali M. Fidopiastis
16. LNCS 11581, Digital Human Modeling and Applications in Health, Safety, Ergonomics and Risk Management: Human Body and Motion (Part I), edited by Vincent G. Duffy

34. CCIS 1033, HCI International 2019 - Posters (Part II), edited by Constantine Stephanidis
35. CCIS 1034, HCI International 2019 - Posters (Part III), edited by Constantine Stephanidis

http://2019.hci.international/proceedings

6th International Conference on Learning and Collaboration Technologies (LCT 2019)

Program Board Chair(s): **Panayiotis Zaphiris and Andri Ioannou,** *Cyprus*

- Ruthi Aladjem, Israel
- Carmelo Ardito, Italy
- Mike Brayshaw, UK
- Scott Brown, USA
- Fisnik Dalipi, Norway
- Paloma Díaz, Spain
- Camille Dickson-Deane, Australia
- Anastasios A. Economides, Greece
- Maka Eradze, Estonia
- Mikhail Fominykh, Norway
- David Fonseca, Spain
- Francisco José García-Peñalvo, Spain
- Preben Hansen, Sweden
- Tomaž Klobučar, Slovenia
- Zona Kostic, USA
- Birgy Lorenz, Estonia
- Ana Loureiro, Portugal
- Antigoni Parmaxi, Cyprus
- Marcos Román González, Spain
- Yevgeniya S. Sulema, Ukraine

The full list with the Program Board Chairs and the members of the Program Boards of all thematic areas and affiliated conferences is available online at:

http://www.hci.international/board-members-2019.php

HCI International 2020

The 22nd International Conference on Human-Computer Interaction, HCI International 2020, will be held jointly with the affiliated conferences in Copenhagen, Denmark, at the Bella Center Copenhagen, July 19–24, 2020. It will cover a broad spectrum of themes related to HCI, including theoretical issues, methods, tools, processes, and case studies in HCI design, as well as novel interaction techniques, interfaces, and applications. The proceedings will be published by Springer. More information will be available on the conference website: http://2020.hci.international/.

General Chair
Prof. Constantine Stephanidis
University of Crete and ICS-FORTH
Heraklion, Crete, Greece
E-mail: general_chair@hcii2020.org

http://2020.hci.international/

Contents – Part I

**Theoretical and Pedagogical Approaches
in Technology-Enhanced Learning**

Cognitive and Psychological Issues in Learning

Technology in STEM Education

Contents – Part II

Virtual Reality and Augmented Reality Systems for Learning

Collaboration Technology

Designing and Evaluating Learning Experiences

Personal Data Broker: A Solution to Assure Data Privacy in EdTech

Daniel Amo[1]([⊠]), David Fonseca[1], Marc Alier[2],
Francisco José García-Peñalvo[3], María José Casañ[2],
and María Alsina[1]

[1] La Salle, Universitat Ramón Llull, Barcelona, Spain
{daniel.amo,fonsi,maria.alsina}@salle.url.edu
[2] Universitat Politècnica de Catalunya, Barcelona, Spain
marc.alier@upc.edu, mjcasany@essi.upc.edu
[3] Universidad de Salamanca, Salamanca, Spain
fgarcia@usal.es

Abstract. Educational technologies (Edtech) collect private and personal data from students. This is a growing trend in both new and already available Edtech. There are different stakeholders in the analysis of the collected students' data. Teachers use educational analytics to enhance the learning environment, principals use academic analytics for decision making in the leadership of the educational institution and Edtech providers uses students' data interactions to improve their services and tools. There are some issues in this new context. Edtech have been feeding their analytical algorithms from student's data, both private and personal, even from minors. This draws a critical problem about data privacy fragility in Edtech. Moreover, this is a sensitive issue that generates fears and angst in the use of educational data analytics in Edtech, such as learning management systems (LMS). Current laws, regulations, policies, principles and good practices are not enough to prevent private data leakage, security breaches, misuses or trading. For instance, data privacy agreements in LMS are deterrent but not an ultimate solution due do not act in real time. There is a need for automated real-time law enforcement to avoid the fragility of data privacy. In this work, we take a step further in the automation of data privacy agreement in LMS. We expose which technology and architecture are suitable for data privacy agreement automation, a partial implementation of the design in Moodle and ongoing work.

Keywords: Smart contracts · Learning Analytics · Moodle · Data privacy ·
Digital identity · Blockchain · Educational data mining · Academic analytics

1 Introduction

In the last decades we have seen a fast-paced evolution in the way information technologies for education (Edtech) are used. This evolution goes from seeing the computer itself as the educational tool in – as first introduced by Seymour Papert in the late 1970's [1] - to software developed specifically with instructional purposes [2, 3], to the usage of computer and other technological devices as content delivery platforms, to

© Springer Nature Switzerland AG 2019
P. Zaphiris and A. Ioannou (Eds.): HCII 2019, LNCS 11590, pp. 3–14, 2019.
https://doi.org/10.1007/978-3-030-21814-0_1

blended and online learning applications like Virtual Learning Environments (VLE) and apps [4], and finally the usage of platforms not specifically designed for learning but providing powerful assets like video streaming, online maps, office tools, calendars, email or social networking. Each of these steps has not deprecated the previous one, but built upon it adding more layers of usefulness and complexity. During the last 15 years there has been a big push for interoperability between systems in education [5–9]. This is allowing for a transformation of the Edtech ecosystem from one based on products (the computer, the software, the content, the VLE …) to an ecosystem of services. These services can be self-provided by the institution, like the back-office management system (enrolment, syllabus and curriculum management, ed-ERP) and the VLE, and can also be services provided by vendors providing learning apps, contents and other services [10–12].

In the first stages of this evolution the learning device was a single computer, unconnected, using software locally executed to perform learning activities or access contents from a tape or disk. But in the early 2000's this shifted to continuous online experience where the device used by the student is just a means to connect to online webapps and content. The software that runs these services is running on servers elsewhere, either by the learning institution or vendors. And all interactions are tracked and logged, generating data, lots of data.

The availability of this data allows for the birth of Learning Analytics, that aims to track and better understand the behaviour of the students at a collective and individual level [13–17]. This knowledge can be given to teachers and instructors in the form of statistics, graphics, dashboards and even recommendations in written form automatically generated [18]. The information can also be given to managers and policy makers in order to make better informed decisions.

What could possibly go wrong? While is reasonable for the learning institution to gather and use data about the learning activities of its students, to a point. When the online learning services are provided by commercial vendors, and especially when minors are involved, there is a clear concern about what data is being gathered and for what purpose [19]. This concern is increased in the current situation where deep learning algorithms are being used to model and influence the behaviour and sentiments of people.

The control of privacy in education has become an important problem to solve in Edtech.

This paper is organized in four additional sections. Section 2 presents the context and the problem authors want to address. Section three explains the solution proposed. Section four describes the software that has been developed as well as the platform authors are using. Section five presents the conclusion of the work and presents future work.

2 The Problem: Data Privacy in EdTech

As we have introduced previously, today the use of Edtech implies that personal information about the students and about their activity is going to be gathered and moved around. This is going to happen in two ways:

1. **Internal data gathering:** The data and metadata about the student and her activity is kept within the servers managed by the learning institution. This information is kept unencrypted and can be accessed by most of the IT personnel with access to the databases and files in the servers. This personal information is highly vulnerable to hacking and lack of proper security. Sometimes a number of schools share an IT provider that hosts their VLE's on a server farm or cloud, and security audits show that in this situations the compromise of one install can spread to the rest of installations.

2. **External data gathering:** The students access a service provided by a vendor outside the learning institution. Sometimes the service is provided through an interoperable service integrated in the VLE – using IMS LTI or another standard [6] -, while there is no direct contract or agreement of terms of service between the student or his legal tutors, some personal information is transferred to the vendor in order to provide the service and the data about the student's interactions are gathered and kept outside the control of the institution, the students and their tutors. Even in the case that the identity of each student is hidden from the vendor, the IP address and cookies from tracking sites can allow the identification of the student via social network profiles and other means.

The students and their legal tutors are all the time agreeing to conditions- they most of the time don't understand the meaning and implications- that allow the collection, management and use – and even selling or sharing with other actors – their personal data and logs. The case of the inBloom schools is a clear example of bad practice with regards to data privacy by the providers of learning online services [20].

Several projects and regulations have been created to deal with data privacy and the current misuses or bad practices. GDPR, data privacy guides such as DELICATE or ethical principles have been created for this purpose [21, 22]. The importance of this issue has made possible the creation of data policies that uses Edtech in micro context (classrooms), medium context (institutions) and macro context (governments).

The formulation of laws, regulations, frameworks for service agreements and ethical codes is important and a step in the right direction to address the problem of data and metadata privacy in education. However, we need to have a technological solution to enforce the agreements and regulations. We need to integrate the privacy management in the very core of the design of our Edtech systems and interoperability standards.

In a previous paper the authors explored the possibility of using Blockchain technologies as a core technology to address this problem. Our findings reveal that most likely the Blockchain [23, 24] is not a good way to go. We also explored the main characteristics of a technological solution that can be introduced in the mix: a software component we have named provisionally Personal Data Broker PDB, outlined in the diagram in Fig. 1.

In the same paper we propose the use of Smart Contracts as technology that can be used to implement the proposed solution. We believe that this technology is a strong candidate to help automate privacy policies in a sound and secure way.

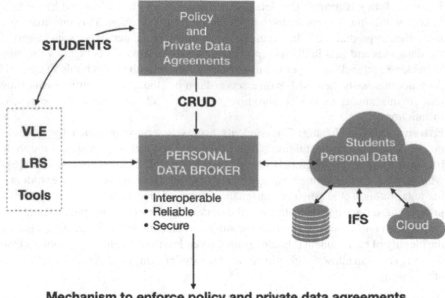

Mechanism to enforce policy and private data agreements automatically by technology in Learning Analytics.

Fig. 1. Personal data broker.

2.1 Research Question, Objectives and Scope

Our research question is: Is possible to implement a secure system that enforces privacy policies and agreements in real time in an Edtech environment?

For one part we are pretty sure that we could design from scratch a new VLE engine, and a family of apps and online services for education with privacy principles embedded in the core of its design. However, our aim is to propose a solution that could be implemented and used in production environments in a short span of time. This means that we have to contend with legacy systems. Fortunately, open source VLEs and interoperability standards can be tinkered with to find a solution and implement prototypes to test our ideas. Hence, our initial scope will be to propose a solution that works for an existing VLE.

Given the author's previous experience and background within the Moodle community we choose Moodle as the host system to implement the PDB.

The objectives we aim for are:

1. **Ensure privacy within the VLE.** The VLE stores personal information and information about the activity of the student in the platform. Our goal is to encrypt this information and make it accessible to software and users only on a need to know basis.
2. **Automate the enforcement of privacy agreements and regulations.** The privacy agreements, regulations and ethical codes of the learning institution need to be enforced by automation. In the same way Creative Commons created sets of legal

choices (licenses) that could be easily communicated to users without legal expertise and read by machines, we aim to define a set of patters of privacy agreements that we can implement with smart contracts within the VLE and its ecosystem of learning apps and services.

This is an ongoing research that has too great a scope to present in a single manuscript. So far we have only developed part of the first goal. The results are presented in the following sections. The development of the remaining part will be presented in future publications due to its greater complexity and extension. However, its approach is exposed and how different development possibilities will be addressed.

To complete the second goal we are conducting an analysis of the current laws and guidelines on data privacy. This will allow us to generate a questionnaire to conduct a series of interviews within the educational context. The results will be presented in future publications.

3   Development

In this section we present the technologies used in PDB as well as the VLE to develop it.

3.1   Smart Contracts

In order to execute policies and privacy agreements, in Edtech and in real time, digital automation technologies are needed. Smart Contracts are the most appropriate technology for this purpose, since their use does not break interoperability and security in the transfer of educational data.

The main goal of a Smart Contract is to automate the business rules between multiple entities, multiple subjects or subjects and entities. This technology is based on small programs whose activation depends on specific conditions.

It has been previously shown that using only laws and regulations is not a valid approach for technological environments. In technological environments, a technological solution is required. Szabo [19] stated in relation to the Smart Contracts: "Smart contracts [...] provide us with new ways to formalize and secure digital relationships, which are much more functional than their paper-based inanimate ancestors." Therefore, the Smart Contracts are useful to solve the problem of the control of the privacy of educational data.

The terms of use of Edtech tools and their data management can be found in the privacy contracts. These contracts are made between students and entities-educational institutions or providers. The Intelligent Contracts must execute the relevant actions declared in the agreements and conditions specified in the privacy contracts.

Intelligent Contracts can be used in VLEs to enforce regulations, laws, principles and good practices. This legal automatism can guarantee the privacy of student data. You can also make secure transfers between interoperable tools or even between independent tools. Therefore, the proposed solution incorporates Smart Contracts.

3.2   Selected VLE

To implement the PDB we are using Moodle. We have selected Moodle following a series of criteria from the research itself, from the knowledge and previous experience of the researchers and time and available resources. We summarize the criteria on which we based our decision as follows:

1. It must be open source.
2. It must be developed in a programming language knows by researchers.
3. It must be widely used by educational institutions.
4. It must have logs and a user table.

The previous criteria reduced the selection of the platform to Moodle and Sakai. After inspecting the source code of both, the architecture of their databases and the architecture of both VLEs, we verified that:

1. **Moodle has a serious problem of queries to the DB user table:** Most are scattered all over the code, visible and used at the discretion of the developers. This means that anyone who has access to the code can know and modify student data. On the other hand, since the queries are direct and built by the developers, serious security breaches can be generated.
2. **Sakai is less mature:** The development of this VLE is more recent. It is demonstrated with some comments inside the code. These comments confirms less maturity than Moodle. For instance "do we need these if we are all-webpack?", "Come up with a better solution for this." Or "these ones are questionable".
3. **Database security:** The Sakai database has an additional level of security because it anonymizes users with an intermediate table. The Moodle user table can be accessed with a direct query without anonymization or encryption.

Finally we decided to use Moodle for the following reasons:

1. It is open source.
2. There is a strong and consolidated community of developers and teachers.
3. It is the most used VLE in Spanish territory and in other countries compared to Sakai.
4. The research team is familiar with the code due to previous developments and direct relationships with the Moodle management team.
5. Moodle Headquarters is located in Barcelona, a city in which researchers develop their activity. This increases the chances of a meeting and faster progress.

We believe that it will be much easier to implement the proposal in Moodle. This will reduce the time, resources and development costs. The widespread use of Moodle will mean that the results of the research will have a greater impact on the educational community.

3.3   Development in Moodle

Our first goal is to ensure the security and privacy of student data in Moodle. After an exhaustive analysis we have detected two possible implementations that affect two different aspects: collection and storage. Our development in Moodle will have to ensure the security and privacy of student data in the data collection models as well as in the available stores.

In Moodle there are two tables related to the collection and storage of personal data of users. On the one hand we find the table where the interactions are stored (logs) and on the other the table where the users own data is stored, such as name or email. Our development focuses on securing these two tables.

Our second goal is the agreements between educational institutions and students. The development of this goal is currently underway. We expose at the end of this section how we are proceeding and what technologies we will use.

Logs

A log is a physical or virtual space where user interactions are stored with tools. The interaction of the students with the VLE generate logs with educational and personal data.

The VLE use a procedure called clickstream to capture the interactions of the students [2]. This procedure consists of saving all the clicks of the students in a table of the database (logs). These clicks are associated with additional information about the course and the student, such as date of interaction, access IP, course, activity, user id or any other related data.

The data collected in this log table allows educational analysts to perform analyzes, visualizations and extractions. With these reports you can act to improve both the learning of students and the environment. This is the foundation of Learning Analytics and the logs table is one of the first resources to analyze.

In Moodle, the logs are a table that is not encrypted. This means that the system administrator and even developers have access. In this table all the interactions of the users are saved. Therefore, anyone who has access to these data can alter, filter, trade with them and use them at their convenience.

Moodle configuration allows logs to be stored outside of your database. This opens up new opportunities for improvement in both the collection and storage of interactions.

Our purpose has been to develop a specific plugin to intervene each user interaction and save it in the Personal Data Broker, a plug-in for Moodle. A plugin is a development that is installed in the VLE and adds new features. The developed plugin captures any interaction by clickstream in Moodle, prevents it from being saved in Moodle's own log and sends it secure to the PDB. This procedure allows to:

1. Keep the data away from possible manipulations and leaks.
2. Secure the data with adequate encryption in the present and future.
3. Keep privacy and prevent unauthorized users from accessing data.

Figure 2 shows the data flow from the moment the user performs an interaction until it is securely and privately stored in the secured logs table of the PDB.

In a first stage we consider Blockchain as a possible solution to the problem. However, we detected a series of limitations that make it an unsafe and unstable candidate. Our new proposal in plugin format improves Blockchain's limitations in the security and privacy of educational data:

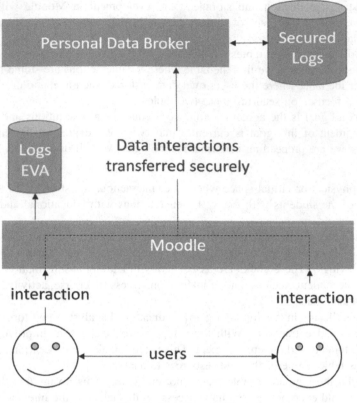

Fig. 2. Data flow PDB.

1. **The immutability of the data:** Blockchain does not allow new encryption algorithms to be applied. This is a danger when the computational capacity can break such algorithms with ease. The PDB plugin can re-encrypt data at your convenience.
2. **The privacy of the data:** in Blockchain all data is public. The users of the network have a copy of all the transactions. This foundation violates the principle of privacy of student data. The PDB plugin enables access to users who have appropriate permissions.
3. **Need for a database:** Blockchain is very bad database. It is very slow writing the blocks, there is no option to delete or modify data, and everyone has access to them. This means that instead of Blockchain we can use a relational database and all these problems are solved automatically. This is the reason why the PDB plugin uses a relational database.

User Table
The Moodle user table contains personal, configuration and relations between tables. In this way we find stored the Moodle user table the internal userId, the name and surnames, the address, an image and even data from social networks. Any access to

these data, manipulation or filtering them is much more serious than doing it in the log table. The log table contains only some user data. The user table contains all the personal data of all users. In addition, the fact of having the social networks data of the each user allows may to extract a lot of intimate information. It is demonstrated that the data stored in the Moodle user table go beyond the academic life of the user.

From the Moodle user table comes out the user data that is displayed in Moodle. Any information, user profile visualization, grades chart, progress visualizations, interactions in a forum or delivery of tasks requires access to this table. Therefore, it is essential to secure and privatize access to the user table.

Despite the security limitations, the Moodle architecture manages to privatize the data through a hierarchy of permissions. A student cannot see students who are not from their course. In the same way, a teacher does not have access to the data of students who are not enrolled in their course. However, anyone can access information on the profiles of the visible users. If we jump at the administrator level, he has the ability to access all user information, without any restriction and without impeding the extraction of them outside of Moodle. Unfortunately, the data is not encrypted, a fact that shows a low security in the protection of personal user data.

The development related to the user table is not trivial. It requires much more advanced techniques that ensure a real security and privacy in accordance with the agreements established in the contracts and data policies. The fact that in the Moodle code there is a high dispersion of queries that Access the user table, makes the solution to be applied more complex. Our mission is not to solve this Moodle problem, but to provide a solution to the problem of data fragility.

In these moments we are developing different prototypes, testing and evaluating their efficiency and adequacy. In general terms, we are going to perform a hack in the Moodle architecture that allows us to add an additional layer of security to any query to the user table. The architecture we propose will be based on the following techniques:

1. **Triggers:** The databases work based on events. Each time one of these events happens, an action (trigger) is triggered. A set of code statements can be assigned to each action. From this point of view, any action of creation, reading, modification or elimination (CRUD) in the user table would be intercepted. Doing so would suppose a control of the security and privacy of the data subedited to the PDB, which would administer accesses and permissions.
2. **Outsourcing of the user table:** This measure is very drastic and consists in outsourcing the user table of the Moodle of the institution. This would require making a modification of the native Moodle code and changing the access system.
3. **Temporary tables:** Consists of creating temporary tables with extracts from the user table. In this way Moodle users would access the temporary table whose content would be the set of users to which they have access.
4. **Triggers and externalization of user data:** This measure is a hybrid between the use of events in the user table and the outsourcing of the same table. It consists in saving the data within the PDB and events would be responsible for retrieving that information that requires the user and also have access permissions.
5. **Triggers, outsourcing and temporary tables:** The complexity of the solution can lead us to implement different approaches at the same time. We are aware that there

is no single approach to solve the problem, since each one solves a specific casu-istry. Therefore, we do not rule out using all the proposed approaches in the final solution.

The review of the possibilities denotes that the solution must be presented at the level of the database and specifically in the user table. We believe that modifying the native Moodle code is not the best option. In this sense, we focus our efforts on finding a solution less intrusive in code, but effective and that acts at the database level.

The complexity and supply of each of the possible solutions can even generate a publication. Therefore, the results of all the tests and final solution will be presented in future publications.

Law Automation

The above situations shows the limitations of laws to solve the detected problem. In addition, the laws are only effective considering a state of good faith on the part of all the actors. Therefore, the need to find a technological solution to the problem of fragility in data privacy is reaffirmed.

For the technological solution to be functional, all the agreements established in contracts and data policies must be applied automatically. In this way we reduce the possibilities of undue access to data and fraudulent uses.

These laws and agreements between students and educational institutions will be automated with the use of Smart Contracts. Before doing so, we must make sure of what must be automated. To achieve this, we will carry out a questionnaire that will allow us to interview different people in the educational field and in different roles. With the answers we can extract patterns to automate.

The questionnaire will be carried out based on the different regulations, frameworks, principles and good practices:

1. **Regulations:** LOPD (Spain) y GDPR (Europe)
2. **Policy frameworks:** DELICATE (LACE), LEA's Box (Europa), NUS, NTU, OU, CSU o Usyd (Australia)
3. **Ethical principles:** Como los expuestos por Abelardo Pardo y George Siemens
4. **Good practices and ethical codes:** SHEILA, ROMA, Jisc (UK)

This process is arduous and involves the participation of different educational agents and EdTech providers. These will be interviewed and their answers will be analyzed to extract automated conditions. These automations will be implemented in the Moodle code to be related to the PDB. The results will be presented in future publications.

4　Conclusions

Throughout the manuscript, we have exposed the biggest current problem in the use of Edtech and how to approach it technologically. The analytical capacity of the different Edtech tools highlights a large amount of educational data collected. These data, including from minors, are vulnerable in terms of their transfer, storage, and use. Consequently, we detected a serious problem of privacy control in education and in the use of Edtech.

Exposure to data can happen in internal and external environments of the educational institutions. The data transfer to Edtech providers increases the risk of misuse and disables the management and control of data by educational institutions.

The laws that regulate the collection and use of data are not enough to avoid leaks, exposures, and misuses. Students and teachers are constantly accepting terms of use and privacy agreements with Edtech tools providers. The content of such contracts is not understood at all or educational roles are not able to glimpse potential risks in some of the contractual conditions.

In the provider's context, there is evidence of entities that ignore the laws. This fact provokes undesirable situations of leaks and marketing of educational data. Therefore, there is a need to apply an automatic regulation system to solve the problem of privacy control.

In a virtual learning environment, there are different places where educational data is stored. We mainly find the logs and the user table. The interactions of the students are stored in the logs. The personal data of the students is stored in the user table. Securing and privatizing these two warehouses is key to avoid the problem detected.

We believe that Smart Contracts are the most appropriate technology to automatically assure the security and privacy of the data stored in the logs and user tables, of any EVA. We succeeded in developing a secure and private logs storage plugin for Moodle. Hence, a technological solution is a manner to solve the problem.

Part of the research is considered a work in process. We are designing the architecture and collecting the necessary information to carry out the following developments. However, throughout the manuscript, we have shown how it is possible to privatize the Moodle logs, from the conception of the architecture to its final functional development.

Acknowledgment. To the support of the Secretaria d'Universitats i Recerca of the Department of Business and Knowledge of the Generalitat de Catalunya for the help regarding 2017 SGR 934.

References

1. Papert, S.A.: Mindstorms: Children, Computers, and Powerful Ideas. Basic Books, New York (1980)
2. Filvà, D.A., Forment, M.A., García-Peñalvo, F.J., Escudero, D.F., Casañ, M.J.: Clickstream for learning analytics to assess students' behavior with Scratch. Futur. Gener. Comput. Syst. **93**, 673–686 (2019)
3. Busquets, F.: Clic: un proyecto cooperativo de producción e intercambio de software educativo. Prim. Not. Comun. y Pedagog. **20**, 40–41 (2000)
4. Calvo, X., Fonseca, D., Sánchez-Sepúlveda, M., Amo, D., Llorca, J., Redondo, E.: Programming virtual interactions for gamified educational proposes of urban spaces. In: Zaphiris, P., Ioannou, A. (eds.) LCT 2018. LNCS, vol. 10925, pp. 128–140. Springer, Cham (2018). https://doi.org/10.1007/978-3-319-91152-6_10
5. Conde, M.Á., García-Peñalvo, F.J., Rodríguez-Conde, M.J., Alier, M., Casany, M.J., Piguillem, J.: An evolving learning management system for new educational environments using 2.0 tools. Interact. Learn. Environ. **22**, 188–204 (2014)

6. Alier, M.F., Guerrero, M.J.C., Gonzalez, M.A.C., Penalvo, F.J.G., Severance, C.: Interoperability for LMS: the missing piece to become the common place for e-learning innovation. Int. J. Knowl. Learn. **6**, 130 (2010)
7. García-Peñalvo, F.J., Conde, M.Á., Alier, M., Casany, M.J.: Opening learning management systems to personal learning environments
8. Casany, M.J., et al.: Moodbile: a framework to integrate m-Learning applications with the LMS (2012)
9. Alier, M., Casañ, M.J., Piguillem, J.: Moodle 2.0: shifting from a learning toolkit to a open learning platform. In: Lytras, Miltiadis D., et al. (eds.) TECH-EDUCATION 2010. CCIS, vol. 73, pp. 1–10. Springer, Heidelberg (2010). https://doi.org/10.1007/978-3-642-13166-0_1
10. Williamson, B.: Decoding ClassDojo: psycho-policy, social-emotional learning, and persuasive educational technologies
11. Hirsh-Pasek, K., Zosh, J.M., Michnick, R., Gray, J.H., Robb, M.B., Kaufman, J.: Putting education in "educational" apps: lessons from the science of learning
12. Merriman, J., Santanach, F.: Next generation learning architecture
13. Amo, D., et al.: Using web analytics tools to improve the quality of educational resources and the learning process of students in a gamified situation. In: Proceedings of 12th Annual International Technology, Education and Development Conference, p. 5 (2018)
14. Peña, E., Fonseca, D., Marti, N., Ferrándiz, J.: Relationship between specific professional competences and learning activities of the building and construction engineering degree final project. Int. J. Eng. Educ. **34**, 924–939 (2018)
15. Campanyà, C., Fonseca, D., Martí, N., Peña, E., Ferrer, A., Llorca, J.: Identification of significant variables for the parameterization of structures learning in architecture students. In: Rocha, Á., Adeli, H., Reis, L.P., Costanzo, S. (eds.) WorldCIST'18 2018. AISC, vol. 747, pp. 298–306. Springer, Cham (2018). https://doi.org/10.1007/978-3-319-77700-9_30
16. Peña, E., Fonseca, D., Martí, N.: Relationship between learning indicators in the development and result of the building engineering degree final project. In: ACM International Conference Proceeding Series (2016)
17. Chatti, M., Dyckhoff, A., Schroeder, U.: A reference model for learning analytics. Int. J. Technol. Enhanc. Learn. **4**, 318–331 (2013)
18. Amo, D., Alier, M., Casañ, M.J.: The student's progress snapshot a hybrid text and visual learning analytics dashboard. Int. J. Eng. Educ. **34–3**, 990–1000 (2018)
19. Lupton, D., Williamson, B.: The datafied child: the dataveillance of children and implications for their rights
20. Singer, N.: InBloom student data repository to close. New York Times **21** (2014)
21. Drachsler, H., Greller, W.: Privacy and analytics: it's a DELICATE issue a checklist for trusted learning analytics. In: Proceedings of the Sixth International Conference on Learning Analytics & Knowledge, pp. 89–98 (2016)
22. Hoel, T., Chen, W.: Implications of the European data protection regulations for learning analytics design (2016)
23. Forment, M.A., Filvà, D.A., García-Peñalvo, F.J., Escudero, D.F., Casañ, M.J.: Learning analytics' privacy on the blockchain. In: Proceedings of the Sixth International Conference on Technological Ecosystems for Enhancing Multiculturality – TEEM 2018, pp. 294–298. ACM Press, New York (2018)
24. Filvà, D.A., García-Peñalvo, F.J., Forment, M.A., Escudero, D.F., Casañ, M.J.: Privacy and identity management in learning analytics processes with blockchain. In: Proceedings of the Sixth International Conference on Technological Ecosystems for Enhancing Multiculturality – TEEM 2018, pp. 997–1003. ACM Press, New York (2018)

Measuring Students' Acceptance to AI-Driven Assessment in eLearning: Proposing a First TAM-Based Research Model

Juan Cruz-Benito[1]([⊠]) [iD], José Carlos Sánchez-Prieto[2,4] [iD],
Roberto Therón[2,3,5] [iD], and Francisco J. García-Peñalvo[2,3,4] [iD]

[1] IBM Research, AI & Q. T. J. Watson Research Center, Yorktown Heights,
NY, USA
juan.cruz@ibm.com
[2] GRIAL Research Group, University of Salamanca, Salamanca, Spain
{josecarlos.sp, theron, fgarcia}@usal.es
[3] Computer Science Department, University of Salamanca, Salamanca, Spain
[4] Research Institute for Educational Sciences (IUCE), University of Salamanca,
Salamanca, Spain
[5] VISUSAL Research Group, University of Salamanca, Salamanca, Spain

Abstract. Artificial Intelligence is one of the trend areas in research. It is applied in many different contexts successfully. One of the contexts where Artificial Intelligence is applied is in Education. In the literature, we find several works in the last years that explore the application of Artificial Intelligence-related techniques to analyze students' behavior, to enable virtual tutors or to assess the learning. However, what are the students' perceptions on this subject of Artificial Intelligence and Education? Do they accept the use of Artificial Intelligence techniques to assess their learning? Are they reluctant to be influenced by non-human agents in such a human process like education? To try to respond to these questions, this paper presents a novel proposal of a research model based on the Technology Acceptance Model. To describe the model, we present its different main constructs and variables, as well as the hypotheses to analyze, adapted to the object of study. Finally, we discuss the main implications of this research model, the opportunities that could come based on this proposal and the future of this research.

Keywords: Artificial intelligence · Technology acceptance model · Education · eLearning · Students

1 Introduction

Artificial Intelligence (AI) is used nowadays in a lot of different contexts [1–8]. It affects millions of humans every day and drives many outstanding innovations around the world. There is no doubt that AI is enabling individuals and companies to accomplish tasks that usually were impossible, even with a large number of people involved in. However, in parallel to the bright side of the advance, we observe that

© Springer Nature Switzerland AG 2019
P. Zaphiris and A. Ioannou (Eds.): HCII 2019, LNCS 11590, pp. 15–25, 2019.
https://doi.org/10.1007/978-3-030-21814-0_2

some part of the society is concerned with the (uncontrollable) advance of AI and its future implications [9–11].

Among the different application areas of the AI, we find the knowledge field of Education. With the appearance of new research tendencies like Learning Analytics, the Smart Classrooms, the Virtual Environments, or the Personal Learning Environments, we are experiencing the mixture of data-driven approaches which include the use of personal data to evaluate the learning process, guide the learning path, etc. [12–15].

Since many years ago, AI has been envisioned as a core part and booster agent of the future in education and human intelligence augmentation [16–20]. However, what are the students' perceptions on this subject of AI and Education? Do they accept the use of Artificial Intelligence techniques to assess their learning? Are they reluctant to be influenced by non-human agents in such a human process like education?

To dig into these questions, it is needed to have the proper tools and methods. This paper deals with these aspects, it is devoted to introducing WIP research which tries to figure out how users perceive the interaction with artificial intelligence in a significant field like the education one. To do so, we use the Technology Acceptance Model (TAM) [21, 22] as the primary basis on where to build our research. Using TAM, we have designed a set of elements composing a survey. This survey will let us know the current status of users' perceptions about AI & Education, their reluctance to be under the scrutiny of intelligent software pieces or their acceptance of this kind of advances.

To present this work, section two introduces background in mixing Artificial Intelligence and in applying TAM models in Education. The third section presents our approach, describing our first proposal of a survey to measure the users' acceptance of this kind of technology. The fourth section depicts the future work to be done and a brief conclusion on our proposal.

2 Background

This section depicts the current state of the art in the fields of AI applied to Education (first subsection) and Technology Acceptance in Education (second subsection).

2.1 AI & Education

As outlined in the introduction, the AI-related algorithms and tools applied to Education are gaining interest in the scientific community [23, 24]. This is not only a perception based on the current general attention and hype around AI. According to the Web of Science, the number of papers published related to the topics "Artificial Intelligence" and "Education" in its core collection is rising since 2008 (Fig. 1). In the last ten years (2010–2019) have been published the 65,56% of all the papers indexed in this database and related to both topics. Even more, during the years 2016–2018, were issued the 34,63% of all the articles published in this context.

The applications of AI in Education, despite the area, is evolving, are varied. Since many years ago, researchers tried to employ artificial intelligence techniques to deal with complex issues like those present in education: analyze students' behavior,

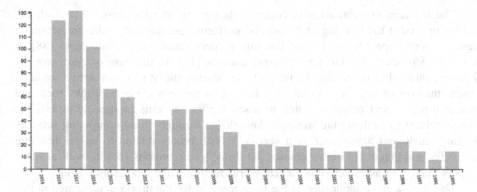

Fig. 1. Papers indexed in the Web of Science in the last 25 years (1995–2019) that contains the topics "Artificial Intelligence" and "Education". Source: Web of Science webofknowledge.com

develop strategies to personalize the learning, detect learning styles, help students during the learning tasks, assess their performance and learning results, etc.

The literature covers a wide range of approaches, solutions, and contexts. We can observe the application of AI in tasks performed in the real world [25], in the virtual one [26], in learning processes that involve K-12 students [27], in other processes with adult learners [28], in smart environments [25], in contexts which include interaction with social robots [29], etc.

To illustrate the impact of AI and related approaches in the field of Education, and according to the literature, we can distinguish different kinds of actuation. One is the application of AI to analyze the humans involved in learning (mainly students), other is the application of AI to improve the learning process, and finally, the use of AI to assess the learning and the results achieved.

In the case of analyzing students' behavior and mental strategies, we find interesting papers about evaluating students' problem-solving strategies [30], about assessing the learning styles of students [31, 32] or predicting the students' mood during online tests and its impact on their results [33].

In the context of improving the learning process can be observed different trends, for example: establish virtual tutors, virtual partners, or the personalization of the learning environments. One of the most common applications of the AI found in the literature is the creation of virtual tutors to guide students during their learning [28]. There are some exciting works related to enable those virtual tutors: from those papers that propose which learn from real teachers and tutors to imitate their behavior when interacting with students to help them [34], to others that try to guide students during specific learning-related tasks to improve their performance [27, 28, 35]. Other papers, rather than create virtual tutors, implement virtual partners for students who advance through the learning process with the students in every moment [36]. Finally, there are some excellent articles on the personalization of the learning environments and students' learning paths. For example, some authors dealt with the personalization of virtual 3D immersive environments [26] or another kind of virtual facilities for learning [37].

The last area of application to comment is the use of AI techniques to evaluate, assess or predict the learning and students' performance. Related to the prediction of results, some papers try to predict the student performance on certain tasks [38] or directly to predict their GPA in different courses [13]. In the case of assessing the learning (instead of predicting the results), we observe that it is a very active sub-area under the area of applying AI into the Education processes. For example, there are research papers and projects related to assessing the students in specific tasks [39], others related to evaluate the students' knowledge through cloud computing services (*a.k.a.* "intelligent assessment as a service") [40], others related to assess learning activities in different environments like 3D immersive scenarios [26], as well as other papers that try to asses activities in real-world facilities like laboratories [41].

This third area of application is the most relevant for the proposal presented in this paper. In the following sections, we will present how to analyze the students' acceptance of being subject of study by artificial intelligence.

2.2   Technology Acceptance in Education

The study of the factors that condition the acceptance of technology among educational users constitutes a large body of research [42] that continues to grow motivated by the fast technological development and the constant incorporation of new devices and information systems e.g. [43, 44] that may offer innovative solutions and contribute to the transformation of the teaching-learning process [45].

One of the primary resources for the study of these factors is the development of technology adoption models. This way we can find a wide variety of researches conducted in the educational field that applies different models such as the Unified Theory of Acceptance and Use of Technology (UTAUT) [46] e.g. [47], the Task-Technology Fit Theory (TTF) [48] e.g. [49] or the Theory of Planned Behavior (TPB) [50] e.g. [51] for the study of the factors that affect the intention of using a given technology of the students.

However, despite this variety of theories TAM rises as the dominant model in the educational context [42, 52]. This theory explains the technology acceptance process through a model (Fig. 2) composed by five factors namely perceived usefulness (PU), perceived ease of use (PEU), attitude towards the use (AU), behavioral intention of use (BI) and actual use (U).

The success of this model is mainly due to its parsimony, given that it can explain a large percentage of the variance of BI and U with a relatively small number of constructs [52] and an instrument composed by 18 Likert-Type items to measure them. This combined with its transferability to different contexts and samples makes TAM the most suitable tool for the development of technology adoption studies in the educational field [42, 52].

However, TAM also has its limitations such as the lack of consideration of the effect of external variables, although their influence is recognized in the model, or its limited explanatory power when is applied in exploratory studies [53, 54].

In order to overcome these limitations, researchers frequently modify the model and expand it to adapt TAM to new contexts and technologies [52]. Some of the findings of

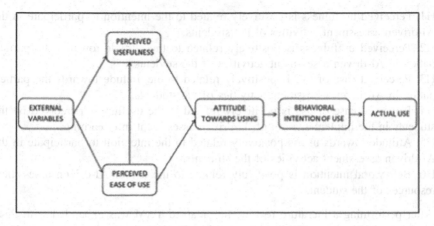

Fig. 2. TAM model [22]

these investigations have been integrated into two subsequent versions of TAM: TAM2 [55] and TAM3 [56].

This way in the educational field we can find examples of the design and application of TAM based models expanded with constructs from other adoption theories such as subjective norm [57], self-efficacy [58] or facilitating conditions [59] to analyze the students' acceptance of technologies including LMSs [57], mobile devices [60] or QR codes [59]. However, to the extent of our knowledge, there is a lack of models specifically designed to examine the acceptance of AI-driven assessment among eLearning students.

3 Proposal

As it has been established, the model presented in this proposal is based on TAM, from this theory we have kept its five main components [43] defined in the model as follows:

- PU: A dimension that measures the perception of the individuals of the degree in which the use of AI-driven assessment would enhance their learning.
- PEU: Defined as the users' perception of the degree of effort necessary to use the new resource.
- AU: A construct that refers to the students' evaluative affect (positive or negative feelings) towards using AI-driven assessment.
- BI: A factor in assessing the students' intention to partake in AI-driven assessment activities.
- U: The endogenous variable of the model, which measures the level of use of AI-driven assessment resources.

Additionally, we also kept the six main hypotheses of TAM [43] adapted to the object of study:

- H1. Perceived usefulness is positively related to the intention to participate in the AI-driven assessment activities of the students.
- H2. Perceived usefulness is positively related to the attitude towards the participation in AI-driven assessment activities of the students.
- H3. Perceived ease of use is positively related to the attitude towards the participation in AI-driven assessment activities of the students.
- H4. Perceived ease of use is positively related to the usefulness perceived by the students in the implementation of AI-driven assessment in eLearning.
- H5. Attitude towards use is positively related to the intention to participate in the AI-driven assessment activities of the students.
- H6. Behavioral intention is positively related to the use of AI-driven assessment resources of the students.

After performing a literature review, the adapted TAM was expanded with three additional variables from other theories with the intention increase the variance explained of the model, namely, subjective norm (SN), resistance to change (RC) and trust (TR).

SN is a variable formulated within the TPB that measures the effect of the social and organizational pressure perceived by the individual towards the performance of a given behavior. This variable is frequently used in investigations focused on the technology adoption of the students [57, 60] with good results and it is included in TAM2 [55] and TAM3 [56]. This way, the existence of an open debate on the convenience of using of AI [9–11] may exert a pressure on the individual that condition both their perception of the advantages of using AI-driven assessment and their intention to use this technology [56], therefore we propose the following hypotheses:

- H7. Subjective norm is positively related to the usefulness perceived by the students in the implementation of AI-driven assessment in eLearning.
- H8. Subjective norm is positively related to the intention to participate in AI-driven assessment activities of the students.

On the other hand, RC refers to the feeling of stress or discomfort experienced by the individuals when they have to face changes [61] and is deemed to have an adverse effect on their technology adoption [62].

The incorporation of AI-driven assessment on eLearning courses entails profound changes in the teaching-learning process including the increase of the human-computer interaction and the decrease of involvement of teachers in assessment activities. These changes may face resistance from the student that may affect their perception of the usefulness of the technology, their feelings towards its use and their subjective probability of participation in AI-driven assessment activities [63]. Thus, we propose the following three hypotheses for this construct:

- H9. Resistance to change is negatively related to the usefulness perceived by the students in the implementation of AI-driven assessment in eLearning.
- H10. Perceived usefulness is negatively related to the attitude towards the participation in AI-driven assessment activities of the students.
- H11. Resistance to change is negatively related to the intention to participate in the AI-driven assessment activities of the students.

- Finally, TR is a construct originated in the field of social psychology [64] nd defined as the willingness of the individual to rely on the other party [65]. This variable has been recognized as a critical element that determines human-automation interaction having a persuasive or dissuasive effect on the use of AI-assisted technologies such as automated vehicles [66].

Although the incorporation of this construct in TAM based models is still in an initial stage of development in the educational field, it is commonly used in other areas such as e-commerce [64], online banking [67] or electronic voting systems [68], showing its effect on the variables from TAM. The model proposal is completed (Fig. 3) with the following hypotheses for this construct:

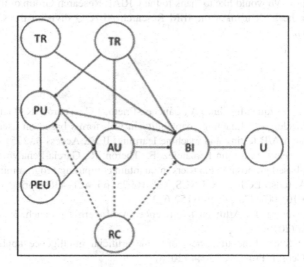

Fig. 3. Research model

- H12. Trust is positively related to the usefulness perceived by the students in the implementation of AI-driven assessment in eLearning.
- H13. Trust is positively related to the attitude towards the participation in AI-driven assessment activities of the students.
- H14. Trust is positively related to the intention to participate in the AI-driven assessment activities of the students.

4   Discussion and Conclusions

As seen in the literature, there is a rising interest in the scientific community about the use of AI-related techniques in education, but there is a lack of studies on what are the effects of the inclusion of these tools among the students. This paper presents a novel research model based on TAM elaborated after an extensive literature review. The purpose of the research model is to study how students accept the use of AI techniques and tools by educators when assessing the learning. The model is composed by 8 constructs that serve to examine the effect of utilitarian motivations, social pressure, dispositional resistance to change and personal conceptions of AI in the disposition of the students to participate in AI-assessed educational activities.

Based on this research model, we have developed an instrument to gather data about students' perceptions of the subject presented. This instrument is currently in the validation stage. Using the validated version of the instrument, we will carry out an empirical study on the acceptance of AI-driven assessment among students. This study aims to provide a solid foundation about subjects' perception on which other researchers could base their future works.

Acknowledgement. We would like to thank to the GRIAL Research Group of the University of Salamanca and to the ETX team at the IBM Research AI & Q division the support received during this research.

References

1. Cruz-Benito, J., Vázquez-Ingelmo, A., Sánchez-Prieto, J.C., Therón, R., García-Peñalvo, F. J., Martín-González, M.: Enabling adaptability in web forms based on user characteristics detection through A/B testing and machine learning. IEEE Access **6**, 2251–2265 (2018)
2. Cruz-Benito, J., Faro, I., Martín-Fernández, F., Therón, R., García-Peñalvo, Francisco J.: A deep-learning-based proposal to aid users in quantum computing programming. In: Zaphiris, P., Ioannou, A. (eds.) LCT 2018. LNCS, vol. 10925, pp. 421–430. Springer, Cham (2018). https://doi.org/10.1007/978-3-319-91152-6_32
3. Russell, S.J., Norvig, P.: Artificial Intelligence: A Modern Approach. Pearson Education Ltd., Malaysia (2016)
4. Shahin, M.A.: State-of-the-art review of some artificial intelligence applications in pile foundations. Geosci. Front. **7**, 33–44 (2016)
5. Zang, Y., Zhang, F., Di, C.-A., Zhu, D.: Advances of flexible pressure sensors toward artificial intelligence and health care applications. Mater. Horiz. **2**, 140–156 (2015)
6. Vasant, P., DeMarco, A.: Handbook of research on artificial intelligence techniques and algorithms. Information Science Reference (2015)
7. Dilek, S., Çakır, H., Aydın, M.: Applications of artificial intelligence techniques to combating cyber crimes: a review. arXiv preprint arXiv:1502.03552 (2015)
8. Papers With Code: Browse state-of-the-art in machine learning. https://paperswithcode.com/sota. Accessed 1 Feb 2019
9. Byrne, E.: From ethics to accountability, this is how AI will suck less in 2019. https://www.wired.co.uk/article/artificial-intelligence-2019-predictions. Accessed 5 Jan 2019
10. Knight, W.: One of the fathers of AI is worried about its future. https://www.technologyreview.com/s/612434/one-of-the-fathers-of-ai-is-worried-about-its-future/. Accessed 15 Jan 2019
11. Hao, K.: Americans want to regulate AI but don't trust anyone to do it. https://www.technologyreview.com/s/612734/americans-want-to-regulate-ai-but-dont-trust-anyone-to-do-it/. Accessed 1 Feb 2019
12. Rodríguez, M.C., et al.: Learning analytics trends and challenges in engineering education: SNOLA special session. In: 2018 IEEE Global Engineering Education Conference (EDUCON), pp. 2066–2070 (2018)

13. Zollanvari, A., Kizilirmak, R.C., Kho, Y.H., Hernández-Torrano, D.: Predicting students' GPA and developing intervention strategies based on self-regulatory learning behaviors. IEEE Access **5**, 23792–23802 (2017)
14. Colchester, K., Hagras, H., Alghazzawi, D., Aldabbagh, G.: A survey of artificial intelligence techniques employed for adaptive educational systems within e-learning platforms. J. Artif. Intell. Soft Comput. Res. **7**, 47–64 (2017)
15. Timms, M.J.: Letting artificial intelligence in education out of the box: educational cobots and smart classrooms. Int. J. Artif. Intell. Educ. **26**, 701–712 (2016)
16. Wenger, E.: Artificial Intelligence and Tutoring Systems: Computational and Cognitive Approaches to the Communication of Knowledge. Morgan Kaufmann, Los Altos (2014)
17. Holland, S.: Artificial intelligence, education and music: the use of artificial intelligence to encourage and facilitate music composition by novices (1989)
18. McArthur, D., Lewis, M., Bishary, M.: The roles of artificial intelligence in education: current progress and future prospects. J. Educ. Technol. **1**, 42–80 (2005)
19. Self, J.: Artificial Intelligence and Human Learning: Intelligent Computer-Aided Instruction. Chapman and Hall, London (1988)
20. Brusilovsky, P., Peylo, C.: Adaptive and intelligent web-based educational systems. Int. J. Artif. Intell. Educ. (IJAIED) **13**, 159–172 (2003)
21. Davis, F.D.: Perceived usefulness, perceived ease of use, and user acceptance of information technology. MIS Q. **13**(3), 319–340 (1989)
22. Davis, F.D., Bagozzi, R.P., Warshaw, P.R.: User acceptance of computer technology: a comparison of two theoretical models. Manage. Sci. **35**, 982–1003 (1989)
23. Jordan, M.I., Mitchell, T.M.: Machine learning: trends, perspectives, and prospects. Science **349**, 255–260 (2015)
24. Roll, I., Wylie, R.: Evolution and revolution in artificial intelligence in education. Int. J. Artif. Intell. Educ. **26**, 582–599 (2016)
25. Mikulecký, P.: Smart environments for smart learning. In: 9th International Scientific Conference on Distance Learning in Applied Informatics, pp. 213–222. Constantine Philosophe Univ Nitra, (2012)
26. McCusker, K., Callaghan, M., Harkin, J., Wilson, S.: Intelligent assessment and learner personalisation in virtual 3D immersive environments. In: European Conference on Games Based Learning, p. 591. Academic Conferences International Limited (2012)
27. McLaren, B.M., DeLeeuw, K.E., Mayer, R.E.: Polite web-based intelligent tutors: can they improve learning in classrooms? Comput. Educ. **56**, 574–584 (2011)
28. Cheung, B., Hui, L., Zhang, J., Yiu, S.M.: SmartTutor: an intelligent tutoring system in web-based adult education. J. Syst. Softw. **68**, 11–25 (2003)
29. Sheridan, T.B.: Human-robot interaction: status and challenges. Hum. Factors **58**, 525–532 (2016)
30. Vendlinski, T., Stevens, R.: The use of artificial neural nets (ANN) to help evaluate student problem solving strategies. In: Proceedings of the Fourth International Conference of the Learning Sciences, pp. 108–114. Erlbaum (2000)
31. Wei, Y., Yang, Q., Chen, J., Hu, J.: The exploration of a machine learning approach for the assessment of learning styles changes. Mechatron. Syst. Control **46**, 121–126 (2018)
32. García, P., Schiaffino, S., Amandi, A.: An enhanced Bayesian model to detect students' learning styles in web-based courses. J. Comput. Assist. Learn. **24**, 305–315 (2008)
33. Moridis, C.N., Economides, A.A.: Prediction of student's mood during an online test using formula-based and neural network-based method. Comput. Educ. **53**, 644–652 (2009)
34. Chin, D.B., Dohmen, I.M., Cheng, B.H., Oppezzo, M.A., Chase, C.C., Schwartz, D.L.: Preparing students for future learning with teachable agents. Educ. Tech. Res. Dev. **58**, 649–669 (2010)

35. Nwana, H.S.: Intelligent tutoring systems: an overview. Artif. Intell. Rev. **4**, 251–277 (1990)
36. Chou, C.-Y., Chan, T.-W., Lin, C.-J.: Redefining the learning companion: the past, present, and future of educational agents. Comput. Educ. **40**, 255–269 (2003)
37. Xu, D., Wang, H.: Intelligent agent supported personalization for virtual learning environments. Decis. Support Syst. **42**, 825–843 (2006)
38. Kuehn, M., Estad, J., Straub, J., Stokke, T., Kerlin, S.: An expert system for the prediction of student performance in an initial computer science course. In: 2017 IEEE International Conference on Electro Information Technology (EIT), pp. 1–6 (2017)
39. Samarakou, M., Fylladitakis, E.D., Prentakis, P., Athineos, S.: Implementation of artificial intelligence assessment in engineering laboratory education. In: International Conference on e-Learning part of Multi Conference on Computer Science and Information Systems (MCCSIS). International Association for Development of the Information Society, Lisbon, Portugal (2014)
40. Stantchev, V., Prieto-González, L., Tamm, G.: Cloud computing service for knowledge assessment and studies recommendation in crowdsourcing and collaborative learning environments based on social network analysis. Comput. Hum. Behav. **51**, 762–770 (2015)
41. Gokmen, G., Akinci, T.Ç., Tektaş, M., Onat, N., Kocyigit, G., Tektaş, N.: Evaluation of student performance in laboratory applications using fuzzy logic. Procedia – Soc. Behav. Sci. **2**, 902–909 (2010)
42. Scherer, R., Siddiq, F., Tondeur, J.: The technology acceptance model (TAM): a meta-analytic structural equation modeling approach to explaining teachers' adoption of digital technology in education. Comput. Educ. **128**, 13–35 (2019)
43. Al-Shihi, H., Sharma, S.K., Sarrab, M.: Neural network approach to predict mobile learning acceptance. Educ. Inf. Technol. **23**, 1805–1824 (2018)
44. Cascales, A., Pérez-López, D., Contero, M.: Study on parent's acceptance of the augmented reality use for preschool education. Procedia Comput. Sci. **25**, 420–427 (2013)
45. Gros, B.: The dialogue between emerging pedagogies and emerging technologies. In: Gros, B., Kinshuk, Maina, M., et al. (eds.) The Future of Ubiquitous Learning: Learning Designs for Emerging Pedagogies. LNET, pp. 3–23. Springer, Heidelberg (2016). https://doi.org/10.1007/978-3-662-47724-3_1
46. Venkatesh, V., Morris, M.G., Davis, G.B., Davis, F.D.: User acceptance of information technology: toward a unified view. MIS Q. **27**, 425–478 (2003)
47. Halili, S.H., Sulaiman, H.: Factors influencing the rural students' acceptance of using ICT for educational purposes. Kasetsart J. Soc. Sci. (2018, in press)
48. Goodhue, D.L., Thompson, R.L.: Task-technology fit and individual performance. MIS Q. **19**, 213–236 (1995)
49. Khan, I.U., Hameed, Z., Yu, Y., Islam, T., Sheikh, Z., Khan, S.U.: Predicting the acceptance of MOOCs in a developing country: application of task-technology fit model, social motivation, and self-determination theory. Telematics Inform. **35**, 964–978 (2018)
50. Ajzen, I.: From intentions to actions: a theory of planned behavior. In: Kuhl, J., Beckmann, J. (eds.) Action Control. SSSSP, pp. 11–39. Springer, Heidelberg (1985). https://doi.org/10.1007/978-3-642-69746-3_2
51. Zhou, M.: Chinese university students' acceptance of MOOCs: a self-determination perspective. Comput. Educ. **92–93**, 194–203 (2016)
52. King, W.R., He, J.: A meta-analysis of the technology acceptance model. Inf. Manag. **43**, 740–755 (2006)
53. Hernández García, Á.: Desarrollo de un modelo unificado de adopción del comercio electrónico entre empresas y consumidores finales. Aplicación al mercado español. Ingenieria_Empresas, p. 422. Telecomunicacion (2012)

54. Legris, P., Ingham, J., Collerette, P.: Why do people use information technology? A critical review of the technology acceptance model. Inf. Manage. **40**, 191–204 (2003)
55. Venkatesh, V., Davis, F.D.: A theoretical extension of the technology acceptance model: four longitudinal field studies. Manage. Sci. **46**, 186–204 (2000)
56. Venkatesh, V., Bala, H.: Technology acceptance model 3 and a research agenda on interventions. Decis. Sci. **39**, 273–315 (2008)
57. Teo, T., Zhou, M., Fan, A.C.W., Huang, F.: Factors that influence university students' intention to use Moodle: a study in Macau. Educ. Technol. Res. Dev. **67**, 749–766 (2019)
58. Moorthy, K., et al.: Is Facebook useful for learning? A study in private universities in Malaysia. Comput. Educ. **130**, 94–104 (2019)
59. Abdul Rabu, S.N., Hussin, H., Bervell, B.: QR code utilization in a large classroom: higher education students' initial perceptions. Educ. Inf. Technol. **24**, 359–384 (2019)
60. Sánchez-Prieto, J.C., Hernández-García, Á., García-Peñalvo, F.J., Chaparro-Peláez, J., Olmos-Migueláñez, S.: Break the walls! second-order barriers and the acceptance of mLearning by first-year pre-service teachers. Comput. Hum. Behav. **95**, 158–167 (2019)
61. Guo, X., Sun, Y., Wang, N., Peng, Z., Yan, Z.: The dark side of elderly acceptance of preventive mobile health services in China. Electron. Markets **23**, 49–61 (2013)
62. Cenfetelli, R.T.: Inhibitors and enablers as dual factor concepts in technology usage. J. Assoc. Inf. Syst. **5**, 16 (2004)
63. Bhattacherjee, A., Hikmet, N.: Physicians' resistance toward healthcare information technology: a theoretical model and empirical test. Eur. J. Inf. Syst. **16**, 725–737 (2007)
64. Shao, Z., Zhang, L., Li, X., Guo, Y.: Antecedents of trust and continuance intention in mobile payment platforms: the moderating effect of gender. Electron. Commer. Res. Appl. **33**, 100823 (2019)
65. Flavián, C., Guinalíu, M., Torres, E.: How bricks-and-mortar attributes affect online banking adoption. Int. J. Bank Mark. **24**, 406–423 (2006)
66. Zhang, T., Tao, D., Qu, X., Zhang, X., Lin, R., Zhang, W.: The roles of initial trust and perceived risk in public's acceptance of automated vehicles. Transp. Res. Part C: Emerg. Technol. **98**, 207–220 (2019)
67. Sharma, S.K., Sharma, M.: Examining the role of trust and quality dimensions in the actual usage of mobile banking services: an empirical investigation. Int. J. Inf. Manage. **44**, 65–75 (2019)
68. Warkentin, M., Sharma, S., Gefen, D., Rose, G.M., Pavlou, P.: Social identity and trust in internet-based voting adoption. Gov. Inf. Q. **35**, 195–209 (2018)

Measuring the Impact of E-Learning Platforms on Information Security Awareness

Tobias Fertig[(✉)], Andreas E. Schütz, Kristin Weber, and Nicholas H. Müller

Faculty of Computer Science and Business Information Systems,
University of Applied Sciences Würzburg-Schweinfurt,
Sanderheinrichsleitenweg 20, 97074 Würzburg, Germany
{tobias.fertig,andreas.schuetz,kristin.weber,nicholas.mueller}@fhws.de

Abstract. Humans play a central role in information security. The behavior of workers at their workplace affects the confidentiality, integrity, and availability of sensitive corporate information. In addition, attackers exploit the "human factor" as a weak point with techniques such as phishing, malware, and social engineering. Exploiting the lack of awareness is often an easy task with minimal risk. To make employees aware of their important role, companies typically carry out security awareness campaigns. Our university created an e-Learning Platform (eLP) to support our awareness campaigns. In order to determine the success, the effectiveness and the impact of such an awareness campaign, suitable measurement methods are needed. A common approach to measure the success of eLPs is to run surveys and questionnaires with the learners. Since the manual evaluation of those surveys and questionnaires is a time-consuming task, we are researching how a possible automation can be achieved. Moreover, the effectiveness is often evaluated through quizzes or knowledge tests. Since knowledge by itself does not improve the behavior of people, the compliant-behavior has to be measured, too. We derived metrics for success and effectiveness but recognized that success can hardly be measured automatically. To reduce the manual effort we decided to only measure the effectiveness automatically. Therefore, we are measuring the behavior and determine if the security-compliance has increased.

Keywords: Information security awareness · Measuring ·
e-Learning Platforms · Success · Effectiveness · Automated measuring

1 Introduction

In information security, humans play a central role. The behavior of workers at their workplace and at their home affects the confidentiality, integrity, and availability of sensitive corporate information. Risks can occur by a lost smartphone, a confidential document accidentally left on a desk, or a strange USB device used

P. Zaphiris and A. Ioannou (Eds.): HCII 2019, LNCS 11590, pp. 26–37, 2019.
https://doi.org/10.1007/978-3-030-21814-0_3

due to missing awareness of potential dangers. In addition, criminals exploit the "human factor" as a weak point with techniques such as phishing, malware, and social engineering [12]. Former social engineer Kevin Mitnick puts it this way: "Cracking the human firewall is often easy, requires no investment beyond the cost of a phone call, and involves minimal risk [18]." To make employees aware of their important role, companies typically carry out security awareness campaigns [11,27].

In order to determine the success, the effectiveness and the impact of such an awareness campaign, suitable measurement methods are needed. In general, experiments or hypotheses cannot be verified without a suitable measurement method. For example, our university aims to increase the information security awareness of employees and students via an e-Learning campaign. To verify that the awareness indeed has increased, a suitable measurement method for security awareness is also required. The awareness level measured before the e-Learning campaign has to be compared with the awareness level measured after the campaign has been finished. In general, measurement results are needed to justify the budget, to identify further opportunities for improvement, and to assess whether actions have been effective.

In order to increase the information security awareness of employees and students, our university created an e-Learning Platform (eLP) about information security to run e-Learning campaigns. The eLP was created as part of a research project and contains slides, lectures and information about security issues and possible attack vectors. Moreover, the platform provides quizzes and other knowledge tests.

Based on related work on measuring the success of eLP, metrics were derived to provide information on whether the participants' security awareness has increased. The derived metrics and results of our research will be used to answer the following research questions:

(Q1) How is the success and effectiveness of eLPs measured in general?
(Q2) How can the impact of eLPs on information security awareness be measured?
(Q3) Is it possible to automate the measurement of success and effectiveness impact?

At the beginning, we summarize related work on security awareness, measuring success and effectiveness of eLPs, and measuring security awareness. In Sect. 3, we evaluate existing metrics to measure the success and effectiveness of eLPs and group them into categories. This evaluation of metrics is based on a literature review. In Sect. 4 we introduce our project in which the eLP and the measuring was executed. Afterwards, we discuss the advantages and disadvantages as well as the limitations of our approach. Finally, we give a short summary of the paper and describe our future work.

2   Related Work

2.1   Security Awareness

Security awareness targets the "human factor" and has established itself as a separate research area within information security. Moreover, security awareness focuses on how IT users can be brought to an information security-compliant behavior. IT users should be motivated to use their theoretical knowledge about information security in practice [2] and should be convinced of the importance of their actions [9]. In practice, information security awareness campaigns mainly do one thing: In lectures, employees receive theoretical knowledge about information security. However, the actual behavior of an employee is hardly influenced by classical training [28].

An additional aspect of information security awareness is organization, which was described by Helisch and Pokoyski [11]. They mention that the organization ensures that employees in the company are able to behave in compliance with information security. Therefore, the organization ensures that no barriers exist, which are in conflict with compliant behavior. For example, a hidden password change link within the depths of the company intranet can be such a barrier. Additionally, organizational measures, such as increasing the usability of applications, can support information security and lead to greater acceptance. The acceptance will then increase the compliant behavior of employees. Information security awareness is thus an interaction of cognition (understanding of the problem and the knowledge to solve it), intention to act (will of the employee to behave in accordance with information security) and the organization [11].

Since the three interactions are not sufficient to define information security awareness, we derived our own Integrated Behavorial Model (IBM) [22]. Our IBM is based on the model of [20]. The IBM describes how compliant behavior of employees is influenced by different factors. Those factors include the knowledge, salience, habit, attitude, perceived norm, personal agency as well as environmental constraints. Using an eLP to increase the information security awareness has to cover the different factors in order to establish a holistic approach.

2.2   Measuring Success and Effectiveness of E-Learning Platforms

The definition of metrics is a prerequisite for measuring the success and effectiveness of eLPs. The metrics are needed to compare the current state with the desired target state. Figure 1 shows the IT controlling cycle of [15]: First, a goal has to be defined - secure behavior of stuff members. Then the metrics for measuring the goal are identified and defined, target values are set. Subsequently, the current state is measured and compared with the target state. In an analysis, conclusions are drawn about actions that are to be implemented to achieve the goal.

There are mainly two different types of metrics for eLPs: those for success and those for effectiveness. Metrics that are focusing on success are often derived from the DeLone and McLean model of information systems success (D&M model)

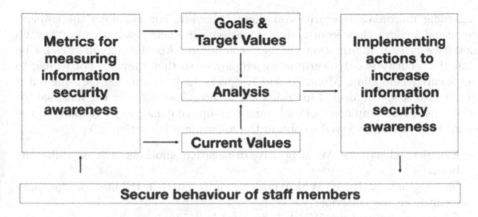

Fig. 1. Controlling cycle for secure behavior [15].

[5]. The derived models focus on the satisfaction of learners besides the other categories. Mainly, because the satisfaction will lead to a better adoption of the eLP by the learners. Adoption means that the learners accept the eLP as a tool to acquire knowledge. The adoption will than generate impact on the outcomes of the e-learning campaign [6,10,16,26]. However, measuring the adoption itself does not necessarily change the behavior of the learners. The Kirkpatrick Evaluation Method describes four levels of learning evaluation [14]. The first level focuses also on learner's satisfaction, whereas the other three levels focus on the results and outcome. Therefore, the Kirkpatrick Evaluation Method can also be divided into the evaluation of success and effectiveness: Satisfaction is part of the success measuring, whereas results and outcome are part of the effectiveness measuring.

The effectiveness of eLPs has to be measured separately to ensure that the adoption of the eLP leads to an improvement of skills. Noesgaard et al. clustered a total of 92 papers according to the definition of effectiveness described within those papers [21]. They distinguish between the effectiveness measured for higher education and for work-related learning. Work-related learning in this case means, that the learners train their knowledge required to fulfill their work or required by their organization. Papers targeting the higher education focused on the learning outcome and compared the grades of e-learners and traditional learners. Papers focusing on work-related learning always defined the effectiveness based on the application to practice.

2.3 Measuring Awareness

We proposed our process to determine how aware the employees are in [22]. Before companies can start influencing the behavioral factors of their employees within the context of an information security awareness campaign, they must carry out an as-is analysis. The aim of this analysis is to find out how strong the individual factors are and which emotions or beliefs prevail in the company regarding information security-compliant behavior. For example, the employees could believe that security is not an issue in their case, because they do not have critical information on their computers. Another example could be that the security is only overhead for employees so that they are not willing to act security-compliant. Montaño and Kasprzyk [20] recommend carrying out a qualitative study in form of interviews. The interviews identify the most salient problems. 15–20 employees of each target group, that has to participate on the eLP, should be interviewed to obtain the following information [20]:

- Experiential attitude: What positive or negative emotions exist regarding the behavior?
- Instrumental attitude: Which positive or negative attributes or outcomes result from the behavior?
- Normative influencers: Which influential individuals or groups support the behavior or are against it?
- Control beliefs and self-efficacy expectations: What situational barriers or supportive factors hinder or support the behavior.

From the findings gathered in the interviews, a questionnaire for a quantitative evaluation can be prepared [13]. A large portion of the employees within the company should answer it. To compose the questionnaire, the beliefs collected in the first step are generalized, transformed into questions and assigned to the four factors knowledge and skills, salience, habit and intention [13]. A question about the normative beliefs could be: "My manager influences me in my working with USB flash drives". A behavioral belief might look like this: "Locking my screen is unnecessary because I have no important data on my computer." Employees respond to a five-point scale ranging from "I disagree" to "I agree" or similar [19]. It is also possible to query the factors knowledge and skills as well as habit (e.g., through the "Self-Report Habit Index" [25]). In order to be efficient, the survey should be computer-aided, and employees should handle it within a reasonable time (e.g., 15 to 20 min). The computer-aided analysis of the survey results provides information about the manifestation of the respective behavioral factors in the company.

3   E-Learning Metrics

Several sources have been reviewed to gather metrics for the success of eLP. Figure 2 shows the updated D&M model [4,5], which is often derived by approaches for measuring the success of eLPs. However, there exist also approaches that are independent of the D&M model. In the following, we will first analyze the approaches that extend the D&M model. In addition, we examine independent approaches to define additional metrics. All approaches are working with questionnaires to obtain the actual values for each metric.

Manisi et al. have produced a literature review summarizing the categories of the D&M model [17]. [16] and [26] both used the D&M model as a basis and defined various metrics for all categories. The first category is 'Intension to

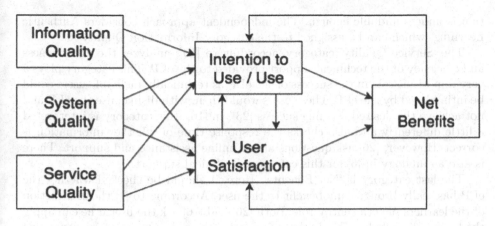

Fig. 2. Updated D&M model based on [5]

Use/Use'. [17] and [10] mention here that the intention of the user can already exist before the actual usage. From a student's point of view, usage also depends on how useful it appears [7, 24]. In this category, [26] measures how often the eLP is being used, whether it is voluntary and whether the user depends on the system. [16] additionally measure the intension of the user: Is the eLP useful and if the user would recommend the eLP to others. In addition, interpersonal statements are also tested: e.g. Users use the eLP to receive rewards. [6] proposed an approach independent from the D&M model. They ask the users about future use.

The next category is 'User Satisfaction'. The D&M model describes the satisfaction of the user after interacting with the system. In addition, [17] and [24] explain that the expectations of the user and the usefulness for the core business also play a role. [16] and [26] each ask three questions about how satisfied the user is with the system, its information, and the interaction. Also, [6] ask questions about the overall satisfaction of the user.

The next category is 'System Quality'. The quality of the eLP depends on the quality of its hardware and software [24]. However, reliability, response time and ease of use are also critical for the System Quality, according to the D&M model. [16] ask questions to get information about reliability, response time and ease of use. [26] extend these factors to include personalized information presentation and attractive features. Moreover, the independent approach of [6] covers the complexity of the eLP within their survey.

The category 'Information Quality' is defined by [10] as the overall quality of the output of the eLP. According to [7], however, security should also be taken into account when measuring information quality. Users are asked if the eLP information is correct, if relevant information is being taught in the lessons, or if the information is up to date [16]. In addition, [26] checks whether the information is communicated at the right time and whether the information is understandable enough. The independent approach considers Authentic Learning, which can be assigned to the category Information Quality [6].

The 'Service Quality' category, according to [10], analyzes the effectiveness and efficiency of the technical support provided to the eLP. This category plays a very important role in the success of the eLP as technically ineligible users could be intimidated by the eLP. These users would then, with dislike, use the eLP and not achieve the desired learning success [23]. In [16], this category is interpreted a little differently and also checks the response time or whether information is correct. However, [26] ask questions about online assistance and support. There is also an analogy in [6] for this category: Technical support.

The last category is 'Net Benefits'. Here, it should be checked whether the eLP has really brought any benefit to the user. According to [1] the satisfaction of the learners plays a central role. Both [26] and [16] ask the user if he can apply the learned knowledge. In addition, [6] queried the age of the users to determine if it had an impact on individual impact.

Another approach that does not depend on the D&M model was shown in [3]. There, both students and staff were interviewed about the eLP. All asked questions can be classified in one of the categories described above and thus no additional metrics result.

4   Project Background

With the widespread use of new, digital services, the importance of information security is increasing. The University of Applied Sciences Würzburg-Schweinfurt has to protect their infrastructure, privacy data, research data and financial data against possible attacks. Moreover, a new e-governance law as well as a new data privacy policy was released. Therefore, our university launched an information security project to increase the security awareness of employees and students. Within the project, the university wants to train security-compliant behavior and to increase the knowledge about security-related topics. To support the project an eLP was created. The purpose of the eLP is to inform users to security risks, and to train them such as being able to better recognize phishing mails. As the creation and management of an eLP requires many resources, the university wanted to know if learners' information security awareness really improved.

Since our research project focuses on the human factor and security awareness in an organizational environment, we are focussing on work-related learning. We try to improve the security awareness so that the learning outcomes can be applied to the practice. Therefore, within our project the effectiveness of eLPs is defined as transfer described by Noesgaard et al. [21]. In order to measure the application to practice, we have to measure the security awareness before the e-learning campaign and afterwards. We can than determine the impact of the eLP on security awareness. However, we have to measure the success of our eLP also, in order to determine if the learners have used the eLP.

5   Research Results

In order to determine if the learners' information security awareness really improved, we had to answer research question Q1 and evaluate how success and effectiveness of eLPs is measured. The literature review showed that many universities and also companies are measuring the success and effectiveness of eLP. Most of the measurements of success are based on the D&M model or can at least be derived from it [5]. Even the proposed models that are not directly based on the D&M model cover related categories with their metrics. All reviewed papers are using surveys or questionnaires in order to determine the success of their eLP. Some researchers are even evaluating the success by interviews. However, many questions rely on the knowledge of the learners, like for example "The information provided by eLP is accurate" [16]. In our opinion, the information quality cannot be measured based on the answers to this questions. A learner who is new to the topic cannot decide properly whether the information is accurate.

Many researchers use surveys and questionnaires also regarding the effectiveness of eLP. The results are then analyzed and evaluated based on different definitions for effectiveness. Companies are defining the effectiveness mainly as the ability to apply the knowledge in practice or transfer of knowledge. Whereas, universities define effectiveness based on the improved grades of their students [21]. In our case, we are not interested in grades of the learners since we want to increase the information security awareness. Therefore, we are defining our effectiveness as transfer of knowledge. However, the general approach to measure the success and effectiveness manually per surveys and questionnaires does not meet our requirements.

Research question Q2 focused on the effectiveness of eLP on information security awareness. In order to measure the effectiveness on information security awareness we need to know the current state of our learners. Therefore, we have to measure the information security awareness of staff and students of our university, which is itself a challenging task. According to our process in Sect. 2.3 we first interviewed about 30 employees for the qualitative analysis. To accomplish the quantitative analysis we run a survey on all our employees and students. The evaluation of results has to be done manually. In order to determine the effectiveness of our eLP, we had to repeat this process. Afterwards, we could determine if the awareness has increased. Nevertheless, a better solution is required, since we defined the effectiveness as application to practice. Based on the answers of our learners we could only draw conclusions about the knowledge but not really about their ability to apply the learned knowledge to practice.

Since measuring the success and the effectiveness manually is a time consuming task, we tried to automate the measuring. Therefore, we determined if the metrics in Sect. 3 are able to be automated for measurement. The first category 'Intention to Use/Use' can be measured automatically. Therefore, the online times of our learners have to be tracked. However, the intention to use itself cannot be measured automatically since the users have to be asked about their intentions. The 'User Satisfaction' cannot be measured without assumptions or without asking the users for their satisfaction. An overall rating could be gathered easily, but no further information about the learners' expectations.

The 'System Quality' which was defined by the reliability, response time and ease of use can also not be measured automatically. A monitoring system could send requests to the eLP to measure the response time, but the ease of use has to be measured by surveys or questionnaires again. The second dimension of 'System Quality' focuses on data accuracy and completeness which is also not possible to measure automatically. In order to measure the 'Information Quality' the learner has to be asked to answer all questions concerning the learners' needs, understandings and requirements. Moreover, metrics focusing on relevance and actual information cannot be gathered automatically. 'Service Quality' is the third quality criteria focusing on online assisstance and support. To measure the satisfaction an overall rating can also be collected automatically. However, for detailed analysis surveys and questionnaires are required also.

The last category of 'Net Benefits' can be measured by measuring the effectiveness of our eLP. An impact during the e-Learning campaign is not expected and therefore, it is sufficient to measure the impact and effectiveness afterwards. To sum up, we can answer question Q3 so that an automated measuring of success is not sufficient since only few aspects can be measured. The effectiveness however, can be measured automatically by measuring the information security awareness before and after the e-Learning campaign. In order to do so, we created a prototype for a monitoring tool. The monitoring tool tracks the behavior of employees and creates anonymous reports within a dashboard.

The prototypical approach was chosen because it helps to formulate the requirements for an information system more precisely and to prove the technical feasibility. Basically, it reduces the number of uncertain assumptions in a software project. Therefore, an explorative prototype was created in the context of our project. The requirements for the prototype were defined within the exploratory preparatory work. In addition, the privacy of personal data introduced further requirements. The prototype tests the measurability of metrics and proves the general feasibility of the approach, including data privacy compliance. For this purpose, a client-server application was developed: The server manages indicators and events that the client has previously collected. The client collects security-relevant data on the workstations of the employees and sends them pseudonymous to the server for evaluation and anonymization by grouping. To enable a pseudonymous login, departmental logins are used. All clients of a department use the same login for authentication. The larger the departments are chosen, the higher the degree of anonymity. By configuring a measurement interval, the metrics are always randomly measured. A complete record of the activities of a person is thus, for privacy reasons, not possible.

An IT admin can configure the login data. The configuration used for the survey is initially downloaded from the server. In a pre-defined interval, the client application now checks to see if thresholds of the active measures have been exceeded. The server refreshes the list of recent events and increases the value of non-critical events as a whole. The server includes a dashboard that provides a quick overview of the number of critical or non-critical incidents. The dashboard also shows a temporal course of the incident frequency in the last week.

The following list summarizes a few of the metrics our prototype can cover:

- The time of inactivity without a locked screen.
- The time interval from receiving an email until opening the attachments.
- The frequency of password changes.
- The installed software. And the installed unauthorized software.
- The amount of external USB devices used.

The combination of metrics can be used to decide whether an event is critical or not: An installation of disallowed software is more critical if an email attachment was opened before. Moreover, if external USB devices have been connected, the installation is also more critical.

We decided to only measure the effectiveness of our eLP, since the effectiveness is the more relevant information to us. Moreover, the effectiveness is part of the success within the category 'Net Benefits'. Therefore, we can reduce the efforts by discontinueing the manual measurements for the success of our eLP. Hagen et al. described that eLP has to be used repetitive in iterations so that the learners' do not forget the security details [8]. The reduced effort is even more helpful if we run repetitive e-Learning campaigns.

However, we have some limitations with this approach. The measuring of effectiveness can only be done before and after the e-Learning campaign. If assumptions about the success should be made, metrics are required, that can be determined during the campaigns. Another drawback is that, the metrics should not be used in isolation. A single metric can improve even if the learners did not use the eLP. Therefore, some usage statistics should be collected to verify that the eLP is useful.

6   Conclusion and Future Work

Our goal was to measure the success, impact and effectiveness of eLP on information security awareness. We evaluated several metrics and determined which metrics can be measured automatically and which require manual efforts. Afterwards, we decided to only measure the effectiveness and the impact of our eLP. Therefore, we can use our prototype that gathers random data about the behavior of our learners.

Our next goal is to run repetitive campaigns and check whether the information security awareness can be steadily increased. Those repetitive campaigns will also help to ensure that the knowledge of our learners becomes stable in the long-term. Moreover, we will run some empirical studies about the impact of eLPs based on the collected data.

Another goal is to evaluate gamification concepts. We assume that it would be easier to derive metrics for the success of our eLP based on the gamification concepts. For example, the character level or the user's achievements can be used. Based on those metrics, we can then verify if a successful campaign will lead to higher impact and effectiveness.

References

1. Aparicio, M., Bacao, F., Oliveira, T.: Cultural impacts on e-learning systems' success. Internet High. Educ. **31**, 58–70 (2016). https://doi.org/10.1016/j.iheduc.2016.06.003. http://www.sciencedirect.com/science/article/pii/S1096751616300367
2. Bada, M., Sasse, A.M., Nurse, J.R.: Cyber security awareness campaigns: why do they fail to change behaviour? In: Global Cyber Security Capacity Centre: Draft Working Paper, pp. 188–131 (2014)
3. Bell, M., Farrier, S.: Measuring success in e-learning-a multi-dimensional approach. Electron. J. e-Learn. **6**(2), 99–110 (2008). https://eric.ed.gov/?id=EJ1098718
4. DeLone, W.H., McLean, E.R.: Information systems success: the quest for the dependent variable. Inf. Syst. Res. **3**(1), 60–95 (1992). https://doi.org/10.1287/isre.3.1.60. http://pubsonline.informs.org/doi/abs/10.1287/isre.3.1.60
5. DeLone, W.H., McLean, E.R.: The DeLone and McLean model of information systems success: a ten-year update. J. Manage. Inf. Syst. **19**(4), 9–30 (2003). https://www.jstor.org/stable/40398604
6. Fleming, J., Becker, K., Newton, C.: Factors for successful e-learning: does age matter? Educ. + Training **59**(1), 76–89 (2017). https://doi.org/10.1108/ET-07-2015-0057. http://www.emeraldinsight.com/doi/10.1108/ET-07-2015-0057
7. Freeze, R.D., Alshare, K.A., Lane, P.L., Wen, H.J.: IS success model in e-learning context based on students' perceptions. J. Inf. Syst. Educ. **21**, 13 (2014)
8. Hagen, J., Ole Johnsen, S., Albrechtsen, E.: The long-term effects of information security-learning on organizational learning. Inf. Manage. Comput. Secur. **19**(3), 140–154 (2011). https://doi.org/10.1108/09685221111153537. https://www.emeraldinsight.com/doi/full/10.1108/09685221111153537
9. Harich, T.W.: IT-sicherheit im Unternehmen. mitp Professional, mitp-Verlags, Frechen, [Germany], 1. auflage edn. (2015)
10. Hassanzadeh, A., Kanaani, F., Elahi, S.: A model for measuring e-learning systems success in universities. Expert Syst. Appl. **39**(12), 10959–10966 (2012). https://doi.org/10.1016/j.eswa.2012.03.028. http://www.sciencedirect.com/science/article/pii/S0957417412004988
11. Helisch, M., Pokoyski, D.: Security Awareness: Neue Wege zur erfolgreichen Mitarbeiter-Sensibilisierung. Vieweg+Teubner Verlag/GWV Fachverlage GmbH Wiesbaden, Wiesbaden (2009). https://doi.org/10.1007/978-3-8348-9594-3
12. ISACA: State of Cybersecurity 2017. Part 2: Current Trends in Threat Landscape. Technical report, Information Systems Audit and Control Association, ISACA, 3701 Algonquin Road, Suite 1010 Rolling Meadows, IL 60008 USA (2017). http://www.isaca.org/Knowledge-Center/Research/Documents/state-of-cybersecurity-2017-part-2_res_eng_0517.pdf
13. Kasprzyk, D., Montaño, D.E.: Application of an integrated behavioral model to understand HIV prevention behavior of high-risk men in rural Zimbabwe. In: Ajzen, I., Albarracin, D. (eds.) Prediction and Change of Health Behavior: Applying the Reasoned Action Approach, pp. 145–168. Psychology Press, London (2007)
14. Kirkpatrick, D.L.: Evaluating Training Programs: The Four Levels. Berrett-Koehler, Oakland (1994)
15. Kütz, M.: Kennzahlen in der IT: Werkzeuge für Controlling und Management. dpunkt-Verlag (2007). Google-Books-ID: bkbXGAAACAAJ
16. Lin, H.F.: Measuring online learning systems success: applying the updated DeLone and McLean model. CyberPsychol. Behav. **10**(6), 817–820 (2007). https://doi.org/10.1089/cpb.2007.9948. https://www.liebertpub.com/doi/abs/10.1089/cpb.2007.9948

17. Manisi, P., Jantjies, M., Kimani, L.: A conceptual integrated model for measuring the success of elearning in developing countries: literature review. In: 2018 IST-Africa Week Conference (IST-Africa), pp. 1–9, May 2018
18. Mitnick, K.D., Simon, W.L.: The Art of Deception: Controlling the Human Element of Security. Wiley, New York (2002)
19. Montaño, D.E., Kasprzyk, D.: Theory of reasoned action, theory of planned behavior, and the integrated behavioral model. In: Glanz, K., Rimer, B.K., Viswanath, K. (eds.) Health Behavior, pp. 95–124. APA PsycNet, Washington, DC (2015)
20. Montaño, D.E., Kasprzyk, D.: Theory of reasoned action, theory of planned behavior, and the integrated behavior model. In: Glanz, K., Rimer, B.K., Viswanath, K. (eds.) Health Behavior and Health Education, pp. 67–96. APA PsycNet, Washington, DC (2008)
21. Noesgaard, S.S., Ørngreen, R.: The effectiveness of e-learning: an explorative and integrative review of the definitions, methodologies and factors that promote e-learning effectiveness. Electron. J. e-Learn. **13**(4), 278–290 (2015). https://eric.ed.gov/?id=EJ1062121
22. Schütz, A.E.: Information security awareness: it's time to change minds! In: Proceedings of International Conference on Applied Informatics Imagination, Creativity, Design, Development - ICDD 2018. Sibiu, Romania (2018)
23. Sun, P.C., Tsai, R.J., Finger, G., Chen, Y.Y., Yeh, D.: What drives a successful e-learning? An empirical investigation of the critical factors influencing learner satisfaction. Comput. Educ. **50**(4), 1183–1202 (2008). https://doi.org/10.1016/j.compedu.2006.11.007. https://linkinghub.elsevier.com/retrieve/pii/S0360131506001874
24. Tate, M., Sedera, D., McLean, E., Burton-Jones, A.: Information systems success research: the "20-year update?" Panel report from PACIS, 2011. Commun. Assoc. Inf. Syst. **34**(1) (2014). https://doi.org/10.17705/1CAIS.03466. https://aisel.aisnet.org/cais/vol34/iss1/63
25. Verplanken, B., Aarts, H.: Habit, attitude, and planned behaviour: is habit an empty construct or an interesting case of goal-directed automaticity? Eur. Rev. Soc. Psychol. **10**(1), 101–134 (1999). https://doi.org/10.1080/14792779943000035
26. Wang, Y.S., Wang, H.Y., Shee, D.Y.: Measuring e-learning systems success in an organizational context: Scale development and validation. Comput. Hum. Behav. **23**(4), 1792–1808 (2007). https://doi.org/10.1016/j.chb.2005.10.006. http://www.sciencedirect.com/science/article/pii/S0747563205000890
27. Weber, K., Schütz, A.E.: ISIS12-Hack: Mitarbeitersensibilisierenstatt informieren. In: Drews, P., Funk, B., Niemeyer, P., Xie, L. (eds.) Multikonferenz Wirtschsinformatik 2018, vol. IV, pp. 1737–1748, Lüneburg, Germany (2018)
28. Wolf, M.: Von security awareness zum secure behaviour. Hakin9 Extra **5**, 18–19 (2012)

An App to Support Yoga Teachers to Implement a Yoga-Based Approach to Promote Wellbeing Among Young People: Usability Study

Alicia García-Holgado[1]([✉]) [iD], Iñaki Tajes Reiris[1] [iD], Nick Kearney[2], Charlotta Martinus[2], and Francisco J. García-Peñalvo[1] [iD]

[1] GRIAL Research Group, Research Institute for Educational Sciences, University of Salamanca, Salamanca, Spain
{aliciagh,inakitajes,fgarcia}@usal.es
[2] Teen Yoga Foundation, Camerton, UK
nickkearney@gmail.com, charlotta@teenyoga.com

Abstract. Many young people suffer from chronic stress and other issues that inhibit the functioning and development of the prefrontal cortex, and this also affects their intrinsic motivation to engage in any activity. In short, unless their well-being is addressed, they cannot engage effectively. The HIPPOCAMPUS project aims to address these issues by promoting the well-being of young people through the practice of a range of techniques derived from yoga. Yuva Yoga app is part of the approach to support the yoga-based practices with young people. It is a multiplatform mobile app developed as Backend as a Service both for Android and iOS. The first public version of the mobile app is part of the pilots implemented in the schools involved in the project, but there is not a special focus on the usability of the app. This work presents the heuristic evaluation of Yuva Yoga for iOS carried out by four experts as part of a major usability study that combines heuristic techniques, both iOS and Android, and empirical methods with users. Some problems were detected during the evaluation, but more of the problems have a low priority rating. They are mainly cosmetic problems that do not need to be fixed unless extra time is available on the project, or minor usability problems. The results have provided an important input to develop a new minor version of the mobile app, in order to improve the user experience in the pilots at schools.

Keywords: Mobile app · Heuristic evaluation · Yoga · Mental health · Wellbeing · Usability · European project

1 Introduction

Mental health is a key issue facing adolescents across Europe. The CAMHEE Child and Adolescent Mental Health in Europe report of 2009, stated that one in five children and adolescents in the EU suffers from developmental, emotional or behavioural problems, and these data do not take into account those who while not yet exhibiting

© Springer Nature Switzerland AG 2019
P. Zaphiris and A. Ioannou (Eds.): HCII 2019, LNCS 11590, pp. 38–49, 2019.
https://doi.org/10.1007/978-3-030-21814-0_4

clear mental health issues suffer from chronic stress or anxiety. These issues tend to fall under the statistical radar but appear to be endemic among today's young people.

Many young people suffer from chronic stress and other issues that inhibit the functioning (and indeed the development) of the prefrontal cortex, and this also affects their intrinsic motivation to engage in any activity. This is a problem that affects all young people to a greater or lesser degree. Though the family environment can provide support to help, unfortunately not all family environments do, which makes it especially important to provide children and young people with approaches to self-management of stress. Unless their well-being is addressed, they cannot engage effectively.

The HIPPOCAMPUS project (https://hippocampusproject.eu) aims to address these issues by promoting the well-being of young people through the practice of a range of techniques derived from yoga. Though the benefits of yoga have been researched extensively, and in some places, these practices are used with young people, they are not always accessible to all sectors of society. Disadvantaged young people mainly are less able to participate, for a variety of financial and other reasons. The Hippocampus programme, though it is available to all, focuses primarily on the needs and requirements of these groups. This project is funded by the Erasmus+ Programme and coordinated by the GRIAL Research Group of the University of Salamanca (Table 1).

Table 1. Project details

Title	Promoting mental health and wellbeing among young people through yoga
Acronym	HIPPOCAMPUS
Funding entity	European Union
Call	European Union. Erasmus+ KA2 – cooperation and innovation for good practices. Strategic partnerships for youth
Reference	2017-2-ES02-KA205-009942
Project leader	Francisco José García-Peñalvo
Coordinator	University of Salamanca (Spain)
Partners	Teen yoga foundation (United Kingdom) IES Venancio Blanco (Spain) Youth for exchange and understanding international (Belgium) Oxfam Italia (Italy) Norges Teknisk-Naturvitenskapelige Universitet (Norway)
Budget	192.914€
Start date	01/10/2017
End date	30/11/2019
Web	https://hippocampusproject.eu

The project has two main outputs. First, a programme to introduce yoga-based practices in youth contexts such as formal education contexts or associations. On the other hand, a mobile app both for iOS and Android in order to give yoga teachers a way to help their students maintain their practice between sessions.

The app, named Yuva Yoga (https://yuvayoga.org), was developed during the first year of the project. The alpha version was launched in March 2018 in order to be validated by the project consortium, in which there are several yoga experts, both yoga teachers and yoga practitioners. The beta version was available in July 2018, and finally the first public version was available on December 2018. The app is part of the pilot experiences carry out in different schools involved in the project to test the programme and use the app to support the yoga-based practices with young people. In particular, it is part of the last phase in which teachers introduce yoga techniques in their daily classroom activities.

The pilots have a set of tasks focused on the evaluation of the HIPPOCAMPUS programme. The evaluation aims to provide empiric data to get a final version flexible enough to adapt to different contexts, mainly schools, across Europe. Although the app is considered part of the processes defined in the programme, it is not directly part of the evaluation methodology. For this reason, there is a need to carry out in parallel an evaluation focused on usability.

The usability study is carried out after launching the first public versions, both iOS and Android. The study combines heuristic techniques with experts and empirical methods with users. This work is focused on the first part of the usability study, the heuristic evaluation by experts in order to apply the heuristic rules defined by Nielsen [1]. The results of this evaluation have been used to develop a new minor version to be tested as part of the second part of the study, to collect empirical evidences.

The work is set out as follow. The second section introduces the multiplatform mobile app. The third section describes the methodology used to study the system's usability. The fourth describes the heuristic evaluation. The sixth section presents the discussion, and the last section concludes the work with its more significant contributions.

2 Yuva Yoga App

The HIPPOCAMPUS mobile app is one of the main outputs of the project. The programme and the app constitute an integral part of the approach proposed in the project. Although it is possible to introduce yoga practices without technological support, experience with other similar social software indicates that this helps to maintain interest and motivation [2–4], and recent research has indicated that it enriches and consolidates the participant's progress [5, 6]. In this sense, the app is a tool for supporting the programme and providing opportunities for participants to continue their practice at home, in addition to the sessions contained in the programme. The app also provides the resources of the programme, and the reminders continue suggestions for activities so that the content is regularly refreshed. A particular requirement was to make the app compatible with different types of devices, taking into account the heterogeneity of young people, also those in disadvantaged situations. For this reason, the app was developed for Android, the most popular smartphone operating system (OS) in the world, and iOS, the second most popular according to the global mobile OS market share report [7].

A native development approach was selected, to ensure a certain quality and the proper functioning of the app. In particular, the development was based on Backend as a service (BaaS), also known as a Mobile Backend-As-A-Service (MBaas), a service that provides a way to link applications to backend cloud storage while also providing features such as user management, push notifications or integration with social networking services [8]. There are two client applications with a cloud server that allows to manage security issues, storage (data and videos), push remote notifications, among other functionality required to ensure the proper functioning of the app. Figure 1 shows the main architecture components. Moreover, to support all offline content related to yoga practices, it was necessary to use local offline databases in client applications. It has been used Realm (in the Android client) and CoreData (in the iOS client).

Regarding the functionality, it is designed to be used to guide personal yoga practice with appropriate yoga sessions and activities. On the other hand, it is also focused on giving teachers, educators and yoga instructors a way to help their students maintain their practice between sessions. With it, you can recommend appropriate sequences of yoga activities for students, depending on their needs.

Fig. 1. Architecture based on Backend as a Service model

The main elements of the app are yoga activities that are postures (*asana*), meditations, reflections and breath (*pranayama*). Each activity has a description and a video without audio in which a yoga expert shows how to do it (Fig. 2a). Inside the app, there is a catalogue composed of more than 100 yoga activities. Although it is possible to have access to a single activity, usually they are organized in yoga sessions (Fig. 2b). The first public version has 15 sessions available. Finally, programs are related to the project aims, promoting the well-being of young people through the practice of a range of techniques derived from yoga. A program is a set of sessions to achieve a set of objectives, such as reduce stress, getting stronger and more relaxed, or waken the body.

The project raised the need to create communication spaces between teens and (yoga) teachers. In response to this need, the app has transferred the classroom concept to support the communication of teachers, educators or yoga instructors with young people. They can create a virtual space for each group of students that they work with and send them different kind of sessions that they must practice at home depending on their needs.

Regarding the language, the first public version was only in English while partners translate the contents and the interface to their languages: French, Italian, Norwegian and Spanish.

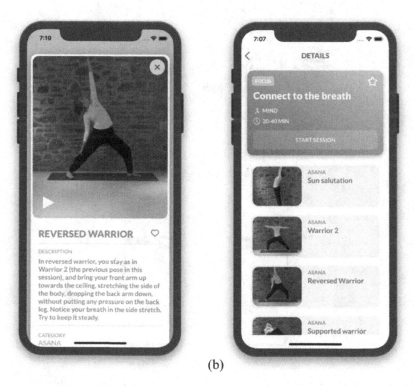

(a)   (b)

Fig. 2. Example of yoga activity interface (a) and yoga session interface (b). Source: screenshots from Yuva Yoga app.

3 Methodology

The heuristic evaluation is a usability engineering method for finding the usability problems in a user interface design so that they can be attended to as part of an iterative design process; it involves having a small set of evaluators examine the interface and judge its compliance with recognized usability principles (the "heuristics") [1, 9].

In this study, the heuristic evaluation was divided into two phases, one focused on iOS client and other on Android client. The following sections are dedicated to the results obtained after analysing the iOS version available in the App Store in January 2019.

3.1 Participants

The heuristic evaluation of iOS client was carried out by four experts, one woman and three men between 32 to 55 years old. None of the experts had used the Yuva Yoga app previously due it was available publicly less than one month before carried out the evaluation. One expert is involved in the HIPPOCAMPUS project, so it can contribute a different point of view than experts that are not familiar with project aims. One of them has participated in yoga sessions, one practices sports frequently, and the rest are sedentary. In addition to these characteristics, the criteria used to select the experts was based on their professional profiles:

- E1: A web developer, mainly focused on frontend, and researcher with ten years of experience whose main research line is the development of technological ecosystems for knowledge and learning processes management in heterogeneous contexts.
- E2: A Java developer expert and professor of human-computer interaction through a human-centred approach with more than 30 years of experience.
- E3: A professor with more than 20 years of experience in teaching and developing graphical user interfaces, from desktop applications for Linux and Windows to mobile apps for Android and iOS, with special emphasis on iOS apps during last 8 years.
- E4: A professor and researcher with 20 years of experience in human-computer interaction, and data visualization in different fields such as cinema and digital humanities.

Furthermore, all experts understand English and use an iOS smartphone daily. Although they are not yoga practitioners, this not influence the usability from a heuristic point of view. The usefulness of the app to practice yoga will be part of the empirical study with final users.

3.2 Instrumentation

The process to carry out the heuristic evaluation was provided to the experts through an electronic document accompanied by HIPPOCAMPUS project description and objectives of the app. A template was provided to the experts in order to get the reports to perform the heuristic evaluation. The template is composed of three fields to collect the name of the evaluator, the name of the tool evaluated and the operating system in which was carried out the evaluation; and a table with one row per each of the heuristic rules proposed by Nielsen [1] and two columns to give a value between 1 to 10, and comment the detected problems or explain the value assigned to the heuristic rule.

3.3   Study Design and Data Collection

The study was developed in three main blocks: preparation, research and evaluation. Each of these blocks has phases which define different tasks of the heuristic evaluation carried out in HIPPOCAMPUS project (Fig. 3).

Thus, the first block is preparation. It consisted of the pre-evaluation training. It has two phases focused on communication between experts and researchers. Only one expert had information about the project before carrying out the study, so the first phase was focused on share information about the project and the main scenarios to use the app. According to Nielsen [1] the evaluators decide on their own how they want to proceed with evaluating the interface, but in this process, the researchers provided a set of guidelines and a report template.

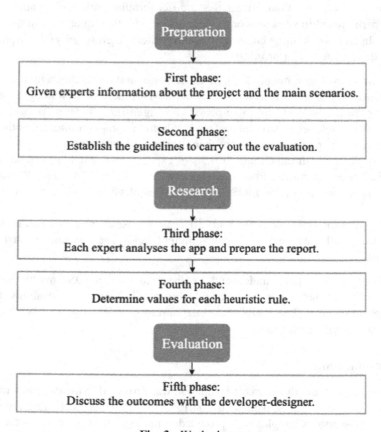

Fig. 3. Work phases

Once the desired information was shared, the second block was conducted. It was characterized by two phases associated with the evaluation itself. First, each expert reviewed the app and took notes about the usability problems detected. The heuristic rules used were those proposed by Nielsen [1]: (1) visibility of system status; (2) match between system and the real world; (3) user control and freedom; (4) consistency and standards; (5) error prevention; (6) recognition rather than recall; (7) flexibility and efficiency of use; (8) aesthetic and minimalist design; (9) helping users to recognize, diagnose, and recover from errors; (10) help and documentation. Data was collected through shared documents in Google Drive. During the second phase of this block, each expert reviewed the problems detected to each heuristic rule and assigned a value from 1 (major usability problems) to 10 (no usability problems).

This study did not have a phase in which each evaluation estimated the severity rating for each problem. On the other hand, they provided a global value for each heuristic and the responsibility to organize how to fix the problems fell in the developer associated with the project. Although a group analysis of the severity rating can provide an input to decide which problems should be solved before, in the project, it is not too much important the severity but the impact to use the app during the pilots.

Finally, in the third phase the heuristic reports were discussed with the developer and designer in order to organize the development of a set of one or more minor versions.

4 Heuristic Evaluation

Experts were identified by a number associated with the profiles provided in the methodology section (E1, E2, E3, E4). Table 2 summarizes the values for each heuristic rule, where 1 indicates that the expert detected a huge amount of serious problems and 10 no problems were found. The average of each heuristic was calculated in order to get a final value for each heuristic, so this value reflect where it is required to prioritize (Fig. 3).

Experts detected problems associated with all heuristic rules. The heuristics that presents the worst value is HR4 (*Consistency and standards*) with 7 points and HR10 (Help and documentation) with 7.5 points. In this sense, 16 usability problems were detected, most of them are inconsistences related to yoga terms and words used to talk about the contents. It should be pointed out one of the main problems identified by E1: "The classroom screens have different design than other parts of the app". This part was added to the app before launching the beta version; it is not designed at the same time than the rest of the app. Also, E3 identified an issue related to the good practices of iOS interaction, the configuration icon should be always available, not only inside one screen.

On the other hand, highlight the low values associated to most of the heuristic, HR8, HR2, HR7, HR3 and HR9, ordered from highest to lowest. All of them are over 9 points and have the lowest number of usability issues detected. Most of these problems are cosmetic or minor, but there is one major problem identified by E4 "The user can start and stop sessions at will. It seems there is no possibility to resume an interrupted session". This problem also was associated to HR4 by E1.

Finally, although it has not the worst value, the heuristic HR1 (*Visibility of system status*) has associated several usability problems with different severity rating according to the time needed to solve them. For example, a major problem is that "the user does not have a notion of the elements of a session. When the cards are piled, there is no way for the user to understand how many parts of the session have been completed and how many are remaining" or "it is not possible to control the videos player inside each activity"; a minor problem, "the visualization of activity stats in the profile is useful but if you want to know exactly which is the percentage of activities that you practice is not possible"; and a cosmetic problem, "it is not possible to know if an activity or session is flag as favorite without entering inside".

Table 2. Assigned values to each heuristic by each expert

Heuristic rule	E1	E2	E3	E4
HR1: Visibility of system status	9	10	6	8
HR2: Match between system and the real world	10	10	9	8
HR3: User control and freedom	10	10	8	8
HR4: Consistency and standards	3	10	8	7
HR5: Error prevention	7	10	10	7
HR6: Recognition rather than recall	9	8	10	7
HR7: Flexibility and efficiency of use	10	10	10	7
HR8: Aesthetic and minimalist design	9	10	10	10
HR9: Help users recognize, diagnose, and recover from errors	10	10	10	6
HR10: Help and documentation	5	10	10	5

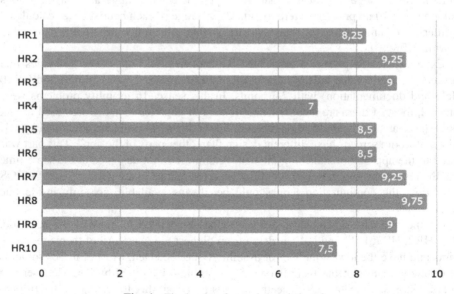

Fig. 4. Final value for each heuristic rule

5 Discussion

Each evaluator identified a set of usability problems, but it is important to highlight some differences between the evaluation carried out by each expert. Figure 4 shows a column graph was prepared in order to compare the values proposed by each expert. First, there are experts that have assigned pretty similar values for some heuristic. This occurs in HR2, HR7 and HR8, although there was no communication between experts during the evaluation.

On the other hand, the lower values and the more significant number of problems were detected by E4, the expert in human-computer interaction and data visualization. Conversely, E2 - Java developer and expert on human-centred design - discovered the lower number of usability problems and assigned the highest score.

It is essential to take into account the low score assigned to HR4 (*Consistency and standards*) by E1, a researcher and web developer mainly focused on the frontend. When the average is calculated, the difference disappears, but the new version of the mobile app should take into account this big difference. Most of the problems are cosmetic and minor usability issues, it is not required to much time to fix them. This evaluator is involved in the HIPPOCAMPUS project, so this experience could influence in the evaluation results.

Finally, there is other important difference between the values assigned by E2 and E3, and E1 and E4 in the HR10 (*Help and documentation*). Both experts agreed that there is not help information associated to the app, such as the meaning of "programs", "sessions", or a frequently asked questions section accessible through the app website (Fig. 5).

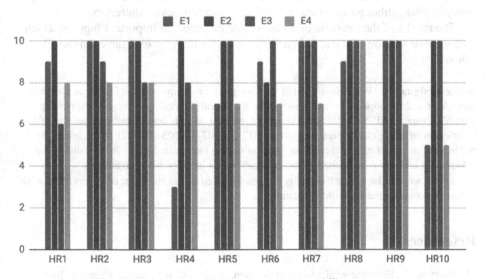

Fig. 5. Distribution of assigned values by usability experts

According to [10], in some areas, the perception of evaluators in using heuristic evaluation method is not consistent with the users' experience with a system. The problems detected by experts can help to improve the usability of the Yuva Yoga app, but it is also required to apply an empirical method to get information about the use of the app by the final users (teachers, yoga instructors, educators and young people).

6 Conclusions

The Yuva Yoga app aims to support teachers and educations to introduce yoga practices as part of school contexts. This app, available for iOS and Android, helps to keep yoga going between sessions. It is designed to be used to guide personal yoga practice with appropriate sessions and activities. Although the app is not associated directly to any yoga teachers, it is important to practice yoga under the supervision of yoga teachers. In this sense, yoga teachers can also use the app to help their students maintain their practice between sessions.

The usability evaluation of Yuva Yoga app combines heuristic techniques with experts and empirical methods with users. The present work is focused on the heuristic evaluation of Yuva Yoga for iOS. In particular, four experts were involved in the evaluation, all of them with different profiles although most are related to human-computer interaction field. More experts could be involved to get different perspective, but the information provided by this study will be completed with the final users' experience.

Although experts did not provide the severity rating for each usability problem detected, the low number of problems have been taken into account to develop a new minor version of the Yuva Yoga app. It is important to highlight that the heuristic evaluation for iOS has influenced in the Android client, because the functionality is pretty similar, although interfaces in iOS and Android have differences.

The results of the heuristic evaluation have provided an important input to develop a new minor version of the app, in order to improve the user experience in the pilots at schools.

Acknowledgments. With the support of the Erasmus+ Programme of the European Union in its Key Action 2 "Cooperation and Innovation for Good Practices. Strategic Partnerships for Youth". Project HIPPOCAMPUS (Promoting Mental Health and Wellbeing among Young People through Yoga) (Reference number 2017-2-ES02-KA205-009942). The content of this publication does not reflect the official opinion of the European Union. Responsibility for the information and views expressed in the publication lies entirely with the authors.

Authors would like to thank usability experts involved in the study for their contribution and support to conduct the heuristic evaluation.

References

1. Nielsen, J.: Heuristic evaluation. In: Nielsen, J., Mack, R.L. (eds.) Usability Inspection Methods, vol. 17, pp. 25–62. Wiley, Hoboken (1994)
2. Ba, S., Wang, L.: Digital health communities: the effect of their motivation mechanisms. Decis. Support Syst. **55**, 941–947 (2013)

3. Wong, C.A., Merchant, R.M., Moreno, M.A.: Using social media to engage adolescents and young adults with their health. Healthcare **2**, 220–224 (2014)
4. Asimakopoulos, S., Asimakopoulos, G., Spillers, F.: Motivation and user engagement in fitness tracking: heuristics for mobile healthcare wearables, vol. 4, p. 5 (2017)
5. Bakker, D., Rickard, N.: Engagement in mobile phone app for self-monitoring of emotional wellbeing predicts changes in mental health: MoodPrism. J. Affect. Disord. **227**, 432–442 (2018)
6. Holzinger, A., Dorner, S., Födinger, M., Valdez, A.C., Ziefle, M.: Chances of increasing youth health awareness through mobile wellness applications. In: Leitner, G., Hitz, M., Holzinger, A. (eds.) Proceedings of USAB 2010. LNCS, vol. 6389, pp. 71–81. Springer, Heidelberg (2010). https://doi.org/10.1007/978-3-642-16607-5_5
7. Statista - The Statistics Portal. https://www.statista.com/statistics/266136/global-market-share-held-by-smartphone-operating-systems/
8. Lane, K.: Overview of the backend as a service (BaaS) space. API Evangelist (2013)
9. Nielsen, J., Molich, R.: Heuristic evaluation of user interfaces. In: Proceedings ACM CHI 1990 Conference, Seattle, WA, 1–5 April, pp. 249–256. ACM, New York (1990)
10. Khajouei, R., Ameri, A., Jahani, Y.: Evaluating the agreement of users with usability problems identified by heuristic evaluation. Int. J. Med. Inf. **117**, 13–18 (2018)

Study of the Usability of the WYRED Ecosystem Using Heuristic Evaluation

Francisco J. García-Peñalvo ⓘ, Andrea Vázquez-Ingelmo ⓘ,
and Alicia García-Holgado$^{(\boxtimes)}$ ⓘ

GRIAL Research Group, Research Institute for Educational Sciences, University
of Salamanca, Salamanca, Spain
{fgarcia,andreavazquez,aliciagh}@usal.es

Abstract. The WYRED ecosystem is a composition of Open Source tools and
the people involved in the project, i.e., partners, stakeholders and young people
between the ages of 7 and 30 years. The main component of this ecosystem is
the WYRED Platform. The WYRED Platform relies on communities, which are
a set of interaction spaces where conversations and research projects are
developed. Every community has a person or persons in charge of its management, which are the so-called facilitators, and also a set of members, mainly
young people, interacting through discussion threads. The high levels of interaction required to accomplish the WYRED Platform's goals lead to the necessity of ensuring that the system is accepted by its final users. Given this need, a
preliminary study was performed to analyze the usability of the Platform from
the point of view of young people. However, it is also crucial that the ecosystem
meets usability criteria for the facilitators, due to their role of encouraging young
people to participate and serving as a guide in the conversations taking place
within communities, as well as in the research projects developed by the young
people about different topics related to the digital society. Therefore, a usability
study targeting facilitators was carried out to reach insights about how these
users value the system's usability. This usability study was performed through a
combination of two techniques, a heuristic analysis by experts and the Computer
System Usability Questionnaire to collect the experience of the real users.

Keywords: Digital society · Heuristic evaluation · Usability · European
project · Technological ecosystem · Software ecosystem · Youth

1 Introduction

There are different terms to talk about current society. The term Information Society
emerged after the Industrial Society, where technological development was boosted to
manage the information. Other authors use the Knowledge Society term as an alternative by some in academic circles to the Information Society [1]. According to
UNESCO, the two concepts are complementary; Information Society is the building
block for knowledge societies [2]. There is a third term used nowadays, Digital Society,
in order to put relevance on how digital technologies have an impact of digitalization
on today's society, culture and politics.

© Springer Nature Switzerland AG 2019
P. Zaphiris and A. Ioannou (Eds.): HCII 2019, LNCS 11590, pp. 50–63, 2019.
https://doi.org/10.1007/978-3-030-21814-0_5

The fast development of digital technologies during the last decades has influenced in all life aspects of the world population. The communication paradigm has undergone a major change; people can interact without temporal or spatial dependence; information and knowledge are available for most of the people at any time in any place. The way to do the shopping, watching TV, listening to music or finding a couple has changed. There are new jobs created by technological advances, such as data engineer, business intelligence analyst or security management specialist; and other jobs have evolved, such as delivery services, bankers or taxi drivers.

Although specific forms of technology uptake are highly diverse, a generation is growing up in an era where digital media are part of the taken-for-granted social and cultural fabric of learning, play, and social communication [3]. The young have emerged as a distinct social group, and with it, an understanding that they have a role in social change, as drivers of new behaviors and understandings [4], but half of them feel that their concerns are not taken into account.

In this context, WYRED project (https://wyredproject.eu) aims to provide a framework for research in which children and young people can express and explore their perspectives and interests concerning digital society, but also a Platform from which they can communicate their perspectives to other stakeholders effectively through innovative engagement processes [5]. WYRED [6] is a European project funded by Horizon2020 programme for three years, from November 2016 to October 2019, in which are involved institutions from Spain, Italy, United Kingdom, Turkey, Ireland, Belgium, Austria, and Israel.

From a technological point of view, WYRED provides a technological ecosystem to support the research framework and boost international conversations among young people from countries directly involved in the project. The ecosystem is composed of a set of Open Source tools and people involved in the project – partners, stakeholders and young people between 7 and 30 years –. The main component of the ecosystem in which the interaction among young people takes place is the WYRED Platform, a private and secure space in which young people can interact inside communities focused on different aspects of Digital Society [7]. Each community has a person or persons in charge of its management, which are the so-called facilitators, and also a set of members, mainly young people, interacting through discussion threads and creating research projects.

It is important than the ecosystem and, in particular, the Platform, being accepted by its final users (young people between 7 and 30 years, facilitators and stakeholders). Given this need, a preliminary study was performed to analyze the usability of the Platform from the point of view of young people [8, 9]. This study applied the System Usability Score [10] after a pilot experience in order to obtain insights about usability of the WYRED Platform. Some technical problems and usability issues detected by the participants during the study were solved before carried out the present work.

Although the main users are young people, facilitators have a crucial role in the ecosystem. They are responsible to engage young people in the international conversations about Digital Society inside the WYRED Platform. Also, they serve as a guide in the conversations taking place within communities, as well as in the research projects developed by the young people about different topics related to the Digital Society.

This work aims to describe the usability study targeting facilitators to reach insights about how these users value the WYRED Platform usability. This usability study was performed through a combination of two techniques. First, a heuristic analysis following the heuristics proposed by Nielsen [11] was executed with four experts with different profiles. This analysis was complemented with the results of the Computer System Usability Questionnaire (CSUQ) (version 3) [12] to collect the experience of real users. The combination of both techniques provides a comprehensive status of the WYRED Platform's usability, to fix any issue and improve its features and engagement.

The work is set out as follow. The second section introduces the WYRED Platform. The third section describes the methodology used to study system's usability. The fourth and fifth sections describes the heuristic evaluation and CSUQ results. The sixth section presents the discussion and the last section concludes the work with its more significant contributions.

2 The WYRED Platform

The Platform is organized in multicultural and interdisciplinary communities where young people can share their ideas and opinions about Digital Society and develop research projects with the support of facilitators from different European institutions and associations. The communities have different tools: forums to support conversations and coordinate research projects; a calendar to share dates and organize events or activities; and a form to give visibility to the research projects. Figure 1 shows a community example within WYRED Platform.

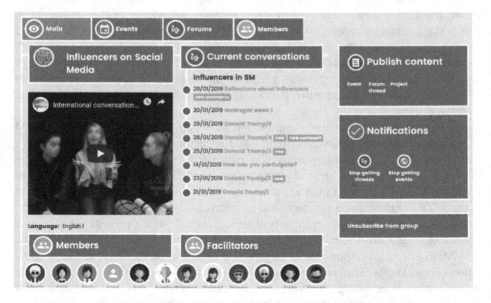

Fig. 1. Community to talk about influencers across Europe

One of its main innovations is the strong commitment to user privacy and security; it is designed as a safe space in which children and young people can express themselves freely. Users need an invitation to register within the Platform and children under 14 years old need parental consent in order to have access after finishing the registration. Besides, privacy policies are established to ensure the anonymity of young people, while allow collecting demographic information.

The users with a facilitator role inside a community are their managers, they can manage user's roles and subscriptions, moderate the conversations, publish research projects created by community members, and invite new members to the community both registered and non-registered users. Moreover, there are users that have the facilitator role in the whole Platform; these users can create new communities and invite new users to register in the Platform.

3 Methodology

3.1 Participants

The heuristic evaluation was carried out by four experts, two women and two men between 25 to 39 years old. Two experts had used the WYRED Platform as facilitators before analyzing it; the other two had access for two weeks before complete the analysis. The experts were selected according to their profiles:

- A Ph.D. student whose doctoral dissertation deals with customizable dashboards to analyze and visualize any kind of data.
- A web developer and researcher with ten years of experience whose main research line is the development of technological ecosystems for knowledge and learning processes management in heterogeneous contexts.
- A researcher with more than ten years of experience in multimodal human-computer interaction.
- A developer and researcher with more than ten years of experience focused on data visualization in different fields such as digital humanities or sports; and also with experience in teaching human-computer interaction in a Computer Science degree.

Regarding the second part of the usability study, a subset of facilitators was invited to answer the CSUQ. There are two profiles of facilitators in the Platform, young people that are involved in some communities as facilitators in order to coordinate, moderate and organize research projects; and members of the consortium of the project that is in charge to involve young people, create communities and manage them. Although there are more than 40 facilitators of both profiles, only those who used the Platform in the last six months were invited to answer the questionnaire. Finally, a total of 30 facilitators were invited to participate in the study and 28 answered the CSUQ. Most of the participants are female (64.3%), 21.4% are male, 3.6% selected another gender, and 10.7% decided not to provide this information. Regarding their profiles, 64.29% are young people (under 30 years old according to the European Union), and 35.71% are over 30 years old.

The WYRED Platform is an online tool so that it can be accessed from different environments. Most of the participants have used several browsers to access the Platform (Fig. 2), taken into account this; Chrome is the most used browser (89.29%). Regarding the device, 10.71% only through a smartphone, 39.29% only access through a computer, 42.86% used both (smartphone and computer), 3.57% access through tablet and computer, an finally 3.57% used all.

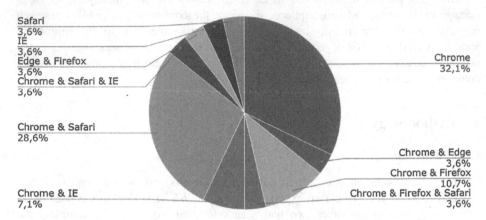

Fig. 2. Browsers used by participants

3.2 Instrumentation

The same template was provided to the experts in order to get the reports to perform the heuristic evaluation. The template is composed of two fields to collect the name of the evaluator, the name of the tool evaluated and a table with one row per each of the heuristic rules proposed by Nielsen [11] and three columns – heuristic rule, points from 1 to 10, and problems detected –.

The chosen tool to measure the usability of the WYRED Platform was the Computer System Usability Questionnaire (CSUQ). This questionnaire is an adaptation of the Post-Study System Usability Questionnaire (PSSUQ), except that the wording of the items does not refer to a usability testing situation [13]. There is three versions of the PSSUQ, the first version had 18 items, the second version was 19 and in the same version, Lewis found that three items did not contribute to reliability of the scale so the version 3 has only 16 items [14].

The CSUQ version 3 contents 16 items rated on a 1 to 7 Likert scale (from "strongly disagree" to "strongly agree", respectively) and a not applicable (N/A) option. The PSSUQ and CSUQ were originally designed to assess the perceived user satisfaction with IT systems; for this study, the term "system" or "computer system" was replaced by "application".

In addition to the 16 items of the CSUQ, a set of variables were also collected by the instrument. First, an open field was provided at the end of the CSUQ to let the users remark any relevant experience during the use of the Platform. Second, a set of questions related to the user environment where included: the language used in the

Platform, the role of the user, the devices used to access – computer, smartphone, tablet –, the operating systems – Android, Chrome OS, iOS, Linux, MacOS, Windows –, and the browsers (Chrome, Edge, Firefox, IE, Safari). Finally, a set of demographic variables: year of birth, gender, country, and any eye diseases of the user that could affect the experience.

The CSUQ was implemented using a customized version of LimeSurvey (https://www.limesurvey.org), an Open Source online statistical survey web application. The instrument was applied in English, but it is also available in Spanish [15].

3.3   Study Design and Data Collection

The heuristic evaluation was carried out by four experts. All experts had access as facilitators to the WYRED Platform in order to analyze all screens. Before starting the evaluation, a brief description of the project and the aim of the WYRED Platform was provided to the experts.

Each expert navigated through the application several times observing all the screens and detecting the usability problems. Each expert has assigned a value of 1 (serious problems) to 10 (no problems) to each heuristic and a brief description of the problems associated in order to justify this value. The heuristic rules used were those proposed by Nielsen [11]: (1) visibility of system status; (2) match between system and the real world; (3) user control and freedom; (4) consistency and standards; (5) error prevention; (6) recognition rather than recall; (7) flexibility and efficiency of use; (8) aesthetic and minimalist design; (9) helping users to recognize, diagnose, and recover from errors; (10) help and documentation. Data was collected through shared documents in Google Drive.

Regarding CSUQ, the participants involved in the study has experience using the Platform in real scenarios; it was not conducted scenario-based usability tests in a laboratory environment. To collect the data, a description of the study and the link to the questionnaire was sent by email to all the participants. Two reminders were sent before the deadline ended (one month after the first message).

4   Heuristic Evaluation

To show the results of the heuristic evaluation, each expert was identified by a number (E1, E2, E3, E4). Table 1 summarizes the values for each heuristic rule, where 1 indicates that the expert detected a huge amount of serious problems and 10 no problems were found. In order to get a final value for each heuristic, the average of each heuristic rule was calculated (Fig. 3).

Experts detected problems associated with all heuristic rules. The heuristic that presents the largest number of usability problems was HR4 (*Consistency and standards*) with 5.75 points. The lowest values assigned by E2, E3, and E4 are related to this heuristic; 19 different medium and serious problems were detected. It should be pointed out one of the main problems identified by E4: "there are two types of roles with a different set of permission using the same word: facilitator, one that is only moderator/community manager inside a community, and one that can create

Table 1. Assigned values to each heuristic by each expert

Heuristic rule	E1	E2	E3	E4
HR1: Visibility of system status	9	7	6	8
HR2: Match between system and the real world	9	10	9	7
HR3: User control and freedom	9	7	7	8
HR4: Consistency and standards	7	5	6	5
HR5: Error prevention	8	8	6	6
HR6: Recognition rather than recall	9	7	7	8
HR7: Flexibility and efficiency of use	8	7	7	7
HR8: Aesthetic and minimalist design	7	7	6	7
HR9: Help users recognize, diagnose, and recover from errors	9	7	6	6
HR10: Help and documentation	7	6	6	9

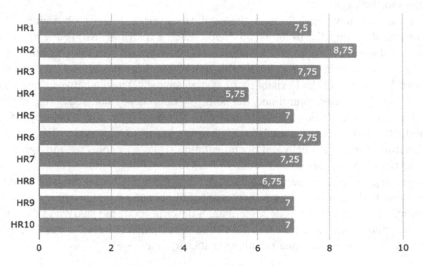

Fig. 3. Final value for each heuristic rule

communities." Also, E2 has detected a serious problem associated to accessibility standards, there are several problems related to color contrast in links (yellow over light grey) and menu (white over blue) according to Web Accessibility Guidelines, the standard proposed by W3C (https://www.w3.org/WAI/standards-guidelines/wcag/).

On the other hand, highlight the low values associated to help users, HR9 (*Help users recognize, diagnose, and recover from errors*) and HR10 (*Help and documentation*). The WYRED Platform has a help section with videos in English, but the application is multilingual, so the contents should be provided with subtitles. Moreover, the display of the content is not clear, the screen should be redesigned according to E1, and E3 indicates that the information is not accessible on demand in text format and there is not a FAQ to make the doubt resolution more straightforward. Also, there is a community for technical support but E2 and E4 comment that it is difficult to find and use it.

The lowest number of usability problems was detected in HR2 (*Match between system and the real world*) with an average of 8.75 points and 6 minor usability problems, one of them related to the concept facilitator, which needs more explanation according to E2 and E4. Regarding the other heuristics, most of the issues detected are minor and medium usability problems, but it is important to highlight several problems associated with search tools in community and projects sections. These problems were detected by E1, E2, and E3, although most of them have low priority to fix them, their combination generates one of the most significant problems. Some of them are:

- "When searching for public projects or communities, there is no straightforward manner of knowing which filter is currently applied" by E3. Associated to HR1.
- "The layout of the search tools is difficult to understand. The search button appears before the search field" by E2. Associated to HR4.
- "When searching for public communities, there are no autocompletion options" by E3. Associated to HR5.
- "It was difficult to find out how to add several tags to the different search bars shown in the Platform. The user has to manually input a comma after the first keyword to be able to insert the second one" by E1. Associated to HR7.

The number of problems identified by each expert is small but the combination of all of them provides an input to improve the WYRED Platform.

5   User Experience

5.1   CSUQ Questionnaire Results

A total of 28 persons answered the CSUQ questionnaire (version 3), which is an enough sample number for the purpose of this evaluation. The mean and a 95% confidence interval were computed for each CSUQ item answer, as well as for the overall and subscales' scores. The results were compared to the PSSUQ norms (Fig. 4) as previous studies indicated that the CSUQ and PSSUQ scales are comparable [14]. To properly compare the results, the PSSUQ norms were reversed, as their original scale indicates that lower values denote higher satisfaction (i.e., 1 means "strongly agree" and 7, "strongly disagree"). The following results were obtained regarding the system quality, information quality, interface quality and overall score:

- System quality: 4.87
- Information quality: 5.02
- Interface quality: 4.82
- Overall score: 4.92

To gain better understanding of these overall scores, each item mean value was also individually analyzed (Fig. 5). This analysis gives hints about the potential causes of the questionnaire overall results. The detailed results are listed in Table 2.

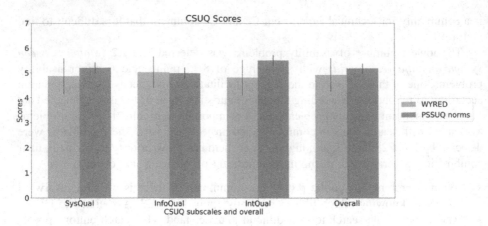

Fig. 4. Overall results regarding the CSUQ results compared to the PSSUQ norms identified in [16]. The overlapped lines represent the 95% interval.

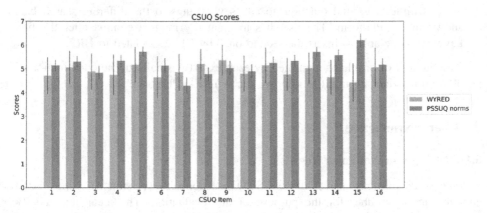

Fig. 5. Individual results of each CSUQ items compared to the PSSUQ norms. The overlapped lines represent the 95% interval.

The distribution of the given scores can be seen at Fig. 6. The figure shows the distribution of values of the CSUQ Likert scale. Through this representation it is possible to understand how the participants rated each item with less granularity.

Finally, as previously mentioned, a set of demographic and technical variables were collected in addition to the CSUQ items. With this data, the main goal is to check whether the employed device or software to access the Platform, the language or other demographic variables were correlated to the finally given CSUQ score.

The Fig. 7 shows the correlation among these variables with the different CSUQ items; yellow cells represent no correlation and more blue cells represent higher correlation. As presented in this figure, there is no relevant correlation among the demographic and technical variables and the CSUQ items, except for the birthdate and the use of the iOS operating system. Younger people and people using the Platform

Table 2. Summary of the CSUQ scores for the WYRED Platform (n = 28).

PSSUQ item/scale	Mean	SD	Margin of error	Confidence interval (95%)
Item 1	**4.71**	2.00	0.77	3.94–5.49
Item 2	**5.07**	1.80	2.05	4.37–5.77
Item 3	**4.89**	1.95	0.76	4.14–5.65
Item 4	**4.75**	2.02	0.85	3.90–5.60
Item 5	**5.18**	1.93	0.75	4.43–5.93
Item 6	**4.65**	2.26	0.88	3.78–5.53
Item 7	**4.86**	1.98	0.77	4.09–5.63
Item 8	**5.21**	1.64	0.64	4.57–5.84
Item 9	**5.37**	1.67	0.65	4.72–6.02
Item 10	**4.81**	1.94	0.75	4.06–5.57
Item 11	**5.16**	1.91	0.74	4.42–5.90
Item 12	**4.78**	1.78	0.69	4.09–5.47
Item 13	**5.04**	1.69	0.65	4.38–5.69
Item 14	**4.65**	1.87	0.73	3.93–5.38
Item 15	**4.43**	2.08	0.81	3.62–5.24
Item 16	**5.07**	2.09	0.81	4.26–5.88
SysQual	**4.87**	**1.88**	**0.73**	**4.15–5.60**
InfoQual	**5.02**	**1.62**	**0.63**	**4.39–5.64**
IntQual	**4.82**	**1.84**	**0.71**	**4.10–5.53**
Overall	**4.92**	**1.73**	**0.67**	**4.25–5.59**

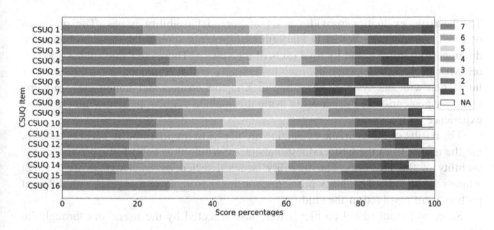

Fig. 6. Distribution of individual Likert values regarding each CSUQ item.

through iOS seem to rate better the Platform. However, this correlation is not very strong (around the 0.3–0.5 interval). Gender has no correlation with the CSUQ items, as previously demonstrated in [14], as well as the language, device and browser employed during the experience with the WYRED Platform.

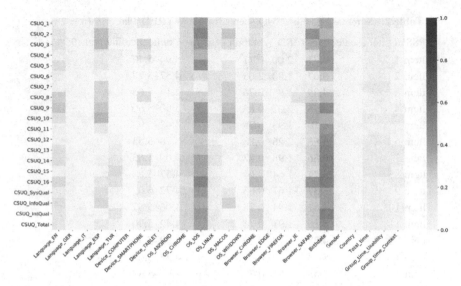

Fig. 7. Heat map showing the correlation among different variables. (Color figure online)

These analyses can be consulted in detain at https://github.com/AndVazquez/wyred-csuq-analysis [17].

6 Discussion

The heuristic evaluation provides a set of potential usability issues. The problems detected can affect the WYRED Platform usability, but sometimes these problems are different from those found by final users of the system. There are some studies focused on what problems detected by usability experts are experienced by users in their interaction with the system. According to Khajouei, Ameri and Jahani [18], in some areas, the perception of evaluators in using this method is not consistent with the users' experience with a system.

The results of the heuristic evaluation are useful to improve the WYRED Platform, but the results from the CSUQ questionnaire are required to get a full overview of the usability of the Platform. The usability issues detected by each expert are a small number of the existed usability problems, for this reason, several experts with different profiles were involved in the study.

Some of the identified problems were also detected by the users, not through the CSUQ questionnaire, but through informal comments provided during the activities that take place inside the WYRED Platform. In this sense, the priority to fix the problems will be defined according to final users, although the experts' opinion will be taken into account.

Regarding the user experience, one of the identified potential issues of the CSUQ questionnaire is the positive nature of the items' statements. The tone of every item elicits agreement (in contrast with the SUS questionnaire, in which positive items are intertwined with negative items [10, 19]), making the answering process more easy, but also being vulnerable to response bias, especially, acquiescence bias [20]. However, there were no evidence of response styles in the PSSUQ data [21], which is almost identical to the CSUQ items, only modifying the wording of the items given its non-lab nature [13].

The obtained results, compared to the PSSUQ norms, show acceptable values, although lower than the references. However, as indicated in [16], these norms are not specially suitable for direct assessment, given the fact that the data came from "a variety of sources that included different types of products at different stages of development and the performance of different types of tasks using systems that were available from the mid-1990s through the early 2000s". Nevertheless, the PSSUQ norms provide a useful reference to compare the obtained scores, and to reach insights about potential weaknesses of the tested Platform.

On the other hand, as presented in Fig. 3, taking as a neutral reference the 4 value, the CSUQ questionnaire responses are mostly positive.

The information quality items are the best-rated items, being even slightly higher than the norms above [16]. These results are directly related to the low number of usability issues associated with the appropriate feedback provided to the users (HR1), the use of real-world conventions such as communities or conversations (HR2), the clear support to undo and redo actions inside the Platform (HR3) and the instructions provided to use the tools (HR6).

The weakest values of the CSUQ questionnaire are related to items 14 ("I like using the interface of this application") and 15 ("This application has all the functions and capabilities I expect it to have"). The potential cause of these lower ratings is the fact that the Platform is still in development, explaining the lack of capabilities and interface maturity. Moreover, usability experts identified several problems associated with these items, in particular, the most significant number of usability issues are associated with the heuristic rule focused on consistency and standards (HR4). Also, during the heuristic evaluation, experts detected several problems related to the layout and the interface elements related to communities. Most of the activity inside the Platform takes place in the communities, so the problems associated with HR8 (*Aesthetic and minimalist design*) could be a potential cause of these lower ratings in the CSUQ.

No strong correlations were found regarding the employed devices or technologies to test the Platform, as well as regarding other demographic values. Only the birth date variable showed that younger people tend to rate better the Platform.

7 Conclusions

A usability evaluation of the WYRED Platform has been executed through two different methods. First, a heuristic evaluation was performed with four experts involved. To complete this information, an evaluation of the Platform using the CSUQ questionnaire was also performed to gain insights about the users' perceived usability of the system.

Having these two points of view of the Platform's usability helped to identify weaknesses of the WYRED interface and interaction methods by comparing them against a set of accepted usability principles (in this case, the Nielsen's Heuristics were chosen), and to identify usability-related issues from the users' perspective by asking a sample to complete the CSUQ questionnaire.

The experts involved in the heuristic evaluation were selected according to their problems in order to get different perspective although all of them has experience with usability issues. Each expert identified a small number of usability issues, but the combination of the results provides relevant information to develop a new version of the WYRED Platform in order to solve the different identified problems and provide a stable final version. It would be interesting to assess this new version through a user testing and a second heuristic evaluation.

Acknowledgments. This research was supported by the Spanish *Ministry of Education, Culture and Sport* under a FPU fellowship (FPU17/03276).

With the support of the EU Horizon 2020 Programme in its "Europe in a changing world – inclusive, innovative and reflective Societies (HORIZON 2020: REV-INEQUAL-10-2016: Multi-stakeholder Platform for enhancing youth digital opportunities)" Call. Project WYRED (netWorked Youth Research for Empowerment in the Digital society) (Grant agreement No. 727066). The sole responsibility for the content of this webpage lies with the authors. It does not necessarily reflect the opinion of the European Union. The European Commission is not responsible for any use that may be made of the information contained therein.

References

1. Burch, S.: Information society and knowledge society. In: Ambrosi, A., Peugeot, V., Pimienta, D. (eds.) Word Matters: multicultural perspectives on information societies. C&F Éditions, Caen (2005)
2. UNESCO: Towards Knowledge Societies. An Interview with Abdul Waheed Khan (2003)
3. Buckingham, D.: Youth, Identity, and Digital Media. The MIT Press, Cambridge (2007)
4. García-Peñalvo, F.J., Kearney, N.A.: Networked youth research for empowerment in digital society: the WYRED project. In: García-Peñalvo, F.J. (ed.) Proceedings of the Fourth International Conference on Technological Ecosystems for Enhancing Multiculturality (TEEM 2016), Salamanca, Spain, November 2–4, 2016, pp. 3–9. ACM, New York (2016)
5. García-Peñalvo, Francisco J., Durán-Escudero, J.: Interaction design principles in WYRED platform. In: Zaphiris, P., Ioannou, A. (eds.) LCT 2017. LNCS, vol. 10296, pp. 371–381. Springer, Cham (2017). https://doi.org/10.1007/978-3-319-58515-4_29
6. García-Peñalvo, F.J.: WYRED project. Educ. Knowl. Soc. **18**, 7–14 (2017)
7. García-Peñalvo, F.J., García-Holgado, A.: WYRED, a platform to give young people the voice on the influence of technology in today's society. A citizen science approach. In: Villalba-Condori, K.O., García-Peñalvo, F.J., Lavonen, J., Zapata-Ros, M. (eds.) Proceedings of the II Congreso Internacional de Tendencias e Innovación Educativa – CITIE 2018, Arequipa, Perú, November 26–30, 2018, pp. 128–141. CEUR-WS.org, Aachen (2019)
8. García-Peñalvo, Francisco J., García-Holgado, A., Vázquez-Ingelmo, A., Seoane-Pardo, Antonio M.: Usability test of WYRED platform. In: Zaphiris, P., Ioannou, A. (eds.) LCT 2018. LNCS, vol. 10924, pp. 73–84. Springer, Cham (2018). https://doi.org/10.1007/978-3-319-91743-6_5

9. García-Peñalvo, F.J., García-Holgado, A., Vázquez-Ingelmo, A., Seoane Pardo, A.M.: Analyzing the usability of the WYRED Platform with undergraduate students to improve its features. Universal Access in the information society in press (2019)
10. Brooke, J.: SUS-A quick and dirty usability scale. Usability Eval. Ind. **189**, 4–7 (1996)
11. Nielsen, J.: Heuristic evaluation. In: Nielsen, J., Mack, R.L. (eds.) Usability Inspection Methods, vol. 17, pp. 25–62. Wiley, Hoboken (1994)
12. Sauro, J., Lewis, J.R. Morgan Kaufmann, Boston (2012)
13. Lewis, J.R.: IBM computer usability satisfaction questionnaires: psychometric evaluation and instructions for use. Int. J. Hum.-Comput. Interact. **7**, 57–78 (1995)
14. Lewis, J.R.: Psychometric evaluation of the PSSUQ using data from five years of usability studies. Int. J. Hum.-Comput. Interact. **14**, 463–488 (2002)
15. Hedlefs Aguilar, M.I., de la Garza González, A., Sánchez Miranda, M.P., Garza Villegas, A. A.: Spanish adaptation of computer system usability questionnaire CSUQ. Revista Iberoamericana de las Ciencias Computacionales e Informática, vol. 4 (2015)
16. Sauro, J., Lewis, J.R.: Quantifying the User Experience: Practical Statistics for User Research. Morgan Kaufmann, Amsterdam (2016)
17. Vázquez-Ingelmo, A.: Code repository that supports the analysis of the usability test (through the CSUQ questionnaire) applied to the WYRED Platform (2019)
18. Khajouei, R., Ameri, A., Jahani, Y.: Evaluating the agreement of users with usability problems identified by heuristic evaluation. Int. J. Med. Informatics **117**, 13–18 (2018)
19. Brooke, J.: SUS: a retrospective. J. Usability Stud. **8**, 29–40 (2013)
20. Schriesheim, C.A., Hill, K.D.: Controlling acquiescence response bias by item reversals: the effect on questionnaire validity. Educ. Psychol. Meas. **41**, 1101–1114 (1981)
21. Salvendy, G.: Handbook of human factors and ergonomics. Wiley, Hoboken (2012)

An Experience Making Use of Learning Analytics Techniques in Discussion Forums to Improve the Interaction in Learning Ecosystems

Luis Magdiel Oliva Córdova[1(✉)], Héctor R. Amado-Salvatierra[2(✉)], and Klinge Orlando Villalba Condori[3(✉)]

[1] Universidad de San Carlos de Guatemala, Guatemala City, Guatemala
moliva@fahusac.edu.gt
[2] Universidad Galileo, Guatemala City, Guatemala
hr_amado@galileo.edu
[3] Universidad Nacional de San Agustín Perú, Arequipa, Peru
kvillalbac@unsa.edu.pe

Abstract. The study discussed in this paper had two principal objectives. The first objective was to stimulate engagement of participants in a virtual learning environment through the invitation to write an application essay on their motivation to be part of the learning experience. This first experience presented a positive reaction in terms of participation in a Massive Open Online Course (MOOCs). The second objective within a subset of the participants in the study was to evaluate the importance of using visual learning analytics to improve and enhance interaction in learning ecosystems, where the participant plays a main role and a visual aid could provide to the teachers different mental models and early alerts related to change of patterns or really low participation. For this, the work presents an analysis of the interaction developed between students and tutors in several types of forums implemented in a virtual course: presentation, doubts, debate, reflection, analysis. Finally, authors performed a comparative study using data and results gathered over two editions in an A/B testing configuration. The results in this study provide evidence that despite the inherent openness behind MOOCs, participants should be encouraged to have a commitment to finish the courses and the standalone discussion forums will not be the only element to consider. In fact the Social Network Analysis will play an important role in a learning ecosystem.

Keywords: Interaction analysis · Engagement · Learning ecosystem

1 Introduction

Interaction is nowadays a cornerstone aspect for knowledge acquisition and a revulsive that constantly creates a sense of engagement within a learning ecosystem. The discussion forums in virtual courses are well known activities that strategically planned, can generate spaces for the construction of knowledge and if they are supported by tools that allow the monitoring, measurement, collection, analysis, and visualization of

© Springer Nature Switzerland AG 2019
P. Zaphiris and A. Ioannou (Eds.): HCII 2019, LNCS 11590, pp. 64–76, 2019.
https://doi.org/10.1007/978-3-030-21814-0_6

interactions between students and tutors, thus then can provide inputs for the peda-gogical reorientation of the teaching and learning action. It is important to mention that Learning Analytics (LA) is highlighting as an emerging discipline, used in educational research, which makes use of technologies to understand the digital contexts in which learning takes place and is being used to provide pertinent information to improve the teaching and learning process. In this sense, virtual tutors can benefit from the appli-cation of LA to know the interactions that are being developed when they propose a forum for the presentation of the participants, discussion, reflection or debate of ideas. In this sense, the authors in [1] presents that there is strong evidence that in well-structured activities, knowledge-building processes reach higher levels of critical thinking, where students are able to establish and sustain cohesive groups. This justifies the need for a broader Social Network Analysis (SNA), taking into account the dis-cussion forums as the first kind of social interaction activity that is evolving into external tools as the different social networks applications available today. For this there is a need to have tools that are capable of providing real-time analysis for tutors and teachers from different external tools.

In this sense, it is worth mentioning that both concepts of Visual Learning Ana-lytics and Social Network Analysis are key factors to the success in Learning Ecosystems. Learning Ecosystems are known as a complex group of elements that interact and coexist with each other to enhance the teaching and learning process with the help of technology. The factor related to interaction is quite important based on the fact that the main actor will be the student. In [2], the authors emphasize that the human factor has a main role in the definition and development of the whole process inside a learning ecosystem and should be taken into account constantly in order to engage the participants in each of the learning activities.

This work presents a study that was carried out at the Faculty of Humanities, University of San Carlos at Guatemala. The purpose of this study is twofold. On the one hand the aim was to stimulate engagement of participants in a virtual learning environment through the invitation to write an application essay on their motivation to be part of the learning experience. This first experience presented a positive reaction in terms of participation in a Massive Open Online Course (MOOCs). The second objective within a subset of the participants in the study was to evaluate the importance of using visual learning analytics to improve and enhance interaction in learning ecosystems. For this, the work presents an analysis of the interaction developed between students and tutors in several types of forums implemented in a virtual course: presentation, doubts, debate, reflection, analysis.

This work is organized as follows: In Sect. 2 the related works on Learning Ecosystems and Visual Learning Analytics are presented. Next, Sect. 3 describes the experience, then Sect. 4 shows the most significant results that are complemented with a discussion and analysis. Finally, Sect. 5 presents the general conclusions and some proposals for future work.

2 Related Work

Learning Ecosystems are known as a complex group of elements that interact and coexist with each other to enhance the teaching and learning process with the help of technology. The factor related to interaction is quite important based on the fact that the main actor will be the student. In [2], the authors emphasize that the human factor has a main role in the definition and development of the whole process inside a learning ecosystem and should be taken into account constantly in order to engage the participants in each of the learning activities. Additionally, authors in literature [3] defined a learning ecosystem metamodel as a platform-independent model to define learning ecosystems based on an architectural pattern [4, 5].

Among the different components of a Learning Ecosystems it is important to mention the process related to Learning Analytics (LA). In a broader sense, one of the leading institutions in the field of Learning Analytics (LA) is the Society for Learning Analytics Research - SoLAR - which since 2011 is organizing events to disseminate scientific research related to the field of engineering and education in subjects related to LA and knowledge. In 2015, the 5th International Conference on Analysis and Knowledge of Learning (LAK 2015) was held. Nested to this event, the First International Workshop on Visual Aspects of Learning Analytics was organized in which a series of questions were discussed and analyzed in an interactive way, such as: What type of data are being visualized? What tools were used to clean up the data (if any)? Who are the visualizations for (student, teacher, manager, researcher, other)? How are the data visualized? What interaction techniques are applied? What tools, are libraries, data formats are being used for technical implementations? What workflow and what strategies are used to develop visualization? These questions represents and active research topic nowadays to provide dashboards and useful representations for the teachers to make decisions and improve the interaction among the participants. In this sense it is possible to affirm that Learning Analytics tools are key players in any learning ecosystem to provide valuable information to decision makers.

The term Learning Analytics has been discussed by several researchers; Siemens expresses that it is the use of intelligent data, data produced by the student and analysis models to discover information and social connections, and to predict and advise on learning [6]; Ferguson considers that LA is the use of Big Data to provide actionable intelligence for students and teachers [7] and Pardo et al. indicates that the LA allows tracking the fingerprints generated in virtual environments to develop practical recommendations that can support student learning [8]. The Society for Learning Analytics Research (SOLAR) at the first International Conference on Learning Analytics and Knowledge (LAK-11) concluded that LA can be considered as the measurement, collection, analysis and reporting of data about learners and their contexts in order to understand and optimize learning and the environments in which it occurs [9]. Also in the Horizon Report in 2016, LA was defined as an educational web analytics application aimed at a learner profile, a process of collecting and analyzing data on the individual interaction of learners with online learning activities [10].

It is evident from literature that in summary Learning Analytics aim to improve the learning processes that are developed in contexts mediated by technology, empowering pedagogical interventions in order to measure, compile, analyze and understand the actions of the tutor and student in their contexts. In other words, LA are based in a systematic process that makes use of digital learning registers to determine the pedagogical and didactic actions required in educational contexts and thus improve learning [11].

Authors in [1] present a model of analysis of educational data based on visual analytics, learning analytics and academic analytics. By means of a system called VeLA that allows analysis of exploratory and confirmatory data, in interaction with the information obtained from a typical learning management system and present them through different graphs. In the scope of a Learning Ecosystem, LA represented by dashboards or visual aids to the stakeholders enhance the overall learning experience. Additionally, authors in [1] highlight that the goal of this techniques is to help users discover unexpected and surprising anomalies, changes in patterns and relationships that are then evaluated to develop new ideas. Overall these visual features make it possible to obtain a mental model of complex data and new knowledge [1].

Considered as a branch of learning analytics, social network analysis is the actual procedure allowing the researchers to study interactions and relations between individuals in a social network [12]. Despite the importance of SNA in learning environments, authors emphasize [12] that there is a clear lack of this feature in most of the current Virtual Learning Environments that make part of a Learning Ecosystem. Related to social networks it is possible to identify the discussion forums in the virtual courses as key elements that are activities that strategically planned can generate spaces for the construction of knowledge and supported by tools that allow the monitoring, measurement, collection, analysis, and visualization of interactions between students and tutors. Forums can provide inputs for the pedagogical reorientation of the tutorial action. Authors in literature describe interesting experiences using LA to identify the influence of leadership on the academic performance of work teams [13], perfectly applied to the scenario of forums. Authors also presented a Comprehensive Training Model of the Teamwork Competence with positive findings [14, 15]. In this sense, virtual tutors can benefit from the application of LA to know the interactions that develop when they propose a forum for the presentation, discussion, reflection and debate of ideas.

In terms of engagement, authors [16] have proposed several strategies to create a sense of belonging and motivation to take part of Massive Open Online Courses (MOOCs), that in the last year are being part of a complex Learning Ecosystem with high drop-out rates and a beginning work to be accessible to all [17, 18].

Within the described works it can be valued that systems and tools have been created for the application of LA in virtual courses learning activities; complex systems supported in the mining of educational data and tools that can be considered complements of existing educational platforms. In addition, it can be determined that these tools can facilitate the work of the virtual tutor in terms of his pedagogical intervention, providing information to be visualized and analyzed in a timely manner.

3   Experience Description

Virtual Learning Environments, have opened new possibilities for the collection of digital records of learning through user interactions in environments, forums, resources, activities, content, among others. In formal online learning contexts, it is well known that the interaction, participation, social exchange and discourse-based knowledge building processes occur essentially in the course forums as the main communication system [19].

There are many advantages to using forums in a virtual course, but one of them is that it is a resource that provides a space for constant feedback from a group as knowledge is exchanged. Unlike an individualized task, forums constitute opportunities for the development of critical thinking through collaborative learning [19]. It is worth to notice the work of Salmon [20] describing a five-stage model for a structured framework that gradually constructs on participants' previous experience. In the different stages the tutor makes use of different activities and tools to guide the student to achieve the learning objectives. It is possible to mention the following stages [20]: Access and motivation, online socialization, information exchange, knowledge construction and development. In this sense, it is important to mention that the social interaction plays a worthwhile role in the whole process in a learning ecosystem.

Thinking about the first stage: "Access and motivation", the scenario that the Massive Open Online Courses is presenting nowadays represents high drop-out rates and some strategies should be prepared to overcome this issue. For this, the first objective of this work envisages to ask to the students a motivation essay in order to be enrolled in the course. This experience will compare the results from two groups.

The Learning Analytics applied to the forums makes it possible to identify the interactions that occur in a virtual course [19], the frequency of participation, as well as to detect patterns associated with social exchange and knowledge management. These digital learning records can be obtained with the use of LA tools focused on data visualization.

The purpose of the second part of the study was to analyze the interaction developed between students and tutors in the types of forums implemented in a virtual course and for this purpose, the Forum Graph tool was applied, which allowed innovation through visualizations and highlighted situations to be improved in virtual tutoring.

As mentioned above, the application of LA tools in virtual course forums can provide relevant information for pedagogical moderation and intervention and peer participation. To carry out the study, two virtual courses were selected, implemented in the Virtual Learning Environment and structured in five learning modules that were developed during five weeks. Each course was prepared with learning content and presented three discussion spaces: technical forum, social forum and academic forums. For this experience Forum Graph was applied as a Learning Analytics - LA - tool for the visualization of intervention actions from the participants.

The research method used was formulated under a quasi-experimental design; because it allowed observing the variables and describing them as they are presented in their natural, cross-sectional environment; because it was done in a certain time and space, with a mixed approach; because digital records of learning were obtained from the Virtual Learning Environment where qualitative and quantitative information was retrieved from the educational event through the forums, and with a descriptive scope; because it allowed describing the context and situations based on the application of LA tools in the types of forums used in the virtual course. On the other hand there was a descriptive scope; because it allowed describing the context and situations based on the application of LA tools in the types of forums used in virtual courses. The process was carried out through six phases: preparation, design, development, analysis, intervention and evaluation, based on the principles of the ADDIE Instructional Design Model [21].

For this experience, regarding the typology of forums, forums have been developed for presentation, doubts, debate, reflection, analysis, cafeteria, etc. [22]. Table 1 presents the classification of forums in three types: Technical, Social and Academic.

Table 1. Virtual forums classification

Classification	Characterization	Purpose
Technical forum	Support and maintenance	Report technical problems
Social forum	Coffee shop	Exchanging ideas outside the course – Off-topic
Academic forum	QA	Share doubts about the proposed activities
	Debate	Discuss an idea
	Reflection	Reflect on theories or events
	Resolution	Raising a solution to a case or problem

The process was carried out through six phases: preparation, design, development, analysis, intervention and evaluation, based on the principles of the ADDIE Model [21] as follows:

Preparation: A review of the internal and external tools of the Virtual Learning Environment to apply Learning Analytics in the forums was carried out, as well as the course planning, the determination of the moments for the development of forums, the bases for the call and the registration form.

Design: In this phase the authors worked on the instructional design of the course, the writing of the forums, the prototyping, graphic elements, multimedia and interactive resources. An initial training was also given to all interested parties who had pre-enrolled in the course, on the use of the educational platform and forms of communication.

Development: With the design of the elements of the course the authors proceeded to the implementation and evaluation of the activities and educational resources in the environment, as well as to the configuration and installation of the plugin selected for the application, in this case Forum Graph. In this phase the course started.

Analysis: After each week of the course, the Forum Graph tool was applied to visualize the interventions of the participants in the support forum, social forum and academic forums. After having the graphs of the forums, the authors proceeded to identify the nodes [23] where the participation took place and to detect the participants with little participation, for decision making.

Intervention: After analyzing the graphics of the forums, the next phase was to make pedagogical interventions through external tools to mediate learning and motivate the participants, in addition some academic forums were adapted to achieve greater interaction.

Evaluation: Finally, in the last week of the experience, the tutors proceeded to verify the trajectory in the participation of the forums and the identification of the forums with greater participation and pedagogical intervention.

4 Results and Discussion

For the first part of the study an A/B testing process was conducted. The course related to soft skills with a focus on technology was open for enrollment. A first phase with a regular enrollment was conducted and then for the second phase the students had to write a short essay expressing the intention and interest to take the course as well as the motivation and time that they will devote to the course.

Using the data of the two phases, information related to the following variables was compiled for each learning experience:

- EP Enrolled participants: indicates the number of participants registered for the learning experience.
- P0 Students that never logged in: indicates the number of the enrolled participants that did not visit the virtual learning environment to begin with the learning experience.
- P1 Students with more than one log in: indicates the number of participants that started the online training course.
- P2 Active students with at least one learning activity submitted.
- P3 Active students that completed half of the learning experience.
- AP Total of approved students.

Another set of variables was defined based on the above data sets in order to have rates for comparisons between groups and to expand the scope of the study:

- P1vEP: This variable indicates the relation expressed from the number of enrolled participants and the number of participants with more than one login. This rate indicate the amount of participants that really started with the learning experience. The aim of this rate is to have rough estimate of real participation in order to have a better resources planning and to encourage student's commitment.
- APvP1: This variable indicates the relation expressed from the number of participants that finished and approved the learning experience divided by the number of students that started with the learning experience.
- APvP2: This variable indicates the relation expressed from the number of participants that finished and approved the learning experience divided by the number of

students with at least one learning activity completed. In MOOC experiences, authors in literature affirm that a group of students enroll to a course for curiosity reasons and to have a sneak-peek of the learning contents but they do not have the intention to complete the course. The aim of this rate is to identify sustained engagement from students, based on the completion of at least one learning activity.

- APvP3: This variable indicates the relation expressed from the number of participants that finished and approved the learning experience divided by the number of students that completed half of the learning experience.

Table 2. Comparison between identified variables for the first experience

Country/Edition	EP	P0	P1	P2	P3	AP
Guatemala	401	55	346	218	117	77

Edition	P1vEP	APvP1	APvP2	APvP3
Guatemala	86%	22%	35%	62%

The identified variables are: P1vEP (rate between students with more than one login and enrolled participants); APvP1 (rate between total of approved and students with more than one login); APvP2 (rate between total of approved and students with at least one activity); APvP3 (rate between total of approved and students that completed half of the training).

From the comparison presented in Table 2, specifically from the P1vEP rate, it is interesting that in average, 13.9% of the participants never started the course. On the other hand, it is really positive that the approval rate of students that completed half of the training is 61.9%. Overall, the approval rate of the first experience was 19.20%.

Table 3. Comparison between identified variables for both learning experience

Edition	P1vEP	APvP1	APvP2	APvP3
Second group (experimental)	94%	56%	61%	69%
First group (control)	86%	22%	35%	62%
Difference	+8	+34	+26	+7

Comparison rate between identified variables is presented Table 3 this group represented the students that completed an essay to be enrolled in the course showing a positive increase in the amount of students that finished and approved the course. Finally students had different opportunities to provide additional feedback about their perceptions and attitude towards the learning experience. In the anonymous survey there was an open question in which students were asked to provide any comment or suggestion. In general we get numerous positive responses.

The second part of the study was conducted by students from the Faculty of Humanities who represented twenty cities in the country of Guatemala: Sololá, Guatemala, Petén, Sacatepéquez, Alta Verapaz, Baja Verapaz, Jutiapa, Jalapa, Retalhuleu and Chiquimula. This was a subset of the second group of participants.

The total number of participants in this particular experience were 55. The group of participants was made up of 76% women and 24% men, ranging in age from 18 to 25 years (17%), 26 to 35 years (52%), 36–45 years (25%) and 46–55 years (6%), who voluntarily decided to participate in the course. The moderation of the course was led by five virtual tutors.

For the Technical Forums developed to raise and resolve doubts related to the use of the platform the Forum Graph presented single node answers. Figure 1 presents the visual analysis from the Learning Analytics tool showing the participation of the tutors as an active player solving particular questions. In this forum the presence of singular nodes is shown and it is evident that there was no need of a further discussion related to the technical support.

The Social Forums, representing the online socialization phase was depicted as a Coffee Shop forum developed to generate a space for free dialogue and the creation of social links among the participants.

Figure 2 presents a visual representation of the active interaction among participants. In this experience more than 80% of the participants took part of the social threads. It is worth noting that the independent comments are also considered as significant contributions within the forum, however, not with the expected transcendence.

The academic forums developed to raise doubts, debate, reflect and give solution to a particular case presented a high volume of participation throughout the course.

Figure 3(a) shows a degree graph indicating that half of the participants in the course raised doubts about a topic during the course. The interaction between the participants is interesting because they were collaboratively helping each other. The graph shows the number of participants and the diameter of each node is proportional to the number of interventions. In this case the central node represents the leadership of the tutor in front of the statements made by the students.

Figure 3(b) shows the participation of more than 85% of the learners who answered the question presented by a tutor, it is possible to identify the horizontal interaction and debate from the students with other participants generating communication nodes. Figure 4(a) shows the participation of the 100% of the participants given that it was an assessment to contribute their opinion. Finally, Fig. 4(b) shows the active participation of the students. It is also visualized that the participation of tutors is lower than in previous forums all based on the type of learning activity designed.

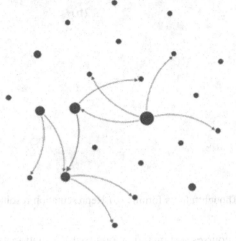

Fig. 1. Visual analytics of technical forum

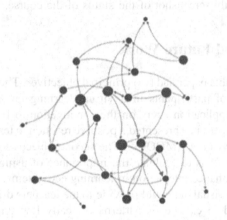

Fig. 2. Visual representation of social forum

(a)   **(b)**

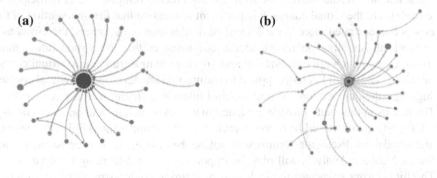

Fig. 3. (a) Visual representation QA forums (b) Discussion forum representation

(a)   **(b)**

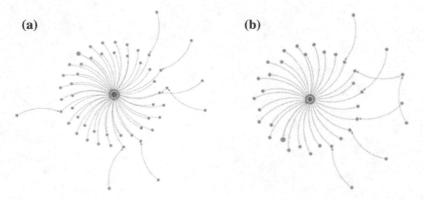

Fig. 4. (a) Thoughtfulness forums (b) Representation resolution forums

The tutors of the courses expressed a positive evaluation on the importance of having the visual aid to help them to make smart decisions to reintroduce learners with troubles and have a daily screenshot of the status of the course.

5   Conclusions and Future Work

The study discussed in this paper had two principal objectives. The first objective was to stimulate engagement of participants in a virtual learning environment through the invitation to write an application essay on their motivation to be part of the learning experience. This first experience presented a positive reaction in terms of participation in a Massive Open Online Course (MOOCs). The second objective within a subset of the participants in the study was to evaluate the importance of using visual learning analytics to improve and enhance interaction in learning ecosystems, where the participant plays a main role and a visual aid could provide to the teachers different mental models and early alerts related to change of patterns or really low participation. It can be concluded that the experience of innovation applying Learning Analytics in forums was satisfactory, it allowed to identify that the academic forums - reflexive, the social forums and the academic - resolutive forums, were the ones that developed greater participation in the students of the virtual course. It is pertinent to mention that the intervention of the tutors was demonstrated more in the forums of doubts than in the others; therefore, as a future work an investigation related to the competences that the virtual tutors must possess to carry out a work of follow-up and appropriate moderation in a virtual course can be raised. The use of LA tools applied to forums that are developed in virtual courses can highlight the interventions of students and tutors in different learning scenarios.

The results in this study provide evidence that despite the inherent openness behind MOOCs, participants should be encouraged to have a commitment to finish the courses and the standalone discussion forums will not be the only element to consider. In fact the Social Network Analysis will play an important role in a learning ecosystem.

The future work envisages the inclusion of a strong component based on different social network tools, not only discussion forums.

References

1. Gómez-Aguilar, D.A., García-Peñalvo, F.J., Therón, R.: Analítica Visual en eLearning. El Profesional de la Información **23**, 236–245 (2014)
2. García-Holgado, A., García-Peñalvo, F.J.: Human interaction in learning ecosystems based on open source solutions. In: Zaphiris, P., Ioannou, A. (eds.) LCT 2018. LNCS, vol. 10924, pp. 218–232. Springer, Cham (2013). https://doi.org/10.1007/978-3-319-91743-6_17
3. García-Holgado, A., García-Peñalvo, F.J.: The evolution of the technological ecosystems: an architectural proposal to enhancing learning processes. In: García-Peñalvo, F.J. (ed.) Proceedings of the First International Conference on Technological Ecosystems for Enhancing Multiculturality, TEEM 2013, 14–15 November 2013, Salamanca, Spain, pp. 565–571. ACM, New York (2013)
4. García-Holgado, A., García-Peñalvo, F.J.: Architectural pattern to improve the definition and implementation of eLearning ecosystems. Sci. Comput. Program. **129**, 20–34 (2016). https://doi.org/10.1016/j.scico.2016.03.010
5. García-Holgado, A., García-Peñalvo, F.J.: A metamodel proposal for developing learning ecosystems. In: Zaphiris, P., Ioannou, A. (eds.) LCT 2017. LNCS, vol. 10295, pp. 100–109. Springer, Cham (2017). https://doi.org/10.1007/978-3-319-58509-3_10
6. Siemens, G.: What is Learning Analytics (2010). http://www.elearnspace.org/blog/2010/08/25/what-are-learning-analytics/. Accessed 10 Mar 2011
7. Ferguson, R.: Learning Analytics: answering the FAQ's. Retrieved from Open University (2014). http://es.slideshare.net/R3beccaF/learning-analytics-fa-qs
8. Pardo, A., Jovanovic, J., Dawson, S., Gašević, D., Mirriahi, N.: Using learning analytics to scale the provision of personalised feedback. Br. J. Educ. Technol. **50**, 128–138 (2017)
9. Ferguson, R.: Learning analytics: drivers, developments and challenges. Int. J. Technol. Enhanc. Learn. **4**(5/6), 304–317 (2012)
10. Horizon Report (2016). http://cdn.nmc.org/media/2016-nmc-horizon-report-he-EN.pdf
11. Oliva-Córdova, L.M., Amado-Salvatierra, H.R., Monterroso, L.: El potencial de aplicar Analíticas de Aprendizaje en Guatemala, creación de una comunidad para desarrollar la investigación educativa en la era digital (2018)
12. Filvà, D.A., García-Peñalvo, F.J., Forment, M.A.: Social network analysis approaches for social learning support. In: Proceedings of the Second International Conference on Technological Ecosystems for Enhancing Multiculturality, pp. 269–274. ACM (2014)
13. Fidalgo-Blanco, Á., Sein-Echaluce, M.L., Esteban-Escaño, J., García-Peñalvo, F.J., Conde, M.Á.: Learning analytics to identify the influence of leadership on the academic performance of work teams. In: García-Peñalvo, F.J. (ed.) Proceedings of the Fourth International Conference on Technological Ecosystems for Enhancing Multiculturality, TEEM 2016, 2–4 November 2016, Salamanca, Spain, pp. 377–382. ACM, New York (2016)
14. Fidalgo-Blanco, Á., Sein-Echaluce, M.L., García-Peñalvo, F.J., Conde-González, M.Á.: Using learning analytics to improve teamwork assessment. Comput. Hum. Behav. **47**, 149–156 (2015)
15. Conde, M.Á., Hérnandez-García, Á., García-Peñalvo, F., Séin-Echaluce, M.L.: Exploring student interactions: learning analytics tools for student tracking. In: Zaphiris, P., Ioannou, A. (eds.) LCT 2015. LNCS, vol. 9192, pp. 50–61. Springer, Cham (2015). https://doi.org/10.1007/978-3-319-20609-7_6
16. Hernández, R., Amado-Salvatierra, H.R.: Towards full engagement for open online education. A practical experience for a MicroMaster. In: Delgado, K.C., Jermann, P., Pérez-Sanagustín, M., Seaton, D., White, S. (eds.) EMOOCs 2017. LNCS, vol. 10254, pp. 68–76. Springer, Cham (2017). https://doi.org/10.1007/978-3-319-59044-8_8

17. Batanero, C., Karhu, M., Holvikivi, J., Otón, S., Amado-Salvatierra, H.R.: A method to evaluate accessibility in e-learning education systems. In: 2014 IEEE 14th International Conference on Advanced Learning Technologies (ICALT), pp. 556–560. IEEE (2014)
18. Martin, J.L., Amado-Salvatierra, H.R., Hilera, J.R.: MOOCs for all: evaluating the accessibility of top MOOC platforms. Int. J. Eng. Educ. 32(5), 2274–2283 (2016)
19. Gottardo, E., Noronha, R.V.: Social networks applied to distance education courses: analysis of interaction in discussion forums. In: Proceedings of the 18th Brazilian Symposium on Multimedia and the Web, pp. 355–358. ACM (2012)
20. Salmon, G.: E-Tivities: The Key to Active Online Learning. Routledge, Abingdon (2013)
21. Molenda, M.: In search of the elusive ADDIE model. Perform. Improv. 42(5), 34–36 (2003)
22. Silveira, I.F., Villalba-Condori, K.O.: An open perspective for educational games. J. Inf. Technol. Res. (JITR) 11(1), 18–28 (2018). https://doi.org/10.4018/JITR.2018010102
23. Vera, J., Villalba-Condori, K., Castro Cuba-Sayco, S.: Modelo de sistema de recomendaciónbasadoen el contexto a partirdclanálisis de códigoestático para el desarrollo del Pensamiento Computacional: Caso de Programación Web. Educ. Knowl. Soc. (EKS) 19(2), 103–126 (2018). https://doi.org/10.14201/eks2018192103126

User-Centered Research and Design
of a K-5 Digital Literacy Curriculum

Jennifer Palilonis[✉]

Ball State University, Muncie, IN 47306, USA
Jageorge2@bsu.edu

Abstract. A research team engaged in a user-centered research and development approach to the creation of "Professor Garfield's 21st Century Literacy
Curriculum," a comprehensive, web-based tool for K-5 teachers. This process
consisted of a four-phase approach that included thorough exploration of the
state-of-the-art in digital literacy tools, a survey of K-5 teachers designed to
understand their technology use and perceptions of digital literacy, design
thinking and empathy research with more than 30 K-5 teachers, and summative
user experience testing with teachers from across the country. This approach
illuminated key requirements for an interactive system that supports digital
literacy instruction, as well as the primary factors that motivate teachers to adopt
new online teaching tools.

Keywords: Digital literacy · User-centered design · E-learning

1 Introduction

Although K-5 students have more access to technology than ever before, few resources
exist that provide teachers with a clear definition of digital literacy, help them
understand how to integrate digital literacy instruction in their classrooms, and allow
them to easily and effectively build digital literacy lesson plans for their students. As
such, digital literacy pedagogy is still relatively undefined and inconsistently executed.
This is largely due to barriers teachers face in integrating technology in the classroom,
including their personal comfort and skill with technology [3], access to professional
development associated with technology use [1], and skepticism about the effectiveness
of technology in the classroom [7]. Although 90% of American teachers recognize the
importance of digital literacy instruction, more than half feel underprepared to implement it in the classroom [12].

A number of online teaching and learning tools exist that offer standards-based
online curriculum [11] or digital literacy lesson plans, activities, games, and videos [5].
However, these tools often fail to provide a comprehensive approach to instruction that
recognizes the complex path to digital literacy. Instead, they often focus on one or two
components of digital literacy, such as using the Internet or e-safety or finding credible
information online. Others fail to address digital literacy at all, assuming instead that
the mere act of using the Internet is enough to effectively engage today's "digital
natives." Moreover, most existing web- or app-based tools fail to provide teachers with

© Springer Nature Switzerland AG 2019
P. Zaphiris and A. Ioannou (Eds.): HCII 2019, LNCS 11590, pp. 77–88, 2019.
https://doi.org/10.1007/978-3-030-21814-0_7

support for effectively implementing them in the K-5 curriculum [8]. As a result, students and teachers alike are left dramatically underserved.

This paper describes, discusses, and illustrates a user-centered research and development approach to "Professor Garfield's 21st Century Literacy Curriculum," a web-based tool created at Ball State University in collaboration with the Professor Garfield Foundation. This novel curriculum is presented as a comprehensive, web-based tool that provides K-5 teachers with (1) content to advance their conceptual understanding of digital literacy; (2) customizable, standards-based, grade-appropriate digital literacy exercises for young learners; (3) lesson plans and supplemental instructional materials; (4) a learning management system that allows teachers to track students' progress toward digital literacy; and (5) a dashboard on which teachers can create and design their own digital literacy lessons.

2   Background

In the late 1990s, Garfield creator Jim Davis began to think about how Garfield's history as a proponent of early childhood literacy might translate in the digital world. Davis soon came upon the idea of the Professor Garfield learning portal and the Professor Garfield Foundation (PGF), a non-profit educational collaboration between Paws, Inc. (the global headquarters for Garfield the Cat) and Ball State University in Muncie, Indiana. Launched in 2004, this collaboration led to the development of professorgarfield.com, a nationally recognized leader in innovative digital learning content with a primary emphasis on children's literacy and creative expression.

However, the national dialog about literacy education has evolved to include the successful use of digital tools for meaning making in online and digital environments. Thus, PGF has begun to explore how the Professor Garfield website might effectively reach beyond traditional notions of literacy by fostering literacy skills central to a learner's success in the digital age.

It is also important to note that although today's students have grown up with technology, digital literacy is not innate. Those skills must be taught incrementally over time through age- and grade-level appropriate methods, just like other subjects. In this context, being digitally literate is the ability to make and share meaning in different modes and formats; to create, collaborate, and communicate effectively in digital environments; and to understand how and when digital technologies can best support these processes [6].

However, research shows that although most teachers understand that technology integration is important to student success, more than half do not feel prepared to use technology in their classrooms. According to Samsung VP Ted Brodheim, "With the increasing popularity of Chromebooks, tablets, interactive whiteboards and apps in classrooms today, it's evident that technology is a critical tool for today's learners. However, our new research highlights that teachers are not yet receiving full support to harness the power of technology and truly transform classroom learning into a 21st century experience" [12].

Thus, the Center for Emerging Media Design & Development at Ball State University partnered with PGF to develop a novel set of online learning tools to support

K-5 teachers and students in their digital literacy efforts. "Professor Garfield's Digital Literacy Curriculum" is grounded in a framework [6] that emphasizes eight key components of digital literacy: functional meaning making, creativity, critical thinking, cultural and social understanding, collaboration, finding and selecting information, effective communication, and e-safety. Moreover, a user-centered approach to the project design identified key requirements to ensure that the Professor Garfield site meets the functional and practical needs of K-5 teachers.

3 Project Design

The development of "Professor Garfield's 21st Century Literacy Curriculum" was based on a four-phase process that included (1) a thorough exploration of the state-of-the-art in digital literacy instructional tools and extant literature related to digital literacy education, (2) a survey of K-5 teachers designed to understand their perceptions of digital literacy and technology use in the classroom, (3) design thinking and empathy research with teachers in two states, and (4) summative user experience testing with teachers from across the country. This user-centered approach allowed us to better understand key requirements for an interactive system that supports digital literacy instruction, as well as the primary factors that motivate teachers to use new web- or app-based teaching and learning tools.

3.1 State-of-the-Art and Extant Literature

In an effort to more fully define digital literacy as a pedagogy and skillset, a number of models for educational technology were explored. Review of these materials was expansive and provided both direction and inspiration for our digital literacy curriculum. The most prominent of these are highlighted in the results section of this paper.

3.2 Digital Literacy Perceptions and Practices Survey

A survey validation study was first conducted in two phases to ensure items were accurate and dependable. First, three digital literacy experts were asked to review the survey and provide feedback via the Questionnaire Appraisal System (QAS-99) [13] to evaluate the wording and accuracy of questions. The expert reviewers were selected because they had similar expertise in digital literacy. To maintain independence of the reviews, all reviewers were asked to conduct the reviews individually. Based on the feedback from each expert, revisions were made to address concerns.

Following the expert review, five elementary teachers from a local laboratory school were recruited to participate in a 30-min validation focus group. This second activity helped ensure questions made sense consistently to members of the target audience. In this session, teachers were asked to review and discuss each question and provide feedback about the nature and content of each question. Based on this feedback, revisions were made and a final *Digital Literacy Perceptions and Practices* survey was developed.

To better understand the specific nature of teachers' perceptions and practices related to digital literacy instruction, a fully-validated survey was distributed to 1,000 K-5 teachers in Indiana and Michigan. For this survey, the Departments of Education for Indiana and Michigan provided email addresses for K-5 teachers in those states.

3.3   Design Thinking and Empathy Research

To form a more comprehensive understanding of teachers' classroom practices and inform the development of digital literacy exercises, the research team engaged in 15 collaborative brainstorming sessions with more than 50 K-5 in-service and pre-service teachers over a six-month period. Teachers were first interviewed about how they integrate technology in their classes. They were also asked what factors contribute to adoption of teaching and learning apps and/or websites. Likewise, teachers engaged in participatory prototyping as a method for brainstorming interactive exercises that foster digital literacy and reinforce language arts concepts, such as phonemic awareness, reading readiness, and storytelling.

Throughout the design and development process, the research team also engaged in iterative usability and user experience research with more than 30 K-5 teachers. Teachers from two schools in Chicago and in Muncie, Indiana were shown exercise prototypes and concepts at both low- and medium-fidelity, and provided valuable feedback about the nature of each exercise, as well as the interaction design of the site.

3.4   Summative User Experience Testing

During the 2017 and 2018 International Society for Technology in Education (ISTE) Conference, attendees were introduced to the Professor Garfield's 21st Century Literacy Project and then asked to sign up to become beta testers for future usability and user experience studies. A total of 100 teachers from 34 states agreed to participate. Participants were divided into five groups, one for each of the five active digital literacy modules that comprise the current iteration of the site. A separate set of questions focused specifically on each exercise module was administered to 20 teachers each.

Participants were contacted via email and asked to complete a remote user experience protocol that engaged them in a systematic walk-through of the Professor Garfield digital literacy offerings using a website testing tool. The task-based survey was also provided as a PDF attachment for teachers who preferred to complete a paper version and return it via postal service or email. The survey included seven key demographic questions and nine tasks that required participants to walk through the site's main sections and provide feedback about the explanatory content, educational merit, and ease of use related to each section and the custom content management functions of the site. Tasks focused on the homepage, digital literacy instructional videos, teacher registration process, course creation, exercise summaries, assignment creation, lesson plans, digital literacy exercises, and grading system. Demographic questions, as well as most task questions, were the same for all participants. However, each of the five groups was given a unique set of questions related to one of the five digital literacy exercises outlined above. The survey was live from June through August 2018.

4 Findings

The following sections provide an overview of what we learned at each stage of the user-centered process.

4.1 State-of-the-Art and Extant Literature

A few notable online solutions for digital literacy education exist. learning.com provides interactive modules designed to "equip students with critical skills including keyboarding, word processing, digital citizenship, and online safety, as well as media and information literacy skills." The site also advertises "a project-based approach to teaching digital literacy and integrating technology into core subject instruction." Likewise, EDSITEment and ArtsEdge provide lesson plans, activities, and online games. Similarly, a number of sites offer resources to help teachers in the classroom, including The News Literacy Project, DigitalLiteracy.gov, Common Sense Media, and Web 20.14. Although they offer an abundance of information and content, they do not address the complexities of teaching and learning digital literacy in K-5.

Additionally, TPACK (Technological Pedagogical and Content Knowledge) [9] emphasizes three types of knowledge instructors need to combine for successful edtech integration. Likewise, the Substitution Augmentation Modification Redefinition (SAMR) Model [10] provides insight about how computer technology might affect teaching and learning. However, neither provides a comprehensive and definitive framework for understanding the broad range of skills a learner must acquire to become digitally literate.

Ultimately, the review of literature revealed that digital literacy is about mastering ideas, not keystrokes. Many scholars and educators have evolved the concept, and according to Hauge and Payton [6], to be digitally literate empowers students to use digital tools – such as online learning environments, software, hardware, etc. – for critical thinking and problem solving. Hauge and Payton's framework identifies eight core components of digital literacy: e-safety, finding and selecting information online, functional technology skills, critical thinking about technology use, creativity in digital environments, the role of technology in their lives, effective communication, and collaboration in digital environments (Table 1). This work underpins the digital literacy curriculum eventually built for this study and informed the development and validation of the perceptions and practices survey outlined in the next section, as it provides a clear operational framework for identifying and defining digital literacy skills. Furthermore, [6] advocates for a cross-curricular, age-appropriate approach to administering essential digital literacy instruction. They note that digital literacy is not a subject, but rather a skillset that students develop.

Table 1. This project is based on eight components of digital literacy [6].

Digital literacy component	Definition
Functional meaning making	Ability to operate software and/or hardware
Finding & selecting information	Ability to find accurate, reliable information online
Effective communication	Ability to communicate online
Collaboration	Ability to work with others using technology and/or effectively collaborate online
Critical thinking	Ability to think critically about technology use
Creativity	Ability to connect ideas and generate creative digital products
E-Safety	Ability to use good judgment, engage in safe in tech use
Effective communication	Ability to appropriately communicate with digital tools
Cultural awareness	Ability to understand how technology shapes the world we live in

4.2   Digital Literacy Perceptions and Practices Survey

A total of 297 teachers started the survey, however, only 249 responded to all survey items. Individuals who didn't complete the survey were removed from the dataset, resulting in a 24.9% response rate. Demographic data, including teaching and/or administrative responsibilities, was collected. Then, participants were asked to respond to 17 questions – including both Likert-scale and open-ended questions – about technology use and digital literacy perceptions and practices. The survey was estimated to take about 20 min to complete.

Respondents were asked a number of general questions about how they approach technology and digital literacy instruction in their classrooms. Most respondents (78%) reported that their schools offer the flexibility and resources needed to teach about technology. Likewise, more than half of respondents (65%) reported that their schools offer the flexibility and resources needed to teach about digital literacy. However, as Fig. 1 illustrates, when asked approximately how many hours per week they dedicate to teaching students how to effectively use digital tools, more than half of respondents reported one hour or less.

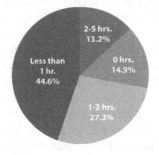

Fig. 1. Teachers' classroom practices related to teaching digital literacy

Respondents were asked whether class time is structured so that students regularly have the opportunity to engage in specific activities related to the eight components of digital literacy: e-safety, finding and selecting information online, functional technology skills, critical thinking about technology use, creativity in digital environments, the role of technology in their lives, effective communication and collaboration in digital environments. Figure 2 illustrates how educators responded to these questions.

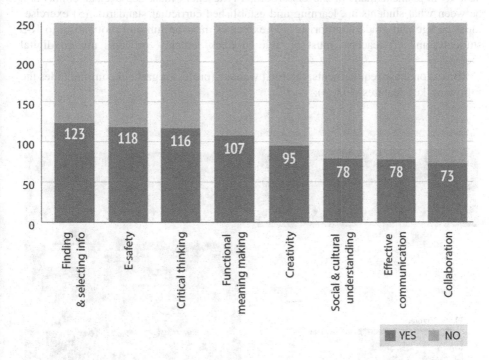

Fig. 2. Teachers' responses to questions about whether class time is structured so that students regularly have the opportunity to engage in specific activities related to the eight components of digital literacy.

Findings also suggested that: (1) professional development opportunities are limited for learning how to teach students how to use digital tools; (2) teachers' understanding of digital literacy is relatively shallow; (3) teachers often focus on tools and software as opposed to underlying principles that govern digital literacy.

4.3 Design Thinking and Empathy Research

Not surprising, the need for a simple design was a key theme during early-stage concept tests. Participants emphasized that both K-5 students *and* teachers require a clean, minimalistic design and clear interaction patterns for the site to be learnable, memorable, and easy to understand. Additionally, teachers indicated that digital literacy exercises must deliver a comprehensive lesson, fun enough to hold a young learner's attention, and brief enough mitigate the chance that they would lose interest.

After several rounds of design thinking, semi-structured interviews, and participatory brainstorming and prototyping, seven key requirements emerged: (1) teachers must have a clear understanding of digital literacy; (2) instructional materials must be grounded in a framework of digital literacy; (3) the site must provide teachers with support materials, such as video tutorials and lesson plans, and offer clear direction for how to implement them in the classroom; (4) teachers must see a clear connection between what students are learning and established curricular standards; (5) exercises must be age and grade appropriate; (6) exercises must be fun and motivating to K-5 students; and (7) teachers must be able to track students' progress toward digital literacy.

Based on these requirements, the final website (professor.garfield.com) includes the following key features (Fig. 3):

Fig. 3. A home page (top left) provides an overview of digital literacy and the site's main offerings. A digital literacy page (right) includes brief instructional videos that define eight components of digital literacy. Videos provide teachers with a clear understanding of each component and exemplify the skills necessary for a student to master digital literacy. Videos are accompanied by an introductory lesson plan that teachers can use at the start of a semester or unit called "Eight Days of Digital Literacy with Professor Garfield." Digital literacy exercises (bottom left) guide students through short tutorial videos prior to engaging in an activity designed to teach one or more of the eight components of digital literacy.

Brief instructional videos define each of the eight key components of digital literacy. These videos provide teachers with definitions of each component and exemplify the skills necessary for a student to master digital literacy. An introductory lesson plan called "Eight Days of Digital Literacy with Professor Garfield" is also included. This comprehensive plan provides teachers with simple activities they can do with students to build a foundation for digital literacy. For example, in one activity, students explore how technology has changed the world. Among the topics discussed are the advent of online schools, online shopping and 24-h access to television, movies, music, and news. Students are introduced to Google Earth to illustrate the global community facilitated by the Internet. Finally, they are asked to search for their school and tour the community surrounding it while the teacher shows some of Google Earth's features.

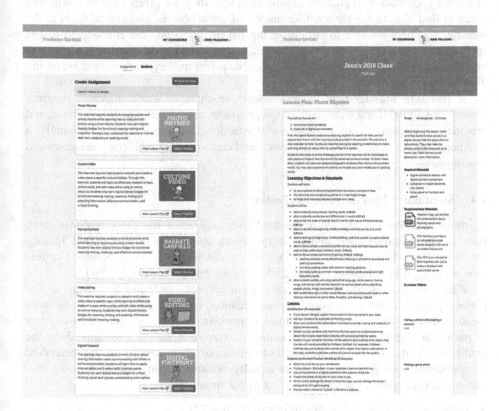

Fig. 4. A teacher dashboard (left) allows teachers to explore exercise descriptions and lesson plans, as well as assign exercises to their class. Cross-curricular lesson plans include downloadable handouts and PowerPoint presentations. Lesson plans also indicate for which grade level each exercise is best suited and the Common Core Language Arts standards and International Society for Technology Educators each lesson covers.

Cross-curricular lesson plans for five exercises include downloadable handouts teachers can print and use, as well as customizable PowerPoint presentations. Lesson plans indicate for which grade level each exercise is best suited (Fig. 4). Lesson plans also indicate which Common Core Language Arts standards [2] as well as which International Society for Technology Educators (ISTE) standards [4] each lesson covers.

Five exercises are each designed to achieve three main goals: (1) teach one or more of the eight components of digital literacy, (2) reinforce concepts related to language arts (e.g., phonemic awareness, reading instruction, storytelling), and (3) leverage the popularity of Garfield in fun, engaging ways.

For example, in an exercise targeted toward first and second graders called "Photo Rhymes," students learn how to tell stories using photos, how to make and edit photos using digital cameras, how to upload photos to a web-based system, and the importance of saving your work in digital environments. Then, they are given a list of words and asked to find objects that rhyme, take photos of those objects, and upload them to the website. Teachers are able to customize the list of words and are encouraged to use spelling or vocabulary words from a language arts lesson. Additionally, students can unlock digital literacy badges and downloadable prizes as they work toward becoming digital literacy masters.

A learning management system allows teachers to track students' progress through the digital literacy curriculum, assign grades and badges for each exercise, and provide comments/feedback on students' digital literacy submissions. Additionally, a dashboard allows teachers to review, select, and customize digital literacy exercises and lesson plans.

4.4 Summative User Experience Testing

Thirty-six teachers participated in the final user experience test (36% response rate). Five sub-groups responded to unique questions about one of five digital literacy exercises: Photo Rhymes (n = 9; 45%), Culture Video (n = 7; 35%), Narrate Garfield (n = 8; 40%), Video Editing (n = 5; 25%), Digital Footprint (n = 7; 35%).

Responses to questions about general system features – including homepage, digital literacy page, teacher registration, course creation, exercise summaries, assignment creation, and grading – were overwhelmingly positive. In nearly all cases, 80% or more of participants responded positively (*strongly agree* or *agree*) to questions about the quality of all areas of the site. Responses to questions about ease of use and perceived appropriateness for K-5 students were equally positive. Open ended responses illuminated several positive attributes and room for improvement:

- Homepage is attractive, and/or informative (n = 22).
- Videos are high-quality, clear, appropriate, informative, easy to understand (n = 17).
- Site is all-in-one resource for digital literacy (n = 24).
- Teachers learned more about digital literacy (n = 12).
- Exercises are fun (n = 17), engaging (n = 4), easy to understand (n = 12), and informative (n = 10).
- Homepage needs more information (n = 16).
- Digital literacy videos might be difficult for younger students to understand (n = 8).
- Younger students may struggle to complete exercises because the videos contain too much talking and not enough explanatory visuals (n = 7).
- Educational standards on the lesson plans should not be state-specific (n = 11).
- Grade levels specified in lesson plans may not be correct (n = 4).

- In several places, videos and/or instructions were difficult to understand/follow (n = 6).

These results have been used to make improvements to the site, including a redesign of the homepage, additional video production, a revised approach to reporting educational standards for each exercise, and simplified instructions for younger children.

5 Discussion

Establishing a user-centered approach that engaged K-5 educators in the design and development process was critical for a number of reasons. First, it allowed the design team to create a positive dialogue throughout the research process with an eye toward developing a curriculum informed by the teachers who might use it. Given the considerable barriers that teachers face when it comes to integrating technology in the classroom, this approach ensured that curriculum and site design decisions will mitigate those barriers. Anecdotal, but certainly important, the feedback we received from teachers throughout this process was extremely positive. Teachers were generally enthusiastic about the content, excited to have comprehensive digital literacy tools for their own development and that of their students, and grateful that we spent a great deal of time with teachers in many different schools and school systems to determine what strategies and tools would work best for them and their students. Many times, teachers expressed to use that all too often, technologists, entrepreneurs, and innovators develop teaching and learning tools based on assumptions they have about how teachers teach and how young people learn. This approach, they said, often leaves teachers feeling undervalued and results in products, services, and methods that are not realistically implementable in the average K-5 classroom.

Additionally, this user-centered approach appropriately respected K-5 teachers' pedagogical content knowledge by giving them a voice in the curriculum development process. By engaging teachers throughout the design process, the team was able to transform their innovative ideas into new digital literacy activities. Furthermore, it allowed us to design a robust digital literacy curriculum that is comprehensive and appropriate for the K-5 audience, as well as motivating for teachers to use and implement in the classroom. Finally, feedback during iterative design, development, and testing phases allowed us to effectively and incrementally build a website that will be useful, relevant, and easy to use. Summative user experience testing uncovered specific ways in which the final product both met and fell short of desired outcomes. Feedback from that research has been used to improve and polish the site. Ultimately, this project has demonstrated the true value of a user-centered approach to web design and development, particularly when there are significant barriers to adoption and highly-specialized domain knowledge among the audience and key stakeholders.

5.1   Conclusion and Future Work

Feedback from user-centered activities informed site improvements, and we are currently developing three more exercises focused on identifying facts vs. opinions and storytelling online. The site will officially launch for free use in Spring 2019. We are currently running a pilot study of the full site with six K-2 teachers and their students (approximately 140 children) at a campus laboratory school to further investigate the efficacy of the site, lessons, and exercises in a live classroom setting. We are also planning a large-scale implementation study in local Muncie schools for Fall and Spring 2019. Finally, we are currently developing a dashboard for creating personalized digital literacy and language arts lesson plans.

References

1. Blackwell, C.K., Lauricella, A.R., Wartella, E.: Factors influencing digital technology use in early childhood education. Comput. Educ. **77**, 82–90 (2014)
2. English Language Arts Standards. Common Core State Standards Initiative. http://www.corestandards.org/ELA-Literacy/. Accessed 2 Oct 2019
3. Ertmer, P.A., Ottenbreit-Leftwich, A.T., Sadik, O., Seneurur, E., Sendurur, P.: Teacher beliefs and technology integration practices: a critical relationship. Comput. Educ. **59**(2), 423–435 (2012)
4. ISTE Standards for Kids. https://www.iste.org/standards/for-students. Accessed 2 Oct 2018
5. Granata, K. (n.d.): Ten digital literacy resources for teachers. Education World. https://www.educationworld.com/a_lesson/ten-digital-literacy-resources-teachers.shtml. Accessed 1 Oct 2018
6. Hague, C., Payton, S.: Digital literacy across the curriculum (2011). http://www.curriculum.edu.au/leader/default.asp?id=33211&issueID=12380. Accessed 8 Apr 2011
7. Inan, F.A., Lowther, D.L.: Factors affecting technology integration in K-12 classrooms: a path model. Educ. Tech. Res. Dev. **58**(2), 137–154 (2009)
8. Instefjord, E.J., Munthe, E.: Educating digitally competent teachers: a study of integration of professional digital competence in teacher education. Teach. Teach. Educ. **67**, 37–45 (2017). https://doi.org/10.1016/j.tate.2017.05.016
9. Koehler, M.J., Mishra, P.: What happens when teachers design educational technology? The development of technological pedagogical content knowledge. J. Educ. Comput. Res. **32**(2), 131–152 (2005)
10. Puentedura, R.R.: Learning, technology, and the SAMR model: goals, processes, and practice (2014). http://www.hippasus.com/rrpweblog/archives/2014/06/29/LearningTechnologySAMRModel.pdf. Accessed 1 Oct 2018
11. Study Island: A proven K-12 practice and assessment tool. http://www.studyisland.com/. Accessed 30 Sept 2018
12. Survey finds majority of teachers do not feel prepared to use technology in classrooms. Samsung Newsroom, 23 June 2015. https://news.samsung.com/us/survey-finds-majority-of-teachers-do-not-feel-prepared-to-use-technology-in-classrooms/. Accessed 15 Sept 2018
13. Willis, G.B., Lessler, J.T.: Question Appraisal System (QAS-99). http://appliedresearch.cancer.gov/areas/cognitive/qas99.pdf. Accessed 15 Sept 2018

Designing a Multimodal Analytics System to Improve Emergency Response Training

Hemant Purohit[1]([⊠]), Samantha Dubrow[2], and Brenda Bannan[3]

[1] Information Sciences and Technology, Volgenau School of Engineering,
George Mason University, Fairfax, VA 22030, USA
hpurohit@gmu.edu
[2] Department of Psychology, College of Humanities and Social Sciences,
George Mason University, Fairfax, VA 22030, USA
sdubrow@gmu.edu
[3] Division of Learning Technologies,
College of Education and Human Development,
George Mason University, Fairfax, VA 22030, USA
bbannan@gmu.edu

Abstract. The role of high-fidelity simulation-based training is critical for preparing first responders to perform effectively in emergency response and firefighting environments. However, training simulation instructors currently rely on direct observation and radio-based audio communication methods to observe behaviors and evaluate interactions of trainees to provide feedback to trainees during debriefing sessions. Such human-driven evaluative methods, while valuable, lose fidelity of information for learning due to working memory limitations and the mind's inability to capture all relevant behavioral information in realtime and to provide relevant detailed information that is easily interpretable to instructors. Thus, there is a need and the potential to explore alternative data collection and processing methods leveraging advanced wireless technologies to attempt to enhance the effectiveness of simulation training process for emergency response, to ultimately help save lives and better prepare our communities building emergency and disaster resilience. In this paper, we present a multimodal streaming analytics system to support learning by leveraging a user-centered design approach in consultation with a regional fire and rescue training academy. This conceptualized system provides real-time collection, visualization, and analysis of heterogeneous data streams including location sensing using Internet of Things (IoT) devices, audio communication, video observations, as well as social media and 911 call log streams. We describe the associated design challenges and lessons learned from the initial prototyping activities to strive toward enhancing the situational awareness and learning of emergency response personnel and leadership instructors with iterative design cycles at the regional fire and rescue training academy.

Keywords: Learning · Realtime streams · IoT · Smart cities ·
Disaster resilience

© Springer Nature Switzerland AG 2019
P. Zaphiris and A. Ioannou (Eds.): HCII 2019, LNCS 11590, pp. 89–100, 2019.
https://doi.org/10.1007/978-3-030-21814-0_8

1 Introduction

Training is an essential component for the successful deployment of any complex socio-technical system, especially those that may involve various types of interactions, specifically between human-to-human, human-to-machine, machine-to-human, and machine-to-machine as well as the interaction among the multiple engaged teams. Emergency management and response is one such type of complex environment, requiring first responders to efficiently and effectively carry out an incident response with multiple teams (e.g. fire and rescue teams, EMS teams, dispatch, etc.) to conduct life-saving operations while leveraging a suite of technologies to assist in their missions. Simulation training provides a key component and process for emergency management and response personnel to help address the inherent uncertainty of a simulated incident toward more efficient task coordination and effective planning and communication (Bannan et al. 2019).

Despite the obvious importance of training, the simulation training process may not always be optimal if the training tools are inefficient to assist the training simulation instructors and the trainees (Buck et al. 2006; Feese et al. 2013). In current practice, the training simulation instructors often primarily rely on direct observation and radio-based audio communication for documenting trainee behaviors and interactions. Such direct observation-based methods can sometimes lose the valuation of information in providing an effective learning feedback to an individual trainee and team during the debrief due to a variety of data-centric limitations (Dubrow and Bannan 2019). For instance, the incompleteness of the observed data, inefficient extraction of behavioral knowledge from the observed data for learning that could be interpretable to instructors, etc.

Therefore, in this paper, we ask the following research questions to help improve the training in the complex environment of emergency management:

- *(RQ1). How is a shared understanding of situation established across personnel within and between teams during an incident response or a training exercise?*
- *(RQ2). What challenges do current practices of human observation and audio-based information collection and processing present when attempting to measure and interpret shared situational awareness and team coordination?*
- *(RQ3). How can we address the identified challenges from the current practices of information processing using the state-of-the-art technologies?*

This research takes a user-centered design approach to address the above questions. In particular, for research questions RQ1 we conducted several iterations of focus groups with our collaborating emergency management trainers at a regional fire and rescue training academy. For answering research questions RQ2 and RQ3 we analyzed the focus group observations in light of the existing literature on data analytics and learning technologies. We found the recent advancement in the multimodal data streams as a unique, unprecedented opportunity to address our challenges in the conceptualization of a human-computer interface for emergency management training.

Recent advancements in video, wearable, and social & web stream technologies present unconventional opportunities to capture and improve multiple streams of information that may be accessible to instructors during simulations and enhance debriefing sessions (Dubrow et al. 2017; Feese et al. 2013; Kranzfelder et al. 2011). The debriefing session concluding a live simulation training event is where prior research indicates the most learning occurs as the first responders view and reflect on their behavioral activities post-event. The capability to mine behaviors from the integration and combination of such non-traditional data streams present a promising method to enrich the information collected, processed, and analyzed in-situ (Bannan et al. 2019). These new combinations of information streams may assist incident commanders and instructors in facilitating relevant pieces of information to provide enhanced situation awareness through replaying targeted episodes that are triangulated and visualized through redundant data sources (e.g. video segments and proximity sensors both recording the proximity of personnel to the patient as the event unfolds). Multiple views of varied streaming information about the specific events during the training exercises provide complementary situational awareness. The improved, integrated data streams optimally visualized to incident command during the live simulation and post-event during the simulation debriefing session could possibly lead to improved awareness for reflection and experiential learning for fire and rescue personnel, as they engage in this complex socio-technical system environment.

We propose a multimodal system design, which provides real-time collection, visualization, and analysis of heterogeneous streams including location sensors, audio communication, video observations, and social media and 911 call streams by building on the redundancy and avoiding split attention effects in the learning science literature.

In the remainder of this paper, we first provide a background on the emergency response and management training with consideration of designing a data streaming and learning analytics system for the first responders audience, followed by presenting the conceptual system design as well as the results from iterative cycles of prototyping in a user-centered design process toward that goal.

2 Background: Emergency Response Training and Stream Data

This section describes the context of our research through the two following related areas.

2.1 Emergency Management and Response Training

There are several types of training exercises utilized in the emergency management domain, ranging from tabletop discussions to high-fidelity in-situ simulations centered around incident management (Buck et al. 2006). There are disparate training forms and each serves unique purposes for team learning, situation awareness, coordination, and improved performance.

Tabletop exercises (TTX) are often used by leaders in emergency management systems when planning future response techniques, such as future assessments of emergency-based damage and potential community recovery (Volunteer Fairfax). Researchers and trainers may want to collect data streams such as audio and video to record discussions during such meetings. Additionally, sociometric and dyadic measures of interactions between leaders may be examined to assess coordination and effort in TTX.

Drill exercises occur when training for a single function, such as applying a tourniquet to a patient. In such exercises, trainers may care more about specific body placement, speed, and proximity to the victim to assess performance (California Hospital Association). Functional exercises are less focused on planning and specific skills, and more focused on the interactions between individuals, teams, and agencies when responding to an event. Functional exercises allow for training and assessment of responders' skills without the costs and risks of in-situ simulations. Thus, data collection in functional exercises should likely be more focused on video, audio, and sociometric sources than on physical sources (e.g., GPS, proximity).

Finally, full-scale in-situ exercises are high-fidelity and as close to real life events as possible (California Hospital Association). Full-scale exercises are the most realistic for first responders, and are better able to create the stress, sense of urgency, and obstacles that come with real life events. Researchers and trainers will want the most information from full-scale exercises, but full-scale exercises are the most challenging to collect data from, due to environmental factors such as noise, vision, and heavy equipment. Thus, data redundancy is especially important in full-scale exercises. Physical, sociometric, audio, and video data are all critical for after-action reviews following full-scale exercises.

Currently, most of the existing approaches to the learning analytics during these variety of training exercises do not exploit the multimodal data streams.

2.2 Streaming Analytics Systems

Researchers and practitioners have designed streaming data analytics systems in a variety of domains. Safety-critical systems in industries have long employed the variety of sensing methods, video surveillance, and audio communication technologies using cyber-physical systems (Rajkumar et al. 2010) for operational and training purposes, which require streaming analytics including signal processing. Likewise, military domain use such technologies, primarily using the simulation based modeling systems that analyze the video data streams for operational training (Buller et al. 2010). Similarly, aviation domain extensively use audio communication and sensor data streams for analyzing team behavior in the training processes. Modern information systems for surveillance and intelligence have extensively mined a variety of open data streams including multiple modalities (Glassman and Kang 2012). These applications of streaming data analytics across different domains suggest the important of studying the diverse data streams, rather than relying on single data stream for any analytical tasks.

However, there is a lack of investigation for designing such streaming analytics system with multimodal data streams in the context of emergency management and response, which provides a strong motivation to our research.

3   System Design: User-Centered Approach

In the current study, we utilize a user-centered design approach (Wallach and Scholz 2012) to ideate, refine, and execute a multimodal analytics software system for supporting the operational training of emergency services. We designed a system to meet the trainer needs, summarized in Fig. 1, that captures multimodal data streams and processes them to identify common behavioral events (e.g., proximity of two personnel from different teams for a common task).

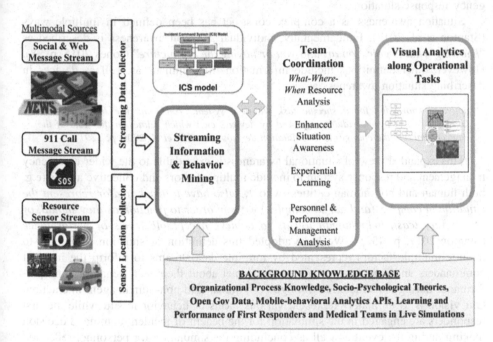

Fig. 1. Overview of the multimodal streaming analytics system for supporting training of emergency personnel.

The system design aims to (a) *save time*, by allowing trainers and incident commanders to browse content from multiple streams on the same visual dashboard, (b) *reduce effort*, by seamlessly aligning common information streams and eliminating the need for trainers and incident commanders to check several different dashboards, and (c) *facilitate scalable monitoring* of trainee learning by allowing more instructor roles to access the same dashboard views. In addition, the system design will also ultimately increase situation awareness to facilitate improved team coordination and experiential learning from the exercise.

3.1 Design Challenges

Our discussions with fire and rescue trainers have highlighted that the lack of access to *redundant* information is a key limitation in current trainee learning practices that leads to missing information and limited situational awareness, which impact learning and team coordination during highly dynamic training exercise environments. To enhance awareness, learning, and team coordination by leveraging streaming analytics, we must align the demands of context and behavioral activity with the identified research constructs and the information processing requirements and challenges in the emergency response situation.

Situation awareness as a complex construct has been defined in multiple ways (Stanton et al. 2017). Fundamentally, individual situation awareness is described as *"knowing what is going on around you or having the big picture"* (Jones 2015, p. 98). However, other definitions include information from humans as well as devices in describing situation awareness as:

> activated knowledge for a specific task within a system....[and] the use of appropriate knowledge (held by individuals, captured by devices, etc.) which relates to the state of the environment and the changes as the situation develops (Stanton et al. 2006, p. 1291).

This expanded view of situational awareness is extendable to the wider emergency management and response system to include multiple factors and collective agents (e.g. both human and non-human entities) who *"...also have to track and/or represent the situation in complex (and not so complex) ways in order to function as they should, or at the very least, help human agents to achieve acceptable levels of performance* (Stanton 2017, p. 452)." We have adopted this definition of situation awareness to include multiple factors represented by multiple data streams to inform the incident commanders and emergency response personnel about their own behaviors and performance during the simulation through both human and non-human agent interaction. Our vision is to ultimately represent various facets of behavior in-situ while the first responders are engaged in the simulation for the benefit of incident command decision making during the event as well as concluding the simulation for personnel reflection during the debriefing session. This would create a common operating picture formed through the captured human-to-human interaction as well as human-to-machine (or device) and then potentially mined for meaningful information through behavior analytics for the observed information by machine (or device) or human. We envision these devices or sensors capturing the dynamic response by multiple teams (e.g., fire and rescue, EMS) and visualizing their different patterns of coordination (e.g. who is near who at what point in time) through a machine learning approach for behavior mining of relevant information in near real-time. This would hopefully, provide the incident commanders, their personnel and observers of the simulation, a common operating picture to form a shared mental model of the event and increase their experiential learning from that event.

However, we identify three key challenges in the training process centered around information processing systems of sensors and other data streams are the following:

1. *Incompleteness*: missing observational data streams.
2. *Miscommunication*: noisy or lossy radio communication channel.

3. *Inconsistency*: across the observational and continuous audio data streams.

During the focus group discussion with our collaborators at the firefighting training academy, we validated the need for solving the above challenges in the data streams across modalities, and the need to minimize uncertainty of information as well as improve the perceived validity of the information using multimodal streaming analytics approach.

3.2   Theory of Redundancy and Split Attention Effect

Our system design is based on the ideas of presenting redundant information through multimodal data streams and purposefully integrating different data streams to avoid the split attention effect to potentially improve first responder awareness, learning and team coordination. The split attention effect occurs when learners are required to divide their awareness between multiple sources of information that have been separated either spatially or temporally and therefore, need to be integrated to avoid cognitive overload. Studies have shown that integrated information is more effective for learning especially if the individual components of information are found to be less intelligible in isolation (Ayers and Cierniak 2012). However, when strategically combined to avoid split attention, an integration of data streams may move toward more intuitive processing of information (Chen et al. 2017). If the same information is physically or spatially (digitally) integrated, this may obviate the need to mentally integrate it, then, potentially reduce the number of interacting elements to minimize extraneous cognitive load.

The split attention effect has been well-documented in multimedia learning. For example, Kalyuga et al. (1999) tested the effect on computer-based instructional materials consisting of diagrams and texts. They found that physically integrated information enhanced learning compared with information split across multiple sources. Al-Shehri and Gitsaki (2010) compared a split attention design with an integrated design for learners' online reading performance. Results supported the view that online integrated materials enhanced students' learning. Similarly, Liu et al. (2012) investigated the split attention effect on mobile learning in the domain of physics. Therefore, we anticipate similar behavior when using a multimodal analytics system design for assisting trainers in complex training environments.

According to Ayers and Cierniak (2012) "*...the split-attention principle says that several separated sources of information should be replaced with a single integrated source of information.*" In our work, we envision multiple modes and streams of data and information aligned in a single, meaningful display for the first responder audience that moves toward optimal information processing in a complex dashboard for simulation training. The incident commanders as well as the fire and rescue trainers must hold a significant amount of information in their working memory during simulation exercise or an actual emergency response incident typically obtained through radio communication. The tendency for information overload is palpable with firefighters during an emergency response with stated concerns related to avoiding cognitive load or adding to their workload with additional, unnecessary information and radio traffic.

Therefore, attempting to reduce the number of information streams in temporal and spatial contiguity is the goal and continuing identified challenge for our system.

Prior research has indicated the first responders desire an overall picture or mental model of the incident at hand typically processed through input gained from various information sources. For example, in a fireground incident, gaining information about the structure of the building, number of occupants, any hazardous materials on-site, etc. would be important information to know immediately upon initial assessment (Xiaodong et al. 2004). Important factors from the Xiaodong et al., study revealed the following design issues that emerged from the field:

1. Accountability of resources and personnel is crucial and should be as simple and accurate as possible.
2. Assessment of the situation through multiple sources of information while avoiding information overload is key.
3. Resource allocation is a primary task for incident commanders and should be a primary focus in designs.
4. Communication support should add reliability and/or redundancy to existing communication channels to ensure that important messages reach the right people (p. 683).

Our study attempts to intersect these core findings with learning science to advance the design of an ubiquitous computing system interface, which adheres to appropriate instructional design principles as well as prior research findings. For example in the same study, tracking individual firefighters in a particular building was perceived as useful, however, incident commanders preferred less granular information and desired broad-levels of information initially such as warnings of imminent dangers (e.g. low levels of oxygen) for their teams. In visualizing their respective team tasks, only presenting information that was necessary or explicitly queried or providing redundancy of important information to validate incoming contextual data was perceived as useful by the firefighters (Xiaodong et al. 2004).

The multimodal learning analytics system is designed to visualize information about the simulation event in-situ but also enhance the debriefing session to improve experiential learning from the live simulation. Learning through *reflection on action* in a simulation experience provides a rich source of objective data that can contribute to effective feedback from the situation. Jenvald and Morin (2004) found that discussion alone in the debrief did not appear to facilitate learning as well as the opportunity to visualize targeted replay information to promote rich reflection in providing relevant details in a calmer environment immediately following the simulation event. Our goal is to provide relevant streams of data to incident commanders and first responder teams that are visualized in the debriefing session with appropriate redundancy and attention to relevant integrated streams of information for this type of enhanced feedback.

3.3 Design Constructs

The specific constructs in our multimodal analytics system are the following:

Data Collection. The rising adoption of mobile technology, Internet of Things (IoT), and social & Web data sources provide emergency management and response organizations a novel opportunity to collect information about incidents from diverse channels, and reduce uncertainty in information for better situational awareness. Social media has enabled citizens to act as "human sensors", who observe, share and update situational awareness information for an unfolding emergency event. Ubiquitous computing and IoT sensors have opened up opportunities to collect field observations from the deployed sensors on resources and personnel in the field, complementing conventional channels of audio communication.

Streaming Information and Behavior Mining. Given, a collection of streaming media sources (e.g., IoT sensor stream, location sensors, wearable biometric sensors, social network streams, news rss feeds, 911 call records), the technical objective is to develop time-series data mining and machine learning approaches with human-machine collaboration to identify the occurrence of a behavioral event of interest that has potential implication for emergency management operations (Pandey and Purohit 2018). We also seek to identify the granular information i.e., specific information from the multitude of streaming outlets that can be considered as supporting evidence for integration within the common operating picture for decision making, such as for personnel management and resource coordination analysis.

Team Coordination Analytics. Our proposed approach of incorporating redundant and complementary information sources, and their unified organization, provides a form of intelligence through selected "smart" capture, integration of data sources with computational intelligence, and timely visualization of these varied information sources for emergency response personnel to consider in extending their situation awareness, decision-making and learning (Dubrow and Bannan 2019). This system design specifically targets team activity by displaying complementary sources of information to improve confidence in, and efficiently support situational awareness analysis for decision making, explicitly addressing the who-what-where of coordination and experiential learning at important inflection points between teams.

Visualization Dashboards. Modeling and visualizing information flow across multiple constituent groups in an emergency scenario to potentially improve situational awareness, coordination, decision-making, and experiential learning requires multidisciplinary expertise and an integrative research approach with attention to the redundancy principle and split-attention effects. Complex interdependencies exist with a focus on actors, processes, and patterns that may be highlighted through the actions of individuals over time responding dynamically in-situ (Zaccaro et al. 2012). We plan custom visualizations such as temporal charts, dynamic networks, and geographical maps that leverage real-time behavioral data for immediate display (and later analysis) from multiple sources, including unconventional data (e.g. physical and biometric sensors on emergency responders, environmental sensors, social media, news feeds) and conventional data (e.g., human-observer checklist, audio communication streams). These visualizations help establish a common operating picture for incident commanders and for reflection by the emergency response teams in the debriefing session. Our primary hypothesis for this design is that viewing these multiple data stream provides important redundant information to reduce uncertainty related to conventional and unconventional data sources for assisting decision-making, coordination, and learning.

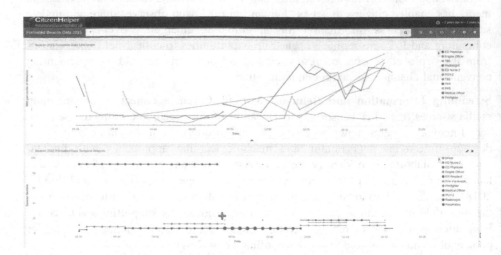

Fig. 2. Snapshot of a dashboard with two widgets from our preliminary prototype for the proposed system design, where the time series data visualization is shown for the movement pattern of diverse trainees during an exercise, which shows the movement pattern of a potential coordinated behavior between multiple actors of different teams (*c.f.* details: Dubrow et al. 2017). The visual dashboard provides the ability to browse the data over time and location, which enables an instructor during debriefing to go back in time and filter all the information across the set of behavioral analytics widgets, which correspond to mining each type of multimodal data streams.

4 Preliminary Prototyping, Lessons Learned, and Conclusion

The proposed system dashboard, shown in Fig. 2, was prototyped for visualizing the movements of fire and rescue exercise participants at our collaborating regional fire and rescue academy. The emergent system continues to evolve testing and integrating multiple sources of information to visualize relevant information about resources, events and actions by location and time. The identified information layers will continue to be designed to deliberately address critical points of team-based interaction related to crisis response decision-making, situation awareness, coordination, and learning during identified interactions or inflection points (such as the effective handoff of the patient from one team to another that involves decisions for routing, awareness of patient condition and environment, coordination and communication between teams, etc.).

The next step is for the system to visualize these selected multimodal information streams into a common operating picture (commonly referred *COP* in the emergency domain), or dashboard, for use in the simulation by the emergency operations center as well as in after-action review, or debrief. Providing visualization of additional unconventional information channels from social media and sensors may offer new information for decision-making and learning to enhance situation awareness, and coordination for participants. Providing additional information channels that are not centralized or accessible in Emergency Operations Centers has been linked to improving understanding of a crisis situation and supporting decision-making of emergency response teams (Van de Walle et al. 2016). However, ensuring that the emergency response professionals are provided the right information at the right time that does not add to their cognitive load and provides validity and improved comprehension with selective redundant information remains a challenge that we plan to address in our ongoing work.

In conclusion, this paper presented a multimodal streaming system design and preliminary findings and challenges from prototyping in a user-centered design process with professionals at a suburban fire and rescue training facility to inform future research.

Acknowledgements. Authors would like to thank undergraduate research assistant Mohammad Rana for implementing the preliminary system and U.S. National Science Foundation grants DRL-1637263 and IIS-1815459 for partially supporting this research. Any opinions, findings and conclusions or recommendations expressed in this material are those of the author(s) and do not necessarily reflect the views of the National Science Foundation.

References

Al-Shehri, S., Gitsaki, C.: Online reading: a preliminary study of the impact of integrated and split-attention formats on L2 students' cognitive load. ReCALL **22**(3), 356–375 (2010)

Ayres, P., Cierniak, G.: Split-attention effect. In: Seel, N.M. (ed.) Encyclopedia of the Sciences of Learning, pp. 3172–3175. Springer, Boston (2012). https://doi.org/10.1007/978-1-4419-1428-6

Bannan, B., Dubrow, S., Dobbins, C., Zaccaro, S., Purohit, H., Rana, M.: Toward wearable devices for multiteam systems learning. In: Buchem, I., Klamma, R., Wild, F. (eds.) Perspectives on Wearable Enhanced Learning: Current Trends Research and Practice, pp. 1–29. Springer, New York (2019, in press)

Buck, D.A., Trainor, J.E., Aguirre, B.E.: A critical evaluation of the incident command system and NIMS. J. Homel. Secur. Emerg. Manag. **3**(3), 1–27 (2006)

Buller, M., Welles, A., Jenkins, O.C., Hoyt, R.: Extreme health sensing: the challenges, technologies, and strategies for active health sustainment of military personnel during training and combat missions. In: Sensors, and Command, Control, Communications, and Intelligence (C3I) Technologies for Homeland Security and Homeland Defense IX, vol. 7666, p. 766610. International Society for Optics and Photonics (2010)

California Hospital Association: Emergency Preparedness: Types of Exercises. https://www.calhospitalprepare.org/post/types-exercises. Accessed 1 Mar 2019

Chen, O., Woolcott, G., Sweller, J.: Using cognitive load theory to structure computer-based learning including MOOCs. J. Comput. Assist. Learn. **33**(4), 293–305 (2017)

Dubrow, S., et al.: Using IoT sensors to enhance simulation and training in multiteam systems. In: Proceedings of the Interservice/Industry Training, Simulation and Education Conference (I/ITSEC) Published, pp. 1–10 (2017)

Dubrow, S., Bannan, B.: Toward improving interagency learning in emergency response simulations contexts with wearable technologies. To be Presented at the 21st Annual Conference of Human-Computer Interaction, Orlando, FL (2019)

Feese, S., Arnrich, B., Troster, G., Burtscher, M., Meyer, B., Jonas, K.: CoenoFire: monitoring performance indicators of firefighters in real-world missions using smartphones. In: Proceedings of the 2013 ACM International Joint Conference on Pervasive and Ubiquitous Computing, pp. 83–92. ACM (2013)

Glassman, M., Kang, M.J.: Intelligence in the internet age: the emergence and evolution of Open Source Intelligence (OSINT). Comput. Hum. Behav. 28(2), 673–682 (2012)

Jenvald, J., Magnus, M.: Simulation-supported live training for emergency response in hazardous environments. Simul. Gaming 35(3), 363–377 (2004)

Jones, D.G.: A practical perspective on the utility of situation awareness. J. Cogn. Eng. Decis. Mak. 9(1), 98–100 (2015)

Kalyuga, S., Chandler, P., Sweller, J.: Managing split-attention and redundancy in multimedia instruction. Appl. Cogn. Psychol.: Off. J. Soc. Appl. Res. Mem. Cogn. 13(4), 351–371 (1999)

Kranzfelder, M., Schneider, A., Gillen, S., Feussner, H.: New technologies for information retrieval to achieve situational awareness and higher patient safety in the surgical operating room: the MRI institutional approach and review of the literature. Surg. Endosc. 25(3), 696–705 (2011)

Liu, T.C., Lin, Y.C., Tsai, M.J., Paas, F.: Split-attention and redundancy effects on mobile learning in physical environments. Comput. Educ. 58(1), 172–180 (2012)

Pandey, R., Purohit, H.: CitizenHelper-adaptive: expert-augmented streaming analytics system for emergency services and humanitarian organizations. In: 2018 IEEE/ACM International Conference on Advances in Social Networks Analysis and Mining (ASONAM), pp. 630–633. IEEE (2018)

Rajkumar, R., Lee, I., Sha, L., Stankovic, J.: Cyber-physical systems: the next computing revolution. In: Design Automation Conference, pp. 731–736. IEEE (2010)

Stanton, N.A., Salmon, P.M., Walker, G.H., Salas, E., Hancock, P.A.: State-of-science: situation awareness in individuals, teams and systems. Ergonomics 60(4), 449–466 (2017). https://doi.org/10.1080/00140139.2017.1278796

Stanton, N.A., et al.: Distributed situation awareness in dynamic systems: theoretical development and application of an ergonomics methodology. Ergonomics 49(12–13), 1288–1311 (2006)

Van de Walle, B., Brugghemans, B., Comes, T.: Improving situation awareness in crisis response teams: an experimental analysis of enriched information and centralized coordination. Int. J. Hum.-Comput. Stud. 95, 66–79 (2016)

Volunteer Fairfax: Fairfax County Community Resiliency Collaboration: Tabletop Exercise Series - Braddock District Situation Manual. http://www.volunteerfairfax.org/individuals/Resilency_Pilot/VolunteerFairfaxBraddockTTX_SITMAN.pdf. Accessed 1 Mar 2019

Wallach, D., Scholz, S.C.: User-centered design: why and how to put users first in software development. In: Maedche, A., Botzenhardt, A., Neer, L. (eds.) Software for People, pp. 11–38. Springer, Heidelberg (2012). https://doi.org/10.1007/978-3-642-31371-4_2

Xiaodong, J., Hong, J.I., Takayama, L.A., Landay, J.A.: Ubiquitous computing for firefighters: field studies and prototypes of large displays for incident command. In: Proceedings of CHI Conference on Human Factors in Computing Systems, Vienna, Austria (2004)

Zaccaro, S.J., Marks, M.A., DeChurch, L.A.: Multiteam systems: an introduction. In: Multiteam Systems, pp. 18–47. Routledge (2012)

SHAUN—A Companion Robot for Children Based on Artificial Intelligence

Tianjia Shen and Ting Han[(⊠)]

School of Design, Shanghai Jiao Tong University, Shanghai, China
1049904168@qq.com, hanting@sjtu.edu.com

Abstract. This article is aimed at providing a design principle for companion robot based on Artificial Intelligence. Taking children at 0–6 years old as target users and their parents as target customers, the author applied methods of investigation and observation to understand their income level, life routine, habit, pain points, consumption capacity and aesthetic level. With these previous researches and some utilization of ergonomics, this paper defined the function, size, material of Companion Robot for children. This paper explores and summarizes the user orientation of Companion Robot for children, its functional definition, material definition and man-machine definition, and shows the design practice under its guidance. This study will provide guidance for future design of companion robots and make the design location clearer by putting forward design concepts and guidelines.

Keywords: Companion Robot · Artificial Intelligence · User experience design

1 Introduction

1.1 Research Background

With the rapid development of Big Data and the Cloud, Artificial Intelligence technology has entered the third development peak. As the solid foundation of the development of many other novel technologies, AI will become the most important technology in the world in the coming decades. The concept of Artificial Intelligence was first presented at a conference held by The Dartmouth Society in 1956. The most important topic is how to imitate human brain with computer and realize some intelligent functions. And AI has now become a subdiscipline of Computer Science. At present, the development of many technologies is related to AI. Today, AI is mainly applied in 7 fields: AI Assistant, Intelligent Security, Unmanned Driving, Healthcare, E-commerce, Finance and Education.

From 2014 to 2017, the scale of Chinese AI market rose from 4.86 billion yuan to 13.52 billion yuan, with an average compound annual growth rate of more than 40%. Among them, the scale of Chinese AI industry reached 9.560 billion yuan in 16 years, an increase of 37.9% over the same period last year. In 2017, it was 13.52 billion yuan, an increase of 41% over the same period last year.

AI currently plays the following functions in the field of education: 1. Helping children learn individually in accordance with their aptitude. 2. Counseling on daily

P. Zaphiris and A. Ioannou (Eds.): HCII 2019, LNCS 11590, pp. 101–114, 2019.
https://doi.org/10.1007/978-3-030-21814-0_9

questions. It has become a supplement to teachers' face-to-face instruction. 3. Intelligent assessment. Reduce the pressure on teachers to correct homework, and achieve large-scale and personalized homework feedback. 4. Teaching with pleasure. AI can establish an entertaining teaching platform. Therefore, Companion Robot for children based on AI becomes a bridge between parents and children and provides a medium for their interaction [1]. In modern time, parents pay more and more attention to the education of children from preschool period, hoping to cultivate children comprehensively, so that children can grow up happily and excellently. Companion robots have gradually become a part of life, relying on the progress of artificial intelligence technology. Companion Robot is a bridge and medium for parents and children to communicate and interact emotionally. With the introduction of second-child policy in China, the market for children has quickly become active. Every year, tens of millions of newborns are born, and the number of children aged between 0 and 8 is about 120 million. Parents are post-80s and post-90s, the main consumers in the current market. They are advanced enough to adapt to globalization. They attach great importance to children's education, especially in early stage and are more willing to invest more in children's development.

1.2 Research Significance

Preschool education is the initial education for children and is especially important for them. Nowadays, the whole society is paying more and more attention to education, various new education methods and tools are emerging. At the same time, according to the survey, nowadays, many young parents are at the peak of their career and they can only spend less than an hour with their children every day. More or less, 60% of parents miss the representative moment when their children grow up. 70% young fathers miss their children's first word because of their business [2]. Only by accompanying the children and giving them optimal education can the children grow up healthily and excellently, and leave a good memory in their childhood life.

Therefore, based on the development of AI technology, Companion Robot is designed to integrate the round and lovely image into children's life. It is easy to be regarded as a close and easy-to-communicate friend by children. Implicitly, it can help children develop good habits, good mentality and make education more interesting, more diverse. Robots are not only partners, but also good teachers. They relieve the parents' burden of education, make up for the deficiencies, and enable children to acquire knowledge and grow up in a happy life.

Taking into consideration the development of AI technology and the psychophysiological characteristics of children aged 0–6 years, this study provides concepts and guidelines for the design of Companion Robot for children.

2 Review of Previous Research

2.1 Academic Research on Companion Robot

In recent years, research on Companion Robot has been under heated discussion. The research scope of companion robots is also quite wide. Meghdari et al. designed a mobile social Companion Robot "A rash" for the education and treatment of children with chronic diseases. It is mainly aimed at children with cancer who suffer from physical pain caused by disease and its treatment. Using robotic partners to interact with sick children in hospital environments can reduce their pain and thus improve the efficiency of cancer treatment [3]. Billard et al. constructed robots with physical characteristics similar to human babies. It has been used as an assistant technology in behavioral research of autistic children [4]. Michaelis et al. designed learning partner robots to increase reading activity and observe the impact of robots on family reading experience [5]. Cavallo proposed a novel method based on reliability and acceptability assessment. This method is used to design, develop and test a personal robot system consisting of a mobile robot platform and an intelligent environment to assist people at home. The viewpoint that robots need to cooperate closely with human beings, so novel interactive engineering design methods are needed to develop service robots [6] that meet the needs of end users and can be used quickly in daily life.

On the AI side, Alpha GO Zero, released by Google, can learn from self-matching and millions of pieces of chess data. Boston Dynamics released SpotMini robots that can quickly adjust leg gait, keep standing, and eventually resume standing to complete tasks. SpotMini is also equipped with a large number of sensors, such as RGBD camera, attitude sensors, and body sensor of the limbs. These sensors can help Spot-Mini perform complex actions and cruise. The goal of Boston Dynamics is to build a robot that is more mobile, agile and perceptive than humans and other animals. At present, their research results show us the breakthrough of AI technology, which will have infinite possibilities and broad application prospects in the future.

2.2 Design Application on Companion Robot

The International Federation of Robots (IFR) released its latest global service robots statistics report in March 2016. Global sales of dedicated service robots in 2014 were 24 207, 11.5% higher than 21712 in 2013, and increased by 3% to $3.77 billion from 2013. However, research on the global service robot market is still in its infancy. The compound annual growth rate of service robot market will reach 17.4% in 2017, and the market scale is expected to reach 46.18 billion US dollars in 2017. It is expected that the annual composite growth rate of service robotics industry in China will reach 40% in the next 5 years, and the market penetration will gradually increase.

In today's robot market, Krund robot-WOW is a new-emerging force of service robot. It can do various interaction with family members through face recognition, sound source localization and voiceprint recognition. At the same time, it can learn independently through the Internet and improve its performance. It also has detection function. Sensors such as temperature, humidity and PM2.5 in the body of the robot can monitor the environment at home in real time, detect whether the elderly fall down and the children are safe, and monitor the situation at home in all aspects. Users can use simple voice passwords to control existing domestic appliances.

ZIB-1S is a dark horse in the field of Companion Robot. It is the first smart robot in China to categorize children's company market. It is especially for children's growth and companionship that each function is subdivided. In order to protect children's hearing, a volume adjustment test was conducted. Radiation is prevented to protect children's health through screen-less design and touch dialogue details.

Buddy is positioned as a family emotional social robot, mainly for young people and the elderly. It is equipped with cameras, voice recognition and face recognition to handle daily household affairs and monitor home security. Drug reminder and drop detection functions are designed for elderly users while nursery rhyme player is designed for children.

AIBO ERS-1000 has advanced and special learning and growth capabilities. Equipped with SONY self-developed ultra-small 1-axis and 2-axis actuators. AIBO has 22 degrees of freedom on its body. At the same time, through fisheye cameras and different sensors, AIBO can recognize and analyze images and sounds, and can respond to the host's voice, and recognize the host's smile and praise. Remember the actions that can make the host happy, etc.

From the point of view of the current application situation, a comprehensive comparison of these representative companion robots is completed (Table 1).

Table 1. Characteristics of present Companion Robots.

Name	Type	Use scenario	Characteristics	Disadvantages
Krund robot-WOW	Service robots	At home, banks, kindergartens, restaurants, supermarkets	Face recognition, sound source localization and voiceprint recognition, interaction, self-learning. Temperature, humidity, PM2.5 sensor in it. Monitoring the family environment. Voice control	Large and tall
ZIB-1S	Companion Robot	At home	Online education, Human-computer interaction and Special features. In order to protect children's hearing, a volume adjustment test was conducted. Radiation is prevented to protect children's health through screen-less design and touch dialogue details	Static and Not vivid
Buddy	Family emotional social robot	At home	It is equipped with cameras, voice recognition and face recognition to handle daily household affairs and monitor home security	Less content for children
AIBO ERS-1000	Pet robot	At home	Equipped with SONY self-developed ultra-small 1-axis and 2-axis actuators. AIBO has 22 degrees of freedom on its body. At the same time, through fisheye cameras and different sensors, AIBO can recognize and analyze images and sounds, and can respond to the host's voice, and recognize the host's smile and praise. Remember the actions that can make the host happy, etc	Realistic image makes people lack imagination. No screen

Summarize their advantages and disadvantages, learn from their strengths and make up for their weaknesses. Companion Robot for children should be considered in such aspects as appropriate size, interesting, functional design for children, modelling that can meet contemporary aesthetics and stimulate purchase.

3 Research Method and Procedure

Firstly, by using literature research method, through reading and referring to many literatures of high quality from international conferences and journals, the research status of Companion Robot is comprehensively understood, which lays a foundation for the research of the design concept of Companion Robot.

Secondly, the qualitative analysis method is used target the user group through investigation and observation. And do in-depth research around the target group of products. Because the target group of this study is children aged between 0–6 years old, and the target consumer group is parents of post-80s and post-90s. Through careful observation of their behavior, life style, habits, pain points, income level, consumption ability, aesthetic needs and so on, the follow-up construction of design concepts is gradually established.

Subsequently, using morphological analysis method, in the definition of shape, a large number of existing children's products and consumer goods with high sales on the market are collected, their main elements and characteristics are analyzed and summarized, these products are divided into several categories by morphological analysis method, and then through in-depth interviews, questionnaires and other methods to summarize the shape suitable for the target group.

Then, by collecting a large amount of data, the performance characteristics of each material are compared, and the human-machine dimensions of the target group are collected, and the materials and sizes corresponding to the target group are defined.

Finally, the design concept and criteria of Companion Robot for children are summarized, and the design practice of this study is guided by the previous research results and methods.

4 Research Outcome and Practical Design

4.1 Research Process

This study first understands the current situation and application fields and scope of AI technology which is becoming more and more mature nowadays. Secondly, the existing academic research and market application in the field of robotics are compared. The design concept and criteria of Companion Robot for children based on AI are proposed, including user targeting, function definition, material selection, modeling definition and ergonomics application, and finally the design practice under its guidance is presented.

4.2   User Targeting

Bill Gates once said, "Robots, ubiquitous screens, voice interaction, all of these will change the way we look at computers." In short, robots will change our world in the future. The degree of segmentation of the robot market depends on the diversity of user needs. UX has always been an important basis for the market in the robotic segment market. If the user experience is good, the market will be good.

Children Aged 0 to 6. This research is aimed at the design of Companion Robot for preschool students of 0–6 years old. It is found that children learn things most quickly during this period. As a partner at home, Companion Robot needs to create an imperceptible learning environment to help children develop the ability of adapting to the society and developing their independence, and also act as a little assistant to take care of their safety.

0–3 years old is the initial stage of human beings. Regarding their language, thought, behavior, balance of limbs and other aspects, they are in the shaping stage. At this time, game is the main activity. 2–3 years old is also the key period of children's oral development. They become very fond of speaking, and their vocabulary increases rapidly. They can express their ideas with simple compound sentences. They can also understand commonly used simple sentences. Their listening and speaking abilities are basically formed. During this period, children will pay attention to and be interested in bright colors, voices and moving things, which can make them familiar with the environment and participate in activities. Many interior changes of three-year-old child emerge gradually. Memory and ideological activities are produced in direct contact with things. At the same time, children will begin to try to imitate and repeat, it is in the repeated interaction of the object, combined with the development of language and action at the same time, that leads to the gradual understanding of the simple relationship of things and generation of imagination.

After the initial stage, children would gradually begin to be independent, they would learn to take care of themselves, but they are slow, clumsy, and still need help. Let's call this period developing period. During this period, children are emotionally unstable, they tend to be affected by the environment. 3–6 years old is exactly the golden period of children's growth and development. Children's mastery of vocabulary has made the fastest progress in this period, and their language ability has developed rapidly. With the rapid development of intelligence, children's personality can form. When children of this age see something interesting, they approach it actively, observe it carefully, touch it, and explore its mysteries. At the same time, we begin to understand the attributes of things around us, such as size, color, length, number, simple shape and so on. The understanding of things is more specific and can only be relied on.

Customer. Companion robots are aimed at the user group of children, but consumers are their parents. At present, the mothers and fathers of children aged 0 to 6 are basically after 80 and 90. They pay more attention to the quality of life and have higher demands in aesthetics and user experience. And in the peak period of career, the level of economic income is continuously rising, and the potential consumption capacity is huge. According to Roy Nielsen's latest consumer confidence index survey, the average monthly income of consumers in the 1980s and 1990s was 3,111 yuan, which was higher than the average of 3,022 yuan.

Compared with people in the 1970s and 1980s, the post-1980s are more casual and have more unplanned shopping. They tend to rely on all sectors of society and choose friends with common values as their social circles.

Function Definition. With the increasing pressure of life, parents tend to use smart devices such as mobile phones and iPads to let their children learn. However, with the development of the Internet and the flood of information, children who lack the ability of discrimination and self-management become more and more addicted to them. Companion robots can just overcome this problem and become a kind of novel education method which is suitable for contemporary children. Based on the application of AI technology, it can realize a diversified learning method with multiple mediums, including games, stories, music, etc. so that children can learn knowledge in a relaxing atmosphere.

The prime demand of parents on Companion Robot is education. Preschool children are not fully developed psychologically and physiologically. Parents are also at the peak of their careers. They can't take care of their children in person for a long time. Under such circumstance, it is necessary for robots to use the rich resources on the Internet instead of parents for heuristic education. Children begin to perceive the world around them and are more sensitive to color and shape. Therefore, they need to provide a great number of picture books for recognizing color and articles. At this time, children's language ability is also beginning to take shape, which is the best time for language exercises. Therefore, companion robots need to communicate with children bilingually to increase their vocabulary and improve their memory.

The second is companionship. Children's companions will influence their behavior and personality in the future. Having good interaction objects will bring them a positive environment. Because children of this age like to touch things, compared with previous robots, it would be way better if Companion Robot for children can let them ride on it. Children can climb up the body of the robot and "ride" at home, so the robot have to own a larger body shape, a stable seat, and intelligent body sensors which can also provide touch feedback. Robots should also be equipped with interactive projection to protect children's eyes and reduce direct use on the display screen. To increase the authenticity of interaction, robots with high-definition cameras and touchable screens can follow children around at home and become good partners.

Considering that children of this age are not separated from their parents, they need to be looked after by their guardians, but they also need to be given independent space. At the same time, parents are also at work, do not know the status of children at home, so companion robots should also be equipped with surveillance cameras, microphones, and speakers, so that parents who are not around their children can clearly understand their every single move and communicate with them in real time, improving the flexibility of their work and life.

It has a preinstalled patrol function. It can map the structure of the home simultaneously, route automatically and interact with children or adults. It stops [7] when people are close to the path of the robot.

In terms of endurance, as a free-moving robot at home, it should have the function of wireless charging. when it detects that the battery is low, it will return to the charging base and charge itself (Fig. 1).

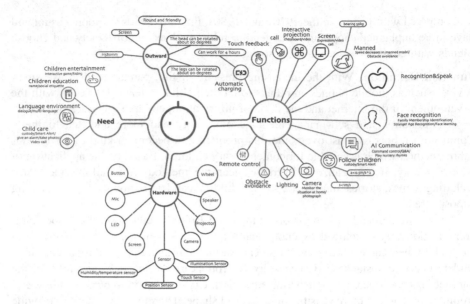

Fig. 1. Function diagram

4.3   Material Selection

In the selection of materials, we should meet the functional requirements of the robot, and consider the safety, load-bearing, environmental protection and other aspects of children. Generally, smooth and flat, environmentally friendly, 3C certified materials should be considered first, and we should also pay attention to fire prevention and so on. After comparison, ABS plastic is selected as the main materials. It is a copolymer of acrylonitrile, butadiene, and styrene. It has the characteristics of chemical resistance, high dyeability, high strength, good toughness, high impact strength, water resistance, inorganic salts, alkali and acid resistance, insoluble in most alcohols and hydrocarbon solvents, and excellent comprehensive performance. It is an ideal material for companion robots.

4.4   Ergonomics

The dimension design of Companion Robot for children needs to consider various users, including children learning to crawl, children who can walk, and adults at home.

When children use the robot, the height is lower than that of the robot's head, which will show a state of looking up to observe the robot's facial expression. Therefore, in order to prevent children from feeling fatigue, the head height is set at about 500–600 mm.

When a child is a little older than one or two years old, he can ride on a robot and play with it. Referring to the size of some mature Trojan products on the market, and considering the safety of children, the height range of his back should be set at about 300–400 mm.

At the same time, as the main interactive medium of the robot, the size of the display screen is also of great importance. Taking into consideration of both the display effect and proportion, the face diameter is set at about 150–250 mm.

Firstly, the overall design semantic of Companion Robot for children should conform to the special target group of children, and use more round shapes to ensure safety and enhance the affinity of the robot, while using fewer square shapes with sharp edges and corners. Secondly, to meet the market demand, the design style needs to be concise and fashionable, with a geometric shape as the main body, mellow and lovely and in line with modern aesthetics.

4.5 Design Practice

Based on the design concept of companion robot proposed in this study, a new type of companion robot, Shaun, is designed based on AI technology. Shaun's black, round head with two handles on both sides is like a sheep's blackface. Its body is white. It has a round curve like a head. It's like a sheep's fat body. Its limbs and legs are oval. It can reduce unnecessary harm to children. The wheels used to move are hidden at the end of the limbs.

Shaun is aimed at children's daily companionship and children's education. It has such basic functions as object recognition, face recognition, riding, interactive projection, automatic follow-up, AI communication, video, touch feedback, calling, automatic charging, remote control and so on.

The robot is about 60 cm high, the back is about 30 cm high, with round and intimate appearance. The head can rotate around 90°, the legs can rotate for up to 40°, reflecting its loveliness and flexibility and has a authentic sense of interaction with children. In order to achieve its rich functions, hardware is equipped with wheels, speakers, projectors, cameras, screens, LED lights, microphones, keys, as well as light, temperature, humidity, location, touch sensors to meet the children's entertainment, education, language environment, child care, growth records and other needs (Fig. 2).

Shaun also has his own wake-up password. When parents or children call "Hey Shaun", Shaun will be waked up and come to you to listen to your next command. It can identify different family members, store memories of relatives and friends, and follow designated members. Shaun can communicate with children in simple words. Children can ask questions like "How far is the Earth to the Moon?" Through the application of AI technology, Shaun can recognize the object in front of him through a camera mounted on his face, such as an apple in his hand. Shaun will tell the child that it is an apple. Children can climb up onto Shaun's body while playing. The antiskid rubber on the back increases friction and prevents falling. When weight sensor on Shaun's back detects gravity, it switches to cycling mode. The pedals on both sides stretch out, the driving speed drops back, and children will route Shaun to enjoy riding on horseback. For parents, the high-definition touch screen on Shaun's face can set up the robot. By default, the screen is Shaun's eyes. After touching, it enters the operation page. At the same time, parents can use the mobile app to control it. For example, you can view the activities of your children through the camera, or you can chat with your children via video. This can alleviate the anxiety that parents can't accompany their children. Shaun can also take photos or videos to record the moments of family life.

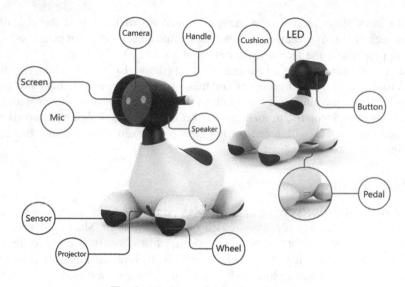

Fig. 2. Hardware distribution diagram

In addition, Shaun can automatically do wireless charging through SLAM technology. In the tail, a wireless charging receiving coil is installed to connect the internal charging battery, and inside the wall at home, a wireless charging transmitting coil is installed to provide the power supply. When the robot senses that the power is insufficient, it will reserve the return power to find the charging base. When Shaun's tail touches the charging base, it can be charged.

The following table shows the main functions for each age group (Table 2):

Table 2. The main functions of each age group:

Functions	1 year old	2 years old	3 years old	4–5 years old	5–6 years old	Parent
Object cognition	•	•				
Color cognition	•	•				
Digital cognition		•				
Interactive projection			•	•	•	
Relationships cognition		•				
Bilingual interaction				•	•	
Reading and writing training					•	
Read a story		•	•	•	•	
Sing a song	•	•	•	•		
Arithmetic training				•	•	
Learning English				•	•	
Develop a habit			•	•	•	
Play a game	•	•	•	•	•	
Riding			•	•	•	
Video chat			•	•	•	•
Security monitoring						•
Take a photo						•

See the ergonomics diagrams below (Figs. 3, 4, 5, 6, 7 and 8):

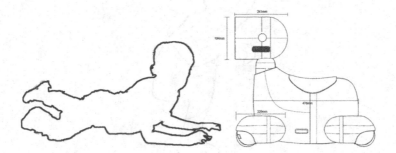

Fig. 3. Ergonomics diagram (Face-to-face) for children below 3 years old

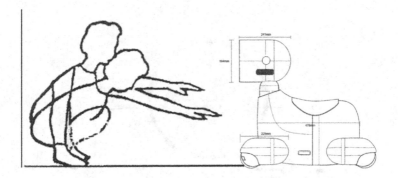

Fig. 4. Ergonomics diagram (Face-to-face) for children aged 3 to 6

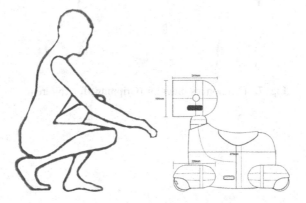

Fig. 5. Ergonomics diagram (Face-to-face) for adults

Fig. 6. Ergonomics diagram (Riding) for children

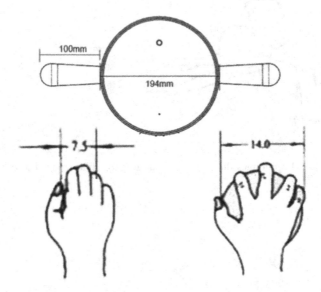

Fig. 7. Ergonomics diagram (Gripping) for children

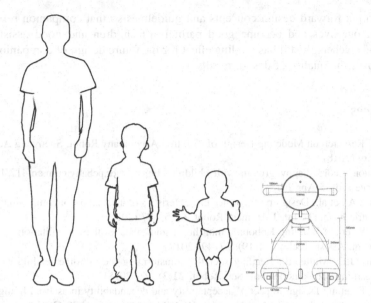

Fig. 8. Ergonomics diagram (Standing) for all ages

5   Conclusion

Owing to the rapid development of AI technology, Companion Robot for children is a hot research topic at present, which involves a lot of knowledge in science and technology. From shape to function to material, the characteristics of children are supposed to be considered in every step.

Based on AI technology and the current status of the mainstream consumer groups, this research systematically puts forward design concepts and guidelines for the design of companion robot from the aspects of user targeting, function definition, material definition, and ergonomics. In terms of dimension, the size of larger service robots and the one of smaller desktop robots on the market are averaged in order to meet more abundant human-computer interaction needs. Different from most of the stationary desktop children's education robots nowadays, a new size is defined. In terms of function, combined with AI technology, some interesting functions that companion robots should have been proposed heuristically, especially the novel interactive mode of riding, which has not appeared in the market at present. Designers can adopt some of the concepts and guidelines to instruct the design of companion robot in the future according to the specific needs and the design background at that time. This research can make the design and orientation of companion robot clearer.

There are still some shortcomings in this study. The threshold of companion robot is not technology, but the content it can provide and the way it interacts with children and parents. The emotional interaction between robots and children is an integral but difficult point. In the follow-up study, we will continue to do in-depth discussion in this area. Let companion robots implicitly help children develop good habits, good mentality, and make education more interesting and diverse. But the significance of this study is to put forward design concepts and guidelines so that companion robots can truly enter our lives and become good partners of children and good assistants of parents and teachers. It still has guiding effect for the future design of companion robot and improves the quality of design results.

References

1. Zhu, X.: Research on Modeling Design of Children Accompany Robot. Shenyang Aerospace University (2018)
2. Companion record, happy growth with children. https://yuer.pcbaby.com.cn/412/4121150.html. Accessed 25 Apr 2018
3. Meghdari, A., et al.: Design performance characteristics of a social robot companion "Arash" for pediatric hospitals. Int. J. Human. Robot. 6(15), P7 (2018)
4. Billard, A., et al.: Building Robota, a mini-humanoid robot for the rehabilitation of children with autism. Assist. Technol. 1(19), 37–49 (2017)
5. Michaelis, J.E., Mutlu, B.: Reading socially: transforming the in-home reading experience with a learning-companion robot. Sci. Robot. 21(3), P2 (2018)
6. Cavallo, F., et al.: Design impact of acceptability and dependability in assisted living robotic applications. Int. J. Interact. Des. Manuf. – IJIDEM 4(12), 1167–1178 (2018)
7. Lichtenthaler, C., et al.: Social navigation - identifying robot navigation patterns in a path crossing scenario. Soc. Robot. J. 8239, 84–93 (2013)

Design Thinking and Gamification: User Centered Methodologies

Eva Villegas[1(✉)], Emiliano Labrador[1], David Fonseca[1],
Sara Fernández-Guinea[2], and Fernando Moreira[3]

[1] La Salle – Universitat Ramon Llull, 08022 Barcelona, Spain
{eva.villegas, emiliano.labrador, fonsi}@salle.url.edu
[2] Universidad Complutense de Madrid, Madrid, Spain
sguinea@psi.ucm.es
[3] Universidade Portucalense, Porto, Portugal
fmoreira@uportu.pt

Abstract. The article presents the analysis of two systems of participatory design that allow to understand collaborative learning as a method of creating strategies and products. Two methodologies are described in order to discuss the possibilities and challenges of its application. The text begins by defining a user experience methodology designed to create with the participation of the user and continues with the definition of Design Thinking, which enhances empathy with the user through active techniques and a proficiency created to enhance the participation of people through the game Gamification. For this, the theoretical basis of each of the systems has been taken into account, the two Frameworks on which they are based on are compared and the design of the sessions with consumers is used as a starting point. It shows a first approximation of the comparison of the two systems through the sample of frameworks in study that mixes the user experience with Gamification. Through this analysis, it is affirmed that the emotional behavior of the user is key to define strategies and products, therefore, it must be designed for the user with the user.

Keywords: Design thinking · Gamification · User centered design · Constructivism paradigm · Creativity · User experience

1 Introduction

The user-centered design is a philosophy that allows the user to be part of the development process, providing motivations, needs and desires during all its stages. The methods used today in which they require this participation, are based mainly on projective techniques [1]. This type of techniques allow emotional connection with the user and active participation in the session. For this, a constructivist paradigm is used [2], leaving all the protagonism to the user and allowing him to build his own thought. The study shown below is based on the analysis of two systems that allow us to work with the emotions of the users who participate in the session and therefore promote a participatory design.

© Springer Nature Switzerland AG 2019
P. Zaphiris and A. Ioannou (Eds.): HCII 2019, LNCS 11590, pp. 115–124, 2019.
https://doi.org/10.1007/978-3-030-21814-0_10

On the one hand, Design Thinking is a methodology that is normally applied in the creation of new products or strategies. On the other hand is Gamification which can be applied in any development or creation process that requires a solution or measurable result with the introduction of a playful attitude [3–5]. In both, it must be based on a working hypothesis and some insights or project objectives. The aim of this study is to analyze the two methodologies, their definitions, phases and objectives, so that their similarities and differences are understood in order to understand which Gamification frameworks are centered on the user and how they apply it.

2   Theoretical Framework

The theoretical framework includes a brief description of the two methodologies used in the study: Gamification and Design thinking, and the two systems in which they are related: participatory design and the constructivist paradigm.

The Gamification [6] is a methodology that is defined as the application of game strategies in non-recreational environments [7]. In 2008, the term was used for the first time, although several documents indicate the use of this system previously by creating several games that were born as a reflection of real life. Nick Pelling in 2002 was the first to use the term as such, but it is not until 2010 that it is disseminated more extensively.

Of the many definitions of the term, it is work with those that are based on the design of the system [8], that is, with those that link the implementation of elements/game components with the requirements or aims to be taken into account in the system. The definition of the method is based in mind by means of three components described by the authors Hunike, Leblanc and Zubec in 2004, the MDA [9]: (M) Mechanics, (D) Dynamics and (A) Aesthetics. Mechanics as rules that define the game system, Dynamics as the relation of the interaction that is established between the system and the users and Aesthetics as the perceptions of the users during the session.

The Design thinking [10] is a methodology that was started, in the case of Gamification in 2008, but it wasn't until in 2009 Tim Brown of IDEO in his book Change by Design [11] that popularized the term. It is a methodology that focuses processes on people and is used mainly to create/define strategies, products or services, so that creativity is enhanced. The participants can be multidisciplinary profiles involved in the proposal allowing them to work in a transversal way.

The two methodologies are based on a participatory design [12] that promotes the active participation of multidisciplinary teams focused on the product to be created or evaluated. In this, it is tried to validate that all the profiles are covered and have contributed their needs and motivations as an important part of the creation process. For this, the constructivist paradigm that conceives knowledge can be used [13] as a construction of the user.

3 Design Frameworks

In the case of Gamification there is no consensus among the authors and it works using different frameworks. Normally, large companies or professionals have published their frameworks and the rest of the community uses them, although there is no record of which is the most used. Below are some of the most commonly used and known frameworks in the field.

3.1 Gamification Design Framework

Gamification Design Framework de Andrej Marczewski
The Gamification design framework is based on establishing the necessary processes to be able to create a gamified system [14] (see Fig. 1).

Fig. 1. Gamification design framework overview [14]

This framework starts from the definition of three components that will be the basis on which the whole system will be built: The definition of the problem, the definition of the users and the definition of the objectives. Within these axes the rest of the elements are included, such as the level of immersion (Discovery/On-boarding/Immersion/Mastery/Replay), the definition of the mechanics that will modify the behaviors, motivators and emotions, and finally, the activities what the users will have to do, as well as the feedback that will be received.

In this type of system, importance is given to three phases: discovery, design and redefine. In the first phase, the problem or aims are defined, the users who will be part of the session and the register of success. In the second phase, the session is designed taking into account the possible motivations and the applicable game mechanics. The final phase works on the actions to act or to give feedback and then, in an iterative way, the necessary improvements can be made. Therefore, we work in a sequential process but iteration is applied when necessary.

Gamification Model Canvas Framework

The Gamification Model Canvas Framework was developed by Sergio Jiménez from the MDS framework and the Business Model Canvas by Alex Osterwalder [15].

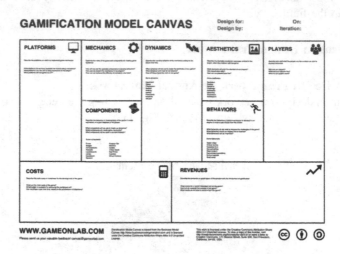

Fig. 2. Gamification Model Canvas by Sergio Jiménez

Like its model the Business Model Canvas (see Fig. 2), this framework bases its structure on the different elements based on when designing a gamified system. Although it takes users into account, it is not a framework centered on the user itself, so it is subsequently redesigned.

The new framework [16] is based on the evolution of Sergio Jiménez's Gamification Model Canvas [17]. In this case, it is worked on the creation of an intrinsic motivation framework for users, the FBM (Fogg Behavior Model). On the one hand, the profiles are analyzed from a difficulty level point of view. In the next step, the types of motivators in which to work with the users are analyzed, and finally the dynamics to be performed are selected. In the following figure (see Fig. 3) the diagram can be visualized.

Gamification Project Design Framework

The framework shown below (see Fig. 4) is based on the process carried out in projects [18]. In the first phase of the process, the objectives of the project are indicated and it is decided if it is appropriate or not to apply Gamification, information is sought about the company for which it is going to work and finally, the target is decided from a possible point of view of the behavior of the user according to certain actions. In the second phase the possible motivators are defined according to what has been studied and decided in the previous phase. In the final phase, the prototype is created and tested with users, it is produced. Moreover, it is still being tested and once the project is delivered, it will be reviewed and possible errors will be solved.

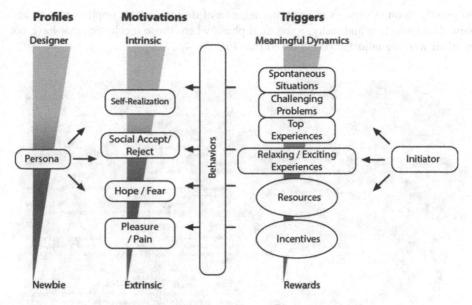

Fig. 3. Gamification Model Canvas Framework [16]

Run a Successful Gamification Project

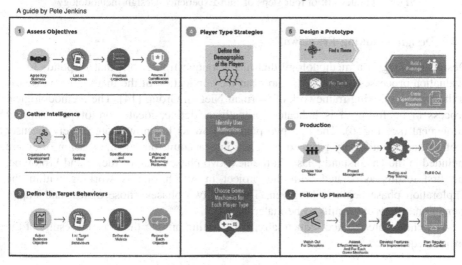

Fig. 4. How to run a successful gamification project [18]

Fun Experience Design Framework

The Fun Experience Design methodology (FED) is an iterative Gamification methodology developed by Emiliano Labrador and Eva Villegas [19] which consists of four phases. One regarding the knowledge of the users to which the system is directed to gamify through surveys or other means, one of design, one of implementation and new data collection and lastly, a redesign phase where those mechanics that have not worked well are adjusted or improved (see Fig. 5) [4, 5, 20].

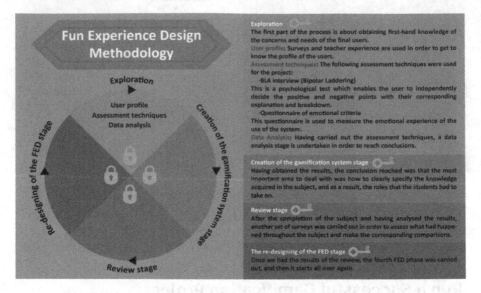

Fig. 5. Framework of four steps of Fun Experience Design methodology

3.2   Design Thinking Framework

Design thinking is a methodology that has a unique framework that responds to the evaluation processes necessary to carry out the application of the methodology. Below is the Design thinking framework of Norman Nielsen Group [14]. The methodological process to be followed is indicated: empathize, define, ideate, prototype, test, and implement (see Fig. 6). The first two phases allow us to know more closely the user profiles and identify any point to be taken into account during the session, they are included in the Understand phase. In the next two phases, that of Ideate and Prototype, the first results associated with the project in which one is working within the Exploration phase begin to be given. The next two phases, those of test and implementation, allow the results to be materialized.

The phases are worked sequentially, but iterating among them as the results of the project require it.

3.3   Comparative

Based on the definitions above, it can be determined that both Design thinking and Gamification use systems based on sequential work processes, but giving consultants the freedom to adapt each of the steps to the needs of the project and according to the results of the projects in previous steps, it can be agreed on that they take into account

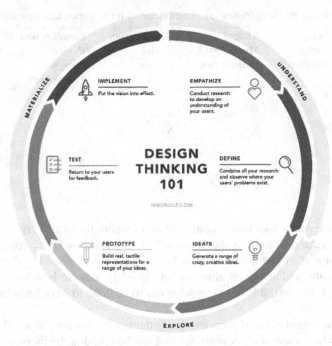

Fig. 6. Design thinking, Norman Nielsen Group

the user, although in different measures where the main objective of the process, the work through the motivators of user behavior is a key point that must always be taken into account. For this, the user profile, the project objective and the insights to be achieved are worked on in the initial phase, which the two methodologies define as the discovery phase. Once the parameters are established, the design and development phase of the process is continued. The exploration phase of the design produced, once there is a defined based on the needs and desires of the users is finalized with a phase of evaluation or testing [21]. This is possibly the most iterative of all since it depends on a large extent on the results of the tests and the opinions of the users. Below is a comparative table of the three phases defined in each of the methodologies (Table 1).

Table 1. Comparison of the phases of the two frameworks

Gamification design framework	Design thinking framework
Discovery	Understand
Design	Explore
Redesign	Materialize

Although all Gamification frameworks have a similar structure, and in turn are somewhat similar to the Design thinking framework, some differences have been observed, as it can be seen in Table 2.

Table 2. Design thinking framework, Gamifications frameworks, and new framework

	Design thinking framework	Andrej Marczewski Framework	Gamification Model Canvas	Gamification Project Design Framework	Fun Experience Design
Empathize	X				X
Define	X	X	X	X	X
Ideate	X	X	X	X	X
Prototype	X			X	X
Test	X			X	X
Implement	X	X	X	X	X

All the frameworks take into account the users whom they call Players, since they define their characteristics not by the traditional demographic and social parameters but by their behavior in a playful environment [22, 23]. However, not all of them define or treat them equally, and above all, they do not explicitly indicate how this information can be obtained. For this, it is not clear what has to be done to have knowledge of one of its central pillars.

In addition, almost none of them explicitly defines the testing phase. This has also been observed in numerous success stories that can be found in the literature, where all the phases of the design and implementation of a gamified system are explained, except for its testing. Thus, a lack of documentation in gamified systems has been detected in a key phase of Design thinking, which turns it into an iterative methodology based on the results of the project.

4   Conclusions

In conclusion, the purpose of the study is to identify the common and divergent points, strengths and weaknesses of two systems that enhance the participatory design. The main point of the two is to situate the user as the key to be able to make a successful design. All frameworks make it clear that it is essential to know who you are designing for, their needs, motivations and above all their behavior. However, a greater consensus is lacking in allowing users to be those who, through their knowledge or action, provide a very real vision of design. Being normally multidisciplinary work teams that develop these systems, the opinions, needs and desires are identified and work from several points of view.

Constructivist psychology helps to understand how people get involved in user experience processes. To do this, the new methodologies shown, that are still in the study phase, enhance user participation through explicit knowledge of the profiles and a session design based on the results obtained. This knowledge should be generated in every design, and therefore all frameworks should incorporate it and also indicate how to obtain this data.

Gamification is an axis that enhances emotional behavior. The user experience is a philosophy of rigor in the collection of data and evaluation of results. The results of the projects that are made through the union of these systems can be used as systems that enhance the emotions and creativity of users, allowing designs to be created from the needs and desires.

As a future line, it will be worked on the detail of knowing in depth the emotional behavior of the user, the time of attention during the session and the empathy of the facilitator with the participants through the analysis of: number of items that are extracted, quality of ideas based on the aim and intervention times. All this by creating a single session target with two different user groups. Intergroup and intragroup.

Acknowledgment. With the support of the Secretaria d'Universitats i Recerca of the Department of Business and Knowledge of the Generalitat de Catalunya with the help of 2017 SGR 934.

References

1. Lilienfeld, S.O., Wood, J.M., Garb, H.N.: The scientific status of projective techniques. Psychol. Sci. Public Interest **1**, 27–66 (2000)
2. Dagar, V., Yadav, A.: Constructivism: a paradigm for teaching and learning. Arts Soc. Sci. J. **7**, 200 (2016)
3. Villegas, E., Labrador, E., Fonseca, D., Fernández-Guinea, S.: Mejora de las metodologías de experiencia de usuario mediante la aplicación de gamificación. Metodología I'm In. In: 13th Iberian Conference on Information Systems and Technologies (CISTI), pp. 1–6, Cáceres (2018). e-ISBN 978-989-98434-8-6, Print-ISBN 978-1-5386-4885-8
4. Labrador, E., Villegas, E.: Unir Gamificación y Experiencia de Usuario para mejorar la experiencia docente. RIED. Rev. Iberoam. Educ. a Distancia. **19**, 125 (2016)
5. Fonseca, D., Torres-Kompen, R., Labrador, E., Villegas, E.: Technology-Enhanced Learning: Good Educational Practices. IGI-Global, Hershey (2018)
6. Prowting, F.: Gamification: Engaging Your Workforce. Prowting, F. (ed.). Ark Group (2014)
7. Deterding, S., Sicart, M., Nacke, L., O'Hara, K., Dixon, D.: Gamification: using game-design elements in non-gaming contexts. In: Proceedings of the 2011 Annual Conference Extended Abstracts on Human Factors in Computing Systems - CHI EA 2011 (2011)
8. Gabe, Z., Cunningham, C.: Gamification By Design. O'Reilly, Newton (2011)
9. Hunicke, R., LeBlanc, M., Zubek, R.: MDA: a formal approach to game design and game research. In: Proceedings of the Association for the Advancement of Artificial Intelligence Workshop on Challenges in Game AI, AAAI 2004 (2004)
10. Brown, T., Wyatt, J.: Design thinking for social innovation. Dev. Outreach **12**, 29–43 (2010)
11. Brown, T.: Change by Design: How Design Thinking Transforms Organizations and Inspires Innovation. HarperCollins Publishers, New York (2009)
12. Spinuzzi, C.: The methodology of participatory design. Tech. Commun. **52**, 163–174 (2005)
13. Harlow, S., Cummings, R., Aberasturi, S.M.: Karl Popper and Jean Piaget: a rationale for constructivism. Educ. Forum. **71**, 41–48 (2006)
14. Marczewski, A.: Gamification: A Simple Introduction. Marczewski, A. (ed.) (2013)
15. Osterwalder, A., Pigneur, Y., Smith, A.: Business Model Generation. Booksgooglecom (2010). https://doi.org/10.1523/JNEUROSCI.0307-10.2010

16. Escribano, F., Moretón, J., Jimenez, S.: Gamification Model Canvas Framework. Evolution (2016). https://gecon.es/gamification-model-canvas-framework-evolution-1/
17. Ruizalba, J., Navarro, F., Jiménez, S.: Gamificación como estrategia de marketing interno. Intang. Cap. **9**(4), 1113–1144 (2013)
18. Hamari, J., Koivisto, J.: Why do people use gamification services? Int. J. Inf. Manag. (2015). https://doi.org/10.1016/j.ijinfomgt.2015.04.006
19. Labrador, E., Villegas, E.: Fun experience design applied to learning. In: ICEILT International Congress on Education, Innovation and Learning (2014)
20. Villegas, E., Pifarré, M., Fonseca, D.: Methodological design of user experience applied to the field of accessibility. In: Proceedings of the 5th Iberian Conference on Information Systems and Technologies, CISTI 2010 (2010)
21. Fonseca, D., Conde, M.Á., García-Peñalvo, F.J.: Improving the information society skills: is knowledge accessible for all? Univers. Access Inf. Soc. **17**, 229–245 (2018)
22. Hamari, J., Koivisto, J., Sarsa, H.: Does gamification work?-a literature review of empirical studies on gamification. In: HICSS, vol. 14, pp. 3025–3034, January 2014
23. Hartmann, T., Klimmt, C., Hamari, J., Tuunanen, J.: Player types: a meta-synthesis. Trans. Digit. Games Res. Assoc. **1**(2), 29–53 (2014)

Theoretical and Pedagogical Approaches in Technology-Enhanced Learning

The Neuro-Subject: A Living Entity with Learnability

Ángel Fidalgo-Blanco[1] , María Luisa Sein-Echaluce[2](✉) ,
and Francisco José García-Peñalvo[3]

[1] LITI Laboratory, Technical University of Madrid, Madrid, Spain
angel.fidalgo@upm.es
[2] Department of Applied Mathematics, University of Zaragoza, Saragossa, Spain
mlsein@unizar.es
[3] GRIAL Research Group, University of Salamanca, Salamanca, Spain
fgarcia@usal.es

Abstract. In the context of an academic subject, students and teachers acquire knowledge and experience, but we must ensure that this experience will be shared and managed. In this way, the learning, acquired in the subject, remains in the subject. A proven way to manage the experience, which has been validated in previous works, is based on considering two dimensions: the conversion of individual knowledge into organizational and the use of a knowledge management system that allows classifying, organizing and finding knowledge based on ontologies and inferences between them. The primary objective of this research work is to join the two dimensions and apply an active method to manage the experience acquired by the teaching staff and students. The combination of the models RT-CICLO, as an active method, and ACCI 3.0 to transform individual and organizational knowledge can be applied so that organizational knowledge and learning are produced in a subject. In this work we have identified the actions in which the students create knowledge, as well as the type of knowledge that is created in each case. Organizational knowledge can be generated from each action, which can also be used to promote individual student learning. In the experience also have been acquired a high perception of usefulness on the part of students with regard to all types of organizational knowledge created.

Keywords: Active methodologies · Collaborative learning ·
Knowledge spiral · Knowledge management system

1 Introduction

In the industry, mainly Japanese, the fact that learning takes place through the interaction of workers has been studied, and that learning must be saved and managed within the organization to improve it [1, 2]. But for the learning to take place in the organization, it is necessary a set of phases of interaction between the implicit knowledge of a person (e.g., their experience) and explicit knowledge (e.g., a technical report that they have made). So, there is a knowledge spiral, called, epistemological spiral [2] that is based on the following phases:

© Springer Nature Switzerland AG 2019
P. Zaphiris and A. Ioannou (Eds.): HCII 2019, LNCS 11590, pp. 127–141, 2019.
https://doi.org/10.1007/978-3-030-21814-0_11

- Acquisition of knowledge, it can come from two types of interaction:
  - Exchanging implicit knowledge of several people through socialization between them. This phase is called *Socialization*.
  - Acquisitioning knowledge from the existing implicit knowledge. It is the phase called *Internalization*.
- Externalization of knowledge. In this phase the person who has acquired knowledge must externalize it. Thus, the person should not keep it, he should transfer it through external support that can be distributed within the organization, even in the absence of that person. This phase is called *Externalization*.
- Combination of explicit knowledge. When there is sufficient explicit knowledge in the organization, mainly produced by its members, it can be combined to produce new knowledge. To get this combination, it's necessary to identify, classify and facilitate the transfer of knowledge wherever it is needed. This phase is called *Combination*.

On the other hand, in the traditional academic teaching, the two main actors are the students and the teachers. The learning that occurs in the subject traditionally affects the students, but also in the teaching staff, since as they work on the subject increases their academic and teaching experience.

Thus, students and teachers learn through the acquisition of knowledge, skills and abilities. If the faculty continues to teach their subject, the experience gained impacts it, improving it. However, when students finish the course, this does not affect the learning acquired in the same since they leave.

In the context of an academic subject, the students and teachers acquire knowledge and experience, but you have to get this experience is shared and managed. The most suitable methodologies for the students to participate, cooperate and share are the active methodologies [3–7].

Numerous authors emphasize that active methodologies produce greater learning in students [8]. Authors, considered as historical, indicate that students learn more "doing" than "listening" [9, 10], the learning must begin with the active participation of the students and, also, this active participation must be doing continually [6]. Some characteristics of the active participation of students are action-reflection [11], cooperation [12], work with real problems [13], decision-making [11], and the creation of knowledge [14].

Likewise, it has been shown that the creation of knowledge itself requires high cognitive abilities on the part of the author, so their level of learning is higher than if they did not create knowledge [3]. On the other hand, the creation of knowledge by students can have different levels of certainty. For this reason, the feedback provided by the teachers to the students who create the knowledge is a key factor for learning occurs in the students, and this feedback should be as immediate as possible after the creation of that knowledge [15].

The main objective of this work is to apply the concept of organizational learning to academic subjects of the university context. For this, the student is considered a member of the organization that can learn and create. For the part of the organization must improve the learning of its members and, for this; it should promote the creation of individual and group knowledge, as well as the management of the same, so that impact both the organization and the own individual.

To get this main objective, it must be met these four objectives:

- Having a conceptual model that considers a subject as an organization that learns.
- Identifying the actions of the students that together with the actions of teachers can produce organizational knowledge.
- Identifying the types of organizational knowledge produced.
- Studying the perceptions of students on the utility for your learning of the different types of organizational knowledge.

The following sections will present the theoretical model on which this proposal is based, the research context that includes the measurement tools, as well as the results obtained, to end with the conclusions.

2 Theoretical Model

The initial theoretical model is based on the model proposed by Nonaka for an organization to carry out learning, this is called epistemological spiral [2]. The first step is based on correlating the different phases of this spiral with a traditional educational model. In this way, the feasibility of applying the model and the actions it carries can be analyzed.

The equivalence between the phases of the epistemological spiral and an educational model are those:

- *Socialization*. During the face to face classes, socialization takes place due to the interaction between the teachers and the students. This type of socialization can be weak (the lecturer holds a master class and the student is passive person) or strong (students and teachers participate in the class actively).
- *Internalization*. It occurs when the students study the notes that have taken personally during the lecture or with another teaching resource provided by the faculty, like notes or recommended books.
- *Externalization*. This phase is unusual among students because traditional methods don't promote the active participation of students, and don't generate teaching resources. In spite of that, there are numerous authors who point out the convenience of the students to create knowledge, as a method to improve their own learning. For example, the elaboration of notes by the students during the master class is an explicit sample of knowledge.
- *Combination*. During this phase the students does a specific academic activity individually. They usually combine explicit knowledge from different sources: their own knowledge, the knowledge of other classmates and that of the teaching staff. For example, in an exam they use the notes that they themselves have taken (explicit since they have generated it themselves), but they will also use notes of other classmates and those of the teaching staff.

From this relationship you can design the characteristics that the model must have in order to allow the subject "learn", that is, to increase organizational knowledge.

Figure 1 shows those characteristics that are described below. The *socialization phase* is very common in educational models. Socialization is weak if the methodology used is passive on the part of the students (for example, a master lesson) and is strong if it is based on an active methodology where the students participate actively in their learning process. Therefore, a first requirement to apply this model is that the methodology must be active (Fig. 1a).

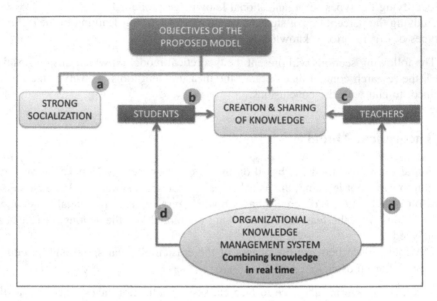

Fig. 1. Characteristics of the proposed model

The *internalization phase* usually occurs in the students, because they usually perform academic activities, such as preparing an exam, through explicit knowledge.

In the *externalization phase* it looks that both students and teachers transform tacit knowledge into implicit knowledge. In order to create organizational learning to occur, the members of the organization must externalize and share their knowledge. Therefore, the model used should motivate students and teachers to make explicit and share their experience. See Fig. 1b and c.

The *combination phase* is essential to do organizational learning. It is based on combining the experience of the students, which they previously shared, with the experience of the teaching staff. For that, we must be a tool that allows this combination of knowledge to be carried out at the time and place where such knowledge is produced. The combined knowledge is part of the subject, but this can also be used by teachers and students in their individual learning. See Fig. 1d.

Thus, the model should be based on active methodologies; this should encourage the creation and sharing of knowledge by students and teachers. And it should allow the combination of knowledge of students and teachers in real time.

In previous research, there have been various models that individually give support to these identified characteristics. The RT-CICLO model [16] supports the features defined in Fig. 1a, b and c and the ACCI 3.0 model [17] supports those described in Fig. 1d. These models are explained below.

2.1 Model RT-CYCLE for Strong Socialization, Creation and Sharing of Knowledge by Students and Teachers

It is based on the fact that students participate actively in the learning process. It would be enough to apply a methodology considered as active, such as Flipped Classroom [18], Project Based Learning (PBL) [19], Gamification [20], or Game Based Learning (GBL) [21].

All of these methodologies have some characteristic processes and procedures that should be applied during the development of the subject. In this work we have used our own model called RT-CICLO (Fig. 2), this uses the basic characteristics of different theories, models and methods of active learning. This model is characterized because it is very simple and can be used punctually or continuously in the development of a subject. For example, you can use it during a 10 min master class or continue in a set of class.

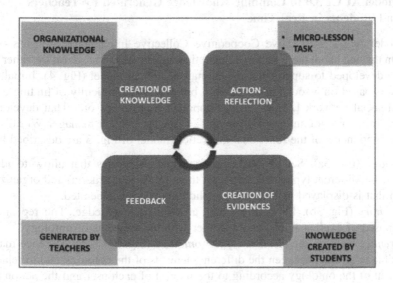

Fig. 2. Model RT-CICLO

The model, described in Fig. 2, is based on five actions grouped into four phases, as follows:

- *Phase 1. Action-reflection.* This set of actions aims to provide a minimum but necessary knowledge (micro-lesson) that guides students in the performance of a specific task. This task is a micro individual or group work, where you must make a reflection and decision making.

- *Phase 2. Creation of evidence.* The evidence is the result of the task, which may be right or wrong. The result must be make explicit and shared online. If the result has been correct, it is considered as evidence that the student has acquired positive learning. If the result has been incorrect, it has also acquired learning because one learns from your own mistakes (as long as they are corrected).
- *Phase 3 - Feedback.* In this phase the teacher selects results that are correct and others that are incorrect. The objective is to improve the learning produced in the previous phase. When feedback is given on a correct result, all students learn from it. The same happens when you make a feedback of the wrong result, all the students will learn, because you are showing an error and how to correct it. This phase gives knowledge to all the students and the learning will improve greater variety of correct or incorrect results. The feedback can be done by the teachers or the students. In any case, the faculty must coordinate the process, selecting the results with which they will work and managing the time.
- *Phase 4 - Knowledge creation.* This phase is based on the students and teachers make explicit the knowledge acquired in the previous phases and sharing it.

2.2 Model ACCI 3.0 to Combine Knowledge Generated by Teachers and Students in Real Time

This model ACCI 3.0 (Active Cooperative Collective Intelligence) consists of two parts. On the one hand, the functional theoretical model (Fig. 3) and, on the other hand, software developed to support this functional theoretical model (Fig. 4). Initially, the model was based on a social network [22], but due to the difficulty of finding content within a social network [23], a self-development was carried out. That development consisted in the programming of a plugin [24] for the content manager WordPress.

The components of the functional theoretical model of Fig. 3 are described below:

- *Ontology* (Fig. 3a). Set of labels grouped into categories that allow to identify (know the different types), classify (sort them by various criteria) and organize (the form that is displayed to users) the explicit knowledge generated.
- *Repository* (Fig. 3b). Physically stores all explicit knowledge. The repository is composed of explicit knowledge together with the elements of ontology.
- *Inferences between the elements of the ontology* (Fig. 3c). The inference makes it possible to interact between the different elements of the ontology and to relate any element of the ontology according to the interest of each user and the action that it wishes to carry out.
- *Semantic search* (Fig. 3d). Use the inferences between the elements of the ontology to define a logical expression that has to meet the organizational knowledge sought. You can do a search by text, but also indicating that it must meet a certain relationship between the elements of the ontology. For example, you can specify that you want to search "integration polynomials" and that it meets the characteristics "that serve to understand the concept" and that also "show an example".
- *Meta-information* (Fig. 3e). Meta-information is added to each of explicit knowledge; the meta-information is the relationship of that knowledge with the ontology. For example, using the previous example, the knowledge "interpolation polynomials" can be associated with the meta-information "explain concept", "example", "2018/19 course", "Mines degree" and "vector data structure".

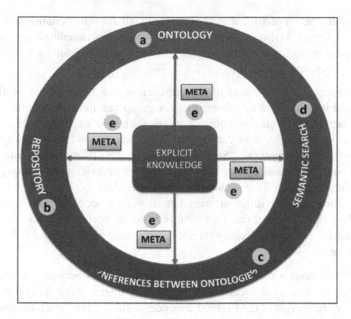

Fig. 3. Model ACCI 3.0

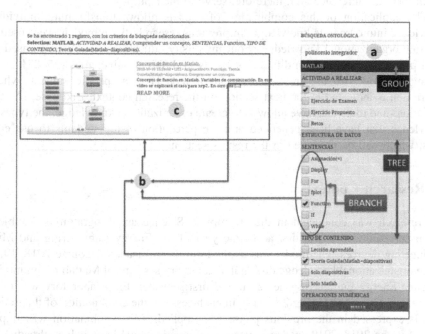

Fig. 4. Semantic search through inferences between the elements of the ontology

The software developed for this model allows all the functionalities of the theoretical model. Figure 4 shows how several of these functionalities are performed. Figure 4a shows an example of the ontology of Fig. 3a. The ontology is composed of the following hierarchical elements:

- *Group*. Represents the context of the application, the figure is the Matlab application used in programming laboratories. A group can have "n" elements "Tree".
- *Tree*. It represents a classification of explicit knowledge. Figure 4a shows five classifications: "Activity to be carried out" (academic action for which knowledge is to be used), "Data structure", "Sentences" used in the different programs, "Type of content" and "Numerical operations". Each explicit knowledge can belong to one to several Tree, and each Tree includes a set of metadata.
- *Branch*. They are the different metadata that is associated with each explicit knowledge. For example, the Tree "Activity to be performed" has the branches "Understand a concept", "Exam exercise", "Proposed exercise" and "Challenge" to be performed.

Figure 4b indicates a semantic search through inferences between the elements of the ontology. In this case, search for the text "Interpolating polynomial". The knowledge has to serve to "Understand a concept" (about the "interpolating polynomial"), that knowledge uses a sentence "Function" and that the content type is "Guided theory (Matlab + slides)", that is, a tutorial. Figure 4c shows the resources found, which meet the inference and, therefore, serve to their purpose.

The application of this combination of models allows transforming individual knowledge into corporate knowledge. In previous research, these models were used to generate organizational knowledge about university educational innovation based on good practices carried out in different subjects of different universities [25–27].

In this work, we use the combination of models in a specific subject, whose description is indicated in the next section on the research context. Likewise, identify the actions and tools that have allowed to create organizational knowledge, the types of knowledge that have been generated and the perception of the students to use each class, which will be presented in the results section.

3   Research Context

The research was conducted in the "Computer Science and Programming" subject, which corresponded to the first academic year of the Energy Engineering and Mine Engineering degrees. The model was applied during the academic course 2018–19, to create organizational knowledge during the laboratory sessions of Matlab programming from the Energy Engineering degree in the first semester. Each laboratory was organized into 12 sessions lasting 2 h each. In each session, the combination of theoretical models expressed in the previous phase was applied. This combination was implemented in the 2018–2019 academic year. The organizational knowledge, already created in the first semester, was applied to one laboratory group during the second semester of 2018–2019 of the Mine Engineering degree, to measure the perception of the usefulness of the organizational learning elements used.

The RT-CICLO model was used in two ways:

- *RT-CICLO Proposed exercise.* Around the realization of a proposed exercise, phases 1, 2 and 4 were carried out in a virtual way (outside the classroom) and phase 3 in person in the classroom. Each cycle lasted a week.
- *RT-CICLO Challenge.* Through the challenges (micro-exercises) carried out in the classroom. All the phases are carried out face-to-face in the same session. The average duration was 30 min. In each session, one cycle was carried out at least.

The ACCI 3.0 model and the software to manage the knowledge created, was applied continuously during all the cycles. In real time, the knowledge produced by the students and the teaching staff was introduced through the software. Based on this added knowledge, the results that we were obtained are: activities that generate organizational knowledge and types of corporate contents created during those actions.

During the second semester of the same course, the organizational knowledge developed was used in the "Computer Science and Programming" subject of the Energy Engineering degree. A laboratory group of that subject completed a survey on "Perception of usefulness for learning the different types of elements of organizational learning". The qualitative results obtained in this work are presented in the next section.

4 Results

The results of this work have been obtained in the following two scenarios within the experience:

- In scenario 1 the students, from the laboratories of the first semester, contributed to create the organizational knowledge (total of 66 students). In this scenario, two types of indicators have been identified that make it possible to assess organizational learning: the first indicator consists of identifying in what activities the students have generated organizational knowledge, and the second indicator is based on the types of organizational knowledge created.
- In scenario 2 the students, of the second semester, used the organizational knowledge of scenario 1 and assessed their perception of the usefulness of this knowledge in their learning.

4.1   Scenario 1: Identification of Actions that Generate Organizational Knowledge and the Type of Knowledge

The active methodology based on RT-CICLO got the students involved in the learning process, generating different types of knowledge through different actions. First, the actions are identified, and then the typology of knowledge created during the various actions is presented.

Identification of Actions. Actions have been of two types: voluntary (in these students have created knowledge spontaneously and unplanned) and involuntary (in these students have created knowledge from the realization of processes planned by the teachers).

Likewise, the contexts where this knowledge has been generated have been taken into account, distinguishing two meanings: during the classroom sessions and outside of them (e.g., at home). Taking into account the type of action and the context where it occurred, the shares are distributed as shown in Table 1.

Table 1. Identification of actions that can originate organizational knowledge

Actions that originate organizational knowledge	Inside the classroom(1)	Outside the classroom(2)
Voluntary (A)	A1 - Doubts and answers	A2 - Tutorials
Involuntary (B)	B1 - RT-CICLO Challenges B1 - Mistakes	B2 - RT-CICLO proposed exercises

The first column of Table 1 represents the type of action carried out by the students. Voluntary actions (second row) are those that are generated spontaneously by students. The involuntary ones (third row) are those created by the application of the model or by the results of mandatory actions (for example, doing an exercise in class).

The second column includes the voluntary and involuntary actions that arise during the teaching of a face-to-face class in the classroom. These actions generate organizational knowledge in real time and synchronously. The third column includes voluntary and involuntary actions that arise outside the classroom. The organizational knowledge created by these actions is carried out asynchronously and for a determined period.

The actions that produced organizational knowledge were the following, to facilitate the placement are assigned a letter A (Voluntary), B (Involuntary) and a number (1) Inside the classroom and (2) Outside the classroom.

A1. The two most common actions were the doubts expressed by the students during the face-to-face sessions and the responses of the students themselves or of the teachers.

A2. The most common action was attendance at face-to-face tutorials in the office of the faculty, where the students also raise questions and answers are given only by the faculty.

B1. Two common actions stand out:

- The application of RT-CICLO during a face-to-face session and which has been called RT-CICLO Challenge.
- The exposure of the common mistakes that students often make in class.

B2. The usual activity is the application of the RT-CICLO model in proposed exercises.

Types of Organizational Knowledge Generated from the Previous Actions. The different types of knowledge originated are described below, associating this with the actions in which it was created (A1, A2, B1 or B2) and these are:

- Collaborative doubts.

- Orientations.
- Mistakes.
- Lesson learned.

Collaborative Doubts (Origin A1). Teachers must make explicit in the classroom the knowledge that is being taught. About this explicit knowledge the student expresses doubts, makes comments and even answers some doubt. This resource is created in real time. Figure 5 shows a concept explained in the classroom (Fig. 5a) and the comments made by the students, together with the questions and answers shown in Fig. 5b.

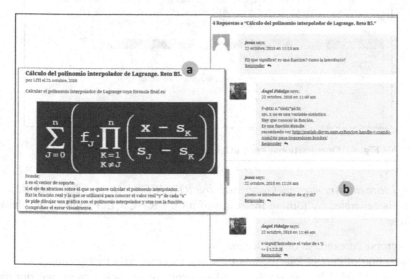

Fig. 5. Organizational knowledge elaborated by uniting the concept with the doubts and answers that it has generated

Orientations (Origin A2). These are prepared synchronously in the last laboratory sessions. A compendium of the concepts that have had to be explained more often in tutorials is made. It consists of collecting information from the tutorials carried out by the students. Two types of knowledge have been generated: those related to the technical part and those that affect the decision-making part (strategy).

Errors (Origin B1). A characteristic example is based on the mistakes that students make during the development of a class exercise. The faculty identifies these, groups these and explains both the error and the way of not committing it. Figure 6 shows a characteristic error to which a code has been assigned, in this case ER # 2. It describes the error, the cause and the way to solve (Fig. 6a) and is accompanied by a visual image that lets us know that the error has been corrected (Fig. 6b).

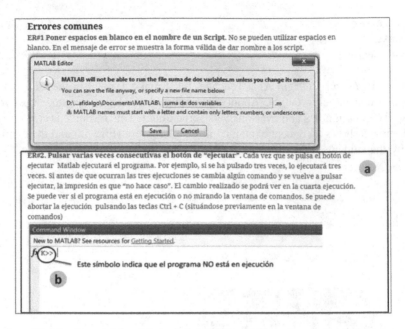

Fig. 6. Organizational knowledge elaborated from the usual mistakes

Lesson Learned. Knowledge Generated by RT-CICLO (Origin B1 and B2). This resource is generated by joining the result of all the RT-CICLO application phases. It combines:

- The proposed exercise or challenge.
- A selection of correct and incorrect results, together with that feedback.
- Comments added by the teachers and students about their experience during the realization (if it was easy or complicated, tips, etc.).

4.2 Scenario 2. Perception of the Students About the Different Elements of Organizational Learning

This test was carried out through a survey of students of the second semester in the 2018–19 course of "Computer Science and Programming" subject. These students study the degree of Energy Engineering and have used the organizational learning generated in the previous semester, with students of the degree in Mine Engineering. The test was completed once the first lab session ended, where they had the opportunity to use organizational learning.

A survey with five questions was carried out. They were asked about the perception of the usefulness (scale Likert 1 - low to 5 - high), for their personal learning, of the following types of organizational knowledge:

- Q1 - Collaborative doubts.
- Q2 - Technical guidance.
- Q3 - Strategic orientation.

- Q4 - Common mistakes.
- Q5 - Lesson learned.

Of a total of 33 people enrolled in the laboratory, the survey was filled out by 27 people (82% of those enrolled). The program R, library R-Commander has been used for the calculations.

The results of the survey are shown in Table 2, with the identifier of the question (Qi), the mean and the standard deviation SD of the answers.

Table 2. Results of the satisfaction survey

Question	Mean	SD
Q1	4.84	0.36
Q2	4.48	0.75
Q3	4.15	0.86
Q4	4.63	0.69
Q5	4.63	0.49

5   Conclusions

The knowledge generated by the students during the learning process in combination with the contributions of the teachers, produces organizational knowledge and for learning purposes, we can affirm that the subject has increased their knowledge, that is, in this case, the subject "has learned".

Organizational knowledge can be obtained through a series of actions by students. The actions identified in this work are:

- The doubts and answers regarding a specific topic.
- The mistakes made when performing exercises.
- Face-To-Face tutoring.
- The activities are implicit in the RT-CICLO process.

Organizational knowledge can be generated from each action. Depending on each action knowledge has been determined by the following types:

- Cooperative doubts. From the actions of the doubts and answers. Organizational knowledge consists in uniting the concept with which one works and the doubts and answers that have originated in its explanation or application.
- Common mistakes. Compilation of the mistakes that students make when performing exercises.
- Technical guidance and decision making. Elaborated from the conceptual, technical and decision-making deficiencies that the students show in face-to-face tutoring.
- Learned lessons. Combination of knowledge generated by each phase of the RT-CICLO model.

All the types of elements described constitute organizational knowledge, and its improvement is associated with increased learning.

Organizational knowledge can also be used to promote individual student learning. The perception survey indicates that for all types of organizational knowledge students have a very high perception of their usefulness. All means exceed 4 points out of 5, with standard deviations less than 1.

It is shown that the combination of RT-CICLO models, as an active method, and ACCI 3.0, to transform individual and organizational knowledge, can be applied to produce that knowledge and organizational learning in a subject.

In this work, organizational knowledge has been generated for the first time in a subject. In future work that knowledge acquired in the subject will be applied with students of a new subject, measuring the impact on the learning of the subject itself (measuring the increase in knowledge) and the effect on the students' own learning (measuring the actions carried out to generate new knowledge, the development of learning and the academic performance of it).

Acknowledgments. This work has been partially funded by the Spanish Government Ministry of Economy and Competitiveness throughout the DEFINES project (Ref. TIN2016-80172-R) and the Educational Innovation Service of the Technical University of Madrid (project Ref IE1819.0602). The authors would like to thank the research groups GIDTIC (http://gidtic.com), GRIAL (http://grial.usal.es) and LITI (http://www.liti.es) for their support.

References

1. Nonaka, I.: A dynamic theory of organizational knowledge creation. Organ. Sci. **5**, 14–37 (1994)
2. Nonaka, I., Takeuchi, H.: The Knowledge-Creating Company: How Japanese Companies Create the Dynamics of Innovation. Oxford University Press, Oxford (1995)
3. Bloom, B.S., Engelhart, M.D., Furst, E.J., Hill, W.K., Krathwohl, D.: Taxonomy of educational objectives: the classification of educational goals. Handbook I: Cognitive domain. In: Taxonomy of Educational Objectives: The Classification of Educational Goals. Handbook I, pp. 201–207. David McKay Company, New York (1956)
4. Ausubel, D.P.: A cognitive theory of school learning. Psychol. Sch. **6**, 331–335 (1969)
5. Piaget, J.: Part I: Cognitive development in children: Piaget development and learning. J. Res. Sci. Teach. **2**, 176–186 (1964)
6. Kolb, D.A.: Experiential Learning: Experience as the Source of Learning and Development. Prentice-Hall Inc, Englewood Cliffs (1984)
7. Fidalgo-Blanco, Á., Sein-Echaluce, M.L., García-Peñalvo, F.J.: APFT: active peer-based flip teaching. In: Proceedings of the 5th International Conference on Technological Ecosystems for Enhancing Multiculturality, TEEM 2017, Article No. 83. ACM, New York (2017)
8. García-Peñalvo, F.J., Alarcón, H., Domínguez, Á.: Active learning experiences in engineering education. Int. J. Eng. Educ. **35**, 305–309 (2019)
9. Dewey, J.: Democracy and Education: An Introduction to the Philosophy of Education. The Macmillan Company, New York (1916)
10. Dewey, J.: Experience and Nature. George Allen & UNWIN, LTD, London (1929)
11. Bonwell, C.C., Eison, J.A.: Active learning: creating excitement in the classroom. School of Education and Human Development, George Washington University (1991)

12. Sein-Echaluce, M.L., Fidalgo-Blanco, A., García-Peñalvo, F.J.: Students' knowledge sharing to improve learning in academic engineering courses. Int. J. Eng. Educ. (IJEE) **32**, 1024–1035 (2016)
13. Honey and Mumford—University of Leicester. https://www2.le.ac.uk/departments/doctoralcollege/training/eresources/teaching/theories/honey-mumford. Accessed 19 Feb 2019
14. Paavola, S., Hakkarainen, K.: The knowledge creation metaphor – an emergent epistemological approach to learning. Sci. Educ. **14**, 535–557 (2005)
15. Chickering, A.W., Gamson, Z.F.: News Seven Principles For Good Practice in Undergraduate Education A Focus for Improvement. Washingt. Cent. News. (1987)
16. García-Peñalvo, F.J., Fidalgo-Blanco, A., Sein-Echaluce, M.L., Sánchez-Canales, M.: Active Peer-based Flip Teaching: An active methodology based on RT-CICLO. IGI Global (2019, in press)
17. Sein-Echaluce, M.L., Fidalgo-Blanco, A., García-Peñalvo, F.J.: Technological ecosystems and ontologies for an educational model based on Web 3.0. Univers. Access Inf. Soc. (2019, in press)
18. Khailova, L.: Flipping library information literacy sessions to maximize student active learning: toward articulating effective design and implementation principles. Ref. User Serv. Q. **56**(3), 150 (2017)
19. Vidoni, M., Montagna, J.M., Vecchietti, A.: Project and team-based strategies for teaching software architecture*. Int. J. Eng. Educ. **34**, 1701–1708 (2018)
20. Rodríguez, M., Díaz, I., Gonzalez, E.J., González-Miquel, M.: Motivational active learning: an integrated approach to teaching and learning process control. Educ. Chem. Eng. **24**, 7–12 (2018)
21. Torres-Toukoumidis, Á., Ramirez-Montoya, M.S., Romero-Rodriguez, L.M.: Valoración y evaluación de los Aprendizajes Basados en Juegos (GBL) en contextos e-learning. Educ. Knowl. Soc. **19**(4), 109–128 (2019)
22. Fidalgo-Blanco, Á., Sein-Echaluce, M.L., García-Peñalvo, F.J.: Micro flip teaching with collective intelligence. In: Zaphiris, P., Ioannou, A. (eds.) LCT 2018. LNCS, vol. 10924, pp. 400–415. Springer, Cham (2018). https://doi.org/10.1007/978-3-319-91743-6_30
23. Santoveña-Casal, S., Bernal-Bravo, C.: Exploring the influence of the teacher: Social participation on Twitter and academic perception. Comunicar: Media Educ. Res. J. **27**, 75–84 (2019)
24. Fidalgo-Blanco, Á., Sánchez-Canales, M., Sein-Echaluce, M.L., García-Peñalvo, F.J.: Ontological search for academic resources. In: Proceedings of the Sixth International Conference on Technological Ecosystems for Enhancing Multiculturality – TEEM 2018, pp. 788–793. ACM Press, New York (2018)
25. Fidalgo-Blanco, A., Sein-Echaluce, M.L., García-Peñalvo, F.: Epistemological and ontological spirals: From individual experience in educational innovation to the organisational knowledge in the university sector. Program **49**(3), 266–288 (2015)
26. Fidalgo-Blanco, Á., Sein-Echaluce, M.L., García-Peñalvo, F.J.: Knowledge spirals in higher education teaching innovation. Int. J. Knowl. Manag. **10**(4), 16–37 (2014)
27. Sein-Echaluce, M.L., Abadía-Valle, A.R., Bueno-García, C., Fidalgo-Blanco, A.: Interaction of knowledge spirals to create ontologies for an institutional repository of educational innovation best practices. Int. J. Hum. Cap. Inf. Technol. Prof. **8**(2), 72–92 (2017)

Information and Communication Science Challenges for Modeling Multifaceted Online Courses

Karim Elia Fraoua[1(✉)], Jean-Marc Leblanc[2], Sarah Charraire[1], and Olivier Champalle[1]

[1] Université Paris Est Marne-La-Vallée, Equipe Dispositifs d'Information et de Communication à l'Ere Numérique (DICEN IDF), Conservatoire national des arts et métiers, Paris-Est Paris-Ouest, EA 7339, Serris, France
{Fraoua, olivier.champalle}@u-pem.fr,
sarah.charraire@gmail.com
[2] Université Paris Est Creteil, Céditec EA 3119, Créteil, France
jean-marc.leblanc@u-pec.fr

Abstract. In this work, we try to demonstrate that the use of the science of information and communication allows the implementation of new tools for online training. In a first reflection we will consider the work on constructivism and socio-constructivism with a look at the work of Hayek and Boudon, to explain the non-normative behavior of learners. This idea will be completed by using the work of Piaget and Vygotsky and the emergence of several models from the SIC, as the linguistic approach to the analysis and the improvement of content. Our work tries to provide some answers, from the theoretical and methodological point of view.

Keywords: Information · Learning process · Constructivism ·
Socio-constructivism · Adaptive Learning Design · Textometry

1 Introduction

In a new societal context related to the evolution of digital uses, how can e-learning tools promote the development of knowledge and skills? It is obvious that today our societies are paving the way for a new more horizontal organization, more centered on the sharing of power where each individual thinks he has his place. If the democratic and open "West" favors individuals and puts freedom, independence and rights at the forefront, other societies have chosen to take a different path, leaving place to democracy and openness and maintaining a preponderant place for social and societal organization, based on an ancestral model still in place, which is the case of Japan.

In so-called collective cultures, priority would be given to group and interdependence; people would accept the roles and positions assigned to them [1]. The forms of learning will be analyzed by comparing the French system to the Japanese system, where the emergence of online courses is still in beginning, Indeed, Japan ranks 18th on the level of online training. According to Aoki, this is due to the lack of educational

P. Zaphiris and A. Ioannou (Eds.): HCII 2019, LNCS 11590, pp. 142–154, 2019.
https://doi.org/10.1007/978-3-030-21814-0_12

innovation in educational institutions in Japan. In the Confucius value system on which Japanese culture and society have been built, teachers are authorities that students should not challenge. In a typical class of a Japanese university, the pedagogical focus tends to be on mastering a specific body of knowledge rather than fostering students' ability to reason and think critically [2]. This can explain the prevalence of the behaviorist approach which is duplicated in the construction of online courses. The technologies are used simply to reproduce the classroom with the advantage that the students can have access everywhere and at any time with supplementing the courses by presentations on this digital space, and which are a kind of tutorial.

For this purpose, we will analyze the foundations of learning, especially the question of the individual and the group. The social aspect of "collective representations" makes community of thought induced by application to a community. It is this reading that can lead to the emergence of multi-faceted approaches inducing a multi-normative reading within the same group, which is the case of a classical class, in which the teacher becomes aware of these different forms and which he must take into account this diversity to organize a course for all learners. We will take these observations into account by analyzing several pedagogical approaches in order to show that the individual first needs to conceptualize things before learning or understanding them and that the interaction within the group is a fundamental element to construct, a learning schema. Our tool and the interface must be the most adapted to this reality. Our main idea is how to anchor e-learning further through the discipline of information and communication sciences, because the diversity of audiences poses an important challenge, and some tools can be issued from this field to enhance user interface.

The first element will be analyzed, is from constructivist perspective. This intellectual approach shows that the learner needs to create his own world in which he will record his learning strategy and consequently emerges the idea of a personalization of the learner. From this perspective, he becomes the actor of his own learning but also of the one who stages the useful phases for his learning. We will also discuss the socio-constructivist model who rely the learner and his social construction, and his interaction with other actors, whether other learners, or the trainer. Vygotsky's work has shown that, whatever the age of learners, we need social interaction to learn [3]. These social interactions are necessary to the cognitive development and the trainer cannot transmit to the learner knowledge or a real know-how without this interaction. Asubel will insist on one essential point, namely the knowledge or methods already acquired by the learner [4]. He criticizes the constructivist approach that learning can only be achieved by confronting the learner with a problem solving. These readings reinforce our conviction, that the learners are not uniform because they all have a different mental structure, but also different assets. To this end, we will outline Boudon approach in the learning process [5] and we will examine Hayek's [6] work to better situate stakeholders, including learners, their strategies for learning and the role of the trainer.

Finally, another observation that emerges is related to the content itself. As a teacher, we realize, based on our experience, that our semantics must evolve sometimes adapting, even within the same class in order to ensure that the content is understood and memorized by all the learners. The challenge is important in an online course, where aside from the feedback; the means of interaction remain low. In this regard, we will use some tools, in order to analyze the text before it goes online, but also the analysis of the feedback of learners to point out if the content does not present any particular difficulties and moreover we will develop the notions of semantics and semiotics, in order to better understand the role of language in the online course.

2 Analysis of the Training Context

The analysis of the public and its motivation to learn and how to mobilize one's attention is the prerequisite before setting up a course and even more for an online training. How the course is done in the absence of a teacher whose main function is mediation, since we consider the role of the trainer as a group animator. Several schools have been interested on teaching models and their organization as Dewey's pragmatic approach [5], Skinner's behaviorist approach [6], or social interactionism [8] and their involvement, which are at the heart of our works and through constructivism, social-constructivism, … These first approaches focus more on processes than on individuals, and encourage group normalization strategies rather than individual consideration, and exclude individuals who fail to integrate groups. We will see in detail the constructivist and socio-constructivist models and their impact on the online tool that we have designed and which is still under evaluation by users.

2.1 Behaviorism

This idea is the first to have emerged [7]. Several authors have put this method in evidence what is turning into an external stimulant on a person with the consequence of the reward or punishment. Watson [8] and then Skinner [9] have developed this model based on animal and human behavior, linking this situation to the learner's behavior, forgetting in passing the way of thinking of the learner. New cognitive approaches will oppose to this model which consider that the learner must listen, remember and reproduce without thinking, in a rather mechanical way. Nowadays, the learner becomes a subject who thinks on the learning that he receives; he also becomes a fundamental player in this learning processes.

2.2 The Constructivist Model

This model makes it possible to conceive that the individual needs to conceptualize things along his learning period. The learner needs to better design and perceive things and the world around him. It is part of a constructivist approach. He needs to build a world of his own and in which he will write his learning strategy. He becomes the actor of his own learning but who also puts in place the useful stages and necessary phases to learn [10]. Asubel indicates that for the learner to assimilate knowledge, it is necessary that the things make sense to him [4] because the knowledge must be integrated in the conceptual schema of the learner. Taking up the idea of Piaget [10], every person has a learning structure stemming from his intellectual progression and the way in which it was constructed. All knowledge is the result of an individual learning experience. Piaget will set different stages during which the individual will be able to build himself through his own progression but also according to his interaction with his environment.

Piaget analyzes the impact of the environment as a whole social, cultural context [11]. One could easily integrate the interactionist approaches and thus get back to the idea of more or less homogeneous groups and that thus justify that the school has built a rather general model which takes less and less account of the emergence of the new society of the world of information and cultural diversities. In this connection, it seemed useful to compare the Japanese system in terms of both structure and linguistic usage in order to show that a system still structured around the notion of group can still function according to a rather procedural approach, as the behaviorist model, and which can give still quite convincing results, for that, it is enough to see the ranking of certain Asian countries in the classification of Pisa. This model leaves little place for the individual and his mental structure, knowledge is defined in terms of observable behaviors expected at the end of learning.

In regard to the constructivist approach, several complexities of learning can emanate from the learner with the consideration that he has undergone, according to Piaget theory. This author shows how the intelligence is the product of a construction through the interactions that the subject has with arrounding objects. These constructions go through the action, operation and then the representation thanks to the assimilation mechanism where the child tries to act on the world according to his sensorimotor patterns, of accommodation where the child himself modifies these sensorimotor patterns, according to the external reality that we will consider to be social interactions and finally of equilibration, which is "the dialectical game between assimilation and equilibration" [12]. This constructivist approach can lead to a form of rigidity in receiving new knowledge that the trainer will moderate, hence its fundamental role as mediator. In fact, it is the learner who learns alone and according to his capacity and speed of receiving data and information, as well as according to the amount of data he can absorb in a given time, and also his ability to change his mental structure on the base of his mental construction. He will often face a phenomenon of cognitive dissonance that results in a form of resistance to the emergence of new knowledge, since it will upset his mental structure, his beliefs, even the norm of the group he frequents daily. In a constructivist pedagogy, there are elements to put in place that are essential [13], first the role of mediation, that the contents must be relevant to the learner, that the teachers serve mainly as animators learning, that multiple representations of content must be encouraged, and that knowledge must be interpreted in the context of prior knowledge.

2.3 Socio-Constructivist Model

This model will complete the previous model taking into account the relationship between learner and its social construction but also its interaction with other actors, of the learning structure even if we will be interested in distance learning, but also with other learners, and the trainer or artifact [14]. Socio-constructivism will give an important role to the social framework and the context in which the learner operates and what others bring as interactions. While constructivism does not consider in the context of learning, even if Piaget has integrated the role of interaction in the mental structure, without however considering its dynamics, and that the individual evolves in a socio-temporal space and that our societies evolve. So, it cannot have learning without taking into account the pedagogical context and unfortunately this aspect was more or less approached when designing online tools. It is this challenge that we try to integrate into this work. In this regard, some authors [15] evoke the idea of interpreting an experience in its context and that it must be the most realistic as possible. With our feedback on personal experience and in some of our courses, we talk about the idea to students that they are doing a job for a client, as considered in situated learning, which can give them, the desire to learn a new knowledge.

We cannot learn without confronting our ideas and debating. The role of social interactions is essential in learning process. The major element is the social interaction is constructive, the learner becoming aware of his own thought and its relativity and therefore he may be able to reconstruct a new mental scheme taking into account this new social representation and ultimately acquire this new knowledge [16]. The language becomes a way to represent our thought and serve to understand as well the thought of others [17]. In the same spirit for Hayek, the agents are moderately rational, which means that they decide to share a little with the hypotheses developed [18]. They are only partially informed, as they base their behavior on limited sequences of observations based on the past behavior of other agents shaping their social environment. And finally, on the socio-constructivist approach, and for Boudon, the implementation of a multi-tool system meets the current needs of agents who appear to be socially or culturally identical, but may ultimately be different and therefore require a different approach [19]. He considers a scale of temporality to build a product in a dynamic way, and consequently presenting a multi-faceted side. Indeed, he considers that our reflection cannot be in a long-term reading, because the modern sociological analysis aims to identify the logic of change in systems of interaction sufficiently restricted to be affordable. The dynamics of change lead to the emergence of the complexity of the groups of learners and the needs are such that we can conceive a static approach with an online course which is only a simple listening of a video or a text.

To complete this reading, we must give the complementary role of the semantic question. According to Piaget, acquisition is a construction, and it is the development that precedes learning and then the learner must experiment and draw consequences. For Vygotsky, acquisition is an appropriation, and objects have a social significance and he specifies that the learner cannot learn alone. The learner can learn and carry out an activity with the support of other, the knowledge is not simply constructed, it is co-constructed and the presence of a mediator is important between the learner and his environment and that the role of the language is primordial whereas for the constructivists it is not or less important. Vygotsky [20] emphasized the role of language and culture in cognitive development and the way that we perceive the world. Like Chomsky, and others, language provides frameworks through which we live, communicate and understand reality [21]. This importance of language in learning suggests that people learn with a sense and meaning, not just by focusing on the facts. Language and conceptual schema conveyed through language are essentially social phenomena.

3   Fundamentals Role of Linguistic Analysis of Contents

In the socio-constructivist model, the notion of language, meaning and signification is unavoidable and therefore the analysis of content is fundamental [17]. We have chosen to first evaluate the effect of context with the notion of semantic rigidity, which can explain the emergence of other forms of learning, notably through online courses in the form of tutorials, or the serious game more technical than educational. We observe this in some disciplines like mathematics or computer science. The language or meta-language used remains within the reach of the general public without seeking to enrich it, in order to develop the concepts necessary for the structuring of the thought, from which the new structuring language elements emerges that leads for learning and memorize this learning.

However, from our experience feedback, in a hybrid course (face-to-face and online), the return of learners is not encouraging, even if many succeed because they have a good foundation, many others fail because the tool is not adapted to their mental structures, also the language used and the lack of interaction with peers or with the trainer. This brings us to a different approach to the issue of linguistics uses and its impact on the emergence of our information system, to emphasize its importance as a concept and to define it rigorously in a multi-faceted approach, to respond to the diversity of our audiences, resulting from this more horizontal approach since places of learning can also be places of debate.

With the emergence of text analysis tools and the sentiments analysis, we can now assess content but also the feeling of learners without technical difficulty. This reading of the role of emotion has been highlighted by several authors; we retain among others Martin-Juchat in the role of emotion in the communication space [22]. The setting up of a forum or feedback at the end of each course, will allow us to build a course that will take into account the differences observed and thus be proposed according to the profile of the learners. But before seeing the benefit of these aspects, it seemed important to us to understand the notion of language and the use of words. When the course is conducted face to face, it is obvious that during the exchange, the teacher can review its wording and correct it in order to capture the attention of the learner, but in an online course this idea disappears to make way for a fixed text and therefore the risk is obvious to lose the attention of the learner.

Moreover, as summarized above, in the socio-constructivist approach, the social meaning of objects, and therefore of words, is important. Saussure provides us with a theoretical framework to better design our tool by understanding this question of meaning and sense [23]. Semiotics and semantics deal with these questions. This notion is also raised by reading due to information and communication sciences in the sense that concomitantly, a process of interpretation is implemented by everyone in the treatment of objects encountered and that sense is manipulated and altered [24]. In the light of Asubel's [4] approach, the learner must be able to create meaning in the knowledge he or she assimilates, allowing knowledge to fit into the learner's conceptual schema. One of the essential tools of learning is communication through language. In structuralism linguistics, we distinguish the language, social object shared by a community, from the speech, individual way of using the language. Before creating meaning, the word is based on a relationship between a sound, called "acoustic image", and a thought, called "concept" [23]. This relationship can also be defined as a relationship between the meaning "acoustic image" and signified "concept". Thus, when we speak about a tree, we evoke at the same time a concept, the idea of a tree, but also the reality of a tree. This "form" of the word tree is identified by its written or oral form, and its symbol is recognized and shared by the members of the linguistic community speaking the French language. On this principle, the sound tree is an imaginary and real tree. The "ideal" concept of a tree makes it possible to group the common characteristics of all the trees, rather than a long list of each existing tree. But the concept must give a simpler and reduced understanding, giving a simple definition: plant composed of a trunk and branches often leafy. Thus, the more the concept has a strong intension, the more one appeals to the understanding of the learner. Indeed, the more the intention of a word is broad, the broader its extension is. From the intention of the word "tree" that has been given, it is possible to group trees and some shrubs when extending the word to real referents.

From this relation between the signifier, the conceptual referent and the real reference, we can see a semiotic relation appearing. To enable the learner to understand what a tree is, he will assimilate his concept by giving it a general definition, which allows him to recognize it in objective reality thanks to his belonging to the tree class. On this principle, there is a tree in its subjective conceptualization and in its objective reality. This makes it possible to define the linguistic sign according to Saussure through the semiotic triangle. It is the relationship of the word between its reading, what means the general sense of the term, and its actual reference. This articulation between thought, language and reality is what creates the meaning, the semantic substance and gives a value to the "form". Thus, the relation between the so-called signifying form, the signified or concept, and the referent creates semiotics. This is the system of the sign, in its expression and content, which can be the study of a semantic unit (a word) or a semantic entity (a sentence) [23].

Tools and methods of text analysis can both be mobilized to analyze the contents of pedagogical devices but also the speech of learners. To do this, several tools are available that provide different and complementary insights into the constituted corpus [25]. All these tools have in common the principle of segmentation of the text in minimal units and the count of these units making it possible either to judge the distribution of the vocabulary in one part of the corpus compared to the others (Author, periods, supports.), the identification of trends (regularities, graphs to evaluate the distance between the texts or parts of the corpus, networks of co-occurrences ...). For example some tools like Lexico 3 or TexObserver allow to compare the vocabulary of the different parts of the corpus, meanwhile, Alceste or Iramuteq allow to emerge the salient themes of a text, or finally Tropes which on the basis of a semantic ontology, makes possible to identify the "reference universes" of a text. This setting up is interesting and it joins the constructivist approach, in the comprehension of the universe of the learners. As an example, we note the difficulties of some students who have little mastery of the language because of their origins. This analysis will enable us to better understand the source of the difficulties and to better correct both the content and the meaning in order to create signifier for each learner [26]. Indeed, the intelligibility of a phenomenon can only be done through the use of metaphors. In fact, a single model cannot alone represent the whole reality, because for Piaget as for Mucchielli the reality in human sciences is the result of an individual construction [27]. This semio-contextual theory of Mucchielli [28] identifies processes of communication and contextualization in relation, through which the meaning of a communication emerges in a given situation, called context. Moreover, this element is close to the classification made by Conole [29]. This context, for an individual, is a subjective reality of which he has a certain image, and it is by influencing this image, through the interaction that he can have with others that the meaning of his conduct may change in the considered context.

4   The Organization of Learning and Its Context

The theory of social constructivism emphasizes the collaborative nature of learning, with the underlying assumption that knowledge is constructed through interaction with others. Traditionally, e-learning has been inherently transmissive. It is teacher-centered, which means that technology provides the knowledge. The learner is passive; he reads, looks, listens and learns. Based on the work of Vygotsky, we learn better through our interactions with others, through discussion and exchange. The Vygotsky concept of the proximal developmental area, which is the difference between what a learner can do without help and what he can achieve with the help of a more experienced peer, is consolidated [30]. This mediator can be the trainer or another learner who understands the content.

These pedagogical approaches were partly taken up by Conole [31] who used a classification that underlaid these approaches, and divided the methods into four categories, Associative, Cognitive/Constructivist, Situationist and finally Connectivist. We clearly find some aspects that interest us, such as the effects of interaction that is also highlighted by Garcia-Penalvo [32], the notion of motivation and the mobilization of learners, ... In the importance of the role of the social field, Garrison et al. [33], also shows the pre-eminence of the social field in the learner's environment. Our approach is to insist on these uses and those we tried to introduce as well the linguistic analysis of the contents and also the emergence of the field of the information and the communication and especially the communication within the organization and the place of individuals and their roles in order to enable this organization to succeed in its educational mission. The constructivist approach already indicates that interaction is necessary. The concept of interaction is a fundamental element in setting up this new training organization, for Mucchielli individuals cannot be solely responsible for this failure, if our learning platform does not work. It is up to us to build an interaction system so that these situations can be solved [34]. To take into account the diversity of learning, learners and their contexts and to facilitate the transmission of knowledge, digital learning platforms (LMS), such as Moodle, Brightspace or Claroline, are used by French universities to support the organization of training and the dissemination of teaching materials. These platforms integrate features and modalities, allowing fostering collaborative interactions between learners.

Within the framework of the notions that we wish to develop to encourage the learning (motivation, interactions, mobilization of the learners, situated learning, etc.), it is necessary to specify, to be complete, that there are also other types of learning, in more specific training environments. These environments are often designed for domains, specific audiences, on a particular knowledge and for specific contexts as programming language, technical gestures, or professional behavior, ... The forms of pedagogy mobilized are also adapted to the learning situation as the virtual reality [35], serious games [36], mobile device use [37], interactive Table [38] and simulation [39], ...

The pedagogical design we have chosen takes this into account and can be more easily implemented in traditional LMS, in our case Moodle, whose current functionalities facilitate online collaboration between learners remotely via, for example, platforms messaging, forum, visioconference and digital sharing [40]. We can point out some indicators that measure the level of interaction in this learning structure, such as the Community Indicators Framework [31], which often depends on the types of platforms used. Whatever the learning environment, hybrid or not, learners need a return on their learning and personal progress. Tracing Learner Interactions in the Learning Environment is a Knowledge Engineering process [41] implemented to provide feedback to the tutor and learner [42]. These traces of interactions are thus perceived as the digital time registration, of a current or past activity, and sources of knowledge about the learner [43]. The research in this area offers a set of answers related to the personalization of learning according to the profile of the learners: according to the traces left by the learners, the profiles can be deduced automatically and then the organization of the courses and the level of exercises adapted, on the basis of the analysis of the interaction of the learners on the platform [44] as well as the exchanges on the forums [45].

Based on these analyzes and observations, we can draw several points that can justify the creation of our tool and that we will consolidate in this paragraph. The general conclusion is that each learner must be considered separately in order to allow better enrollment in an online course. On this basis, we have considered a scenario that takes into account this approach, especially with specific applets that will be chosen by the learner during the constitution of his educational path that he has decided. These choices are part of a rewarding approach that also allows the learner to make alternative choices that will allow him to optimize his learning path. Our approach is already tackled by several authors, called Adaptive Learning Design, which takes into account the profiles of learners, by setting up a model à la carte [46]. This approach will define in advance with the learners, the objectives, the prerequisites that we have set up, in the form of a Quiz to guide the learner to the right content but also if the content adapted and through a textometric analysis of the feedback from the learner. García-Peñalvo et al., compare this approach to a Lego method [47]. Thus, a scenario will be proposed at the beginning of each course with a sequence to be chosen by the learner. In this sequence, we will offer each learner a series of slides, a document to read and a video with a recommendation of sequencing, but free for the learner to organize it. The duration of each element of the sequence will be the subject of an in-depth analysis taking into account the speed of reading a text, of the order of 100 words by minute, and the length of the video that will be around 2 min, in order to keep the learner vigilant. In the educational offer, we have integrated textometric and lexicometric tools that allow at the end of each sequence to analyze the feedback of each learner. This allows to improve the content of the course, or to provide new video that will allow a better understanding of the proposed courses. We will also be able to analyze corpus of forum that we will put in place and which will serve as a place of exchange in this learning structure between the learners but also with the trainer. Moreover, we will put in place a portfolio that will contain all the elements that concern the exercise of the profession and therefore the skills to be acquired, which is part of the "situated learning" approach. Authors such as Noy and Mucchielli, among other principles that they state, go in this direction and indicate that the processes of elaboration of knowledge are directed towards the ends of action, as well as the principle of the experimentation of knowledge [48]. In fact, individuals act with regard to things according to the interpretive meaning that these things have for them. We find here again easily the concept of constructivism.

We have also planned the implementation of this portfolio to allow the learner to enter any questions that may arise and that are not contained in the offered online training and thus allow him to situate his own learning. The creation of a scalable, digital, web-based learning platform that is innovative and responsive in a pedagogical and interactive way seems easy, but it must be the consequence of deep reflections that must be carried out before any implementation of a learning platform. This cross-cutting project covers information technologies, teaching methods, interactivity with learners, validation of the understanding of skills and permanent optimization of format and content. We applied these approaches to a new course that is being evaluated, namely a course offered to students but also to employees. The course is presented by a teacher who will talk to the learners through a video. As a mediator, he will help develop the knowledge and understanding of these learners. He will encourage them to apply the content of the course in their own context, hence the implementation of several certi-fication levels and whose semantic level has been analyzed according to the level of adequacy of these learners. We have in our tool created three levels to better get closer to the sociology of groups. Each lecture starts with a Quiz in order to analyze the notion of the object and meaning of the learner in order to offer him the best path and avoid putting him in a situation of failure from the beginning, because even if the scenario and the platform take into account our approach, the content and therefore the language can be incomprehensible and so it can put him in a situation of avoidance and thus ultimately lead to failure. Indeed, many existing courses consist of a series of PowerPoint screens, with voiceovers, based simply on the reading of the learner. This is the model that would be closer to the behaviorist model and which unfortunately causes a recurring failure. Our approach takes the candidates into a narrative story that reinforces the learner's engagement and our entire linguistic analysis shows the importance of this aspect.

5 Conclusion

Our work complements previous work that we have evoked by highlighting the importance of learning models and makes it clear that LMS today make it possible to implement these reflections from a practical point of view. It opens us real prospects afterwards, after the feedback of the learners on questions like the importance of the linguistic analysis, of the scenario to the map but other reflection that we will begin on the duration of each sequence of learning.

References

1. Hofstede, G.: Dimensionalizing cultures: the Hofstede model in context. Online Readings in Psychol. Cult. **2**(1), 8 (2011)
2. Aoki, K., Bray, E.: Learning Styles of Distance Learners in Japan: Cultural Considerations. Eric Bay (2007). Accessed 3 Nov 2016
3. Vygotsky, L.: Interaction between learning and development. Readings Dev. Child. **23**(3), 34–41 (1978)
4. Ausubel, D.P., Novak, J.D., Hanesian, H.: Educational Psychology: A Cognitive View, vol. 6. Holt, Rinehart and Winston, New York (1968)
5. Boudon, R.: Le juste et le vrai: études sur l'objectivité des valeurs et de la connaissance. Fayard (1995)
6. Von Hayek, F.A.: Economics and knowledge. Economica **4**(13), 33–54 (1937)
7. Schwartz, B.: Psychology of Learning and Behavior, 3rd edn. W W Norton & Co., New York (1989)
8. Watson, J.B.: Psychology as the behaviorist views it. Psychol. Rev. **20**(2), 158–177 (1913)
9. Skinner, B.F.: Are theories of learning necessary? Psychol. Rev. **57**(4), 193 (1950)
10. Piaget, J.: Part I: Cognitive development in children: Piaget development and learning. J. Res. Sci. Teach. **2**(3), 176–186 (1964)
11. Blake, B., Pope, T.: Developmental psychology: incorporating Piaget's and Vygotsky's theories in classrooms. J. Cross-Discip. Perspe Fictives Educ. **1**, 59–67 (2008)
12. Piaget, J.: Problems of equilibration. In: Appel, M.H., Goldberg, L.S. (eds.) Topics in Cognitive Development. TOPCOGDEV, pp. 3–13. Springer, Boston (1977). https://doi.org/10.1007/978-1-4613-4175-8_1
13. Carwile, J.: A constructivist approach to online teaching and learning. Inquiry **12**(1), 68–73 (2007)
14. Palincsar, A.S.: Social constructivist perspectives on teaching and learning. Annu. Rev. Psychol. **49**(1), 345–375 (1998)
15. Brown, J.S., Collins, A., Duguid, P.: Situated cognition and the culture of learning. Educ. Res. **18**(1), 32–42 (1989)
16. Bauersfeld, H.: Interaction, construction, and knowledge: alternative perspectives for mathematics education. Perspectives on research on effective mathematics teaching (1988)
17. Gergen, K.J.: Social constructionist inquiry: context and implications. In: Gergen, K.J., Davis, K.E. (eds.) The Social Construction of the Person. SSSOC, pp. 3–18. Springer, New York (1985). https://doi.org/10.1007/978-1-4612-5076-0_1
18. Hayek, F.A.: Individualism and Economic Order. University of Chicago Press, Chicago (1948)
19. Fraoua, K.E., Bourret, C., Amar, C., Mouly, S.: Theory and tools in learning methods for medical doctors. In: Zaphiris, P., Ioannou, A. (eds.) LCT 2016. LNCS, vol. 9753, pp. 607–615. Springer, Cham (2016). https://doi.org/10.1007/978-3-319-39483-1_55
20. Goodman, Y.M., Goodman, K.S.: Vygotsky in a whole language perspective. In: Making Sense of Learners Making Sense of Written Language, pp. 98–114. Routledge (2014)
21. Chomsky, N.: Language and Mind. Cambridge University Press, Cambridge (2006)
22. Dumas, A., Martin-Juchat, F.: Approche communicationnelle des émotions dans les organisations: questionnements et implications méthodologiques. Revue française des sciences de l'information et de la communication (9) (2016)
23. De Saussure, F.: Course in General Linguistics. Columbia University Press, New York (2011)

24. Zacklad, M.: Classification, thésaurus, ontologies, folksonomies: comparaisons du point de vue de la recherche ouverte d'information (ROI). In: CAIS/ACSI 2007, 35e Congrès annuel de l'Association Canadienne des Sciences de l'Information. Partage de l'information dans un monde fragmenté: Franchir les frontières, sous la dir. de C. Arsenault et K. Dalkir. Montréal: CAIS/ACSI, May 2007
25. Leblanc, J.-M.: Approches textométriques du web: corpus et outils" (Pierre Fiala, Christine Barats, Jean-Marc Leblanc) Dans Manuel d'analyse du Web (Dir Christine Barats), Armand Colin (2013)
26. Lebart, L., Salem, A., Berry, L.: Exploring Textual Data, vol. 4. Springer, Heidelberg (1997). https://doi.org/10.1007/978-94-017-1525-6
27. Mucchielli, A.: L'Identité individuelle et les contextualisations de soi. Le Philosophoire 1, 101–114 (2015)
28. Mucchielli, A.: La nouvelle communication: épistémologie des sciences de l'information-communication. Armand Colin (2000)
29. Conole, G.: E-learning: the hype and the reality. J. Interact. Media Educ. 12, 1–18 (2004)
30. Chaiklin, S.: The zone of proximal development in Vygotsky's analysis of learning and instruction. Vygotsky's Educ. Theory Cult. Context 1, 39–64 (2003)
31. Conole, G.: Learning Design: A Practical Approach. Routledge, London (2014)
32. García-Peñalvo, F.J. (ed.): Advances in E-Learning: Experiences and Methodologies: Experiences and Methodologies. IGI Global (2008)
33. Garrison, D.R., Anderson, T.: E-Learning in the 21st Century: A Framework for Research and Practice. RoutledgeFalmer, New York (2003)
34. Mucchielli, A.: Deux modèles constructivistes pour le diagnostic des communications organisationnelles. Communication et organisation 30, 12–46 (2006)
35. Amokrane, K., Lourdeaux, D., Burkhardt, J.-M.: Learner tracking in a virtual environment. Int. J. Virtual Reality 7(3), 23–30 (2008)
36. Hussaan, A.M., Sehaba, K., Mille, A.: Helping children with cognitive disabilities through serious games: project CLES. In: The Proceedings of the 13th International ACM SIGACCESS Conference on Computers and Accessibility, pp. 251–252. ACM (2011)
37. Kearney, M., Maher, D.: Mobile learning in maths teacher education: using iPads to support pre-service teachers' professional development. Aust. Educ. Comput. 27(3), 76–84 (2013)
38. Bachour, K., Kaplan, F., Dillenbourg, P.: An interactive table for supporting participation balance in face-to-face collaborative learning. IEEE Trans. Learn. Technol. 3(3), 203–213 (2010)
39. Theureau, J.: Nuclear reactor control room simulators: human factors research and development. Cogn. Technol. Work 2, 97–105 (2000)
40. Gros, B., García-Peñalvo, F.J.: Future trends in the design strategies and technological affordances of e-learning. In: Spector, M., Lockee, B., Childress, M. (eds.) Learning, Design, and Technology, pp. 1–23. Springer, Cham (2016). https://doi.org/10.1007/978-3-319-17727-4_67-1
41. Bachimont, B.: Arts et sciences du numerique: Ingenierie des connaissances et critique de la raison computationnelle. Memoire d'habilitation à diriger des recherches, Universite de Technologie de Compiegne (2004)
42. Champalle, O., Sehaba, K., Mille, A.: Facilitate sharing of training experience by exploring behavior discovery in trainees traces. In: Conole, G., Klobučar, T., Rensing, C., Konert, J., Lavoué, É. (eds.) EC-TEL 2015. LNCS, vol. 9307, pp. 28–41. Springer, Cham (2015). https://doi.org/10.1007/978-3-319-24258-3_3

154   K. E. Fraoua et al.

43. Lund, K., Mille, A.: Traces, traces d'interactions, traces d'apprentissages: definitions, modeles informatiques, structurations, traitements et usages. In: Marty, J.C., Mille, A. (eds.) Analyse de traces et personnalisation des environnements informatiques pour l'apprentissage humain, IC2 - Serie Informatique et Systemes d'Information, chap. 1, pp. 21–66. Hermes Sciences Publications, Juin 2009
44. Djouad, T., Mille, A.: Observing and understanding an on-line learning activity: a model-based approach for activity indicator engineering. Technol. Knowl. Learn. **23**(1), 41–64 (2018)
45. May, M., George, S., Prévôt, P.: TrAVis to enhance online tutoring and learning activities: real time visualization of students tracking data. Int. J. Interact. Technol. Smart Educ. (ITSE) **8**(1), 52–69 (2011)
46. Berlanga, A., García, F.: Learning technology specifications: semantic objects for adaptive learning environments. Int. J. Learn. Technol. **1**(4), 58–472 (2005)
47. Berlanga, A., García-Peñalvo, F.-J.: J. Univ. Comput. Sci. **14**(22), 3627–3647 (2008)
48. Mucchelli, A., Noy, C.: Communication Studies: Constructivist Approaches. Éditions Armand Colin, Paris (2005)

Let's Talk About Tools and Approaches for Teaching HCI

Adriano Luiz de Souza Lima$^{(\boxtimes)}$ and Fabiane Barreto Vavassori Benitti

Universidade Federal de Santa Catarina, Florianópolis, SC, Brazil
{adriano.lima,fabiane.benitti}@ufsc.br

Abstract. Human-computer interaction (HCI) is an important knowledge field in the program of most computer-related majors, but not many studies on HCI teaching at undergraduate level can be found. This paper presents a systematic mapping study carried out in order to get an overview of HCI classes at undergraduate level, with the objective of investigating how HCI is being taught and what tools are being used to support the process. The study selected 17 papers to analyze the teaching approach being applied and the supporting tools, if any, being used to help teaching HCI. As a result, most of the papers mentioned or described an active learning approach and only two specific tools to support HCI teaching have been identified, which comes as a future work opportunity.

Keywords: Human-computer interaction · Computing education · HCI education

1 Introduction

In the last 20 years, the development of technology considerably changed the way people interact to each other. Before that time, mobile phones had very little use besides making calls, fewer people had Internet access and most of online communication was done by email. Today people communicate with each other by sending and receiving messages through various forms such as text, audio, images, video or symbols, synchronous or asynchronously.

During this period, education has always kept its doors open to the use of new technologies such as simulators, just to mention a single example. In spite of that, communication between teachers and students in class seem not to have taken full advantage of the possibilities the advances of technology have brought. Most of the classes are still based on oral lectures, using few visual aids, where teachers just speak and students ask their questions when they think something is not clear [1]. This type of class hardly draws students' attention [2] and they, as a result, usually have a low rate of content retention [3].

Students commonly feel little involved in the communication process of more traditional teaching methods since, in general, they allow them have a more passive posture towards their teachers that, on the other hand, must be very

© Springer Nature Switzerland AG 2019
P. Zaphiris and A. Ioannou (Eds.): HCII 2019, LNCS 11590, pp. 155–170, 2019.
https://doi.org/10.1007/978-3-030-21814-0_13

active in their classes in order to keep students motivated [3]. Also, those methods do not usually offer the students many opportunities to apply that recently acquired knowledge to real life situations, leading to a superficial learning level that could be represented by the initial categories of the cognitive domain of Bloom's taxonomy [4], for instance.

Receiving considerable attention over the past several years, active learning has found many advocates among faculty looking for alternatives to traditional teaching, even though there may still exist some that regard it as just an educational fad [5].

Human-Computer Interaction (HCI) is an important area in computer related degree programs, such as computer science [6], information systems [7] and software engineering [8]. Despite its importance, there seems to be a lack of literature on practice-level issues about its implementation in the classroom [9]. Likewise, technological tools specifically designed to aid HCI teaching are practically nonexistent [10]. Considering this scenario, the present paper conducts a systematic mapping study that aims at checking how HCI is being taught and if any tools to support the process are being used.

The remaining of this paper is organized as follows: Sect. 2 presents related work. Section 3 describes the systematic mapping with the presentation of its results. Section 4 discusses the implication of the results, answering the research questions and presenting the threats to the validity of the study. Conclusions and comments on future work are described in Sect. 5.

2   Background

The importance of HCI can be stated when looking at the Curriculum Guidelines for Undergraduate Degree Programs for Computer Science [6], for Information Systems [7] and for Software Engineering [8]. Computer science students are expected to have at least 6.4 lecture hours of HCI core topics and have a choice of some other elective ones [6]. When majoring in information systems, the students might take *Introduction to HCI* as an elective course, though it brings significant coverage to the application developer and user interface designer career tracks, whereas the program for software engineering [8] considers that it is essential that students have 10 hours of HCI.

By looking at those programs, and understanding the role HCI plays on interface designing, one might think that a considerable number of software developers have at least been initiated on the matter. Edwards et al. [11], however, argues that this might be true, but teachers are failing at HCI education. As an evidence of his position, he points out the abundance of poorly designed interfaces and great number of papers published in the HCI literature that do not offer much more than criticisms of interface designs. He concludes that there is a vast scope for improvement in HCI teaching.

Battistella and Wangenheim [12] carried out a systematic review of the literature to understand what kind of games are available for teaching computing in higher education. They encountered a considerable number of 107 games, indicating that there exists a trend to game-based learning also in computing education. However, only one ranked match in the HCI area was found. The game called "3DAR Lego Game" provides a tool to improve spatial ability for a wide range of ages [13].

In 2012, Sommariva [14] conducted a systematic mapping study to search for games or simulators specifically developed to support usability teaching, and also to understand what usability topics were being taught and how. His study found no games developed to support usability teaching. He later developed and proposed a game to help teach usability engineering life cycle [10]. When it comes to usability teaching, his study focused on the activity proposed by the teacher, without mentioning the underlying teaching approach. Later, in 2014, Ferreira et al. [15] presented a game to teach Jacob Nielsen's heuristic evaluation. The game makes use of analogies to reinforce the heuristics understanding, building a story to motivate the students during their learning process.

Nevertheless, systematic reviews (or systematic mappings) that analyzed approaches and computational solutions specifically for teaching HCI were not identified. Therefore, this article proposes: "Let's talk about tools and approaches for teaching HCI".

3   Systematic Mapping

This work presents a systematic mapping study carried out to get an overview of HCI classes at the undergraduate level. A systematic mapping is usually used to investigate a wider research area than a systematic literature review when little or no evidence on a topic is known [16]. The interest here is to get an indication of the quantity of that evidence and classify it for further studies.

3.1   Planning and Conducting the Mapping

The phase of planning the mapping consists of developing a review protocol which defines the methods to undertake a specific systematic review. Having a well defined protocol reduces the possibility that this review can be driven by research expectations.

Review Objective and Research Questions. The main objective of this mapping is to identify how HCI is being taught to undergraduate students. In order to guide this analysis towards its achievement, it is important to know what are the teaching approaches that are mostly used in class and what tools, if any, are used to support it. With this in mind, three research questions are proposed:

RQ1 What are the main approaches used to teach HCI to undergraduate students?
RQ2 What are the available technological tools specifically developed to support HCI teaching?
RQ3 How have the approaches or technologies used to teach HCI been evaluated?

Search Strategy. An automated search strategy was used in three different scientific databases: ACM Digital Library[1], IEEE Xplore Digital Library[2], Google Scholar[3]. These results were complemented with manual search on selected conferences:

- International Conference on Applied Human Factors and Ergonomics and the Affiliated Conferences, AHFE 2015 [17] and AHFE 2017 [18];[4]
- HCI International 2013–2017 [19–25];[5]

The search string used is divided into three parts:

Part1 This part of the string used expressions relating HCI and teaching. By using only the expression "HCI", without relating it to teaching, most of the studies returned by the search discussed on the applications in the area, but outside the education context. If on one hand the search was restricted, on the other hand, it was extended by adding term "usability". The choice for this term is supported in [26], that states "Usability and HCI are becoming core aspects of the system development process to improve and enhance system facilities and to satisfy users' needs and necessities."

Part2 Here the string was limited to search for papers that dealt with teaching undergraduates.

Part3 The last part had the intention to find among those papers the ones that explicitly mentioned how their teaching was conducted, using some kind of tool, approach or both.

In this way, the string used for the search was:

("teaching hci" OR "hci teaching" OR "hci education" OR "teaching usability" OR "usability teaching" OR "usability education") AND undergraduate AND (software OR game OR simulation OR tool OR environment OR methodology).

To complement the automated procedure, a snowballing search, backward and forward, was conducted following the guidelines in [27]. All the works selected from the automated search were used as seeds.

---

[1] dl.acm.org.

[2] ieeexplore.ieee.org.

[3] scholar.google.com.

[4] When searching in the proceedings of International Conference on Applied Human Factors and Ergonomics (AHFE), only the conferences held in 2015 and 2017 were considered since those were the only years when the affiliated conference "Advances in Human Factors in Training, Education, and Learning Sciences" took place. AHFE was not held in 2013.

[5] The search in HCI International conference, in 2013, aimed at the affiliated conference "Design, User Experience, and Usability (Part II: Health, Learning, Playing, Cultural, and Cross-Cultural User Experience; and Part III: Information and Interaction for Learning, Culture, Collaboration and Business"), whereas in the years 2014–2017, it aimed at the affiliated conference "Learning and Collaboration Technologies". The conference was not held in 2012.

Inclusion and Exclusion Criteria. Some inclusion and exclusion criteria were defined for selecting papers for the final review.

The mapping should only include:

- Peer-reviewed publications appearing in journals, conferences, and workshops;
- Publications written in English;
- Papers published from 2012 to 2017;
- Papers that discussed about or presented a methodology or an approach for teaching HCI on undergraduate level;
- Papers describing computational solutions to support HCI teaching.

The following works should be excluded from the mapping:

- Presentation documents, such as PowerPoint slides, and short/extended abstract papers;
- Papers that did not relate to undergraduate HCI courses;
- Papers that, although related to HCI teaching undergraduates, discussed about other aspects of the course or program, such as curriculum proposal, for instance;
- Papers that described computational solutions applying concepts related to HCI area, but that did not focus on teaching those concepts.

Data Extraction and Data Synthesis Strategies. The mapping was conducted from December 2017 to February 2018 with the execution of the protocol, and resulted in the selection of 21 papers for data extraction. However, during the data extraction process it was observed that in three selected studies there was no consistent information for extraction, that is, the information was not sufficient to respond to the RQs. So these 3 papers were excluded. The number of retrieved, examined and selected papers from each resource is summarized in Table 1. The selection process is illustrated in Fig. 1.

Data were extracted from each selected paper following 15 previously defined information items (Table 2).

Results. Table 3 summarizes the data extracted for the 17 articles selected considering some information from groups 1 and 2 of Table 2:

- The *Context* column indicates where the research described in the paper was conducted, i.e., which course, with its major in parenthesis;
- The *In-Text Topics* column presents those HCI topics the authors mentioned they had worked with the students during their research;
- The *HCI Topics* column classifies the topics surveyed by considering an HCI course in a curriculum guideline for undergraduate degree programs [7];
- The methodologies/approaches used to teach HCI are in the column *Approach*;
- The last column, *Tools*, indicates the tools used during the teaching process that were mentioned in the text.

Table 1. Search result

Resource	# Papers found	# Papers examined	# Papers selected
ACM	6	6	2
IEEE	24	24	4
Google Scholar	353	100	9
AHFE	938	938	0
HCI International	439	439	0
Backward snowballing	421	421	2
Forward snowballing	51	51	0
Total selected	2,232	1,979	17

Table 2. Data extracted from each primary study selected

Group	Information item
Group 1: Publication identification	II1. Publication ID
	II2. Publication title
	II3. Year of publication
	II4. Authors' name
	II5. Publication source
Group 2: Context reported in the publication	II6. Context of research (course/major)
	II7. Specific topics being taught
	II8. HCI topics [7]
	II9. Approach applied
	II10. Justification for use of approach
	II11. Technological tool used
	II12. Use of the tool
Group 3: Evaluation described in the publication	II13. Research type classification [28]
	II14. Evaluation
	II15. Sample

During the period researched, the publication of selected studies seemed to have been fairly regular, with 3 to 7 papers being published a year. The exception was in the 2013–2014 period, when no papers were published (Fig. 2).

From the 17 selected papers, 12 (70.5%) conducted their research in a HCI course, whether mandatory or elective, whereas 5 of them (29.5%) had their researches in some other courses (technical communication [TC], system design [SD], interaction design [ID] or winter school), where some topic of HCI was taught.

Table 3. Selected papers summary

ID	Ref.	Context*	In-Text Topics	HCI Topics [7]	Approach	Tools
1	[30]	HCI (CS)	Usability lifecycle; Requirements analysis; Prototyping; Heuristic evaluation	Development; Evaluation methods	Serious game	Computer game (UsabilityGame)
2	[31]	SD (CS)	Task analysis	Special HCI issues	-	ConcurTaskTrees Environment (CTTE)
3	[32]	HCI (CS)	User interface design project	Development	Studio-based learning	Simple art supply; Prototyping tools (WOZ Pro); HTML
4	[33]	HCI (CS)	User-centered design process with emphasis on interface design	User-centered design	Problem-based learning	Virtual world platform (OpenSimulator)
5	[34]	HCI (CS, IS)	Usability testing	Evaluation methods	Active learning	Student Centered e-Learning Environment (SCELE)
6	[35]	winter school (Eng)	Interaction design, usability, user experience, prototyping, data collection and analysis	User-centered design; Development	Action research approach	-
7	[36]	HCI (SE)	Basic Foundation, Requirement Analysis, Interaction Design, Usability Evaluation	Principles in HCI design; Development; Evaluation methods	Project development	-
8	[37]	HCI (not informed)	Prototyping; Evaluation; Usability testing	Development; Evaluation methods	Blended learning model	sLearn
9	[9]	TC (S, T, Eng, M)	Usability testing	Evaluation methods	User-centered approach	-
10	[38]	TC (Eng, CS, B)	Usability testing	Evaluation methods	Service-learning projects	-
11	[39]	HCI classes (P, D, Eng)	Core HCI design cycles	Development	Scaffolding approach	-
12	[40]	HCI (CS, ISc)	Principles of design and usability, with an emphasis on the human-side of interactions	User-centered design	Hands-on experiential activities	-
13	[41]	HCI (MIS)	Interface design with emphasis on the users	User-centered design	Studio-based learning	-
14	[42]	HCI (CS)	Single-modal and multiple modal cognitive theories	Principles in HCI design	Interest-Based Learning	-
15	[43]	HCI (CS)	Requirement collection and analysis; Interface design; Interface evaluation	Development; Evaluation methods	Realistic projects approach	-
16	[44]	HCI (CS)	HCI4D (HCI for Development)	Development	Student-centered, hands-on approach	-
17	[45]	ID (not informed)	Design thinking	Development	Design thinking approach; studio-based teaching	-

* Legend of abbreviations: [CS] Computer Science; [M] Mathematics; [HCI] Human-Computer Interaction; [IS] Information Systems; [B] Business; [SD] System Design; [Eng] Engineering; [P] Psychology; [TC] Technical Communication; [SE] Software Engineering; [D] Design; [S] Science; [ISc] Information Science; [T] Technology; [MIS] Management Information Systems; [ID] Interaction design

4   Discussion

With the data extracted from the selected papers it is possible now to answer the research questions.

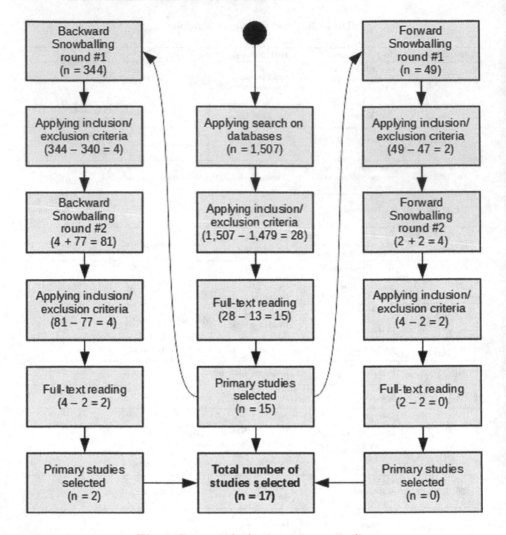

Fig. 1. Process of selecting primary studies

RQ1 What are the main approaches used to teach HCI to undergraduate students?

From the data extracted here, a wide variety of teaching approaches or techniques can be identified (Fig. 2).

Most articles mentioned the use of a specific approach (blue dots in the graph of Fig. 2). However, some articles did not cite a specific approach, and in this case, they were ranked from the analysis of the text (red dots in the graph of Fig. 2):

– Experiential activities: experiential learning is a guided process of questioning, investigating, reflecting, and conceptualizing based on direct experiences.

Fig. 2. Approaches used in selected studies

In this learning process, the learner is actively engaged, has freedom to choose, and directly experiences the consequences of their actions [45].
- Hands-on experiences: development of projects with real users, that is, real-world cases.
- Project development: development of projects without considering real users.
- Serious game: use of serious game (educational game) to support teaching.

Among the articles that did not mention a specific approach, the teaching of HCI through the development of group projects using as case study real needs, that is, real-world cases [33,37,42] can be highlight as the most recurrent.

Nine different approaches were cited in the selected studies. For Zaharias et al. [32] problem-based learning develops "experiential and social learning and calls for an active rather than passive approach to learning that leads to the development of critical thinking skills". Jeon [38], on the other hand, defends that although a problem-solving approach may not work for novices (i.e., under-graduates), "they are still encouraged to be involved in the overall design process, but they start with a focus on part of the problem with well-defined guidance based on the scaffolding approach." Culén [44] proposes the use of design think-ing that "stands firmly on three main pillars: empathy with users and human centeredness, rapid prototyping to generate large number of alternatives in order to solve the right problem rather than a problem right, and last, but not least, their synthesis leading to best viable and feasible solutions that incorporate desired values" [44].

Chong [9] mentions the use of user-centered approach, whereas, Taylor et al. [43] prefer student-centered learning which are research-led, problem-based and flexible, where students can focus on the topics and content delivery methods which are most interesting and useful to them. Alnuain et al. [36] apply blended learning model "a learning approach that contains different types of education techniques and technologies. This learning model aims to provide more effective education experiences by combining features and functions of well-known learning and teaching techniques" [46].

Studio-based learning was the most cited approach [31,40,44]. Adapted from architecture and art education, as well as from collaborative problem-solving pedagogies, studio-based learning has shown great promise for computing education [47]. Key elements of studio based learning include exploring multiple solutions to a problem, justifying the choice of one solution, and being subject to, as well as providing, peer reviews [47].

Yang et al. [41] propose a new approach, called interest-based learning, in this approach "students are guided to organize teams by same personal hobbies or specialties, e.g. music or sports, and conduct research on HCI in these familiar and interested topic."

It can be observed from this analysis that the teaching of HCI to undergraduates has used some kind of active learning approach, considered here as "any instructional method that engages students in the learning process"[5]. The popularity of active learning among HCI teachers seems to be clear when assuming that this approach tries to involve the students in a way that is closer to the professional environment. Most of the importance of HCI for the IT industry is related to practical activities such as interface prototyping and development or usability testing, for instance. The approaches identified on the selected papers try to actively involve the students at doing something rather than passively receiving information. For Hundhausen et al. [31], giving the students a more central participation "is akin to the situation of an expert designer presenting a user interface design to a design team in a real-world company."

RQ2 What are the available technological tools specifically developed to support HCI teaching?

Although HCI is closely related to computers and some other technological devices, the use of tools specifically developed for HCI teaching does not seem to be very widespread. From the selected papers, only 6 mentioned some kind of tool during the process and, among them, only 2 described tools that were specifically designed for the purpose.

One of those tools is a serious game, called UsabilityGame [29], that offers the students the opportunity to practice the usability lifecycle by addressing requirement analysis, prototyping and heuristic evaluation. When playing the game, the students have to select the correct set of requirements for each scenario presented, develop a prototype to be evaluated by the teacher and evaluate real-world interfaces by choosing one of Nielsen's heuristics [48] that would correctly improve the detected usability issue. The main role of the teacher, during the game, is to set up the game according to the student's learning objectives, to conduct the evaluation of the prototypes, and monitor the performance of the class.

The other tool is WOZ Pro (Wizard of Oz Prototyper) [31], a low-fidelity prototyping environment that was developed to support prototyping creation and wizard of oz testing. Although it was conceived to be used by college students who are first learning about interaction design, this tool could also be used outside the educational context [49].

A few other tools such as an environment for editing and analysis of task models (CTTE – ConcurTaskTrees Environment [30]), an e-learning environment (SCELE – Student Centered e-Learning Environment [33]), a virtual world platform (OpenSimulator [32]) and even simple art supply [49] were mentioned to be used during the teaching process and they can all be as valuable as the computer-based tools described above. However, HCI teachers seem not to have many choices when picking out some supporting tool that could meet their educational purposes.

RQ3 How have the approaches or technologies used to teach HCI been evaluated?

The selected studies were also classified following the research type classification proposed by [28]. According to this study, most of the primary studies (76%) were classified as experience papers, presenting the authors' experiences in class. The importance of these papers rely in the relevance of the lessons learned by the author from that experience [50]. Three other studies (18%) were classified as evaluation research, with the proposal of a novel piece of knowledge in HCI education. At last, 1 study (6%) was classified as an opinion paper (see Table 4).

Despite the importance of experience papers, that contribute with experiences of in-practice approaches, revealing their results when applied in real contexts, the number of studies evaluating new developments in HCI education does not seem to be very large. This high percentage of experience studies on HCI education seems to indicate that researchers are mostly concentrated on applying their efforts to understanding the area, producing data to pave the road of further developments.

When evaluating the result of the applied approaches: (i) a simple survey was used in 7 studies [9,34–37,41,44] without statistical tests; (ii) 4 studies applied statistical analysis to evaluate their results (Wilcoxon test [29], Pearson Product-Moment Correlation Coefficient [40], Kruskal-Wallis, Mann-Whitney [42], chi-squared test and ANOVA [31]); (iii) interview [9,40] and structured interviews were used by [32]; (iv) observation was the technique used by [32,36,40]; and (v) content analysis (video) used by [31].

The size of the sample used by the researchers ranged from 8 [44] to approximately 1,150 [35] students participating in the process. When analyzing the mean and the median numbers (159 and 40, respectively), they are considerably higher than those of the studies published at CHI2014 [51].

4.1 Threats to Validity of the Mapping

One of the major problems with systematic reviews is finding all the relevant primary studies (evidence). In this case, three search strategies were used to

Table 4. Research type classification [28]

Research type	Papers
Experience papers	[9,30,32–37,39–41,43,44]
Evaluation research	[29,31,42]
Opinion paper	[38]

ensure that the largest number of related studies would be found: (i) Automatic search in 3 different databases; (ii) Manual search in specific proceedings of two conferences of HCI area not indexed on the searched databases; and (iii) backward and forward snowballing.

In addition, our search strings were designed to find the maximum number of relevant papers. Nonetheless, it is possible that they have missed studies that used different terminology to describe any part of the string.

The search resulted in some papers that, in spite of having their titles and abstracts in English, were actually written in other languages. Those papers were excluded from the selection, but, due to language limitations, it was not possible to assess whether they had relevant information or not.

Readers must consider that a systematic review is by definition limited by the search date, the electronic sources and key terms used in the search. Therefore, it is possible that other papers may be included in a future replication of the study. The results are limited by the previous features, and by the evolution of the HCI education area itself.

5   Conclusions

Although HCI teaching is present in many computer-related programs, it seems that HCI teaching in undergraduate level has not been drawing enough attention from researchers, what is evidenced by the small number of selected papers. This conclusion gets patent when looking at the dates of the publications and realizing that for two years in a row there were no selected publications on the theme. The lack of selected papers from the proceedings of prestigious conferences shows that the road is still open for research in HCI education.

Most of the selected papers presented researches on either development or evaluation methods teaching. Nevertheless, the teaching of some topics, such as *Relevance of HCI* and *Devices*, was not mentioned. The lack of research on those topics does not mean they are less important than others, it simply means that there is a field ahead to be explored.

Active teaching approaches as a whole seem to be the main option when teaching HCI to undergraduate students. The present study did not try to categorize the multitude of approaches or evaluate its results when applied to this area of knowledge, because the prevalence of one approach over the others could not be stated in small number of primary studies found. This categorization might eventually become an object of future work.

HCI teachers have very few options when choosing a supporting tool exclusively developed for their classes. The same does not happen in other areas of knowledge on computer field. On a paper of 2009, for example, Wangenheim and Shull [52] found 16 games used in software engineering education, most of them computer-based, but also card or board games. Although the paper concludes that more research in the area is necessary, it is clear that there were a higher number of educational games on software engineering 10 years ago than there are of educational tools for HCI today. Future work on these tools would bring great benefit for HCI teachers and students.

Finally, it is noted that few empirical studies have been conducted to verify the results obtained by the different teaching approaches and tools used. Thus, this paper suggests that more empirical studies be performed with sufficient rigor to improve the body of evidence in the HCI education field.

References

1. Djajalaksana, Y.M.: A National Survey of Instructional Strategies Used to Teach Information Systems Courses: An Exploratory Investigation. Doctor of Philosophy, University of South Florida, Tampa (2011)
2. von Wangenheim, C.G., von Wangenheim, A.: Ensinando Computação com Jogos, 1st edn. Bookess Editora, Florianópolis (2012)
3. Brabrand, C.: How to make sure your students learn what you want them to. Palestra (2010)
4. do Carmo Marcheti Ferraz, A.P., Belhot, R.V.: Taxonomia de Bloom: revisão teórica e apresentação das adequações do instrumento para definição de objetivos instrucionais. Gestão e Produção 17(2), 421–431 (2010)
5. Prince, M.: Does active learning work? A review of the research. J. Eng. Educ. 93(3), 223–231 (2004)
6. Joint Task Force on Computing Curricula, Association for Computing Machinery (ACM) and IEEE Computer Society: Computer Science Curricula 2013: Curriculum Guidelines for Undergraduate Degree Programs in Computer Science, 999133. ACM, New York (2013)
7. Topi, H., et al.: Curriculum Guidelines for Undergraduate Degree Programs in Information Systems. ACM/AIS Task Force (2010)
8. The Joint Task Force on Computing Curricula: Curriculum guidelines for undergraduate degree programs in software engineering. Technical report, ACM/IEEE, New York (2015)
9. Chong, F.: Implementing usability testing in introductory technical communication service courses: results and lessons from a local study. IEEE Trans. Prof. Commun. PP(99), 1–10 (2017)
10. Sommariva, L.W.: Usabilitygame. Mestrado em computação aplicada, Universidade do Vale do Itajaí, São José (2012)
11. Edwards, A., Wright, P., Petrie, H.. HCI education: we are failing-why. In: Proceedings of HCI Educators Workshop (2006)

12. Battistella, P.E., von Wangenheim, C.G.: Games for teaching computing in higher education - a systematic review. IEEE Technol. Eng. Educ. (ITEE) **1**, 8–30 (2016)
13. Do, T.V., Lee, J.-W.: A multiple-level 3D-LEGO game in augmented reality for improving spatial ability. In: Jacko, J.A. (ed.) HCI 2009. LNCS, vol. 5613, pp. 296–303. Springer, Heidelberg (2009). https://doi.org/10.1007/978-3-642-02583-9_33
14. Benitti, F.B.V., Sommariva, L.: Investigando o ensino de ihc no contexto da computação: o que e como é ensinado? In: Anais do III Workshop sobre Ensino de IHC (2012)
15. Ferreira, B.M., Rivero, L., Lopes, A., Marques, A.B., Conte, T.: UsabiliCity: Um Jogo de Apoio ao Ensino de Propriedades de Usabilidade de Software Através de Analogias. In: Anais do Simpósio Brasileiro de Informática na Educação, Dourados, MT, Sociedade Brasileira de Computação - SBC, pp. 1273–1282 (2014)
16. Kitchenham, B., Charters, S.: Guidelines for performing Systematic Literature Reviews in Software Engineering. Technical report EBSE 2007–001, Keele University and Durham University Joint Report, Durham, UK (2007)
17. Ahram, T., Karwowski, W., Schmorrow, D.: 6th International Conference on Applied Human Factors and Ergonomics (AHFE 2015) and the Affiliated Conferences. Procedia Manufacturing, vol. 3, p. 6660 (2015)
18. Andre, T.: Advances in Human Factors in Training, Education, and Learning Sciences. AISC, vol. 596, 1st edn. Springer, Cham (2018). https://doi.org/10.1007/978-3-319-60018-5
19. Marcus, A.: Design, User Experience, and Usability: Health, Learning, Playing, Cultural, and Cross-Cultural User Experience. LNCS, vol. 8013, 1st edn. Springer, Heidelberg (2013). https://doi.org/10.1007/978-3-642-39241-2
20. Yamamoto, S.: Human Interface and the Management of Information: Information and Interaction for Learning, Culture, Collaboration and Business, LNCS, vol. 8018, 1st edn. Springer, Heidelberg (2013). https://doi.org/10.1007/978-3-642-39226-9
21. Zaphiris, P., Ioannou, A.: Learning and Collaboration Technologies: Designing and Developing Novel Learning Experiences. LNCS, vol. 8523, 1st edn. Springer, Cham (2014). https://doi.org/10.1007/978-3-319-07482-5
22. Zaphiris, P., Ioannou, A.: Learning and Collaboration Technologies: Technology-Rich Environments for Learning and Collaboration. LNCS, vol. 8524, 1st edn. Springer, Cham (2014). https://doi.org/10.1007/978-3-319-07485-6
23. Zaphiris, P., Ioannou, A.: Learning and Collaboration Technologies. LNCS, vol. 9192, 1st edn. Springer, Cham (2015). https://doi.org/10.1007/978-3-319-20609-7
24. Zaphiris, P., Ioannou, A.: Learning and Collaboration Technologies. LNCS, vol. 9753, 1st edn. Springer, Cham (2016). https://doi.org/10.1007/978-3-319-39483-1
25. Zaphiris, P., Ioannou, A.: Learning and Collaboration Technologies: Novel Learning Ecosystems. LNCS, vol. 10295, 1st edn. Springer, Cham (2017). https://doi.org/10.1007/978-3-319-58509-3
26. Issa, T., Isaias, P.: Sustainable Design, pp. 19–36. Springer, London (2015). https://doi.org/10.1007/978-1-4471-6753-2_2
27. Wohlin, C.: Guidelines for snowballing in systematic literature studies and a replication in software engineering. In: Proceedings of the 18th International Conference on Evaluation and Assessment in Software Engineering, EASE 2014, pp. 38:1–38:10. ACM, New York (2014)
28. Petersen, K., Vakkalanka, S., Kuzniarz, L.: Guidelines for conducting systematic mapping studies in software engineering: an update. Inf. Softw. Technol. **64**, 1–18 (2015)

29. Benitti, F.B.V., Sommariva, L.: Evaluation of a game used to teach usability to undergraduate students in computer science. J. Usability Stud. **11**(1), 21–39 (2015)
30. Marçal de Oliveira, K., Girard, P., Gonçalves, T.G., Lepreux, S., Kolski, C.: Teaching task analysis for user interface design: lessons learned from three pilot studies. In: Proceedings of the 27th Conference on L'Interaction Homme-Machine. IHM 2015, pp. 31:1–31:6. ACM, New York (2015)
31. Hundhausen, C.D., Fairbrother, D., Petre, M.: An empirical study of the "prototype walkthrough": a studio-based activity for HCI education. ACM Trans. Comput.-Hum. Interact. **19**(4), 26:1–26:36 (2012)
32. Zaharias, P., Belk, M., Samaras, G.: Employing virtual worlds for HCI education: a problem-based learning approach. In: CHI 2012 Extended Abstracts on Human Factors in Computing Systems, CHI EA 2012, pp. 317–326. ACM, New York (2012)
33. Santoso, H.B., Sari, E.: Transforming undergraduate HCI course in Indonesia: a preliminary study. In: Proceedings of the Asia Pacific HCI and UX Design Symposium, pp. 55–59. ACM (2015)
34. Lazem, S.: A case study for sensitising Egyptian engineering students to user-experience in technology design. In: Proceedings of the 7th Annual Symposium on Computing for Development, p. 12. ACM (2016)
35. Feng, G., Luo, B.: An experience of teaching HCI to undergraduate software engineering students. In: 2012 IEEE 25th Conference on Software Engineering Education and Training, pp. 125–129, April 2012
36. Alnuaim, A., Caleb-Solly, P., Perry, C.: Enhancing student learning of human-computer interaction using a contextual mobile application. In: 2016 SAI Computing Conference (SAI), pp. 952–959, July 2016
37. Chong, F.: Teaching usability in a technical communication classroom: developing competencies to user-test and communicate with an international audience. In: 2012 IEEE International Professional Communication Conference, pp. 1–4, October 2012
38. Jeon, M.: What to teach in HCI?: How to educate HCI students to envision the future of human being, not the future of technology? Proc. Hum. Factors Ergon. Soc. Ann. Meeting **59**(1), 362–366 (2015)
39. Scialdone, M., Connolly, A.J.: A creative approach to devising non-technical, meaningful exercises in human-computer interaction undergraduate education. In: Proceedings of the EDSIG Conference ISSN, vol. 2473, p. 3857 (2016)
40. Or-Bach, R.: Design and implementation of an HCI course for MIS students-some lessons. Issues Inf. Sci. Inf. Technol. **12**(unknown), 153–163 (2015)
41. Yi, Y., Shengjin, W., Jiasong, S., Xian, Z.: Interest-based learning for teaching a human-computer interaction course: media and cognition course. In: Proceedings of the 2017 International Conference on Frontiers in Education: Computer Science and Computer Engineering (FECS 2017) (2017)
42. Urquiza-Fuentes, J., Paredes-Velasco, M.: Investigating the effect of realistic projects on students' motivation, the case of human-computer interaction course. Comput. Hum. Behav. **72**, 692–700 (2017)
43. Taylor, J.L., Tsimeris, J., Zhu, X., Stevenson, D., Gedeon, T.: Observations from teaching HCI to Chinese students in Australia. In: Proceedings of the ASEAN CHI Symposium 2015, pp. 31–35. ACM, New York (2015)
44. Culén, A.L.. HCI education: innovation, creativity and design thinking. In: Proceedings of the The Eighth International Conference on Advances in Computer-Human Interactions, ACHI 2015 (2015)
45. Obrenović, Z.: Rethinking hci education: teaching interactive computing concepts based on the experiential learning paradigm. ACM Interact. **19**(3), 66–70 (2012)

46. Köse, U.: A blended learning model supported with web 2.0 technologies. Procedia
    - Soc. Behav. Sci. **2**(2), 2794–2802 (2010). Innovation and Creativity in Education
47. Hendrix, D., Myneni, L., Narayanan, H., Ross, M.: Implementing studio-based
    learning in CS2. In: Proceedings of the 41st ACM Technical Symposium on Com-
    puter Science Education, SIGCSE 2010, pp. 505–509. ACM, New York (2010)
48. Nielsen, J.: 10 usability heuristics for user interface design (1995). https://www.
    nngroup.com/articles/ten-usability-heuristics/. Accessed 25 July 2017
49. Hundhausen, C.D., Balkar, A., Nuur, M., Trent, S.: WOZ pro: a pen-based low
    fidelity prototyping environment to support wizard of OZ studies. In: CHI 2007
    Extended Abstracts on Human Factors in Computing Systems, CHI EA 2007, pp.
    2453–2458. ACM, New York (2007)
50. Wieringa, R., Maiden, N., Mead, N., Rolland, C.: Requirements engineering paper
    classification and evaluation criteria: a proposal and a discussion. Requir. Eng.
    11(1), 102–107 (2006)
51. Caine, K.: Local standards for sample size at CHI. In: Proceedings of the 2016 CHI
    Conference on Human Factors in Computing Systems, pp. 981–992. ACM (2016)
52. von Wangenheim, C.G., Shull, F.: To game or not to game? IEEE Softw. **26**(2),
    92–94 (2009)

Four-Dimensional Learning, a Response to Social Responsibility in Learning

Rafael Molina-Carmona[1,3]([☒]), Pilar Arques-Corrales[2],
and Faraón Llorens-Largo[3]

[1] Unidad Científica de Innovación Empresarial "Ars Innovatio",
University of Alicante, Alicante, Spain
rmolina@ua.es

[2] Department of Computer Science and Artificial Intelligence,
University of Alicante, Alicante, Spain
arques@ua.es

[3] Cátedra Santander-UA de Transformación Digital,
University of Alicante, Alicante, Spain
faraon.llorens@ua.es

Abstract. Corporate Social Responsibility can be considered as the integration in an organisation of social and environmental concerns in their operations and in their interaction with their stakeholders on a voluntary basis. Universities, as leaders in higher education and scientific advancement, have long adopted this social responsibility from several points of view, particularly training their students. Our research focuses on effectively introducing the social factor in the training of engineers. In order to do this, four principles or dimensions define our proposal: Project-Based Learning, that uses an engineering project as a central element of learning; Transversal Learning, that uses a project defined between several disciplines; Professional Learning, which takes place in an environment that is very close to the professional context; and Service Learning, in which the academic results not only benefit the learner but also the society. In short, we propose a transversal project-based learning experience developed in collaboration with an external organisation that contributes its problems and collects the solutions developed by the students. As a consequence of this collaboration, the students are introduced to a real professional environment, and provide both a strategic vision of the organisation and innovative solutions to their problems. In addition, the institution has a social character as it is a non-profit organisation that works with disadvantaged people (Spanish Red Cross), which turns the experience into a service learning experience. The result is encouraging and very positive, as evidenced by the opinions of students, teachers and the organisation that hosts the experience.

Keywords: Corporate Social Responsibility in Universities ·
Project-Based Learning · Transversal Learning ·
Professional Learning · Service Learning

© Springer Nature Switzerland AG 2019
P. Zaphiris and A. Ioannou (Eds.): HCII 2019, LNCS 11590, pp. 171–190, 2019.
https://doi.org/10.1007/978-3-030-21814-0_14

1   Introduction

Although there is no unique definition of Corporate Social Responsibility (CSR), it can be considered as the integration in an organisation of social and environmental concerns in their operations and in their interaction with their stakeholders on a voluntary basis [1]. For the European Commission, CSR provides the foundations of an integrated approach that combines economic, environmental and social interests to their mutual benefit. It opens a way of managing change and of reconciling social development with improved competitiveness.

Other terms used for CSR in specialty literature are corporate responsibility, corporate citizenship, corporate sustainability or corporate sustainable development [2]. It is important to note several issues about CSR: it covers both social and environmental aspects, it must be aligned with the organisational strategy, it has a voluntary character and it concerns how the organisation interacts with their internal and external stakeholders.

Universities, as leaders in higher education and scientific advancement, have long adopted this social responsibility from several points of view. The social dimension of the University is adopted through its teaching, research and cultural extension functions. For this reason, it must comprehensively incorporate aspects relating to professional ethics, the development of key competences and entrepreneurial initiatives, as well as the impact of technologies and processes in terms of social and environmental sustainability, being a driving force for change for future professionals [3].

Our research focuses on the field of engineering, although it can be extended to any other field. Since engineers must be socially responsible, but they must also know how to operate in a professional environment, we make a proposal to effectively introduce the social factor in the training of these professionals. In order to do this, four principles or dimensions define our proposal (hence the name Four-Dimensional Learning):

- Project-Based Learning, as a teaching methodology that uses an engineering project as a central element of learning.
- Transversal Learning, which uses a project defined between several disciplines, which brings it closer to a real project, in which transversal concepts participate.
- Professional Learning, which takes place in an environment that is very close to the professional context in which future engineers will develop their work once they have finished their studies.
- Service Learning, as a way of endowing the project with a social character, in which the academic results not only benefit the learner but also the society.

In order to incorporate social responsibility in the training of future computer engineers, we propose the coordination of transversal subjects, developed through a project that articulates all the activities of the subjects. In short, it is a transversal project-based learning experience.

In addition, this project is developed in collaboration with an external organisation that contributes its problems and collects the solutions developed by the students. As a consequence of this collaboration, the students are introduced to a real professional environment, and provide both a strategic vision of the organisation and innovative solutions to their problems. In addition, the institution has a social character as it is a non-profit organisation that works with disadvantaged people (Spanish Red Cross), which turns the experience into a service learning experience.

As a consequence of their project, the students develop their skills related to the social responsibility that every engineer must have.

The result, after several years of experience is encouraging and very positive, as evidenced by the results of satisfaction of students, teachers and the organisation that hosts the experience.

The document is organised as follows: Sect. 2 presents the background of the research, including a short review on the main concepts. The context is presented in Sect. 3, with a brief description of the subjects. Section 4 is devoted to explain our proposal in depth. Finally, some conclusions are highlighted in Sect. 5.

2 Background

2.1 Social Responsibility and Higher Education

In recent years, social responsibility has gained prominence in many fields, and particularly in university environments. The university governance is becoming aware of this need and there is a proliferation of actions related to CSR, organic units dedicated to these actions and specialised training in this field. However, there is no consensus on the concrete definition of this concept or on how to implement it through specific strategies and actions. Each institution and each author determine its own orientation.

For example, [4] tries to facilitate understanding of the concept of CSR as a strategic challenge for universities and conducts a literature review in which he detects three major perspectives for this concept: managerial, transformational and normative. The management approach is concerned with analysing the impact of university work in society, especially through accountability of their actions and decisions to their stakeholders. The transformational approach, however, focuses on reviewing the university's contribution to debate and reflection to achieve a more sustainable and just society. Finally, the normative approach focuses on the development of normative frameworks from the university as an axis to do the right thing in life in society, through the establishment of national or global university networks around social responsibility.

The transformational perspective is especially interesting to us because it is the one we have taken in our work. Gaete Quezada [4] classifies the different initiatives into four areas: training, research, social leadership and social commitment. In the area of training, in which our proposal is included, the main actions are related to Service Learning and the relationship of the university with society. Service Learning favours the preparation of students so that they insert themselves into society as responsible citizens and contribute to its sustainable development for mutual benefit.

For its part, González Alcántara et al. [3] consider it important to integrally incorporate aspects relating to professional ethics, the development of key competencies and entrepreneurial initiatives, as well as the impact of technologies and processes in terms of social and environmental sustainability. This author has studied the situation of CSR in Spanish universities and has identified a set of good practices for four axes: academic and pedagogical training, research and dissemination, organisation management and social participation. For the academic and pedagogical training axis, it considers as good practices the existence of degrees in Social Responsibility, or subjects that promote the values of citizenship, responsibility and social commitment in other degrees. With regard to research and dissemination, good practices are considered to be research actions aimed at achieving benefits for society (collaboration with companies, research groups in CRS and the existence of ethical committees), and dissemination actions (websites, journals, conferences and other publications). The good practices related to the axis of organisation management include dialogue with interest groups, commitment with workers, integration of CSR in management or transparency. Finally, on the axis of social participation, good practices are identified as actions that allow society to be participants in the university, not requiring them to be students or staff, as well as measures to encourage volunteerism and cooperation.

Particularly, the University of Alicante, in which this proposal is framed, is a public and socially responsible institution, whose mission is the integral training and development of its students. Not only in knowledge and disciplines, but also the promotion of the critical awareness, social responsibility, health and sustainability principles, to contribute effectively to the welfare of the society where it is inserted. It should also be added the guarantee of personal dignity, the free development of persons, without any discrimination, and finally, the right to effective equality between women and men. Research is another basic principle to increase improvement of knowledge. On the one hand, by its transfer through teaching. On the other hand, the direct contribution of the University to the society through its inescapable commitment to the cultural, scientific and technological development. In this way, thanks to the collaboration with other social agents, such research can be realised in innovation for sustainable development and the improvement of the quality of life [5]. The references that guide the values of the University of Alicante are designed in order to foster the quality of a public university. Among these, it can be found solidarity and sustainability.

This initiative is part of the curriculum of Masters Degree in Computer Engineering, among which the following competences stand out [6]:

- Ability to project, calculate and design products, processes and installations in all areas of computer engineering.
- Ability to manage works and computer systems installations, complying with current regulations and ensuring service quality.
- Ability to manage, plan and supervise multidisciplinary teams.

– Capacity for the elaboration, strategic planning, direction, coordination and technical and economic management of projects in all areas of Computer Engineering following quality and environmental criteria.
– Capacity for the implementation, direction and management of manufacturing processes of computer equipment, with a guarantee of safety for people and goods, the final quality of products and their homologation.
– Ability to understand and apply the ethical responsibility, legislation and professional deontology of the activity of the profession of Computer Engineer.
– Ability to apply the principles of economics and management of human resources and projects, as well as legislation, regulation and standardisation of information technology.
– Capacity for strategic planning, elaboration, direction, coordination, and technical and economic management in the fields of computer engineering related, among others, with: systems, applications, services, networks, infrastructures, or computer facilities and software development centres or factories, respecting the proper compliance with quality and environmental criteria and in multidisciplinary work environments.
– Ability to manage research, development and innovation projects in companies and technology centres, guaranteeing safety for people and goods, the final quality of the products and their homologation.
– Ability to design, develop, manage and evaluate certification mechanisms and guarantee security in the treatment and access to information in a local or distributed processing system.
– Capacity to contribute to the future development of information technology.
– Ability to integrate knowledge and deal with the complexity of making judgements based on information that, being incomplete or limited, includes reflections on the social and ethical responsibilities linked to the application of their knowledge and judgements.

The concepts of ethical, social and professional responsibility, deontology, regulations, sustainability, safety, standardisation, resource management, innovation, service, and transference are present in every subject and area of the curriculum. In this context, the aspects of CSR in a wide sense are fully justified in the curriculum of Computer Engineering. A good way to complete the training of these future professionals may be the development of transversal projects as a service for non-profit organisations and we already have some previous experiences about this question. For instance, we have experience in achieving the social inclusion of disabled people, as part of the social responsibility of future engineers, through the realisation of the final degree project in collaboration with associations of disabled users, in particular through the design and development of adapted video games [7]. The students are trained in the social responsibility but also solving some problems of inclusion in the collective of disabled users (such as the access to digital entertainment) and carrying out an in-depth study about the interaction problems for these users, providing concrete and practical solutions. As a result, the experience has served to introduce the aspects of social responsibility in the curricula of engineers in a very effective way.

2.2   Project-Based Learning

The vertiginous evolution of today's society is demanding increasingly new skills from professionals. These professionals of the future, among other skills, need to manage change appropriately, collaborate and cooperate with other professionals, integrate different points of view, operate in technological, multidisciplinary and multicultural environments or be autonomous in the search for information and learning. In short, they must be prepared to adapt to changing environmental conditions with high uncertainty.

One of the teaching methods that best adapts to these characteristics is Project Based Learning (PBL) since it allows to cover the key aspects of which we have spoken, with a professional project as objective, with an active role of the student, cooperative and interdisciplinary, and with an adequate use of technological resources.

There are numerous successful works of application of the PBL methodology in Engineering studies. The PBL develops skills such as encouraging teamwork, encouraging autonomous learning, reinforcing oral and written communication, and improving the ability to plan time, among others [8,9]. In addition, the PBL allows an approximation to the professional practice of future engineers and to develop a finished product that can be included in their personal portfolio [10].

2.3   Transversal Learning

Traditionally, curricula are divided into subjects that divide knowledge into stand-alone partitions. However, knowledge is not compartmentalised, and real problems always need the help of different branches of knowledge. In contrast to this classical division into subjects, transversal and multidisciplinary learning enriches the formative work in such a way that it connects and articulates the knowledge of the different disciplines and establishes connections between mere instruction and integral formation.

Multidisciplinary refers to the broad spectrum of scientific fields that are collectively employed to provide heterogeneous training experiences for learners [11]. Several studies have proven that multidisciplinary projects have made a positive difference in both teachers and students, increasing their motivation [12,13].

Transversality is a related and wider concept. It seeks to see the entire educational experience as an opportunity for learning to integrate its cognitive and formative dimensions, which has an impact not only on the established curriculum, but also on the educational culture and all the actors that are part of it [14].

The transversal dimension of learning not only implies a change in educational practice, but it must play a fundamental role in the profile of the future citizen. In this sense, one of the most innovative options of the current educational proposals lies in firmly advocating an integral formative action that takes into account both the intellectual and moral aspects in a balanced manner and promotes the harmonious development of the students' personalities, without forgetting the problematic social context in which they live. At this point, the direct involvement of learners with social agents through Transversal and Service Learning implies a decisive humanising orientation of educational practice. Some authors define this Transversal Learning from a triple perspective [15]): in the attitudinal contents of each curricular area, in some optional subjects and through the so-called transversal axes, teachings or subjects. In our case we achieve transversality through the integration of several subjects, proposing unique projects that deal with different aspects and analyse common cases from different perspectives [10].

2.4   Professional Learning

Profession is defined as a vocation requiring specialised knowledge and often long and intensive preparation including instruction in skills and methods as well as in the scientific, historical, or scholarly principles underlying such skills and methods, maintaining by force of organisation concerted opinion high standards of achievement and conduct, and committing its members to continued study and to a kind of work which has for its prime purpose the rendering of a public service [16].

Professional Learning is a cognitive-affective process of the human being or a collective, through which the appropriation and systematisation of the professional experience and technological culture is produced, favouring that the learner develops his labor competences, immersed in the real processes of activity and communication of a company [17].

Professional Learning has the advantage that the learner obtains the work and professional skills necessary to perform successfully in the work activity, but it does so immersed in that work context significant for him, assimilating, appropriating and systematising the organisational culture of the companies and the work experiences accumulated in them. In addition to the obvious relationship between the learner and the company with which he or she is trained, relationships are created between the teacher and the company, between the educational center and the productive entity, between the teaching process and the productive process, and between academic education and professional training.

To achieve the learning of professional skills, Project-Based Learning is especially useful as it introduces the student to a realistic project [10,18]. If in addition, this project is performed with the collaboration of a real organisation, the project in addition to being realistic is also real, and you get the development of professional skills of which we spoke.

2.5   Service Learning

There are several points of view when defining the Service Learning concept. Some approaches emphasise the roles of faculty and community members in the process, and others make social justice or systems change an explicit objective [19].

The Corporation for National and Community Service emphasises the fact that with this type of learning, students develop through active participation in experiences that meet the real needs of the community. These experiences need to be integrated into the students' academic curriculum and provide structured time for reflection. In this way learning goes beyond the classroom and extends into the community [20].

An important nuance that distinguishes Service Learning from other types of experiential learning (school volunteering, community service, field activities or internships) is the fact that there must be reciprocal benefits, i.e. Service Learning only occurs when there is a balance between learning objectives and service outcomes. In short, in true Service Learning the results of the experience must benefit both the service provider (the student and the educational institution) and the receiver (the social organisation) and the two facets of the process (as a learning process for the student and as a service for the organisation) must be balanced [19,21,22].

This is our approach in this work. We are interested in a reciprocal Service Learning, since the first goal is using a project to make the students learn, but this project is performed for a social organisation which is, in turn, interested in receiving a final product. Moreover, there is a third facet in Service Learning: in addition to the acquisition of the specific technical skills of each degree, this methodology (complemented with PBL) also reinforces the training of the transversal skills that all students must develop in order to be good professionals: critical and reflective thinking, decision making, teamwork, communication and negotiation, problem solving and initiative. This way, the possibilities of labor insertion are multiplied, as these skills are among the most demanded by employers.

3   Context

Originally, the master's programme was designed as a face-to-face course. Subsequently, the course became a blended-learning course [23], so the subjects had to be modified to include a part of non-classroom work with a significant workload. In this section we explain how the subjects were after their transformation to become blended-learning, but before the experience presented here.

The two subjects that take part in this experience are *Strategic Direction of Information Technologies* and *Applied Technological Innovation*. Both are compulsory first-year subjects, taught in the first semester, and their design is based on the principles of *teaching by example* (for the teacher) and *learning by doing* (for students). For this reason, the principles and techniques specific to each discipline (management skills and instruments for direction and innovation) as well as the principles and diversity of teaching innovation tools were taken into account. Thus, the subjects were made up of different pieces fitted together making a puzzle, and with the evaluation as the backbone of the teaching proposal, indicating to the students the path to follow.

The fundamental blocks of the design, applying the principle of task-centred learning, are:

- Lessons: devoted to expose the theoretical contents of the subject.
- Workshops: devoted to organise a hands-on session about specific techniques or methods.
- Deliverables: that students must hand over in order to success the subject and fulfill the learning outcomes.

Following the philosophy of Flipped Learning, the classroom hours were invested in the tasks that best took advantage of the interaction, both between the teacher and the students and between the students themselves. And the student's autonomous work consisted of preparing for the face-to-face sessions: watching videos, reading documents, searching information, interpreting infographics and figures or navigating through websites.

For the evaluation of the students' learning, different instruments depending on the subject were used as a cocktail, which made it possible to measure the students' learning from different perspectives. In addition, in the last session the subject and the teacher were evaluated by means of a satisfaction survey.

This modular and task-based design has allowed us to evolve the subjects throughout the seven academic years that they have been teaching and make the coupling between both subjects and the adaptation to the Spanish Red Cross organisation in a simpler way. In the following sections, we present each of the subjects in more detail.

3.1   Strategic Direction of Information Technologies

The subject is organised in four main blocks: IT governance, Technology foresight, Managerial skills and Strategic planning, with the CIO (Chief Information Officer) as the centre of the subject. The task-based approach allows the students to acquire the knowledge corresponding to one or several of the four blocks of the subject through the performance of these tasks. In addition, they develop different skills, depending on the type of task (lesson, workshop or deliverable). Figure 1 presents in a schematic way the structure of the course and the different tasks proposed.

A key element was introduced in the course: learning minutes. They ensured the proper organisation of all this educational architecture and helped the students to be aware of what they were doing at each moment and what they had yet to do. A more detailed description of the design of the subject can be consulted in [24].

The evaluation of the students' learning has been carried out through different instruments (questionnaires, conceptual map, practical work, participation and preparation of workshops, oral presentation of the works, defence of an IT trend...) in order to have a multifaceted vision of the students' learning results. Throughout the course, at the end of each activity (a whole block) there was a brief debate about the positive and negative aspects of the activity.

Satisfaction surveys carried out at the end of each year show that the students, in a time sustained manner, have valued the subject very positively. In terms of content, they essentially report that this model has allowed them to

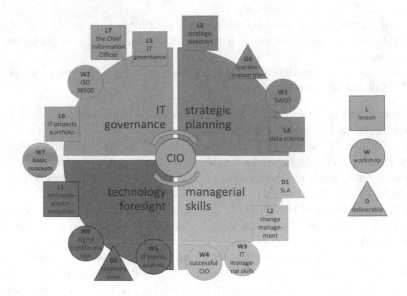

Fig. 1. Structure of *Strategic Direction of Information Technologies*

do more research on the subjects as well as helping them to delve deeper into certain concepts. And as relevant aspects, they say that it is good to spend time studying at home and debating in class and that the blended-learning model has helped them to combine studies with work.

3.2   Applied Technological Innovation

Since its inception, the subject has introduced Project-Based Learning as a differentiating element. Therefore, the main objective of the subject is to acquire knowledge, skills and abilities in a proactive way, carrying out an innovation project from its conception, covering the different stages necessary for its correct design and implementation.

The subject can be divided into four main thematic blocks (Fig. 2): Creativity, Innovation Management, Innovation Implementation, and Ethical and Legal Aspects. In some of the didactic units these aspects are seen from more than one perspective. Specifically, the units dealing with the issues of SMEs, Technology Alliances and Financing are seen from an innovation management approach (through case studies, trends and possible improvements), from an innovation implementation approach (how the specific project can be financed, or which is the best alliance to carry it out) and from an ethical and legal approach (defining the legal requirements and social responsibility aspects that must be considered to carry out and implement the project in question).

The subject begins with sessions in which the origins of innovation are evaluated and workshops are held to generate, defend and evaluate ideas, already

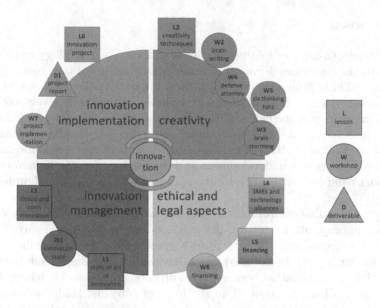

Fig. 2. Structure of *Applied Technological Innovation*

focusing on a specific project. The tasks of the students in the successive sessions
are:

- Define the objectives and value proposition of their project, its strengths and
  weaknesses, as well as the innovation it represents for society.
- Describe in detail the whole project, evaluate the risk management and study
  the impact it would have, both at the innovation level, as well as at the ethical
  and social level.
- Present a plan for dissemination and exploitation of the project.
- Detail the estimated budget for the implementation of the project.
- Specify the most appropriate financing plan for the project, weighing the
  different types of public and private financing.
- Search for possible alliances that would be convenient for the real implementation of the project.

At the end of the term, the project is fully defined and only its implementation and real deployment are missing, aspects that are beyond the scope of our
subject.

The evaluation of the subject is made from small deliveries that must be
made during the course and, mainly, from the project. The project is assessed by
teachers and by peer evaluation. The aspects that are assessed are: the communication capacity of the team, the technical quality of the project, the innovation
it implies, the viability of the project and the quality of the presentation, in such
a way that both specific and transversal skills are evaluated.

4 Proposal

The Master in Computer Engineering [6] trains future technology directors, in contrast to the Bachelors degrees and other Masters degrees that basically train technicians. These professionals must have a broad scientific, technological and socioeconomic training that allows them to direct and manage development and application projects in the field of Computer Science. To this end, the degree has, among others, objectives such as training for strategic planning; management and coordination of multidisciplinary teams; technical and economic management of projects; research, development and innovation projects; human resource management and application of ethical responsibility, legislation and professional ethics.

In this demanding environment of professionals with high management skills, it was not appropriate to develop the subjects in the traditional way. For this reason, this proposal was put forward as a result of the needs identified.

The starting point is the need to transversalise learning. That is why we started with a collaboration between two subjects. In classical teaching, knowledge has always been fragmented, in the form of subjects. Each subject focuses on its own content and rarely communicating vessels between subjects are considered. However, the reality is that the real problems are not compartmentalised. Problems do not belong to a single subject. Our students, particularly at the level of Master, really know how to solve problems when they are able to integrate the knowledge of the different disciplines. The two subjects chosen develop the aspects of strategy and innovation that are indeed the two highest level elements in organisations.

The second element is the decision to articulate the learning around a project, due to the success of this methodology in the separate subjects and in some previous experiences of the teachers in other subjects [8–10]. This way, learning is based on *learning by doing* in which skills, attitudes and knowledge are acquired as a consequence of action. This methodology fosters skills such as autonomous learning and work, self-evaluation and self-criticism, time planning, leadership, oral and written expression skills, and so on. Moreover, the project is tackled as a team, which allows, in addition, to acquire other transversal skills related to group work, preparing the students for a social environment. The final consequence is that the PBL improves student performance and motivation.

The third element we introduced into the equation was the use of a real case to setup the project. Academic projects that are often used in the PBL are often far from the reality of actual organisations. This means that the conditions for project development are artificial and very controlled. In a real environment the requirements tend to be much stricter and the situation much more uncertain. The introduction of a real organisation has allowed us to develop a Professional Learning, i.e., subject to the rules, the time and economic constraints, and the uncertainty of a real professional environment.

Finally, we decided that the organisation that hosted our course should be a non-profit institution with a social character. This has allowed us to approach the learning process as Service Learning, so that the project resulting from the subject had a double objective: to serve as learning for the students but also to serve as a service to a third party and to society in general. On the other hand, the fact of introducing students into a social environment, with interdisciplinary teams made up of technologists and social agents, reinforces transversality, the need to look for solutions in contexts very different from the usual ones and learning in CSR matters.

Figure 3 presents the structure of the learning proposal. The project is the centre of the process and involves both subjects and the organisation being studied. In the following sections a deeper explanation of the proposal is presented.

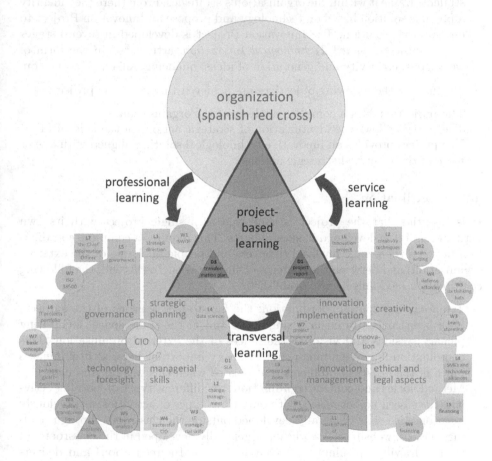

Fig. 3. Structure of *Four Dimensional Learning*

4.1   Project

The project becomes the centre of learning and the main deliverable of both subjects. Although the project is unique, it develops the contents of both subjects in two distinct parts:

- The Digital Transformation Plan: it is nourished by the different workshops of *Strategic Direction of Information Technologies* subject, in which an in-depth analysis of the organisation is carried out in order to identify strengths, weaknesses, opportunities and threats and generate the SWOT analysis. This analysis continues with the definition of objectives and actions to define the strategy of the organisation. The identification of the main IT trends and the development of managerial skills also contribute to the definition of the Digital Transformation Plan.
- The Innovation Project: The Spanish Red Cross defines a problem and the students frame it within the organisation's strategies. From there they identify a possible solution based on technology and propose an Innovation Project to develop that solution. The Innovation Project is developed in several stages in the subject *Applied Technological Innovation*, articulated in the form of workshops: creativity and generation of ideas, financing, alliances, and so on.

In this way the following objectives are achieved thanks to the project:

- The project enables a complete analysis of the organisation.
- The project allows the identification of strategic actions in the field of IT.
- The project provides an innovative technological solution aligned with one or more of the identified strategic actions.

4.2   Coordination

It is essential that the project is conceived as a single project with its own entity, even if it is developed in several parts. This requires a complete coordination between the people involved (teachers and people in charge of the external organisation) and between the contents of the subjects. To this end, the following coordination mechanisms are established:

- Temporal and spatial coordination: the face-to-face sessions of the subjects have been concentrated in a single day and in the same space, facilitating plenary sessions and visits to the offices of the external organisation. This coordination may seem minor, but it is very important because it eliminates much of the logistical problems that existed when this was not fulfilled.
- Methodologies and content coordination: the different types of learning activities have been homogenised, with only three types of activities, as previously mentioned: lessons (generally developed outside the classroom through readings, videos, websites...), workshops (generally developed in the classroom, in teams, drawing up minutes of what is done and agreed upon) and deliverables (products that are developed in teams or individually, mostly carried out outside classroom hours).
- Tools coordination: beyond the tools specific to each activity, the same Learning Management System is used to make the materials available to the students, as well as the same tools for collaborative work.
- Teacher coordination: the teachers meet weekly for the joint follow-up of the course development. In many cases, all teachers attend the same work session (this always happens in plenary sessions).

- Organisation coordination: teachers and the heads of the external organisation have several previous work sessions to define the objectives of the projects for each academic year, to determine the departments of the organisation that will participate in that course, and to agree on the dates of the plenary sessions.
- Evaluation coordination: the evaluation of the project is joint, which implies in itself a coordination mechanism between the subjects. The evaluation is discussed in more detail in a later section of this article.

4.3 Sessions

The course is developed over 15 weekly sessions of 8 h, of which 4 are non-classroom work and 4 are face-to-face work. The non-classroom work is perfectly scheduled and consists mainly of lessons and the development of deliverables, while the face-to-face sessions focus on teamwork in the form of workshops most of the time. Moreover, the face-to-face sessions of the subjects are of two types: plenary and ordinary.

The plenary sessions are joint sessions of both subjects in which all the students participate (as they are independent subjects, there may be some students enrolled in only one of them, although this is a very infrequent case), all the teachers and the heads of the Spanish Red Cross. Although 4 h are available, they last between 2 and 3 h, depending on the number of projects developed. There are three plenary sessions throughout the course:

- Initial plenary session: It is a session of presentation of the subjects and of the organisation. It is usually organised in a classroom at the University of Alicante, in the first week, to which the Spanish Red Cross leaders are invited. In this session the subjects are presented and an overview of the organisation is given. In addition, a specific problem is presented, that students must specify and frame in a strategic line within their Digital Transformation Plan. In addition, this problem will serve as the basis for the Innovation Project, in which they must find a technological solution.
- Intermediate plenary session: Before the end of the first half of the course (towards the sixth or seventh week), a working session is organised at the headquarters of the external organisation. At this time, the plans for Digital Transformation and the Innovation Projects are outlined, but not specified. It is time to resolve the doubts with the organisation. In addition, this session serves to get to know the organisation and its headquarters, with the presence of the heads of the different departments that give a complete view of the Spanish Red Cross.
- Final plenary session: The last session of the course consists of the presentation of the projects and of their evaluation. The session takes place at the Spanish Red Cross headquarters. The presentation allows the development of communication skills and the joint presentation of the results of all the work of the term. Doing so at the organisation's office provides a professional framework, facilitates the assistance of the members of the Spanish Red Cross,

gives it an institutional character and facilitates that the project is seen as a service for this institution. The evaluation of the project is carried out by peers and with the participation of the teachers and the organisation's heads. In a later section we delve into the evaluation issue.

The ordinary sessions last 4 h (2 h dedicated to each subject) and basically the workshops proposed in each subject are developed, as previously mentioned. Some of these workshops include the participation of members of the Spanish Red Cross. Sometimes these persons travel to the classrooms of the University of Alicante, other times are the students who move the offices of the organisation and most times the communication is established through videoconference.

The sessions of the first half of the course (between the initial and the intermediate plenary sessions) are aimed at developing basic skills, getting to know the organisation in general, and generating ideas that will allow the development of an innovative solution to the proposed problem. As a result, the intermediate plenary session is reached with an outline of the Digital Transformation Plan and two or three alternative solutions for the Innovation Project. The intermediate plenary session allows to solve doubts and prepare for the final development of the project.

After the intermediate plenary session, the first version of the Digital Transformation Plan has been validated and the Innovation Project has identified the criteria that allow defining a specific solution. From then on, and until the end of the course, the ordinary sessions are dedicated to the complete development of the project, deepening its contents and resolving punctually the problems that arise directly with the Spanish Red Cross in specific work meetings.

4.4   Participation of the External Organisation

The participation of an external organisation and its involvement in the learning process is fundamental to the success of such an experience. The organisation has three fundamental roles in the process: it is the organisation being studied, so it must be willing to share internal information that allows students to know it in depth; it is the service beneficiary, so it must be able to provide a problem that is strategic or at least of high interest to it; and it is the center of the development of the project, so it must be willing to meet the needs of the students, participating in the different work sessions.

A committed participation of the organisation has a high impact on the four dimensions of learning that we have proposed. In this sense, the participation of the Spanish Red Cross has been fully satisfactory.

4.5   Evaluation

Each subject is evaluated through different instruments such as questionnaires, participation in class, short oral presentations, occasional deliveries and, of course, the whole project. The aim is obtaining a multifaceted vision of the students' learning results.

In the evaluation result, the main facet is, however, the project, in accordance with the time devoted to its design and development. The project is assessed by the students (peer evaluation), by the teachers and by the member of the Spanish Red Cross.

The evaluation is carried out at the end of the course, in the final plenary session, through a rubric, which is identical for all evaluators. The rubric assesses the following aspects:

- Communication capacity of the team and quality of the presentation
- Team work and collaboration
- Quality of the strategical analysis of the organisation
- Quality of the innovative solution and its impact
- Technical quality of the project and its implementation
- Ethical and legal aspects
- Viability of the project, budget and financing.

Each aspect is evaluated at four possible levels:

1. Deficient
2. Enough
3. Good
4. Excellent

In addition, evaluators are asked to highlight the strengths and weaknesses of the project and to offer their opinion freely.

4.6 Satisfaction and Opinions

At the end of the term, the opinion of the students and the Spanish Red Cross heads is gathered through a questionnaire. The following are the most generalised opinions regarding the learning model presented here.

The students value in a very positive way the dynamics of the subjects and the project development within a real and social organisation. Their specific opinions are focused on highlighting the following aspects:

- The project seems to them to be a perfect tool to practice all the aspects studied in the subjects.
- The study of real cases is an attractive way for them to learn about the contents of the subjects and to project them into the world of work.
- This way of working gives them new knowledge in order to approach their professional projects from a different perspective. Thus, they perceive that these subjects will be useful in the future.

From the Spanish Red Cross organisation, the people who collaborate in these projects perceive very positively the way in which the students get involved in a facet, the social scope, so foreign to the technological field. The comments that they suggest to us after the experience can be summarised in:

- They are attractive projects with a good technological solution.

- They are very innovative projects.
- The projects involve large collectives that the organisation deals with, so they can be very useful for them and give practical solutions to some of their problems.
- The impact that projects would have on society is very positively valued.

5   Conclusions

We have presented an approach called Four-Dimensional Learning, based on the following four dimensions:

- Project-based learning: The project becomes the central component of the learning process. We adopt the PBL as the central element, and the other three dimensions of learning contribute to improving the project and the own learning, as we want to represent in Fig. 3.
- Professional Learning: The project is based on a real case, but not only that, the students have a direct contact with the organization: they know what is their daily life, what are their real needs and particularities of the organization (their priorities are probably different from those of a business, so they can compare it with other examples they see throughout the degree).
- Transversal learning: The project is seen as a whole. Not only must a problem be solved, but it is necessary that the project is framed in the strategy of the organization. In this way they learn to satisfy the requirements of several parts: the subjects (on the one hand, the strategy and on the other, the innovation) and the organization itself.
- Service learning: The result of the project becomes a service to the organization and, by extension, to society.

This approach makes it possible to develop several facets of a technology manager in an organization:

- The role of the CIO, knowing all the aspects of the organization and taking part in its governance. Its role, therefore, is to identify strategic actions of the organization in the field of technology, always aligned with the rest of the organization.
- The role as the person responsible for innovation, knowing how to conceive an innovation project (for this reason special attention is paid to the development of creativity) and how to manage it (at a more technical level).
- The role as the person in charge of prospecting, to identify new technologies that allow solving the organization's problems.

In addition, all this proposal contributes to developing a learning imbued with social responsibility. This theme is not only a set of explicit lessons, but is implicit in all learning. In this way, the need to attend to the social responsibility of future engineers is much more set, as the students have faced the problem in a real case and in a professional environment.

Acknowledgments. We would like to express our gratitude to the Spanish Red Cross organisation, and particularly to its staff at the headquarters of the organisation in Alicante, for the facilities for the development of this initiative and their continued involvement.

This research is partially supported by *Unidad Científica de Innovación Empresarial "Ars Innovatio", Agència Valenciana d'Innovació* and University of Alicante, Spain.

References

1. Commission of the European Communities: Green Paper. Promoting a European framework for Corporate Social Responsibility. Technical report, Commission of the European Communities, Brussels, Belgium (2001)
2. Vasilescu, R., Barna, C., Epure, M., Baicu, C.: Developing university social responsibility: a model for the challenges of the new civil society. Procedia - Soc. Behav. Sci. **2**(2), 4177–4182 (2010)
3. González Alcántara, O.J., Fontaneda González, I., Camino Pérez, M.Á., Revilla Gistain, A.: Responsabilidad Social en las Universidades: Del conocimiento a la acción. Pautas para su implantación, Forética (2016)
4. Gaete Quezada, R.: La responsabilidad social universitaria como desafío para la gestión estratégica de la Educación Superior: el caso de España - The university social responsibility as a challenge to the strategic management of Higher Education: the case of Spain. Revista de Educación **355**, 109–133 (2011)
5. de Alicante, U.: Plan Estratégico UA 40, February 2014
6. de Alicante, U.: Master's Degree in Computer Engineering, February 2012
7. Molina-Carmona, R., Satorre-Cuerda, R., Villagrá-Arnedo, C., Compañ-Rosique, P.: Training socially responsible engineers by developing accessible video games. In: Zaphiris, P., Ioannou, A. (eds.) LCT 2017. LNCS, vol. 10296, pp. 182–201. Springer, Cham (2017). https://doi.org/10.1007/978-3-319-58515-4_15
8. Reverte Bernabeu, J., Gallego, A.J., Molina-Carmona, R., Satorre Cuerda, R.: El aprendizaje basado en proyectos como modelo docente. Experiencia interdisciplinar y herramientas groupware. In: Actas XIII Jornadas de Enseñanza Universitaria de la Informática, JENUI'07, Teruel, Spain, Thomson Paraninfo, July 2007
9. Villagrá-Arnedo, C.J., Gallego-Durán, F.J., Molina-Carmona, R., Llorens Largo, F.: ABPgame+: siete asignaturas, un proyecto. In: Actas de las XX Jornadas sobre la Enseñanza Universitaria de la Informática (Jenui 2014), Oviedo, España, pp. 285–292, July 2014
10. Villagrá-Arnedo, C.J., et al.: ABPgame+ o cómo hacer del último curso de ingeniería una primera experiencia profesional. In: El reconocimiento docente: innovar e investigar con criterios de calidad. Universidad de Alicante. Vicerrectorado de Estudios, Formación y Calidad, pp. 1384–1399 (2014)
11. Dinov, I.D.: Integrated, multidisciplinary, and technology-enhanced science education. In: Seel, N.M. (ed.) Encyclopedia of the Sciences of Learning, pp. 1591–1593. Springer, US, Boston, MA (2012). https://doi.org/10.1007/978-1-4419-1428-6_1704
12. Díez-Higuera, J.F., et al.: Adapting the telecommunication engineering curriculum to the EEES: a project based learning tied to several subjects. In: IEEE EDUCON 2010 Conference, pp. 1307–1313, April 2010
13. Wicklein, R.C., Schell, J.W.: Case studies of multidisciplinary approaches to integrating mathematics, science and technology education. J. Technol. Educ. **6**(2), 59–76 (1995)

14. MINEDUC: Qué es la transversalidad educativa?. Ministerio de Educación del Gobierno de Chile (2018)
15. Reyzábal, M.V., Sanz, M.I.: Aprendizajes para la vida: los ejes transversales. Escuela Española, July 1995
16. Kemper, J.D., Sanders, B.R.: Engineers and Their Profession, 5th edn. Oxford University Press, New York (2001)
17. Ortiz Ocaña, A.: Metodología del Aprendizaje Significativo. Hacia una Didáctica Integradora y Vivencial. EAE, Problémico y Desarrollador, May 2017
18. Wang, J., Fong, Y.C., Alwis, W.: Developing professionalism in engineering students using problem based learning. In: Proceedings of the 2005 Regional Conference on Engineering Education, Johor, Malaysia (2005)
19. García-Peñalvo, F.J., Llorens-Largo, F.: Design of an innovative approach based on service learning for information technology governance teaching. In: Proceedings of the 3rd International Conference on Technological Ecosystems for Enhancing Multiculturality - TEEM 2015, Porto, Portugal, pp. 159–164. ACM Press (2015)
20. Corporation for National and Community Service: National and Community Service Act of 1990 (1990)
21. Sigmon, R.: Service-learning: three principles. Synergist **8**, 9–11 (1979)
22. Sigmon, R.: Serving to Learn, Learning to Serve. Linking Service with Learning. Technical report, Council for Independent Colleges (1994)
23. Satorre-Cuerda, R., Compan-Rosique, P., Molina-Carmona, R., Arques-Corrales, P., Llorens-Largo, F.: Algunas claves para el diseño de asignaturas en modalidad semipresencial. ReVisión (Revista de Investigación en Docencia Universitaria de la Informática) **9**(3), 49–63 (2016)
24. Llorens Largo, F., Molina-Carmona, R., Satorre-Cuerda, R., Compan-Rosique, P.: Dirección estratégica de la asignatura Dirección Estratégica de las Tecnologías de la Información. In: Actas de las XXI Jornadas sobre la Enseñanza Universitaria de la Informática (Jenui 2015), Andorra La Vella, pp. 193–200, July 2015

Learning Translation in Geometric Transformations Through Digital and Manipulative Artefacts in Synergy

Antonella Montone[1], Michele Giuliano Fiorentino[2(✉)], and Maria Alessandra Mariotti[2]

[1] Department of Mathematics, University of Bari Aldo Moro, Bari, Italy
Antonella.montone@uniba.it
[2] Department of Information Engineering and Mathematics Science,
University of Siena, Siena, Italy
michele.fiorentino@uniba.it, mariotti2l@unisi.it

Abstract. In this paper we report a study that aims to highlight the potentialities of the combined use of both digital and manipulative artefacts to construct and conceptualize mathematical meanings related to the notion of translation. The research hypothesis of our study is that, the alternating use of a digital and a manipulative artefact foster synergically the construction of mathematical meanings. Both the design and the analysis of data is framed by the Theory of Semiotic Mediation in a Vygotskijan perspective. The study involved a class of 20 students, aged 13–14, of a secondary school in the Apulia Region, Italy. Data collection of the study is based on student interaction transcriptions during experimental task execution, written answers to given questions, and finally the transcripts and video analysis of the collective discussions concluding each experimental cycle.

Keywords: Semiotic mediation · Digital artefact · Translation · Interaction · Synergy

1 Introduction and Rationale

Technology is almost everywhere in our lives and there is no process, even educational, that does not deal with it. Moreover, technological resources have been combined with already existing instrumental resources and used in didactic practices supporting the construction of mathematical meanings. In recent years, a considerable corpus of research has focused on the ways in which technologies can influence mathematics learning, in particular how technology could offer new ways to interact with mathematical thinking and generate new kinds of mathematical experiences for students [1–3]. However, the digital technologies do not eliminate the need of a synergic relationship between all the educational artefacts, each of them bringing different possibilities and supporting the process of incorporation and conceptualization in a different way [4–8].

Moreover, one of the mathematical topics that need to be supported by artefact is the geometric transformation. In Italy, as in other countries, geometric transformations

© Springer Nature Switzerland AG 2019
P. Zaphiris and A. Ioannou (Eds.): HCII 2019, LNCS 11590, pp. 191–205, 2019.
https://doi.org/10.1007/978-3-030-21814-0_15

appear in the curriculum, at different school levels, nevertheless, they do not receive much attention by teachers. Also, in math research geometric transformation has not been a popular topic. More recently, the advent of new technologies and specific micro world for Geometry brought this topic to the forefront, mainly at secondary school level [9].

We think that geometric transformations can become a powerful and effective tool in solving geometrical problems only if they are introduced in a mathematically consistent way, in other terms, if intuitive meanings emerging from actions and observation are suitably formalized into appropriate and well defined mathematical properties.

On the basis of a recent research on the use of two artefacts for the construction of the axial symmetry meaning [10], we report a study that aims to highlight the potentialities of the combined use of both digital and manipulative artefacts for the construction of the meaning of the translation. The study design is based on the Theory of Semiotic Mediation (TMS), developed by Bartolini Bussi and Mariotti [11] in a Vygotskijan perspective, which deals with the complex system of semiotic relations among fundamental elements involved in the use of artefacts to construct mathematical meanings: the artefact, the task, the mathematical knowledge that is the subject of the activity, and the teaching/learning processes that take place in the class.

Our didactic assumption claims that the process of formalization characterizing a geometrical transformation, such as the translation, can be achieved through the mediation of specific artefacts. The TSM provides a reference for the design and the implementation of a teaching sequence, as well as the analysis of the data resulting from the experiment.

The research hypothesis of our study is that, during the resolution of a translation task, the alternating use of a digital and a manipulative artefact generates in students a cognitive interaction between the schema use of one of the two artefacts and the signs exhibited while using the other artefact. This fosters a suitable and coherent construction of the translation meaning and its properties.

In this paper we present the design and implementation of a teaching experiment centered on the combined use of two artefacts. We will focus on the role played by the theoretical frame analyzing the key moments of the teaching sequence where the combination between the two artefacts was assumed to trigger the unfolding of the expected mathematical meanings. The study involved a class of 20 students, aged 13–14, of a Secondary School in the Apulia Region, Italy.

Our research is framed in a broader projection that, exploiting the teaching experimental methodology, it aims at validating the hypothesis regarding the possible synergic effect of the use of the two artefacts [10, 12].

2 Geometric Notion of Translation

The geometric concept referred to is that of translation. It is understood as an isometric transformation of the plane itself. Specifically, it is intended to point out that the translation is a point-to-point correspondence between points of the plane. Therefore it is the domain of the function, which transforms straight lines into congruent/super imposable segments. It also keeps the parallelism and the width of the angles.

Moreover, closer attention will be paid to the properties of the translation through which it is possible to construct the translated point of a given point with respect to a vector, i.e. the parallelism between the joining of the corresponding points and the direction of the vector as well as the preservation of the distance between the point and its translation, and the form of the vector.

3 Theoretical Framework

According to Vygotskian view, the Theory of Semiotic Mediation (TSM) concerns the complex system of semiotic relations between the elements taking part in the construction of mathematical meanings through the use of artefacts: the artefact, the task the artefact is used in, the mathematical knowledge which is the objective of the didactic intervention and the teaching/learning processes that take place in the classroom [11].

The concept of artefact used here is consistent with the distinction between artefact and instrument that was introduced by Rabardel [13] and re-elaborated by Bartolini Bussi and Mariotti [11]: an artefact is any device created and realized by human beings for any objective. The notion of artefact and that of schema of utilization [13] is the main focus of the TSM's construct of semiotic potential, that is the twofold relationship that the artefact has with the personal meanings emerging from its use and the mathematical meanings that might be evoked by such use:

> [...] on the one hand, personal meanings are related to the use of the artefact, in particular in relation to the aim of accomplishing the task; on the other hand, mathematical meanings may be related to the artefact and its use. This double semiotic relationship will be named the semiotic potential of an artefact [11, p. 754].

The study of the semiotic potential will describe what could emerge in the classroom, in particular actions and signs produced by the student and its relationship with the mathematical meanings. This is why, it is the main focus of any teaching sequence and it is the fundamental reference for the analysis of any experimental realization of the didactic intervention. In particular, meanings related to the use of the artefact can be referred to the schema of utilization that is shown by the students during a specific task. Consequently, the design of the tasks develops on the base of a fine grain a-priori analysis of the solution processes, and specifically on the identification of the schema of utilization that are expected. According to the TSM, during semiotic activities various signs are produced.

Personal meanings are expressed by the "artefact signs", that often have a highly subjective nature and are linked to the learner's specific experience with the artefact and the task to be carried out; these signs may evolve into mathematical meanings expressed by the "mathematics signs"; finally the "pivot signs", with their hybrid nature, show the evolution between artefact signs and mathematics signs, through the linked meanings. Such an evolution can occur together with specific semiotic activities, in particular, in the peer interaction during the task and in the collective discussions, accompanied by the expert guidance of the teacher. The collective construction of shared mathematical meanings is a complex process, where it is possible to distinguish evolution paths (semiotic chains) described by the appearance and chain of different types of signs: artefact signs, mathematical signs and pivot signs [11].

Finally, the notion of didactic cycle [11, p. 754] constitutes the unit of design: the didactic cycle organizes the coordination between activities with the artefact and semiotic activities finalized to make the expected evolution of signs occur. According to this structure, the description of the sequence will be framed by an iteration of didactic cycles.

4 The Artefacts

As described above, a digital and a manipulative artefact have been employed.

The digital artefact is Geogebra (GG) with some specific tools that correspond to particular elements of the manipulative artefact. To be more specific, the tools chosen are those that allow the construction of some geometric objects (point, straight line, segment, vector, perpendicular and parallel line, and intersection point), the 'Translation' artefact and the 'Trace' tool. A very important role is also played by the dragging function, boosted by the 'Trace' tool that allows observing the invariance of the properties characterizing the figures.

The manipulative artefact consists of a sheet of paper, with a vector line drawn on it marking where to fold it, a transparent sheet of paper used to copy the initial figures and a pin used to pierce both the sheets at the right points in order to construct their translated points (Pa+T+Pi). This artefact allows a translation to be directly created because the sheet naturally models the plane, the transparent sheet of paper allows moving the figure on the plane and sliding the transparent sheet allows the production of translated points using the pin.

The original aspect of this study concentrates on the choice of two different artefacts and of the didactic assumption that by using these two artefacts in an intentionally combined way, it is possible to create a fruitful synergy between them [10].

To be more precise, it is possible to design a teaching sequence so that it can connect the semiotic potential of one artefact with the semiotic potential of the other, in a way that the semiotic potential of an artefact can potentiate the semiotic potential of the other.

5 Research Methodology

According to the TSM and the main assumption concerning the possible synergy between the two artefacts, a teaching sequence following the general scheme of successive 'didactic cycles' has been formed; the main hypothesis, however, consists of alternating activities that involve the use of one or the other artefact, and of formulating tasks that could exploit the complement of their semiotic potentials.

All the pupils involved were at an average mathematical level. Data collection of the study is based on student interaction transcriptions and videotapes during experimental task execution, written answers to given questions, and finally the transcripts and videotapes of the collective discussions concluding each experimental cycle. A specific lens of analysis is related to the identification of key elements supporting our synergy hypothesis.

The semiotic potential related to each of the two artefacts and how a synergy between them can influence the construction/conceptualization of translation and its properties, will be shown by the analysis of some episodes.

In this paper we will analyze the data coming from the first two of these cycles and we will demonstrate the unfolding of the semiotic potential related to each of the two artefacts, and how a synergy between them can influence the construction of mathematical meanings.

6 Focus on the First and Second Didactic Cycles

In this section, we present in detail the first and second didactic cycle describing the tasks and the semiotic potentials of the artefacts involved.

6.1 Description of the Tasks of the First Cycle

The first didactic cycle involves two tasks (Task 1 and the Task). Given a figure (convex quadrilateral) drawn (in black) on a sheet, at the moment while handing over the sheet a red vector is drawn on it. The task is:

TASK 1 – first part
Draw in red the translated figure of the black one, with respect to the red vector, with the help of a transparent sheet of paper and a pin:

* Fold the sheet along the line identified by the red vector so that the folded sheet portion overlap the white sheet;
* Overlap the transparent sheet of paper over the white sheet, putting it into the fold;
* Trace the black figure on the transparent sheet of paper and make a notch on it at the point where the vector begins;
* Slide the transparent sheet into the fold until the notch reaches the tip of the vector arrow;
* Pierce the transparent sheet and the white sheet by piercing with a pin on the figure on it;
* Remove the transparent sheet and join the holes by using a red marker.

After completing this task, on the same paper, the teacher draws a blue vector. The task is:

TASK 1 – second part
Draw in blue the translated figure of the black one, with respect to the blue vector, with the help of a transparent sheet of paper and a pin:

* Fold the sheet along the line identified by the blue vector so that the folded sheet portion overlap the white sheet;
* Overlap the transparent sheet of paper over the white sheet, putting it into the fold;

- Trace the black figure on the transparent sheet of paper and make a notch on it at the point where the vector begins
- Slide the transparent sheet into the fold until the notch reaches the tip of the vector arrow
- Pierce the transparent sheet and the white sheet by piercing with a pin on the figure on it;
- Remove the transparent sheet and join the holes by using a blue marker.

In the final task, the pupils are asked:

TASK 2

Observe what you have done and write the answers to the following questions:

- How many times did you point the pin to draw the red figure?
- Where did you point the pin?
- How many times did you point the pin to draw the blue figure?
- Where did you point the pin?
- Describe how you drew the translated figure obtained by folding the sheet along the direction identified by the vector and sliding the transparent sheet of paper.
- Look at the red figure and the blue figure. What looks the same about them? Explain why.
- What looks different? Explain why.

6.2   Analysis of the Semiotic Potential and the Schemes of Utilization of the Artefacts P+T+P in Relation to the Described Tasks

According to the TSM, we assume that the meanings' construction and their emergence through signs' production are based on the development of utilization schemes related with both the artefact and the specific task [11, p. 748].

The artefact Pa+T+Pi, related to Task 1, evokes four important mathematical meanings:

1. The idea of the vector of translation (direction, modulus and orientation), expressed by folding the paper along a line; by sliding the transparent sheet of paper along the straight line for a fixed distance, by sliding the transparent sheet along the straight line in one of the orientation indicated by the arrow;
2. The idea of translation as correspondence of points, expressed by the holes in the paper made by piercing it with a pin;
3. The idea that the translated figure depends on the vector of translation, expressed by comparing what changed and what didn't change in two translated figures when drawn on different vectors after folding the paper;
4. The idea of translation as a one-to-one correspondence that transforms segments into other congruent and parallel segments: as a matter of fact, this property corresponds to the fact that joining the points obtained with the pin produces a figure that is the translation of the original one.

Taking into account previous results [14] and with the aim of fostering the emergence of specific signs related to the task, some particular expressions, words and phrases, have been chosen purposefully in the formulation:

- *To fold along a line*, is used to refer to the direct action when using the vector;
- *Overlap* transparent sheet of paper over the white sheet, *trace* black figure over the transparent sheet and *make a notch* on the transparent sheet at the point where the vector begins, *slide* the transparent sheet into the fold until the notch reaches the tip of the vector arrow, with the aim to refer to transfer the original figure on a plane which moves following the direction and orientation vector actions;
- *To point*, is used to refer to the direct action when using the pin to point and pierce to find the translated point;
- *To join*, is used to refer to the direct action when drawing a segment between two corresponding points;
- *Translated figure*, is used to refer to the direct outcome of the six actions (folding along a line, overlap, trace, slide, pointing/piercing on the vertexes of the figure, joining the points/holes);
- *What looks different*, is used to refer to the direct action when comparing two translated figures obtained by the same figure with respect to two different vectors.

Let's now describe the semiotic potential of Pa+T+Pi artefact referring to conceptualizing vector of translation and the point-to-point correspondence. For this we will analyze the possible schema of utilization relating to previous tasks. Given a drawn black figure on the white sheet on which a red vector is drawn consequently, we want to obtain the translated figure of the already given one, with respect to the red vector, by using the fold along the line of the given vector, the transparent sheet on which to trace the black figure and translate it into a new position by sliding it along the fold, with respect to the orientation and modulus of the vector and by using a pin to recognize translated points obtained by piercing the sheets, both the white and the transparent one.

When this task is accomplished, on the same sheet we will draw a further blue vector, giving the same task. So the previously defined parts of Task 1 will be given separately. In Task 2 pupils will be asked to answer some questions.

6.3   Description of the Tasks of the Second Cycle

The second didactic cycle involves two tasks (Task 3 and Task 4) to be carried out using the digital artefact GG and by using the buttons/tools "translation" and "trace" as well as the dragging function.

Task 3

- Open in a new Geogebra file, graphic view without axis and grid;
- Draw a quadrangle and call it "t", then name its vertices A, B, C and D;
- Draw a vector outside the quadrangle and call it "s";
- Using the button/tool 'translation', construct the translated figure of figure "t" with respect to the vector "s" and call it "t'";
- Call the corresponding vertices respectively A', B', C' and D'.

With new assignments students go on:

- Activate 'Trace' on point A and point A'. Drag point A. What moves? What does not move? Why?

- Drag point A'. What moves? What does not move? Why?
- Deactivate "Trace" on point A and A'. Drag side "a" of the figure. What moves? What does not move? Why?
- Drag "s". What moves? What does not move? Why?

According to the notion of 'didactic cycle' within the TSM, Task 4 aims at fostering the pupils' personal production of signs related to Task 3. For this reason, the pupils are asked to:

Task 4:
Write down in the summary table below the answers to the questions asked in Task 3:

Drag	What moves?	What does not move?	Why?
Point A			
Point A'			
Side a			
Vectors			

6.4 Analysis of the Semiotic Potential and the Schemes of Utilization of the Artefacts GG in Relation to the Described Tasks

The artefact GG, related to Task 3 and Task 4, evokes the following mathematical meanings:

1. The idea of translation as a point-to-point correspondence, expressed by clicking on the tool/button "Translation";
2. The idea that the translated figure depends on the figure of origin, in particular the idea that the translated vertex of the figure depends on the figure vertex of origin expressed by clicking on the tool/button "Trace" for the point of origin and the translated point, and by dragging the point of origin;
3. The idea that the translated point depends on the vector, expressed by clicking on the tool/button "Trace" for the point of origin and the translated point, and by dragging the vector;
4. The idea that the translated point depends on both the point of origin and the vector, expressed by dragging the translated point.

The use of the dragging function in the task 3 allows us to introduce the meanings of co-variation, by means of the dragging action and the observation of the resulting correlated movement of the points. In particular, the request to drag the vector could allow the distinction between independent and dependent variation to emerge. This is related to the different nature of the mutual movements of the points: some points move as a result of the direct action on them that the user achieve with the mouse, and other points indirectly move as the result of the movement of those points from which they have been constructed [15].

Moreover, the request to drag the translated point, allows the user to underline its specific behavior with respect to all the other objects of the configuration. When dragging the translated point, indeed, it can be observed a resulting no movement of the entire configuration. The difference in the movements between the translated point and the point of origin can be compared to the distinction between a dependent variable and an independent variable.

7 Data Analysis

The following episode refers to the class discussion at the end of the first cycle. When Task 1, using a manipulative artefact, was carried out, one student, G., was absent. The following day, during the discussion, the teacher asked others students to tell G. what they did. This teacher's intervention is a case of "back to the task" which opens up a discussion and aims at pointing in the story the emergence of signs that refer to the activity carried out with the artefact.

The first to speak is A. who says: "First we copied the figure on a transparent sheet of paper and we folded the white sheet on the…". The teacher focuses attention on an aspect that was drifting away, in an attempt to re-emerge the importance of the vector, asking: "What was the first request, before copying the figure on the transparent sheet?".

The teacher's attempt is successful because the importance of the vector is confirmed in the words of C. who answers: "the first request was to fold the sheet on the vector, make a notch at the beginning of the vector" and A. adds: "and then we had to copy the figure on the transparent sheet" and finally M. goes on: "and after make it move along the arrow of the vector".

The discussion continues and the teacher intervenes by drawing attention to the artefact, bringing out at the same time the point-to-point correspondence (Table 1).

This episode shows the unfolding of the semiotic potential, as expected, but it also illustrates a first evolution towards the mathematical meanings that are the aims of the teaching intervention. The intervention of the teacher is fundamental in inducing the students to express their personal meanings, and the different reformulations showed how such meanings evolved from the description of the action to the idea of point-to-point correspondence. During the discussion another translation characterizing property emerged, the parallelism among the segments joining correspondent points and the vector of translation.

Indeed F says: "go all along the same direction… that is the arrow goes always on the same direction of the vector". The sign "go all along the same direction" evokes the idea that the original figure moves following the vector direction. This artefact sign evolves in the mathematical sign "parallel" (Table 2).

Following episode refers to the collective discussion started after the second cycle, which consists in the Task 3 and Task 4 instructions, in which the students have built the translated figure from an original figure relative to a vector, using the "Translation" tool of the digital environment and dragging for first the original figure's vertex A, then one side of the original figure and finally one of the translating vector on the display. With the aid of the "trace" tool they have observed what moves and what does not.

Table 1. Episode 1

Transcript	Analysis of actions and signs
(9:45) T: Ok, let's go to the second step. Do you remember what you had to do?	
Little group: to point (Italian translation of "puntare") the pins	"to point" is a pivot sign because it evokes both the piercing action and the mathematical sign "point"
G.: … and then a notch and we slide transparency sheet along the vector	"slide" is an artefact sign which evokes the translating over a plane idea; "along the vector" is a mathematical sign which indicates movement by following direction, modulus and orientation of the vector
T: where did we stop?	
Little group: at the arrow's tip	
T: and now?	
(10:55) F: At the figure's angles, we took the pin and we did some signs, we remove the transparent sheet and… we have …ehm… trace the figure	"trace" is a pivot sign because it evokes the action to join corresponding points and the translation property to transform segment in congruent segment and so to create isometric figures
T: Where did you point the pin?	The teacher mirrors the word "point" that in Italian is both a verb and a noun. As a verb it means pierce, while as a noun it means point. "To point" can function as a pivot sign because it evokes the position where to pierce and the piercing itself
M: On the point…	
Ins: On the point! Which point?	The teacher aims to foster the sign "point" being made explicit
M.: The vertex!	The meaning of correspondence among figures is emerging by correspondence among points
T: so you have pointed the pin on the vertices, you have pierced… what?	The teacher mirrors the sign "pointed the pin on the vertices" and pose provocative question to push pupils to explain. She makes explicit the relationship between the artefact and the math. It is an artefact-interpretation action
All students: both transparency and white sheet	
(12:41) Am.: we needed it to draw the translated figure… because if we didn't make the points with pin, we shouldn't…	The point-to-point correspondence obtained by piercing the paper with the pin at the vertices is therefore, in Am.'s view, the thing that makes it possible to obtain a translated figure. The meaning of correspondence among figures has emerged

Table 2. Episode 2

Transcript	Analysis of actions and signs
(33:43) T.: Francesca said that the three lines, which connect the figures' vertexes and the vector, go along the same direction. Why?	Here the teacher invites the students to make the correspondence explicit between the directions of the lines connected the figures' vertexes and the vector. She reflects the sign "along the same direction" and asks them to summarize
M.G.: The orientation changes, but the direction stays the same	M. summarizes making a distinction between orientation and direction and highlighting that the direction is set, it cannot change, the orientation could change
T.: Meaning what?	
M.G.: That the direction stays the same, while the orientation changes, it goes the opposite way	M. confirms her thesis on the translation's direction, which is the vector that cannot change, while she pinpoints the two possible travelling orientations on the vector. She uses two different artefact signs: "direction" and "orientation"
An.: Meaning that the paper fold implicates... how can I put it... the direction is determined from where we direct the arrow. So if you move the arrow, the figure will move as well and change direction, but the... the position does not change because the direction causes the variations in the paper fold	Anna is confused even though in her speech, she justifies the direction by relying on the paper fold along the vector, and she tries to support the translated figure's dependence of position by relying on the travelling orientation of the vector
(35:44) T: Let us try to rephrase what An is saying. She started saying that the paper fold suggests us something. What does that add up to?	Summary request
M.G.: The direction	This is an artefact sign connected to the paper folding action and to the tracing paper's panning action into the fold
G.: The direction	
T: Meaning what? Why do you say they have the same direction? How are they to each other?	Back to the task. The teacher will let the pupils intervene to make the different personal senses emerge
G.: Parallel	G. uses the evolved Mathematical sign, which states one of translation's characteristic properties
T.: Do you agree?	The teacher involves all of student to share the emerging sign "parallel"
All students: yes...	

The video analysis in the discussion highlights two aspects:

- In the first one, it is possible to recognize the arising of the digital artefact's semiotic potential;
- In the second one, it is also possible to detect an early reminder to the experience already had with the manipulative artefact, in terms such as "like what we did on the sheet", coupled with gestures referring to something previously occurred.

Moreover, with the aid of the "trace" tool, the dependence of the translated point A' from the original point A and the translating vector became clear for the students.

Furthermore, the cross-references about the two artefacts' employment support the mathematical meaning's structure of the functional dependence between a translation's points.

Now let us consider the transcription of the discussion's second phase (Table 3).

An. is dragging point A', derived from point A's translation. Therefore, she can observe nothing moving.

When the teacher asked, *"What is moving? And what is not moving?"*, M.G. answered confidently, *"If I move A, A' will move too. If I move the vector, A' moves; and if I move A'... well... it does not move... nothing!"*.

Table 3. Episode 3

Transcript	Analysis of actions and signs
T.: So, who wants to elucidate this further?	The teacher asks to justify what happened on the whiteboard's display
G.: The translated figure is the same of the original figure, even though it is located differently. So, if something moves from the original figure, something will move from the translated figure as well	G. summarizes the dependence of the translated figure from original one
(6:35) T.: And if I move something of the translated figure?	
G.: It will not move... It will not move not even if... I mean, no point nor line segment will move...but... I don't know why!	G. observes what happens on the whiteboard's display but is confused in relation to the various objects' dragging behavior
T.: Why?	Request for explanation
G.: ...because...	G. doesn't know how to explain what she's observing yet
Am.: Because this figure is not the original one, but is linked to the original one.	Am. uses the artefact sign "is linked" to point at the translated figure's dependence from the original one. Moreover, she uses the pivot sign "this", which refers to the translated figure and its position on the display

(continued)

Table 3. (*continued*)

Transcript	Analysis of actions and signs
M.G.: Because it <u>depends on</u> the original one	The expression "depends on" M.G. uses reinforces Am.'s idea: the dragging on the free objects causes the dependent objects' movement At this stage, the "depends on" is a pivot sign, for it expresses both the dragging action and the mathematical meaning of functional dependence The signs found because of the synergy between the two artefacts are evolving on a joint basis: M.G expresses, through the expression "depends on", the common significance of the relation linking the different objects: the original figure and the translated one
G.: Exactly. The translated figure depends on the original one	G. knowingly reuses the expression "depends on"
F.: The vector <u>does not depend on</u> the original figure, therefore it does not move On the other hand, the translated figure depends on the vector because…	F. uses the "does not depend on" sign to refer to independent objects
(8:05) T.: Alright, let us try to lengthen the vector and see what happens	The teacher keeps examining what changes the vector's modification could cause
M.G.: The translated figure moves	
(8:42) An.: Yes, this is the same thing we did with the sheet, the tracing paper and the pin, the example of different vectors Meaning that if I lengthen the vector, the translated figure will move further away from the original one… It's like there were a new vector On the sheet, the red figure was closer because the red vector was shorter; the blue figure was further because the blue vector was longer	An. attempts to explain what she's observing. She mentally retrieves the experience had with the manipulative artefact and clarifies it when she says, "this is the same thing we did with the sheet", and to that expression follows a hand gesture, which refers to something previously occurred She connects the figure's movement on the display (due to the modification of the vector's modulus) to the two blue and red vectors with which she worked on the sheet, linking the conjured significance in the two experiences Emphasis is given to An.'s description which focuses on the actions which took place. She uses "if I lengthen" the vector as if she were actually moving a real object The digital artefact's strength lies in the fact that it requires an action to perform with one's finger or a mouse
T.: Are we all on the same page?	The teacher seizes the hint referring to the sheet's use and reopens the discussion between the two experiences

(*continued*)

Table 3. (*continued*)

Transcript	Analysis of actions and signs
G.: The figure moves as much as the vector lengthens	
M.G.: But here we move it (the vector) with the computer... with the mouse	MG. highlights the digital artefact's strength using the "move" sign as if she were moving a real object

This episode shows how when using the digital artefact the meanings of the correspondence between figures and that of the vector of translation emerge once more. In particular, the argumentation by A. in the second part of Table 3, concerning the impossibility of a free movement of translated figure, shows how effective is the cross-reference to the use of the two artefacts, accompanied by an explicit interpretation of the experiences made with them, led to a consolidation of the mathematics meaning of functional dependence.

Finally, the meaning emerges most strongly not through the unfolding of the semiotic potential of the two different artefacts, but through the synergy activated by the comparison between the experiences with them.

8   Concluding Remarks

This paper, in continuity with the research on axial symmetry [11], reported on some preliminary results concerning the validity of the hypothesis about the potentialities of using the combination of artefacts as tool of semiotic mediation.

The analysis of the data coming from a teaching experiment clearly shows how the potentialities of each single artefact can be exploited and combined for constructing and developing some mathematical meanings concerning translation.

A careful analysis of the semiotic potential of each of the two artefacts and the didactical activity goals, guided the design of the tasks.

The results highlight the development of a synergy, created at a cognitive level, in the use of the two artefacts that is capable of enhancing the semiotic mediation functions of each of them. Moreover, we have shown how in passing from the use of manipulative artefacts to virtual artefacts, a synergy is created so that each experience enhances the potential of the other.

The study is still in progress but the results obtained encourage us to go forward and develop a long-term teaching experiment to confirm them. In accordance with the TSM, and in particular with the didactic cycle model, we intend to verify the efficacy of the observed synergy in a longer sequence of didactic cycles.

References

1. Hoyles, C., Lagrange, J.-B.: Mathematics Education and Technology—Rethinking the Terrain: The 17th ICMI Study. Springer, New York (2010). https://doi.org/10.1007/978-1-4419-0146-0
2. Drijvers, P., Kieran, C., Mariotti, M.A.: Integrating technology into mathematics education: theoretical perspectives. In: Hoyles, C., Lagrange, J.-B. (eds.) Mathematics Education and Technology—Rethinking the Terrain: The 17th ICMI Study, pp. 89–132. Springer, New York (2010). https://doi.org/10.1007/978-1-4419-0146-0_7
3. Drijvers, P., Tacoma, S., Besamusca, A., Doorman, M., Boon, P.: Digital resources inviting changes in mid-adopting teachers' practices and orchestrations. ZDM 45(7), 987–1001 (2013)
4. Santi, G., Baccaglini-Frank, A.: Forms of generalization in students experiencing mathematical learning difficulties. PNA 9(3), 217–243 (2015)
5. Calder, N., Campbell, P.: Using mathematical apps with reluctant learners. Digit. Exp. Math. Educ. 2(1), 50–69 (2016)
6. Hegedus, S., Tall, D.: Foundations for the future: the potential of multimodal technologies for learning mathematics. In: English, L.D., Kirshner, D. (eds.) Handbook of International Research in Mathematics Education, 3rd edn, pp. 543–562. Routledge, New York (2016)
7. Sinclair, N., Chorney, S., Rodney, S.: Rhythm in number: exploring the affective, social and mathematical dimensions of using TouchCounts. Math. Educ. Res. J. 28(1), 31–51 (2016)
8. Faggiano, E., Ferrara, F., Montone, A. (eds.): Innovation and Technology Enhancing Mathematics Education. MEDE, vol. 9. Springer, Cham (2017). https://doi.org/10.1007/978-3-319-61488-5. ISBN 9783319614878. ISSN 2211-8136
9. Hollebrands, K.F.: The role of a dynamic software program for geometry in the strategies high school mathematics students employ. J. Res. Math. Educ. 38(2), 164–192 (2007)
10. Faggiano, E., Montone, A., Mariotti, M.A.: Synergy between manipulative and digital artefacts: a teaching experiment on axial symmetry at primary school. Int. J. Math. Educ. Sci. Technol. (2018). https://doi.org/10.1080/0020739x.2018.1449908
11. Bartolini Bussi, M.G., Mariotti, M.A.: Semiotic mediation in the mathematics classroom: artifacts and signs after a Vygotskian perspective. In: English, L. (ed.) Handbook of International Research in Mathematics Education, 2nd edn, pp. 746–783. Routledge (2008)
12. Faggiano, E., Montone, A., Rossi, P.G.: The synergy between manipulative and digital artefacts in a mathematics teaching activity: a co-disciplinary perspective. Je-LKS: J. e-Learn. Knowl. Soc. 13, 33–45 (2017). https://doi.org/10.20368/1971-8829/1346. ISSN 1971-8829
13. Rabardel, P.: Les hommes et les technologies; approche cognitive des instruments contemporains. Armand Colin, Paris (1995)
14. Mariotti, M.A., Maracci, M.: Resources for the teacher from a semiotic mediation perspective from text to 'Lived' resources: mathematics curriculum materials and teacher development. In: Gueudet, G., Pepin, B., Trouche, L. (eds.) Mathematicsteacher Education, Part 1, vol. 7, pp. 59–75. Springer, Dordrecht (2012). https://doi.org/10.1007/978-94-007-1966-8_4
15. Mariotti, M.A.: Transforming images in a DGS: the semiotic potential of the dragging tool for introducing the notion of conditional statement. In: Rezat, S., Hattermann, M., Peter-Koop, A. (eds.) Transformation - A Fundamental Idea of Mathematics Education, pp. 155–172. Springer, New York (2014). https://doi.org/10.1007/978-1-4614-3489-4_8

Fables for Teachers and Pupils

Incrementally Defined Scenario-Based, Interactive and Spatial Stories

Andrea Valente[1]([⊠]) ⓘ and Emanuela Marchetti[2] ⓘ

[1] Maersk Mc Kinney Moller Institute, Embodied Systems for Robotics
and Learning, University of Southern Denmark (SDU), Odense, Denmark
anva@mmmi.sdu.dk
[2] Media Studies, Department for the Study of Culture,
University of Southern Denmark (SDU), Odense, Denmark
emanuela@sdu.dk

Abstract. The Fables project is grounded on an ecological approach to
e-learning, where we analyze the practice of e-learning as an information
ecology, centered on the interaction among teachers, pupils and their tools,
placed within the classroom. A simple Fable represents one of Schön's exemplars; a Fable can be interacted with digitally, as a simulation, to help understand
and predict the behavior of a real-world system or scenario. In schools Fables
can be used to represent the knowledge that pupils have, to be shared/showed
interactively to others, and they are experienced as a more dynamic version of
presentation slides. In this paper we strengthen the formal definition of Fables,
and we investigate Fables' expressive power. A new version of the online Fables
tool F4BL3s has been implemented and used in the evaluation. The main new
features of this version are: better visualization of Fables in playback, possibility
for the authors to associate custom images to the characters in their Fables, and
new export functions to convert a Fable into Twine stories and Microsoft
PowerPoint compatible slides. According to our knowledge of the needs of
teachers and pupils, the last feature is needed to improve interoperability of
F4BL3s with other standard tools, which is in turn a key factor for the acceptance of the tool. Future work includes an improved visual editor as suggested
by the data from our evaluation, and continue in-classroom tests.

Keywords: Scenario-based learning · Education · Knowledge management ·
Simulation · Visualization

1 Introduction

In our previous work [11] we started an exploration of more natural ways of expressing
behavior to create digital simulations, usable by primary school teachers and pupils.
Instead of focusing on programming concepts, we looked at soft methods like *rich
pictures* [5], and formalisms like *concept maps* and *mobile ambients* [4]. In [11] we
define the concept of **Fables** and present an alternative and novel way to simplify
digital game design and programming, aimed at a central problem in this area: how to

© Springer Nature Switzerland AG 2019
P. Zaphiris and A. Ioannou (Eds.): HCII 2019, LNCS 11590, pp. 206–224, 2019.
https://doi.org/10.1007/978-3-030-21814-0_16

express knowledge about interactive digital systems in a simple yet powerful enough way, so that new digital games or interactive simulations can be generated automatically by teachers (especially with non-technical background) and pupils descriptions.

E-learning classically relates to *"learning delivered fully online where technology mediates the learning process, teaching is delivered entirely via Internet, and students and instructors are not required to be available at the same time and place"* [26], however here we are interested in any blending of technologies for learning, classroom and home activities. In this paper we discuss how the fables project is grounded on an ecological approach [12] to e-learning; we analyze e-learning practice as an information ecology, centered on e-learning practice, defined by the relationships and interactions emerging between teachers, pupils and their tools. Tools are analyzed in this perspective as active participants in the ecology, acting as mediators, contributing to learning [15].

This e-learning ecology, present in Danish schools, involves the use of digital and analog media as well as other strategies in active learning practices. Fables are envisioned to support teachers in authoring digital branching scenarios for and with their pupils, and also for pupils to create contents for other pupils and teachers. A simple fable represents one of Schön's *exemplars* [3], and multiple fables can be composed together to create what Schön calls *repertoire of exemplars*. A fable can be interacted with digitally, as a simulation, to help *"achieving understanding and predicting the behavior of systems"* [2]. In schools Fables can be used to represent the knowledge that pupils have, to be shared/showed interactively to others, and they are experienced as a more dynamic, scenario-oriented version of presentation slides.

Fables are implemented as a web-based tool called F4BL3s, conceived to accommodate the different roles of teachers and pupils. This means that differently from current studies like [16], the roles of users are recognized and translated into distinct, interconnected working environments, hence partially reproducing the interactional ecology involving the participants and their different roles. In this respect, F4BL3s is designed to fit within e-learning practice seen as a social, transformative practice that teachers and pupils co-design through forms of distant and in person interactions, where the targeted result is mainly a learning experience for the pupils.

In the following sections we discuss related work and theoretical background for this study (Sect. 2), then we provide a formal syntax and semantics for Fables (Sect. 3); our latest prototype is presented in Sect. 4, and the evaluation is discussed in Sect. 5. Section 6 presents conclusions and future work.

2 Related Work and Theoretical Background

In our previous studies (see [1]) we found that the digitization of learning practice in Denmark has led towards the exploration of available digital media to enrich pupils' learning experience. As a consequence, the teachers have creatively explored how to engage in digitally mediated forms of learning and communication with their pupils, such as individual or shared assignments in which the pupils have to edit stories and slide-based presentations through free systems like Google Docs. A common aspect to these assignments is storytelling, that enables the pupils to creatively synthetize and communicate in the classroom their understanding of the learned topics. Starting from these storytelling-oriented practices, we have analyzed e-learning practice in Danish schools as an information ecology [12], consisting an organized set of digital and analogue artefacts and individuals (teachers and pupils) engaging in shared learning related practices. We created F4BL3s as mediating tool, encouraging teachers' and pupils' self-expression through the simple creation of interactive forms of storytelling; the tool also aims at reflecting the roles played by teachers and pupils in their e-learning ecology, to better fit their mutual interaction. In the following subsections we present our theoretical framework (2.1) and related work from the field of interactive storytelling and scenario-based learning (2.2).

2.1 E-Learning as Information Ecology

The concept of information ecology was proposed by Nardi and O'Day [12] in a book published in 1999, in which the authors analyzed the roles of librarians in using the available digital artefacts to provide a service to the citizens coming to the local library. The concept of information ecology was defined as a biological metaphor to analyze the relationships among people, tools, and their practices. The notion of ecology was chosen to evoke an image of complex relations, interdependences and dynamics involving different species within a given environment. An ecology is defined as a complex system [12], characterized by diversity, coevolution and locality, as the ecology is formed by the co-presence of different species or actors, playing different roles, within a specific environment. These actors are in a dynamic balance of coevolution, as whatever major change might affect one of the species will affect the whole ecology, while minor changes might simply go unnoticed [15]. Analyzing e-learning as an information ecology, we find teachers and pupils sharing a flow of information through different tools. Interestingly the e-learning ecology is localized within two main environments: the classroom, where the pupils and their teachers interact directly with each other, and the home, where their interaction is indirect. In the latter case, the role of digital tools is more crucial, for instance when the pupils have to edit a story online through Google Docs, the pupils interact with each other through the document that they are editing together. At the same time, the teachers can access the same document and check the progress, discussing in class how are the pupils doing with the assignment and provide help. We see this ecology as experiencing an on-going co-evolution, as new tools and practices are being experimented by teachers and pupils, affecting their mutual interactions and the practices they participate in.

Tools and human actors within an ecology are seen as active and capable of producing changes within the different practices in which they participate. Latour [15] insists on the notion that tools can act as mediators, mediating and altering meaning among the human actors, facilitating or inhibiting specific exchanges and communications. In this sense tools act as means of translation, which can suggest different meaning to the different individuals. In our view, e-learning digital tools, like games or simulations, act as means of translation for complex meaning, which can be experienced by the learners, eliciting reflections and individual understanding. F4BL3s is in this sense supposed to act as a mean of translation between pupils and teachers, enabling them to communicate their understandings of the topic in individualized and creative ways, creating simple stories, or Fables, on the learning content.

According to Schön's notion of *exemplars* [3], learners acquire new knowledge by participating in active learning activities, which reproduce real world situations, such as in his example of the architecture student dealing with the planning of a school building. In this way learners engage in a *reflection in action*, in which they reflect concretely on the situation at hand and practice forms of problem-solving. Each of these situations act as an exemplar, which the learners collect through their studies, becoming prepared to face new similar challenges in the future. In our view, each Fable should play the role of an objectified exemplar, interactive stories embodying the pupils' reflections and problem-solving strategies on complex topics.

In conclusion, we see e-learning as a complex information ecology, centered on an information exchange between teachers and their pupils as they engage in a variety of practices, such as: lecturing, hands-on and playful activities, and assignments. In the terms of Schön, all these practices are contributing to eliciting forms of reflective in action, hence providing exemplars for the application of knowledge. Teachers have recently engaged in exploring the affordances offered by a variety of digital platforms like Youtube, Kahoot and Google, and media like images, videos, and presentations, with the goal of enriching their pupils experience while dealing with children challenged by autism or dyslexia (as in [25]). We see F4BL3s entering this ecology, offering the possibility to pupils and teachers to create interactive exemplars of knowledge, to be shared and played with; hence contributing to the ongoing exploration of digital platforms conducted by teachers.

2.2 Storytelling and Scenario-Based Learning

Since our preliminary data suggests that storytelling is an emergent component of digitally-mediated learning practices in Danish schools, our design process aims at exploring how we can support digital storytelling, from the perspective of both teachers and students. As discussed in [4] our F4BL3s tool supports the creation of non-linear stories and branching scenarios, for scenario-based learning. Our goal is to support teachers and pupils to generate creative representations of knowledge, and taking full advantage of digital media without being limited by lack of coding skills. These representations are envisioned as resources for the teachers to show and explain abstract concepts in a more effective way than with textbooks only, also meeting the need for authorship expressed by the teachers we communicated with in our previous studies (see the attitudes of teachers towards technologies we found in [1]). The creation of these representations can also be an assignment given to the pupils, enabling them to express their knowledge in more creative and interactive ways, bridging school with young people's daily media engagement.

The use of storytelling and scenarios has been investigated in primary and secondary education, through the creation of simulations which might recreate scenarios taken from actual practice. For example a rich use of simulation has emerged in the field of medicine and other healthcare related educations. According to Bennet et al. [22] the use of scenarios and simulations has become widespread in the education of occupational therapy, including: simulated patients, through virtual simulations or physical mannequin, video or written case-based scenarios, and role-play. The use of simulation has been defined as a particular learning technique, in which selected aspects of a phenomenon are reproduced (see Bennet [22] and Simon [2]), and in some cases that involves the creation of interactive scenarios taken from real life practice. This form of learning is aimed at fostering critical thinking and forms of hands-on-interaction with the learning material. An interesting example is [21] where Hook et al. discussing how occupational therapy students experienced a virtual environment in Second Life. The students had to navigate with an avatar through a house and had to reflect on the house physical barriers, which hindered occupational performance for a patient moving on a wheelchair. Interesting applications come also from a case-study in genetic analysis [23], in which a "laboratory scenario" is given to students, consisting of a series of locations, each containing actions, items or quizzes.

According to Broadbent et al. in [24] the use of digital simulations or scenarios within blended learning, has lead students in healthcare education to become more engaged with their study material, becoming self-regulated learners. By self-regulated learning it is meant an independent attitude towards learning, in which students engage in learning through a cyclical process applying cognitive, metacognitive and resource management strategies. The authors of [24] argue that through blended learning supported by simulations and scenarios, students become active agents in their learning, planning and setting goals for themselves, therefore, becoming self-reflective on their learning path. Hence, scenario-based learning has been acknowledged as a valuable form of learning, enabling students to become more independent and self-reflective. However, we find that there is a need to also investigate how teachers can be empowered in the creation of relevant scenarios for their own subject and their personal way of teaching.

Finally, we find scenario-based learning also outside the school context, and in particular in the domains of e-learning and digital games. Examples of scenario-based e-learning games are *Connect With Haji Kamal*, discussed by the author Moore in her book [7] and blog[1], and *LIFESAVER* an interactive film by Martin Percy freely available online[2]. *Connect With Haji Kamal* is a non-linear visual novel with the look of a comic book and the goal of is to support US Army soldiers to prepare for their missions in Afghanistan, and in particular to become aware and sensitive to the inter-cultural problems they will be facing once abroad. The game was developed using Twine, and the pace of the story is controlled by the player, as it would be in a turn-based game. By contrast LIFESAVER is an interactive move, where choices need to be made in real-time to help people suffering from heart attacks. We consider fables related to games like *Connect With Haji Kamal*, since manipulation of video footage seems too complex for primary school pupils, even if it is being currently considered in a related project discussed in [13]. Furthermore, a discussion of some of the most widely used authoring tools related to our F4BL3s is presented in Sect. 4.4.

---

[1] http://blog.cathy-moore.com/2010/05/elearning-example-branching-scenario/.
[2] https://life-saver.org.uk/.

3   What Are Fables: A Formal Definition

In this paper we strengthen the definition of Fables by better formalizing their syntax, what are their operations and semantics. We also investigate Fables' expressive power: from a formal stand-point Fables can only express a specific kind of non-linear story where in a world with fixed, eventually nested, rooms, a set of people move around picking up and dropping objects. In spite of this apparent limitation, we have a working hypothesis that states that many kinds of stories can in fact be expressed in the form of a Fable.

From a formal point of view, Fables are related to mobile ambients [4] without processes. A Fable can be thought of as semi-structured data, therefore it can be expressed as a tree of nodes (like an XML document). More precisely we define a Fable as a collection of slides forming a graph, and a palette composed of 3 lists: persons, things and rooms.

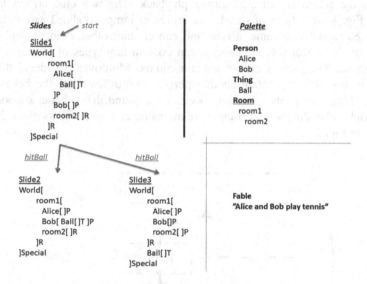

Fig. 1. Example of Fable "Alice and Bob play tennis". The Fable starts at Slide1 then the user will have to choose to go to Slide2 or Slide3. (Color figure online)

Figure 1 shows a Fable about Alice and Bob playing tennis. Inside each slide of the Fable, there is a single ambient-like container called World and inside it a list of rooms. Each room in turn can contain other rooms, persons or things. In the example in Fig. 1 Alice has a ball, and that is represented as follows: **Alice[Ball[]T]P**. The superscripts that follow the closing square brackets are indication of the type of the item: R stands for room-type, P for person-type and T for thing-type. The World has a special type, since it is similar but not the same as a room. The syntax for Fables is defined as in Table 1.

Table 1. Formal syntax for Fables. The syntax is inspired by Typed Ambients.

Fable := title slide* palette
slide := slideId description World[element*]^{Special} action$_1$ action$_2$ action$_3$
action$_i$:= *no-action* | label slideId
element := name[element*]^{type}
type := R | P | T
palette := personName* thingName* roomsTree
roomsTree := *empty* | roomName → (roomsTree) roomsTree

According to Table 1 a Fable has a title, a list of slides, and a palette; each slide has a unique identifier, a description, a world that contains a list of elements (possibly empty), and up to 3 actions. An action is just a label and a slide id, to which the Fable will jump if the action is activated during playback. The two blue arrows labeled "hitBall" in Fig. 1 are actions of slide1, and represent jumps to slide2 and slide3.

A Fable element has a name, a type and can contain other element, with some semantic restrictions. Room-type elements can contain any types of elements, while People- elements Thing-types cannot contain rooms. Moreover, we decided that a person should not directly contain another person. We differentiate the behavior of Person- and Thing-type elements mainly because we found that it better supports the intuition of our authors/users. The complex relationship among elements of the 3 types is explained in Fig. 2.

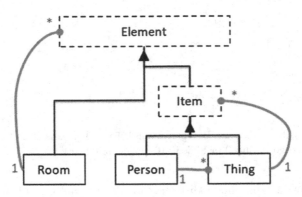

Fig. 2. The relationship among the 3 types of elements of a Fable: room, person and thing.

A palette has 3 elements: a list of person names, a list of thing names and list of rooms. The list of rooms can be empty or it can have a multiple rooms; each room can in turn have nested rooms (i.e. children rooms). Consider for example a house with a living room and a kitchen, and a broom closet in the kitchen; the representation as a *roomsTree* would be: **house→(living_room kitchen→(broom_closet))**, which corresponds to the following indented, nested list:

House
   living_room
   kitchen
     broom_closet

Finally, all slides must have the same tree of rooms as the *roomsTree* in the palette, eventually populated with different people and things (see slide1 and slide2 in Fig. 1 as an example). Hence, the rooms are immovable elements in a Fable.

3.1 Operations and Semantics

We want Fable authors to be able to create interactive scenario-based stories in an incremental way, therefore we provide operations to create/clone, rename, move and delete any element of a Fable, at any moment during editing.

Table 2. Semantics of Palette-related operations.

Operation	Palette
Create	(room) Add room in same relative position in all slides
	(person/thing) Just add to the palette, no changes in any slide
Rename	Rename element in all slides (substitution)
Move	(room) Same move of the room in all slides, nested rooms follow
	(person/thing) NOT POSSIBLE or MEANINGLESS
Delete	(room) Remove the room in all slides, nested elements also deleted
	(person/thing) Remove in all slides

Table 3. Semantics of operations on a single slide.

Operation	Slide
Create/clone	(slide) local effect
	(room) global effect, same as create at Palette level
	(person/thing) to room of current slide: add to Palette, add to room
Add from Palette	(person/thing) local effect, check not present in slide, then add to room
Rename	global effect, same as rename element at Palette level
Move	(room) global effect, same as move room at Palette level
	(person/thing) local: from source element to destination element
Delete	(room) global effect, same as delete room at Palette level
	(person/thing) local: delete element and nested elements
Pickup	A pickup B: select any item B in same room as A, move B inside A
Drop	A drop B: select an item B nested inside A, move B outside A

Moreover, we distinguish between global and local operations, because palette operations have global effects across slides, while manipulation of individual slides only has localized effects (see Tables 2 and 3). In our definition of the semantics we assume that in each Fable all names are unique, i.e. rooms, people and things all have distinct, unique names across all slides.

The last operations in Table 3 are special, specific to a person picking up a thing or a thing being inserted inside another. They are inspired by the classic mobile ambients operations of *in* and *out*.

3.2 Expressive Power

Fables are incrementally defined scenario-based, interactive and spatial stories. By this we mean that the authors (a primary school teacher, a pupil or group of pupils) are able to create a story step-by-step, eventually defining and re-defining rooms, people and things as they like, while the Fable's palette keeps a consistent overview of all the elements and their relationships. For instance how the rooms are nested is kept coherent globally by the operations of a Fable, which accounts for these stories to be considered spatialized. Since each slide can be connected to a maximum of three slides via labeled actions (including looping back to the same slide if needed), Fables are clearly non-linear stories with a branching factor of 0 to 3. Therefore, Fables can be used to define interactive scenarios, where the actions chosen by the user of the Fable during playback lead to potentially different storylines and possibly alternative endings.

An important question in this project is: what can you express with a Fable? At first glance every Fable just is a non-linear story where, in a world with fixed nested rooms, a set of people move around picking up and dropping objects. Persons and things that are in the Fable's palette can appear or disappear from rooms, from one slide to the next.

It is our working hypothesis that many kinds of scenarios and stories can be assimilated to a Fable. Our first argument in favor of the hypothesis is that narration in different media is described in terms of locations, actors and objects, and their interplay. For example, a theatrical play is described by locations where the action takes place, characters and props (or theatrical property). In [18] the Drammar ontology is defined with the goal of annotating and formally reasoning about drama; the ontology is defined as follows: *"Drammar consists of two components, encoding respectively the conceptual model and the SWRL rules. The conceptual model, mainly grounding in AI theories, represents the major concepts of drama, such as agents, actions, plans, units, emotions and values."* As for drama itself, [18] explains it as this: *"[...] it is well known that in dramatic media (drama) the audience engages the story via the character's behavior [...] rather than via the literary values; indeed the cause–effect chain results from a complex interplay of agents, objects and events, well known in playwriting techniques [...]"*

The authors of [18] also argue that drama is not exclusively related to theatrical performances and they use the term *dramatic media* to cover *"[...] media that display characters performing live actions, such as theatre, cinema and videogames."*

To further investigate the expressive power of Fables we created a number of different stories, some inspired by the actions of characters in children books, others based on the typical daily life of historical characters. We found quite possible to express instructions (for recipes for instance) in the form of Fables, and in those cases we took advantage of the branching to cover alternative storylines with typical errors and their consequences. Finally, in Sect. 5 we discuss how the evaluation of F4BL3s (the web-based tool implementing Fables) also shed light on the expressive power of Fables.

The main limitation we can see in Fables is that rooms are immovable and must be the same in every slide. Therefore, game-like scenarios in which rooms or locations are created and/or destroyed dynamically as the game progresses will be impossible to express. Even a Fable where a room only exists in a slide but not in all others would be impossible; furthermore, all rooms must be present and the same in all slides also across all alternative branches of the same Fable. In our brainstorming sessions and experiments with Fables we have not found this a major limitation; moreover, the kind of dynamic narrative that we are excluding is perhaps mostly found in digital games, while Fables focuses on interactive scenario-based stories, which are naturally more *static* (like the game/novel by Moore [7]).

Another problem we encountered is with the current terminology we adopted for Fables; for instance, consider a fairy tale with a talking wolf as a character. In Fables the wolf could be represented by an element of type Person or Thing, depending on whether the wolf is an active character or a passive item in the story. Being the wolf an animal, some Fable authors might find it illogical to associate the Person type to it; situations like this (e.g. stories involving robots, magical animals or animated objects in general) led us to consider a possible renaming of all categories of elements in Fables. **Room** seems so far a general enough name, which is clearly related to theater, movies and computer games, so it could be left as is. However, **Person** and **Thing** might be changed to **Character** and **Prop** (or perhaps **Item**), adopting a more theatrical metaphor for Fables. This change in terminology is still under discussion, and might be implemented in a future version, provided evaluation by our users (both teachers and pupils) supports its usefulness.

4 Extended Implementation

A new version of the online Fables tool F4BL3s has been implemented and used in the tests. The main new features of this version of F4BL3s are:

- possibility for the authors to associate custom images to the characters in their Fables (i.e. *skins* for Fables),
- better visualization of Fables in the playback page,
- and export function to convert fables into Twine stories and Microsoft PowerPoint compatible slides (PPT for short).

4.1 Skins and the New Playback Page

A *skin* is a collection of small, icon-like images that the author of a Fable can upload in her Fable via a special page of the F4BL3s web tool. The images, if present, will be used when the Fable is played back, in the playback page of F4BL3s. In the current implementation rooms have a static background image associated with them, but the author can customize the image representing any person or thing (see Fig. 3, created with free icons from www.flaticon.com).

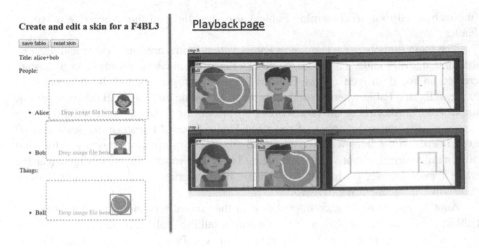

Fig. 3. Skin editor (on the left) and playback page for the Alice and Bob Fable (right).

Technically the image is loaded in the webpage via an input file-upload HTML element; the image is then transferred to a temporary canvas and converted in a string using base64 using the standard toDataURL method. Since the F4BL3s tool is a serverless web application, and all data is stored locally using localStorage, also the skin is stored in localStorage, in the same object that is associated to its Fable. This is done via the standard JSON API, therefore only small images can be used in the current version, up to 20 kilobytes per image.

4.2   Exporting to Twine and PPT

Twine file format is HTML-based with special tags, and it is well documented, so we simply implemented a Javascript library that saves a text file in the right HTML format, with data representing a textual rendition of a Fable. The file can be saved locally and uploaded via the free Twine online editor (at http://twinery.org/2). Once the exported Fable is opened it the Twine editor shows a bubble for each slide in the Fable, and clicking on a bubble it is possible to edit the contents. A bubble (i.e. a passage in the Twine jargon) can contain text, HTML tags and images; the exported Fables use HTML DIVs to represent the nesting of rooms, people and things in each slide. Navigation in Twine works by defining buttons with links that connect all passages into a graph. Taking advantage of this, we simply map the actions that each slides of a Fable can have (with up to three actions out-going from each slide) into Twine button-links. Twine users can then click on the play button and navigate interactively through the slides, in the same way the playback page in F4BL3s allows to interact with the Fable. We also implemented non-deterministic choice in our export function: in case multiple actions with the same label lead away from a slide in a Fable (for instance in Fig. 1, the two *hitBall* actions), the corresponding Twine button-links are automatically replaced by a short *Harlowe* script[3] that rolls a die to randomly jump along one of the possible alternatives. And this is exactly the same that happens in the playback web-page of F4BL3s.

We also wanted to export to Microsoft PowerPoint slides, since they are a commonly used format for school teachers, and it was in our requirements for F4BL3s to interoperate well with PowerPoint and Google Sheets. For the creation of PPT files from Javascript we adopted the PptxGenJS library, which has simple commands to:

- create a presentation from within a webpage,
- save it as a PPT file, by downloading it
- create and a slide to the presentation,
- add shapes, text and hyperlinks to a slide at specific coordinates.

The resulting PowerPoint presentation is still editable and behaves exactly as a manually created presentation would, allowing teachers and pupils to further alter their exported Fable. Our implementation exports a Fable to a PPT file by creating an initial PowerPoint slide with the title of the Fable and three lists of elements in the Fable: rooms, people and things. Then for each Fable slide a PPT slide is generated, with a visual rendition of the tree of elements. More details about the layout of the slides can be found in the next subsection about visualization. The actions (which represent jumps from slide to slide, in a Fable) are converted to PPT hyperlinks: during presentation, these hyperlinks can be clicked like buttons and will make the PowerPoint presentation jump to a new slide, hence implementing the semantics of our actions. Contrary to the Twine export, we could see not simple way to implement non-deterministic choice for multiple actions with the same label (such as the two *hitBall* actions in Fig. 1), therefore, we decided to map each action directly to a PPT hyperlink. The user interacting with the PowerPoint presentation will have to decide manually which of the multiple hyperlink with the same label to click. Finally, we believe that having a PPT export file supports printing, cutting and tinkering with a paper version of a Fable, hence, it fits very well with the activities in the typical Danish primary classroom.

4.3 Visualizations

Most new features in F4BL3s have to do with better visualization of Fables. For the new playback page and for the export to PPT we explored many possible visualization styles. Figure 4 shows the best three visualization styles, that we call *nested sticky notes* version 1, version 2 and *fixed minimal size* (respectively the second, third and fourth column in Fig. 4). The problem of rendering a Fable closely resembles that of creating a responsive layout for a webpage, where scaling works automatically across a large range of possible dimensions and number of elements in the page; however, especially for PPT export, we could not rely on style sheets (such as CSS), so we decided to develop custom layout algorithms.

---

[3] Twine's internal scripting language.

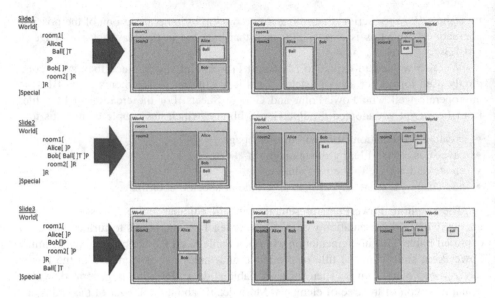

Fig. 4. The first column from the left is the textual representation of Fable slides; the second column is the rendering according to nested sticky nodes version 1, and the next two columns are rendered according to version 2 and the export to PPT layout algorithm.

For *nested sticky notes version 1* we used the following rules:

- if a room has *n* room-type children, then each room-child takes up (100/n) percent of the parent area (e.g. in Fig. 4 first row and second column, *room1* in slide 1 is the only child of *world*, so it takes up 100% of *world*)
- if any item present:
  - items take 30% of their room's area; items are vertically stacked, with nesting if it is the case
  - sub-rooms equally share the remaining 70% left

Nested sticky notes version 2 uses simpler rules:

- place rooms before persons and things (left-to-right),
- divide horizontal space equally among children.

Nested sticky notes version 2 is used in the playback page of F4BL3s, as visible also in Fig. 3 on the right; this visualization style works best when there are few rooms, and limited nesting, which is typically the case with a Fable.

Both versions of the *nested sticky notes* layout algorithms display a problem: as visible in Fig. 4 the same item (for example the ball) changes size significantly from slide to slide, in the second and third column. We call this problem **variable scale problem** and we found that it is distracting and somewhat confusing for our users, as well as being aesthetically unpleasing. To solve this problem and also to explore more natural-looking layout methods, we developed a completely different layout for the PPT export, called *fixed minimal size*.

The idea is that for each slide:

- all rooms are arranged first, recursively. At each level of the rooms' tree, a grid is defined, as *square* as possible. For example 3 rooms at the same level will be arranged in a 2-by-2 grid, with a bit of space left over.
- then for each room: all persons and things are arranged (i.e. placed and resized).

To avoid the problem of variable scale present in the other two layout methods discussed above, we compute the first step (i.e. arranging all rooms) in order to discover the size of the smallest room in our rendered slide, and we call that *minimal size*. Then we define the size of all persons and things to be fixed at 1/6 of the minimal size, in all rooms of the slide: this offers a nice visual consistency for persons and things, as visible in the Fig. 4, last column.

4.4   Existing Tools and F4BL3s

During the development of F4BL3s we investigated various related tools, and we focused on Twine and Ren'py [9] since they are most commonly and widely used. As discussed in [8] Twine is a free web tool for authoring hypermedia and it is aimed at non-technical people as well as game developer. The main mechanism of Twine is the definition of paragraph of text that can be connected to other paragraphs by labeled links. Since each paragraph can contain text, images and audio, the created games can be quite sophisticated. Twine also has a scripting language called Harlowe to support more complex behavior by the part of the game, than simply allowing the player to navigate the paragraphs, e.g. score can be kept or certain links might only work after the player has collected some specific item. Another similar tool is Ren'py [9], a visual novel engine that runs on computers and mobile devices; it allows authors to use text, images and audio to create tell interactive stories such as visual novels and simulation games. Ren'py uses Python scripting to program the behavior of potentially large and complex novels and games. Interestingly in [10] an e-learning tool based on Ren'py is defined, and some limitations of the use of Ren'py are discussed.

Contrasting F4BL3s with tools like Twine and Microsoft PowerPoint, we find that F4BL3s offer more semantic support to create scenario-based, interactive and spatial stories. Fables have both *visual* and *spatial* semantics, where a story is constructed of actors like rooms, people and things; the author of a Fable works explicitly with an ontology (the palette in the F4BL3s tool), where actor roles are clearly defined. For instance rooms do not move during playback, while people move from room to room, and things move when picked up by people. We modeled these roles on natural ways of describing stories exhibited by our informants, and formally on type systems for mobile ambients (as discussed in [17]). In comparison to Ren'py, F4BL3s does not support scripting but instead it leverages on direct manipulation and definition of structured data, such has rooms and items. However, there are similarities: for example a Fable can be played as a interactive visual novel, and the visual aspect of a Fable are customizable in F4BLs, by defining a skin.

5   Evaluation: Method and Results

This study is conducted via a research through design approach [14], aimed at gaining new knowledge on the needs of teachers regarding how new digital tools could support them in expressing their creativity and arranging new e-learning experiences for their pupils. Our analysis focuses on functional, experiential and informational values, in order to evaluate how Fables could concretely fit within the e-learning ecology. However, being engaged in a research inquiry, we see the design of F4BL3s as a design exemplar, embodying our understanding of the inquiry at hand [14]. Moreover, through our inquiry we have conducted a participatory design process, rooted in findings from previous studies (see [1]). Hence, our idea of Fables emerged from previous studies and from the knowledge we gathered on how Danish teachers were responding to the digitization of learning. In accordance with the participatory design agenda, our goal is to empower our user groups [6], leveraging on their skills and desires for their practice.

As it is typically done with research through design and participatory design, we are integrating our design process with ethnographic methods [20], such as observations and situated interviews with potential users. All the sessions were video-recorded, with permission from the participants, so that we could analyze their needs and responses to our concept. Moreover, we are conducting an iterative design process [20], in which prototypes are made to foster creative thinking within our creative team and in the users. We started from low-fi prototypes [11]: simple, semi-interactive visualizations to imagine the interface and the interaction. Currently we are at the second iteration, and this time our F4BL3s prototype is moving towards a hi-fi prototype, as the key features have all been implemented and most of the graphic interface is functioning. Since F4BL3s is a tool addressed to teachers and pupils to develop interactive stories, we found it challenging to rely on paper-based prototypes, as we feared that the users would be confused and expect a pre-made simulation or another PowerPoint-like application. For this reason, we started testing our prototype only when it could communicate its purpose, an agile technique usually called *minimum viable product*.

At this stage we have conducted a preliminary evaluation with a focus-group of 3 teachers from a local primary school in Odense. It was our goal to conduct a test with a small group of teachers and their classes, however, we decided together with the teachers that we will involve their pupils with a more mature version of the prototype, that incorporates teachers' suggestions.

5.1   Discussion and Results

We conducted our evaluation with a group of three primary school teachers. The participants included two male teachers, one teaching Danish language and literature, geography, and social sciences, the other teaching mathematics and history. A female teacher was also involved and she was teaching Danish language and literature, English, mathematics and physical education.

The evaluation involved a shared semi-structured interview (a technique discussed in [19]), during which we showed our prototype. We both took ethnographic notes and video-recorded the interview, so that we could store their comments for the design of the new prototypes. The interview took place inside a meeting room at the school and we planned it to be centered around three main themes: to find out if they saw a purpose for F4BL3s in their classes, possible future scenarios of use that they might see in our prototype, and possible desired or missing features.

We started by presenting ourselves and our concept, showing our prototype on a large wall-mounted television from our laptop. In order to effectively communicate the use of F4BL3s, we live-edited three different stories, which were supposed to act as demos, fostering ideas on possible use and features for the tool. During the start of the interview the teachers seemed confused on the nature of F4BL3s. We hoped that after we explained the scenario we had in mind and after having shown the stories we edited, the teachers could take control of the prototype, trying to edit the existing stories or creating a new one. However, they did not seem confident in doing that, so we continued an open conversation on how the prototype could be improved. We planned about 30 min for the test, and instead as the conversation went on we actually used about 1 h.

We identified three main themes in our analysis of the video recording: technical functionalities, learning applications, and multimodal communication. These three themes emerged one after the other during the interview. During the first 15 min circa, the teachers tried to make sense of how F4BL3s worked technically and its purpose, with the Danish language male teacher taking the lead in their dialogue with us. Afterwards the teachers tried to figure out how our prototype could contribute to their own teaching practices. Hence, we all shifted into a shared brainstorming which lasted for the rest of the time, on possible applications and on which functions could be useful in concretely supporting their teaching practice. During this brainstorming, the teachers expressed their desire for more support for multimodal communication.

Regarding the technical functionalities, the male Danish language teacher commented on the interface: "We would like to have coding in other classes than just sciences and this looks like block coding!" and then he asked more about how he was supposed to relate to the interface. All the teachers had previous experience with coding workshops held for their pupils by external instructors, who showed systems like MIT Scratch and they could identify similarities with our tool. As we explained that it might look like *block coding*, but that the interface is mostly inspired by PowerPoint and Unity and centered on drag-and-drop actions, they seemed to have understood that coding was not central in our case. Then the male Danish language teacher said: "I see, so it resembles block coding, but its meaning is subjects-based!" This comment provided a needed clarification for the teachers and created a more relaxed atmosphere. From an ecological perspective, the teachers were concerned about which changes F4BL3s would introduce in their evolving e-learning practices and how it fitted with their own needs, more concretely the teachers seemed worried that we were going to "sell them" yet another application for learning coding, which they did not want. Hence the teachers showed a different attitude: in the start they appeared very focused and quiet, leaning forward on their chairs, but as it became clear that F4BL3s was not a coding tool they leaned back and smiled. They became also eager to share their ideas, freely intervening in conversation and interrupting us.

Regarding possible applications, the teachers discussed how a tool like ours could be fruitfully used to demonstrate in class mathematical calculations step-by-step in the form of a multiple choice story, showing which mistakes can be made and how to avoid them. Other interesting applications were discussed, like the representation of historical events and the articulated process through which laws are being passed in a democracy. The focus shifted then to the pupils' as makers of Fables for assignments in class and at home. The feature of automatic generation of Fables from a written text was particularly appreciated by the female teacher, who suggested a possible task in which the pupils would have to convert a script, from a story or theatre piece in English or Danish, into a Fable and enrich it with details and branching.

These comments suggest to us that the teachers have correctly framed the tool, in terms of supporting the creation of exemplars (as in Schön [3]) through mini projects, which the pupils can solve in their assignments. Moreover, our prototype, although at an early stage, was seen as a reflective tool, potentially enriching the current flow of information between teachers and pupils. In this regard, the teachers readily expressed their desire for more support for multimodal communication; in particular they would like to be able to include sound and video footage, instead of just image and text.

Open questions must be addressed in relation to how correctly frame the interaction between teachers and pupils and how can F4BL3s contribute to it. Moreover, we need to investigate how F4BL3s fit within the other tools which are used in the school, if it can be part of a valuable tool chain, hence enriching expressive opportunities. Therefore, it is our plan to incorporate the teachers' suggestions in a new version of our tool and test this with the same teachers and their pupils during actual classes in the coming months.

6 Conclusions

Fables were introduced to explore ways to simplify digital game design and game programming for primary school teachers and their pupils. In this paper we refine our concept of Fables, by providing a more formal definition; furthermore, we discuss the second iteration in the development of the F4BL3s web tool. In F4BL3s an author can create a Fable (i.e. an objectified version of Schön's exemplars), starting from a textual description as well as by directly manipulating the rooms, people and things that appear in the Fable. The Fable can then be *run* as a digital, interactive scenario-based story, exemplifying abstract concepts or step-by-step problem-solving processes, for instance in mathematics. F4BL3s effectively allows Fable authors to create interactive digital media without coding, a need that was expressed by the teachers we cooperated with in previous studies [1].

In the present study, we approach e-learning as an information ecology [12], in which teachers and pupils are engaged in sharing information on learning content, subjective understandings, individual challenges, and feedback. This exchange of information is mediated through a series of analogue and digital tools. In recent years, Danish schools have been engaging in a digitization of learning practice, hence emphasizing the role of digital tools within the ecology. Teachers are actively contributing to this process exploring the learning affordances offered by existing digital tools, such as Kahoot, Google Docs, Microsoft PowerPoint and others. Through this process, teachers and pupils are becoming increasingly competent in communicating through digital tools, to edit simple stories, presentations, and paper-based games. In ecological terms we see this process as a form of co-evolution, a complex dynamics affecting our teachers and pupils engage and experience their daily practices. Issues emerge when teachers and pupils wish to create interactive media, like games or interactive animations, as these require coding skills. In our experience it is not realistic to expect primary school teachers to learn to program digital games, especially teachers with non-technical backgrounds. The responses we gained from the teachers participating to our study confirmed our expectation that they did not want another coding tool, but they welcomed the idea of evaluating a tool targeting their subjects, and in fact we designed F4BL3s to contribute to the ongoing co-evolution in e-learning ecologies, offering new affordances for existing storytelling, scenario-based learning practices.

In conclusion, although our prototype is still in the form of a minimum viable product and for this reason it could not be tested with pupils yet, it was nonetheless positively evaluated by teachers. More specifically the teachers responded positively to our envisioned scenario where Fables empower teachers and pupils and let them communicate and learn by creating their own digital scenario-based stories. They also liked the fact that Fables can easily support subject-related narratives, without imposing coding in the class, but actually mirroring the roles of teachers and pupils in their daily mediated interaction. From what we know now about the needs of teachers and pupils, we consider interoperability with other standard tools (such as Twine and PowerPoint) a key element in the acceptance of the Fables tool. Finally, building on the data gathered so far, future work includes an improved visual editor for F4BL3s, and we are considering importing standard file formats, such as those used in Microsoft Power-Point or Google Docs. This will allow our users to work full-cycle, starting from whatever tool they find best, and finishing their Fables within the F4BL3 tool-chain.

References

1. Marchetti, E., Valente, A.: It takes three - re-contextualizing game-based learning among teachers, developers and learners. In: Connoly, T., Boyle, L. (eds.) Proceedings of the European Conference on Games Based Learning, pp. 399–406. Academic Conferences International (2016)
2. Simon, H.A.: The Sciences of the Artificial. MIT Press, Cambridge (1996)
3. Schön, D.A.: The Reflective Practitioner: How Professionals Think in Action. Ashgate, Farnham (1986)
4. Sangiorgi, D., Valente, A.: A distributed abstract machine for safe ambients. In: Orejas, F., Spirakis, P.G., van Leeuwen, J. (eds.) ICALP 2001. LNCS, vol. 2076, pp. 408–420. Springer, Heidelberg (2001). https://doi.org/10.1007/3-540-48224-5_34
5. Love, S., Gkatzidou, V., Conti, A.: Using a rich pictures approach for gathering students and teachers digital education requirements. In: Little, L., Fitton, D., Bell, B., Toth, N. (eds.) Perspectives on HCI Research with Teenagers. HCIS. Springer, Cham (2016). https://doi.org/10.1007/978-3-319-33450-9_6
6. Björgvinsson, E., Ehn, P., Hillgren, P.A.: Participatory design and "democratizing innovation". In: Proceedings of the Participatory Design Conference, pp. 41–50. ACM (2010)
7. Moore, C.: Map It: The Hands-On Guide to Strategic Training Design. Montesa Press (2017)

8. Friedhoff, J.: Untangling twine: a platform study. In: Proceedings of the 2013 DiGRA International Conference (2013)
9. Rothamel, T.: Visual novel engine Ren'Py. https://www.renpy.org/. Accessed 1 Feb 2019
10. Prastowo, B.N.: Design and implementation e-learning system using Ren'Py based visual novel. Doctoral dissertation, Universitas Gadjah Mada, Yogyakarta (2017)
11. Valente, A., Marchetti, E.: Fables – exploring natural ways of expressing behavior to create digital simulations. In: Marcus, A., Wang, W. (eds.) DUXU 2018. LNCS, vol. 10919, pp. 110–126. Springer, Cham (2018). https://doi.org/10.1007/978-3-319-91803-7_9
12. Nardi, B.A., O'Day, V.: Information Ecologies: Using Technology with Heart. MIT Press, Cambridge (1999)
13. Marchetti, E.: Occupational therapy and RPG games: a playful, ecological approach to healthcare education. In: ECREA 2018, the 7th European Communication Conference, Digital Library, Lugano, Switzerland (2018)
14. Zimmerman, J., Forlizzi, J.: Research through design in HCI. In: Olson, J., Kellogg, W. (eds.) Ways of Knowing in HCI, pp. 167–189. Springer, New York (2014). https://doi.org/10.1007/978-1-4939-0378-8_8
15. Latour, B.: Reassembling the Social. An Introduction to Actor-Network-Theory. Oxford University Press, Oxford (2005)
16. Benamar, L., Balagué, C., Ghassany, M.: The identification and influence of social roles in a social media product community. J. Comput. Mediat. Commun. **22**, 337–362 (2017)
17. Barbanera, F., Bugliesi, M., Dezani, M., Sassone, V.: Space-aware ambients and processes. Theoret. Comput. Sci. **373**(1–2), 41–69 (2007)
18. Lombardo, V., Battaglino, C., Pizzo, A., Damiano, R., Lieto, A.: Coupling conceptual modeling and rules for the annotation of dramatic media. Semant. Web **6**(5), 503–534 (2015)
19. Drotner, K., Iversen, S.M.: Digitale Metoder. At skabe, analysere og dele data. Samfudslitteratur (2017)
20. Kensing, F., Blomberg, J.: Participatory design: Issues and concerns. Comput. Support. Coop. Work (CSCW) **7**(3–4), 167–185 (1998)
21. Hook, A.D., Bodell, S.J., Griffiths, L.: A pilot project of the learning experience of undergraduate occupational therapy students in a three-dimensional virtual environment in the United Kingdom. Br. J. Occup. Ther. **78**(9), 576–584 (2015)
22. Bennet, S., Rodger, S., Fitzgerald, C., Gibson, L.: Simulation in occupational therapy curricula: a literature review. Aust. Occup. Ther. J. **64**, 314–327 (2017)
23. Breaky, K.M., Levin, D., Miller, I., Hentges, K.E.: The use of scenario-based-learning interactive software to create custom virtual laboratory scenarios for teaching genetics. Genetics **179**(3), 1151–1155 (2008)
24. Broadbent, J.: Comparing online and blended learner's self-regulated learning strategies and academic performance. Internet High. Educ. **33**, 24–32 (2017)
25. Marchetti, E., Valente, A.: A tangible digital installation in the classroom: role play and autistic children. In. Munkvold, R., Kolås, L. (eds.) Proceedings of the 9th European Conference on Games Based Learning, pp. 346–353. Academic Conferences and Publishing International (2015)
26. Gros, B., García-Peñalvo, F.J.: Future trends in the design strategies and technological affordances of e-learning. In: Spector, M., Lockee, B., Childress, M. (eds.) Learning, Design, and Technology. An International Compendium of Theory, Research, Practice, and Policy, pp. 1–23. Springer, Cham (2016). https://doi.org/10.1007/978-3-319-17727-4_67-1

Cognitive and Psychological Issues in Learning

Proposing an Estimation Method of Mental Fatigue by Measuring Learner's Leg Movement

Daigo Aikawa, Yasutaka Asai, and Hironori Egi$^{(\boxtimes)}$

Graduate School of Informatics and Engineering,
The University of Electro-Communications,
1–5–1 Chofugaoka, Chofu, Tokyo 182–8585, Japan
{daigo.aikawa,y.asai,hiro.egi}@uec.ac.jp

Abstract. In this research, we propose a method to estimate the mental fatigue of learner by measuring leg movement. Generally, fatigue of a learner in a class gradually increases with time. Taking short breaks can effectively mitigate this problem. However, it is challenging to conduct short breaks at an appropriate timing in consideration of the learner's mental state. In this research, we focus on the movement of learner's legs and propose a method to estimate learner's fatigue from the number of transitions. Experiments were conducted to investigate whether fatigue estimation is possible. A 10-min mental arithmetic task was imposed on the subjects and repeated multiple times. We recorded the movement of legs during the task. Also, we administered a questionnaire to measure the subjective degree of fatigue every time the mental arithmetic task is completed. The result of analysis of the leg movement and the answer to the questionnaire, revealed that there was a significant correlation between the number of transitions of leg posture and the subjective degree of fatigue. From these results, we concluded that fatigue of the learner could be estimated by measuring leg movement.

Keywords: Learner's fatigue · Leg movement · Break during a class · Class orchestration · Classroom sensing

1 Introduction

Having a short break during classes is essential. Mental fatigue of a learner is tends to increase over time during a class. In Watanabe et al. [1], the concentration of learners can be kept for only about 40 min, so it is important to take a break at appropriate intervals in order to conduct efficient learning.

Also, taking breaks at appropriate intervals or changing topics during classes can reduce the fatigue of learners. A study conducted on the efforts of teachers during a class showed that taking breaks during classes were valuable to the learners [2]. However, when a teacher conducts a short break during a class, the decision to conduct the break is based on the experience of the teacher.

© Springer Nature Switzerland AG 2019
P. Zaphiris and A. Ioannou (Eds.): HCII 2019, LNCS 11590, pp. 227–236, 2019.
https://doi.org/10.1007/978-3-030-21814-0_17

The proficiency of the teacher is necessary to decide the appropriate timing for the break.

The conception of our research is that teachers can decide the appropriate timing to take a break by understanding the degree of fatigue of the learners. To evaluate the psychological state, there are several questionnaires, such as Profiles of Mood States (POMS) [3]. However, answering the questionnaires often hinders the progress of the class and learning activity. Another method of evaluating psychological state is measuring neurophysiological signals by attaching devices. However, the devices attached to the learner's body also influence the mental state of the learner and hinder the learning activity.

Physical motions have been reported to represent a specific mental state, one example is leg movements [4]. In this study, we focused on the learner's leg movement. It is possible to measure the learner's leg movement without interfering with the progress of the class or attaching measuring devices to the learner. In this research, we propose a method for estimating mental fatigue by measuring the leg movement of the learner.

2   Related Work

There are several studies on estimating human mental fatigue. In [5] mental fatigue is Event related potential (ERP) P300 induced by the oddball task. However, it takes a certain amount time to implement the oddball task and measure the ERP. For this reason, it is difficult to measure ERP during class.

Other studies worked on the estimating the mental fatigue of drivers and pilots using neurophysiological signals such as electroencephalogram (EEG), electrooculography (EOG), heart rate. A review revealed the accuracy of using neurophysiological signals to estimate mental fatigue in drivers and pilots is close to 90% [6]. However, in each measurement, it is necessary to attach a multiple electrodes to the head of the subjects. In addition, it is stated that the number of electrodes is too much for the subjects to be measured comfortably.

Since attaching measuring instruments inhibits learner's activity, design of a contactless estimation method is needed.

3   Leg Movement for Mental Fatigue Estimation

In the educational setting, the movement of the upper body of a learner in the sitting position in a class changes significantly depending on activities. For example, the expected behavior of the upper body greatly varies between writing and discussing. In such a case, it is difficult to obtain effective measurements of mental fatigue using contactless measurements of upper body movement, due to the variety of tasks.

With regards to lower body posture, there are substantial differences in leg posture. For example in size and physique of a cahir can hinder a specific posture of a learner. And the effect hinder a specific posture of a learner.

Therefore, it is necessary to use measurements that are not easily influenced by the conditions of chairs, as indicators of mental fatigue in the leg movement. As a result, we focused on the number of transitions of leg posture. The definition of a leg posture transition is when a learner starts moving legs and then stops the legs, forming a specific posture. The merit of introducing the transitions of leg posture is that it applies to subjects independently of the physical condition of the subjects.

4   Experiment

The experiment was conducted for 15 undergraduate and postgraduate students (A,...,O) of a science and engineering university. The subjects tackled a 10-min mental arithmetic task (Calc-n) and answered a questionnaire (VAS-n) using the VAS (Visual Analogue Scale) to measure subjective fatigue level. This experiment was repeated for seven repetitions (n = 1,..., 7). The mental arithmetic tasks and the questionnaires are conducted on a desktop computer. We did not inform the subjects in advance of the time required and the number of repetitons of the mental arithmetic task that would be conducted during the experiment.

After finishing the tasks (Calc-7 and VAS-7), the subjects took a 20-min break, and then answered the questionnaire again (VAS-break). After that, they tackled the same mental arithmetic task again (Calc-post) and answered the questionnaire (VAS-post).

Before the start of the experiment, a time period for practice was established, to allow the subjects a period to become familiar with answering the mental arithmetic tasks and the questionnaire. This adaptation phase was conducted until the subjects felt that they were fully accustomed (Adaptation Phease). After the practice, the subjects took a 10-min break to dissipate any mental fatigue that might have accumulated during adaptation. Then the subjects answered the questionnaire (VAS-pre) and started the experiment.

The procedure of the experiment is shown in Fig. 1.

The subjects were instructed not to take a meal and not to look at the clock. The subjects were also instructed not to touch mobile devices such as smartphones during the break to eliminate the influence on the subjects' mental state by external information. We restricted eating except drinking water during the break, in order to prevent drowsiness.

In order not to hinder the occurrence of mental strain, those that could infer the current time were excluded from the experimental environment so that subjects could not obtain information on the current time. The subjects were instructed to remove their watch. The mental arithmetic tasks were carried out in an unmanned room except the subject so as not to influence the mental state of the subject by the existence of another person.

The leg movement of the subjects during the experiment was recorded on a video except for during the breaks. The number of transitions of the leg posture was counted by observation of the recorded video. The analysis was conducted according to the following rules.

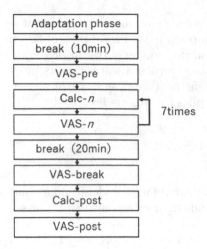

Fig. 1. The procedure of the experiment

- It is assumed that a transition happens when the legs move from a stationary state and stop again within 4 s.
- If the movement stops for 2 s or longer, it is regarded as a stationary state.
- If the legs keep moving for more than 4 s, it is regarded as a new transition every 4 s.

The mental arithmetic task used in this experiment was to judge whether the calculation formula displayed on the screen was correct or not. The answer from the subject was collected with the mouse connected to the computer. If the calculation formula was thought to be correct, the subjects clicked the left button of the mouse. If the calculation formula was thought to be wrong, the subjects clicked the right button of the mouse. The screenshot of the mental arithmetic task is shown in Fig. 2.

In this experiment, VAS was used as a method for evaluating subjective mental fatigue. A questionnaire using VAS was shown on the computer display consisting of the following two questions.

- Please answer the following questions about your current fatigue.
  - Question 1: Please move the marker to the appropriate place as a degree of "mental" fatigue.
  - Question 2: Please move the marker to the appropriate place as a degree of "physical" fatigue.

The response was made using a slide bar simulating VAS, between the left end of "no feeling of fatigue" and the right end of "maximum imaginable fatigue". The answer is acquired in 21 steps from 0 to 20 and stored in a CSV file.

The screenshot of the questionnaire is shown in Fig. 3.

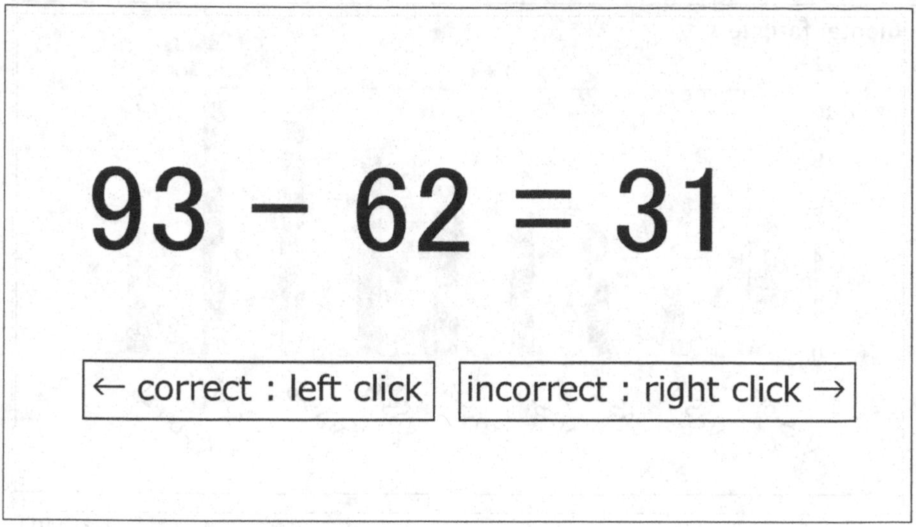

Fig. 2. The screenshot of the mental arithmetic task

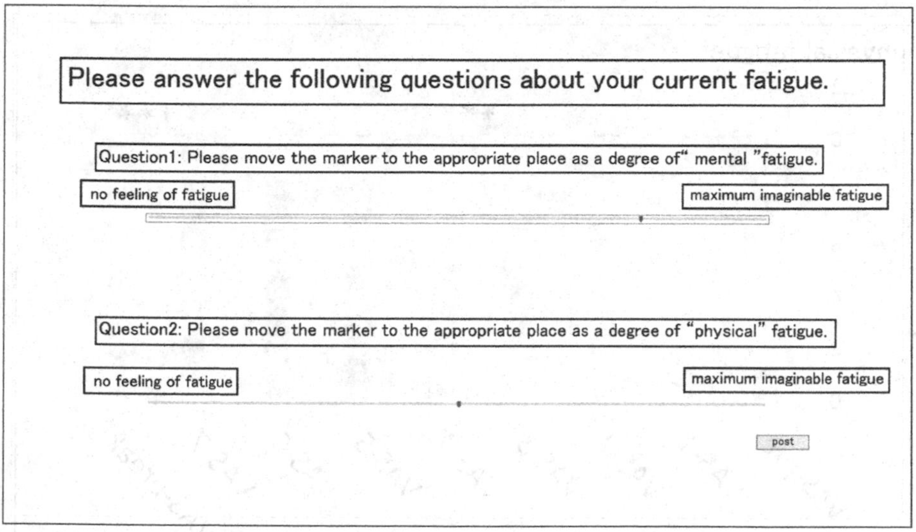

Fig. 3. The screenshot of the questionnaire

5   Results and Discussion

It is necessary to confirm whether the mental arithmetic task used in this study is mental stress that induces a sufficient mental strain on the subjects. The subjective average of the mental and physical fatigue value of the subjects in the questionnaire is shown in Figs. 4 and 5 respectively.

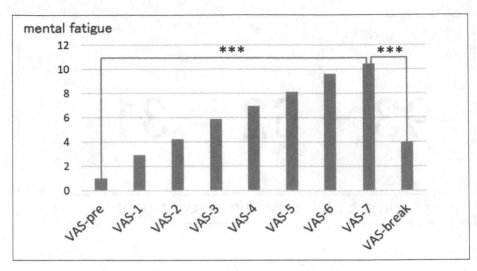

(*** : p < .001)

Fig. 4. Average value of the mental fatigue by questionnaire

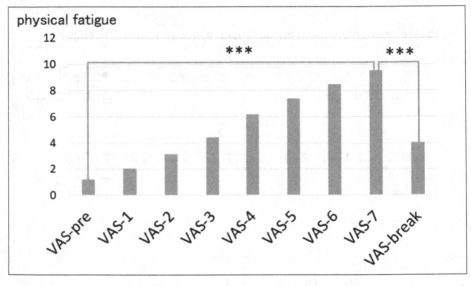

(*** : p < .001)

Fig. 5. Average value of the physical fatigue by questionnaire

Both subjective mental and physical fatigue were significantly increased prior to the mental arithmetic task (VAS-pre) and after finishing VAS-7. Moreover, there was a significant decrease in the result after a 20-min break (VAS-break).

Therefore, it is clear that the mental arithmetic task was appropriate as a mental stress and a physical stress to cause strain on subjects. Also, the subjects recovered by taking a break.

Figure 6 shows the average number of transitions of the leg posture in each mental arithmetic task. The average number of transitions of leg posture in the Calc-7 was significantly higher (p < .001) compared to the calc-1. Moreover, the average number of transitions of leg posture in the Calc-post was significantly lower (p < .05) compared to the Calc-7. Although the average number of transitions decreased from the Calc-6 to the Calc-7, there was no significant difference during this period. From these results, it can be considered that the number of transitions increases due to the strain of the mental arithmetic task and decreases due to the break.

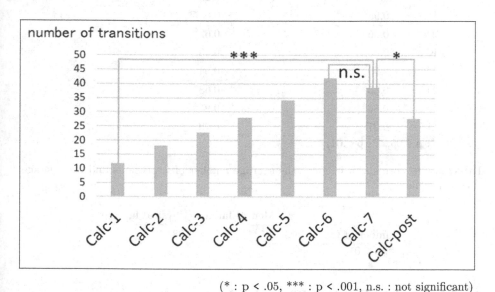

(* : p < .05, *** : p < .001, n.s. : not significant)

Fig. 6. Average number of transitions of the leg posture

Next, Spearman's rank correlation coefficient was calculated for the number of transitions of leg posture in Calc-n (n = 1,...,7 post) and the fatigue of VAS-n (n = 1,...,7 post) in each subject. The results are shown in Table 1.

There was a strong correlation (r > .60, p < .05) with 10 out of 15 subjects in the number of transitions of leg posture and mental fatigue. There was also a strong correlation (r > .60, p < .05) with ten subjects in the number of transitions of leg posture and physical fatigue.

Spearman's rank correlation coefficient was calculated for the average number of transitions of leg posture in the Calc-n (n = 1,...,7, post) and both the mental and physical fatigue in VAS-n (n = 1,...,7, post) of the subjects. The results are shown in Table 2.

Table 1. Correlation between the number of transitions and the fatigue of each subject

Subject	Transition & mental fatigue	Transition & physical fatigue
A	0.81**	0.80**
B	0.97**	0.95**
C	0.55	0.60*
D	0.63*	0.64*
E	0.91**	0.88**
F	0.08	0.29
G	0.65*	0.80**
H	0.42	−0.23
I	0.93**	0.85**
J	0.66*	0.62*
K	0.46	0.53
L	0.90**	0.54
M	0.85**	0.68*
N	0.86**	0.95**
O	0.27	0.29

(*: $p < .05$, **: $p < .01$)

Table 2. The correlation between the average number of transitions and the average of each fatigue

	Mental fatigue	Physical fatigue
Number of transitions	.95**	.98**

(**: $p < .01$)

6   Measuring Device: ThinkingLeg

We designed a device named "ThinkingLeg" to detect leg movement automatically. The device is intended to be placed under the foot of a learner. The developed device is shown in Fig. 7.

ThinkingLeg is a base-like device made up of a large number of photo reflectors and controlled by Raspberry Pi. The detail of the ThinkingLeg is shown in Fig. 8.

The photo reflectors detect foot through the acrylic board. Foot-ground positions are measured every two seconds. By analyzing the change of foot's ground positions, the number of leg transitions is counted automatically.

Fig. 7. ThinkingLeg

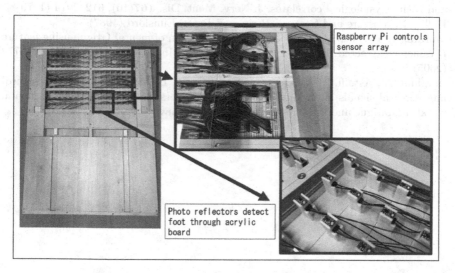

Fig. 8. Design of ThinkingLeg

7 Conclusion

In this study, we propose a method to estimate mental fatigue by measuring the leg movement of a learner, andwe also conducted an experiment to evaluate the usefulness of the method. A mental arithmetic task was carried out by test subjects in an effort to cause a mental strain. The number of transitions of leg posture was counted. A questionnaire was administered to measure subjective fatigue.

As a result of the experiment, it was found that there was a strong correlation between the number of transitions of the leg posture and subjective fatigue.

Therefore, it was revealed that there is a possibility of estimating the fatigue of learners from their leg movement.

As a next step, the number of transitions of the leg posture will be analyzed by multiple persons to improve the objectivity of the results. Also, the performance of ThinkingLeg will be evaluated, and a system that estimates mental fatigue with ThinkingLeg will be developed.

References

1. Watanabe, Y., Ikegaya, Yuji.: Effect of intermittent learning on task performance: a pilot study. J. Neuronet 38, 1–5 (2017)
2. Olmsted III, J.: The mid-lecture break: when less is more. J. Chem. Educ. **74**(4), 525–527 (1999)
3. Pollock, V., Cho, D.W., Reker, D., Volavka, J.: Profile of mood states: the factors and their physiological correlates. J. Nerv. Ment. Dis. **167**(10), 612–2014 (1979)
4. Bull, P.E.: Posture and Gesture. Pergamon Press, Elmsford (1987)
5. Murata, A., Uetakeb, A., Takasawab, Y.: Evaluation of mental fatigue using feature parameter extracted from event-related potential. Int. J. Ind. Ergon. **35**, 761–770 (2005)
6. Borghini, G., Astolfi, L., Vecchiato, G., Mattia, D., Babiloni, F.: Measuring neuro-physiological signals in aircraft pilots and car drivers for the assessment of mental workload, fatigue and drowsiness. Neurosci. Biobehav. Rev. **44**, 58–75 (2014)

Collaborative Meaning Construction in Socioenactive Systems: Study with the *mBot*

Ricardo Caceffo[1]([⊠]), Eliana Alves Moreira[1,5], Rodrigo Bonacin[2,3],
Julio Cesar dos Reis[1,4], Marleny Luque Carbajal[1], João Vilhete V. D'Abreu[4],
Camilla V. L. T. Brennand[1], Luma Lombello[1], José Armando Valente[4,6],
and Maria Cecília Calani Baranauskas[1]

[1] Institute of Computing, UNICAMP, Campinas, SP, Brazil
{caceffo,jreis}@ic.unicamp.br,
marleny.carbajal@students.ic.unicamp.br,camillatenorio123@gmail.com,
lumalombello@gmail.com, c.baranauskas@gmail.com
[2] UNIFACCAMP, Rua Guatemala, 167, Campo Limpo Paulista,
SP 13231-230, Brazil
[3] Center for Information Technology (CTI), Rodovia Dom Pedro I, Km 143,6,
Campinas, SP 13069-901, Brazil
rodrigo.bonacin@cti.gov.br
[4] Nucleus of Applied Informatics to Education (NIED), Campinas, SP, Brazil
joao.vilhete@gmail.com
[5] Federal Institute of Education, Science and Technology of São Paulo (IFSP),
Guarulhos, SP, Brazil
eliana.moreira@ifsp.edu.br
[6] Institute of Arts, UNICAMP, Campinas, SP, Brazil

Abstract. The design of interactive systems concerned with the impact of the technology on the human agent as well as the effect of the human experience on the technology is not a trivial task. Our investigation goes towards a vision of socioenactive systems, by supporting and identifying how a group of people can dynamically and seamlessly interact with the technology. In this paper, we elaborate a set of guidelines to design socioenactive systems. We apply them in the construction of a technological framework situated in an educational environment for children around the age of 5 (N = 25). The scenario was supported by educational robots, programmed to perform a set of actions mimicking human emotional expressions. The system was designed to shape the robots' behavior according to the feedback of children's responses in iterative sessions. This entails a complete cycle, where the robot impacts the children and is affected by their experiences. We found that children create hypotheses to make sense of the robot's behavior. Our results present original aspects related to a social enactive system.

Keywords: Enactive · Educational · Robots · Interactive design ·
Evaluation · Ontologies · Emotions · HCI

P. Zaphiris and A. Ioannou (Eds.): HCII 2019, LNCS 11590, pp. 237–255, 2019.
https://doi.org/10.1007/978-3-030-21814-0_18

1   Introduction

Advanced interactive systems entail complex interaction scenarios as well as research challenges demanding the consideration of new factors to design and guide the interaction. Kaipainen *et al.* [12,13] have drawn the outlines of a multidisciplinary research agenda focusing on a dynamically coupled human and technological processes. They defined the concept of **enactive system**, based on a ubiquitous approach [18,19] of the Bruner's enactment idea [1].

This approach is recursive by nature, involving the impact of the technology on the human agent as well as the effect of the human experience on the technology. Our investigation expands this concept to a **socioenactive vision**, which goes further by supporting and identifying how a group of people can dynamically and seamless interact with the technology. The conception and experimentation of such a system presents several open research questions. For instance, how to adequate the design of socioenactive systems in specific domain scenarios.

Our research scenario is an environment of complementary education for children around the age of 5, enrolled in the Division of Early Childhood and Complementary Education of the University of Campinas [3]. In this context, we worked with educational robots, in particular the mBot [4], a robot kit that enables programming via Scratch.

In this paper, we propose a set of socioenactive design guidelines and apply them to a system in the educational environment. We assume that the system's behavior must be driven and shaped according to users' input and sense making. For this particular purpose, we adapted Kaipainen's *et al.* [12] set of objectives to design enactive systems, establishing a series of guidelines for the socioenactive systems design. Following the guidelines, we mapped 6 human expressions (happiness, sadness, disgust, surprise, anger and despise) to emojis and their respective technological representation in the educational robot.

On this basis, we designed and evaluated a first version of a socioenactive system, in which a series of iterative sessions were performed, consisting of the following steps: a child secretly performs one of the mapped expressions to a camera; the expression is identified and input into the system; the system identifies, for that moment, which action must be executed by the robot; other children hypothesize which expression led the robot to take that action; responses are inserted into the system, influencing the next cycle of interaction.

We analyzed the study's data relying both on systems' behavior and the participants' responses. Our study explains how children created meaning to the performed actions as a group working collaboratively. We found patterns related to the diversity (lack of unanimity) on the robot's expressions identified by the children; a clear preference for an expression (happiness) and that children have better performance when identifying the robot's expression than the expression performed by the child in the cardboard box.

Although recent literature has presented alternatives to tailor system's results according to students' performance [9] and improved Educational Robotics (ER) [16], we advance the state-of-the-art in the design and evaluation of systems with dynamic interactive coupling between people interaction and the systems' behavior.

The remainder of this article is organized as follows: Sect. 2 presents the foundations and related work. Section 3 thoroughly describes the defined methodology by presenting the experimental design, the participants and the studied application scenario. Section 4 presents the results and Sect. 5 discusses the obtained findings. Finally, Sect. 6 presents the conclusion remarks and our envisioned future work.

2   Background

Kaipainen *et al.* [12] defines as enactive a system that *"is recursive by nature, involving the impact of the technology on the human agent as well as the effect of the human experience on the technology"*. The following research questions were considered to lead the design of enactive systems [12]:

- What if the interaction experience would modify the content, thus constituting a self-controlling system?
- What would be the proper metadata ontologies to account not only for pre-existent content categories, but for those that can emerge in such a recursive system dynamics?

Kaipainen *et al.* [12] further defined several objectives that could be used to lead the development of such systems. In this investigation, we organized the objectives into guidelines (named here from G1 to G4) as follows:

- **G1:** definition of a database or rule set to support the generation of behavior in real time;
- **G2:** definition of technologies supported by sensors to detect and track participants behavior;
- **G3:** mapping between psycho-physiological dimensions of content;
- **G4:** an algorithm to manage the narrative montage in real time.

We propose to include **social** aspects into the model to expand the original enactive concept defined by Kaipainen *et al.* [12]. In this sense, our proposal considers not only the individual—traditional key in the interaction process with technology—but the impact of the social interactions performed by a group of individuals in such environment. We defined this concept as **"socioenactive"**[1].

A key research challenge to achieve socioenactive systems refers to the difficulties of capturing, modeling, and interpreting human aspects such as emotion

---

[1] The current research is part of a broader project, supported by the São Paulo Research Foundation (FAPESP), grant #2015/16528-0, that aims to study, build and evaluate socioenactive conceptual frameworks for different scenarios, like the educational, health and museums. The complete project description is available at: https://interhad.nied.unicamp.br/projetos/socio-enactive-systems Accessed: February, 2019.

and social environment. The use of ontologies stands for an alternative to achieve this goal, once they represent semantics in computational systems, by describing concepts and interrelationships among them.

To represent semantics in computational systems, Web Ontologies have been designed to provide rich machine-decidable semantic representation [6–8,10]. They refer to a formal specification of a domain, formalizing a conceptualization of a domain in terms of classes, properties and relationships between classes.

Soft Ontology is another conceptual approach, in which, in contrast to Web Ontologies, with fixed hierarchies described in Web Ontology Language (OWL) [14], refers to flexible set of meta-data [12,13]. This is useful to represent dynamically evolving information domains, as well as for representing and interpreting psycho-physiological states by including, for instance, the emotions [15] from the involved participants in the interaction. These ontologies present individual elements associated with values in a non-structured a priori hierarchy. They should evolve according to the recursive cycle, thus impacting the human agent and being affected by the human experiences.

With the objective of implementing these flexible solutions, ontology-based enactive systems are frequently based on fuzzy models [17]. Other studies propose the use of ontology networks, which conciliate models of several types of ontological representations, including soft and hard ontologies [5].

In this work, we rely on the concept of Soft Ontology to develop a behavior matrix representing the meaning of robot's actions. We assume that the robot's behavior is based on the children' collective assignments by round to round from the interaction in the environment.

3   Methodology

This investigation aims to answer the following research questions:

- **RQ1:** how to adapt the enactive guidelines proposed by Kaipainen *et al.* to the design of socioenactive system?
- **RQ2:** what would be the first impressions of the execution of a socioenactive system in an educational environment?

In the following, we present the experimental design of a socioenactive system (Subsect. 3.1), followed by the educational application where the study was conducted and the description of the participants in our study (Subsect. 3.2). Subsection 3.3 presents the workshops environment and dynamics. Subsection 3.4 presents how data collected from the study was analyzed.

3.1   Experimental Design

The experimental research design was organized to adapt the enactive systems' goals proposed by Kaipainen *et al.* [12] as guidelines to support the design of socioenactive systems. Table 1 presents the 4 proposed key guidelines (G1, G2, G3 and G4) underlying our experimental design.

Table 1. Guidelines for the socioenactive design. Adapted from the guidelines proposed by Kaipainen *et al.* [12] to support the design of enactive systems.

Guideline	Socioenactive design guideline
G1	Defining a database or rule set to support the generation of behavior in real time: *Definition of a behavior matrix to support the generation of real-time feedback. From a given input, the system analyzes the behavior matrix, processes the data, and provides the appropriate output*
G2	Defining technologies supported by sensors to detect and track participants' behavior: *We adopt the mBot [4], a robot based on Scratch programming to support this study. The mBot has a wide range of sensor that can be used to detect and track participants' behavior*
G3	Mapping between psycho-physiological dimensions of content: *The mapping between psycho-physiological dimensions of content through human facial expressions, like happiness, sadness, etc. We define 3 mapping levels: closer to humans, represented by the used emojis; intermediate, through the representation of the expression in the mBot software and; hardware, in which each facial expression was showed in the mBot's display (cf. Fig. 5)*
G4	Defining an algorithm to manage the narrative montage in real time: *The algorithm to manage the real-time narrative was defined as an internal mBot's programming: for each facial expression, it was programmed to perform a specific action through a series of joint actions of its locomotion and sound sensors (cf. Table 4)*

Figure 1 shows an adaptation of an enactive system' scheme [12,17] towards a **socioenactive** system's organization explored in this study. It shows the socioenactive feedback cycle, starting with G1, used to support the implementation of the socioenactive system instance (*cf.* Subsect. 3.2). The guidelines were mapped to a behavior matrix (G1), the mBot [4] (G2 and G4) and the mapping of human facial expressions (G3). The social component is represented by the children themselves.

3.2 Study Scenario and Participants

In total, 25 children, aged 4 to 5 years old, participated in this study. All children were enrolled in the Division of Early Childhood and Complementary Education of the University of Campinas [3]. The children came from two separated classes, morning and afternoon—referenced from now on as Group 1 and Group 2—with respectively 13 and 12 students each. Each group had a different teacher.

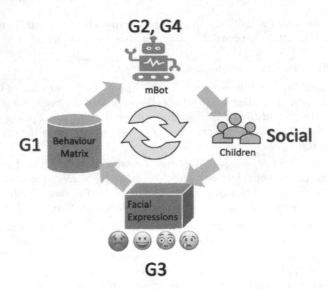

Fig. 1. Socioenactive feedback cycle mapped to the proposed guidelines. Adapted from the enactive system proposed by Tikka *et al.* [17] and organized by Kaipainen *et al.* [12].

In this study, all parents signed a Term of Consent[2], allowing the participation of children, and data collection through video and images. All children assented to participate and signed the Term of Agreement with the help of teachers.

Initially, in a brainstorming session with teachers, we defined 6 expressions that would make sense for the children' related context: happiness, sadness, disgust, surprise, anger and despise. Each expression was associated to an emoji[3] expression (*cf.* Fig. 2).

In order to contextualize each emojis expression to children, the teachers mapped parts of an adapted version of the "Little Red Riding Hood" story to each of the emojis. The teachers then organized storytelling sessions with the children, showing to them the respective emoji plaque when required (associated to specific parts of the story). For example, a plaque with the "surprise" emoji was shown to the children in the scene that the wolf revealed his disguise to the Little Red Riding Hood. Table 2 illustrates how some parts of the story were mapped to the emojis:

---

[2] This research was approved by the Research Ethics Committee of the University of Campinas with number 72413817.3.00000.5404.

[3] Ideograms and smileys used in electronic messages and web pages. Definition retrieved from: https://en.wikipedia.org/wiki/Emoji Accessed: January, 2019.

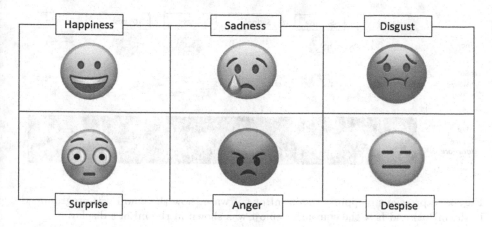

Fig. 2. Representation of the emoji expressions used in this study, portraying happiness, sadness, disgust, surprise, anger, despise. The emojis were retrieved from the public list of Unicode 11.0 emoji characters [11]. Although very similar, the original images used in this study were not reproduced here as they were retrieved from several internet websites.

Table 2. Example of how some parts of the adapted version of the "Little Red Riding Hood" were mapped to the emoji expressions.

Emoji expressions	Parts of the story
Happiness	*"Little Red Ridding Hood looked back and saw the magic tree swinging its branches from side to side, she was HAPPY because unraveled all the charades ..."*
Surprise	*"After walking a little, Little Red Ridding Hood was SURPRISED to see a castle haunted! ..."*
Sadness	*"... the children were very SAD! How do we find our way back? ..."*
Anger	*"... trapped inside the castle. Little Red Ridding Hood was ANGRY at that. How could she leave? ..."*
Disgust	*"With the rain, a DISGUSTING super toad appeared ..."*
Despise	*"Then the magic tree say with a tone of DESPISE : I'm not going to open now ..."*

Related to the guideline G3 (*cf.* Table 1), Fig. 3 shows the expressions mapping, in which each emoji (first row) was mapped as a segment display image, programmed in the mBot software (second row). The third row shows the mBot display mapped to each one of the emojis.

Related the guideline G1 (*cf.* Table 1), our behavior matrix represents domain concepts and ontology dimensions. This matrix is based on the idea of ontological dimensions (ontodimensions) and ontospaces as proposed by Kaipainen *et al.*

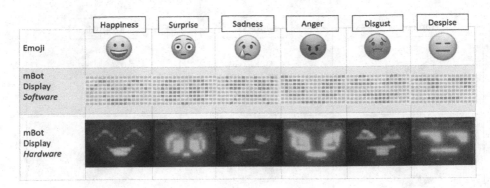

Fig. 3. Expressions mapping: emoji; mBot software (how the emoji was programmed in the mBot) and how the equivalent emoji was shown in the mBot's display.

[12]. Their proposal focused on the representation of collaborative tagging practices, with the tags representing ontodimensions and the tag space, ontospaces.

The behavior matrix is our ontological solution to represent knowledge about the emotional expressions and a set of behaviors that can be performed by the robot. Table 3 shows our solution exploring a probability matrix to represent the association of the robots' actions (rows) and emotional expressions (columns). Each cell represents a weighted probability value of the robot to execute an action for a given emotional expression. The matrix provides flexible and fuzziness behavior to our robot solution. New actions can be dynamically included by inserting new rows, and new emotional expressions can be inserted including new columns in runtime.

Table 3. Behavior matrix (initial state). Cells represent weighted probability values of the robot to execute an action (rows) for a given expression performed by a child.

	Despise	Happiness	Anger	Sadness	Disgust	Surprise
Action 1	1.00	1.00	1.00	1.00	1.00	1.00
Action 2	1.00	1.00	1.00	1.00	1.00	1.00
Action 3	1.00	1.00	1.00	1.00	1.00	1.00
Action 4	1.00	1.00	1.00	1.00	1.00	1.00
Action 5	1.00	1.00	1.00	1.00	1.00	1.00
Action 6	1.00	1.00	1.00	1.00	1.00	1.00

Here, the concepts refer to the defined emotional expressions and the ontology dimensions to the robot's actions. Each matrix element stands for a probability of relating the concept with an ontology dimension. All values of the matrix were initialized with an initial default probability. Along the execution of the workshop dynamics (*cf.* Subsect. 3.3) and the input answers from children, the probabilities are adjusted representing the children' understanding of the correlation between concepts and ontology dimensions. This dynamic behavior of the matrix based on participants' input can be seen as a socioenactive system because the association of the robot's actions with the emotional expression are modeled according to the social interaction context and people's contribution.

Related to the guideline G4 (*cf.* Table 1), the mBot was programmed to perform a set of actions for each one of the expressions. The set of actions for each expression was designed with the help of teachers aiming to give a realistic emotional aspect to the mBot. Table 4 shows the algorithm related to each action programmed in the mBot. Guideline G2 was not adopted on this study (*i.e.*, the robot's sensors were not employed).

Table 4. Algorithm (actions to be executed) programmed in the mBot related to each emoji expression.

Action	mBot's programmed algorithm
Action 1 *Happiness*	Display changes to happy expression
	mBot dances (go forward for 2 s, them turn left and right several times
Action 2 *Sadness*	Display changes to sadness expression
	Go slowly forward and stops (repeat three times)
Action 3 *Disgust*	Display changes to disgust expression
	mBot moves away slowly. Stops
Action 4 *Surprise*	mBot goes fast forward for 4 s. Stops
	Display changes to surprise expression
Action 5 *Anger*	Display changes to anger expression
	Zig zags forward; Stops
Action 6 *Despise*	mBot goes fast forward for 4 s. Stops
	Display changes to despise expression
	Turn 180°; Go forward for 4 s

3.3 Workshops Environment and Dynamics

We conducted workshops for evaluating of our socioenactive system. The study environment was composed by a cardboard box, presented to the children as a "telepathic box", equipped with a camera and isolated from the other parts; a stage for the robot to perform its actions; a children audience area; and a table for the children to choose (vote) which expression they thought their friend made inside the "telepathic box". Figure 4 shows the workshop environment organization.

The workshop dynamics was organized in the following steps:

- **Step 1:** Each child is randomly selected to mimic an emotional expression in the "telepathic box". Overall, each child is selected once.

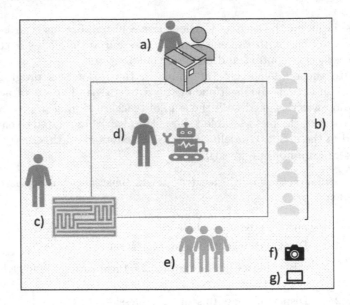

Fig. 4. Workshop environment. Part (a) relates to the "telepathic box", a cardboard box where in each iteration a child draw and performed an expression; part (b) relates to the children in audience; part (c) relates to the table in which the children, each one on his/her turn, chose which expression (identified through RFID emojis) they thought his/her friend made inside the "telepathic box"; part (d) relates to the stage in which the robot performed its actions; part (e) relates to the researchers who watched the study; part (f) refers to the camera that recorded the entire study; and part (g) relates to the notebook in which the robot was connected.

- **Step 2:** The selected child choose a plaque and mimic an emotional expression in front of a camera.
- **Step 3:** The system triggers an action in the robot based on the recognition of the expression performed by the child. Considering the difficulties related to real-time image processing and facial recognition, we adopted a Wizard of Oz approach [2]: after the child in the "telepathic box" mimics the expression, a researcher signals to the other researchers which expression was performed.
- **Step 4:** Children in the audience area watch the robot performing the action.
- **Step 5:** Teachers ask the children in the audience area: "What expression do you think your friend made in the telepathic box that triggered this action on the robot?". Each child selects, privately and in his/her own turn, an emoji expression from a pool with the 6 available expressions. Each emoji was internally identified with an RFID.
- **Step 6:** The data collected in the step 5 is used to update the system's behavior matrix.

Figure 5 shows the "telepathic box" (left) and a child selecting an emoji expression (equipped with a RFID tag) as they thought his/her friend performed inside the "telepathic box".

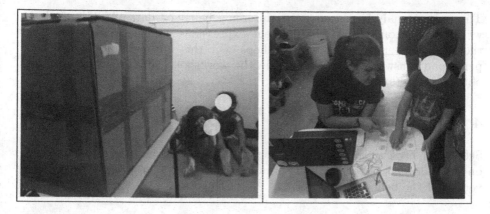

Fig. 5. On the left, the "telepathic box"; on the right, a child selecting an emoji expression.

The behavior matrix was initially configured to select aleatory actions (Step 3) for a given emotional expression (all ontological dimensions present an equal probability). In such a case, it is initialized with default values (*cf.* Table 3), which is adjusted according to the children's behavior. The fuzziness behavior is provided by the weighted random selection of the robot' actions. For this purpose, we used weighted values associating actions to emotion expressions (*i.e.*, the values of a column). The weighted value is adjusted according to the children' feedback during the Step 6 in the workshop. This complete a cycle, where the robot impacts the children and is affected by their experiences.

As the rounds proceed, our defined algorithm balances the probabilities among the robot's actions according to audience feedback (Steps 5 and 6). For instance, given an "action x" performed by a child in the "telepathic box", if most of the children selected a "happy emotion" to such action, the system would increase the probability of association between "happy emotion" and "action x". In this sense, the robot's behavior is based on the children' collective feedback, as it relies on the assignments received in each round.

As mentioned earlier, we carried out studies with two groups, Group 1 and Group 2, respectively, related to the morning and afternoon classes. The study with Group 1 was used to calibrate the behavior matrix, test it, and correct errors. The matrix was really put into practice only during the study with Group 2.

3.4 Employed Analyses

All workshop sections were filmed and produced data recorded for analyses. We emphasize two distinct analyses. The first concerns the behavior matrix data. For this purpose, we stored the matrix status for each iteration related to the children's answers to understand the consistency and convergence of concepts related to the ontology dimensions (Subsect. 4.1 presents the obtained results).

The second analysis concerns the children's behavior data. At this analysis, we aimed to comprehend the different expressions assigned by children over the different iterations in the workshops. For this purpose, we counted each participant answer in each iteration in the workshop (Subsect. 4.2 presents the obtained results).

4   Evaluation Results

Section 4.1 presents an analysis of the behavior matrix data. Section 4.2 focuses on the children's behavior during Group 2 study, once this group used a stable version of the behavior matrix.

4.1   Behavior Matrix Analysis

Table 5 presents the status of the matrix after the first iteration (with Group 2). For example, in Table 5 there is a lower probability of the robot to execute *action 1* in response to a child that performed the disgust expression in the "telepathic box".

Table 5. Behavior matrix after first iteration. Cells represent weighted probability values of the robot to execute an action (rows) for a given expression performed by a child in the "telepathic box" (columns). $*^i$ cell's value was changed by iteration i

	Despise	Happiness	Anger	Sadness	Disgust	Surprise
Action 1	1.00	1.00	1.00	1.00	0.71^{*1}	1.00
Action 2	1.00	1.00	1.00	1.00	1.00	1.00
Action 3	1.00	1.00	1.00	1.00	1.00	1.00
Action 4	1.00	1.00	1.00	1.00	1.00	1.00
Action 5	1.00	1.00	1.00	1.00	1.00	1.00
Action 6	1.00	1.00	1.00	1.00	1.00	1.00

Table 6 presents the matrix values after four iteration rounds. In the first iteration a child expressed *disgust* in the "telepathic box", leading the robot to execute *action 1*, related to *happiness*, as presented in Table 4. Then, in average, the other children chose, through the RFID emojis, a **different expression** of the one performed by the child in the "telepathic box". Thus, the weight for *action 1* was **decreased**, *i.e.*, it was not a good action to be associated to the disgust expression for this group of children.

In the second iteration, a child expressed *happiness* in the "telepathic box", leading the robot to execute *action 3*, related to *disgust*. Similarly to the first iteration, in average the other children chose, through the RFID emojis, a **different expression** of the one performed by the child in the "telepathic box". Thus, the weight for *action 3* was **decreased** in the *happiness* column of the matrix.

Table 6. Behavior matrix after the fourth iteration. Cells represent weighted probability values of the robot to execute an action (rows) for a given expression performed by the child in the "telepathic box" (columns). ^{*i} cell's value was changed by iteration i

	Despise	Happiness	Anger	Sadness	Disgust	Surprise
Action 1	1.00	1.00	0.60^{*3}	1.00	0.71^{*1}	1.00
Action 2	1.00	1.00	0.60^{*3}	1.00	1.00	1.00
Action 3	1.00	0.71^{*2}	0.60^{*3}	1.00	1.00	1.00
Action 4	1.00	0.71^{*4}	0.60^{*3}	1.00	1.00	1.00
Action 5	1.00	1.00	1.40^{*3}	1.00	1.00	1.00
Action 6	1.00	1.00	0.60^{*3}	1.00	1.00	1.00

In the third iteration, a child expressed *anger* in the "telepathic box", leading the robot to execute *action 5*, related to *anger*. Then, in average, the other children chose, through the RFID emojis, the **same expression** of the one performed by the child in the "telepathic box", *i.e.*, the *anger* expression. Therefore, the behavior matrix had increased the value related to *action 5* in the *anger* column, also decreasing the values of the other actions in the same column, once there was a correspondence between the expression performed by the child in the "telepathic box" and the expression chosen by the other children.

In the fourth iteration a child expressed *happiness* in the "telepathic box", leading the robot to execute *action 4*, related to *anger*. Then, in average, the other children chose, through the RFID emojis, a **different expression** of the one performed by the child in the "telepathic box". Thus, the weight for *action 4* was **decreased** in the *happiness* column.

After 12 iterations, the behavior matrix presented a slow but consistent convergence, by attributing higher weights to the actions that represent the emotional expressions, as planned by the researchers. It is important to mention that this (12) is still a low number of iterations for convergence purpose. Scenarios with larger number of actions, including various action alternatives for a given emotion expression, are necessary to a more precise evaluation of the behavior matrix.

4.2 Children's Behavior Analysis

In the Group 2 study, 12 children were present, thus leading to 12 iteration rounds. For each iteration, 11 children should choose what facial expression they thought the child in the "telepathic box" had performed. They used RFID emojis to indicate their choices (*cf.* Sect. 3.3).

Figure 6 shows the number of different emoji expressions chosen by the children in Group 2 in each of the 12 iterations. It is possible to observe that none of the iterations had an unanimity in the expression's choice. Iterations 1 and 8 presented the lowest diversity in the choices with 3 different expressions chosen.

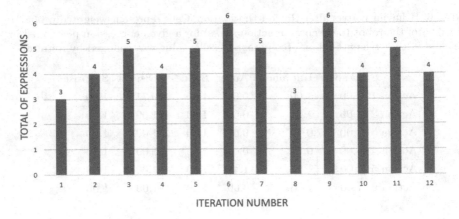

Fig. 6. Number of different expressions chosen by the children in Group 2 in each iteration. For example, in iteration 8 a total of 3 different expressions were chosen by at least one child through the RFID emoji. On its turn, in iteration 6 all possible expressions were chosen.

Figure 7 presents (in blue) the total number of choices related to each expression, considering all iterations. The max number (132 choices), was calculated multiplying the number of iterations (12) by the number of choices in each iteration (11). It also presents (in orange), the total number of iterations in which each expression was chosen by at least one child.

On its turn, Fig. 8 shows the frequency of children's choices related to each expression in each iteration. For each iteration, the expression drawn and performed by the child in the "telepathic box" is indicated in a black label, whereas the action performed by the robot is indicated in a blue label. For example, the disgust expression was performed by the child in the "telepathic box" in iterations 1 and 9, and the robot did not execute this action in any iteration. Also, in iterations 1 and 9, respectively 3 and 2 children chose RFIDs emojis related to the disgust expression, meaning they believed the child in the "telepathic box" had performed the disgust expression.

Additionally, also through the analysis of Fig. 8, it is possible to infer that the expression with the highest number of votes was equivalent to the one performed **by the child** in the "telepathic box" in 25% (3 of 12) of the cases (specifically iterations 3, 7 and 10). On the other hand, in 75% (9 of 12) of the cases (specifically iterations 1, 2, 3, 4, 7, 8, 9, 10 and 11) the expression with the highest number of votes was equivalent to the one performed **by the robot**.

Finally, we observe that in three iterations (4, 8 and 11) a consensus was reached, *i.e.*, the majority of children chose the same RFID emoji. In all of these iterations the emoji chosen corresponds to the action performed by the robot.

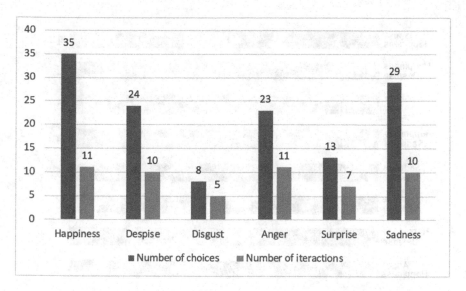

Fig. 7. In blue, the total number, considering all iterations, that each expression was chosen by the children in Group 2 (max = 132). In orange, the number of iterations in which that expression was chosen by at least one child (max = 12). (Color figure online)

5 Discussion

Kaipainen *et al.* [12] proposes, as a contrast to the standard conceptualization of human-computer interaction, an **enactive** relationship between the individual and technology. On that approach, an enactive system would consider the impact of the technology on the human agent as well as the effect of the human experience on the technology [12]. This relates to the ubiquitous computing approach proposed by Weiser [18,19], which predicts a seamless interaction with technology, that adapts itself accordingly to the environment characteristics.

Pushing forward the state-of-the-art, this investigation aimed at understanding how a group of people can dynamically and seamlessly interact with technology underlying socioenactive systems enriched by ontology aspects regarding emotional expressions (research question **RQ1**). For this purpose, our research scenario involved an educational environment with two different groups (Group 1 and Group 2) of 4–5 years old children (N = 25 in total) participating in proposed activities supported by an educational robot. Our robot was programmed to perform a set of actions mimicking some emotional human expressions: happiness, sadness, disgust, surprise, anger and despise.

In the carried out workshops, a series of iterative sessions were conducted, consisting of the following steps: a child secretly performs one of the mapped emotional expressions to a camera; the expression is identified and is input into the system; the system identifies, for that moment, which action must be executed by the robot; other children hypothesize which expression led the robot

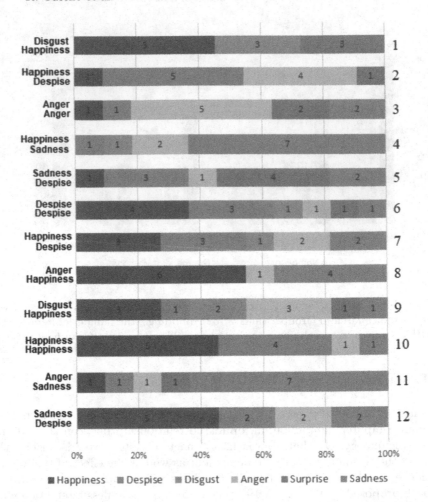

Fig. 8. For each iteration (1 to 12), the horizontal bars represent the number of participants whom chose each expression. The left labels indicate the expression drawn for each iteration (in black) and the action executed by the robot (in red). For example, in iteration 1: the expression performed by the child in the "telepathic box" was disgust; the action executed by the robot was happiness; 5 children chose happiness and; 3 children chose disgust and other 3 chose surprise. (Color figure online)

to take that action; responses are inserted into the system, starting another iterative cycle.

In summary, answering the research question **RQ2**, we observed in Group 2 some patterns in the actions and behavior performed by the children as our key findings:

- **Diversity of choices for the emotion expression done by the robot:** We observed a lack of unanimity in the interpretation of the expression made by the robot. For instance, the group had 4 and 5 different emotion expressions chosen in 8 iterations (out of 12). This result could be attributed in part to the difficulty of the task, considering emotion and its expression through interpretation of the behavior of a robot is not trivial, especially for children of that age. Moreover, there was the complexity of the ontology algorithm in getting input from the audience to rebuild the robot's behavior in the iterative feedback cycle, which could have made the emotional situation even harder to grasp.

- **Happiness is the king/queen!** The choice of happiness as a response for interpreting the robot's action (or the expression supposedly made by the child in the telepathic box to be reproduced by the robot) was present in 11 of the 12 iterations. This could be interpreted in part as a reflex of the pleasure and excitement children were experiencing in the activity, with the robot's actions in the narrative scenario presented to them. It seems that children tended to see happiness more frequently than the other emotions.
- **Capturing the robot's emotion expression:** A relevant result relative to the interpretation of the robot emotion was observed. Instead of guessing the emotion the kid in the telepathic box did, children were very good in guessing the expression the robot was expressing. In nine, out of 12 iterations, the expression most chosen by the children was the same actually performed by the robot. This means the action of the robot as a system output was characterizing very well the intended emotion in its behavior.

Overall, several lessons could be learned from this study, that should be addressed in further investigations. Some approaches should be useful in dealing with the many complexities present in our research scenario. The scenario was created for children's interaction with a robot, who learns with the children's interpretation of the emotion expressed in the robot's behavior. This is clearly a socioenactive system scenario, as the enactive and the social aspects of children's enaction are present.

Although the system enactive loop was very consistently performed as there were actions coming from the audience that fed the system, shaping the next system's actions, some fine tuning in the algorithm is still needed. The social aspect of interaction in the enactive loop was consistently considered by the ontology algorithm to deal with what that specific group understands as a particular emotion expression. Nevertheless, some adjustments in parameters are still required to cope with the learning aspect of the algorithm.

Besides the ontology system algorithm, other aspects deserve our attention. Working with emotions and their expression, especially in children context might need more granular treatments. For example, reducing the set of emotions could help in making more visible the children's responses. The joint behavior of children in expressing or interpreting emotions should be another aspect to explore, going further in understanding their 'choices' of the emojis which better represent the robot's action.

This work contributed to understanding some socioenactive aspects of interaction in technology-enhanced scenarios. The lessons learned in this investigation is certainly helpful for informing new scenarios and going further to thoroughly advance the state-of-the-art.

6 Conclusion

The way of designing coupled interactive systems integrating technology and humans in a less deterministic fashion deserves huge research efforts. This paper expanded the enactive concept to a socioenactive vision. Based on the features for enactive systems, we defined a set of guidelines to design socioenactive systems. An instance of such system was implemented in an educational scenario, in which several iterations generated data to shape the behavior of the system according to the meaning given by the children in the conducted workshop dynamics, leading to a non-deterministic behavior of the system. We found several patterns in the children's actions and behaviors. We consider this study as a first of several efforts in investigating socioenactive systems in practice, shedding light and supporting further development related to this topic. Future work involves further analyses over the user experience in the context of our study. The analysis of such data might provide additional support and evidences to conduct additional studies in the design and development of socioenactive systems.

Acknowledgments. This research is supported by São Paulo Research Foundation (FAPESP)[4], grants #2015/16528-0, #2014/07502-4, #2018/06416-8 and #2017/02325-5. Additional support was provided by the Brazilian Federal Agency for Support and Evaluation of Graduate Education (CAPES), the National Council of Technological and Scientific Development (CNPq) under grant #306272/2017-2, the University of Campinas (UNICAMP), the Nucleus of Informatics Applied to Education of the University of Campinas (NIED), and the Federal Institute of Education, Science and Technology of São Paulo (IFSP).

References

1. Bruner, J.S.: Toward a Theory of Instruction, 177 p. Belknap Press, Cambridge (1966). $3.95. Bull. Natl. Assoc. Second. Sch. Princ. **50**(309), 304–312 (1966). https://doi.org/10.1177/019263656605030929
2. Critical acclaim for research methods in human computer interaction. In: Lazar, J., Feng, J.H., Hochheiser, H. (eds.) Research Methods in Human Computer Interaction, 2nd edn, pp. v–viii. Morgan Kaufmann, Boston (2017). http://www.sciencedirect.com/science/article/pii/B9780128053904099866
3. Division of early childhood and complementary education of the university of campinas (dedic), January 2019. http://www.dgrh.unicamp.br/dedic/prodecad
4. mBot: Ideal robot for children to build and code, January 2019. https://www.makeblock.com/steam-kits/mbot

---

[4] The opinions, hypotheses, and conclusions or recommendations expressed in this material are the responsibility of the authors and do not necessarily reflect the views of FAPESP.

5. Bonacin, R., Calado, I., dos Reis, J.C.: A metamodel for supporting interoperability in heterogeneous ontology networks. In: Liu, K., Nakata, K., Li, W., Baranauskas, C. (eds.) ICISO 2018. IAICT, vol. 527, pp. 187–196. Springer, Cham (2018). https://doi.org/10.1007/978-3-319-94541-5_19
6. Dos Reis, J.C., Bonacin, R., Baranauskas, M.C.C.: A semiotic-based approach to the design of web ontologies. In: 12th International Conference on Informatics and Semiotics in Organisations (ICISO 2010), pp. 60–67 (2010)
7. Dos Reis, J.C., Bonacin, R., Baranauskas, M.C.C.: An assisted process for building semiotic web ontology. In: 13th International Conference on Informatics and Semiotics in Organisations (ICISO 2011), pp. 167–174 (2011)
8. Dos Reis, J.C., Bonacin, R., Baranauskas, M.C.C.: Constructing web ontologies informed by semantic analysis method. In: 13th International Conference on Enterprise Information Systems (ICEIS 2011), pp. 203–206 (2011)
9. Effenberger, T., Pelanek, R.: Towards making block-based programming activities adaptive. In: Proceedings of the Fifth Annual ACM Conference on Learning at Scale, L@S 2018, pp. 13:1–13:4. ACM, New York (2018). https://doi.org/10.1145/3231644.3231670
10. Gruber, T.R.: Toward principles for the design of ontologies used for knowledge sharing. Int. J. Hum. Comput. Stud. **43**(5–6), 907–928 (1995)
11. Unicode Inc.: Unicode 11 emoji fonts (2019). http://www.unicode.org/emoji/charts-11.0/emoji-list.html
12. Kaipainen, M., Normak, P., Niglas, K., Kippar, J., Laanpere, M.: Soft ontologies, spatial representations and multi-perspective explorability. Expert Syst. **25**(5), 474–483 (2008)
13. Kaipainen, M., et al.: Enactive systems and enactive media: embodied human-machine coupling beyond interfaces. Leonardo **44**, 433–438 (2011)
14. Kalyanpur, A., Golbeck, J., Banerjee, J., Hendler, J.: OWL: capturing semantic information using a standardized web ontology language. Multiling. Comput. Technol. Mag. **15**(7) (2004)
15. Pittermann, J., Pittermann, A.: A data-oriented approach to integrate emotions in adaptive dialogue management. In: IUI (2007)
16. Pöhner, N., Hennecke, M.: The teacher's role in educational robotics competitions. In: Proceedings of the 18th Koli Calling International Conference on Computing Education Research, Koli Calling 2018, pp. 34:1–34:2. ACM, New York (2018). https://doi.org/10.1145/3279720.3279753
17. Tikka, P., Vuori, R., Kaipainen, M.: Narrative logic of enactive cinema: obsession. Digit. Creat. **17**(4), 205–212 (2006)
18. Weiser, M.: Some computer science issues in ubiquitous computing. Commun. ACM **36**(7), 75–84 (1993). https://doi.org/10.1145/159544.159617
19. Weiser, M.: Human-computer interaction. In: The Computer for the 21st Century, pp. 933–940. Morgan Kaufmann Publishers Inc., San Francisco (1995). http://dl.acm.org/citation.cfm?id=212925.213017

Gender Difference in Language Learning with Technology

Yen-ju Hou[⊠]

Shu-Zen Junior College of Medicine and Management, Kaohsiung City, Taiwan
yunju@ms.szmc.edu.tw

Abstract. Nowadays, mobile-assisted technology has been widely adopted to promote learning outcomes in various realms. This study sought to determine how gender affects students in evaluation of the use of mobile-assisted tools, such as Kahoot!, Socrative and Classdojo on English learning. It involved in 143 learners of English as a foreign language (EFL) at a junior college in southern Taiwan. Regarding to feedback about the use of Kahoot!, female students strongly agreed its benefits than male students, especially in helping organize important information from reading texts. Compared to Kahoot!, female students felt less stressful than males because they can respond to questions via Socrative by their own speed. In addition, females showed higher agreement than males that everyone is required to answer questions helps them check their comprehension. In terms of overall perception of using mobile-assisted tools, students showed positive attitudes of using them in reading courses. The finding is interesting that females reported higher agreement and expectation in various situations than males on learning with mobile-assisted tools. For instance, females showed more positive perceptions than that of male students on helping them pay more attention in lectures, perform better learning outcomes, build confidences to study well in class and receive better scores on exams, understand the lectures well, and monitor their learning performance instantly. Despite of benefits of mobile-assisted tools in education, another important element for such tools on creating effective and efficient teaching is the ease of use, which reduces both teachers and students' loads and time on familiarizing the applications. Mobile-assisted tools mentioned in the study, including Kahoot!, Socrative, and Classdojo, provide easy functions that increase users' acceptance level. In addition, those applications were free of charge that increases accessibility and application for teachers to integrate into their teaching practice.

Keywords: Gender difference · Mobile-assisted learning · Kahoot! · Socrative · EFL

1 Introduction

1.1 Background of the Study

The study was conducted in at a junior college in Southern Taiwan, and participated students are English major students who took literacy course from the researcher. Since

© Springer Nature Switzerland AG 2019
P. Zaphiris and A. Ioannou (Eds.): HCII 2019, LNCS 11590, pp. 256–265, 2019.
https://doi.org/10.1007/978-3-030-21814-0_19

the normal class size is about 50 to 60 students in an English classroom, it makes it challenging for the teacher to monitor all students' learning. Moreover, reading involves complex and cognitive process that requires advanced level of thinking skills [1]. The complexity of reading text might have negative impacts on learners of English as a Foreign Language (EFL), and decrease their interest on reading. Thus, increasing English learners' motivation on literacy reading and comprehension is the purpose of the study.

To this purpose, Kahoot! was adopted in the English classroom. Kahoot! is a game-based learning platform that assesses learning by answering different types of questions correctly. In addition to motivation, questions are used as major classroom task to enhancing students' comprehension since it was proved to improve students' motivation and comprehension [2, 3]. Studies have proved significant effects of Kahoot! on promoting learning motivation [4–6]. However, after researching current studies that are done in Taiwan, it is found that most studies on teaching with technology have centered on elementary and junior high school students, especially in the area of science, social science and computer. How game-based platform affects language learning has not been discussed much in this decade.

As game-based learning gains more and more attention among educational institutions, this article sought to determine how gender affects students in evaluation of the use of Kahoot! and their comprehension from game-based learning.

1.2 English Education in Taiwan

In Taiwan, English has been officially recognized as core subject that is taught since third grade. Therefore, learning English becomes a trend among students and is considered an essential skill either in school or at workplace. However, English achievement seems not to be enhanced steadily as educators expect [7], and educators begin to investigate the reason why overall English skill is not promoted. English education during junior and senior high stage is mainly text-oriented, that students learn to memorize language rather than to use language. Thus, students show less motivation on learning English or show more desires to enhance English [7]. Educators points out that the lack of educational resources and inputs lead to a learning gap because at-risk students might not have opportunities to involve intensively in English environment and receive better education [7].

1.3 Gender, Language Learning, and Technology

Nowadays, how technology integrates into classroom receives much attention, and more and more teachers are trying to adopt game-based software as a means in teaching language. However, certain software might favor particular goals in language learning. Student learning could be affected by their perception and attitudes toward the use of technology in learning [7].

As English has treated as the lingua franca around the world, it plays essential role in various fields of our lives, including workplace and education [8]. People arises interest and intention in enhancing their English proficiency. In terms of language development, second language learning could be influenced by various factors, such as readers, text, the teacher, sociocultural [1, 9, 10]. Among, gender has been one of the most common investigated factors that affect foreign language learning [11].

Science has proved men and women think and process information differently [12]. Studies showed that female students performed better in language learning than male students [13]. Delić et al. [11] synthesized a number of studies on the effects of gender, confirmed that female students are more motived than male students in learning foreign language and obtaining better scores. Despite better achievement of female students, gender difference seems not to be significant in certain language learning process. That is, female and male students favor particular strategies in learning language, which might contribute to their greater performance in the process of language learning [11, 14, 15]. It is saying that both females and males have preferences.

When it comes to technology, gender has been an important issue that determines the success of integration of technology in learning [16]. In addition, high portion of females enters in the workplace, and females seem to receive disadvantage in certain area, such as education and workplace, because of discrimination and less skills in technology and engineer [16, 17]. In Venkatesh and Morris's [18] study investigated employees about using technology model, it found that females seem to use the technology that needs less effort and difficulty since they report high level of anxiety in computer than males. Gender difference exists in the way they use the technology. Females was found to spend more time in social network than man, and use social media as productive tool, whereas male students use it for the purpose of entertainment [19, 20].

Apart from the gender difference in technology preference, studies have been done to investigate how technology is helpful on various fields of learning performance [21, 22]. Schools plays essential role in developing students' learning performance because of environment where they negotiate and interact with peers. Through computer programs, it creates "a nonthreatening language learning environment where second language learners will not feel insecure to practice the target language and to make and correct their errors without embarrassment or anxiety" [23, p. 86]. However, based on Krashen's input hypothesis, when learners are given advanced level of comprehension, they can gain the meaning and structures without instruction. That is to say that effective learning requires inputs from both the level the learner is at and the advanced level.

Studies on the benefits of teaching with technology, synthesized by Jian [7], showed that technology-assisted teaching delivers information fast and effectively, and increases motivation on language learning by integration of words and visual graphs. Visual resources, such as logo and simulations, help to raise and build children's level of understanding on concepts more quickly. Visualization is helpful to increase retention [24] and to make connections to the prior knowledge for storing in long-term memory. For instance, software programs can help beginning-level ESLs to connect words and sentences to pictures or animations in context of a specific setting to assist comprehension [23].

Among various educational online platforms, game-based platforms are adopted for creating interactions between teachers and students. Such game-based platforms were found beneficial in classrooms, include helping teachers monitor students' learning progress, adjusting teaching speed and methods, creating teacher-student or student-student interactions [22], and offering student-centered learning environments [25]. In Taiwan, game-based platforms, such as Kahoot! and Plickers, have been proven to increase students' motivation and satisfaction and concentration [5, 26, 27]. That is, it appears common for teachers to adopt technology in their teaching to promote class participation and learning achievement.

2 Methodology

2.1 Research Design and Participants

Surveys were used in the study in order to investigate students' language learning motivation and feedback toward the use of mobile-assisted tools in English reading courses. The study was conducted at a private five-year medical junior college in Southern Taiwan in the spring of 2018. Students who enroll in the five-year junior college are normally between 16 and 20 years of age. Approximately 145 students taught by the researcher participated in the study. Participants were all English majors with lower-intermediate to intermediate English level (CEFR A2-B1 level). By removing the uncompleted surveys, valid samples were reduced to a total of 136 students, including 30 (22%) males and 106 (78%) females. The reading courses were taught for 2 h a week for 16 weeks. The participants were around 16 to 19 years old, and Chinese is their native language.

2.2 Instruments

The research designed a 31-item questions dealing with students' experience about using mobile-assisted technology in reading class, such as difficulty in applying the technique or support in understanding reading material. In addition, the research adopted 16 out of 21 questions designed by Wang [5] to find out learners' feeling toward teaching through such mobile-assisted technologies, with teaching interaction, engagement, self-efficacy and degree of learning satisfaction. Participants responded to each statement by using 5-point scale, from 1(not at all describes me) to 5 (best describes me). The questionnaire was done in the end of the semester.

2.3 Mobile Assisted Tools

Mobile-assisted tools, including Kahoot!, Socrative and Classdojo were used mainly to access students' comprehension and to enhance their participation and attention on reading through Kahoot!, Socrative and Classdojo. Kahoot! was mainly used to access student's comprehension by responding to multiple-choice questions, and used as review games for less than 10 min before the end of class. Socrative was used to train students' thinking and creativity by collecting short answers to questions, whereas Classdojo was used as a tool for classroom management and individual learning progress by marking students' performance in classroom.

2.4   Procedures

A 16-week period of teaching using mobile-assisted tools was given to literacy courses with English-major students. In order to know the feedbacks toward the use of Mobile-assisted tools, a self-reported survey was given to students at the end of semester. At the first week, the teacher introduced of mobile-assisted tools used in the study. Students were asked to preview assigned text every week, and expected to complete a set of questions during class discussion session. The questions contain different level of cognitive skills to check their comprehension. During discussion, all students were expected to offer their own ideas and come out a conclusion. Then, the teacher led the discussion for each question, and asked further questions or feedbacks toward students' response. The choice to pick specific mobile-assisted tool could be adjusted depends on what learning output the teacher intends to create.

3   Findings

3.1   Gender Difference of Attitudes Toward the Use of Kahoot!, Socrative and Classdojo in Literacy Reading

Regarding to feedback about the use of Kahoot!, female students strongly agreed its benefits than male students, especially in helping organize important information from reading texts ($p < .01$, item 2). Compared to Kahoot!, female students felt less stressful than males because they can respond to questions via Socrative by their own speed ($p < .05$). In addition, females showed higher agreement than males that everyone is required to answer questions helps them check their comprehension ($p < .01$, item 27). In terms of using mobile phones in learning, the finding failed to revealed significant difference on gender, but it showed that females seem to express greater level of acceptance using smartphones to complete classroom tasks (item 17). Apart from responding tools, more females agreed that Classdojo increased desires of getting higher score through competition ($p < .05$, item 21) (Table 1).

Table 1. Frequency summary of student attitudes toward the use of Kahoot!, Socrative and Classdojo in reading class

Item	Gender	M	SD	Sig.
I think Kahoot! helps me organize important information from reading texts (item 2)	Male	4.25	.45	.000
	Female	4.53	.50	
I am not familiar or unfavorable using smartphone to answer questions (item 17)	Male	2.91	1.16	.796
	Female	2.23	1.31	
Classdojo increases desires of getting higher score through accumulating scores I earn in class (item 21)	Male	4.16	.38	.021
	Female	4.33	.56	
Compared with Kahoot!, answering questions at their own speed using *Socrative* was less stressful (item 26)	Male	3.25	1.35	.039
	Female	3.77	1.03	
Socrative that everyone being required to answer questions helps me check whether I understand the story (item 27)	Male	3.41	1.08	.005
	Female	4.14	.71	

3.2   Students' Overall Attitudes Toward the Use of Mobile-Assisted Tools in Reading Class

In terms of overall perception of using mobile-assisted tools, most students showed positive attitudes on using mobile-assisted tools in reading courses. The finding is interesting that females reported higher agreement and expectation in various situations than males on learning with mobile-assisted tools. For instance, females showed more positive perceptions than that of male students on helping them pay more attention in lectures ($p < .01$, item 39), perform better learning outcomes ($p < .05$, item 41), build confidences to study well in class ($p < .05$, item 42) and receive better scores on exams ($p < .01$, item 43), understand the lectures well ($p < .01$, item 44), and monitor their learning performance instantly ($p < .01$, item 46).

When it comes to interaction between the teacher and students, females reported higher agreement than males on mobile-assisted tools to attract their attention in class lectures ($p < .01$, item 32). Besides, both female and male students thought integration of MALL tools into their learning made it a diverse teaching method ($p < .05$, item 45) (Table 2).

Table 2. Frequency summary of student attitudes toward the use of mobile-assisted tools

Item	Gender	M	SD	Sig.
Teacher-student interaction				
mobile-assisted tools attract my attention(item 32)	Male	4.16	.38	.000
	Female	4.36	.48	
I would love to answer teacher's questions when using mobile-assisted tools (item 34)	Male	4.16	.38	.000
	Female	4.36	.48	
Learning engagement				
I will pay more attention on lectures when teacher uses mobile-assisted tools (item 39)	Male	4.16	.38	.000
	Female	4.42	.49	
Self-efficacy				
I can perform better learning outcomes when teacher uses mobile-assisted tools (item 41)	Male	4.25	.45	.012
	Female	4.39	.49	
I have confidences on learning the content well when teacher uses mobile-assisted tools (item 42)	Male	4.25	.45	.014
	Female	4.41	.49	
I have confidences to get better scores on exams when teacher uses mobile-assisted tools (item 43)	Male	4.25	.45	.001
	Female	4.42	.49	
Learning satisfaction				
The content becomes easier to understand when teacher uses mobile-assisted tools (item 44)	Male	4.16	.38	.000
	Female	4.44	.50	
The teaching method is diverse when teacher uses mobile-assisted tools (item 45)	Male	4.25	.45	.012
	Female	4.39	.49	
I can monitor my learning progress instantly when teacher uses mobile-assisted tools (item 46)	Male	4.16	.38	.000
	Female	4.42	.49	

4 Discussion and Conclusion

Literacy reading involving complexity and lexical difficulty could be challenging for English learners, and makes learner less motivated in reading [4]. Since the motivation has always contributed to language learning [28], the study adopted three kinds of mobile-assisted tools in reading courses to promote students' motivation as well as comprehension. The findings showed that females reported higher mean than males on how mobile-assisted tools are helpful in their learning. In particular, they stated that Kahoot! helps organizing information from reading texts, and Socrative is less stressful than Kahoot! when responding questions at their own speed. The finding is not surprising that students reported higher level of desires and attitudes toward the use of technology in language learning. In addition, participating students, particularly female students, embraced mobile-assisted tools in their learning for promoting teacher-student interaction, class engagement, and self-efficacy, and this finding was supported by Teng's [29] and Ke's [30] study. In Ke's [30] study on junior high students in Taiwan, Kahoot! was found essential to improve engagement and motivation on learning English. Moreover, it's not surprise that females showed positive attitudes toward mobile-assisted tools in English learning more than male students because female students are confirmed to be more motived than male students in learning foreign language and obtaining better scores [11].

As for smartphone comfort level of use in learning, gender difference was not significantly appeared. Still, female students perceived more acceptability than males on using smartphone to answer multiple choice questions since males are often considered to have advantage in technology and engineer [18]. However, Kay's [31] study found gender differences disappeared in computer comfort level of use and male students showed more positive attitudes than females on overall learning process. Though most students perceived favorable attitudes about using Kahoot! or Socrative, some of them reported unfamiliar or unfavorable attitudes toward using mobile phones to respond questions. Thus, it raised concerns about anxieties suffered by mobile phone users [32]. Students might be anxious and frustrated because of no access to the Internet, or phone with insufficient functioned to run programs well. As studies have proved that the benefits of Kahoot! or Socrative on learning [21, 22], such mobile-assisted tools were used as a mean to engage students in lectures and offer students opportunity to interact with peers. In the study, the research found the ideal time for better learning and classroom management was about 10 min on mobile-assisted application, and has it done as review game on the last part of lessons. Moreover, it is suggested to invite students to design questions and use in Kahoot! platform to promote students' thinking and comprehension and engagement [33]. Kahoot! is beneficial for learning because it combines several elements, including game-based competition, music, and visual resources, that are helpful to raise attention to the concept and to make impression to the concept. Music has been considered an effective and powerful element that affects emotional and intellectual simulation, and then facilitates learning and cognitive process [24]. As students are involved in learning process, they are likely to engage actively in learning. As for those without mobile phone or Internet access, they were allowed to submit answers by pairs. In this way, it also created student interaction and helped encourage shy students' participation in sharing answers.

Technology and education are largely converging on this new technological era and many of strategies and study have been proposed about the essential of computer in promoting learning and the need of computer competence [34]. For students we are facing now are so-called Z generation who stands for young age with widespread usage of Internet [6], Internet-related activities become essential part in their daily life. Thus, emerging educational technology into curriculum and embedding certain level of the sense of technology are the demands and enforcements for faculty, educators, and students.

References

1. Celce-Murcia, M.: Teaching English as a Second or Foreign Language, 3rd edn. Heinle & Heinle, Boston (2001)
2. Choi, I., Land, S.M., Turgeon, A.J.: Scaffolding peer-questioning strategies to facilitate meta-cognition during online small group discussion. Instr. Sci. **33**(5–6), 483–511 (2005)
3. Zillmann, D., Cantor, J.R.: Induction of curiosity via rhetorical questions and its effects on the learning of factual materials. Br. J. Educ. Psychol. **43**, 172–180 (1973)
4. Hou, Y.: Integration of Kahoot into EFL classroom. In: Stephanidis, C. (ed.) HCI 2018. CCIS, vol. 852, pp. 31–37. Springer, Cham (2018). https://doi.org/10.1007/978-3-319-92285-0_5
5. Wang, C.C.: Correlations of teaching through interactive response system with teaching interaction, engagement, self-efficacy and degree of learning satisfaction. Unpublished Master's thesis, National Taipei University of Education, Taiwan (2017)
6. Kuo, C.L., Chuang, Y.H.: Kahoot: applications and effects in education. J. Nurs. **65**(6), 13–19 (2018). https://doi.org/10.6224/JN.201812_65(6).03
7. Jian, Y.F.: The impact of teachers' adoption and integration of information and communication technology into english teaching on seventh graders' motivation, learning strategies, and academic achievement. Unpublished Master's thesis, Chung Hua University, HsinChu, Taiwan (2014)
8. Wu, Y.A.: English language teaching in China: trends and challenges. TESOL Q. **35**(1), 191–194 (2001)
9. Cook, V.: Second Language Learning and Language Teaching, 3rd edn. Arnold, London (2001)
10. Maria, K.: Reading Comprehension Instruction: Issues and Strategies. York Press, Parkton (1990)
11. Delić, H., Bećirović, S., Brdarević-Čeljo, A.: Effects of grade level and gender on foreign language learning process in Bosnian high schools. Int. J. Educ. Policy Res. Rev. **5**, 83–89 (2018). https://doi.org/10.15739/IJEPRR.18.010
12. Collom, K.: Does Gender Impact Language Learning? (2015). https://www.languagetrainers.co.uk/blog/2015/11/05/does-gender-impact-language learning/. Accessed 7 Dec 2018
13. Voyer, D., Voyer, S.D.: Gender differences in scholastic achievement: a meta-analysis. Psychol. Bull. **140**(4), 1174–1204 (2014)

14. Bećirović, S., Brdarević-Čeljo, A., Sinanović, J.: The use of metacognitive reading strategies among students at international Burch University: a case study. Eur. J. Contemp. Educ. **6**(4), 645–655 (2017)

15. Lee, M.L.: A study of the selection of reading strategies among genders by EFL college students. Procedia-Soc. Behav. Sci. **64**, 310–319 (2012)

16. Shin, I.S., Go, E., Harbke, C.R., Ravikumar, P., McDonald, B., Zbeeb, K.: Evaluations of interactive learning tools among engineering students: effects of grit and gender (2018). https://docs.lib.purdue.edu/aseeil-insectionconference/2018/assess/3.   https://doi.org/10. 5703/1288284316861. Accessed 7 Dec 2018

17. Brussevich, M., Dabla-Norris, E., Kamunge, C., Karnane, P., Khalid, S., Kochhar, K.: Gender, technology, and the future of work. Staff Discussion Notes No. 18/07 (2018)

18. Venkatesh, V., Morris, M.G.: Why don't men ever stop to ask for directions? Gender, social influence, and their role in technology acceptance and usage behavior. MIS Q. **24**(1), 115–139 (2000)

19. Ananya, G., Sraboni, D.: Gender differences in technology usage - a literature review. J. Bus. Manag. **4**, 51 59 (2016)

20. Flad, K.: The influence of social networking participation on student academic performance across gender line. Counselor Education Master's theses: 31 (2010)

21. Wu, T.H.: Exploring pre-service elementary teachers' intention toward using interactive response system in teaching: a technology acceptance model approach. Unpublished Master's thesis, National Taipei University of Education, Taipei, Taiwan (2017)

22. Huang, C.P.: A study of IRS integrated instruction design-implemented with Minnan dialect course in elementary school. Unpublished Master's thesis, Hsing Wu University, New Taipei City, Taiwan (2016)

23. Butler-Pascoe, M.E., Wiburg, K.: Technology and Teaching English Language Learners. Allyn and Bacon, Boston (2003)

24. Sousa, D.A.: How the Brain Learns. Corwin Press, Thousand Oaks (2006)

25. Chiang, Y.F.: Effects of the flipped classroom model of elementary students with interactive response system on math learning. Unpublished Master's thesis, Chung Hua University, HsinChu, Taiwan (2016)

26. Lee, C.C.: The research on the learning effect by integrating an online instant response system into earth science teaching-a case study for the middle school students from the rural area. Unpublished Master's thesis, National Taiwan Normal University, Taipei, Taiwan (2017)

27. Yang, T.H.: An elementary educational study on chinese stroke real-time response system. Unpublished Master's thesis, National Taichung University of Education, Taichung, Taiwan (2017)

28. Dörnyei, Z., Ushioda, E.: Motivation, language identities and the L2 self: future research directions. In: Dörnyei, Z., Ushioda, E. (eds.) Motivation, Language Identity and the L2 Self, pp. 350–356 (2009)

29. Teng, S.J.: Study on effects of mathematical learning with interactive response system on first graders in elementary school. Unpublished Master's thesis, National Changhua University of Education, Changhua, Taiwan (2016)

30. Ke, T.H.: Integrating Kahoot! to improve student engagement: an action research study on an EFL junior high class. Unpublished Master's thesis, National Chengchi University, Taipei, Taiwan (2018)

31. Kay, R.H.: Examining gender differences in attitudes toward interactive classroom communications systems (ICCS). Comput. Educ. **52**(4), 730–740 (2009). https://doi.org/ 10.1016/j.compedu.2008.11.015

32. Dixit, S., Shukla, H., Bhagwat, A., Bindal, A., Goyal, A., Zaidi, A.K., Shrivastava, A.: A study to evaluate mobile phone dependence among students of a medical college and associated hospital of central India. Indian J. Community Med.: Official Publ. Indian Assoc. Prev. Soc. Med. **35**(2), 339–341 (2010)
33. Bryant, S.G., Correll, J.M., Clarke, B.M.: Fun with pharmacology: winning students over with Kahoot! game-based learning. J. Nurs. Educ. **57**(5), 320 (2018). https://doi.org/10.3928/01484834-20180420-15
34. Pearson, G., Young, A.T.: Technically Speaking: Why All Americans Need to Know More About Technology. National Academy of Engineering. National Research Council. National Academy Press, Washington, DC (2002)

Cognitive Load Levels While Learning with or Without a Pedagogical Agent

Madlen Müller-Wuttke[1]([⊠]) and Nicholas H. Müller[2]

[1] Technische Universität Chemnitz, Thüringer Weg 11,
09126 Chemnitz, Germany
madlen.mueller-wuttke@phil.tu-chemnitz.de
[2] Socio-Informatics and Societal Aspects of Digitalization,
Faculty of Computer Science and Business Information Systems,
University of Applied Sciences Würzburg-Schweinfurt, Würzburg, Germany
nicholas.mueller@fhws.de

Abstract. An eye-tracking study examining the benefits of a proactive human-computer-interaction has been conducted. Regarding the beneficial aspects of knowledge transfer, the data shows a clear benefit once the system has been enhanced by the so called electronic educational instance which tracks a user's gaze and thereby infers whether or not someone is actually looking at a screen while the e-learning software is conveying its knowledge. To further show how a physiological input might be used as a form of input, current literature of smoothing pupillary response data is discussed and a preliminary tool is presented. Due to this, pupillary data can be used to indicate cognitive load levels while learning and would therefore allow a proactive system to change the e-learning program accordingly.

Keywords: Pedagogical agent · E-learning · Proactive system · Cognitive load

1 Introduction

Forms of interaction with a learning system are still mostly limited to traditional forms of human computer interaction, like a keyboard and a mouse. Although there are a number of new technologies available to interact with a computer system and they are getting more affordable day by day, equipment like VR goggles, haptic interfaces or gestures in midair are still confined to specific niches. And while there are numerous advances in regards to how a topic is framed or in what way it is presented to the user, the main areas of research activity in electronic learning [1] and the validation of an e-learning application is most often limited to an analysis about the framing of given information, the appearance of the learning system or certain elements inside the environment (e.g. [2–4]).

But according to the media equation theory [11], humans have a tendency to actually use and behave in front of and towards a computer system, like within a human-to-human-interaction. Reeves and Nass tested this assumption by having participants work with a computer and then asked them to rate the system, once on the same system as they have previously worked with and another group on a different

© Springer Nature Switzerland AG 2019
P. Zaphiris and A. Ioannou (Eds.): HCII 2019, LNCS 11590, pp. 266–276, 2019.
https://doi.org/10.1007/978-3-030-21814-0_20

computer. This lead to the result of people being more 'nice' in their answers as long as they had to give their rating on the same as they worked on.

As our previous conceptual research has shown [8], human-computer-interaction should be able to profit from a non-verbal backchannel to the learning environment. This would enable a learning application to take environmental information into account. If a user is distracted or the environment is too noisy, this should be taken into account by the learning system – leading to pausing the conveyance of information or by offering to repeat a section, which might not have been sufficiently understood due to outside disturbances.

With this in mind we developed an electronic educational instance [9, 10] which is working as a plug-in component for already established applications. Due to this, the learning application is capable of checking for the gaze of a user and determine the focus of attention regarding the screen. Furthermore, by checking microphone levels, the application is able to analyze the noise level of the surroundings and decide whether or not it would be enough to just dial up the volume levels of an explanatory video- or audio-stream or if it would be beneficial for the learning success to pause the learning session, until the noise-level decreases.

Therefore, the system possesses an environmental-feedback-channel, leading to the inclusion of non-verbal human-computer-interaction possibilities and thereby leading to an interaction experience which is more closely related to a human-to-human-interaction, as stated in the media equation theory by Reeves and Nass [11]. The system would then be capable to analyze a situation as any real-world teacher would do and react to user specific deviations from the learning session. This is realized by using a common webcam and microphone, as is most of the time already built into current notebooks and tablets. For the presented study, the camera checks for the presence of two eyes and interprets this as being attentive towards the screen while the microphone filters out the audio from the learning application and is focused on background noises. As soon as one of the two criteria for pausing the application occurs, gaze away from the screen or noise levels too high, the content on screen is paused. In order to check for the persona effect, as discussed by Lester et al. [12], we used an SMI eye-tracker to reliably check for the specific areas of interest by the users, specifically our own pedagogical agent. The use of an eye-tracker in order to gain insights into user behavior during a learning session have often been used to validate the position of certain elements of learning applications.

One of the most commonly recorded metrics while recording eye-tracking-data is that of a pupil dilation. As Rosch and Vogel-Walcutt states [5], there appears to be a link between the size of a pupil and the current cognitive load level of a subject. Based on the research of Mathot et al. [6, 7], their algorithm for the extrapolation of cognitive load based pupil dilation was used to re-analyze the data of our study with 139 participants. Building on our earlier publications [8–10] we are going to report the results of the cognitive load levels while learning with our enhanced learning system. In theory, once being able to apply this calculation in real-time, which it is currently not, this could function as a third non-verbal feedback channel, enabling the system to check in real-time whether or not the current form of presentation is suitable for the individual learner. So, in theory, this would allow for the system, for example, to switch to another, more time consuming and more detail-oriented form of explanatory knowledge conveyance.

2 Eye-Tracking Study Regarding Pedagogical Agents

In order to test for this possibility of a cognitive load feedback channel, we re-examined data from a previous experiment about knowledge of the Dreamweaver software, during which we recorded the eye tracking data to check for the 'did-they-or-did-they-not' focus attention towards the pedagogical agent. In addition, we used this to test for the persona effect [12] by Lester et al., which should lead to a higher learning success as soon as there is a depicted agent visible on the screen. Four groups were tested (see Table 1 and Fig. 2).

Table 1. Experimental groups

Group 1	Depicted agent, with proactivity
Group 2	Depicted agent, without proactivity
Group 3	Audio-only agent, with proactivity
Group 4	Audio-only agent, without proactivity

The data is based on N = 74 undergraduate students from a study conducted in 2014 [13]. Participants were asked to take part in a second-task wizard-of-oz-experiment during which the proactive system of the EEI (see Fig. 1) would stop the e-learning software whenever the study participants were distracted by the second task. Once the training was completed, the volunteers had to apply their gained knowledge during a practical task session.

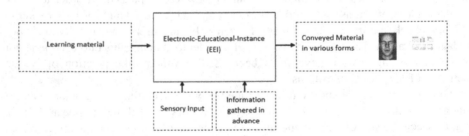

Fig. 1. The Electronic Educational Instance [9, 10] (EEI)

During the learning part of the study, we recorded the eye tracking data and during the apply knowledge phase of the study, we recorded whether or not the participants chose were able to apply their gained knowledge correctly or incorrectly and we recorded the mouse-track-distance in pixels, number of mouse clicks as well as the time until the subjects ended the experiment. In addition, participants took part in a multiple-

Fig. 2. Learning material and the group variations regarding the pedagogical agent [14]

choice questionnaire regarding their previous knowledge about the Dreamweaver software as well as a learning success test once the experiment was completed.

When checked with a Kruskal-Wallis test, the data shows a significant group difference regarding the AOI (Area-of-Interest) of the pedagogical agent ($H_{Agent}(3) = 41.74$, $p < .001$), but not regarding both the other, much bigger, AOIs regarding the learning material or the white space, meaning everything else on the screen ($H_{LerningMaterial}(3) = 3.46$; $H_{WhiteSpace}(3) = 2.83$). In addition, we checked with a Mann-Whitney test whether or not the two groups with a depicted agent showed a difference regarding their fixations towards the pedagogical agent, but they showed none ($U = 93$, $r = -.31$). Meaning, both groups with a depicted pedagogical agent did actually look at the agent while the groups with a blank space at the position of the agent did not.

Interestingly enough, the results (see Table 2) showed a significant group difference regarding the correct solution of the applied knowledge task ($H_{Solution}(3) = 9.55$, $p < .05$) but not regarding the mouse track or the time until completion ($H_{MousePath}(3) = 1.17$; $H_{Time}(3) = 5.44$; $H_{Clicks}(3) = .77$).

Table 2. Overview regarding mousepath, time, clicks and correct/incorrect solution [13]

	Mousepath	Time	Clicks	Correct	Wrong
Group 1	93917,34	00:07:32	120,43	16	5
Group 2	103404,83	00:08:54	116,7	9	11
Group 3	99358,96	00:06:28	116,7	18	2
Group 4	101946,50	00:07:34	124,8	11	9

It can be deduced that the two groups 1 and 3 (group 1 with the depicted agent and proactivity components activated, group 3 without a depicted agent, audio only, but proactive behavior as well) showed the best learning performance with the proactive behavior. In a comparison of these two groups, group 3, with no depicted agent, but with proactive behavior, appears at first sight to be the best group result. However, a Mann-Whitney test shows no significant differences between the two groups 1 (depicted and proactive) and 3 (audio only and proactive).

Therefore, it can be confirmed that the proactive system component has had an essential influence on the learning success and the ability to apply knowledge in practice. Also, as shown for example by Louwerse et al. [15], it could be confirmed that subjects with a visualized pedagogical agent also fixated them in their field of vision.

The results concerning the mouse distance, time and the number of clicks seem to be interesting in that they do not statistically show a group difference. A purely descriptive analysis of the data (see Table 2) shows that the respective peer groups were faster in terms of proactivity (1, agent with proactivity, and 2, agent without proactivity, as well as 3, audio only with proactivity, and 4, audio only without proactivity), insofar as the system acted proactively. However, this was not done to a statistically significant extent. Accordingly, statistically speaking, all groups had an equal period of time, which is why a similar pixel-track was searched for clues to the solution and a comparable number of clicks were used to bring about a solution. In the case of non-proactive groups, however, this was more likely to be unsuccessful, although the groups without a proactive component also had correct solutions to the practical task.

An in-depth examination of the knowledge difference in the pre- and post-test with regard to the depiction of the agent reveals no significant group difference in the previous knowledge test when distinguishing between group 1 and group 2 ($U_{PreTestKnowledge} = 183$, $p = .668$) but during the post knowledge test ($U_{PostTestKnowledge} = 127$, $p < .05$). Meaning, since both groups have a depicted agent, but group 2 does not have the proactive component, this shows that it is not the agent that is responsible for the knowledge gain but rather an information transfer based on the proactive component. Accordingly, there should be no significant differences between the two proactivity groups 1 and 3, confirmed by the following results ($U_{PreTestKnowledge} = 145$, $p = .082$; $U_{PostTestKnowledge} = 174$, $p = .254$).

As a result of the study's knowledge test before the experiment, it can be concluded that the basic knowledge of HTML code, its components and the knowledge about the function and operation of the Dreamweaver software, can be considered negligible, since currently web content is mainly used by content management systems or as service software offered by aggregators. Knowing the background of CSS layouts and tags is no longer necessary for the active distribution of content online, which is why it could be expected that this knowledge was not to be found during the pre-experiment knowledge test. Having it established at the end of the experiment speaks to the effectiveness of the original e-learning tool (see Fig. 3).

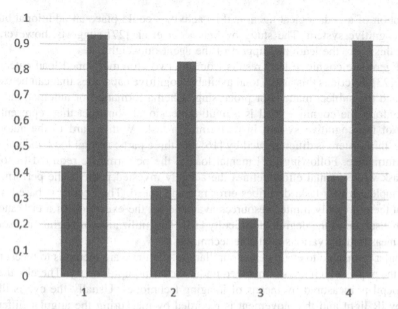

Fig. 3. Knowledge before (left bars) and after the experiment (right bars) of the four groups

3 The Cognitive Load Analysis

In the context of information acquisition, cognitive capacity is of essential importance
and also of interest in the context of pedagogical agent research [25]. Starting point in
the considerations on the cognitive load theory [23] is that the working memory, which
plays an essential role in the acquisition of knowledge, is limited. In order to avoid
cognitive overload when learning or linking new information, it is necessary that
learning materials are prepared by an appropriate design. Sweller [23] identifies in this
context three different forms of cognitive load in the learning process, which can be
added to a continuum of the available cognitive capacity resources.

The intrinsic cognitive load is conditioned by the learning material or the
complexity/difficulty of the matter to be taught. This can be broken down into suitable
information units by segmentation or by a suitable form of instruction design [26].
However, this only influences the amount of the knowledge itself, as each learning
material has an intrinsic complexity that can not be further reduced. Insofar as it is
accordingly necessary that different areas of knowledge must be understood simultaneously in order to enable further conclusions, this can only be achieved by segmenting
the necessary elements of prior knowledge.

The extraneous cognitive load is considered as the part necessary for the understanding of the presentation or design of the learning material. The previous section on
intrinsic cognitive load addressed the possibility of segmentation. For example, if such
a didactic presentation of the subject matter is missing, or if crucial foundations have
been disregarded in the design of learning environments [26], the learner needs a great
deal of effort to acquire the knowledge. In this context, it could be assumed that the

presentation of a pedagogical agent and its activities could place an additional burden on the cognitive system. The study by Schroeder et al. [27] suggests, however, that even in this case, the learning support of the agent outweighs.

The germane cognitive load results from the two aforementioned load categories. Sweller [23] describes this as the total available cognitive capacities that can be used to understand the subject matter, for processing, schema formation or automation.

Therefore, the cognitive load is a multi-dimensional construct that represents the activity of the cognitive system in performing a task. With regard to the automatic analysis, this system is differentiated by [16] into three parts: mental load, mental effort and performance. Following [17] mental load is the performance required to solve a given task while mental effort defines the actually invested power. The performance, after completion of a task, describes error rate and speed. This theory is based on the fact that there are only limited resources available for the execution of a task and that these are used up to the degree of difficulty [18]. This utilization of cognitive resources can be measured by various available techniques.

In order to be able to evaluate the pupillary reflex, there are methods to measure the size of the pupil, which are summarized under the term pupillometry. Thereby the size of the pupil is measured by means of imaging techniques. Usually the eye is illuminated by IR light and the movement is recorded by measuring the angular difference between the center of the pupil and the IR reflection spot on the eye. So, by measuring the eye-movements, the pupil size is a by-product.

For this reason, a contact-free gaze-measuring device is used in the present experimental setup, which uses infrared lamps to image a so-called Purkinje reflection [19] on the cornea. This measurement method is suitable for media psychology research practice through the non-contact configuration [20].

Therefore, we used an infrared-based eye movement apparatus from SMI for the implementation of the study [21]. The infrared illumination and the camera for eye movement detection are mounted by a bracket below a 21" wide-screen display and we measured the infrared reflection on the cornea and the distance to the pupil center (see Fig. 4). Although regarding this specific article, we only focused on the dilation measurements of the pupil during the learning phase of the experiment, regardless of the fixation or saccade of the eye itself.

Possibly the main challenge by analyzing pupillary reactions in order to infer cognitive load, is the problem of rapid pupillary dilations, blinks and other artifacts from differences in lighting. Therefore, pupillary response data has to be smoothed over time in order to be able to find relevant differences and to be able to identify actual increases or decreases in cognitive load. We chose the procedure described in [6, 7] in order to smoothen the data-set and implemented them into a prototypical software. By using maximum and minimum pupil-dilation diameters, we normalized the single-user data into a spectrum of 0 to 1. Future iterations of the software will also include a z-transformation to allow for a comparison of different user data.

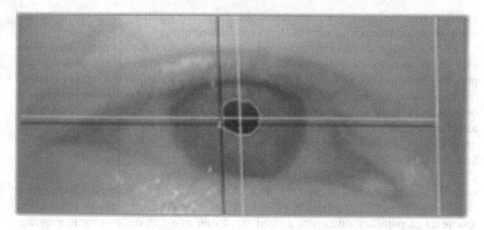

Fig. 4. IR reflection on an eye with the measured pupil-diameter

4 Cognitive Load Data

Using the aforementioned method, we smoothed the pupillary responses of our subjects. Looking at the data, there are still numerous variances visible in the data stream
(see Fig. 5).

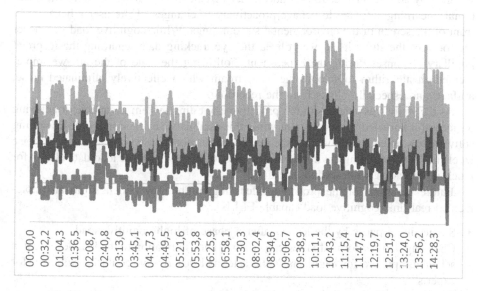

Fig. 5. Three random participants pupil dilations after smoothing of the data

Interestingly enough, the first two streams seem to be running pretty much in
unison, while the third shows variations. Nevertheless, since the lighting was kept
constant during the trial, the smoothed data is free of artifacts like blinks or lost

pupillary tracking, Therefore, we are now able to gain an insight into the cognitive load while users are interacting with the learning system.

Our next steps will be to overlay the data stream onto the recorded videos of the experiment and to check where during the knowledge conveyance peaks in the pupillary response are visible. In addition, we are going to collate the area of interests (pedagogical agent, learning material and white-space) with the cognitive load data in order to get a better understanding of how different aspects of the learning environment might influence the cognitive load in general. Maybe this could lead to a better understanding of the relationship between intrinsic, extraneous and germane cognitive load [22–24].

The proactive EEI (see Fig. 1) could now use this data in real-time to analyze the cognitive load levels and change the mode of knowledge presentation, if and when it should be necessary. For example, when looking at the data, there seems to be a very low level of pupillary dilation at around the 4 min mark of the e-learning program. While on the other hand there appears to be a very demanding task at around the 10 min mark.

5   Conclusion

We presented a study utilizing eye-tracking data while our participants learned with a tried and tested e-learning software. Our goal was to enhance the knowledge conveyance by adding an Electronic Educational Instance (EEI) which enables the traditional e-learning software to behave proactively to changes of the user's behavior in front of the screen or the environmental surroundings. While cognitive load was never the focus of the study itself, we utilized the eye tracking data regarding the recorded pupillary responses during the experiment. Following the state of the art, we implemented an algorithm to smooth the data stream which effectively eliminated noise, artifacts and especially blinks from the recording.

As the study was able to show, a proactive e-learning system is capable of ensuring a successful knowledge transfer. But while this establishes a reaction by the e-learning software to stop and pause while either attendance is not focused on the screen or noise levels in the surrounding environment were too loud, the cognitive load data allows for much more varied actions while learning.

Future iterations of the proactive e-learning might now benefit from an implemented real-time cognitive load capable EEI by:

- Suggesting a pause by the learner after a phase of high cognitive load
- Choosing another form of knowledge conveyance in relation to the load level, e.g. a schematic picture for beginners while a textual description could be sufficient for experts
- Explanation of a certain topic with multiple examples
- Adapting the learning-success-test to the obviously harder to learn topics.

The next iteration of our cognitive load module for the EEI will be tested regarding these and other aspects of possible beneficial actions while learning in conjunction with the cognitive load level.

References

1. Heidig, S., Clarebout, G.: Do pedagogical agents make a difference to student motivation and learning? Educ. Res. Rev. **6**, 27–54 (2011)
2. Lusk, M.M., Atkinson, R.K.: Animated pedagogical agents: does their degree of embodiment impact learning from static or animated worked examples? Appl. Cogn. Psychol. **21**, 747–764 (2007)
3. Wang, N., Johnson, W.L., Mayer, R.E., Risso, P., Shaw, E., Collins, H.: The politeness effect: pedagogical agents and learning outcomes. Int. J. Hum.-Comput. Stud. **66**, 98–112 (2008)
4. Veletsianos, G.: How do learners respond to pedagogical agents that deliver social-oriented non-task messages? Impact on student learning, perceptions, and experiences. Comput. Hum. Behav. **28**, 275–283 (2012)
5. Rosch, J.L., Vogel-Walcutt, J.J.: A review of eye-tracking applications as tools for training. Cogn. Technol. Work **15**(3), 313–327 (2012)
6. Mathot, S., et al.: Safe and sensible preprocessing and baseline correction of pupil-size data. Behav. Res. Methods **50**(1), 94–106 (2018). https://doi.org/10.3758/s13428-017-1007-2
7. Mathot, S.: A simple way to reconstruct pupil size during eye blinks (2013). https://doi.org/10.6084/m9.figshare.688001.v1
8. Wuttke, M., Heidt, M., Rosenthal, P., Ohler, P., Wuttke, M., Müller, N.H.: Proactive functions of a pedagogical agent – steps for implementing a social catalyst function. In: Zaphiris, P., Ioannou, A. (eds.) LCT 2016. LNCS, vol. 9753, pp. 573–580. Springer, Cham (2016). https://doi.org/10.1007/978-3-319-39483-1_52
9. Wuttke, M.: Pro-active pedagogical agents. In: Fakultät für Informatik (ed.) Proceedings of International Summer Workshop Computer Science, pp. 59–62, July 2013
10. Wuttke, M., Heidt, M.: Beyond presentation - employing proactive intelligent agents as social catalysts. In: Kurosu, M., Ioannou, A. (eds.) HCI 2014. LNCS, vol. 8511, pp. 182–190. Springer, Cham (2016). https://doi.org/10.1007/978-3-319-07230-2_18
11. Reeves, B., Nass, C.: The Media Equation. How People Treat Computers, Televisions, and New Media Like Real People and Places. Cambridge University Press, New York (1996)
12. Lester, J.C., Converse, S.A., Kahler, S.E., Barlow, S.T., Stone, B.A., Bhogal, R.S.: The persona effect: affective impact of animated pedagogical agents. In: Pemberton, S. (ed.) Human Factors in Computing Systems: CHI 1997 Conference Proceedings, pp. 359–366. ACM Press, New York (1997)
13. Wuttke, M.: Proaktive Agenten im Lernkontext. Die Auswirkungen neuer Inputkanäle in der lernstoffvermittelnden Mensch-Computer-Interaktion. Dissertationsschrift. Universitätsbibliothek Technische Universität Chemnitz, Chemnitz (2018)
14. Wuttke, M., Völkel, S., Ohler, P., Müller, N.H.: Analytical steps for the validation of a natural user interface. In: Zaphiris, P., Ioannou, A. (eds.) LCT 2017. LNCS, vol. 10295, pp. 55–63. Springer, Cham (2016). https://doi.org/10.1007/978-3-319-58509-3_6
15. Louwerse, M.M., Graesser, A.C., McNamara, D.S., Lu, S.: Embodied conversational agents as conversational partners. Appl. Cogn. Psychol. **23**(9), 1244–1255 (2008)
16. Yeh, Y.Y., Wickens, C.D.: Dissociation of performance and subjective measures of workload. Hum. Factors: J. Hum. Factors Ergon. Soc. **30**(1), 111–120 (1988)
17. Paas, F.G.W.C., Merrienboer, V., Jeroen, J.G.: Instructional control of cognitive load in the training of complex cognitive tasks. Educ. Psychol. Rev. **6**(4), 351–371 (1994)
18. Just, M.A., Carpenter, P.A., Miyake, A.: Neuroindices of cognitive workload: neuroimaging, pupillometric and event-related potential studies of brain work. Theor. Issues Ergon. Sci. **4**(1-2), 56–88 (2003)

19. Duchowski, A.T.: Eye Tracking Methodology Theory and Practice. Springer, London (2007). https://doi.org/10.1007/978-1-84628-609-4
20. Bente, G.: Erfassung und Analyse des Blickverhaltens. In: Mangold, R., Vorderer, P., Bente, G. (eds.) Lehrbuch der Medienpsychologie, pp. 297–324. Hogrefe-Verlag, Göttingen (2004)
21. SMI - SensoMotoric Instruments: SMI - SensoMotoric Instruments (2008). RED/RED250: http://www.smivision.com/en/gaze-eye-tracking-systems/products/red-red250.html. Accessed 01 May 2017
22. Sweller, J., Chandler, P.: Why some material is difficult to learn. Cogn. Instr. **12**(3), 185–233 (1994)
23. Sweller, J.: Cognitive load theory, learning difficulty, and instructional design. Learn. Instr. **4** (4), 295–312 (1994)
24. Sweller, J.: Element interactivity and intrinsic, extraneous, and germane cognitive load. Educ. Psychol. Rev. **22**(2), 123–138 (2010). https://doi.org/10.1007/s10648-010-9128-5
25. Schroeder, N.L.: The influence of a pedagogical agent on learners cognitive load. Educ. Technol. Soc. **20**(4), 138–147 (2017)
26. Niegemann, H.M., Domagk, S., Hessel, S., Hein, A., Hupfer, M., Zobel, A.: Kompendium multimediales Lernen. Springer, Heidelberg (2008). https://doi.org/10.1007/978-3-540-37226-4
27. Schroeder, N.L., Adesope, O.O., Gilbert, R.B.: How effective are pedagogical agents for learning? A meta-analytic review. J. Educ. Comput. Res. **49**(1), 1–39 (2013)

Where the User Does Look When Reading Phishing Mails – An Eye-Tracking Study

Kevin Pfeffel[(✉)], Philipp Ulsamer, and Nicholas H. Müller

University of Applied Sciences Würzburg-Schweinfurt, Würzburg, Germany
{kevin.pfeffel, phillip.ulsamer,
nicholas.mueller}@fhws.de

Abstract. To detect phishing mails, various strategies based on a reliable cryptography-based security framework exist. Nevertheless, the user themselves still provide a greater opportunity for phishing attacks. Therefore, it is crucial to understand how the user deals with phishing mails when confronted with them. This study limits itself to visual stimuli of phishing mails and therefore uses an eye-tracking procedure to determine the gaze behavior. Twenty-one different mails were used for this experiment, of which fourteen were phishing mails. The task of the users was to decide whether it was a phishing mail or a real mail. For the evaluation, the individual mails were provided with Areas of Interest (AOIs). This is similar to the usual components of a mail that would be attachment, body, footer, header and signature. Thereafter, three artificial groups were formed. There was one group with a low score of correct answers, one with a middle score and one with a high score. These three groups were then compared and showed differences in processing time. This led to the assumption that knowledge and time are two important factors in recognizing phishing mails.

Keywords: Phishing · Awareness · Security · Eye-tracking · Human factors

1 Introduction

In the course of digitization, information technologies play a crucial role. Accordingly, information security in companies is particularly important. New digital business processes are creating new challenges, such as an increased demand for information security awareness. Security awareness has established itself as a separate research area within information security. It targets the human factor and wants to convey an information security-compliant behavior to IT users.

Said so, employees play a crucial role as attackers target the human factor with techniques such as phishing, malware, and social engineering [1]. For any attacker, it is easier to learn a password from an employee than to hack it through a compute-intense brute-force attack. In the case of phishing, the majority of enterprises even face attacks on a daily basis [2]. This suggests that the effectiveness of security is highly dependent on the behavior of employees at the workplace because they have a big influence on the confidentiality, integrity and availability of sensitive corporate information.

© Springer Nature Switzerland AG 2019
P. Zaphiris and A. Ioannou (Eds.): HCII 2019, LNCS 11590, pp. 277–287, 2019.
https://doi.org/10.1007/978-3-030-21814-0_21

According to the FBI's 2017 Internet Crime Report [3] Business email compromise scams cost organizations $676 million in 2017. If one also counts the private attacks, the victim losses exceeded $1.4 billion in 2017. To this day, mail is a main source for malware.

Therefore, many attempts have been made to use machine learning to classify incoming emails as phishing mails [4–6]. One possible solution for phishing mails or websites is to blacklist them [7, 8]. Users are warned directly from their web browser or their mailing services should a URL be on the blacklist. There are also other technical solutions such as whitelists and spam filters. Nevertheless, there is a big problem. These technical solutions are not always sufficient to provide full protection. Oftentimes there is a small amount of time in which technical solutions are not yet responding, and in that time the user is on his own. Therefore, the user needs own knowledge and skills to prevent becoming a victim of a phishing attack. Unfortunately, most users are lacking this knowledge to detect such attacks, and there is a lack of awareness that such attacks even exist and therefore warnings are often ignored [9].

Therefore, this study aims to examine how users try to distinguish phishing mails from real mails, by using an eye-tracking method. Of special interest are those phishing mails that are perceived only with great difficulty or not at all as such.

This paper is organized as follows. Section 2 presents related work and gives an overview of the term phishing and in the process, applied attack strategies are discussed in more detail. Section 3 introduces the datasets that are used in this study as well as the metrics that we will use in order to examine the eye-tracking data. Section 4 shows the eye-tracking results of what users care about most about mails, when trying to identify them. In Sect. 5 a discussion about the results of the study will be conducted, where also the own limitations will be discussed. We conclude in Sect. 6.

2 Related Works

In this part of the study, the term phishing should be explained exactly. Furthermore, phishing attack strategies should be presented.

2.1 Phishing

A phishing attack is a combination of "social engineering" and technical manipulation methods to convince Internet users to receive sensitive information of their own to give away [10].

Mostly these are web pages or e-mails that have the goal to get the users sensitive data such as username and the associated password. With this data, the attacker can then make money, for example, by logging in to the online bank account of the user and transferring money [10]. Most of the time a phishing mail is modeled to closely resemble an original mail. In this phishing mail, the user is usually asked to update or change user data. The phishing mail contains a link that leads to a phishing page. Again, a custom website that is very similar to the original website, so users will not suspect foul play and feel safe. This phishing site usually uses the original design, as well as any logos. Personal information such as credit card details, social security number, PayPal username and password and the like are then asked to be entered on the phishing page. Once the user clicks on a confirm-button, their data will be sent to a hostile server, on which the attacker saves the data in order to use it.

In terms of social engineering aspects, it is important to note that most phishing mails try to intimidate the user, create fear and build up time pressure to access their data. An example is "we need you to confirm your account details or we must shut your account down" [11]. This suggests that time is a very relevant factor why phishing mails are efficient.

2.2 Phishing Attack Strategies

In a study from Dhamija, Tygar, and Hearst [12], various attack strategies were collected and then hypothesized how lay users respond to these attack strategies. Three factors were described that are used by the attacker: 1. Lack of knowledge about computer and security systems, 2. Visual illusion with fake pictures, texts and input windows and 3. Lack of attention and low awareness of security indicators. These will be described in more detail below.

(1) Lack of Knowledge: One problem is that only a few users can identify enough indicators to recognize secure web pages. Many have problems to interpret them correctly. For example, initial Internet users rarely know that a web page is secured with SSL encryption when the icon of a closed padlock appears in the browser bar. Another problem are SSL certificates. Few know how to verify them or understand the content properly.

(2) Visual Deception: Another pervasive method of attacking is the interchanging of individual resembling letters in the domain name. For example, at the domain www.paypal.com the lower case letter "l" could be exchanged with the number "1" (www.paypa1.com) or the capital letter "I" (www.paypaI.com). Only by an increased attention, users have the chance to recognize such a fake link. Some attackers also use images of hyperlinks that lead to a fake website that looks confusingly similar to the originals.

(3) Bounded Attention: Another major problem is that protection against attacks on internet users is often a secondary goal for them. If the user is too absorbed in his work, alerts or their absence can quickly go unnoticed. Even users who actually know that they have to pay attention to encryption symbols are often deceived, because they pay attention to them but do not pay close attention to their position. Some attackers deliberately place visual security warnings on their websites, which users interpret as genuine.

Therefore, this is a fight between phishers and anti-phishing around the interface. The attacker's goal is to present a victim a credible website, so that any security risks are ignored [12].

This study focuses on the point of visual deception and attempts to find out which features users utilize for their decision making process and in what time they apply them.

3 Methods

In the empirical part of this paper, an eye-tracking experiment will be used to investigate on what basis users make a decision about whether they are confronted with a phishing mail or a real mail.

For the evaluation, we built areas of interests (AOIs) within the mails. AOIs are a tool to select specific areas of a visible stimulus, and to extract metrics specifically for those areas. An AOI itself is not a standalone metric, but defines the scope in which other metrics are calculated. The metrics are the time to first fixation (TTFF), which indicates the amount of time that takes respondents to look at a specific AOI from stimulus onset. The time spent, which quantifies the amount of time that respondents have spent looking at a particular AOI. The ratio, which provides information about how many of your respondents, actually guided their gaze towards a specific AOI. The sheer number of fixations in a given AOI and the revisits, which provides information about how many times participants, returned their gaze to a particular spot, defined by an AOI.

3.1 Participants

All data were collected in a laboratory at the University of Applied Sciences Würzburg-Schweinfurt and the subjects were taken directly from there. It involves both technical staff, scientific staff and students of computer science and e-commerce. 25 people participated in the study, but three of them had to be excluded from the final analysis due to poor gaze sampling. Thus, 22 records remained for the final analysis. Of these 22 valid records, three were female subjects. In total, the 22 valid records consist of 5 subjects from the technical staff, 7 subjects from the scientific staff and 10 subjects were students.

3.2 Materials and Measuring Instruments

During the work process, the subjects wear eye-tracking glasses. These glasses are the Tobii Pro Glasses 2. It consists of a head unit with a head strap and a recording unit. The glasses are able to record with a measurement frequency up to 100 Hz. The high definition scene camera captures a Full HD video of what is in front of the participant and the eye tracking sensors records eye orientation e.g. the direction of the eye gaze.

Overall, subjects had to identify 21 different mails. 14 of them were phishing mails and 7 were real mails. The mails were divided into the following AOIs: header, attachment, body, signature and footer. Not every mail could have all AOIs. However, a test mail always consisted of at least two of the created AOIs.

3.3 Procedure

First, the subjects were welcomed and got a detailed guide to further action. Afterwards, the subjects were put on the eye-tracking glasses. Then the eye-tracker was calibrated. After a successful calibration, the subjects were referred to a link on the desktop of the computer. By pressing on the link, they got to a survey. Here again there was an instruction about the further course of the study. If the subjects had no more questions, the test started. After a few demographic questions were collected, the actual test began.

During the test, the subjects were shown test mails. The task of the subjects was to decide whether the mail shown was a phishing mail or a real mail. If the subjects were very uncertain, they also could answer with no answer. This was done trying to exclude any guessing.

4   Results

The results are divided into the descriptive results and Visualizations and the univariate ANOVA. The descriptive results are first presented with all the key figures for the AOIs, while the univariate ANOVA are used to determine the correlations between the AOI total fixation duration of the single AOIs and the group affiliation. Group affiliation means that the subjects were artificially divided into one of three groups based on their test result. There is the group 1 - novice, which reached 0–9 points from 21, then there is the group 2 intermediate, which reached 10–14 points, and lastly the group 3 - experts, which reached 15–21 points.

4.1   Descriptive Results and Visualization

The following Table 1 gives a summary of the AOI total fixation duration for each mail.

Table 1. AOI total fixation duration

	Header	Attachment	Body	Signature	Footer
mail001	5,63		18,14		7,05
mail002	4,1	5,11	8,76	3,12	
mail003	6,52		12,24	2,64	
mail004	6,44		18,7	2,35	3,83
mail005	4,27		17,51	0,76	2,02
mail006	4,23		10,37	0,73	0,69
mail007	3,28		16,13		1,84
mail008	2,96	0,83	6,16	0,83	
mail009	3,63		16,39		
mail010	2,26		9,04	1,05	
mail011	2,52		10,6	1,66	
mail012	4,22		15,45	1,08	1,55
mail013	3,27		16,43	1,67	0,66
mail014	2,62		24,45	0,83	2,02
mail015	2,11		16,22	0,95	2,35
mail016			9,28		0,5

(continued)

Table 1. (*continued*)

	Header	Attachment	Body	Signature	Footer
mail017	20,3		7,77		0,43
mail018	2,57	1,64	13,02		
mail019	3,34		5,34		
mail020	2,61		7,47		0,9
mail021	2,97		10,07	0,87	0,89
Average	4,49	2,53	12,84	1,43	1,90

It is shown that the subjects spend most of their time with the body of the mail. After that, the header got the most attention. If an attachment was present, this was followed in third place. The footer, as well as the signature received on average rather less attention.

The same results can be seen in the AOI fixation count, the AOI total visit duration and the AOI visit count. Furthermore, this becomes recognizable if ones considers the heat maps of the single mails (see Fig. 1).

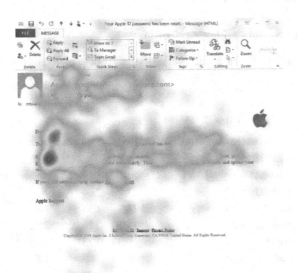

Fig. 1. Presentation of a heat map on an exemplary mail.

The Table of the AOI time to first fixation showed that most subjects started at the body or the header and then processed the mail consistently from top to bottom. After one pass, however, it was possible to jump or repeat. This can also be seen in an exemplary gaze plot (see Fig. 2).

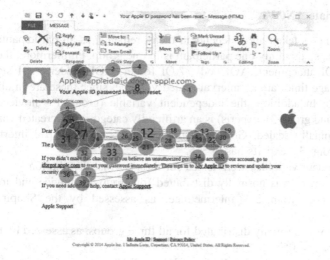

Fig. 2. Presentation of a gaze plot on an exemplary mail

Therefore, it can be stated once more, that most of the subjects focus their attention towards the body and header of a mail and try to find out whether this is a phishing mail or not. If there is an attachment, this is also attributed a great importance. The signature as well as the footer of the message tend to be neglected.

Table 2 gives a further overview of the distribution of AOI total fixation duration within the three groups.

Table 2. Overview of AOI total fixation duration

	Attachment	Body	Footer	Header	Signature	Sum
Group 1 Average	2,01	11,91	1,50	2,58	1,27	19,27
Group 1%	10,43%	61,77%	7,81%	13,41%	6,59%	100%
Group 2 Average	3,04	16,04	2,47	4,11	1,91	23,10
Group 2%	11,03%	58,19%	8,94%	14,91%	6,92%	100%
Group 3 Average	2,14	8,09	1,27	3,76	0,84	16,10
Group 3%	13,27%	50,23%	7,91%	23,35%	5,24%	100%

This shows that group 3 - experts are paying more attention to the attachment and especially towards the header areas than the other two groups. In addition, on average group 3 - experts needed the least amount of time to process. The biggest difference between group 1 – novice and group 2 – intermediate seems to be the total time. Where the group 2 - intermediate has consumed a little more time in the processing. The next step is to see if these differences are statistically significant.

4.2   Univariate ANOVA

The measurements taken are independent measurements, as all participants were only collected once, so that only one participant is in one group. Furthermore, the dependent variables (AOI attachment, AOI body, AOI footer, AOI header, AOI signature and summed average time) are an interval-scaled variable, since these are in all cases time measurements. In addition, the independent variable (group 1 - novice, group 2 - intermediate and group 3 - experts) is an artificially categorically created variable and is therefore nominally scaled. Group 1 - novice has N = 6, group 2 intermediate has N = 9 and group 3 - experts has N = 5.

The dependent variables were tested for their normal distribution.

AOI attachment was normally distributed for group 1 - novice and for group 3 - experts, but not group 2 - intermediate, as assessed by the Shapiro-Wilk test (alpha = .05).

AOI body was normally distributed for all three groups, as assessed by the Shapiro-Wilk test (alpha = .05).

AOI footer was normally distributed for all three groups, as assessed by the Shapiro-Wilk test (alpha = .05).

AOI header was normally distributed for group 1 - novice and for group 3 - experts, but not group 2 - intermediate, as assessed by the Shapiro-Wilk test (alpha = .05).

AOI signature is normally distributed for group 1 - novice and for group 2 - intermediate, but not for group 3 - experts, as assessed by the Shapiro Wilk test (alpha = .05).

The sum of average time was normally distributed for all three groups, as assessed by the Shapiro-Wilk test (alpha = .05).

Although the normal distribution assumption was partially violated at this point, a parametric test should nevertheless be used, as we assume that the one-factorial ANOVA is relatively robust to violations of the normal distribution. Extreme outlier values are only for the AOI attachment, but they should not be removed for further calculations.

Homogeneity of variances was asserted for all dependent variables using Levene's test, which showed that equal variances could be assumed.

We then conducted a one-way ANOVA to assess the effects of AOI total time fixation within every single AOI on the group affiliation based on the test points. The following Table 3. Gives a complete overview over the univariate ANOVA.

The AOI Body differed statistically significant for group affiliation, $F(2, 17) = 5,971$, $p < .05$.

The AOI Signature differs statistically significant for group affiliation, $F(2, 17) = 6.998$, $p < .01$.

The sum of average time difference statistically significant for group affiliation, $F(2, 17) = 5.546$, $p < .05$.

For the other variables, no statistically significant difference could be determined. Therefore, the Tukey post-hoc analysis will not be discussed here.

Table 3. The univariate ANOVA

Einfaktorielle ANOVA

		Quadratsumme	df	Mittel der Quadrate	F	Signifikanz
Attachment	Zwischen den Gruppen	1,118	2	,559	,095	,910
	Innerhalb der Gruppen	99,846	17	5,873		
	Gesamt	100,963	19			
Body	Zwischen den Gruppen	222,980	2	111,490	5,971	,011
	Innerhalb der Gruppen	317,437	17	18,673		
	Gesamt	540,417	19			
Footer	Zwischen den Gruppen	6,626	2	3,313	3,281	,062
	Innerhalb der Gruppen	17,163	17	1,010		
	Gesamt	23,789	19			
Header	Zwischen den Gruppen	6,224	2	3,112	,901	,425
	Innerhalb der Gruppen	58,696	17	3,453		
	Gesaml	64,920	19			
Signature	Zwischen den Gruppen	6,070	2	3,035	6,998	,006
	Innerhalb der Gruppen	7,374	17	,434		
	Gesamt	13,444	19			
SumAvgTime	Zwischen den Gruppen	381,063	2	190,531	5,546	,014
	Innerhalb der Gruppen	583,997	17	34,353		
	Gesamt	965,059	19			

5 Discussion

This study illustrates that even in the best-case scenario, when users expect phishing mails to be present and are motivated to discover them, many users cannot distinguish a legitimate mail from a phishing mail. In our study, the best phishing mail was able to fool 40% of participants. All of which had a technical background knowledge as being either staff member of the university or students of computer sciences.

The results have shown that subjects mainly look at the body and the header of an e-mail. This sounds logical considering that the body of the mail contains most of the text or content of the mail and that the header is a good source to detect phishing mails. However, statistically significant differences between the groups were found only in the AOI body, AOI signature and the summed average time. A closer look reveals this in group 3 - experts received the highest scores, but needed least time for it. Apparently, these users already have a great deal of knowledge in dealing with phishing mails. Therefore, the factor knowledge was crucial to solve the tasks. On the other hand, it seems that non-experts will benefit from allowing more time to process mails. If one compares the summed average time of group 1 - novice and group 2 - intermediate, then the summed average time was a noticeable difference. This leads to the assumption that the processing time for non-experts is an important factor.

Thus, the two most important factors that help users recognize phishing mails are the knowledge about phishing mails and the processing time. Therefore, users should at best become experts or encourage them to spend more time processing mails.

5.1 Limitations

This study has some limitations. First of all, the sample should be mentioned, as it is all about employees or students at the University of Applied Sciences Würzburg-Schweinfurt. Thus, it is not assumable that this sample is also transferable to a larger population.

Another limitation is the setting itself. The subjects were explicitly told that there are phishing mails and real mails and they should make a decision. Better would be a test in that the subjects just have to process mails as a secondary task. In this setting, you could sprinkle phishing mails repeatedly and look at which users would give out the data. In addition, it could be tested how pressure and anxiety in the context of social engineering affect users in the management of work.

A third limitation is that in this test all mails were classified into AOI areas. A useful modification of this could be to form AOIs only where phishing mails can also be detected and to check whether users perceive these explicit recognition features and how long it takes them to find these features.

6   Conclusion

The results suggest that users especially need a better understanding of phishing mails and making this understanding more intuitively to naïve users. No automated system will ever be foolproof. Therefore, the user always remains a weakness, which the phisher is trying to exploit. As mentioned, the best phishing mail was able to fool 40% of participants. It is therefore never sufficient to rely solely on traditional cryptography-based security frameworks, instead, a training program is important that the user heavily involves.

References

1. Semba, B., Eymann, T.: Developing a model to analyze the influence of personal values on IT security behavior. In: Nissen, V., et al. (eds.) Multikonferenz Wirtschaftsinformatik (MKWI) 2016, TU Ilmenau, Ilmenau, pp. 1083–1091 (2016)

2. ISACA: State of Cyber Security 2017: Part 2: Current Trends in the Threat Landscape (2017)
3. FBI Gov Homepage. https://pdf.ic3.gov/2017_IC3Report.pdf. Accessed 15 Feb 2019
4. Bergholz, A., Paaß, G., Reichartz, F., Strobel, S., Chung, J.H.: Improved phishing detection using model-based features. In: Proceedings of the International Conference on E-mail and AntiSpam (2008)
5. Fette, I., Sadeh, N., Tomasic, A.: Learning to Detect Phishing Emails, Technical Report, Institute for Software Research International, School of Computer Science, Carneige Mellon University (2006)
6. Toolan, F., Carthy, J.: Phishing detection using classifier ensembles. In: Proceedings of the 4th ECrime Researchers Summit, Tacoma, WA (2009)
7. Ma, J., Saul, L.K., Savage, S., Voelker, G.M.: Beyond blacklists: learning to detect malicious web sites from suspicious urls. In: 15th ACM SIGKDD International Conference on Knowledge Discovery and Data Mining, pp. 1245–1254. ACM, New York (2009)
8. Prakash, P., Kumar, M., Kompella, R., Gupta, M.: Phishnet: predictive blacklisting to detect phishing attacks. In: IEEE INFOCOM 2010, pp. 1–5. IEEE, San Diego (2015)
9. Wu, R., Miller, R.C., Garnkel, S.L.: Do security toolbars actually prevent phishing attacks? In: SIGCHI Conference on Human Factors in Computing Systems, pp. 601–610. ACM, New York (2006)
10. Kirda, E., Kruegel, C.: Protecting users against phishing attacks. Comput. J. **49**(5), 554–561 (2006)
11. Jakobsson, M.: Modeling and preventing phishing attacks. In: Patrick, A.S., Yung, M. (eds.) FC 2005. LNCS, vol. 3570, p. 89. Springer, Heidelberg (2005). https://doi.org/10.1007/11507840_9
12. Dhamija, R., Tygar, J.D., Hearst, M.: Why phishing works. In: Proceedings of the SIGCHI Conference on Human Factors in Computing Systems, pp. 581–590. ACM (2006)

Automated Behavioral Modeling and Pattern Analysis of Children with Autism in a Joint Attention Training Application: A Preliminary Study

Tiffany Y. Tang$^{(\boxtimes)}$ and Pinata Winoto

Media Lab, Department of Computer Science, Wenzhou-Kean University,
Wenzhou, China
{yatang, pwinoto}@kean.edu

Abstract. Although recent research works have highlighted and demonstrated the applicability of the activity and behavioral pattern analysis mechanisms in offering early windows of opportunities in the assessment and intervention for individuals with autism spectrum disorder (ASD), the computational cost and sophistication of such behavioral modeling systems might prevent these automatic and semi-automatic systems from deploying, which might in turn restrict its actual use. As such, in this paper, we proposed an easily deployable automatic system to train joint attention (JA) skills, characterizing and evaluating JA and reciprocity patterns (i.e. the frequency and degree of reciprocity, initiating and responding to JA bids). Our proposed approach is different from most of earlier attempts in that we do not capitalize the sophisticated feature-space construction methodology; instead, the simple designs and in-game automatic data collection offers hassle-free benefits for such individuals as special education teachers and parents to use in both classrooms and at homes.

Keywords: Joint attention skills · Children · Pattern · Autism ·
Behavioral modeling · Puzzle · Training application

1 Introduction

Imagine John, a four-year-old boy and his mother, Alice, are eating at a local McDonalds when John points to the ketchup on the table (referred to as *initiating joint attention bids*, IJA) while looking at Alice, and saying "here is the ketchup". In responding to John's initiation, Alice looks at the ketchup and then back at John uttering "oh, yes, ketchup" (referred to as *responding to joint attention bids*, RJA). The eye shifting behaviors that Alice engaged between the ketchup and John are also included in such daily social interaction.

IJA and RJA are two key aspects of joint attention (JA) which must occur in social interaction [1]. It is regarded as the executive form of information processing from early in infancy through adulthood: it is predictive of later language development [2–4], theory of mind abilities [5] and social communicative skills [6]. Raver's study on the social interaction between typically developing (TD) toddlers and their mothers

© Springer Nature Switzerland AG 2019
P. Zaphiris and A. Ioannou (Eds.): HCII 2019, LNCS 11590, pp. 288–300, 2019.
https://doi.org/10.1007/978-3-030-21814-0_22

revealed the link between JA and emotion regulation [7]. It is notably known that children with autism spectrum disorder (ASD) often exhibit atypical JA behaviors [8]. Specifically, they engage in fewer joint attention behaviors, including eye-gaze shifting [9], initiating and responding to joint attention bids [10], etc. Due to its criticality and motivated by the following two facts, we proposed the present study:

- The ecological validity of an intervention

As White et al. argued that "Joint attention behaviors may vary across ethnicity, language, family structure, or socioeconomic status, and currently there is no assessment of how those vary" (pp. 1293 [11]); hence, there is a necessity of assessing (and charactering) such skills in a Chinese special education classroom.

- Current assessment protocols are more inclined to focus on the more abstract and higher-level social skills where JA skills precede.

For example, mutual planning and joint performance in [12], turn-taking and negotiating in [13]. In our present study, the evaluation is measure in the context of the tasks—puzzle-making in a loosely coupled collaborative play environment to engage children with ASD so as to minimize their cognitive loads without enforced collaboration (EC) [14].

Our proposed approach presented in this paper is different from most of earlier attempts in that we do not capitalize the sophisticated feature-space construction methodology; instead, the simple designs and in-game automatic data collection offers hassle-free benefits for such individuals as special education teachers and parents to use in both classrooms and at homes.

The organization of this paper is as follows. In Sect. 2, relevant research will be presented; followed by the detailed descriptions of our training application including the defined IJA and RJA bids which can be utilized for behavioral pattern recognition. In Sect. 3, we will show the detailed in-game pattern analysis module. Section 4 includes a pilot testing in the lab with two typically developing (TD) adults for evaluating the feasibility of our behavioral pattern modeling module. We conclude our paper in Sect. 5 with discussions on our future research along this avenue.

2 Previous Works

Two indirect lines of past research are relevant to our present study.

2.1 IJA, RJA and Best Practices in Teaching JA Skills

Aligning with the two JA bids, Whalen and Schreibman [15] documented two phases of joint attention intervention in a non-computerized setting which has prevailed in such intervention: initiation and response training. The former includes coordinated gaze shifting and pro-declarative pointing. The latter sponsors five levels of responses as "response to hand on object", "response to showing of object", "eye contact", "response to object being tapped", "following a point", and "following a gaze". In addition, physical (i.e. touching a child's hand to remind), verbal (utterances such as "you can drag the puzzle to here") and gestural prompts were adopted to further assist children to engage with others during the response training phase [15]. Both IJA and RJA behaviors to JA bids had also been studied in a parent-child intervention setting (i.e. Parent-Mediated Communication-Focused Treatment in Children with Autism (PACT) [16]) and caregiver or parent mediated behavioral intervention (i.e. Joint Attention-Mediated Learning (JAML) [17, 18]).

Over the past years, computerized JA training applications have emerged, and many of them had been deployed in a collaborative play environment in a tabletop which allows larger space to afford joint performance [12–14, 19–22]. The majority of these earlier systems engage children in a tightly coupled collaborative play environment where only one work-space is deployed [1, 13, 19–22] except for [14] which does not enforce collaboration by providing private workspace for each child. These earlier works investigated the feasibility, usability and usefulness of the play environment in training JA skills, while the present study focuses on the automated pattern and data analysis to facilitate personalized training and intervention.

2.2 Behavioral Modeling and Pattern Analysis for Technology-Based ASD Intervention and Training

Users' interaction and engagement in a virtual and physical space (including in a computerized application space) offers rich information on profiling and modeling the users in user-centered computing. In the pattern recognition and computer vision area, activity and behavioral analysis based on multimodal data has been much studied for a long time (for example among many references, [23–26]). The majority of these prior works focus on the recognition of single user activities and behaviors which often spans a considerable temporal duration. Recently, many works had focused on characterizing group activities at a coarse level [27–31, 34].

Among them, [28, 29, 31–33] targeted at children with ASD. For example, Chong et al. [28] attempted to measure and predict eye contact of infant with ASD via eye-gaze tracking during interaction sessions with the examiner who wears a pair of commercially-available glasses to capture infants' face and head poses; such automatic system is beneficial and efficient to characterize atypical gaze behavior involving children with ASD in natural social settings. Anzulewicz et al. [29] focused on obtaining gesture data during ASD children's (touch-sensitive) tablet gameplay sessions; the unique touch-sensitive screens and embedded inertial movement sensors are programmed to record movement kinematics and gesture forces. Winoto et al. [34] proposed to feature users' movements in a naturalistic space which had been captured using depth-camera in the form of temporal skeleton data; and they argued that such data, if combined with other ambient sensing data could provide social-meter to predict social relationships. Prabhakar and Rehg [31] segmented and analyzed real-world social interaction videos to characterize turn-taking interactions between individuals. [32] documented a detailed study on the computational analysis of children's social and communicative behaviors based on video and audio data in the dyadic social interaction between adults and children with ASD.

These recent earlier works demonstrated the applicability of the activity and behavioral pattern analysis mechanisms in the computer vision and pattern recognition area to assist therapists, care-givers and individuals with development disorders including ASD [32, 33].

Two recent studies focused on visualizing the behavioral patterns (including eye-gaze direction) during the social interaction between a child with ASD and a therapist [35, 36]. In both studies, sophisticated data capture system had been deployed. For example, in [36], the eye-gaze direction data were retrieved and analyzed via a high-definition video-recording system, followed by gaze-analysis based on facial landmark and head movement data. The computational cost of the system is inherently high; however, the authors claimed that compared with the manual rating and evaluation based on videos by therapist, the system can facilitate the medical specialist's evaluation [36]; it is unclear, however, whether such behavioral visualizing system can easily be deployed. Unlike video-based data capturing system in [36], Kong et al. [35] utilizes Abaris to allow therapists using Anoto digital pen and paper technology and Nexidia voice recognition to create meaningful indices to videos [37].

Despite earlier efforts, however, the computational cost and sophistication of behavioral modeling systems in most of these works might prevent such automatic and semi-automatic systems from deploying, which might in turn restrict its actual use. Our proposed approach is different in that we do not capitalize the sophisticated feature-space construction; instead, the simple designs and in-game automatic data collection offers hassle-free benefits for such individuals as special education teachers and parents to use in both classrooms and at homes.

In the next two sections, detailed description of our system and the in-game data collection and automatic behavioral analysis model will be presented.

3   Our Joint Attention Training Application

3.1   The Training Application at a Glance

The two-player game is deployed on a 27 inches tabletop as a puzzle game (see Fig. 1, 2 for two screenshots). Figure 2 shows the general application design.

Fig. 1. Application screenshots where two players have a separate work space. (Color figure online)

Fig. 2. Application screenshots where two players have a separate work space where one puzzle piece belonging to the left player is in the right player's work space (with puzzle border color in orange). (Color figure online)

Each child has her/his own work space, where he/she needs to piece the puzzles together; the blue button (i.e. the help button) with a question mark can be tapped when either play cannot find a piece in his/her workspace (Figs. 1, 2 and 3). Upon tapping the help button, the puzzle will be blinked to prompt to alert the child to pass the puzzle that does not belong to his/her space to another. When the puzzle is being blinked in a child's work space, he/she can ignore it or take actions to swipe it to another space. The border color of each puzzle corresponds to the color of each player's work space (Figs. 1, 2 and 3), which serves two purposes: (a) providing visual cues for each player; (b) initiating JA bids for a player when he/she points to a puzzle piece in another player's workspace (see Fig. 4).

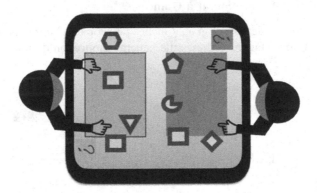

Fig. 3. Application screenshots where two players have a separate work space; a help button can be pressed for players to seek help. (Color figure online)

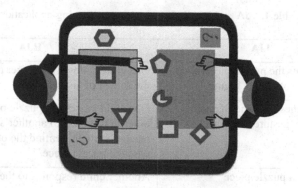

Fig. 4. The left player is seen pointing to the puzzle piece in another player's space (IJA). (Color figure online)

3.2   The IJA and RJA Bids Defined in Our Application

As we discussed in the previous section, a help button has been placed at the right bottom of the screen for children to ask for help (see Fig. 3). Once they click the button, the puzzle piece on his/her own working space will be automatically moved to the correct place, the piece on other working space will blink to prompt another user to share it to his/her. Such blinking puzzle piece, in the form of a visual pattern provides visual cues to prompt for RJA. When the piece is in being blinked, the other child can ignore or take action to deliver the puzzle piece. As such, as a unique design in our training application, the behavior of clicking the help button is defined as a IJA bid. RJA bid occurs when the puzzle piece is blinking and (a) the player notices it; (b) the player passes the blinking piece to another play. Obviously, a child might have noticed a puzzle piece that does not belong to his/her works space, and swipe it to the other child, which is regarded as a indicative evidence of proactive help.

Table 1 below lists key IJA and RJA bids in the puzzle training game, where the ones below the green bar shows the unique designs in our application where such bids can be objectively assessed.

These bids can best be evaluated based on behavioral and speech analysis of their actions (recorded in a video) during the interactions. In cases that either child failed to initialize or respond to each other's attention bids, such reminders can come from the teacher/parents who are present, in the form of verbal and bodily cues [15].

Table 1. IJA and RJA bids in our puzzle training application

IJA	RJA
One child points the puzzle piece(s) on another's workspace (see Figure 4)	One child follows the finger pointing on the screen of another child
One child touches the hand of another child/a teacher (gesture clue)	One child passes the puzzle piece to another in response to another's touch)/the teacher verbally remind the other child the pass the puzzle piece
One child taps a puzzle piece	Another child responds to the piece being tapped
One child taps a help button	Another child responds to the piece being tapped
One child taps a puzzle piece that does not belong to his/her own work space	Another child responds to the piece being tapped

4   Behavioral Modeling and Preliminary Analysis in Our Joint Attention Application

4.1   In-Game Data Collection Module

It includes a built-in game data collection module to indirectly assess the quantitative degree of reciprocity as well as the overall performance of each children. The help button is specially designed as a visual cue and objective measurement of proactive help.

Figure 5 shows these parameters. Each player has 12 puzzle pieces, the pieces for left and right player is labelled from L1 (R1) to L12 (R12) respectively. X and Y

In-game Parameter	Explanation	Notes	Description	Bids type
notAskRGiveL	R gives the piece to L without being asked	proactive help	The frequency that R offers L help without being asked	RJA
notAskLGiveR	L gives the piece to R without being asked	proactive help	The frequency that L offers R help without being asked	RJA
askRGiveL	R gives the piece to L when being asked		The frequency that R offers L help when being asked	RJA
askLGiveR	L gives the piece to R when being asked		The frequency that L offers R help when being asked	RJA
lAskHelp	L asked for Help	visual cue (blinking puzzle piece)	The frequency that L pressed the help button	IJA
rAskHelp	R asked for Help	visual cue (blinking puzzle piece)	The frequency that R pressed the help button	IJA

Fig. 5. In-game data related to the help behavior.

represent the 2D index of each puzzle piece (see the image in Figs. 1, and 2 for the user interface of this version of the application).

Proactive help is essential for mutual planning and better joint performance. Each player's behavioral data will be collected and stored as a data book. The data reflects the temporal movement of the puzzle pieces registered to each player (Left and Right player respectively). For each movement of a puzzle piece, the following data will be automatically collected: the piece's index, the time stamp of the attempt, the duration of the operation, the final location of the piece and the wrong place that the piece was placed, if any, respectively. Figure 6 shows such a data example of player's behaviors for further user modeling and analysis.

Parameter	Data Example	Description
piecesIndex	pcsL1	The index of the puzzle is L1
moveTimes	1	The moving frequency of the puzzle is 1 time
spanTime	2.52	The duration of moving a puzzle piece is 2.52 second
pcsLocX	340	The X coordinate of the puzzle
pcsLocY	465	The Y coordinate of one puzzle
wrong@	L2	The puzzle piece was wrongly placed on L2

Fig. 6. An example of player behaviors for user modeling and analysis

The data shown in Fig. 6 records the temporal manipulations of a puzzle piece by a given player (L or R). They are computed to measure the overall performance of the task and can be used to obtain the behavioral pattern of both players.

When all puzzle pieces had been placed on the correct place, our in-game data collector will generate one row of data which contains the performance of each player at a given level with the following additional behavioral data (Fig. 7).

Parameter	Exemplary value	Description
autoFillL	2	L asks Help to auto fill the puzzle twice
autoFillR	1	R asks Help to auto fill the puzzle for one time
wrongTimesL	2	L place the puzzle at the wrong place for twice
wrongTimesR	1	R places the puzzle at the wrong place for one time
askLGiveR	1	L passes a puzzle piece once When being asked
notAskLGiveR	2	L passes a puzzle piece twice without being asked
askRGiveL	1	R passes a puzzle piece to L once when being asked
notAskLGiveR	2	R passes a puzzle piece to L twice without being asked

Fig. 7. Overall behavioral data (by user).

Notice that in order to reduce stress for low-functioning ASD children, an advance help has been added: when such a button is pressed, the puzzle-filling operation will be automatically finished. Such a design is important in that individuals with ASD (including children) are much less reluctant to engage in eye-contact and close encounter of the face [38]. Hence, when such automatic operation is observed, the ASD child's JA skills might need to be further trained.

4.2   The Feasibility Study: Preliminary Analysis

In order to assess the usability of the module before deploying it in a special education classroom, we conducted an in-lab study involving two TD adults (see Fig. 8). The test environment is similar to that in [14].

Fig. 8. Preliminary feasibility testing in the lab.

Due to limited space, in this paper, we focus on the RJA and IJA skills in terms of both proactive and non-proactive helps. To this end, we measure the quantity of these skills (see Fig. 5).

Two students were invited to participate in the study. They completed six levels of the games which consists of 6 (from level one to five) and 12 puzzle pieces (level six) respectively. We followed the study protocol as in [14].

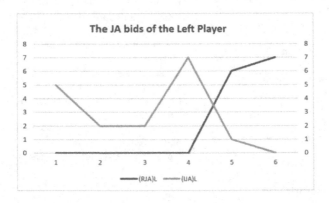

Fig. 9. The JA bids of the left player.

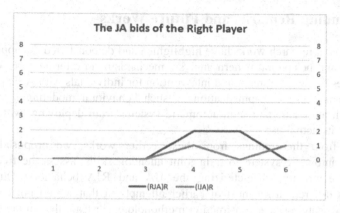

Fig. 10. The JA bids of the right player.

Figures 9 and 10 show the temporal JA bid pattern of both players respectively. Some quick assessment of the quantity of the JA bids can be easily drawn from the figures. For example, the IJAs and RJAs of both players tend to show opposite patterns; overall, the left player is more socially active in terms of both IJAs and RJAs; more joint attention and proactive help patterns can be observed in when both players entered level four, five and six., etc.

Obviously, these behavioral marks provide rich information for therapists to assess the appropriateness of game activities as well as the social interaction patterns of players. The data collection and analysis can automatically be conducted at the background to allow tele-therapy and facilitate live behavioral marking by therapists in different physical location [37, 39, 40]. Our system has the advantage over the previous ones, including [28, 29, 31–33, 35, 36], in that it is lightweight and easily deployable, which thus made it an ideal use at home.

4.3 Discussion

Our in-game data collection module has been carefully designed to assess the performance of the tasks, measurement of reciprocity which is key to social interaction and JA skills [41].

We speculate that a good performance on a given level could indicate an intact or typical JA skill sets reflect compensatory strategies such as pressing the 'auto-finish' button. The preliminary in-lab study demonstrated the high feasibility of such an automated system from data collection to analysis.

Further sophisticated analysis such as finer-tuned eye-tracking is expected. However, such game design to facilitate compensatory strategy is necessary to avoid the melt-down of the child. A more challenging research path to pursue is to provide adaptive and personalized visual support based on such behavioral pattern recognition and analysis so as to enhance the quality of therapy and intervention [42].

5 Concluding Remarks and Future Works

Although recent research works have highlighted and demonstrated the applicability of the activity and behavioral pattern analysis mechanisms in offering early windows of opportunities in the assessment and intervention for individuals with ASD [32, 33], the computational cost and sophistication of such behavioral modeling systems might prevent such automatic and semi-automatic systems from deploying, which might in turn restrict its actual use.

Drawn from the findings from these earlier works, we proposed an easily deployable automatic system to train joint attention skills, assess the frequency and degree of reciprocity, characterizing the IJA and RJA behaviors. Our proposed approach is different from most of earlier attempts in that we do not capitalize the sophisticated feature-space construction methodology; instead, the simple designs and in-game automatic data collection offers hassle-free benefits for such individuals as special education teachers and parents to use in both classrooms and at homes. The preliminary in-lab study demonstrated the high feasibility of such an automated system from data collection to analysis.

The design of the game and activities followed our previous approach [14]; the revised system described in this paper (including the integration of the automated data collection and analysis module) had been developed based on our interview with the special education teachers.

We expect the system to be deployed in Chinese special education classrooms to evaluate its usability and applicability over an extended use of period.

Acknowledgements. The authors gratefully acknowledge financial support from Zhejiang Provincial Natural Science Foundation of China (LGJ19F020001). Our thanks to Aonan Guan for implementing the system; Haoyu Yu for her design of the pictures used in the application. Thanks also go to Jie Chen, for participating in the preliminary test.

References

1. Winoto, P., Tang, T.Y.: A multi-user tabletop application to train children with autism social attention coordination skills without forcing eye-gaze following. In: Proceedings of the 16th ACM Interaction Design and Children Conference (ACM IDC 2017), pp. 527–532. ACM Press (2017)
2. Brooks, R., Meltzoff, A.N.: The development of gaze following and its relation to language. Dev. Sci. **8**, 535–543 (2005)
3. Mundy, P., Block, J., Delgado, C., Pomares, Y., Van Hecke, A.V., Parlade, M.: Individual differences and the development of joint attention in infancy. Child Dev. **78**, 938–954 (2007)
4. Kasari, C., Paparella, T., Freeman, S., Jahromi, L.B.: Language outcome in autism: randomized comparison of joint attention and play interventions. J. Consult. Clin. Psychol. **76**(1), 125–137 (2008)
5. Nelson, P.B., Adamson, L.B., Bakeman, R.: Toddlers' joint engagement experience facilitates preschoolers' acquisition of theory of mind. Dev. Sci. **11**, 847–852 (2008)
6. Van Hecke, A.V., et al.: Infant joint attention, temperament, and social competence in preschool children. Child Dev. **78**, 53–69 (2007)

7. Raver, C.: Relations between social contingency in mother–child interaction and 2-year-olds' social competence. Dev. Psychol. **32**, 850–859 (1996)
8. Bruinsma, Y., Koegel, R.L., Koegel, L.K.: Joint attention and children with autism: a review of the literature. Ment. Retard. Dev. Disabil. Res. Rev. **10**, 169–175 (2004)
9. Carpenter, M., Pennington, B.F., Rogers, S.J.: Interrelations among social-cognitive skills in young children with autism. J. Autism Dev. Disord. **32**, 91–106 (2002)
10. Stone, W., Ousley, O.Y., Yoder, P.J., Hogan, K.L., Hepburn, S.L.: Nonverbal communication in two- and three-year-old children with autism. J. Autism Dev. Disord. **6**, 677–695 (1997)
11. White, P.J., et al.: Best practices for teaching joint attention: a systematic review of the intervention literature. Res. Autism Spectr. Disord. **5**(4), 1283–1295 (2011)
12. Giusti, L., Zancanaro, M., Gal, E., Weiss, P.L.T.: Dimensions of collaboration on a tabletop interface for children with autism spectrum disorder. In: Proceedings of the SIGCHI Conference on Human Factors in Computing Systems (CHI 2011), pp. 3295–3304 (2011)
13. Gal, E., Lamash, L., Bauminger-Zviely, N., Zancanaro, M., Weiss, P.L.T.: Using multitouch collaboration technology to enhance social interaction of children with high-functioning autism. Phys. Occup. Ther. Pediatr. **36**(1), 46–58 (2016)
14. Winoto, P., Tang, T.Y., Guan, A.: "I will help you pass the puzzle piece to your partner if this is what you want me to": the design of collaborative puzzle games to train Chinese children with autism spectrum disorder joint attention skills. In: Proceedings of the 15th ACM Interaction Design and Children Conference (ACM IDC 2016), pp. 601–606. ACM Press (2016)
15. Whalen, C., Schreibman, L.: Joint attention training for children with autism using behavior modification procedures. Phys. Occup. Ther. Pediatr. **44**(3), 456–468 (2003)
16. Green, J., Charman, T., McConachie, H., PACT Consortium, et al.: Parent-mediated communication-focused treatment in children with autism (PACT): a randomized controlled trial. Lancet, **375**, 2152–2160 (2010)
17. Kasari, C., et al.: Randomized controlled trial of parental responsiveness intervention for toddlers at high risk for autism. Infant Behav. Dev. **37**(4), 711–721 (2014)
18. Schertz, H.H., Odom, S.L., Baggett, K.M., Sideris, J.H.: Effects of joint attention mediated learning for toddlers with autism spectrum disorders: an initial randomized controlled study. Early Child. Res. Q. **28**(2), 249–258 (2013)
19. Battocchi, A., et al.: Collaborative Puzzle Game: a tabletop interactive game for fostering collaboration in children with Autism Spectrum Disorders (ASD). In: Proceedings of the ACM International Conference on Interactive Tabletops and Surfaces (ITS 2009), pp. 197–204 (2009)
20. Goh, W.B., Shou, W., Tan, J., Lum, G.T.: Interaction design patterns for multi-touch tabletop collaborative games. In: Proceedings of CHI 2012 Extended Abstracts on Human Factors in Computing Systems (CHI 2012), pp. 141–150 (2012)
21. Piper, A.M., O'Brien, E., Morris, M.R., Winograd, T.: SIDES: a cooperative tabletop computer game for social skills development. In: Proceedings of the 20th Conference on Computer Supported Cooperative Work (ACM CSCW 2006), pp. 1–10 (2006)
22. Silva, G.F.M., Raposo, A., Suplino, M.: Exploring collaboration patterns in a multitouch game to encourage social interaction and collaboration among users with autism spectrum disorder. J. Comput. Support. Coop. Work **24**, 149–175 (2015)
23. Ke, Y., Sukthankar, R., Hebert, M.: Volumetric features for video event detection. Int. J. Comput. Vis. **88**(3), 339–362 (2010)
24. Laptev, I., Marszalek, M., Schmid, C., Rozenfeld, B.: Learning realistic human actions from movies. In: Proceedings of 2008 IEEE Conference on Computer Vision and Pattern Recognition (CVPR 2008), pp. 1–8 (2008)
25. Messing, R., Pal, C., Kautz, H.: Activity recognition using the velocity histories of tracked keypoints. In: Proceedings of IEEE 12th International Conference on Computer Vision (ICCV 2009), pp. 104–111 (2009)

26. Tran, D., Sorokin, A.: Human activity recognition with metric learning. In: Forsyth, D., Torr, P., Zisserman, A. (eds.) ECCV 2008. LNCS, vol. 5302, pp. 548–561. Springer, Heidelberg (2008). https://doi.org/10.1007/978-3-540-88682-2_42

27. Choi, W., Shahid, K., Savarese, S.: Learning context for collective activity recognition. In: Proceedings of 2012 IEEE Conference on Computer Vision and Pattern Recognition (CVPR 2012), pp. 3273–3280 (2012)

28. Chong, E., et al.: Detecting gaze towards eyes in natural social interactions and its use in child assessment. In: Proceedings of the ACM on Interactive, Mobile, Wearable and Ubiquitous Technologies, vol. 1, no. 3, Article No. 43 (2017)

29. Anzulewicz, A., Sobota, K., Delafield-Butt, J.T.: Toward the autism motor signature: gesture patterns during smart tablet gameplay identify children with autism. Sci. Rep. **6** (2016). Article number 31107

30. Lan, T., Wang, Y., Yang, W., Mori, G.: Beyond actions: discriminative models for contextual group activities. In: Proceedings of NIPS, pp. 1216–1224 (2010)

31. Prabhakar, K., Rehg, James M.: Categorizing turn-taking interactions. In: Fitzgibbon, A., Lazebnik, S., Perona, P., Sato, Y., Schmid, C. (eds.) ECCV 2012. LNCS, vol. 7576, pp. 383–396. Springer, Heidelberg (2012). https://doi.org/10.1007/978-3-642-33715-4_28

32. Rehg, J.M., et al.: Decoding children's social behavior. In: Proceedings of 2013 IEEE Conference on Computer Vision and Pattern Recognition (CVPR 2013), pp. 3414–3421 (2013)

33. Rehg, J.M., Rozga, A., Abowd, G.D., Goodwin, M.S.: Behavioral imaging and autism. IEEE Pervasive Comput. **13**(2), 84–87 (2014)

34. Winoto, P., Chen, C.G., Tang, T.Y.: The development of a kinect-based online socio-meter for users with social and communication skill impairments: a computational sensing approach. In: Proceedings of IEEE International Conference on Knowledge Engineering and Applications (ICKEA 2016), pp. 139–143 (2016)

35. Kong, H.K., Lee, J., Ding, J., Karahalios, K.: EnGaze: designing behavior visualizations with and for behavioral scientists. In Proceedings of 2016 ACM Conference on Designing Interactive Systems (ACM DIS 2016), pp. 1185–1196 (2016)

36. Higuchi, K., et al.: Visualizing gaze direction to support video coding of social attention for children with autism spectrum disorder. In: Proceedings of 23rd International Conference on Intelligent User Interfaces (ACM IUI 2018), pp. 571–582 (2018)

37. Kientz, J.A., Boring, S., Abowd, G.D., Hayes, G.R.: Abaris: evaluating automated capture applied to structured autism interventions. In: Beigl, M., Intille, S., Rekimoto, J., Tokuda, H. (eds.) UbiComp 2005. LNCS, vol. 3660, pp. 323–339. Springer, Heidelberg (2005). https://doi.org/10.1007/11551201_19

38. Zwaigenbaum, L., et al.: Early identification and interventions for autism spectrum disorder: executive summary. Pediatrics **136**(Suppl), S1–S9 (2015)

39. Cason, J., Richmond, T.: Telehealth opportunities in occupational therapy. In: Kumar, S., Cohn, E. (eds.) Telerehabilitation. Health Informatics, pp. 139–162. Springer, London (2013). https://doi.org/10.1007/978-1-4471-4198-3_10

40. Peretti, A., Amenta, F., Tayebati, S.K., Nittari, G., Mahdi, S.S.: Telerehabilitation: review of the state-of-the-art and areas of application. JMIR Rehabil. Assist. Technol. **4**(2), e7 (2017)

41. Redcay, E., Kleiner, M., Saxe, R.: Look at this: the neural correlates of initiating and responding to bids for joint attention. Front. Hum. Neurosci. **6**, 169 (2012)

42. Tang, T.Y., Winoto, P.: Providing adaptive and personalized visual support based on behavioural tracking of children with autism for assessing reciprocity and coordination skills in a joint attention training application. In: Proceedings of the 23rd International Conference on Intelligent User Interfaces Companion (ACM IUI 2018), Article No. 40. ACM Press (2018)

Student Emotion Recognition in Computer Science Education: A Blessing or Curse?

Dustin Terence van der Haar[✉]

Academy of Computer Science and Software Engineering,
University of Johannesburg, Gauteng, South Africa
dvanderhaar@uj.ac.za

Abstract. One of the key skills in the fourth industrial revolution is the ability to program. To attain this skill, many prospective students study for a degree in computer science or a related field. An important skill in computer science is the ability to solve for a particular problem by programming an application. However, some challenges exist that make teaching this skill difficult, which leads to student frustration and a decrease in grades. These challenges can be attributed to a lack of access to appropriate skill-building or disjoint teaching methods that are not applicable to the student, which is especially prevalent with some inexperienced educators. Using teaching methods, which a student cannot relate to can lead to distance between the taught skill and the student. The article aims to address this distance by proposing a model that derives user sentiment with affective computing methods and leveraging the sentiment outcome to support the educator by providing feedback relevant for teaching. The technology will then allow the educator to adjust teaching and provide a more personalized teaching experience cognizant of classroom concepts with a lower level of understanding or that evoke certain emotions. It can also provide an informal assessment of content delivery by using student sentiment to infer whether concepts are well received. The preliminary prototype shows there is value in using assistive technologies in the physical classroom to achieve adaptive student learning. However, the onus is still on the educator to be able to react correctly to compensate for the lack of understanding for it to be an effective tool.

Keywords: Computer science education · Affective computing · Computer vision

1 Introduction

The ability to program is an important skill that is slowly becoming a critical skill in the 21st century. The ability to systematically solve a problem by implementing an application has thus become a requirement to contribute to digital

© Springer Nature Switzerland AG 2019
P. Zaphiris and A. Ioannou (Eds.): HCII 2019, LNCS 11590, pp. 301–311, 2019.
https://doi.org/10.1007/978-3-030-21814-0_23

society. Computers and smart devices have become ubiquitous, and the Internet of Things (such as smart devices and appliances) have been integrated into our daily lifestyles. Thereby increasing the amount of data being generated and subsequently increasing the demand for individuals that can program [1]. Although education programs that target the programming skill set have come a long way, it is still plagued by many issues that hinder computer science education. Although there exist fundamental stumbling blocks, such as a lack of numeracy skills [2] and resources, there exist more subtle issues that make it difficult to learn to program. Students learn in different ways, and something needs to be done to take these differences into account.

Traditional teaching methods [3] attempt to maximize learning by targeting the attributes shared by the majority of the classroom. However, each student is more receptive to particular teaching methods and may not engage with other methods. Another problem is that the turnaround time for finding out which students are not engaging and how to address it can be quite high. Some educators (especially inexperienced educators) only ask for student feedback at the end of each semester when all the content has been completed, instead of more frequent feedback during the semester. The author argues the educator should align student feedback with their teaching methods and adapt accordingly, but if the feedback is sparse, so is its applicability to current students in the classroom.

The rise of ubiquitous computing allowed for students to access content in more flexible ways, thereby promoting more adaptive student learning [4]. However, current methods show the benefits are limited within a physical classroom setting, where the traditional passive-student approach still prevails. Access to a computer or technology becomes a prerequisite in this setting, thereby excluding the students who do not have access to these technologies. There is a need for adaptive teaching and learning methods that do not incur a great deal of cost for the student, but still, provide the personalized student experience which is conducive to more effective learning.

The article introduces such an approach by applying affective computing (where the student's emotion is derived using a sensor, some processing and machine learning) to achieve adaptive teaching and learning in a physical classroom while limiting the cost to the educator's side. It begins by defining the problem background, where the underpinning issues in computer science education are briefly unpacked, followed by an outline on adaptive learning and where adaptive teaching is relevant. Background to affective computing methods are then introduced, which is relevant for the proposed model that is subsequently discussed, along with a discussion on the preliminary results and recommendations for the implemented prototype. The article ends with a conclusion and future work.

2   Problem Background

Technology has progressed well, and the near prospects show even more potential in various domains. It has especially opened opportunities within the space of higher education. There is also evidence that shows there is improved access to education and satisfaction through distance learning [5]. More recently we can also see that blended learning has enhanced both the effectiveness and efficiency of more meaningful learning experiences [6]. Thereby showing there is a continuing inquiry into how best to use technology in higher education.

The fourth industrial revolution is characterized by the fusion of technologies that blur the lines of the physical, digital and biological spheres of our world, which have evolved at an exponential rate [7]. Emerging technology breakthroughs such as mainstream artificial intelligence, the Internet of Things and 3-D printing have disrupted certain industries such as manufacturing, logistics or commerce and the disruption of education is not far behind. The breakthroughs have to lead to a great deal of demand for the creation of new technologies and subsequently the programming skill, along with other skills within the space of computer science. Thereby making the education of computer science a crucial component in higher education.

2.1 Computer Science Education

Several challenges exist in computer science education and more needs to be done to cater for the current and upcoming demand for computer science within higher education. Teaching and learning methods exist that directly attempt to address these issues found in computer science education, but certain issues remain open problems. Fundamental stumbling blocks are still present in certain institutions (especially in third world institutions). There is a lack of resources, such as access to equipment, human capital [8], along with low levels of motivation and mathematical competency levels [2] which hinder the delivering of computer science graduates. If these fundamentals are not understood or accommodated, the student will find difficulty in learning anything. Innovative teaching methods that are cognizant of these constraints need to be introduced for us to provide for the fourth industrial revolution.

In the past decade, in response to proposed science education reform [9], there has been an increase in the use of active as opposed to passive teaching methods to improve computer science education. Historically, participatory teaching methods have always been seen as a critical component in the teaching of computer science [10]. However, the way we have engaged with the student has changed. Research [11] has shown that there is value in using constructivism in teaching computer science, where knowledge is constructed by the student instead of merely receiving it from the educator. Thereby shifting course design to include certain teaching methods to provide for both the effective and non-effective novice [12]. These teaching methods include pair programming [13], game-based learning [14] and using more accessible programming languages, such as Scratch [15]. However, an educator can introduce these learning methods within their context, but it may only benefit certain students, leaving the rest in the lurch.

2.2   Adaptive Teaching and Learning

Adaptive teaching and learning methods aim to maximize learning for the target student base by using information derived from the student to adapt teaching to their learning style, which in turn improves the learning process [4]. Adaptive learning can be defined as a learning system that monitors user behavior, interprets it according to a domain-specific model and acts on these interpretations to dynamically facilitate the learning process. Traditional learning methods have shown to be ineffective in achieving this individual or personalized learning experience [16], and this has lead to a pursuit of various teaching methods that may be able to achieve adaptive learning.

Adaptive learning methods discussed in the literature can be divided into four categories [16]. The first category of adaptive learning systems is called *adaptive interaction* and achieves adaptive learning by changing the way the user interfaces with the e-learning setting by changing aspects, such as color or font schemes to accommodate the user. The second category and most commonly used category is *adaptive course delivery* systems where course content is changed to make the student feel more comfortable, such as accommodating subjective assessments and providing the student with alternative paths or selections for course material. The third category consists of systems with *content discovery and assembly* where a concerted effort is made to tailor content based on historical student information and behavior during every course design phase. The final category includes *adaptive collaboration support* where continuous social interaction or communication is used to support the learning process [17].

All the above categories of adaptive learning are enacted within a specific environment, which comply with specific models in adaptive learning. The models in adaptive learning environments include the domain model, the learner model, group models and the adaptation model [16]. The *domain model* (also known as the application model) focuses on adaption efforts within the context of roles, relationships and course elements found in the intended application domain. The *learner model* adapts when changes occur in student behavior, demographics and achievements. *Group models*, are similar to the learner model, where they glean information from the characteristics for a group of similar students (instead of an individual) in a dynamic manner. The last model, the *adaption model*, facilitates adaption in various layers of abstraction to determine what, when and how certain aspects can be adapted.

Pea discusses two key dimensions required in the teaching process: the social dimension and technological dimension [18]. Historically much research has targeted the social dimension for facilitating more effective teaching. We are now beginning to understand how to best leverage the technological dimension of effective teaching, especially in computer science. Adaptive teaching and learning can be seen as the bridge between these two dimensions, and there is value in exploring where the two intersect. Thereby showing there is also value in exploring the varying levels of student input and new attributes that can be leveraged to facilitate better adaptive teaching in the classroom.

The area we explore is similar to the adaptive collaboration support category applied to the learner model, but we explicitly look at how support can be provided to the educator specifically for them to adapt their teaching during a class. The feedback delivered to the educator is derived in a novel way by using affective computing to gain student sentiment on specific content delivery to infer whether teaching is well received, while it is being delivered to the students.

2.3 Affective Computing

Picard defines affective computing as computing that relates to, arises from or influences emotions [19]. One of the key points Picard brings up when proposing the concept of affective computing is its benefit within a teaching and learning setting. The affect derived in these systems provides a key attribute that promotes learning: the ability to determine if the user is exhibiting enthusiasm, excitement or experiencing confusion, frustration and anxiety.

The premise is that certain emotions portrayed by a user are more conducive to learning and potentially negative emotions, which detract from learning. Educational psychologists have recently determined that emotions intertwined in teacher responses and student actions are an integral part of the teaching and learning process [20]. Their pursuit has lead to new theoretical frameworks that deviate from focusing on either individuals or environments without any social interactions, but rather leverage them to understand the classroom better learning context. Most of the research focuses on the educator emotions and their impact on learning. Emotions that include frustration when a student cannot grasp a concept or disappointment with a lack of effort from the student negatively impact the student and some research attempts to find ways of regulating these emotions [21, 22]. While more recent research explores student emotions, such as enjoyment, pride and hope and their relationship with the learning process [23]. However, the primary instrument used to capture or determine the emotions using surveys or interviews, which make insights derived from the classroom a more "offline" exercise.

Thankfully, technology has progressed to a point where a machine can be used to determine the emotion of a user, thereby automating the capture of these user emotions. Thereby opening up an avenue of research that leverages the capturing of emotion within an educational setting in a more "online" manner within the context of a physical classroom.

2.4 Similar Work

New entrants within this context attempt to derive emotion from students in a physical classroom setting using various physiological sensors. There are physical manifestations or attributes a user portrays when they experience emotion, and by capturing these attributes, one can derive their approximate emotion. Historically, physiological signals, such as skin conductance or heart rate have been used to determine user emotion in various contexts, such as lie detection. However, they come with their limitations [24]. One of these constraints being the requirement of special sensor equipment for each participant and the lack of portability the equipment exhibits, which limit its practicality within a physical classroom setting.

Shen, Wang and Shen use a collection of biofeedback devices to collect physical data such as heart rate, skin conductance, blood volume pressure and brain waves for every student [25]. Using labelled positive and negative emotion data from these sensors to train a Support Vector Machine (SVM) and K-Nearest Neighbor (KNN) classifier, they achieved between 60.8% and 86.3% accuracy depending how many sensors you factor in. However, some users are not very comfortable with wearing these sensors or providing these attributes, because they feel it is quite intrusive and it may not be yet practical within the physical classroom context.

Wu, Tzeng and Huang capture eye movements, brain waves and heartbeat while the student is playing a digital game designed to teach Newton's law of motion [26]. They specifically outline there is a significant relationship between these physiological attributes and effective learning. However, similar to other work, it too suffers from privacy, hardware and practicality issues. More work needs to be done that introduces models, which capture student emotion in a less intrusive manner with minimal overhead.

3   Experiment Setup

The study serves as exploratory research that allows for further insights on deriving emotion within the domain of the physical classroom without being too intrusive. Once sufficient background on the problem domain and methods is explored, a model is formed, along with a basic implementation for a pilot study to derive insights relevant on whether there is value in using computer vision methods to derive emotion within a physical classroom.

3.1   Data Collection

In the pilot study, video footage of a small group of computer science lab students was captured using a Canon 80D placed in front of the classroom for three classes, which is set to capture video at a resolution of 1920 by 1080 at 60 frames per second. In the environment nominal lighting was provided and any occlusions within the scene were kept to a minimum. Each video sample contained footage from the beginning of the class until the end of the class with an average time of 80 min.

3.2   Data Analysis

Once the video was collected, the methods described in the following section are applied to capture, process and classify the emotions relevant to the study. The emotion results are plotted for the observer, along with the emotional mean. The emotions measured include:

- anger
- contempt
- disgust
- fear
- happiness
- neutral
- sadness
- surprise

The classification outcomes at various stages in the video footage are then observed and any important shifts are noted and collated to derive insights for the study.

4 Model

In order to derive emotion from the students in the physical classroom computer vision methods are employed to derive each student's emotion as depicted in Fig. 1. Once captured, each video frame is sent for the region of interest (ROI) segmentation, where in this case is face detection in the scene using pre-trained Haar cascades. Any ROI sub-images less than 40 by 40 pixels are discarded because it is difficult to derive an emotion on such a low resolution with the current emotion classification method. Each ROI is then processed further to derive emotion scores for each category using Microsoft's Cognitive Service Face API (version 1.0). The emotion scores for each ROI is then returned and consolidated to a mean emotion score for each category for a predefined time window, which can be set by the observer. The scores and significant events are then displayed with the report module and provides a brief notification on whether a class is going well or if the educator should adjust their teaching accordingly.

Fig. 1. A model for achieving adaptive teaching and learning using computer vision methods to derive emotion.

5 Results and Recommendations

The pilot implementation successfully derived the emotion scores for each of the students in the physical classroom. As shown in Fig. 2, even at a side profile view, the faces for most of the students in the classroom that are participating

Fig. 2. An example of the lab class group used for the pilot study, where the face ROI have been removed for privacy reasons.

can be captured for further processing. Once the ROI images are sent to the Microsoft API the emotion scores are successfully returned in JSON format as seen in Fig 3. The emotion scores are then consolidated and parsed by the report module for display to the observer or educator. The observer can then use the report module to view the current and mean emotion scores and adjust teaching accordingly in future classes delivered to the same student class.

```
"scores": {
        "anger": 0.00473169656,
        "contempt": 0.0002789871,
        "disgust": 4.001353E-05,
        "fear": 4.643466E-05,
        "happiness": 2.00395989E-05,
        "neutral": 0.99336195,
        "sadness": 0.00115420332,
        "surprise": 0.000366691558}
```

Fig. 3. An example of the emotion scores for one captured face in the class, depicting the neutral emotion.

Although the pilot implementation showed that it is possible to derive emotion in a physical classroom and use it to adjust teaching, some issues were encountered that hinder the capturing of student emotions in the classroom. These issues are mostly attributed to environmental or hardware constraints. For the students further back in the classroom ROI segmentation would fail at times and in some cases when they would be captured, deriving the emotion for them would be unsuccessful due to the low resolution of the ROI. The number of frames processed within a period was also limited by the API and bandwidth available, which can slow down processing of the frames, thereby warranting the investigation of a local emotion recognition method for further implementations in the study.

5.1 Privacy and Ethical Considerations

Deriving emotion for adapting teaching also comes with privacy and ethical implications. As with any computer vision technology that involves humans there is a chance that it can potentially be infringing on one's privacy. The use of emotion score information beyond the scope of the work also presents problems. For example, general strain theory (GST) posits that strain or stressors increase the likelihood of negative emotions such as anger and frustration, which can lead to crime and delinquency [27]. If institutions use the data collected in the classroom to screen for potential criminals, it may not sit well with society. More so, laws such as the EU General Data Protection Regulation (GDPR) have a set a precedent of how data is processed within the public sector [28]. Care would need to be taken with regards to where and how information, such as students in a physical classroom, is being sent and used.

5.2 Insights

In the pilot study, there was also a residual impact when using the model within a classroom setting. Students were willing to participate in the pilot, because it may benefit their learning experience. The model brings about a certain amount of educator awareness that would normally only be seen in a seasoned educator. However, some aspects could be surprising even to a seasoned educator, such as students that maintain one emotional state may not be necessarily good for learning too or the surprise indicator may portray a relationship with attentiveness. However, the future adjustments as a result of prolonged negative sentiment do promote more interactivity on the educator's part. The report model also confirms that student interaction does increase with more positive emotions in a classroom. Thereby showing there is value in using the model with less experienced educators that can not intuitively get a "feel" for the classroom.

5.3 Computer Science Education

Participatory teaching methods within the space of computer science education are on the rise. Evidence suggests there is a need for a shift in course design that addresses the unique methods of learning for each student [12]. The methods introduced thus far adjust content such as the type of programming language or the target problem to maximize learning [13–15], but this is not the only dimension that should be pursued for more personalized learning. There is room for deriving other student attributes, such as emotion or weak areas using technology that serve to assist the educator, especially in the sciences. Being able to quantify the extent to which student learning takes place is a promising value proposition and may be useful in the future.

Overall one can ask is there value in pursuing emotion recognition for computer science education or education as a whole. Although one has to be cognizant of the constraints experienced within this context, it still achieves the use case and it opens up a further avenue of research that may assist educational psychologists and educators alike in determining conducive conditions for student learning.

6   Conclusion

Changing the education landscape to include more participatory teaching methods to maximize student learning has been a challenge especially in the sciences. It is further complicated by the fact that certain students do not engage with certain participatory methods. An experienced educator can pick up any distance between these teaching methods and their students to facilitate adaptive teaching and learning.

Advances in the field of computer vision have shown potential in other domains, and an attractive inventory of methods have been identified, which warrant the investigation of using these technologies to achieve collaborative support-based adaptive teaching and learning for a physical classroom of students. By leveraging innovation within the field of computer vision, many application domains can benefit from insights derived in a scene to promote user effectiveness.

Although automation efforts within the fourth industrial revolution are typically not well received because it can lead to job loss, this study shows there is also potential in using the technology as an assistant mechanism for fields that require the "human touch". The current and potential benefits cannot be ignored, as we endeavor to find the next generation of learning, which is aware of ideal conditions necessary for individual student learning.

References

1. Yin, S., Kaynak, O.: Big data for modern industry: challenges and trends [point of view]. Proc. IEEE **103**(2), 143–146 (2015)
2. Wilson, B.C.: A study of factors promoting success in computer science including gender differences. Comput. Sci. Educ. **12**(1–2), 141–164 (2002)
3. Hake, R.R.: Interactive-engagement versus traditional methods: a six-thousand-student survey of mechanics test data for introductory physics courses. Am. J. Phys. **66**(1), 64–74 (1998)
4. Jones, V., Jo, J.H.: Ubiquitous learning environment: an adaptive teaching system using ubiquitous technology. In: Beyond the Comfort Zone: Proceedings of the 21st ASCILITE Conference, Perth, Western Australia, vol. 468, p. 474 (2004)
5. Phipps, R., Merisotis, J.: What's the difference? A review of contemporary research on the effectiveness of distance learning in higher education (1999)
6. Garrison, D.R., Vaughan, N.D.: Blended Learning in Higher Education: Framework, Principles, and Guidelines. Wiley, Hoboken (2008)
7. Schwab, K.: The fourth industrial revolution. In: World Economic Forum (2016)
8. Teferra, D., Altbachl, P.G.: African higher education: challenges for the 21st century. High. Educ. **47**(1), 21–50 (2004)
9. Handelsman, J., et al.: Scientific teaching. Science **304**(5670), 521–522 (2004)

10. Jones, J.S.: Participatory teaching methods in computer science. In: ACM SIGCSE Bulletin. vol. 19, pp. 155–160. ACM (1987)
11. Ben-Ari, M.: Constructivism in computer science education. In: ACM Sigcse Bulletin. vol. 30, pp. 257–261. ACM (1998)
12. Robins, A., Rountree, J., Rountree, N.: Learning and teachingprogramming: a review and discussion. Comput. Sci. Educ. **13**(2), 137–172 (2003)
13. Williams, L., Kessler, R.: Pair Programming Illuminated. Addison-Wesley Longman Publishing Co., Inc., Boston (2002)
14. Papastergiou, M.: Digital game-based learning in high school computer science education: impact on educational effectiveness and student motivation. Comput. Educ. **52**(1), 1–12 (2009)
15. Meerbaum-Salant, O., Armoni, M., Ben-Ari, M.: Learning computer science concepts with scratch. Comput. Sci. Educ. **23**(3), 239–264 (2013)
16. Paramythis, A., Loidl-Reisinger, S.: Adaptive learning environments and e-learning standards. In: Second European Conference on e-learning, vol. 1, pp. 369–379 (2003)
17. Brusilovsky, P., Peylo, C.: Adaptive and intelligent web-based educational systems. Int. J. Artif. Intell. Educ. (IJAIED) **13**, 159–172 (2003)
18. Pea, R.D.: The social and technological dimensions of scaffolding and related theoretical concepts for learning, education, and human activity. J. Learn. Sci. **13**(3), 423–451 (2004)
19. Picard, R.W., et al.: Affective computing (1995)
20. Meyer, D.K., Turner, J.C.: Discovering emotion in classroom motivation research. Educ. Psychol. **37**(2), 107–114 (2002)
21. Sutton, R.E., Mudrey-Camino, R., Knight, C.C.: Teachers' emotion regulation and classroom management. Theory Pract. **48**(2), 130–137 (2009)
22. Fried, L., et al.: Teaching teachers about emotion regulation in the classroom. Aust. J. Teach. Educ. (Online) **36**(3), 1 (2011)
23. Titsworth, S., McKenna, T.P., Mazer, J.P., Quinlan, M.M.: The bright side of emotion in the classroom: do teachers' behaviors predict students' enjoyment, hope, and pride? Commun. Educ. **62**(2), 191–209 (2013)
24. Lisetti, C.L., Nasoz, F.: Using noninvasive wearable computers to recognize human emotions from physiological signals. EURASIP J. Appl. Signal Process. **2004**, 1672–1687 (2004)
25. Shen, L., Wang, M., Shen, R.: Affective e-learning: using "emotional" data to improve learning in pervasive learning environment. J. Educ. Technol. Soc. **12**(2), 176 (2009)
26. Wu, C.H., Tzeng, Y.L., Huang, Y.M.: Understanding the relationship between physiological signals and digital game-based learning outcome. J. Comput. Educ. **1**(1), 81–97 (2014)
27. Agnew, R.: Building on the foundation of general strain theory: specifying the types of strain most likely to lead to crime and delinquency. J. Res. Crime Delinq. **38**(4), 319–361 (2001)
28. Albrecht, J.P.: How the gdpr will change the world. Eur. Data Prot. L. Rev. **2**, 287 (2016)

Technology in STEM Education

Creative Learning and Artefacts Making: Promises and Challenges in Practice

Eliana Alves Moreira[1,2(✉)], Marleny Luque Carbajal[2],
and Maria Cecília Calani Baranauskas[2]

[1] Federal Institute of Education, Science and Technology of São Paulo,
Guarulhos, SP, Brazil
eliana.moreira@ifsp.edu.br
[2] Institute of Computing, University of Campinas (UNICAMP),
Campinas, SP, Brazil
marleny.carbajal@students.ic.unicamp.br,
cecilia@ic.unicamp.br

Abstract. In an increasingly technological world of constant change, encouraging the development of skills such as creativity is becoming increasingly important. In this sense, Creative Learning and Maker Movement can be explored to enrich the learning process in subjects such as science, mathematics and computing. In this paper we explore and discuss the use of electronic components to create physical objects in support for science teaching. We investigate how children and their teachers make sense of the technological concepts and aspects involved in the object's construction. We carried out eight Workshops where we worked out four different scenarios. At the end of each Workshop, the children and teachers assessed their affective states regarding the activities. In general, children were very happy and motivated with the maker activities, but not all of them felt in control of the activity. Teachers showed less motivation in the activities whose construction was more elaborate, and showed less control, suggesting that the technological aspects are still a challenge for them.

Keywords: Creative learning · Maker movement · School

1 Introduction

In a technological world of constant change, encouraging the development of skills such as creativity is becoming increasingly important. Creative people are curious and enjoy exploring ideas, so they are more innovative in problem solving. Creative Learning is an emerging concept which has been explored by researchers [1–3] and it is often referenced as a learning style or a culture, a pedagogical approach that uses contemporary and imaginative forms of enquiry to make access and knowledge construction a highly engaging, relevant, and rewarding experience. Sefton-Green *et al.* [4] explain the Creative Learning as a "teaching that allows student to use their imaginations, have ideas, generate multiple possible solutions to problems, communicate in a variety of media and in general think outside the box". Creative Learning is a style of

P. Zaphiris and A. Ioannou (Eds.): HCII 2019, LNCS 11590, pp. 315–331, 2019.
https://doi.org/10.1007/978-3-030-21814-0_24

"learning by doing" [5] and it involves creation [3], that in this theory means the successive emergence of discoveries. Modern technological tools and applications should be incorporated into the school environment, to enrich the learning process and promote the creation of things that are concrete and shareable. Papert [6] in his constructivist approach, had already argued that the teaching-learning relationship is most effective when the learner tries to construct a product that is meaningful to him/her. Creative Learning is active learning, and therefore it is so successful at building student engagement. It recognizes that we all learn in different ways that we learn better when there is relevance, and that learning can be collaborative and social. Five key behaviors that Creative Learning seeks to encourage include "asking questions, making connections, imagining what might be, exploring options and reflecting critically" [7]. In stimulating imagination and curiosity other capacities are discovered and strengthened too, like the ability to take risks, to think independently and empathically, and to be collaborative.

On another front, there is the Maker Movement, which broadly refers to the growing number of people who are engaged in the creative production of artefacts in their daily lives [8]. Martinez and Stager [9] credit Seymour Papert as "the father of the maker movement", implying that constructionism is the theory of learning that undergirds the maker movement's focus on problem solving and digital and physical fabrication. Hatch [10] highlights the importance of the construction of physical objects as a feature of the Maker Movement that distinguishes it from the earlier computational and Internet revolutions. Making encourages students to share ideas and projects and show off their creations. Failure is celebrated as a positive function of progress [11]. Many have commented on the potential of the Maker Movement to support, enliven, change, or even revolutionize children's education in subjects such as science, mathematics and computing [12]. Making enables learning to be more relevant and meaningful as it features a learning-by-demand model, rather than the more traditional just-in-case model that covers a curriculum fixed in advance to include something that might hopefully be useful later [13].

Several authors have proposed activities based on Creative Learning and Maker Movements, which encompass most commonly three main technological areas: Electronics, 3D digital fabrication and Programming or Computation [14].

Paper electronics is the construction of circuits on paper [15] using conductive foils, tapes, or inks to make connections between electronic components such as lights, sensors and programmable microcontrollers. Creators can express themselves by creating circuit patterns with the conductive materials and by decorating their circuits with traditional paper craft media.

Story-Making [16] is a process that cultivates creative learning by combining innovative forms of storytelling and new forms of making with novel technologies. The author proposes a constructionist process designed to engage children in creating multiple representations of their personal experiences and integrating them into a coherent narrative. The author describes experiences with children creating stories using paper electronics, programmable projections and sewable circuits (circuits made on textiles using conductive threads and fabrics to create connections between electronic components).

In this work, we aimed at exploring and understanding the potential of using the approach of Maker Movement as support in activities that promote the Creative Learning in the school context. In the next sections, we provide details about a set of workshops that we have engaged with elementary school students and their teachers to explore creative classroom learning. This paper is structured as follows: Sect. 1 introduces context, the research problem, related works and our objectives; Sect. 2 presents the research methodology; Sect. 3 presents the workshops conducted; Sect. 4 reports on the results and discusses our findings; Sect. 5 presents conclusions and suggests future work.

2 Method

2.1 Participants

We carried out four Workshops with 6-14-year-old children and four others with teachers in an educational environment, throughout 2017. The Workshops' purpose was introducing children to different technologies through creative and meaningful experiences, and in addition, support teachers on methods and materials that could be used autonomously in classes involving creative learning. The activities were approved by the Ethics Committee on Research from the University of Campinas (UNICAMP), under the number 55678316.4.0000.5404.

Each Workshop lasted ninety minutes and took place separately for children and teachers in the Division of Child and Supplementary Education (DedIC, acronym in Portuguese of *Divisão de Educação Infantil e Complementar*) at UNICAMP, inside the unit of Program for the Development and Integration of Children and Adolescents – PRODECAD[1] – acronym in Portuguese of *Programa de Desenvolvimento e Integração da Criança e do Adolescente*. This unit provides complementary education to children, out of shift to the regular education.

2.2 Pre-workshops Activities

Before the first Workshop, a presentation was made, mainly to the children, for elucidating the basic characteristics of electric circuits and safety issues. Firstly, the safety aspects, such as "Don't use electric devices next to water", "Don't touch outlet with wet hands", "Don't touch the metallic parts of the plug", "Don't put scissors, pens, fingers or conductors of electricity into outlets", "Pay attention to the warnings", among others, were shown and discussed. In a second part of the presentation, we presented and discussed how electric power gets into our house, pointing out the electric conduction by wires and the lights being turned on through the switch. During the presentation, the children were asked to think about certain key questions such as "What do you think it is happening when the light in our house doesn't turn on?". Afterwards, we discussed how the unplugged devices work, such as the ones that use AA batteries or rechargeable batteries, like mobile phones.

---

[1] http://www.dgrh.unicamp.br/dedic/prodecad.

Sequentially, we presented to the audience three series electric circuits sketches: a switchless circuit – Fig. 1(a) – and switch-controlled circuit with the switch in the "on" state – Fig. 1(b) – and a switch-controlled circuit with the switch off – Fig. 1(c).

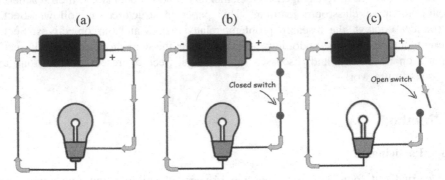

Fig. 1. Examples of serial electric circuits: (a) switchless circuit; (b) and (c) switch-controlled circuits with a closed switch and open switch, respectively.

We also introduced parallel circuits, explaining how they differ from their serial counterparts. We provided further explanations, to the teachers, related to specific characteristics of each kind of topology, specifically, how current and voltage divide in both cases (Fig. 2).

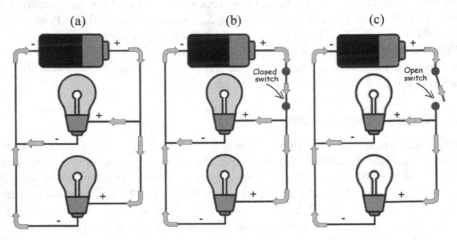

Fig. 2. Examples of parallel electric circuits: (a) switchless circuit; (b) and (c) switch-controlled circuits with a closed switch and open switch, respectively.

2.3 Evaluation

At the end of each Workshop, the participants assessed their affective states regarding the activities performed, using the Self-Assessment Manikin (SAM) instrument [17], and issuing opinions and suggestions that were used as a feedback for subsequent

Pleasure

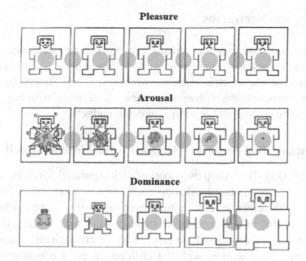

Arousal

Dominance

Fig. 3. Self-Assessment *Manikin* (SAM), reproduced from [17].

workshops. To the affective state evaluation, SAM was used as a pictorial evaluation, that reports pleasure, arousal and dominance regarding the activity performed by the user (see Fig. 3). In the SAM, each participant was supposed to rank from 1 to 9 their pleasure, arousal and dominance about the activity; nine represents very high pleasure, very high arousal and very high dominance and one represents very low pleasure, very low arousal and very low dominance.

At the beginning of the second Workshop, we handed the kids a sheet of paper with a set of objects printed. Then we asked them to choose the ones that would be used to make the electric circuit, so that we could evaluate whether the children had understood the electric circuit concepts shown and used in the first Workshop (see Fig. 4). Furthermore, they would name other materials they thought would be required.

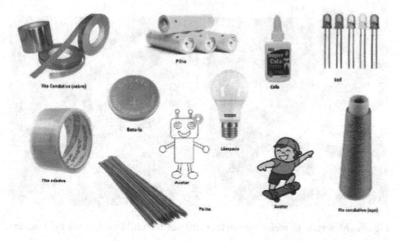

Fig. 4. Objects listed for the children to choose the ones would be used on circuit building.

3   The Designed Scenarios

Four different scenarios were created during the Workshops, with increasing levels of difficulty. The intention was for the participants to gradually build an understanding of the characteristics of the electric circuits, while they built them. In the following subsections, we introduce the different scenarios that were worked, describing the materials used, the dynamic and how to make the gadgets.

3.1   The Lightning Dog Scenario – Origami with Electric Circuit

In the Lightning Dog Workshop we worked with parallel circuits. Following our incremental strategy, in this first workshop each child would work individually with a circuit. Inspired by the creative learning and learning-by-doing approaches, we decided that it would be useful to associate the electric circuits with a familiar subject to the children. Therefore, we associated origami with electric circuits, since the former subject had already been worked with the children in prior educational activities. In order to make the gadget work, the participants should make their own circuit and fold the paper.

Materials. Each participant received a set (see Figs. 5 and Fig. 6), which contained all the necessary materials to make the gadget. Each set had a 60 cm of conductive copper tape, a paper compartment to hold the battery, a 3-volt lithium CR2032 battery (coin-shaped), two Light Emitting Diodes (LEDs), three metallic paper clips and a sheet of origami paper with a sketch of the dog and the electric circuit printed on both sides (Fig. 6). The only difference between the sets for children – Fig. 5(a) – and for the teachers – Fig. 5(b) – was that, for the children, we bent the anode of the LEDs into a square and the cathode into a circle; we thought it would be better, at the current point, to aid the identification of the polarity of the LEDs in such way.

(a)   (b)

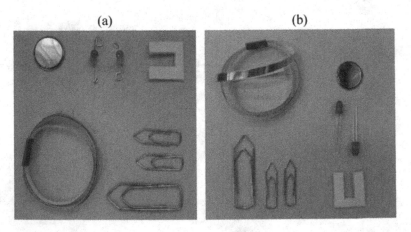

Fig. 5. Materials to make the artefact: (a) set for children; (b) set for teachers.

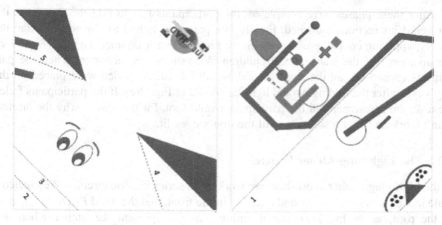

Fig. 6. Material to make the artefact: Sketch for parallel electric circuit origami.

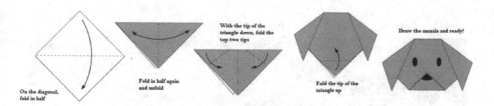

Fig. 7. Instructions for the dog head origami. Adapted from [18].

Dynamic. The first activity assigned to the participants was making a dog's head in origami, as in Fig. 7.

The artefact making consisted of, firstly, covering the green paths (positive side) and the red ones (negative side) in the sketch with the tape of conductive copper, as shown in Fig. 8(a), emphasizing that the LEDs should be placed on their corresponding spaces. We pointed out to the participants that both the batteries and the LEDs had polarities which should be respected; the positive pole of the battery with the positive pole of the LED; the same for the negative poles.

Fig. 8. (a) and (b) Teachers and children, respectively, making the artefact; (b) artefact correctly made by a child. (Color figure online)

After these phases were completed, the participants had to fold the sketch, as the numbered instructions indicated. Finally, the participants had to clip the ears and the battery, applying enough pressure to ensure proper electric contact. The Fig. 8 shows a few moments of the teachers and children Workshops, respectively. When the participants carried out all the steps accurately, all the LEDs, which were placed on the dog's eyes after the folding, would light, as shown in Fig. 8(c). If the participants failed the task, the researcher and the participant would look for the reason why the artefact didn't work and find a solution until the dog's eyes lit.

3.2   The Lightning Atelier Scenario

In the Lightning Atelier Workshop, we worked on series electric circuits. We created a scale model featuring a house and a garden in the front, and the word *PRODECAD* next to the roof, as in Fig. 9(a); our intention was to represent the atelier where the Workshops took place and the educational area attended by the children who participated in the research.

(a)   (b)   (c)

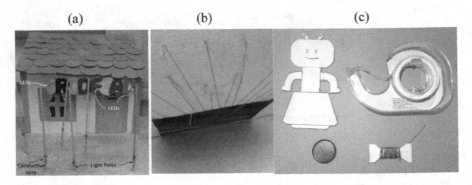

Fig. 9. (a) and (b) Atelier scale model with wood skewers with a conductive wire - *Part B* of the circuit; (c) Materials to make the Part A (Avatars, in a robot shape) of the artefact.

Each letter of the word PRODECAD had a LED; the goal of this activity was to turn on these lights by connecting robot-shaped *avatars* – Fig. 9(c) – to the scale model. Each letter was part of an independent series circuit, which was initially open and became closed when the avatar was connected to the scale model, because each avatar had a part of the circuit (named *Part A*, in order to simplify the explanation). On the other hand, in the Atelier scale model there were several pairs of *light poles* (wood skewer with a conductive wire) placed on it, which had the *Part B* of the circuit. The avatar would be connected to the light poles, closing a circuit (*Part A* + *Part B*), which would make one of the LEDs light.

In our incremental workshops approach, kids worked in pairs, this time, to make an avatar. In order to turn all the lights on, it was necessary that all the teams made their avatars correctly.

Materials. The Lightning Atelier Scenario design involved the initial creation of the scale model where the avatars would be connected. The model was developed by the researchers using conductive wire, tape, Styrofoam, paper, wood skewers and LEDs. Each pair of wood skewers was connected to a LED by a conductive wire; one of them was on the positive pole and the other on the negative pole, see Fig. 9(a). There were two layers of Styrofoam, placed one over the other. The wood skewers were pinned on the top layer. The wire went down the light pole and reached the LED between the layers of Styrofoam, see Fig. 9(b). In order to make the avatar, each participant received a set – see Fig. 9(c) – containing a 40-cm conductive wire segment, avatars, a 3-volt lithium CR2032 battery (coin-shaped) and tape.

Dynamic. At the beginning of the Workshop activities, we explained the goal and how the avatars would be used. Each pair of children chose their avatar. The second task that the children had to perform was to design their avatar, using paper and pencils, in order to create the electric circuit of the atelier; only after this design phased would they continue with the hands-on part. Figure 10 shows some moments of the Workshop and the "Lightning Atelier" with a few lights on.

| (a) | (b) | (c) |

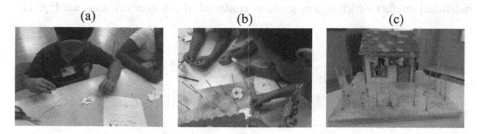

Fig. 10. (a) Children making the Part A of the circuit; (b) Children connecting the Part A to the light poles; (c) The Atelier with a few lights on.

3.3   The Electrical Garden Scenario

In the Electrical Garden Workshop, we carried out the activity using the parallel circuit concept in an electric garden shape, in which the flower cores consisted of LEDs that lit. Each child made an artefact individually. We continued applying the origami activity with electric circuits. All the participants should make their own circuit, fold the origami and join it to the whole artefact, so the garden would light up. In our incremental approach, each of these artefacts would be joined with a larger set in order to make the circuit work only after adding all the parts.

Materials. The electrical garden design involved the initial creation of a base where each individual artefact would be connected, implemented by the researchers using conductive copper tape, adhesive tape, 3-volt CR2032 lithium batteries (coin-shaped) and E.V.A (Ethylene-vinyl Acetate). The base consisted of two parts: a support, on which the circuit was built using sections of conductive copper tape – see Fig. 11(a) – and a layer that covered the circuit, shown in Fig. 11(b), where parts of the underlying copper tape were made to protrude, thereby forming one side of an electric switch.

(a)   (b)   (c)

Fig. 11. (a) and (b) Base where each individual artefact would be connected; (c) Materials for the artefact making.

To build the individual artefacts the participants received a set, as Fig. 11(c). Each one included 20 cm of conductive copper tape, one LED (with the legs in a U-shape so they would fit on the conductive tape path), a paper clip and two sheets of paper to fold. One of the sheets had a drawing showing where to lay the conductive tape. The sheets were joined together using common adhesive tape.

Dynamic. In order to carry out the activity, each participant had to build his/her individual artefact which in this scenario consisted of a flower origami, see Fig. 12.

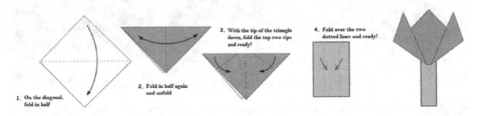

Fig. 12. Instructions for the flower petals and stem origami. Adapted from [18].

The artefact construction started by placing the LED on top of the stem, covering the black marks with conductive tape and folding the origami, as shown in Fig. 13(a). Afterwards, the participant would fold the flower petals, punch a hole where the LED would fit and join the stem and the petals with adhesive tape. With the individual artefact ready, each participant would place his/her flower onto one of the slots, in the garden, where the underlying conductive tape protruded and was exposed, as shown in Fig. 13(b). The garden had ten slots for flowers; nine of them connected in parallel to each other, and one connected in series with the battery. Placing a flower onto a slot would close that part of the circuit. Electric current would only flow through the circuit when the series slot was closed. We, therefore, purposely left that slot to be connected the last, so all the LEDs would light up simultaneously only after the last flower was placed on the garden, for an enhanced effect. Figure 13(c) shows the fully lit garden, with all the flowers connected in it.

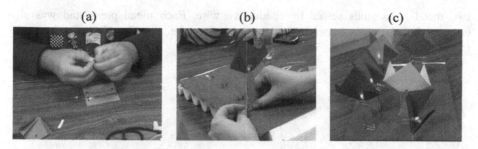

Fig. 13. (a) Individual artefact making (flower); (b) Connecting the flower to the base artefact (garden); (c) Garden after the connection of all the flowers.

3.4 The Fashion Bracelet Scenario

In the Fashion Bracelet Workshop, each child made a fabric bracelet. It contained a series circuit (sewed onto the fabric) that turned on a LED. In our incremental approach of activities, the making of the serial circuit, formerly built with paper, is now in a wearable artefact.

Materials. Each participant received a set, as Fig. 14 shows, featuring all the necessary materials to make the Workshop's artefact. In each set, there were two 20 × 6-cm pieces of fabric (felt), a needle, a sewing thread, LEDs (only one for children and two for teachers), 50-cm steel conductive wire (for sewing), 3-volt CR2032 lithium batteries (coin-shaped), two metal press studs, a 6 × 6-cm piece for the battery casing, a felt clipping flower or spaceship and a model to make the bracelet. In order to facilitate the identification of the LED poles, the negative and positive poles of the model had been marked with a circle and a square, respectively. The same identification had been physically made on LED poles.

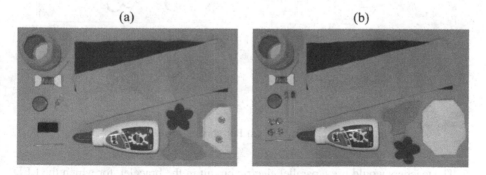

Fig. 14. Materials for the artefact making: (a) for children; (b) for teachers.

Dynamic. The bracelet design involved the construction of a case where the battery would be placed. The children were handed a readymade case by the researchers. For the teachers, the dynamic included the case making. It consisted of a felt casing with two metal press studs sewed by conductive wire. Each metal press stud was also connected to one of the battery poles by conductive wire. The Fig. 15 shows the model to the case making.

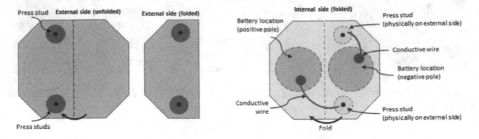

Fig. 15. Battery case diagram.

Each participant made his/her own bracelet, out of the provided felt. The kids would use a series electrical circuit in the bracelet which would light up when a battery was placed in the case. Thus, the kids had to sew the LED's legs to the inner side of the bracelet using the conductive wire, and each leg to their corresponding pole on the battery case using the same conductive wire. On the external side of the bracelet the kids had to make a hole in order to pass the LED and sew either the flower or the spaceship around it. The bracelet was tied off with Velcro. Figure 16(a) shows the bracelet diagram for kids.

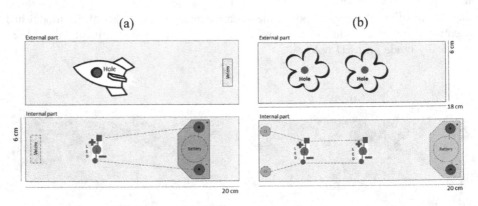

Fig. 16. Bracelet diagram. (a) For children; (b) For teachers.

The teachers would use a parallel electric circuit in the bracelet, for which the LED would light up when the press studs were buttoned. As Fig. 16(b) shows, the battery case in the teachers' bracelet was connected to two press studs whereas the LEDs were connected to their respective press studs placed in the opposite side, so that the electrical circuit would close when the bracelet was buttoned. Figure 17 shows a bracelet completed and some Workshop moments.

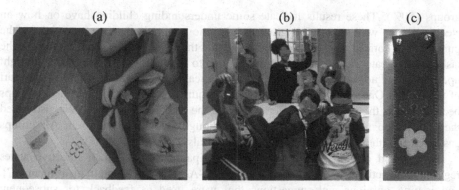

Fig. 17. (a) Children sewing the bracelet; (b) Children showing their bracelets; (c) ready bracelet.

4 Workshops Results and Discussion

As we mentioned above, at the beginning of the second Workshop (see Sect. 3.2 - The Lightning Atelier Scenario), we asked the children to choose, among a set of objects, the ones that would be used to make the electric circuit and complete the task so that we could evaluate whether the children had understood the electric circuits shown and used in the first Workshop. Figure 18 depicts the available objects and the numbers in brackets next to each object are the quantity of groups that judged the respective object to be necessary for lighting up the LED. In total, four groups answered.

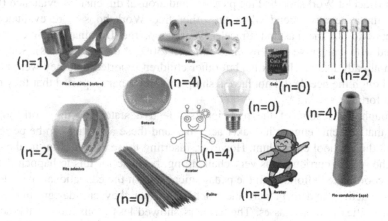

Fig. 18. Objects and respective number of groups (n) that marked the object as needed to create the electrical circuit.

The material needed to create the electrical circuit and complete the second Workshop' task consisted of a battery, conductive wire, avatar and tape, as shown in Fig. 9(c). The first three objects were chosen by all the groups and the last one by two groups (50%). These results indicate some understanding children have on how an electric circuit works, since all groups chose the materials that are essential for the purpose. We noticed that two groups marked that they would need LEDs. Although the task was to create the avatars and connect them to the light pole for the LEDs to light up, they would not be on the part of the circuit created by the children since it was part of the model. One group noted that it would require conductive copper tape, perhaps because it was the conductive material used in the previous workshop. We also asked the children to name other materials they thought would be required. All groups answered that they would not need other materials.

At the end of each Workshop, the participants assessed their affective states regarding the activities performed, using the Self-Assessment Manikin instrument [17], and issuing opinions and suggestions that were used as feedback for subsequent workshops. For the analysis of the results we used a scale of 1 to 9 to represent the affective state chosen by the respondent, where nine means total pleasure, total arousal or total dominance over participation in the activity, and one means total displeasure, total disinterest or lack of control. The frequencies of responses are expressed in Fig. 19(a) and (b) for children and teachers, respectively. Responses with negative trends are expressed in blue tones (left) and responses with positive trends are expressed in shades of orange (right); the central item of the SAM (normal pleasure, normal arousal and normal dominance) is presented in gray (marked with a vertical line). Over each of the frequencies we present the number of people who chose it.

In general, the children were very happy and motivated with the maker activities, but not all of them felt in control of the activity. We observed that the activities that involve artistic skills (crafts) were those with poor evaluation and therefore, these had the evaluations with more negative trend – see Fig. 19(a). For instance, only the Fashion Bracelet Workshop had the pleasure and arousal dimensions evaluated (by one child) with a negative trend while the other tree Workshops were evaluated with positive trend. In the Fashion Bracelet Workshop, the Dominance dimension was evaluated with a negative trend by three children (30% of the participants). Some of the children already had sewing skills, but other children reported that they were afraid to sew (although the needle did not have a sharp tip) and others reported that they did not feel comfortable sewing.

Through the results of the participants affective states for the workshops, we noticed that students engage in maker activities and these activities can be perfectly in line with their school curriculum. However, inserting these activities in the day-to-day and in the school curriculum is very challenging, because for this to happen there is a need of coordinated efforts from the pedagogical staff in the educational space to adapt teachers practices and to prepare the teachers so that they can design and offer the maker activities in their classes. The teachers showed less motivation in the activities whose construction of the artifacts was more elaborate in terms of the complexity of electrical circuit making (*i.e.* Fashion Bracelet). Regarding their control of the learning situation, the teachers presented a response of normal to lack of control, suggesting that the technological aspects are still a challenge for them. The incremental method applied in our Workshops could be added to some special training with the basics of the science behind the scenarios' construction, as an alternative to face this challenge.

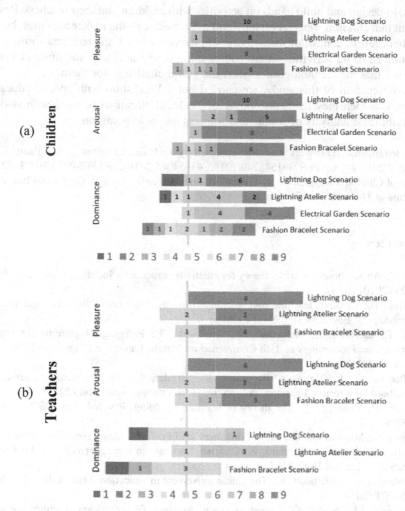

Fig. 19. Self-assessment: (a) Children; (b) Teachers. Responses with negative and positive trends are expressed in blue (left) and orange tones (right), respectively; the central item of the SAM is presented in gray (marked with a vertical line). Over each frequency we present the number of people who chose it. (Color figure online)

5   Conclusion

Modern technological tools and applications should be incorporated into the school environment, to enrich the learning process and to promote the creation of things that are concrete and shareable. Nevertheless, a path into these technologically-enriched new learning spaces must be constructed as well. In this work, we present our efforts in designing scenarios to explore the benefits and challenges of joining maker ideas to the creative learning approach. We explored the use of technologies, specifically electrical circuits, to design and build hands on activities with children and their teachers. Results point out that children were very happy and motivated with the maker activities, but not all of them felt in control of the activity. On the other hand, the teachers showed less motivation in those activities where construction of the artifacts was more elaborate, suggesting that the technological aspects are still a challenge for them.

In continuation of this study, we carried out a Workshop with special education teachers, in which they learned to build an electrical circuit to be used with students with disabilities; analysis of results and impacts are now going on.

Acknowledgments. This work was also supported by the Federal Institute of São Paulo, CNPq (# 306272/2017-2), CAPES (#1545149/2015, #1654045/2016), FAPESP (#2015/16528-0), Division of Child and Supplementary Education, Social Benefit Manager Group and Institute of Computing at University of Campinas.

References

1. Iba, T.: An autopoietic systems theory for creativity. Procedia - Soc. Behav. Sci. **2**(4), 6610–6625 (2010)
2. Jeffrey, B.: Creative teaching and learning: towards a common discourse and practice. Cambridge J. Educ. **36**(3), 399–414 (2006)
3. Iba, T., Ichikawa, C., Sakamoto, M., Yamazaki, T.: Pedagogical patterns for creative learning. In: Proceedings of 18th Conference on Pattern Language Programs - PLoP 2011, pp. 1–6 (2011)
4. Sefton-Green, J., Thomson, P., Jones, K., Bresler, L.: The Routledge International Handbook of Creative Learning, vol. 35, no. 3. Routledge, Abingdon (2011)
5. Anzai, Y., Simon, H.A.: The theory of learning by doing. Psychol. Rev. **86**(2), 124–140 (1979)
6. Papert, S.: Mindstorms: Children, Computers, and Powerful Ideas, New York (1980)
7. Craft, A., Cremin, T., Burnard, P.: Creative learning: an emergent concept. In: Creative Learning 3-11: and How We Document It (2008)
8. Halverson, E.R., Sheridan, K.: The maker movement in education. Harv. Educ. Rev. **84**(4), 495–504 (2014)
9. Martinez, S.L., Stager, G.: Invent to Learn: Making, Tinkering, and Engineering in the Classroom. Constructing Modern Knowledge Press, Torrance (2013)
10. Hatch, M.: The maker movement manifesto. Mak. Mov. Manif. 1–31 (2014)
11. Martin, L.: The promise of the maker movement for education. J. Pre-College Eng. Educ. Res. **5**(1), 4 (2015)
12. Chu, S.L., Schlegel, R., Quek, F., Christy, A., Chen, K.: 'I Make, Therefore I Am'. In: Proceedings of 2017 CHI Conference on Human Factors Computer Systems - CHI 2017, pp. 109–120 (2017)
13. Gershenfeld, N.: Fab: The Coming Revolution on Your Desktop–from Personal Computers to Personal Fabrication. Basic Books Inc., New York (2007)
14. Chu, S.L., Deuermeyer, E., Quek, F.: Supporting scientific modeling through curriculum-based making in elementary school science classes. Int. J. Child-Comput. Interact. **16**, 1–8 (2018)
15. Qi, J., Buechley, L.: Sketching in circuits: designing and building electronics on paper. In: Proceedings of Human Factors Computer System, pp. 1713–1721 (2014)

16. Panjwani, A.: Constructing meaning: designing powerful story-making explorations for children to express with tangible computational media. In: Proceedings of 2017 Conference on Interaction Design and Children, pp. 358–364 (2017)

17. Bradley, M.M., Lang, P.J.: Measuring emotion: the self-assessment manikin and the semantic differential. J. Behav. Ther. Exp. Psychiatry **25**(1), 49–59 (1994)

18. Revolução Artesanal, "Cachorro-Origami". https://www.revolucaoartesanal.com.br/serie-do-fazer-manual-brincando-e-criando/origami-cachorro/. Accessed 02 Feb 2017

Effects of Teaching Methodology on the Students' Academic Performance in an Introductory Course of Programming

Patricia Compañ-Rosique$^{(\boxtimes)}$, Rafael Molina-Carmona$^{(\boxtimes)}$, and Rosana Satorre-Cuerda$^{(\boxtimes)}$

Cátedra Santander-UA de Transformación Digital, Universidad de Alicante, Alicante, Spain
{patricia.company,rmolina,rosana.satorre}@ua.es

Abstract. The work of a teacher is dynamic. Year after year it is necessary to adjust the contents and the methodology to the features of the students and the changes in the profession. The authors of this paper are aware of these needs and have been adapting over time a basic programming subject of the degree in Computer Engineering. The objective of this work is to analyse how the different teaching methodologies used in an introductory course to programming during several academic years affect the students' performance. For this purpose, the students' academic performance has been collected (the final grade in the first call of the subject) and they have been confronted with different input variables: methodology used (three methodologies: lecture, flipped learning, hybrid methodology), gender and university access grade. The article shows the results of this analysis and establishes the possible correlations between the variables studied.

Keywords: Programming teaching · Teaching methodologies · Flipped learning · Lecture

1 Introduction

The teaching-learning process is highly complex as many factors influence its success. Basically it involves two agents, teachers and students [1].

From the point of view of teaching, the main protagonist is the teacher while the student acquires all the protagonism considering the facet of learning. In any teaching-learning model, a structured plan must be drawn up that can be used to configure a syllabus, to design teaching materials and to guide teaching in the classroom. Many authors present different classifications of teaching methodologies [2]. Among them, Bruce Joyce and Marsha Weil [3] argue that there is no perfect or unique methodology, as there is no model capable of coping with all learning styles. It is evident that each person has a different learning

© Springer Nature Switzerland AG 2019
P. Zaphiris and A. Ioannou (Eds.): HCII 2019, LNCS 11590, pp. 332–345, 2019.
https://doi.org/10.1007/978-3-030-21814-0_25

style according to his or her individual abilities. This means that the teacher must be aware of these differences and establish different teaching strategies in order to reach each student [4]. Even so, within a course the same activity is seen differently by each student.

These characteristics oblige the teacher, and in our case the university teacher, to try to improve not only their knowledge on the subject, but also the way of teaching it. Year by year, they research and put into practice different methodologies and techniques so that their students can better assimilate the knowledge, competences and skills corresponding to the subject [5]. This motivation on the part of the teacher is important because as time goes by it improves the way in which the subject is taught.

This continuous change in teaching methodologies generally leads to greater success in student learning. Although this is the case in most situations, it is important to analyse the academic results of students year after year. In recent times, lecture have been widely denigrated in favour of more active methodologies such as project-based learning, gamification or flipped learning [6].

Computer programming is a basic subject in any computer curriculum. In the specific case of an introductory course to programming, the teacher asks many questions about how to teach it. Many doubts arise about which programming language to use, which paradigm, and so on. The teaching methodology to be used is no exception: lecture? flipped learning? project-based learning? Regardless of the methodology used, it is essential to analyse the results obtained with it. Sometimes, it is thought that more modern techniques are better than more traditional procedures. This is not always so, it is important to review the results obtained to see if effectively using new methodologies makes students learn better.

This paper analyses different teaching methodologies that have been used from the academic year 2011-12 to the academic year 2017-18 to determine if there is a correlation with the academic results obtained. Although the main objective of this work is to determine whether the methodology influences the results, other possible influencing factors have also been analysed, such as the university access grade or the student's gender.

The document is organised as follows. Section 2 presents the context of the research. The teaching methodologies are presented in Sect. 3. Section 4 is devoted to explain how each methodology has been applied. The studies carried out to determine the possible relationships between the variables analysed (methodology, gender, access grade) and the results obtained (subject grade) are shown in Sect. 5. Finally, the conclusions resulting from this work, as well as the possible lines of future work, are presented in Sect. 6.

2   Context

The subject of this research is an introductory subject to programming. It is taught in the first year of the Bachelor's degree in Computer Engineering. It is a degree with a large volume of students, so there is a wide variety of data, about a thousand samples. With these data, a study is developed in which the results obtained in the subject are analysed according to the access grade, the gender and the main focus of this study, the methodology used.

This subject is the first contact of many students with computer programming. Some of the students, a minority, have notions of this subject because they have taken a programming course before starting university studies. However, for most students this subject is the first encounter with this field. This study will focus on the latter, that is to say, on those students who come from secondary school and who, therefore, have had little or no contact with the subject analysed in this work.

It is an introductory subject with the following objectives:

- Ability to solve problems with initiative, decision making, autonomy and creativity.
- Analyze problems that can be solved by computer and design algorithms to solve them.
- Implement algorithms using structured programming techniques.
- Understand and know how to use a high level language.
- Understand the implications of the work of a programmer, individually and as a member of a team.

The content of the course includes data types, control sentences (conditionals and loops), modular programming, recursion, arrays, records and basic notions of how to measure the computational cost of an algorithm. The programming language used is C. Development environments are not used because the subject teachers are interested in students learning to differentiate basic concepts such as source code, executable code, compiler, and so on. A Linux terminal is used, using the commands to call the compiler and to run the program. Although the use of an integrated development environment would be more comfortable for them, from the point of view of the teachers, the student learns better the basic concepts using this system.

The essential objective of the course is that students learn to solve problems and are able to propose an efficient solution by means of a high level language.

3 Teaching Methodologies

There are multiple teaching methodologies that can be put into practice in the classroom: flipped classroom [7], micro flip teaching [8], project-based learning [9], cooperative learning [10], gamification [11], problem-based learning [12], design thinking [13], thinking-based learning [14], and so on. Normally, the teacher chooses the methodology that he or she believes will work best with the students. This would be the ideal case but it is not always possible and does not always work as expected. The teacher is subject to a number of constraints that also determine the methodology that can be used:

- Temporary restrictions: the time dedicated to the subject, as well as the moment in which it is taught, cannot be modified.

– Quantitative restrictions: the number of students per classroom limits in many cases the methodology to be used.
– Spatial constraints: for instance, the configuration and location of the tables in the classroom often does not facilitate the use of some methodologies.

For example, more active and participatory methodologies on the part of students often require small groups. There are also methodologies that, by their nature, require the student to have a significant amount of time to research and usually it is necessary to adhere to an academic calendar that severely restricts deadlines.

In the subject Programming 1, since the academic year 2011-12, two well-differentiated teaching methodologies have been used and a combination of both. The main characteristics of these methodologies are listed below.

3.1 Lecture

This method could be defined as the set of theoretical or practical knowledge given to apprentices by the master of a science, art or craft [1].

The lecture is the traditional method used in teaching. Although it has drawbacks [15] (it favours passivity in the student, reduces information sources to the teacher's word etc.), it also offers the advantage that it allows the quick transmission of a large volume of knowledge. In addition, it facilitates the comprehension of complex knowledge, since the teacher is in charge of simplifying the concepts to adapt them to the students' level of knowledge. Part of the teacher's job in preparing the lectures is to document himself or herself in an appropriate manner by consulting various authors on the subject. Therefore, although the student does not consult other sources of information, the teacher will have done so and the lessons should show this diversity in knowledge. Another important advantage of the lecture is that the students usually feel more secure in the knowledge conveyed by the teacher than in their own research on the subject.

A good lecture consists of four phases:

1. Preparation and design: objectives formulation, contents organization, activities preparation for students. This phase would be prior to classroom action.
2. Introduction: capturing the audience's attention, establishing relationships with the group, arousing interest, motivating towards the task, objectives presentation, introductory general summary, and so forth.
3. Body: content structuring, maintenance of attention and interest, adequate speed and rhythm, expressiveness, etc.
4. Conclusion: intensified retention, emphasis on main ideas, questions, summary, etc.

3.2 Flipped Learning

Flipped learning is a methodology widely used today [16,17]. With this type of technique, students are provided with a series of materials to prepare the course.

Normally, face-to-face sessions are left to solve doubts or do exercises. Before the face-to-face session, the student must have worked on the subject in order to be able to ask the teacher any doubts that may have arisen. It is also common practice to establish some milestones (report delivery or exercises) during the teaching period of the subject. These methodologies rely on techniques that actively involve students and give them a leading role in their own learning.

By means of flipped learning techniques, the student can establish his own work rhythm. In the specific case of a subject belonging to a university degree, as it is the subject we are talking about, this is so to some extent. The student is provided from the beginning with all the teaching materials (both audiovisual and written). It is obvious that the student can establish a learning rhythm higher than the one initially set by the teachers, but it is also true that the student has to respect a minimum speed set by the different deliverable activities, each of which has a deadline.

4   Practical Implementation

The authors of this work have been teaching programming for more than twenty years. This section explains in a concrete manner the way in which the subject has been taught from the academic year 2011-12 to the academic year 2017-18. Different methodologies and approaches have been followed in each academic year. All this with the very complicated aim of ensuring that students acquire the knowledge, skills and abilities involved in computer programming. Different techniques have been used in both theory and practice over the years, but the main changes have occurred in theory. The practical classes have always been taught in a similar way: the students are dedicated to doing programming exercises, so that from a given problem, they find an efficient solution in which they use the appropriate structures, asking the practice teacher when they have doubts. From one course to another there are some variations in the way of evaluating the practice. There are always two practice exams, but in addition, some years some additional control has been incorporated. In addition to this, there have been courses in which a competition of practices has been organised to foster the motivation of the students. Table 1 shows in a schematic way the methodology used in theory and practice classes, as well as other data related to the way of teaching the subject.

4.1   Lecture

Computer programming is an eminently practical subject. In addition, it is characterized by a double aspect: it presents a rigorously technical character with methods characteristic of an engineering as well as requiring an important creative component, as Andy Hertzfeld, co-designer of Macintosh, comments in Programmers at Work [18]. These characteristics of programming make the lecture, in its strictest sense, not the most appropriate methodology for this discipline.

Table 1. Methodology used each academic year

Year	Theory	Practice	Competition
2011/12	Lecture	-5 paper controls -2 practice exams	No
2012/13	Lecture	-3 paper controls -2 practice exams	No
2013/14	Lecture	-peer reviewed paper control - access to a practice requires that a particular exercise of the previous practice has been delivered -2 practice exams	No
2014/15	Lecture	-peer reviewed paper control -2 practice exams	Yes
2015/16	Lecture	-peer reviewed paper control -2 practice exams	Yes
2016/17	Flipped learning	-2 practice exams	No
2017/18	Hybrid methodology	-2 practice exams	No

It is necessary to incorporate multiple examples during the exposition, as well as to intercalate practical activities to be developed by the students.

From year 2011/12 to year 2015/16 the lecture with examples and practical exercises has been the methodology used for the theoretical sessions of the subject. It is important to point out that although all teachers share the same teaching material, the characteristics of the specific group of students to whom the session is addressed, as well as the character of the teacher, greatly influence the way the session is given. Working with a small group of 20 students is not the same as working with a group of 100 students. Similarly, the attitude of the students, which has a great influence on the final result, may also be very conditioned by their profile: age, access studies, family situation, etc.

Although the lecture usually requires little or no student participation, this is not really how it develops in our classes. During the session, concepts are explained and student participation is encouraged through exercises, comparisons with real situations, comments on habits and even exposition by students of their own proposed solutions.

4.2   Flipped Learning

A class based on flipped learning requires prior involvement of the students, which seems to be ideal for this subject. For this reason, in the academic year 2016/17 the teaching staff of the subject decided to implement this methodology for the theory sessions. At the beginning of the course all materials were provided, as well as the planning of deliverables. Approximately every week, the students had to deliver some basic programming exercises corresponding to the theoretical concepts on which they were going to work during the face-to-face session. It is important to point out that the students had to review the materials and send the deliverables before the face-to-face session, that is, without the teacher having explained anything about this topic. The first part of the session was dedicated to solving doubts, as well as to commenting on the main errors detected in the deliverables sent. This meant that the teacher had to review the deliverables before the face-to-face session in order to be able to address errors in the exercises. The second part of the session was devoted to solving more difficult exercises. Specifically, 12 deliverables were planned for the period between September and December.

An important part of the teacher's task during the correction was based on providing feedback to the student. This task was very laborious, given the volume of students enrolled in the subject, but very useful in motivating the delivery of the exercises.

4.3   Hybrid Methodology

The implementation of flipped learning during the 2016/17 academic year presented some drawbacks. The first topics corresponding to simple concepts such as conditionals or loops did not present much difficulty. The students managed quite well with the supplied materials and were able to solve the deliverables without major problems. The complications started when they started working with the modular programming materials. In spite of the fact that the materials had a special emphasis on the parameter passing, as well as on the decomposition into modules, the students did not assimilate it correctly and had difficulties in making the deliverables. It is also true that in previous courses, in which lecture were used, this topic had always generated many complications.

The other major problem that arose was due to the enormous amount of exercises that the teacher had to review before each face-to-face session in order to be able to address the main faults detected.

Given the volume of students each teacher had, an excessive amount of time had to be devoted to reviewing deliverables properly and providing students with feedback on their work. As mentioned above, individualised feedback is essential for the students to learn from their mistakes and be able to progressively improve.

The main problem, though, arose when students, lacking the habit in this type of methodology, considered that it was essential to provide correct exercises and frequently resorted to copying them from other classmates or other sources. They had been strongly insisted that the important issue was to perform them, even if they were not functioning well, since the aim of this type of task is to think, to analyse the problem and thus see whether or not one is capable of providing a solution. However, if the student did not make his own developments, the main advantages of this methodology were completely lost. Actually, the problem of applying this methodology is not the methodology itself, but the fact that since they have started school they have been taught to memorise and then release what has been memorised. Rarely have they been taught to think [19].

Analysing the problems derived from the use of this methodology, it was decided to implement in the academic year 2017/18 a hybrid methodology in which for the initial topics (conditionals and loops) the flipped learning scheme was followed. Two deliverables corresponding to these two topics were programmed. For the rest of the topics of the subject, a lecture scheme was followed, complemented with 4 deliverables corresponding to modular programming, recursion, arrays and records. In addition, the students were provided with an automatic corrector that they could apply to the modular programming and recursion deliverables. If they used the template supplied for these deliverables they could run their programs with different test cases and the corrector indicated whether or not there were operating errors.

Both teachers and students have perceived that this hybrid methodology provides more satisfactory results. However, the problem of copying was still present. This is an issue for which no solution has been found, since the aim of the deliverables is for students to work and make mistakes, but they prefer to copy an exercise that works from another colleague.

5 Results

This section shows a detailed analysis of the results obtained by students from the academic year 2011-12 to 2017-18. Although each course has followed different techniques to teach the subject, it could be said that basically three techniques have been used:

- Lecture: from year 2011-12 to 2015-16. Data are available for 888 students.
- Flipped learning: year 2016-17. Data are available for 148 students.
- Hybrid methodology: year 2017-18. Data are available for 141 students.

The technique followed to find out if there is a relationship of dependence between two variables has been the technique ANOVA (ANalysis Of VAriance) [20,21]. Following the terminology of this technique, the independent variable will be called factor and the dependent variable will be denoted as response. In this work, a one-way ANOVA will be applied since only one factor is analysed for each case presented. The application of the ANOVA technique is based on a hypothesis contrast. The null hypothesis that is contrasted is that the population means are equal:

```
H0: means are equal
H1: means are not equal
```

If the null hypothesis is accepted, it means that the population groups do not differ in the mean value of the dependent variable and therefore the mean value can be considered independent of the factor. In order to contrast the null hypothesis, the value of Snedecor's distribution F is calculated and if it is greater than the critical value, the null hypothesis is rejected [22].

Given that there are three methodologies to be analysed, the data have been grouped into three groups: one for the years in which lectures have been used, another for the year in which flipped learning was used and another for the hybrid methodology.

The objective of the study is to detect whether the teaching methodology is related to the results obtained in the subject. In addition, it also aims to analyse other factors of possible influence such as the student's gender and the university access grade. In order to be able to apply the ANOVA technique, the groups under study must follow a normal distribution. Figure 1 shows the distributions of the grades for the three teaching methodologies and for the gender of the student. As can be seen, the distributions of population groups can be assumed to be normal.

Each academic year there are two calls to pass the subject, so that students who fail the first call have the opportunity to pass in the second. In order to make the contrast in the most similar conditions between years, only the first call of each academic year analysed has been considered. In addition, repeat students have not been considered, since they could affect the result since the second year they take the subject they already have knowledge that the rest of the students do not have.

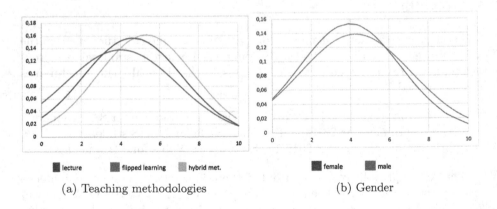

(a) Teaching methodologies   (b) Gender

Fig. 1. Grade distributions

5.1   Teaching Methodology - Final Grades

This section shows the study carried out between the teaching methodology used and the final grade obtained by the student.

Applying the ANOVA technique gives a value F = 14.6742124, the critical value is 3.0033766. Since the value F is greater than the critical value, the null hypothesis is rejected and it is concluded that there is a relationship between the teaching methodology used each academic year and the grades obtained by the students. Figure 2 shows a diagram representing the final grade for the three methodologies analysed. The line joins the average grade obtained for each methodology. It can be seen that the average grade has increased slightly with the hybrid methodology.

These results confirm the initial impression of the teachers of the subject that the use of a combined methodology presents the advantages of the two methodologies used and at the same time compensates for their shortcomings. This subject is developed during the first four-month period of the first year. The students have just begun their university life, are a little disoriented and do not know how the University works. A pure flipped learning methodology is too radical for them, while the lecture makes them maintain a too passive attitude. After trying different strategies, it seems that what works best is to combine both techniques to take advantage of the lecture for complicated concepts while simpler concepts can be assimilated with a more student-dependent methodology. In addition, the fact of introducing some content through flipped learning prepares the students so that in later courses they can introduce this methodology in a more complete way.

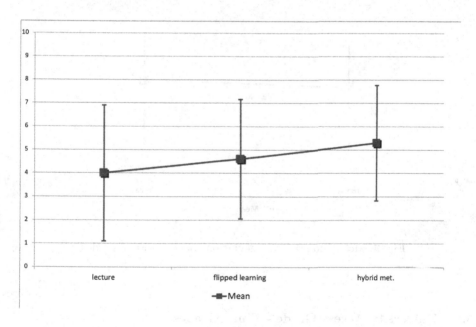

Fig. 2. Mean and standard deviation: Teaching methodology - Final grades

5.2   Gender - Final Grades

In this case, the study carried out between the student's gender and the final grade obtained is shown. Data are available for 162 women and 1015 men. Computer Engineering is a degree whose students are mostly men, due to this fact there is so much disparity in the number of samples.

When applying the ANOVA technique, a value of F 1.43 has been obtained, the critical value being 3.84. Given that the value of F is lower, the null hypothesis is accepted, which means that the population groups do not differ in the mean value of the dependent variable and therefore this mean value can be considered independent of the factor.

Figure 3 shows a diagram representing the mean and standard deviation obtained in the subject grade for the two population groups: men and women. There are no significant differences between the two groups.

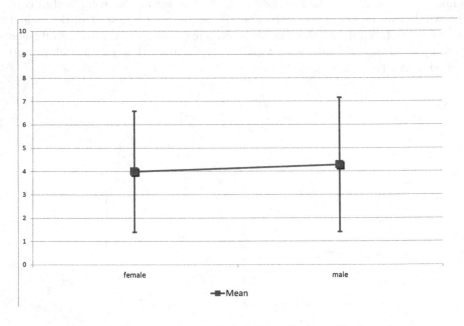

Fig. 3. Mean and standard deviation: Gender - Final grades

5.3   University Access Grade - Final Grades

This section shows the study that has been carried out between the student's university access grade and the final grade obtained by the student. The number of samples available is 1177.

In this case, since both variables are quantitative, a linear correlation analysis has been performed to detect possible relationships between the variables [23].

There are several coefficients that allow quantifying the degree of linear relationship between two variables. In this case the correlation coefficient of Pearson [24] has been used. The value obtained was 0.5. This is a middle value that indicates that there is a moderate linear relationship.

Figure 4 shows a diagram made for the two variables object of this analysis: university access grade and final grade obtained in the subject. Students who have a very high access grade (12–13 points), obtain high grades in the subject. On the other hand, students with low access grades (5–7) obtain low average results in the subject. In the latter cases, the variance has high values. This may be due to the fact that there are students who have a low access grade because the access grade measures the average of the subjects that the students have taken in their pre-university stage, where there are subjects that they do not like or they are not good at. When the students begin their university stage, they are taking a discipline closer to their preferences.

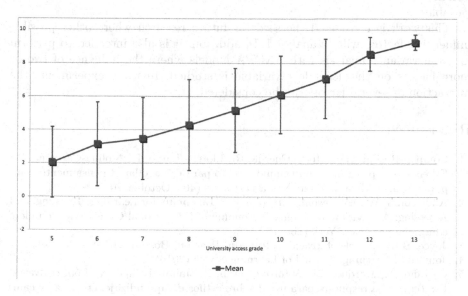

Fig. 4. Mean and standard deviation: University access grades - Final grades

6   Conclusions and Further Work

This study has served to verify possible factors of influence on the final grades obtained by the students in a course of introduction to programming.

In order to carry out the study, the ANOVA technique was used, based on a hypothesis contrast. After compiling the data of the students of the degree in Computer Engineering from the academic year 2011-12 to the academic year 2017-18, different analyses have been carried out to determine the relationship between the final grade obtained by the students and variables such as the teaching methodology used, the gender of the students and the university access grade.

The first study has shown the results of the ANOVA technique between the teaching methodology and the final grade. Analysing the results obtained, it is detected that the use of a hybrid methodology (lecture and flipped learning) seems to be more convenient for the subject under consideration.

The second study analysed the relationship between the gender of the students and the final grade. In this case, there is a great difference in the number of samples between both populations, since it is a degree in which the majority of students are men. However, the analysis carried out allow us to state that there are no significant differences in the subject grade between both groups.

The last case shown analyses the relationship between the university access grade and the final grade. For this last study, a linear correlation analysis has been carried out since both variables are quantitative. The correlation coefficient obtained indicates that there is a moderate linear relationship between both variables.

This work is considered the seed for future research where other possible influencing factors will be analysed. In addition, it is also intended to perform factorial variance analysis with ANOVA models where the influence of two or more factors on the dependent variable is studied. In these experiments the interaction of several factors can be considered.

References

1. Compañ-Rosique, P., Satorre-Cuerda, R., Llorens-Largo, F., Molina-Carmona, R.: Enseñando a programar: un camino directo para desarrollar el pensamiento computacional. Revista de Educación a Distancia (46), October 2015
2. Anderson, L.W., Krathwohl, D.R. (eds.): A Taxonomy for Learning, Teaching, and Assessing: A Revision of Bloom's Taxonomy of Educational Objectives, Complete edn. Longman, New York (2001)
3. Joyce, B.R.: Models of Teaching, 9th edn. Pearson, Boston (2015)
4. Journal of Learning: Journal of Learning Styles (2016)
5. Castaño, A., Marquós, M., Satorre Cuerda, R., Jaume i Capó, A., López Álvarez, D.: Tengo una respuesta para usted sobre estilos de aprendizaje, creencias y cambios en los estudiantes, Universidade de Santiago de Compostela. Escola Técnica Superior d'Enxeñaria, pp. 275–282, July 2010
6. Knight, K.: Book Reviews: The Manual of Learning Styles Peter Honey and Alan Mumford, 83 p. Peter Honey, Maidenhead (1982). £25.20, ISBN 0 9508444 0 3. Manag. Educ. Dev. 14(2), 147–150 (1983)
7. Bloom, B.S., Hastings, J.T., Madaus, G.F.: Handbook on Formative and Summative Evaluation of Student Learning. McGraw-Hill, New York (1971)
8. Fidalgo-Blanco, Á., Sein-Echaluce, M.L., García-Peñalvo, F.J.: Micro flip teaching with collective intelligence. In: Zaphiris, P., Ioannou, A. (eds.) LCT 2018. LNCS, vol. 10924, pp. 400–415. Springer, Cham (2018). https://doi.org/10.1007/978-3-319-91743-6_30
9. de Los Ríos, I., Cazorla, A., Díaz-Puente, J.M., Yagüe, J.L.: Project-based learning in engineering higher education: two decades of teaching competences in real environments. Procedia - Soc. Behav. Sci. 2(2), 1368–1378 (2010)

10. Spencer, K.: Kagan Cooperative Learning. Kagan Publishing, San Clemente (2009)
11. Llorens-Largo, F., Villagrá-Arnedo, C., Gallego-Durán, F., Satorre-Cuerda, R., Compañ-Rosique, P., Molina-Carmona, R.: LudifyME. In: Formative Assessment, Learning Data Analytics and Gamification, pp. 245–269. Elsevier (2016)
12. Delisle, R.: How to Use Problem-based Learning in the Classroom. ASCD, Alexandria (1997)
13. Naiman, L.: Design thinking as a strategy for innovation
14. Yusuf, M.: Infusing thinking-based learning in twenty-first-century classroom: the role of training programme to enhance teachers' skilful thinking skills. In: Amzat, I.H., Valdez, N.P. (eds.) Teacher Empowerment Toward Professional Development and Practices, pp. 211–220. Springer, Singapore (2017). https://doi.org/10.1007/978-981-10-4151-8_14
15. Fidalgo, A.: Metodologías. Lección Magistral: Qué es y cómo mejorarla (2016)
16. Lage, M.J., Platt, G.J., Treglia, M.: Inverting the classroom: a gateway to creating an inclusive learning environment. J. Econ. Educ. 31(1), 30–43 (2000)
17. Fidalgo-Blanco, A., Sein-Echaluce, M.L., García-Peñalvo, F.J.: APFT: active peer-based flip teaching. In: Proceedings of the 5th International Conference on Technological Ecosystems for Enhancing Multiculturality - TEEM 2017, Cádiz, Spain, pp. 1–7. ACM Press (2017)
18. Lammers, S.M.: Programmers at Work: Interviews with 19 Programmers who Shaped the Computer Industry. Tempus Books of Microsoft Press, Redmond (1989)
19. Swartz, R.: ENSEÑNAR A PENSAR: 9 PRINCIPIOS BASICOS-IX - INED21
20. Sthle, L., Wold, S.: Analysis of variance (ANOVA). Chemom. Intell. Lab. Syst. 6(4), 259–272 (1989)
21. Smalheiser, N.R.: ANOVA. In: Data Literacy, pp. 149–155. Elsevier (2017)
22. Yoo, S.K., Cotton, S.L., Sofotasios, P.C., Matthaiou, M., Valkama, M., Karagiannidis, G.K.: The Fisher-Snedecor $\mathcal{F}$ distribution: a simple and accurate composite fading model. IEEE Commun. Lett. 21(7), 1661–1664 (2017)
23. Taylor, R.: Interpretation of the correlation coefficient: a basic review. J. Diagn. Med. Sonogr. 6(1), 35–39 (1990)
24. Sedgwick, P.: Pearson's correlation coefficient. BMJ 345, e4483–e4483 (2012)

Adaptive Learning Case Studies Implementation at Architectural BIM Construction Courses

Jose Ferrándiz[1](✉) and David Fonseca[2](✉)

[1] Department of Technology, Norfolk State Universty, NSU, Norfolk, VA, USA
jaferrandiz@nsu.edu
[2] GRETEL- Grup de Recerca en Technology Enhanced Learning,
La Salle Universitat Ramon Llull, Barcelona, Spain
fonsi@salle.url.edu

Abstract. This paper aims to detail the changes in two BIM construction courses of the architecture degree at the American University of Ras Al Khaimah (AURAK), and the process of analyzing the data collected from them. At the course level we explain the changes effected in the grading criteria and the adaptive approach of the teaching material. At the methodology level we describe the types of data collected and the statistical analysis methods. These elements will establish a clear reproducible pedagogical methodology, clarifying its benefits and scientific, reproducible and proven analysis method.

Keywords: BIM · AEC · Curriculum · Higher education · Mixed methods · Enhanced learning · User centered evaluation · Motivation · Satisfaction · User profile

1 Introduction

Universities in the United Arab Emirates (UAE) are facing a challenging problem in terms of lack of effort, rigor and punctuality from the students, specifically within the architecture program as it is a creative degree which has less structure than other engineering processes. Additionally, Business Information Modelling (BIM) is an innovative development in the AEC industry that is increasingly in demand and more gradually being implemented in AEC curricula, which adds a layer of complexity to the problem. The usual result in such a circumstance is that the faculty are forced to lower expectations within their courses in order to create an environment where these expectations are in sync with the amount of work produced by the students.

In order to improve this situation and create a more competitive environment while improving student motivation, the authors changed grading and project submission policies in order to encourage students to take on the responsibility and ownership of creating their own schedule tailored to their abilities and interests. In this way the students will develop their knowledge at their own speed, allowing advanced students

P. Zaphiris and A. Ioannou (Eds.): HCII 2019, LNCS 11590, pp. 346–356, 2019.
https://doi.org/10.1007/978-3-030-21814-0_26

to progress faster and those needing more time to build confidence by giving them the tools to complete the course at their own pace.

In this experiment we created two different approaches, one linear approach where the students are required to follow a single path sequentially, with each step more challenging than the last; and another adaptive approach which has two paths – a linear one which encompasses the basics of the course and must be completed by every student, and optional assignments which will deepen student knowledge of each course segment and will allow for more credit to improve overall grades.

2   Related Work

2.1   Building Information Modelling (BIM)

Building Information Modelling (BIM) has been recognized as a pivotal point in the development of the Architecture, Engineering and Construction (AEC) industry. Whereas traditionally the various stakeholders involved in the design, construction and management of a building worked largely independently, BIM allows these parties to have real-time access to shared information in order to develop and produce a project cooperatively. It is not a single tool, rather it is a centralized database where information on a single model/project is uploaded, used, and downloaded using different tools. Common factors in different definitions of BIM include a common database; interoperable information; a whole-life informational model (from a building's design to its demolition); and demonstrable advantages, namely increased efficiency and productivity [1].

In 2009 Farid stated, "Twenty years ago, AutoCAD pushed designers into a new era; BIM represents a new generation of virtual model already widely accepted by the industry" [2]. The adoption of BIM within the AEC industry has expanded, such that now many governments globally require the use of BIM, recognizing the clear benefits to costs and workflow [3]. Consequently focus has turned to academia, as AEC graduates and professionals need BIM skills and experience, however most curricula have not fully adopted the BIM methodology [4, 5].

One challenge for institutions in implementing BIM (and the new BIM Information Technology (IT) tools) in their departments has been logistical – whether it should be introduced in an individual course or across the entire curriculum. There is limited data on the practical implementation of BIM within the curriculum; [6–10] however some have suggested a tiered approach where BIM is introduced in a single subject, then across disciplines with subsequent emphasis on the collaboration and teamwork that BIM demands, culminating in actual construction projects in conjunction with AEC professionals in the final year [11, 12].

The demand for BIM in the AEC industry, the unique and innovative nature of BIM, and the lack of concrete data as to its implementation within the AEC curricula make this study of critical importance for further integration of BIM in academia.

2.2 Mixed Methods Research

A mixed method methodology is ideal for gathering and analyzing data from a smaller pool of subjects, as encountered in this study. As the name suggests, this method combines quantitative and qualitative aspects to accomplish a deeper understanding. Quantitative methods use objective questions to generate "hard" data that is useful on a large scale to generate statistics and create graphs or tables of the resulting analysis. Traditionally these methods are more associated with the natural sciences, statistics and other related studies.

The data from qualitative methods is more subjective, generated by observation, case studies, interviews, etc. which are commonly associated with the social sciences. The collection of the data is more labor-intensive, both in formulating the questions and collecting and analyzing the information generated. Because of this complexity, qualitative methods are usually conducted on a smaller scale. The advantages of using a mixed method over either method individually is that the two methods can work together to fill any gaps and produce more refined results [13]. Quantitative methods can enable the researcher to determine the critical elements that warrant further investigation, allowing the qualitative research to focus on those significant areas and provide richer data [14].

2.3 Adaptive Learning

The focus of adaptive learning is a customized learning experience that is *adapted* to each individual student, in order to give students a central role in their learning experience to boost motivation and maximize learning potential [15]. The student and instructor cooperate and interact to create the ideal learning environment, individually personalized. There is a range of possible approaches, but all are focused on tailoring the learning experience to each student in order to "stimulate his learning process and to encourage his involvement in this process [15–18]".

Importantly, while latitude is given to students to shape the course to maximize their experience, the role of the instructor/tutor is still necessary for setting the criteria and configuring the course elements that are required; modification can include a range of elements, such as content covered, time needed to complete assignments, order in which topics are learned, assessment methodologies, interface options for introducing course material, etc. [15].

The interest in adaptive learning includes motivation of the student. Pintrich and De Groot propose three components to self-regulated learning – cognition (planning, monitoring and modifying), effort (management and control of focus), and cognitive strategies (methods students use to learn, remember and understand) [19]; however they likewise acknowledge the need for student motivation in order for a self-regulated, or otherwise individually-adapted, learning environment to be successful. They identify three motivational elements: expectancy, a student believes himself capable of completing a task (self-efficacy); value, a student understands and believes in the importance of, or has interest in, a task; and affective, or emotional reaction (e.g. test anxiety) [19].

Milosevic et al. addressed adaptive learning and motivation directly in a study where course material was designed to be delivered online and adapted to individual student's learning style preferences and level of motivation. Motivation was determined by similar elements – intrinsic motivation, self-efficacy, engagement and test anxiety. Students with greater motivation and interest were designed lessons with more content covering multiple learning outcomes at greater depth at once, whereas those with less motivation were given core content material only, with additional in-depth material optional.

An adaptive learning system developed at the college level was shown to be effective in improving learning achievements and performance by Tseng et al. [20]. They designed a course in two manners – a traditional, sequential framework and an adaptive modular framework consisting of individualized sections of 38 learning objectives in total. Sixty-four students were given a pre-test to establish equivalency, then they were divided into two groups, experimental (adaptive, modular course) and control (traditional course). After completing the course a post-test was given, in which the experimental group showed a "significantly better" academic performance, and 91% of whom found the adaptive course material "suitable". After completing the course analysis, and conducting a qualitative interview, results "concluded that the adaptive system is innovative, helpful, and well-developed enough to foster students' learning" [20].

3 Data Analysis Methodology

The main objective of this study is to create, compare and analyze two similar adaptive learning methodologies, and compare and contrast them with previous traditional methodologies used in prior semesters. Two BIM construction courses (Construction II and IV) from the Architecture curriculum are redesigned and serve as the subjects of this study. Each course was changed from a BIM Project-Based Learning (PBL) format with a traditional methodology, to an adaptive learning process where the student can work their own path at their own speed, depending on their skills and interests, to complete the different assignments.

The analysis and comparison will be defined using a well-established mixed method (as more fully explained in the journal articles of Fonseca and ourselves [7, 13, 14, 21, 22]), using two surveys, grades, graded samples from course files and student interviews. All data gathered will be combined in a quantitative and qualitative methodology. The quantitative statistical analysis for short samples will be complemented by a qualitative analysis which supplies supporting and explanatory data. The combined analysis measures student motivation, satisfaction and performance in the courses, comparing and noting any improvements from previous semesters. It will also provide the student point of view throughout each process in order to highlight any strengths and/or weaknesses from the adaptive learning method.

3.1 Statistical Analysis Tools for This Research

The quantitative data obtained in this research will come from the surveys and grades, mentioned previously and explained in the referenced journals [7, 14]. In order to analyse the data, we need first to understand the type of data we will collect. The size of the classes is fewer than 25 people in each; such small samples cannot be tested correctly for normality, so it cannot be assumed. If normality of the sample is not proven, we are not able to use the P-test, T-test or ANOVA, as all these statistical tests are only accurate when used with normal distribution samples. Therefore non-parametric tests are utilized, which are more accurate for non-normal samples.

It must be noted that two kinds of data will be gathered in this study for analysis:

- Different groups of students in the same course, re-designed with a different (non-traditional) methodology, in order to understand the pros and cons of adaptive learning in the course.
- Different student groups at different points in their construction courses, to compare both of the adaptive learning methods proposed, in order to understand which one would be more successful in raising student motivation and performance.

This kind of data should be considered as independent samples, as we are testing the results in different study subjects. It will be tested two-by-two (as pairs), using the two samples comparison test developed by Wilcoxon (1945) [23] and Mann-Whitney (1947) [24], and as recommended by Fay, Proschan, Depuy and Neuhaser [25–28]. The described test will be used for analysis of the day-to-day study throughout the course.

For documents, requiring the analysis of a larger amount of data and comparing it in a common margin, we will follow a multiple pairwise comparison using the Steel-Dwass-Critchlow-Fligner procedure/two-tailed test. This test compares the median/means of all pairs of groups using the Steel-Dwass-Critchlow-Fligner pairwise ranking nonparametric method, and controls the error rate simultaneously for all $k(k + 1)/2$ contrasts [29].

In this manner we can test all the values for one variable at the same time for all the courses, thereby achieving an understanding of the overall evolution of the variable.

3.2 Qualitative Data

There are three kinds of qualitative data which we collect in this research: first, feedback extracted from the questionnaires; second, interviews after all students have finished their construction courses; and third, the graded samples.

In both pre-test and post-test questionnaires we introduce one final qualitative section where we will receive varying inputs from the students. In the pre-test this section will inquire about the different tools students think should be used to teach construction, design and other courses. In the post-test, it was initially decided that the students would be given the opportunity to highlight the best and worst elements in the course and how they could be (further) improved; however, ultimately we removed this section from the post-test. The reality is that most students are reluctant to answer these questions, and if included as mandatory in the online questionnaire most of them would write either very few things or comments that are not relevant; truly relevant issues will likely be the same as would appear during student interviews. This consideration prompted us to delete the qualitative questions on the post-test, and to focus the post-course qualitative data mainly in the interviews where there is a more accurate, genuine and relevant interaction with the students [30, 31].

It is important to highlight that the post-test questionnaires will also be administered after students finish the course, so that the students can be more sincere, honest, and open to talking about any issues encountered. The questions are directed to discover and understand: student opinions about the course; suggested improvements to the course; ideas for how to coordinate the use of different Information Technology (IT) tools within the course; their satisfaction towards BIM tools; their motivation and intention to use Revit in their future studies and work; and the need to implement Revit as a BIM software in the university.

Student interviews will be performed after finishing the course, so that the students can be more sincere, honest, and open to talking about any issues encountered. The interviews will be conducted in a relaxed environment at the AURAK campus under the direction of researcher Jose Ferrandiz. In these interviews the students will have the opportunity to explain their feelings and opinions about the course, their performance, and the new IT and why they believe they were successful (or not) in using it. The responses collected in the quantitative tests are on a scale of 1 to 5, without the possibility to explain (qualitative data); so after finishing the construction courses, when students have a comprehensive view and experience of the entire program, they are then given the opportunity to provide feedback and their sincere opinion about the process, the course, BIM and related new IT tools, how they dealt with these tools, and whether they will continue using them after this stage.

During the interviews the interviewer will note any comments, and immediately afterwards read them back to the interviewee to confirm accuracy, allowing for rectifications or modifications in the notes to ensure that all opinions are accurately represented. Following the interviews, all statements are categorized and organized in a way to generate meaningful conclusions and calculate percentages of the students interviewed who held one opinion or another.

Student graded samples will be collected and organized by course, group, grade and assignment. These samples are to be used to double check the grading, but most importantly it will provide a database allowing the comparison of completed courses and the introduction of BIM in other courses which were not a subject of this study.

The qualitative data is a critical element in a mixed method research because it provides a measure of depth to the consequences of our study that a purely quantitative data approach could not provide.

4   The Case Studies

As mentioned above two courses were re-developed for this study – Construction II and Construction IV, changing from traditional methodology BIM Project Based Learning (PBL), to an adaptive learning process. In actuality we created two different methodologies of adaptive learning in order to compare the data from both and determine which is more effective.

1. The first design has two paths. Two types of assignments are created for each chapter: type A are basic assignments providing concepts, fundamental understanding of the elements and basic skills; type B will provide advanced knowledge and skills in the same subject area.

    a. When a student completes and passes a type A assignment, a type B assignment will be released from the same chapter in addition to the next type A (related to the next lecture).

2. The second design is linear. Course chapters will be arranged by complexity and each assignment will lead to the next one on a linear basis.

With the first design the student is able to develop basic skills for all the chapters studied, and obtain advanced knowledge on those topics where he has the interest and/or motivation to improve; in the second the student can use as much time as needed to complete each task but they must all be finished in order, therefore if a student has difficulty with one assignment it can negatively impact the rest of the course. Each method has its benefits, and their individual effect on student performance, motivation and satisfaction will be measured in order to understand which one would be more effective, and to determine the relative benefits and disadvantages of each.

4.1 Changing the Grading Criteria

In order to improve student motivation and effort, the grading criteria will be changed from the traditional way, where the students are not fully informed of their status and feel that they are losing critical points with each assignment, to a simplified grading system where students increase their grades depending on the knowledge acquired. This is stated in the syllabus as follows:

- This course will be evaluated on a basis that is different from the rest of the courses. We will be using an adaptive learning environment, where the assignments will not have a specific due date. Every assignment will be evaluated from 1–10, and the student will need to earn at least 7 points in order to be able to continue and open the next assignment.
- Each one of you can use the time you need to properly complete each task, depending on its requirements and your skills. You will need to learn and understand each chapter before advancing to the next task, assessed by the assignments. You won't be able to advance to the next level until you complete the current one.
- You must fulfil at least 60% of the assignments in order to pass the course, constituting a minimum of six assignments and the portfolio; after assignment 6, any completed assignment will increase your grade. The grading criteria will consider all grades, but it will always align with the following Table 1:
- For those who seek to earn an A grade, all the assignments but one should be finished and graded with a minimum score of 9. There will be other optional assignments which will help to improve your grade, but these will not count as one of main ten.

Table 1. Comparison of the phases of the two frameworks

Assignments fulfilled	As1–5	As6	As7	As8	As9	As10
Maximum grade possible	F	D+	C	B−	B+	A
Minimum grade possible		D	C−	C+	B	A−

Using this grading criteria the students will know their course standing and grade at all times throughout the course, and will know what they need to do in order to get a higher grade; it is anticipated that this will improve the organizational and self-responsibility skills of the students, who will have more ownership over their course performance and grading and a clear awareness of how to earn the desired grade.

The students will need to reach a minimum level at each stage in order to continue with the next concept; if they have not reached that level, they can review extra material that will be provided or ask for help from the instructor until they reach it. By this method it is suggested that student motivation will increase, while assuring that any student who passes the course has at a minimum a clear understanding of the basic concepts.

There are two possible benefits from these changes: first, this process will provide the student time to fully understand each concept at his or her own pace, as explained; second, and importantly, instead of potentially losing points with each assignment, which can frustrate some, students move forward and their grades progress as they advance in their studies, which should encourage them to work harder. While in the traditional system a student who earned a poor grade on initial assignments may find it difficult to get good grade in the course, by this adaptive process we will help them until they complete each assignment properly and earn the required marks, while ensuring they have a solid foundation in the course material.

4.2 Works Submission, Lectures, Examples and Extra Information

It is expected that the students will attend all the course lectures, and cover the same chapters. In order to accomplish this, although the assignments are related to the lectures these elements will be disconnected. Everyone in the class will experience the same lectures at the same time, but each student will work on the assignments to cement the understanding of each concept on their own path. This process doesn't evaluate the student by their assignments, but by how much knowledge they have acquired during the semester.

In order to help in this process, the assignments are released only when the student has acquired the knowledge from the prior lesson, which will help them to advance. We have also prepared a complete package to help the student on the learning process, comprised of several items:

- Lecture pdf, which allows the students to review the concepts explained during the class;
- Examples of previous students' work, which we also review and explain during the lecture, including the strengths and the weakness of each;
- Checklist of the minimum requirements for the assignment to be completed;

- Video tutorials of additional skills which could be helpful for the assignment;
- Additional material – such as construction process videos, real examples, codes related to the assignment or any other relevant information available.

All this material is shown as a package at the same time as the assignment. Most of it is not new, as it will already have been discussed during the lectures and will be reviewed again during the lab sessions as one-to-one training with each student. It is very important to provide the material only for the current and previous assignments, so the student can use it without distractions or overload of materials/information. A lack of information can be a problem, but too much information without filters is likewise problematic and can overwhelm and/or distract the student from the target.

By this methodology the student can focus on one concept at a time until they reach mastery and then advance to the next step, while providing each student with their own time to take in the information and cement the knowledge as the foundation for the next step.

5   Conclusions

In furtherance of this research, we have created two different adaptive methodologies to be introduced in construction BIM courses at the degree of architecture, in order to improve student motivation, effort and performance/results. These methodologies provide the students the opportunity to learn and work at their own speed, allowing more advanced students to gain further knowledge while affording every student enough time to properly learn and internalize each concept.

These methodologies are analyzed using a mixed-method methodology which uses both quantitative and qualitative data in order to provide statistical analysis and greater understanding of the underlying causes.

The application of adaptive learning to the architectural degree, and mainly in a BIM project-based learning experience, is unique; therefore this research can lead to the improvement of the learning process at the Architectural program.

References

1. Miettinen, R., Paavola, S.: Beyond the BIM utopia: approaches to the development and implementation of building information modeling. Autom. Constr. **43**, 84–91 (2014)
2. Sabongi, F.J., Arch, M.: The integration of BIM in the undergraduate curriculum: an analysis of undergraduate courses, pp. 1–4 (2009)
3. McAuley, B., Hore, A., West, R.: BICP Global BIM Study (2016)
4. Chasey, A., Pavelko, C.: Industry expectations help drive BIM in today's university undergraduate curriculum (2010)
5. Nejat, A., Darwish, M., Ghebrab, T.: BIM teaching strategy for construction engineering students, p. 25.262 (2012)
6. Barison, M.B., Santos, E.T.: BIM teaching strategies: an overview of the current approaches. In: Proceedings of the ICCCBE 2010 International Conference on Computing in Civil and Building Engineering (2010)

7. Ferrandiz, J.: The implementation of BIM in the introductory building construction course at the United Arab Emirates University, pp. 130–137 (2016). https://doi.org/10.13140/rg.2.2. 30575.02725

8. Barison, M.B., Santosi, E.T.: BIM teaching: current international trends. Des. Manag. Technol. **6**, 67–80 (2011)

9. Bastos, B.A., Fonseca, J.Á.L., Gomes, A.V.M.S., Santos, A.A.: Implantação de tecnologia BIM na incorporação imobiliária. In: TIC 2011: V Encontro de Tecnologia de Informação e Comunicação na Construção (2011)

10. Mitchell, D.: 5D BIM: creating cost certainty and better buildings, pp. 1–9 (2012)

11. Hietanen, J., Drogemuller, R.: Approaches to a university level BIM education. In: IABSE Conference (2008)

12. Kymmell, W.: Building Information Modeling: Planning and Managing Construction Projects with 4D CAD and Simulations. McGraw-Hill Construction Series. McGraw Hill Professional, New York (2008)

13. Fonseca, D., Redondo, E., Villagrasa, S.: Mixed-methods research: a new approach to evaluating the motivation and satisfaction of university students using advanced visual technologies. Univ. Access Inf. Soc. **14**, 311–332 (2015)

14. Ferrandiz, J., Fonseca, D., Banawi, A.: Mixed method assessment for BIM implementation in the AEC curriculum. In: Zaphiris, P., Ioannou, A. (eds.) LCT 2016. LNCS, vol. 9753, pp. 213–222. Springer, Cham (2016). https://doi.org/10.1007/978-3-319-39483-1_20

15. Burgos, D., Tattersall, C., Koper, R.: Representing adaptive eLearning strategies in IMS learning design. Educational Technology Expertise Centre (OTEC) (2006)

16. Burgos, D., Ruiz-Mezcua, B.: Building an interactive training methodology to develop multimedia (2003)

17. He, S., Kinshuk, H.H., Patel, A.: Granular approach to adaptivity in problem-based learning environment. In: Proceedings of ICALT, pp. 3–7 (2002)

18. Fredericksen, E., Pickett, A., Shea, P., Pelz, W., Swan, K.: Student satisfaction and perceived learning with on-line courses: principles and examples from the SUNY learning network. J. Asynchronous Learn. Netw. **4**, 7–41 (2000)

19. Pintrich, P.R., De Groot, E.V.: Motivational and self-regulated learning components of classroom academic performance. J. Educ. Psychol. **82**, 33 (1990)

20. Tseng, S., Su, J.-M., Hwang, G., Hwang, G., Tsai, C.-C., Tsai, C.J.: An object-oriented course framework for developing adaptive learning systems. J. Educ. Technol. Soc. **11**, 171–191 (2008)

21. Ferrandiz, J., Banawi, A., Peña, E.: Evaluating the benefits of introducing "BIM" based on Revit in construction courses, without changing the course schedule. Univ. Access Inf. Soc. **17**, 491–501 (2017)

22. Fonseca, D., Villagrasa, S., Valls, F., Redondo, E., Climent, A., Vicent, L.: Engineering teaching methods using hybrid technologies based on the motivation and assessment of student's profiles, pp. 1–8 (2014)

23. Wilcoxon, F.: Individual comparisons by ranking methods. Biom. Bull. **1**, 80–83 (1945)

24. Nachar, N.: The Mann-Whitney U: a test for assessing whether two independent samples come from the same distribution. Tutor. Quant. Methods Psychol. **4**, 13–20 (2008)

25. Neuhäuser, M.: Wilcoxon–Mann–Whitney test. In: Lovric, M. (ed.) Anonymous International Encyclopedia of Statistical Science, pp. 1656–1658. Springer, Heidelberg (2011). https://doi.org/10.1007/978-3-642-04898-2_615

26. Fay, M.P., Proschan, M.A.: Wilcoxon–Mann–Whitney or t-test? On assumptions for hypothesis tests and multiple interpretations of decision rules. Stat. Surv. **4**, 1–39 (2010)

27. McElduff, F., Cortina-Borja, M., Chan, S., Wade, A.: When t-tests or Wilcoxon–Mann–Whitney tests won't do. Adv. Physiol. Educ. **34**, 128 (2010)

28. DePuy, V., Berger, V.W., Zhou, Y.: Wilcoxon–Mann–Whitney test (2005)
29. Analyse-it: Multiple comparison procedures for the means/medians of independent samples (2018). https://analyse-it.com/docs/user-guide/comparegroups/multiplecomparisonprocedures. Accessed 23 Feb 2018
30. Ferrandiz, J., Gonzalo, F.D.A., Sanchez-Sepulveda, M., Fonseca, D.: Introducing a new ICT tool in an active learning environment course: performance consequences depending on the introduction design. Int. J. Eng. Educ. **35**, 360–371 (2019)
31. Ferrandiz, J.: BIM* implementation in the AEC* curriculum: a quasi-experimental case study of the Architectural Engineering (AE) Bachelor's degree at the United Arab Emirates University (UAEU). Dissertation, Etsab (universidad politecnica de catalunya) (2018)

Case Studies of Applications to Encourage Students in Cyber-Physical Environment

Yuko Hiramatsu[1]([✉]), Atsushi Ito[2]([✉]), Miki Kakui[3]([✉]),
Yasuo Kakui[3]([✉]), Kazutaka Ueda[4]([✉]), and Rina Hayashi[5]([✉])

[1] Chuo University, 742-1 Higashinakano, Hachioji, Tokyo 192-039, Japan
susana_y@tamacc.chuo-u.ac.jp
[2] Utsunomiya University, 7-1-2 Yoto, Utsunomiya, Tochigi 321-8505, Japan
at.ito@is.utsunomiya-u.ac.jp
[3] Sanze Co., Ltd., 2-3-6F, Kanda-Jimbocho, Chiyoda-ku,
Tokyo 101-0051, Japan
{m-kakui,y-kakui}@sanze.co.jp
[4] Graduate School of Engineering, Department of Mechanical Engineering,
University of Tokyo, 7-3 Hongo, Bunkyo-ku, Tokyo 113-865, Japan
ueda@design-i.t.u-tokyo.ac.jp
[5] Okinawa Prefectural Government, 1-1-2 Izumizaki, Naha 900-8570, Japan
rina.h.1218@gmail.com

Abstract. People became to have convenient lives in ICT society using the Internet. However, convenience is not the purpose to live. It is only the method to get something or know something quickly. Especially for learning, students have to overcome many obstacles actively to know and get knowledge. How we make an attractive point to be interested in the object? For active learning, we have researched applications to make some attractive points for students using psychological methods. Also, we had to arrange much information to make a point in cyber-physical environments. This paper explains about 2 kinds of applications. One is an application for inside studying using a Player versus Player (PvP) game. Another is for outdoor studying using Bluetooth Low Energy (BLE) beacon at the national park in Nikko. We developed applications of e-learning not for convenience but to feel beyond the smartphone screen. According to our experiments, such application makes students active to know about the subject.

Keywords: Computer aided education · Active learning · BLE beacon ·
PvP game · Cyber-physical environment

1 Introduction

1.1 Tools for Active Learning at the Convenient Society

Education level in Japan is high. According to the results of TIMSS 2015, which continues the long history of international assessments in mathematics and science conducted by IEA – the International Association for the Evaluation of Educational Achievement [1], Japanese students were in the grade of top 5 average score in the

© Springer Nature Switzerland AG 2019
P. Zaphiris and A. Ioannou (Eds.): HCII 2019, LNCS 11590, pp. 357–369, 2019.
https://doi.org/10.1007/978-3-030-21814-0_27

fields of mathematics and science both at elementary schools and at junior high schools. However, the research also told that they did not enjoy such works. For example, only 52% of Japanese students, the 8th grade, answered mathematics was joyful (cf. International average 71%). 66% of Japanese students answered science was joyful (cf. International average 81%) [2]. It is a problem that Japanese students have less motivation for learning. It is crucial to consider how we can improve students' ability and raise their motivation for learning.

Nowadays, people enclosing young students connect many intangible objects at the ICT society. However, it is difficult for young students to imagine intangible things. Many websites contain useful information for students. However, they tend to look over such information passively. What are the practical methods for young students to add information to their stock of knowledge? Make a point which students focus on, and they are interested in it. We have studied applications for that purpose. If students notice something that is not perfect (someplace is lacked), they urge to know complete one and would be attractive to know it. Human beings tend to be interested in something unfinished, and students tend to know about the lack points to finish their learning. We aimed to create applications to connect other place or other time using psychological approach. Then they can learn such expanse of space and time with our applications. Figure 1 shows the map of our case studies. There are two axes; one is "Space-Time," another is "active-passive."

In the following parts of this paper, we explain each case study. After explaining about related works in Sect. 2, we mention our two applications in Sect. 3. Then Sect. 4 tells the results of our researches. Finally, we mention conclusions and our research for the future.

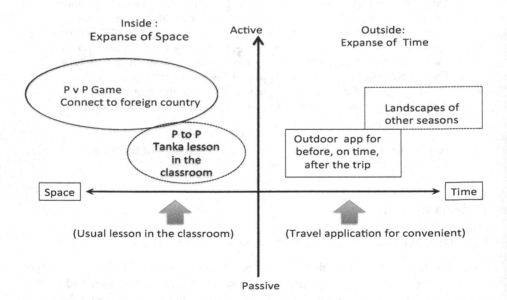

Fig. 1. Case studies of inside and outside

2   Related Works

2.1   Game (for Inside Studying)

We created an application for active learning in the classroom or house using a PvP (Player versus Player) game. The use of game thinking and game mechanics is getting more attention as a means of self-motivated and sustained behavioral change.

Gamification is not equal game. However, there are common elements. "Gamification Platform for Supporting Self-motivated and Sustained Actions" [3] indicates the effectiveness of the games. The Researchers had experiments at the elementary school [4]. In the paper, young students enjoyed the lesson using animation with a mission for them.

McGonigal told that the failures in the game are very light and players can make many failures in "Reality is Broken: Why Games Make Us Better and How They Can Change the World" [5]. Also, the success in the game is visible as some items such as a treasure, extraordinary powers that encourage players and make players active. Using these elements, we designed our application.

2.2   Psychology for Tourism (for Outdoor Studying)

Students visit famous places for several days with their classmates and teachers in Japan. We created another application using psychology in such few days outdoor studying. There are several works about psychology and tourism. Pearce and Stringer [6] studied from the viewpoint of physiology, cognition, and individual variation. Fridgen [7], van Raaij [8], Sasaki also studied this field. Especially, Sasaki mentioned that trip had three scenes: before the trip, during the trip, and after the trip [9]. It means that a trip is not only enjoying the trip itself but also planning to increase expectation before the trip and remember the memory of the trip after returning home.

3   Our Case Studies

3.1   Inside Use Case: Expansion of the Space

At first, we have developed an application for young students using SNS, which was a closed system in the school. Using this system, students talked to each other and created a lot of traditional Japanese poems, TANKA. Students created TANKA, and then they sent comments to other authors. Some comments were written with rhymes naturally. This process is similar to Japanese olden methods to write TANKA [10–12]. In the course of this experiment, it was found that young students who belonged to acquirement failed a lot to do their works. However, they learned how to use the system among making failures. We had to tolerate to make such mistakes for their acquirements. However, even the slightest mistake can be fatal in the ICT society. Then for usage in the classroom or at home, we created a PvP game for learning, named Fevordio, Sanze Learning System [13] (Refer to Fig. 2 and Table 1).

Students check the knowledge using the card game. They sometimes fail. However, it is not such a big problem to fail in the game. They can fail in the game. They study the subject themselves and then remotely battles with the other members using questions which they choose. "the win and loss records" describes the battle score (Refer to Fig. 3). The characteristic points of this battle learning are as followings.

- Self-study: The results of each personal usage; accuracy rate and frequency of use, are recorded. The database is designed to follow the results and choose the degree of cards by AI to study low percentages of attendance.
- After using the card several times, students not only answer or choose the cards but also can make questions. They become positive parts of this battle.
- 3D database shows relations of cards visually. (Refer to Fig. 4). The cards are increasing and become big data because teachers and students create new ones using this application. Many data is arranged and became 3 databases by AI. For example, if the same word is found in 2 cards, they are connected in this database. By using this system, cross-curriculum learning becomes possible, and students can learn the subject multilayered.
- Create membership groups and members can sharing content within the groups.

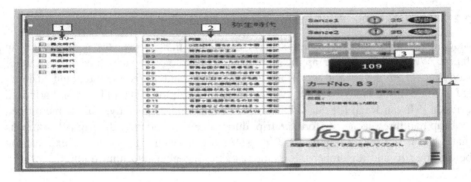

Fig. 2. The screen to choose the card (quiz)

Table 1. The explanation of numbers at Fig. 2

No.	Item	Description
1	Card list category	Click category name to display cards in each category
2	Card list	Display card information (card no., question and card type) of selected category. Click on list to select a card
3	OK button	Submit selected card to the sever
4	Card thumbnail	Display thumbnail of selected card

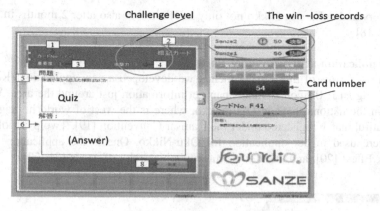

Fig. 3. Question & answer screen (on PC)

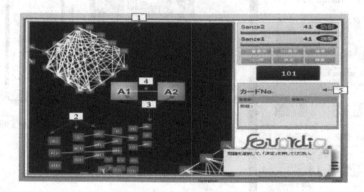

Fig. 4. The screen to choose quiz cards in 3D display

3.2   Outside Use Case

3.2.1   Our Previous Orienteering Application

We developed an application for outdoor studying using Bluetooth Low Energy (BLE) Beacon in Nikko, the world heritage site in Japan. At the quiz function in this application, we urged students to attend traditional objects actively. The quiz function made students look at one point in the landscape. This function provides a new learning model for outdoor studies using Zeigarnik effects; human beings take an interest in uncompleted or interrupted tasks [14]. Some desire or some stress, which includes the uncompleted part, can keep memory longer until the desire is fulfilled. In other words, the tasks that have been completed are recalled less well than tasks that have not been completed. In the case of school trips, if there is something uncompleted and know the answer, the memory of the point may remain longer. Students become active to the object using this smartphone application. For example, after answering the animal written in a famous picture, they looked up the building and ascertained the animal in the picture. The results of experiments students remembered the objects and evaluated great history and culture in Nikko not only in Nikko but also after 2 months in 2016–2017 [15–18].

3.2.2   Application at the National Park

Based on the results of those experiments, we developed a new application (Refer to Fig. 5) Using BLE Beacon, students can get information just around the area. We set beacons in the national park in Oku-Nikko, where is the west of world heritage area with beautiful marsh registered under the Ramsar Convention [19]. Two psychological effects were used in our application for Oku-Nikko. One is the application of the Zeigarnik Effect [20], and another is Maslow's hierarchy of needs [21, 22].

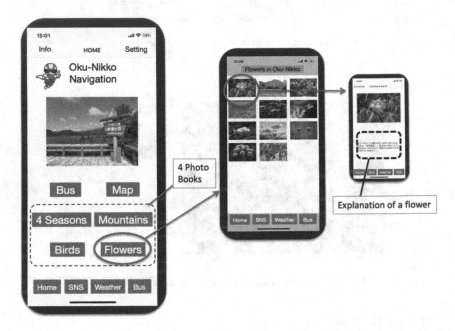

Fig. 5. Screens of Nikko application (top screen and an example of photo books. The details of the design process are described in [18].)

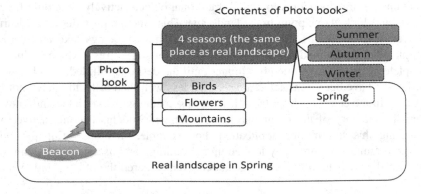

Fig. 6. Contents of photo book (the case in spring)

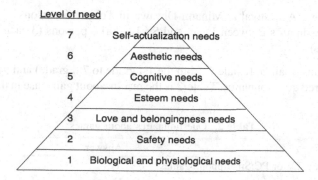

Fig. 7. Maslow's hierarchy of needs

We use the Zeigarnik Effect as followings. If students visit Oku-Nikko in autumn, the application display shows photos of scenery filled with cherry blossoms in spring or that covered by white snow with a footprint of a fox in winter, too. Those photos may attract the students, and it is expected that the memory of Oku-Nikko becomes stronger and the visitor becomes repeaters. Students may imagine other seasons. Figure 6 shows an example in spring. The white parts of the Fig. 6 are visible and the grey ones are invisible parts in spring. (Students are not always able to find the birds. So it is painted grey a bit) Looking at the beautiful landscape and know the objects around there using explanation of photos in our contents. Also, they look at photos of other seasons, they know there are other landscape which they have looked at them yet.

This application is used in nature. Information about map and timetables of an autobus is necessary for safe walking. Students are making groups, and they walked around the area within a designated time. Also, they collect photos and record their research.

A lot of information are set on the application. It seems that the developer sometimes set too many functions for users. Our most basic need is for physical survival, and it is the first thing that motivates the behavior. After one level is fulfilled, the next level up is what motivates us, and so on. The lower need is more critical and has higher priority. Maslow developed different types of the hierarchy of need such as five layers model and eight layers model. In our research, we used seven layers model (Fig. 7), since this model meets the classification of information required for outdoor studying. Having experiments as the next Sect. (4.2), we decided the arrangements at the interface of our application. Using Maslow's hierarchy of needs as the Cyber-Physical System (CPS). Maslow stated that people are motivated to achieve individual needs and that some needs take precedence over others.

4 Experiments and the Results

4.1 Fevordio, Application for Inside

We had questionnaires and experiments using mathematics battles in 2018.

(1) 23 on Nov. (A Festival at Minami-Ohsawa in Tokyo) 6 persons
(2) 5 on Dec. (houses Between Japan and Sri Lanka) 6 persons (3 each in Japan and Sri Lanka)

Total: 12 persons (male 5, female 7, from the 1st grade to 7th grade) and 9 parents of 12 persons answered questionnaires. Table 2 is the results about game use in their daily life.

Table 2. Questionnaires about games

Question	Answer		
Do you play TV or PC/Smartphone games?	Yes		11
	No		1
How many days do you play games (per week)?		4.95 days	(Average)
How long do you play games?	Week day	0.75 h	(Average)
	Holiday	1.29 h	(Average)

11 out of 12 children answered to play games every day (41%). The parents answered the same questionnaire as only 6 or 7 children play the game. (1 person had 2 children.) 4 parents answered that their children did not play the TV or PC game. The answers didn't match. Children, whom parents consider as no game users, did not have any rules for playing games with their parents.

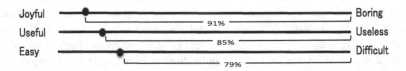

Joyful ——————————————————— Boring
                        91%
Useful ——————————————————— Useless
                        85%
Easy ——————————————————— Difficult
                        79%

Fig. 8. The evaluation by children using Fevordio

The answers after using Fevordio, children evaluated it was "joyful" as 91/100 points (average), "useful" 85/100 points (average). It was a high score. We asked them whether they liked Mathematics or not as the same way as Fig. 8, in advance. The scores of "like" were followings. Math class was 82/100 points, and Math drills were 66/100 points. They liked less drills than the subject itself. No children answered to prefer Math drills to Math class. However, they enjoyed our card battle named Fevordio, in spite of the same contents as Math drills. Children evaluated far higher this game than calculation Math drills (25 points higher). They answered this battle was "useful" and also was "easy". If it was useful for them to practice calculations, did we have to guess cards for the battle were too easy? Games are regarded to give players to feel happiness or well-being from easy battles. Sonija Lyubomirsky writes about such games, "We obtain maximum happiness when we take on flexible and appropriate goals" [22].

According to the data analysis, there was not a correlation between whether they liked Math drills and whether they enjoyed this card battle (r = −0.08). On the other hands, there was a positive correlation between the question "How many days do you play games in a week?" and their feelings of "joyful" (r = 0.64). The difficulty level and "joyful" did not have correlation (r = 0.16).

Parents inclosing who answered their children did not play games, looked at their children playing the game, wrote comments as "Children look fun," "It is Interesting. Children are stimulated", "This concept is good" and "Good!". They evaluated this game positively.

At the Festival in Minami-Ohsawa on November 23, children sat next to each other in a single row and had the card battle. An elder child taught her opponent who couldn't answer the card. Though she met him for the first time then, it seemed to have friendly communication using the same game. This is a prosocial emotion named "naches". McGnigal explained the term "This is a Yiddish word for the bursting pride we feel when someone we've taught or mentored succeeds" [5]. Players sometimes feel a kind of vicarious pride from giving advice and encouragement to the opponent on games. Ekman also told, "it encourages us to contribute to someone else's success, and achievements from networks of support from which everyone involved benefit" [23]. This scene in festival at Minami Ohsawa was an example of naches and they studied together with communication.

On the battle between Japan and Sri Lanka on December 5, comments of the children both Japanese and Sri Lanka were "Joyful (n = 6)", "Useful (n = 1)" at the experiment. 2 children answered to be interested in Sri Lanka after playing the game in Japan. Also, a student at a higher grade of the elementary school became to notice news about Sri Lanka and remembered the long name of capital, "Sri Jayawardenepura Kotte". When children start to learn English as a foreign language at the elementary school, they connected directly using a Math game on the first hand. It is just a start point to communicate with each other. It is difficult to sense of foreign countries for young students in a stage of concrete operations. However, using such a system, they have chances to know other persons beyond the PC screen.

The results of our experiments, students made calculations (Math drills) with fin and also some of them were interested in opponents. They will learn each other using the game not only mathematics drills but also quizzes of cultural or historical subjects in future. We aim to develop the battle game, Fevordio, to bring up the feeling of real connection among the students. Young students feel the world and people in other countries directly and quickly. It is a game inside. However, students become to fell the extent of space.

4.2   Oku-Nikko Application for Outside

Setting BLE beacons in the national park of Oku-Nikko, we had an experiment from February 19 to 21 in 2018, at Utsunomiya University (n = 20).

We listed up required elements of trips at the setout and categorized into ten elements. Based on Maslow's hierarchy of needs, we added priority to the functions of a mobile phone application and designed it for Oku-Nikko. Students evaluated the effectiveness of our designs. For example, all higher priority functions are accessible from the home screen, and some of them are in the tab bar to be accessible from all screens of the application. We added a photo book of seasons on the home screen to use the Zeigarnik Effect in order to encourage students to revisit Oku-Nikko in other seasons. We expected that the photos of nature (mountain, flower, bird) might cause a similar effect at the national park, too.

The results of the classification about the functions are as followings (Refer to Table 3).

Table 3. Mapping among elements of information, Maslow's hierarchy of needs

Elements of sightseeing (Oku-Nikko)	Hierarchy of needs						Function of App
	1	2	3	4	5	6	
Weather		O					Weather
New information (weather, disaster, bear, event etc.)		O			O	O	Information
Transportation, access		O					Bus (timetable and route)
Restroom, present location, model courses	O	O			O		Map
High light, guidance, transportation, food (shops)	O	O			O		Pop-up
High light, photos of seasons						O	Seasons photo
Guidance, origin, photos of animals, flowers, mountains					O	O	Photo books
Event					O		Stamp rally
SNS, "Like"			O	O			SNS
Multi lingual		O					Setting

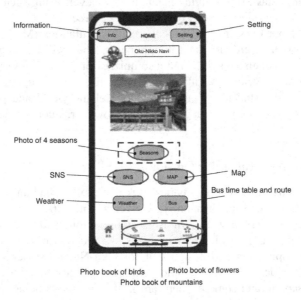

Fig. 9. New version user interface

The Weather, Map, Information (disaster, bear notification etc.) Bus routes and timetables were mapped as level 1 and 2. SNS was Level 3 and 4. Photo books and a part of information and a part of map were mapped as level 5 and 6. After basic needs (Level 1, 2) are fulfilled, human beings can think about higher levels. Therefore, after the experiments, the interface of our application was arranged mainly those basic needs (refer to Fig. 9.). Exceptionally photos of 4 seasons are not the basic needs. However, using basic information around the functions, we set "Seasons" in order to make students to be interested the other landscapes they cannot see real then.

After the experiments, the interface of our application was arranged as Fig. 9.

We had another test to use BLE beacon in the deep snow. In addition, we set a beacon by the pot spring source. The result of the test, it is possible to use beacon in a closed box in such areas. We have continued to research the condition of beacons in the forest or near hot springs. The reception of signals of a mobile phone is terrible in the forest so that it is not easy to get information about the direction. However, there are limited several paths that people can walk in the national park for the act of conserving nature. Therefore we can design the scene which people get signals of the beacon easily. We have an experiment in Oku-Nikko in 2019 to check the signals from BLE beacons and to know what kind of function is useful or joyful for people.

5   Conclusion

According to the researches, we concluded that the case studies about both inside and outside e-learning, studies in cyber-physical environments continue to urge students to have some active point for their learning. To connect some points invisible (Time or Space), young students imagine the objects beyond the PC or smartphone's screen and are interested in them. These applications express the expanse of time and space. Those applications are useful is not for convenience but imagination.

Why students have to learn foreign languages? Students may consider the reason for learning and get motivation for learning foreign languages. Connecting with foreigners is essential. One of the characteristic points of Fevordio is "Create membership groups, and members can share content within the groups" (Refer to Sect. 3.1). We try to bring up children's motivation. Also, such motivation brings them from virtual communication using games to real communication. Contents of Fevordio are increasing, and children would like to play card battles such as English, history, and science. Then 3D database's display has not used our experiments yet. We have other experiments using the function. That will make students learn multi-layered related subjects.

For outdoor studying, it is an excellent time to develop a new application in Oku-Nikko. The Ministry of the Environment has been promoting "the Project to Fully Enjoy National Parks [24]" at eight national parks in Japan since 2016, and the Nikko National Park is one of the selected areas. A mission of these projects is to support the national park by ICT. Our application will support it. We would like to have an experiment and evaluate the effect of our design method in the real field in Oku-Nikko before service-in.

Those 2 applications we developed have different systems and are used in different scenes. However, they have the same aim. These 2 applications make students to imagine some objects. They become actively imagine other persons beyond the screen or landscapes of other seasons. Students get not only some information positively, but also the information which they get, operates them beyond the space or the time. This effort is a step to active learning. In the ICT society, a great deal of information tends to make people passive. It is too much to be active users. We have to make some entrance points to focus on learning.

We continue to experiment for active learning both inside and outside to encourage active learning and bring up students' imagination.

Acknowledgments. Authors would like to express special thanks to Mr. Yoshihiko Sato (Metatechno Inc.) and members of Metatechno Lanka Company (Pvt) Ltd.) to test PvP game between Sri Lanka and Japan. Authors thank students who joined the experiment at Kami-ichibukata Elementary School.

Also, authors would like to thank to all members of the committee for increasing satisfaction of tourists in Nikko. They provided us with information of Oku-Nikko and valuable advice. Authors thank to students who joined the experiment in Nikko.

JSPS Grant-in-Aid for Scientific Research Grant Number JP17H02249 and supports this research, and, the basis of this research was performed as a project of SCOPE (142303001).

References

1. TIMSS & PIRL. http://timss2015.org/#/?playlistId=0&videoId=0. Accessed 18 Jan 2019
2. The Results of TIMSS 2015: Minister of Education, Culture, Sports, Science and Technology Japan (Japanese only). http://www.mext.go.jp/component/a_menu/education/micro_detail/__icsFiles/afieldfile/2016/12/27/1379931_1_1.pdf. Accessed 18 Jan 2019
3. Nemoto, K., Takahashi, M., et al.: Gamification platform for supporting self-motivated and sustained actions. Trans. Inf. Process. Soc. Jpn. **55**(6), 1600–1613 (2014)
4. Fujioka, D.: Development of teaching programs for children to learn by highly concentrated using gamification. Bull. Fac. Educ. Chiba Univ. **64**, 143–149 (2016)
5. McGonigal, J.: Reality is Broken: Why Games Make Us Better and How They Can Change the World, p. 87. Penguin Books, New York (2011)
6. Pearce, P.L., Stringer, P.F.: The effect of task interruption and closure on perceived duration. Ann. Tour. Res. **18**, 136–154 (1991)
7. Fridgen, J.D.: Environmental psychology and tourism. Ann. Tour. Res. **11**(1), 19–39 (1984)
8. Van Raaij, W.E.: Consumer research on tourism: mental and behavioral constructs. Ann. Tour. Res. **13**, 1–9 (1986)
9. Sasaki, T.: Psychology of Tourism, Kitahojishobou, Kyoto, pp. 51–59 (2007)
10. Hiramatsu, Y., Ito, A., Sato, F.: A study of teaching digital literacy for children: moral education to use the internet on mobile phones. In: ADIS International Association for Development of the Information Society, Rome, vol. III, pp. 337–340 (2011)
11. Hiramatsu, Y., Ito, A., Sato, F.: A study of mobile application for children's learning-based on study of Japanese old poetry. In: IADIS International Association for Development of the Information Society e-Learning 2012, Lisbon, Portugal, pp. 161–168 (2012)
12. Ito, A., Hiramatsu, Y., Shimada, F., Sato, F.: Designing education process in an elementary school for mobile phone literacy. J. Green Eng. **30**, 307–324 (2013)

13. United States Patent No. US8,702,434B2 by Sanze Co., Ltd., Yasuo Kakui

14. Zeigarnik, B.V.: On finished and unfinished tasks. In: Ellis, W.D. (ed.) A Sourcebook of Gestalt Psychology. Humanities Press, New York (1967)

15. Hiramatsu, Y., Ito, A., Sato, F.: The site-specific learning model on mobile phones using Zeigarnik effect - designing collaboration tool for outdoor studying. In: HCII International Conference on Human-Computer Interaction, HCII 2013, Las Vegas, Posters, Part II, pp. 43–47 (2013)

16. Hiramatsu, Y., et al.: Recovering the traditional street with BLE beacons base on classification of travelers. In: The 3rd World Congress on Computer Applications and Information Systems 2016 (3rd WCCAIS 2016), Dubai, United Arab Emirates (2016)

17. Hiramatsu, Y., et al.: A service model using Bluetooth low energy beacons—to provide tourism information of traditional cultural sites. In: Service Computation 2016, Roma, Italy, pp. 14–19 (2016)

18. Ito, A., Hayashi, R., Hiramatsu, Y., Sasaki, A.: A study of designing process for tourism support mobile application applying psychological effects. IJRET: Int. J. Res. Eng. Technol. **7**, 58–70 (2018)

19. OkuNikko. http://nikko-travel.jp/english/attract/oku_nikko.html. Accessed 8 Jan 2019

20. Schiffman, N., Greist-Bousquet, S.: The effect of task interruption and closure on perceived duration. Bull. Psychon. Soc. **30**(1), 9–11 (1992)

21. Maslow, A.H.: Motivation and Personality, 3rd edn. Pearson Education, Delhi (1987)

22. Lyubomirsky, S.: The How of Happiness: A New Approach to Getting the Life You Want, p. 213. Penguin Books, New York (2008)

23. Ekman, P.: Emotion Revealed: Recognizing Face and Feelings to Improve Communication and Emotional Life. Times Books, New York (2003)

24. Visit National Park, Minister of Environment. http://www.env.go.jp/en/nature/enjoy-project/index.html. Accessed 18 Jan 2019

Supporting the Teaching and Learning for Subject of Computer Sciences

Ana Ktona[1(✉)], Anila Paparisto[1], Alda Kika[1], Verina Çuka[2],
Denada Çollaku (Xhaja)[1], and Jezuina Koroveshi[1]

[1] Tirana University, Tirana, Albania
{ana.ktona, anila.paparisto, alda.kika, denada.xhaja,
jezuina.koroveshi}@fshn.edu.al
[2] Ibrahim Rugova High School, Kamëz/Tirana, Albania
verinacuka@gmail.com

Abstract. Obtaining good knowledge in computer science area before university education is considered a necessity in the most developed countries of the world. Decision makers in Albania have embraced this initiative. Currently, in Albania, ICT education starts from the fourth grade of primary school. But, what difficulties do institutions and interest groups currently face in teaching and learning the Computer Science' subject? Secondary and primary data were analyzed to find the actual situation of technology used in High Schools and challenges the pupils and teachers face during teaching and learning the subject of Computer Science. It was found that currently there are some difficulties in using ICT in schools. As a result, the teaching and learning of Computer Science' subject, is affected. Is there any appropriate emerging technology that could be alongside school infrastructure to support the teaching and learning process of Computer Science? Such technologies used in teaching and learning were identified through analysis of secondary data. By analyzing primary' data we found that "Bring Your Own Device" policies in combination with learning technologies would be feasible in Albania. A prototype is made, by implementing a LMS with lessons and quizzes in one of the Computer Science' Area. The prototype was tested in one of the High Schools of Tirana District. The pupils and the teacher participating in the test expressed a very positive attitude regarding the effectiveness of the prototype.

Keywords: Computing education · Bring Your Own Device ·
Learning Management System

1 Introduction

Technology is driving major changes in the way people interact, work, learn and access knowledge and information [1, 2]. And furthermore, this power has been seen as a major and sustainable source in the development contribution of economic activity in every country [3–6].

The development power of technology has been well understood by policy decision maker authorities in Albania and is strongly emphasized the extended use and

© Springer Nature Switzerland AG 2019
P. Zaphiris and A. Ioannou (Eds.): HCII 2019, LNCS 11590, pp. 370–379, 2019.
https://doi.org/10.1007/978-3-030-21814-0_28

penetration of ICT in medium-term Pre-universities and Digital Agenda' document strategies [7, 8].

Information and communication technologies are seen by the Albanian Government, as essential to enhancing the opportunities of economic development across the country [9]. Effects and influence of ICT implementation is extended on all social and economic sectors of the country [8]. During 2008–2013, a series of laws were prepared and adopted in compliance with the European Union standards [8]. Actually, the Albanian government is offering a series of e-services to its citizens resulting in the improvement of the general index of readiness for the electronic governance [8]. While in the field of education there have been investments for building up computer laboratories, internet network installation in schools [8].

Albanian Government, via its document on the "Digital Agenda's Strategy 2015–2020" points out the need for more investments and attention for the ICT in education in order to provide a society based on knowledge and to widely increase the skills of ICT utilization [8]. The strategy stresses, also, that Albanian society needs to be prepared for new challenges which emphasize the acquisition of trends in information technologies [8]. While the strategy for the Development of Pre-University Education emphases the need for the integration of ICT in teaching and learning in order for the educational institutions to prepare students to live in "a knowledge society" and to enhance quality [7].

Obtaining good knowledge in computer science area before university education is considered a necessity in the most developed countries of the world [10–13]. Decision makers in Albania have embraced this initiative. Currently, in Albania, ICT education starts from the fourth grade of primary school [14]. But, what difficulties do institutions and interest groups currently face in teaching and learning the Computer Science subject? Is there any appropriate technology that supports the teaching and learning process of Computer Science?

2 Methodology

Technologies used in teaching and learning were identified through analysis of secondary data. Secondary and Primary data were analyzed to find the actual situation of technology used in High Schools and challenges the students and teachers face during teaching and learning the subject of Computer Science. Study reports, guidelines and strategy documents from different sources like Ministry of Education, Sport and Youth, Ministry of Innovation and Public Administration, UNESCO, World Bank etc. were analyzed. Two online questionnaires which were distributed in Tirana' High Schools were created one for High School pupils and one for teachers. These questionnaires were filled out by 294 pupils and 57 teachers where only 17 were ICT teachers. Also, interviews were conducted with 95 Computer Science students who were from almost all of Albania's districts. A prototype is made, by implementing a LMS with lessons and quizzes in one of the Computer Science' Area. The prototype was tested in "Qemal Stafa" High School of Tirana' District.

3   Findings and Results

3.1   Actual Situation of Technology Used in High Schools

Knowing the development power of technology in every area, including education, different actions are undertaken by Albania Government to include ICT into the teaching and learning process. E-School program was introduced in December 2005 by the government [15]. Considered as a core component of the major initiative that the government has embarked on to include Albania into the digital age, the program' main objective was to create an environment in which students, both rural and urban, can learn the use of Information Technologies and communication [15]. Under the E-School program was made possible equipment with computer labs to all high schools and a considered number of schools in primary education, the connection of these labs to internet, training of ICT' teachers and started the improvement of the ICT curricula in pre-university education [15]. Pre-University Education Development Strategy [7] emphasized the priority of government on curriculum reform, which is expected to lead to the equipment of schools with a secure and functional infrastructure that provides opportunities for the use of digital content in the learning process. Aiming the students being prepared for the labor markets is promoted the extensive introduction of ICT in the teaching process. In this context a contemporary Computer Science curriculum is developed, aiming at enabling students to comply with European standards. This will be accompanied by the improvement of technological infrastructure and the support for internet connections in schools that are not connected to [7].

One of the main priorities set it up in the Cross-cutting Strategy for the Information Society 2008–2013 [15] was the implementation of ICT in education and knowledge spread. According to different sources the ratio computer per pupils is improved significantly. In 2006 the ratio was one computer per 61 pupils [16], in 2008 the number of pupils for one computer was 45 [15], in 2009, the number of pupils for one computer was 25 [16] and in 2015 the ratio was one computer per 27 pupils [8]. Some of the computers distributed in pre-university education are not functional. Even in the major part of the schools have a dedicated broadband connection it remains only in computer labs [8]. The spread of broadband connection all over the school will facilitate the utilization of different information sources.

According to Pre-University Education Development Strategy [7], Digital Agenda [8] and National Strategy for Development and Integration [9] ICT in Education and curriculum development and reform still remains some of the top priorities for Albania. One of the main objectives set it up in Digital Agenda related to ICT in Education is: "Digitalization of the education system in order to increase the quality of education and contribute in the establishment of a society based on knowledge through the increase of access into digital curriculums and the facilitation of their internet connectivity up to 100%" [8 p. 32]. Integration of ICT utilization in a contemporary level in teaching and learning remains the main step for a gradual transition toward a knowledge based society, is emphasized in Digital Agenda [8 p. 32]. The guideline, "Learning with Examples, Constructivism and Technology" [17] prepared by the Institute of Educational Development, supports this objective. This guideline' aim is the use of technology and ICT to improve the learning process through the implementation of modern methodologies. It emphasizes that using technology in the classroom makes the teaching process more effective and more attractive when developed according to appropriate teaching theory and methodologies. This guideline brings concrete examples of effective technology integration through the use of appropriate teaching/learning methodologies for different curriculum subjects.

Albania government, with the purpose of supporting the country's vision for educational reform in the context of its national, regional, and international aspirations, had initiated in 2015 the Education Policy Review [18]. This review seeks to identify relevant policy issues, to conduct in-depth analysis, and to formulate evidence-based recommendations within three key policy domains including information and communication technology (ICT) in education. One of the ICT in education policy issues found in EPR is: "The lack of a stable, responsive and widely available infrastructure and digital learning resources hinders the use of ICT in schools" [18 p. 60].

3.2 Technologies Used in Teaching and Learning

Every year started in 2009 till 2017 reports from New Media Consortium and Consortium for School Networking were created with the aim to examine emerging technologies for their potential impact on and use in teaching, learning, and creative inquiry in schools [19]. Key trends like Collaborative Learning Approaches and Redesigning Learning Spaces, challenges like Improving Digital Literacy and Integrating Technology in Teacher Education and important developments like digital strategies i.e. Bring Your Own Devices practices or learning technologies like learning analytics and mobile and online learning are very likely to impact changes in K-12 education across the world not beyond that the next five years [20–22]. New Media Consortium and Consortium for School Networking reports [19] show evidences about implementations of important developments that have direct implications for K-12 education settings.

3.3 Feasibility of Emerging Technologies in Albania

As the analysis of secondary data found actually there are difficulties in using ICT in schools in the process of teaching and learning. As a result, difficulties arise in the implementation of Computer Science curriculum. Is there any key trends or important developments that could be used alongside to school technology in teaching and learning? Introducing emerging technologies in teaching and learning is a challenge even to developed countries [23]. What about Albania? Is there any emerging technology suitable to be implemented here? With the drop in prices for desktops, laptops and mobile phones, learning technologies like mobile and online learning and digital strategies like Bring Your Own Device looks possible for Albania. There are evidences that implementing BYOD digital strategy alongside to school technology allows students to have better access to technology in the classroom, a greater range of learning activities involving technology, and more useful and meaningful peer and teacher feedback [24].

Two questioners were created to find out the feasibility of implementing learning technologies or digital strategies. One of them was intended to be filled out by pupils. Some of the questions in this questionnaire are:

- Do you have any digital devices in your home? (See Fig. 1 for the graphic of the answers)
- Do you have internet in your home?
- Could you bring any digital device in school from home? (See Fig. 2 for the graphic of the answers)
- Do you use technology to help you with homework/projects?

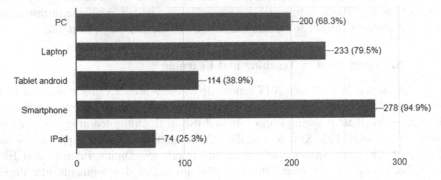

Fig. 1. Answers on the question: do you have any digital devices in your home?

Almost all the pupils answered they have internet in their home (97.3% of the pupils answered yes).

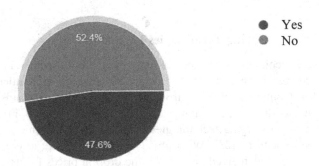

Fig. 2. Answers on the question: could you bring any digital device in school from home?

Almost all the pupils answered they use technology to help them with their homework/projects (99% of the pupils answered yes).

The other questionnaire was intended to be filled by the teachers. Some of the questions teachers answered were:

- How often do you integrate computer technologies into your teaching activities? (see Fig. 3 for the answers from ICT teachers)
- Please read the following descriptions of computer skill levels. Determine the level that best describes you. (see Fig. 4 for the answers from ICT teachers)
- Preferred Methodology of Teaching (see Fig. 5 for the answers from ICT teachers)

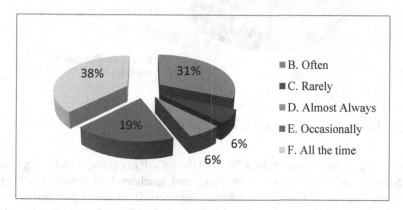

Fig. 3. Answers from ICT teachers: how often do you integrate computer technologies into your teaching activities?

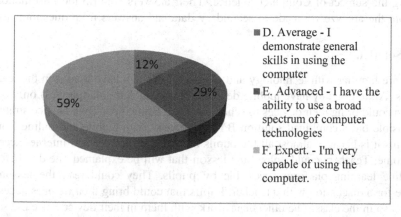

Fig. 4. Answers from ICT teachers: determine the level that best describes you.

The questionnaires were distributed in Tirana district. To get an overview of other districts in Albania 95 student that were from all over Albania's Districts were interviewed.

Interviews were conducted by some of the authors with 95 Computer Science students, including students from study program Master of Science in Computer Science' teacher, who were from almost all of Albania's districts. The students were asked about their experience in High School on learning ICT subject. The objective of these

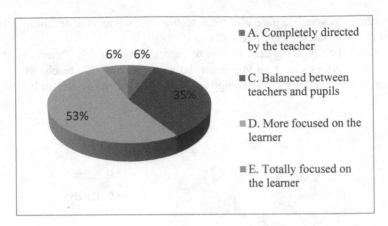

Fig. 5. Answers from ICT teachers: preferred methodology of teaching.

interviews was to get an information for all Albania's districts about technology used in High Schools and challenges the students and teachers face during teaching and learning the subject of Computer Science. Students from study program Master of Science in Computer Science' teacher were asked also about the situation they found, during their internship in the High Schools, about the actual situation of technology used in High Schools and challenges the students and teachers face during teaching and learning the subject of Computer Science. Their answers confirm the information we got from the analyze we made to secondary data and answers from questionnaires.

3.4 Solution

Pupils are familiar with technology and almost all of them have used it in the learning process. Although they have mobile devices (laptop, tablets smartphones) only 47.5% of them could bring their devices to school. A fully Bring Your Own Device strategy is not feasible but a combined solution BYOD strategy with mobile and online learning platforms it is because almost all the pupils have digital devices and internet access in their home. Teachers could upload the lesson that will be explained one day before in an online learning platform accessible by pupils. They could read the lesson and prepare for a discussion with a teacher. Pupils that could bring their devices access the lesson also in the class. The others can work with them in their devices, use the school technology or work in a traditional way in the class. To better manage the class we suggest allowing pupils to bring only a laptop in the Classroom. Other devices like smartphones or tablets could be used outside the class. As an online learning platform we propose a free Learning Management System. Lessons and quizzes prepared by Teachers uploaded in a Learning Management System, web-based systems that enable teachers and students to share materials [25], could be accessible from pupils via their devices or school devices. With such a system, teachers can create and integrate the course materials, assess and create personalized tests for pupils. LMS allows communication of learning objectives and organizes learning deadlines. Such systems distribute course contents directly to students and include both student progress and assessment. Thus, pupils can see their progress in real time and instructors can monitor and communicate the learning effectiveness. Important for LMS is to try to create a simple communication between students and instructors. Such systems, in addition to facilitating online learning, tracking the progress of learning, providing digital learning tools and communication management, can be used to provide different communication functions. Introducing this solution for teaching and learning will modernize teaching methods [26].

A prototype is made, by implementing a LMS with lessons and quizzes in one of the Computer Science' Area. The pupils at any time and place can access and consult with the learning material. For any new material, added in the system, an email is sent. Materials can not only be viewed online but also downloaded directly from the site in order to have it stored in the device if there is no internet access. Most importantly, the tests are in the system and the result of the test is taken immediately as soon as it ends up seeing also the correct answers. The teacher also has many facilities, no worries as to whether or not the pupils have taken the teaching materials, and should not spend hours indefinitely manually correcting them. Teacher can look at the pupils' results in the system and through the reports that the system generates evidences the problems the students have and where the focus should be on their work.

The prototype is tested in "Qemal Stafa" High School in Tirana district. About 48 high school pupils from 10-th grade of the gymnasium "Qemal Stafa" participated in the testing. After creating the accounts for each of them they entered into the system to attend a one-hour class about the next topic they had in ICT subject. All the necessary materials, video (mp4) and power point materials related to the topic were uploaded in the system. By the end of the class-hour, students received a mini test with 5 questions on the topic, 100% of students reached the minimum target of the classroom.

The students and the teacher participating in the test expressed a very positive attitude regarding the effectiveness of the prototype and showed their commitment to involve them in this system.

4   Conclusion

Albania, as a lot of other countries, considers important to expose pupils to Computer Science knowledge since primary school and has developed a contemporary curriculum of Computer Science subject. Since 2005, different initiatives of Albania government, has improved the schools' ICT infrastructure in function of teaching and learning process. Although, currently there are some difficulties in using ICT during the teaching and learning process, which also affect the teaching and learning of Computer Science' subject. Important technological developments could be used alongside the school infrastructure to support the teaching and learning process. Bring Your Own Device strategy in combination with learning technologies was found appropriate for Albania. The prototype made, by implementing a LMS with lessons and quizzes in one of the Computer Science' Area, resulted interesting and productive. The use of appropriate technologies to support the teaching and learning process will introduce an innovative, more productive and more interesting way of learning and teaching. By combining these new technologies with teachers' pedagogical methods and tools, we believe that the students' knowledge, attitudes, and skills will be increased. As a result, students and high school pupils will be more competent, as we are living in an information technology age and will gain lifelong learning skill.

5 Future Work

We will implement the prototype for three months in a High School of Tirana district to test it and improve it if necessary.

In the future, established incubators and cooperation with enterprises will support the use of Emerging Technologies in better teaching and learning by allowing investigation, acquisition, testing, prototyping, piloting, researching, and evaluation of emerging technologies that have the potential to transform education, enhance teaching, and increase student success and retention.

We strongly believe that on the long run time frame this will contribute on improvement on the labor skills of the Labor Market in Albania which in turn is fully in line with not only the Digital Agenda's Strategy of Albanian Government but the regional countries as well and even broader.

References

1. The World Economic Forum. https://www.weforum.org/agenda/2017/01/technology-is-changing-the-way-we-live-learn-and-work-how-can-leaders-make-sure-we-all-prosper/. Accessed 13 Feb 2019
2. JoomlaLMS. https://www.joomlalms.com/blog/expert-interview/how-has-technology-changed-the-way-we-learn-matt-harris.html. Accessed 13 Feb 2019
3. Heeks, R.: The ICT4D 2.0 manifesto: where next for ICTs and international development? (PDF). Development Informatics Group Institute for Development Policy and Management University of Manchester (2009)
4. The World Economic Forum. https://www.weforum.org/agenda/2013/04/five-ways-technology-can-help-the-economy/. Accessed 13 Feb 2019
5. Pohjola, M.: Information Technology, Productivity, and Economic Growth: International Evidence and Implications for Economic Development In: WIDER Studies in Development Economics. Oxford University Press, Oxford (2001)
6. https://www.weforum.org/agenda/2016/01/the-fourth-industrial-revolution-what-it-means-and-how-to-respond/
7. Ministry of Education and Sports (MES): Strategy on pre-university education development 2014–2020, Tirana (2014)
8. Ministry of Innovation and Public Administration: Cross-Cutting Strategy "Digital Agenda of Albania 2015–2020" (2015)
9. National Strategy for Development and Integration NSDI 2014–2020 Ministry of Innovation and Public Administration
10. The White House. https://obamawhitehouse.archives.gov/the-press-office/2016/01/30/fact-sheet-president-obama-announces-computer-science-all-initiative-0. Accessed 13 Feb 2019
11. The Royal Society. https://royalsociety.org/topics-policy/projects/computing-in-schools/report/. Accessed 13 Feb 2019

12. Sturman, L., Sizmur, J.: International Comparison of Computing in Schools. NFER, Sloughf (2011). https://www.nfer.ac.uk/publications/cis101/cis101.pdf. Accessed 13 Feb 2019
13. Jones, S.P.: Computing at School: International Comparisons. Microsoft Research UK, November 2011. https://community.computingatschool.org.uk/files/6710/original.pdf. Accessed 13 Feb 2019
14. Ministry of Education and Sport: Kurrikula Bërthamë. Për Klasën Përgatitore Dhe Arsimin Fillor. http://izha.edu.al/new/wp-content/uploads/2017/03/Kurrikula-berthame-1-5.pdf. Accessed 13 Feb 2019
15. Ministry of Innovation and Public Administration: Cross-Cutting Strategy 2008–2013 http://shtetiweb.org/wp-content/uploads/2014/05/Information-Society-strategy_printed_version_en1.pdf. Accessed 13 Feb 2019
16. World Bank. http://web.worldbank.org/archive/website01337/WEB/0__CO-27.HTM. Accessed 13 Feb 2019
17. Institute of Education Development, Ministry of Education and Sport: Të nxënit me situata, konstruktivizmi dhe teknologjia. Udhëzues për mësuesit, Tiranë (2015). http://dartiraneqark.edu.al/images/Udhezuesi-me-situata-te-te-nxenit-me-TIKun.pdf. Accessed 13 Feb 2019
18. UNESCO: Education Sector (2017). https://ec.europa.eu/epale/sites/epale/files/albania_education_policy_review_issues_and_recommandations_april_2017.pdf. Accessed 27 Feb 2019
19. The Archived Website of New Media Consortium (NMC), https://www.nmc.org/nmc-horizon/. Accessed 27 Feb 2019
20. Johnson, L., Adams Becker, S., Estrada, V., Freeman, A.: NMC Horizon Report: 2015 K-12 Edition. The New Media Consortium, Austin (2015)
21. Adams Becker, S., Freeman, A., Giesinger Hall, C., Cummins, M., Yuhnke, B.: NMC/CoSN Horizon Report: 2016 K-12 Edition. The New Media Consortium, Austin (2016)
22. Freeman, A., Adams Becker, S., Cummins, M., Davis, A., Hall Giesinger, C.: NMC/CoSN Horizon Report: 2017 K-12 Edition. The New Media Consortium, Austin (2017)
23. Consortium for School Networking: Driving K-12 Innovation/2019 Hurdles (2019)
24. NSW Department of Education. https://education.nsw.gov.au/teaching-and-learning/professional-learning/scan/past-issues/vol-33,-2014/enhancing-learning-and-collaboration-with-byod. Accessed 27 Feb 2019
25. de Oliveira, P.C., de Almeida Cunha, C.J.C., Nakayama, M.K.: Learning management systems (LMS) and e-learning management: an integrative review and research agenda. JISTEM – J. Inf. Syst. Technol. Manag. 13(2), 157–180 (2016)
26. Mc Quiggan, S., Kosturko, L., Mc Quiggan, J., Sabouri, J.: Mobile Learning. A Handbook for Developers, Educators, and Learners. Wiley, Hoboken (2015)

Programming Teaching Tools Feature Assessment Associated with Brazilian Curriculum Base Obtained Through BPL Platforms Analysis

Aléssio Miranda Júnior(✉) ⓘ, Deisymar Botega Tavares(✉) ⓘ,
and Jordana Caires Carvalho(✉)

Centro Federal de Educação Tecnológica de Minas Gerais,
Belo Horizonte 35180-008, Brazil
{alessio,dbotegatavares}@cefetmg.br,
jordana.caires.carvalho@gmail.com

Abstract. Learning programming isn't only important for programmers. Studies show that learning computation is useful for logical reasoning development, which leads to an easier learning in mathematical fundamentals and language skills. Because of this, several computation platforms have emerged for children and teenagers. These tools can be used by teachers from several fields of knowledge to stimulate their student's learning. However, these platforms don't include topics from the Brazilian National Curricular Joint Base (BNCC), which make them difficult to use for this specific purpose. Looking to the relevance of creating or remodeling a platform for this goal, the first step is to survey for necessary features. The LORI method was used by students from elementary public school, using Code and Blockly platforms. This paper describes which and how features were studied during the exploration of two platforms, while analysing the audience. Computer education platforms directed to young people can highlight some important characteristics: daily use and cultural aspects of students in order to approach the platform, giving feedback with enough information for them to understand their error and the possibility for the teacher to visualize and measure in what aspect and how often the students make a mistake.

Keywords: Cultural issues in learning with collaboration technologies ·
Programming for children · E-learning · LORI · Education ·
Programming with education

1 Introduction

Logical reasoning is the basis of cognitive maturation and it supports the development of other skills. Several studies consider it one of the foundations for critical thinking skills development, as its absence can hamper linguistic learning abilities, like Portuguese and mathematics fundamentals [1].

P. Zaphiris and A. Ioannou (Eds.): HCII 2019, LNCS 11590, pp. 380–389, 2019.
https://doi.org/10.1007/978-3-030-21814-0_29

Logical reasoning is also the basis of computation, as this area covers and reaches most other fields of knowledge and has steady growth in the professional market. However, unlike the others, this is neither predicted nor taught in the Brazilian National Curricular Joint Base (BNCC).

If a future professional doesn't need programing, it will still bring benefits by developing logical reasoning, critical thinking, and linear thinking in problem-solving. Furthermore, understanding how technologies are being developed and having the ability to develop oneself may grant opportunities [2].

The teaching of programming for children and teenagers aims to encourage not only logical reasoning development, but also other areas of knowledge so that solutions may be created to their own desires while checking if it is something they like [2].

The main objective is not to teach a specific programming language, but to show that logic is the same for all languages. It should be noted that not all students will become programmers, but with a differential, they will have a greater ability to think and be more creative, since learning programming logic develops various skills that are often hidden [3].

Although current programming teaching platforms are widely used and easily accessible, with playful methodologies and didactic resources aimed at children and teenagers, there is no perspective of targeting or customize based on cultures. Citing the example of Code platform, "there are some problems that are limited to being solved by requiring little study, but is not possible to fit them into a format to be used in a classroom, respecting the BNCC".

The proposal is to create or remodel a tool available to this target audience, involving both programming learning and the BNCC, jointly. That is, as long as the person has a problem in basic disciplines, its solution will be through programming and prior knowledge of the discipline itself. The intention isn't to replace classroom teaching in schools, but to be an instrument of support and fixation, while gaining the ability of programming.

The creation or remodeling of a tool is an extensive and complex work, for the initial steps are significant. One of them is the study of existing and non-existing features on the main platforms, that are essential to the proposed tool.

The Problem Based Learning (PBL) methodology emphasizes learning through problem solving. Through this method the student is the main actor of his learning, as when faced with a problem presented by the teacher, they should actively seek the solution, without theoretical classes or previous examples of resolution given by the teacher. The teacher's function becomes that of an instructor, indicating sources where students can research problem solutions and follow their reasoning, being able to redirect it if they escape the goal, except it is up to the student to research, develop and present a solution. In this method some concepts of collaborative work are also employed, since the students are separated in small groups of a maximum of six, where they discuss and analyze together the solutions to the problems.

Zanatta [4] shows some programming educational platforms where the author mention history, aspects, and purpose. The text called *"Programação de Computadores para Crianças: Metodologia do Code Club Brasil"* (Computer Programming for Children: Code Club Brazil Methodology) has the experience of building and applying the Code Club to students and observe its methodology. The difference in this work is that Zanatta (2015) doesn't apply any method to validate the other platforms, (like Learning Object Review Instrument) [5], there is no intention of listing the characteristics of each of them and the purpose to join the Brazilian National Curricular Joint Base (BNCC).

This article describes what these characteristics are and how they were examined. Section 2 clarifies the methods used to scan the features and Sect. 3 presents the result obtained by the assessment.

2 Construction of the IPC and Application of the Methodology

An extension project was created at CEFET-MG (*Centro Federal Tecnológico de Minas Gerais*), called Introduction to Programming and Competitions (iPC), with the purpose of involving elementary and high school students that don't study in CEFET into logical learning, with oriented use in the current platforms.

The project started in 2017 and attended until 2018 a total of 84 students. The team involved 15 undergraduate students, three Computer Engineering teachers and two students from the Informatics technical course. Through this project, it was possible to accomplish actions that allowed the study of existing and/or non-existing features of the current programming platforms for children and teenagers. The actions were (i) choice of platforms and activities, (ii) Code and Blockly analysis with LORI method: results in the Sect. 3.3, (iii) invitation of the students, (iv) use and analysis of Code and Blockly with the students.

2.1 Choice of Platform(s) and Activities

The first step was the selection of existing platforms, as well as verification of which of them possessed the elements that would facilitate compliance with the BNCC. It was decided not to show code lines and advanced concepts to beginner students in programming. Bau et al. [6] demonstrated that the goal should be focused on logic and avoid complicated elements in the educational environment.

We adopted Blockly in the first group of students and it has been more explored by the iPC development team to see and test the possibilities. Thus, Code was applied in a primary plan for students, as to evaluate the aspects that are appropriate or not to the iPC purpose.

Noticing the experience of the iPC team and seeking for a platform that could be used as a test with its own method and what would the students think about it, Code and Blockly were analyzed by the LORI (Learning Object Review Instrument) [4]. The results are in the Sect. 3.2.

Visualizing the games in Code, by experience in computer teaching, the one that demonstrated to be completer and more suitable for young people aged between 14 and 15 years old was the "Accelerated Intro to CS Course".

2.2 Inviting Students

Over two years of project, 84 students were invited and distributed in four classes, as shown in Fig. 1. The first group was composed of ninth grade students from municipal schools personally invited in each school, accompanied by the Education Secretary of the municipality of Timóteo.

Teachers, principals, and students from the ninth-grade elementary school proposed were introduced to the purpose of the project and informed how it would work. The Education Secretary was requested to select 21 students, analyzing math punctuation, personality, talking with the teachers about the responsibility of each one and considering the equal distribution of representant by school.

After the first class finished the course with 21 students (Fig. 1), the next two classes were composed of first year students from municipal and state high schools. The students made a subscription by form and each group was composed between 18 and 25 people each (Fig. 1), having about two to three dropouts individually.

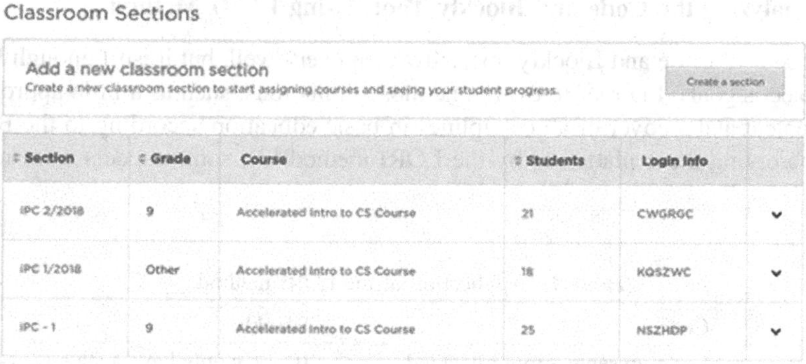

Classroom Sections

Add a new classroom section				
Create a new classroom section to start assigning courses and seeing your student progress.				Create a section

Section	Grade	Course	Students	Login Info	
iPC 2/2018	9	Accelerated Intro to CS Course	21	CWGRGC	⌄
iPC 1/2018	Other	Accelerated Intro to CS Course	18	KQSZWC	⌄
iPC - 1	9	Accelerated Intro to CS Course	25	NSZHDP	⌄

Fig. 1. Three classes of the iPC project

2.3 Use and Analysis of Code and Blockly with Students

The recruited students were submitted to various activities from the accelerated course of Code (all classes) and some activities of Blockly (only the first class).

There was one weekly meeting of three hours each for the first group and two weekly meetings of two hours for the second and third classes.

During the meetings, the instructors (students from the Informatics technical course and the Computer Engineering course) coordinated the activities by teaching students how to use the platforms and asking questions. During this follow-up process, several interventions were needed since the students were sometimes euphoric or couldn't progress, or could not properly exploit the platform's resources. In addition, in some instances the resources of the platforms were not sufficient for the students' progress, and therefore intervening with more practical teaching strategies were necessary, mainly in the teaching of programming concepts, such as function for example.

As the instructors were monitoring the class, it was possible to perceive several characteristics on the platforms, and if they were sufficient or not. Section 3.3 presents these raised characteristics.

3   Results of the Platforms Analysis and Students

The process of arriving to a tool that can combine the learnings of Code and Blockly and show the user basic study elements in a motivational way is long, since a lot of detailed perception is needed and the students behavior especially counts. With the application of the LORI method, the chosen platforms and their use by the groups of students in a monitored way, it was possible to raise series of important features for a platform that has the final design to be an instrument of assistance in learning the contents of the BNCC through practice. The following sections highlight these raised characteristics.

3.1   Analyzing the Code and Blockly Tools Using LORI Method

The purpose of Code and Blockly normally attend very well, but it isn't enough for the iPC project's goals. In order to overcome those limitations, such as a little approach of math content and a cover of all disciplines in basic education according to the BNCC, while observing these platforms by the LORI method [4], some aspects were noticed (Table 1).

Table 1. Application of the LORI method.

Item	Code	Blockly
Content quality	Code presents a more detailed content with explanations in each game. There are also videos for more context	Blockly only have a statement of the problem
Learning objectives alignment	Both have the purpose to teach logic programming for children and teenagers. But, for the iPC's goal, it is not enough	
Feedback and adaptation	Code sends feedback to the user with different sounds; a message on top of a statement informs a mistake and offers a help	Blockly only have a message in the screen center when a mistake has occurred, there isn't a note to click for help or any box with more information
Motivation	Code conducts the user in all screen games and the characters are distributed in levels, as they come back to reinforce the knowledge as time goes	The games are presented with little information on screen and a message appears if the exercise is correct. The platform has motivation, but doesn't give enough feedback

(continued)

Table 1. (*continued*)

Item	Code	Blockly
Presentation design	Both have animations and sounds to encourage the student to continue the exercises	
Interactive usability	The screens are colorful and the explanation videos lead the user to have an easy experience with the platform	Blockly has a screen focusing on the game as a way not to compete with functionalities
Accessibility	Disapproved. Both don't have resource for low vision or blind people	
Compliance with the pattern	Doesn't apply in this case	

3.2 Lessons Adaptation

Through observation during the three months of classes with the selected students in CEFET, by the students questions, monitoring of reasoning improvement, the perception the teenagers resolution for the most difficult exercises, some aspects in terms of functional and non-functional requirements were regarded.

As cited in Sect. 2.3, some theoretical classes were taught. It occurred in view of the teenagers' anxiety, with regard to new concepts and situations, and also because Code doesn't analyze code quality. For example, the tool counts blocks (Code uses drag-and-drop code blocks), but not which of them was put by the student in the solution. In other words, if the student in a repeated loop lesson doesn't bring any repeat loop block, but instead puts less or the correct number of blocks to execute, and the execution solves the problem, Code accepts the student's solution.

The interventions in each classes had the purpose of alerting the students about it and reinforce computational concepts according to Brazilian culture. The instructors had the responsibility to create appropriate activities taking into account a close observation of harder exercises in classroom and conversations at the end of activities with the teenagers. Those exercises could be a presentation, word research, a game to write a story with algorithm words (if, do, while, etc.), an explanation of "functions" using cake shapes with equal shapes but with different sizes, and others of this type.

Therefore, the explanatory resources: video-lessons, since textual explanations on these platforms are not enough to solve the students' doubts, due to their generic nature and not contextualized with the national reality. In this way, a mechanism that allows the insertion of more video-lessons is necessary as well as textual explanations in these platforms are a relevant resource, based on the lived experience.

3.3 Learning and Teaching the Students

Through the follow-up of students during the execution of the activities and by the necessary interferences performed in this process, series of situations were perceived and make a difference for a better growth of the student's learning. Among them:

- Empathy - Understanding how the students felt about the new situation at the end of each class, asking and dialoguing about how were the exercises, the difficulties and changes for a better adaptation, and if they had enjoyed it. This conversation made possible to spot the empirical aspects in the Sect. 3.4. This empathy could be exposed with an AI resource that would talk to the user about their experience and enable the user to asks about their doubts, as the tool would analyse this data, like a chat boot. It would show and repeat the exercises that the person had difficulties, and over the exercise display, some interesting facts about the tool and how logical reasoning can be helpful day by day, in life in general, and applied at school.

- Simple thinking - Showing a student a farmer that digs a field doesn't approach the teenagers to the tool, because it's possible that someone has never been into a field. Simple things like the weather are general subjects that anyone knows, and it doesn't involve a cultural or regional point of view. When the scenarios of the activities are closer to the reality of the students, their understanding of the problems, as well as their solution, becomes simpler. Consequently, it is important to adapt the problems to the knowledge and competences foreseen in the BNCC, in order to make an expected use of the learning resource.

- Together is funnier than alone - Code and Blockly are tools to learn by oneself. But altogether, having healthy competitions and to be able to ask for help is a way to support other people. A specific screen (Fig. 2) was found harder by the students, and when they spoke to each other while the instructors were observing, they understood that the problem wasn't so difficult, which leads to questioning whether the tools available or to be created should have at least some group activity.

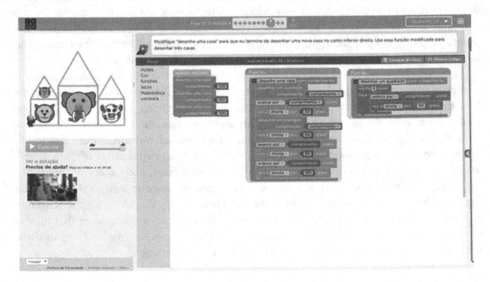

Fig. 2. A screenshot of an exercise

- The tool is important, but knowledge goes far beyond - The purpose of Code and Blockly is to teach logic to children and teenagers. However, like the screen shown on Fig. 2, if the person doesn't know the basic concept, the computational matter stays on a second plan. Mathematical concepts had to be reviewed and even taught, as well as notions of right and left and text interpretation. Even though Code has explanatory videos and some interventions with offline exercises, it was perceived by practice that it is not enough, and there must be other means of explanation for the students. And some of these could be through the intervention of teachers in classroom, via platform, by video-lessons to deal with specific subjects of each activity when necessary and/or through a chatbot that the student could receive some other explanation, one that could be more comfortable, choosing a text, a video, a book, a game or other kinds of educational resources.

3.4 Analyzing the Code and Blockly Tools After an Application in a Classroom

With these experiences and observations, the final goal is to think and prototype a platform with the search and development teams. Beyond that, it is required that

Table 2. Analysis result of Code and Blockly platforms.

Platforms	Positive aspects	Negative aspects
Code	• It presents playful elements that are familiar to students • It is self-explanatory • It does not present student-ready resolution, forcing them to create their own reasoning • It has several modules that deal with different concepts and characters from movies or games • There is a quality evaluation of the student's code	• There is no view of the student progress history (hits and misses) • There is no way to communicate with the student through this tool • The administrative part, mainly the possibility of creating questionnaires for the students shows to be inefficient and is a difficult understanding functionality, with little support for such • The simultaneous translation into Brazilian Portuguese go through deformations, hindering communication • It doesn't obligate the student to complete modules with perfection, giving the possibility to obtain a certificate of completion without this requirement
Blockly	• The exercises have a more complex level than code, such as the music game and the geometric game, that include time variables • The interface is visually clean	• There is no option to log in by storing progress • Problems have insufficient instructions for the student's understanding • There is no return guidance information after some programming error is committed • There is no evaluation of the student's code

teachers and other professionals of education, computing and pedagogy create, analyze and approve each step according to the level of difficulty, the learning method, the content of disciplines simultaneously as making the code and the Software Engineering tests.

After analyzing the selected platforms, it was possible to list a set of positive and negative aspects (Table 2). Such aspects should be considered in order to create or remodel future platforms to integrate the contents of the disciplines governed by BNCC in programming.

3.5   Empirical Result by the Teenagers

The monitoring of the use of the Code and Blockly platforms by the students has led teachers and monitors to perceive a series of aspects that aren't fully aligned with the purpose of this article, but deserve attention considering that they are experiences that motivate more and more the improvement of the tool for the use of programming for children and teenagers, as well as the advancement of pedagogical practice's that include computation as an instrument of teaching and learning. These aspects were:

- Improvement of logical and mathematical reasoning.
- They made new friends.
- They met and were immersed into CEFET-MG teaching institution, demonstrating the interest in entering of computer courses.
- Personal progress.
- Discovery of a possible new career.
- Greater interest in mathematics and programming.
- Reflection of the project as learning content in the school environment.
- Development of concentration, attention, reasoning and patience.
- The perception that reading is important and makes a difference.

Attentive to this opinion, the search team surveyed the third class with two questionnaires application (one at the beginning of the project and one at the end) to measure the transformations in reasoning. The method and results will be shown in another paper.

4   Conclusion

In this report about the first two years of the project, we have done evaluations of programming teaching tools for children and teenagers, looking for features that adapt to the reality of the BNCC.

Using the LORI method, we can make a comparative analysis of the two tools within the requirements placed. These results serve as guides for the analysis of the empirically collected features.

We indicate that the obtained results are preliminary but important to demonstrate the need and guidance for the improvement of the educational development of the tools. Mainly due to the fact that no tools are already in the desired state, and that when fitting, the results become detachable.

The teaching of programming logic focusing on pre-existing problems in the students' disciplines facilitated the learning of both. Complementing cognitive and interpersonal development of students in working in groups to solve problems was also presented in the reports.

We recognize that more formalism is needed in the next stages of validation. A step of municipal analysis of each raised feature and an amplification of the tests bases must reinforce the purpose of this work.

In addition, there is a consistent space for a new proposition that really adapts these educational environments to the Brazilian educational model.

References

1. García, J.N.: Manual de dificuldades de aprendizagem: linguagem, leitura, escrita e matemática, 1st edn, 274 p. McGraw Hill – Artmed, Brasil (1998). ISBN 8573073128
2. Fernandes, C.S.: Ciência da computação para crianças. Dissertação (Mestrado em Computação) - Instituto de Informática. Universidade Federal do Rio Grande do Sul., Rio Grande do Sul., 156 p. (2002). https://lume.ufrgs.br/handle/10183/6843. Accessed 01 Jan 2019
3. Garlet, D., Bigolin, N.M., Silveira, S.R.: Uma Proposta para o Ensino de Programação de Computadores na Educação Básica. Universidade Federal de Santa Maria (UFSM) – Campus de Frederico Westphalen, Brasil, pp. 1–25 (2016)
4. Zanatta, A.C.: Programação de Computadores para Crianças: Metodologia do Code Club Brasil. Universidade Federal de Santa Catarina Campus Araranguá, Brasil, 102 p. (2015). https://repositorio.ufsc.br/xmlui/handle/123456789/158762. Accessed 01 Jan 2019
5. Nesbit, J., Belfer, K., Leacock, T. (ed.). Instrumento para a Avaliação de Objectos de Aprendizagem (LORI): Manual do Usuário, 2nd edn. [S. l.: s. n.], 14 p. (2009). http://www.avu.org/avuorg/images/Documents/ODeLPD/lori_pt.pdf. Accessed 01 Jan 2019
6. Bau, D., et al.: Learnable Programming: Blocks and Beyond. arXiv, USA, ano 2017, pp. 1–8 (2017)

How E-Learning Can Facilitate Information Security Awareness

Andreas E. Schütz[✉], Tobias Fertig, Kristin Weber, and Nicholas H. Müller

University of Applied Sciences Würzburg-Schweinfurt, Würzburg, Germany
{andreas.schuetz,tobias.fertig,kristin.weber,nicholas.mueller}@fhws.de

Abstract. Users of information systems are increasingly being attacked and exploited by cyber criminals. Information Security Awareness addresses how users can be convinced to behave compliantly to a company's information security policies. This paper explores the potential of e-Learning as a tool to increase the information security awareness of users. The factors that ultimately lead to information security-compliant behavior are the factors knowledge, habit, salience, and behavioral intent. By looking at the peculiarities of e-Learning, the chances and limitations of influencing these factors are examined exploratory. The basis for this is Bloom's Taxonomy from learning theory. The paper shows that e-Learning can help influencing knowledge and habit of a person. The salience and intention of a person, however, can only be influenced in combination with other factors. Especially with affective emotions and beliefs, e-Learning can also have negative effects. The paper also gives an outlook on how further quantitative research could help to ultimately shape effective e-Learning courses.

Keywords: Information security awareness · E-Learning platforms · Learning · Bloom's Taxonomy

1 Introduction

As digitization progresses, the demand on the security of the data and information processed grows as well. To protect the confidentiality, integrity, and availability of information, technical security controls such as firewalls and virus scanners are established. Attackers, however, increasingly attack and exploit the human factor in information systems: the user [12,29]. The main types of attacks today are phishing, malware, and social engineering [14]. With the help of these attacks, the hackers are not only able to harm private users, but also companies, research institutions, or even whole countries.

The research area Information Security Awareness (ISA) addresses how people can be convinced to behave in accordance with information security policies, guidelines, or best practices. High ISA should minimize the risk that users are exploited as weak spots in the information security concept. Especially in companies, security awareness campaigns are utilized to sensitize employees towards

P. Zaphiris and A. Ioannou (Eds.): HCII 2019, LNCS 11590, pp. 390–401, 2019.
https://doi.org/10.1007/978-3-030-21814-0_30

their role in securing their companies' information assets. ISA is a complex result of a multitude of factors [3,11,27]. In addition to knowledge, salience and habit it consists of the intention of a person to behave properly and the necessary organizational aspects enabling people to behave securely. Proper security awareness measures should therefore consider all aspects: knowledge, salience, habit, intention, and organization [27].

E-Learning is a popular way to teach people. Forecasts assume that the e-Learning market will continue to grow in the next years [26]. Policy makers are tempted by the many benefits of e-Learning, such as increasing economic competitiveness, cost effectiveness, or more generally the opportunity for better education [5]. Companies regard compliance and IT expertise as potential contents that can be conveyed via e-Learning [18]. Hagen et al. [21] investigate the effects of an e-Learning tool that has been used to improve ISA. They were able to see significant changes in attendees' awareness and behavior after using e-Learning. Therefore, e-Learning can be an easy, low-priced method to familiarize people with information security in addition to posters, flyers, or offline training. To generate insights about the benefits of e-Learning regarding improving employees' ISA, this study follows an exploratory approach. Based on the factors presented by [27], this paper evaluates the possibilities and limitations of e-Learning in order to influence the behavior of employees with regard to information security. As a result, the paper shows that e-Learning is basically suitable for influencing cognitive, psychomotor, and also affective factors. While knowledge and habits are easy to convey in the digital field, it is only to a limited extent true for salience and the behavioral intention of a person.

The paper is structured as follows: In the second chapter we introduce the research field of ISA and explain the basics of learning and e-learning. In the next chapter, Analysis, we examine e-learning for its suitability for influencing the ISA. In the fourth chapter we discuss these findings and give an outlook on future research on this topic.

2 Basics

2.1 Information Security Awareness

Information Security Awareness has been established as a separate research area within information security. It targets the "human factor" and how IT users can be brought to an information security-compliant behavior. Attackers now prefer to attack the user to gain access to proprietary information [14]. This approach requires less effort than technically attacking IT systems, using classical methods such as brute-forcing. In addition to technical security controls, it is therefore also important to actively involve the user in the information security concept of a company. One commonly realized method for this involvement are security awareness campaigns. These campaigns aim for motivating IT users to use their theoretical knowledge about information security in practice [3] and for convincing them of the importance of their actions. Today, ISA campaigns mainly do one thing [2]: In lectures, employees receive theoretical knowledge about information

392   A. E. Schütz et al.

security. However, the actual behavior of an employee is hardly influenced by classical training [34].

Hänsch and Benenson [11] describe three possible perspectives of the term security awareness. The simplest perspective is that employees know which threats to information security exist and recognize them ("perception"). Another perspective adds that employees also know how to protect themselves and their organization against those threats ("protection"). And the third perspective is that employees know what a threat is, what they can do about it and that they behave accordingly ("behavior"). Only the last approach promises an actual increase in information security in the company. Altogether, information security awareness means that employees know how to behave in compliance with information security policies and standards (e.g., choosing a secure password), what consequences they and the company may face in the event of non-compliant behavior (e.g., loss of image and financial loss due to loss of customer data) and that they actually apply this knowledge in critical situations.

Schütz [27] describes information security compliant behavior as a result of a person's knowledge, habit, salience, and behavioral intention in relation to a particular behavior. A particular behavior might be, for example, locking the screen when leaving the workplace. Beside the knowledge and the habit, the salience describes how tangible a behavior in the current situation is for a person. But the most complex and influential factor is the behavioral intention. The intention to behave is formed from various emotions and beliefs of a person. If a person is afraid of choosing a password or believes secure passwords are useless, the person will hardly form an intention to choose a secure password. Emotions and beliefs can be divided into three groups. The attitude towards a certain behavior, the perceived norm regarding a behavior in the environment of the person (for example colleagues or family members) and the personnel agency, which describes whether a person is confident in the execution of the behavior in the given circumstances. Despite a positively pronounced security awareness, however, the final execution of a behavior can still be prevented by organizational restrictions in the environment of a person. This is the case, for example, if the IT service for changing a password is not accessible to the user. With the knowledge of the individual factors of a person, it is possible to influence these, in order to change an unwanted behavior or to strengthen a desired behavior.

2.2   Learning

A common method to change behavior is learning [16]. The famous Bloom's Taxonomy differentiates into three learning domains: Cognitive Domain, Affective Domain and Psychomotor Domain [7]. Figure 1 shows that individual domains are subdivided into levels that differ in their complexity and are followed by the learner one after the other.

The *cognitive domain* describes mental skills or the intellectual capability of a person. The revised version of Blooms Taxonomy divides this domain in the dimensions Knowledge and Cognitive Process. The dimension Knowledge

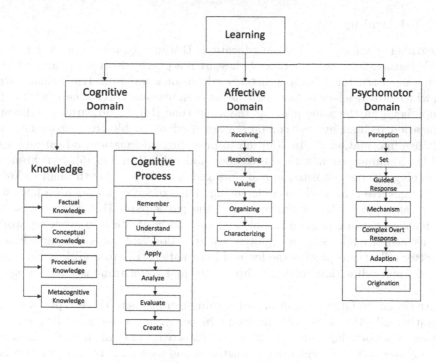

Fig. 1. The three domains of Bloom's Taxonomy

distinguishes four different types of knowledge: Factual Knowledge (basic elements of a knowledge area), Conceptual Knowledge (interrelations between the basic elements), Procedural Knowledge (knowledge of how to do something) and Metacognitive Knowledge (awareness and knowledge of own cognition). The expression of the individual types of knowledge in a person can be assessed on the basis of the cognitive process dimension. This dimension consists of the following hierarchically structured levels: Remember (retrieving knowledge from long-term memory), understand (determine the meaning), apply (carrying out in a given situation), analyze (breaking material into parts and detecting the relation), evaluate (making judgments), and create (putting elements together to create something new) [19].

The *affective domain* describes feelings and emotions, such as an attitude towards a certain thing. It consists of the hierarchically structured levels: Receiving (willingness to pay attention), responding (react to the objective), valuing (attach value to an objective), organizing (organize values into priorities), and characterizing (having a value system that controls behavior) [7].

The *psychomotor domain* describes manual or physical skills. The domain consists of the hierarchically structured levels: Perception (using sense organs to guide activity), set (mental, physical and emotional readiness to act), guided response (imitating, and trial and error), mechanism (responses are habitual), complex overt response (performing activity skillfully), adaptation (well developed skills), and origination (creating new movement patterns for specific situations) [30].

2.3 E-Learning

E-Learning is a form of distance education. Distance education is designed to enable learners to learn, even though they are not physically in one place with the teacher or instructor. This sets distance education apart from traditional learning, which provides face-to-face sessions between teachers and learners, with both groups being in the same place at the same time [16]. In e-Learning, telecommunication technology and computers are used to enable the participants to exchange information [5]. In addition to providing information, e-Learning also enables communication with the teacher and other learners [5]. Synchronous e-Learning can be completed in real time and is made possible through technology such as live chat or video conferencing. The synchrony allows for a personal participation and a better motivation of the participants [13]. However, asynchronous e-Learning is more flexible and easy to integrate into everyday work. The asynchrony allows for a cognitive participation and helps the participants to better reflect and process the learned information [13]. In addition, there are hybrid approaches that work synchronously and asynchronously at the same time [13].

According to Ghirardini et al., e-Learning can promote three types of skills: Cognitive skills (i.e., knowledge or comprehension), interpersonal skills (i.e., presenting or negotiating), and psychomotor skills (e.g., movements) [10]. Blended learning combines different learning methods and uses both traditional learning and e-Learning approaches [8]. For example, a traditional face-to-face lecture can be enriched by combining it with an online course to deepen the learning content.

3 Analysis

A person's Information Security Awareness is made up of several factors that influence the person's behavior. This chapter analyzes these cognitive and affective factors and assesses how they can benefit from e-Learning.

3.1 Knowledge

Knowledge is the sum of facts, information, and skills of a person. A person acquires knowledge through experience or education. The revised version of Bloom's Taxonomy (cf. Chapter 2) separates the knowledge of the cognitive domain and differentiates between factual knowledge, conceptual knowledge, procedural knowledge and metacognitive knowledge. We take the knowledge of secure passwords as an example. Factual knowledge is the knowledge that user accounts and passwords exist. Knowing that a password, consisting of more than eight characters and special characters, can secure a user account is conceptual knowledge. Knowing where to change the password, is procedural knowledge. Metacognitive knowledge is when a person knows they find it difficult to remember secure passwords and therefore use a password manager.

How It Affects ISA: Behavioral research declares knowledge in general as an important component to effect behavioural change. Even a strong behavioural intention is useless, if the necessary knowledge for implementing the behavior was missing [24]. A lack of knowledge is also an obstacle when developing compliant behavior regarding information security [17]. User who do not know the rules for secure passwords will not be able to behave compliantly, though they may want to. This is in line with Hänsch & Benenson's view of the concept of ISA that the perspective behavior builds on knowledge of threats and the protection against these threats. In most cases, the knowledge needed in the information security environment requires also background knowledge about the technical functioning of information systems. Looking at the perspectives of Hänsch & Benenson shows that in the area of ISA, factual knowledge (perspective perception) and conceptual knowledge (perspective protection) are needed. In many cases, also procedural knowledge is needed to fulfill the perspective protection (e.g., requesting a certificate for secure e-mail traffic). The imparting of this quite technical knowledge can be complex depending on the behavior and the prior knowledge of the users.

How e-Learning Can Facilitate It: The acquisition and use of knowledge is the main objective of e-Learning [22]. Therefore, it is a suitable tool to strengthen the knowledge factor in the field of information security. In order to promote individual learning and convey content that is really relevant for the user, the topics to be treated should be adapted to the prior knowledge of the user. As an initial analysis, for example, the execution of a test is suitable. To accomplish this, approaches for semi-automated generation of course content can be used [10]. For the general content design of e-Learning, it should be noted that factual knowledge and conceptual knowledge are promoted equally. Procedural knowledge can be practiced through interactive simulation. The digital nature of e-Learning makes it easy to simulate digital environments needed for information security, as users already have the system at their fingertips. In addition, interactive e-Learning activities help teaching people how to use methods in new situations [10]. Similarly, it is important to consider the cognitive process dimension. In order to increase the knowledge of one person, the other levels of the process should be promoted in addition to the levels "remember" and "understand". Knowledge can be applied in subsequent tests or simulations or can be analyzed by case studies. Evaluation of the learned can be promoted in discussion boards. The level "creating" is again very difficult to implement in e-Learning [32].

3.2   Habit

A habit is a learned sequence of actions that has become an automatic response to specific triggers [33]. The more often a behavior is carried out, the more it becomes habitual [31]. With increasing habit, the influence of the behavioral intention on the performance of the behavior eventually decreases [31]. When the impact of other factors that affect the performance of a behavior is less, the whole process of building compliant behavior is less complex.

How It Affects ISA: A habit can be used to strengthen the execution of information security compliant behavior. Studies show, that habit influences the compliance of employees with information security policies [25]. Habit is influenced by the repetition of a behavior and, in turn, a habit also positively influences the performance of a behavior. Locking the computer when leaving the workplace is an example of a frequently performed activity. After being executed a few times, employees will unconsciously lock their computer as soon as they leave the office chair, without worrying about it. The behavior became a habit. However, there are also behaviors that are performed less frequently, such as reporting a security incident. Those behaviors hardly become a habit. If employees notice an incident, they will probably first need to think about how they should behave in this situation.

How e-Learning Can Faciliate It: Before content is created for e-Learning, a fundamental check should be made as to whether it is possible to strengthen the habit for each type of behavior. If a behavior requires a lot of attention, such as the detection of phishing e-mails, or if, as mentioned earlier, the behavior needs to be performed rather rarely, there is only a limited way to increase habit. In order to habituate a suitable behavior, it must be rehearsed repeatedly. According to [10] e-Learning is actually less likely to be used for practicing psychomotor skills. However, thanks to the special characteristics of digital domains, the computer is nevertheless a suitable medium here, since everything is in reach. Habitual behaviors on computers, such as locking the screen, are rather simple tasks. E-Learning must ensure that the habit is repeated on a regular basis and linked to the necessary triggers (for example, getting up from the workplace triggers screen locking). In the classification of [30] the achievement of habitual responses corresponds to the level "mechanism".

3.3 Salience

Something is considered salient when it stands out from its immediate environment [6]. A salient behavior must be so prominent and important for a person that they translate their behavioral intent in action. Especially when a longer period of time has elapsed after the intention to behave, salience gets even more important, so that the person remembers the behavior when it matters [24].

How It Affects ISA: For example, we assume that employees have already been persuaded not to use any external USB drives on the company computer. However, the situation does not become reality until three months later, when a representative of a supplier gives them a USB drive. Now it is important that the employees still remembers the correct behavior of not using the USB drive. The behavior must be salient for the employees. Methods from social marketing, such as the use of posters or flyers, are a suitable means to increase the salience against an information security compliant behavior [4,27].

How e-Learning Can Faciliate It: E-Learning can be used to support social marketing campaigns. When users complete e-Learning, they already devote their attention to the content. For example, funny-looking videos could help anchoring proper behavior in the memory. However, the content of e-Learning should be coordinated with the entire marketing campaign.

3.4 Intention

The intention to behave or motivation happens before the actual behavior and ultimately influences the actual execution. With the formation of such an intention a person decides bindingly for a certain action goal. This decision can be weakened if there is a long period of time between grasping behavioral intent and actual behavior [28]. This means that after a campaign in which a behavioral intention has been formed, employees also need the opportunity to apply the desired behavior as quickly as possible in the working environment. The behavioral intent is very complex and is made up of three constructs: the attitude, the perceived norm, and the personal agency of a person.

How It Affects ISA: The intention is an important construct in terms of ISA and, in contrast to the other factors, is strongly dominated by a person's affection. The attitude results from the experiential attitude ("What have I experienced while performing the behavior in the past?"), which is influenced by feelings, and the instrumental attitude ("What are the consequences of the execution of the behavior?"), which is affected by beliefs regarding the effects of the behavior. For example, if a person assesses their own behavior as irrelevant ("Nobody cares about what I have on my computer."), they will also have a rather negative attitude towards the behavior. The perceived norm is also subdivided into two areas: the injunctive norm (reflects the person's beliefs about what behavior their social environment expects of them), and the descriptive norm (describes the beliefs of how the environment itself behaves). If managers expect their staff to lock the screen when leaving the workplace, but do not follow the rule themselves, the employees' injunctive and descriptive norm will diverge. The personal agency is formed by the perceived control ("Is the execution of the behavior simple or difficult in view of the circumstances?"), and the self-efficacy ("Do I dare to perform the behavior with my abilities?"). These, too, are created by the beliefs of a person.

How e-Learning Can Faciliate It: To influence a person's intention to behave in compliance with information security, An e-Learning course should address the person's feelings and beliefs [24]. In order to influence the beliefs of a person, they can vary in their strength, that is, strengthened or weakened depending on the desired behavior, or changed [1]. Beliefs, for example, may change if contradictory information is presented to the person who believes [15]. When a person is told how much important data is on their computer, or how an attacker can use the computer to access other systems in an organization, their opinions change that their careless behavior makes no difference. Interactive multimedia, such as e-Learning, is generally considered useful in the affective domain [20]. By conducting e-Learning, the user has already reached the first level of the affective domain of the Bloom Taxonomy "receiving". E-Learning can be used to promote the achievement of the other levels. Through active participation in an e-Learning course and the use of synchronous components, it is possible to initiate discussions in live chats, the second stage "responding" is encouraged. At the same time, the perceived norm is influenced. The following stages are more difficult to influence [9] and can be achieved, for example, through moderated discussions. But this should be more feasible in a discussion in which the participants are on site. [23] found that e-Learning can produce both positive and negative consequences in the affective domain. Negative consequences may arise from failing technology, too little emotional support, or simply the difficulty of self-regulated learning. If a participant bothers about failing the e-Learning, they might associate the negative emotion with the behavior. For participants, it is therefore also important to have a synchronous or asynchronous contact with a real person during the execution of an e-Learning course. This can alleviate the negative consequences and at the same time encourage the participants to strengthen personal agency.

4   Discussion

In the previous analysis, e-Learning could generally be identified as a suitable tool for ISA campaigns. E-Learning was invented for the communication of knowledge and, consequently, clearly has its strengths in this regard. Especially factual, conceptual, and procedural knowledge can be taught via e-Learning. However, due to the digital nature and the isolated learning environment, it is difficult to reach all levels of Bloom's Taxonomy. E-Learning is a suitable training tool to build habits for digital behaviors. However, it should be examined if a specific behavior is suitable for becoming a habit. In the area of salience, e-Learning cannot replace, but certainly support, social marketing measures. In the area of forming an intention, e-Learning can also help influencing affective factors, such as emotions and beliefs about a behavior. However, a large part of the success depends on the quality of the synchronous and asynchronous discussion options. If discussions or support are insufficient, e-Learning can also have negative effects [23]. As a consequence, in order to reach the higher levels of a person's affective domain, e-Learning cannot sufficiently replace face-to-face events.

It should be noted that the analysis of the individual situation of a person is a basic requirement for the design of a targeted ISA e-Learning course. The purpose of such an analysis is to identify which information security behaviors are a relevant content to be presented in the e-Learning. For example, if a user is already well versed in password security, they may not need to attend an e-Learning about the topic. The analysis also provides for attitudes a user has regarding these behaviors [27].

For the initiator, organizing e-learning offers some advantages. E-Learning has great scalability and allows for many people attending a course at the same time. In addition, an e-Learning course involves less organizational effort compared to classroom sessions. For example, no rooms need to be reserved or appointments arranged. For the users themselves, e-Learning has the big advantage that they can freely organize their time. However, this could be a disadvantage, if users are not able to motivate themselves for self-responsible learning.

This paper examines the suitability of e-Learning from a purely exploratory point of view and using common learning theories. Only the basic suitability can be examined and theses generated, which should be evaluated quantitatively as a next step. Based on quantitative results concrete recommendations for the design of an e-Learning for security awareness can be given. In order to enable quantitative checks, however, it is being necessary to further research the success and effectiveness measurements of e-Learning in particular and information security awareness in general.

Acknowledgments. Andreas E. Schütz was supported by the BayWISS Consortium Digitization.

References

1. Ajzen, I.: Behavioral interventions based on the theory of planned behavior: brief description of the theory of planned behavior (2006). https://people.umass.edu/aizen/pdf/tpb.intervention.pdf
2. Allianz fuer Cybersicherheit: Awareness-Umfrage 2015. Technical report, Bonn, May 2016
3. Bada, M., Sasse, A.M., Nurse, J.R.: Cyber Security Awareness Campaigns: Why do they fail to change behaviour? In: Global Cyber Security Capacity Centre: Draft Working Paper, pp. 131–188 (2014)
4. Baranowski, T., Cullen, K.W., Nicklas, T., Thompson, D., Baranowski, J.: Are current health behavioral change models helpful in guiding prevention of weight gain efforts? Obesity **11**(10), 23–43 (2003). https://doi.org/10.1038/oby.2003.222
5. Bates, T.: Technology, E-Learning and Distance Education. RoutledgeFalmer Studies in Distance Education, 2nd edn. Routledge, London (2005)
6. Baumeister, R.F.F., Vohs, K.D.D.: Encyclopedia of Social Psychology. SAGE, Thousand Oaks (2007). http://gbv.eblib.com/patron/FullRecord.aspx?p=996937
7. Bloom, B.S., Krathwohl, D.R.: Taxonomy of educational objectives; the classification of educational goals by a committee of college and university examiners. In: Handbook I: Cognitive Domain. Longmans, Green (1956)
8. Bonk, C.J., Graham, C.R. (eds.): The Handbook of Blended Learning: Global Perspectives. Local Designs. Pfeiffer Essential Resources for Training and HR Professionals, 1st edn. Pfeiffer, San Francisco (2006)
9. Boyd, B.L., Dooley, K.E., Felton, S.: Measuring learning in the affective domain using reflective writing about a virtual international agriculture experience. J. Agric. Educ. **47**(3), 24–32 (2006). https://doi.org/10.5032/jae.2006.03024
10. Ghirardini, B., Food and Agriculture Organization of the United Nations, Germany, Bundesministerium für Ernährung, L.u.V.: E-learning methodologies: a guide for designing and developing e-learning courses. Food and Agriculture Organization of the United Nations, Rome (2011). oCLC: 805047485
11. Hänsch, N., Benenson, Z.: Specifying IT security awareness. In: 2014 25th International Workshop on Database and Expert Systems Applications, pp. 326–330, September 2014. https://doi.org/10.1109/DEXA.2014.71

12. Hirshfield, L., et al.: The role of human operators' suspicion in the detection of cyber attacks. Int. J. Cyber Warfare Terrorism **5**(3), 28–44 (2015). https://doi. org/10.4018/IJCWT.2015070103

13. Hrastinski, S.: Asynchronous and synchronous e-learning. Educause Quarterley **31**(4), 51–55 (2008)

14. ISACA: State of Cybersecurity 2017. Part 2: Current Trends in Threat Landscape. Technical report, ISACA, 3701 Algonquin Road, Suite 1010 Rolling Meadows, IL 60008 USA (2017). http://www.isaca.org/Knowledge-Center/Research/ Documents/state-of-cybersecurity-2017-part-2_res_eng_0517.pdf

15. Kabay, M.E., Robertson, B., Akella, M., Lang, D.T.: Using social psychology to implement security policies. In: Computer Security Handbook, pp. 50.1–50.25. Wiley (2012). https://doi.org/10.1002/9781118820650.ch50

16. Kahiigi, E.K., Ekenberg, L., Tusubira, F.F., Danielson, M.: Exploring the e-learning state of the art. Electron. J. e-Learn. **6**(2), 77–88 (2008)

17. Khan, B., Alghatbar, K.S., Nabi, S.I., Khan, M.: Effectiveness of information security awareness methods based on psychological theories. African J. Bus. Manage. **26**(5), 10862–10868 (2011)

18. mmb Institut - Gesellschaft für Medien-und Kompetenzforschung mbH: Weiterbildung und Digitales Lernen heute und in drei Jahren: Erklärfilme als Umsatzbringer der Stunde Ergebnisse der 12. Trendstudie mmb Learning Delphi". Technical report (2018)

19. Krathwohl, D.R.: A revision of bloom's taxonomy: an overview. Theory Into Pract. **41**(4), 212–218 (2002)

20. McFarland, D.: Multimedia in higher education. Katharine Sharp Rev. **3**(3) (1996)

21. Merete Hagen, J., Albrechtsen, E.: Effects on employees' information security abilities by e-learning. Inf. Manag. Comput. Secur. **17**(5), 388–407 (2009). https:// doi.org/10.1108/09685220911006687

22. Meyen, E.L., Tangen, P., Lian, C.H.: Developing online instruction: partnership between instructors and technical developers. J. Special Educ. Technol. **14**(1), 18–31 (1999). https://doi.org/10.1177/016264349901400102

23. Moneta, G.B., Kekkonen-Moneta, S.S.: Affective learning in online multimedia and lecture versions of an introductory computing course. Educ. Psychol. **27**(1), 51–74 (2007)

24. Montaño, D.E., Kasprzyk, D.: Theory of reasoned action, theory of planned behavior, and the integrated behavior model. In: Glanz, K., Barbara, K., Viswanath, K. (eds.) Health Behavior and Health Education, pp. 67–96. Wiley, Hoboken (2008)

25. Pahnila, S., Siponen, M., Mahmood, A.: Employees' behavior towards is security policy compliance. In: 2007 40th Annual Hawaii International Conference on System Sciences (HICSS 2007), p. 156b, January 2007. https://doi.org/10.1109/ HICSS.2007.206

26. Reportlinker: Global E-Learning Market Outlook (2014–2022) (2015). https:// www.prnewswire.com/news-releases/global-e-learning-market-outlook-2014- 2022-300146534.html

27. Schütz, A.E.: Information security awareness: it's time to change minds! In: Proceedings of International Conference on Applied Informatics Imagination, Creativity, Design, Development - ICDD 2018. Sibiu, Romania (2018)

28. Schwarzer, R.: Psychologie des Gesundheitsverhaltens: Einführung in die Gesundheitspsychologie. Hogrefe, Göttingen, 3, überarb. aufl. edn. (2004)

29. Semba, B., Eymann, T.: Developing a Model to Analyze the Influence of Personal Values on IT Security Behavior. In: Tagungsband Multikonferenz Wirtschaftsinformatik 2016, pp. 1083–1091. TU Ilmenau, Ilmenau (2016)
30. Simpson, E.J.: The classification of educational objectives in the psychomotor domain. Technical report, University of Illinois, Urbana (1966)
31. Triandis, H.C.: Interpersonal Behavior. Brooks/Cole, Monterey Calif (1977)
32. Tulsiani, R.: Applying bloom's taxonomy in eLearning, July 2017. https://elearningindustry.com/blooms-taxonomy-applying-elearning
33. Verplanken, B., Aarts, H.: Habit, attitude, and planned behaviour: is habit an empty construct or an interesting case of goal-directed automaticity? Eur. Rev. Soc. Psychol. **10**(1), 101–134 (1999). https://doi.org/10.1080/14792779943000035
34. Wolf, M.: Von Security Awareness zum Secure Behaviour. Hakin9 Extra **5**, 18–19 (2012)

Learning with Trees:
A Non-linear E-Textbook Format for Deep Learning

Eric Spero[⊠], Milica Stojmenović, Ali Arya, and Robert Biddle

Carleton University, Ottawa, Canada
{eric.spero,milica.stojmenovic,ali.arya,robert.biddle}@carleton.ca

Abstract. A "deep" approach to education requires considering the non-linear connections between concepts, which is difficult to do with the standard linear textbook format. Guided by the cognitive science literature, we designed a format for a new, non-linear e-textbook format, and implemented a high fidelity prototype. We tested this prototype with end-users, measuring its pedagogical efficacy, usability, and overall likability, in comparison with a linear control. We found no significant differences in learning outcomes between the two conditions, but a significantly greater number of participants preferred the non-linear interface. We suspect that many potential advantages of the non-linear format were negated by our short study. Future work should study the effects of the non-linear interface over a longer period of use.

Keywords: Human-computer interaction · Educational technology · Cognitive science

1 Introduction

Educators are calling for a "deeper" coverage of learning material—one that focuses more on the interactions between concepts, within and across domains [20]. This is a proposed departure from the present dominant "broad" approach, which prefers to instead focus on covering a large number of concepts in relative isolation from each other.

Textbooks are important tools in formal education, and making significant changes to textbooks is a prerequisite for making changes to education as a whole [27]. Textbooks today are designed to support the broad approach [2,22,30,33]: there is a need for deep textbooks.

The relationships between concepts have a non-linear structure: they are hierarchical [1,25,36,39], associative [10,17,31], and multidimensional [15,40]. Communicating non-linear relationships is possible in linear texts, but we think it comes with a cost. For example, hierarchy can be signalled with language and with headers, but we think that organizing concepts into a visual hierarchy would make the relationships more salient to the learner. We think that a non-linear textbook format would better support the deep approach to education.

© Springer Nature Switzerland AG 2019
P. Zaphiris and A. Ioannou (Eds.): HCII 2019, LNCS 11590, pp. 402–422, 2019.
https://doi.org/10.1007/978-3-030-21814-0_31

In this paper, we describe the design and study of a novel e-textbook format which is guided by the cognitive science literature on knowledge representation and organization. Our non-linear format deviates from the standard linear format in two key ways. First, we separate content into two types: core and peripheral, as seen in Fig. 1. Core content corresponds to domain concepts, and peripheral content grounds these domain concepts in the real world. Second, content is arranged non-linearly. Core elements are organized in a hierarchy, and each core element is flanked to the left, right, and bottom by up to three types of peripheral content. Our format more explicitly communicates the relations between concepts, reducing extraneous cognitive load [34], which frees up mental resources for learning.

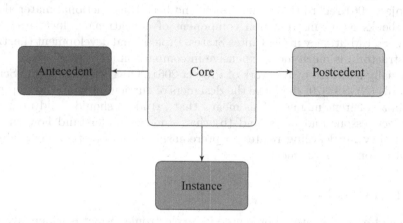

Fig. 1. Our version of a page: a core concept surrounded by grounding concepts

Our research questions were:

1. Can we create a non-linear e-textbook that accords with the cognitive science literature?
2. Does this non-linear textbook better support learning?
3. Do users prefer the proposed non-linear format?

To address the first question, we first conducted a review of the cognitive science literature. Highlights of this literature review are presented in Sect. 2. This section also reviews the relevant literature on e-textbooks. Guided by this literature review, we then designed and implemented a prototype, which is described in Sect. 3. After designing the prototype, we came across a study which suggested that our e-textbook interface may present difficulties for certain kinds of learners. In Sect. 4 we describe this study, and our attempts to examine the challenge it presents. To address the second and third research questions, and to examine the just-mentioned challenge, we designed a study to test the effectiveness of our non-linear interface compared to a linear control. We describe the methodology of the study in Sect. 5, our findings in Sect. 6, and discuss their implications in Sect. 7. Finally, we present concluding remarks in Sect. 8.

2   Background

2.1   Project 2061 and the Next Generation Science Standards

Project 2061 is a research and development initiative aimed at improving literacy in science, mathematics, and technology through educational reform. The project was created in response to middling scores [11] in science, math, and technology literacy among students in the United States [8]. Project 2061 believe that the science curricula focus too much on breadth, and call for a "radical" reduction in the total number of concepts students are asked to learn [22]. They believe that real science literacy requires making connections between science, mathematics, and technology, with the arts, humanities, and the vocational subjects.

Project 2061 regard the design of new and better instructional material such as textbooks as an instrumental component of educational reform needed to improve STEM literacy in the Unites States. Professional development (i.e. training instructors) is much more expensive in comparison [27].

Partially informed by the work of Project 2061, The Next Generation Science Standards (NGSS) [20] challenge the designers of curriculum material to present ideas in a coherent manner. This means that (a) ideas should build upon each other over lessons and units, and (b) that students understand how the new content they are learning relates to prerequisite ideas, or other ideas already present in long-term memory.

2.2   E-Textbooks

Although textbook material presented in an electronic format is widely available through retailers like Apple, Amazon, and Google, e-textbooks have not enjoyed the same success as e-books [9]. The typical e-textbook in use today is structurally very similar to print texts, with some additional features added such as the ability to search the text, and support for multimedia content. Studies comparing these kinds of electronic texts and standard print texts typically show no differences in learning outcomes, but a preference for using standard print texts [24,29,35]. Four out of five students prefer print texts to digitized texts despite print being more expensive and less portable, because they are more familiar, and they better afford highlighting, dog-earing, and annotation [24]. In a study by Daniel and Woody [9], students using e-textbooks spent significantly more time reading than those using print texts. In general, it seems that the drawbacks of the typical e-textbook compared to print texts do not outweigh the benefits. Authors like Toukonen [35] have argued the current incarnation of e-textbooks do not properly leverage the advantages of digital media technology such as dynamicity and non-linearity.

More recently, in response to the issues with this first type of e-textbook, efforts have been made to create e-books that leverage the interactive nature of computers. Interactive texts (i-texts) contain less text, and add animations of key concepts, more questions, and interactive tools [13]. A new system proposed by Miller and Ranum [19] incorporates video, code editing, execution, and visualization inside the textbook. A commercial line of i-texts called zyBooks [13] have recently gained popularity [41]. zyBooks present text interleaved with interactive examples of the learning material. The approach taken by i-texts is complementary to our approach: our non-linear text could one day accommodate—and may well benefit from—interactive material.

DeStefano and LeFevre [12] review studies on hypertext reading, and discuss the advantages and disadvantages relative to linear texts. Hypertext is more demanding of working memory resources than linear text because it requires that readers make a decision before selecting a link. The researchers do not specify if this additional load is extraneous (i.e. unnecessary), or if it aided learning. They note that in many cases where hypertexts appear to impair learning, it is because these hypertexts exceed the working memory capacity of the reader. Many hypertexts used visual overviews of the content to reduce the cognitive load burden placed on readers, but these visual overviews were helpful only when their structure matched the inherent structure of the domain. Structuring texts hierarchically seemed to aid learning, whereas other structures (e.g. allowing readers to navigate a semantic network of concepts) seemed to impair learning.

2.3 Review of Cognitive Science Literature on Concepts

E-textbooks should make use of the advantages of dynamicity and non-linearity. To do this in a way that does not overwhelm readers' working memory capacity, e-textbook designers should strive for harmony between the text's format and the mind. We conducted a review of the cognitive science literature on concepts, and this subsection summarizes some key findings.

Knowledge Is Categorical. Concepts are a unit of knowledge about the world. Through concepts we divide the complex, continuous world into simple, finite categories, thereby lightening the load of perception [5,26]. Concepts form the basis for thought and communication [16]. A fundamental property of knowledge is its categorical nature [4]. A conceptual system is not a collection of holistic images like a camera. Rather, it is a collection of category knowledge, where each represented category corresponds to a component of experience, not to an entire holistic experience.

Knowledge Is Hierarchical. There is evidence that concepts are subdivided hierarchically in two ways: taxonomically, and partonomically [36]. A taxonomy organizes things by kind: a McIntosh is a kind of apple, and an apple is a kind of fruit, but the reverse is not true. A partonomy organizes things by part: a piston is a part of an engine, and an engine is a part of a car, but the reverse is not true. This is true of abstract concepts as well, such as governments: a democracy is a kind of government, and a government consists of the legislative, judicial, and executive branches. Events have a hierarchical structure as well [1,39].

Meaning and Use. Philosophical pragmatists hold that, phenomenologically speaking, the meaning of objects and categories is subjective and situation-dependent [6]. Objects get their meaning from their relation to a goal. For example, a chair is canonically viewed as a tool used for seating, but in other situations it can have a different meaning: it can be a tool used for standing-on, or an obstacle that impedes motion. This idea underlies a number of important intellectual works of the last century, including Gibson's Affordance Theory [14]. Gibson argues that the act of perceiving leads one toward a course of action: when we perceive a door handle, we do not perceive the object in-itself, but rather the ways in which we can interact with it.

Grounding Abstract Concepts. Traditionally, there is thought to be a sharp distinction between concrete concepts and abstract concepts. This view is supported by so-called concreteness effects, which are well-established cognitive processing advantages for concrete concepts over abstract concepts: concrete concepts are linked to stronger memories, and they are accessed and comprehended more quickly than abstract concepts [5]. However, research by Schwanenflugel, Shoben, and colleagues (e.g. [28]) showed that this processing advantage for concrete concepts disappears when people are provided with an instantiating situation for abstract concepts. Providing concrete examples of abstract concepts has also shown to be an effective teaching tool [3, 23].

Cognitive Load Theory. Cognitive load theory describes the role that working memory limitations play in the learning process [34]: learning is an information processing activity, humans are limited information processors, and so it is important to manage the information workload placed on students.

Some workload is necessary and desirable, and some is not. What makes workload desirable is whether or not it contributes to the acquisition of new concepts and skills. *Intrinsic* load is the workload inherent to the material being learned; it is the minimal workload associated with learning a given piece of information. The driving force behind this type of workload is element interactivity, which is the total number of elements that must be considered at one time in order to understand some piece of information. Learning a concept that is high in element interactivity requires that a number of elements are held in working memory simultaneously. *Extraneous* load is workload that is unnecessary and therefore detrimental to learning. An example of this type of workload is requiring that students search for some piece of information when it could just be provided for them. The crucial management of extraneous workload becomes especially important when element interactivity is high, because the learning task will test the capacity of working memory. Good instructional texts should keep extraneous cognitive load to a minimum.

The deep approach to education is high in element interactivity, so minimizing extraneous workload is even more important than in the broad approach.

3   Design and Implementation

Our primary design goal was to harmonize the structure of our text with the conceptual structure of its content. We think this will aid the learning process by reducing extraneous workload in two ways.

The first is by *offloading mental work onto the environment*. Concepts are complex—they are multidimensional, hierarchical, and categorical—and the interrelations between domain concepts and other concepts are brought to the forefront in the deep approach. If the information regarding how concepts relate to each other can be represented in the visual environment, it will free up cognitive resources which can be spent on some other aspect of the learning task at hand, thereby enhancing learning.

The second is by *minimizing thought about the text's structure that is not also thought about its content*. To navigate instructional materials, students must consider its structure. Wherever the structure of the instructional material matches the structure of the content, any effort exerted thinking about the structure of the instructional material is also effort spent learning the content. Conversely, wherever there is disharmony between the two structures, the student will be exerting effort that does not help them learn the content. For this reason, we think that the designers of instructional materials should strive for structural harmony between texts and content.

3.1   Key Features

This goal of harmonizing the structure of the text and its content is realized in our design in two major ways: we (i) divide content into two major categories: *core* and *peripheral*; and (ii) allow for the non-linear navigation of content.

Core and Peripheral Content. We identify two broad categories of content in instructional materials. The first type of content pertains to domain concepts. Examples of domain concepts from psychology include: operant conditioning, behaviorism, and working memory. We call these concepts *core* concepts because we believe they are the focus of an educational unit, and that learning them is the primary goal. Since we believe that domain concepts have a important status in the classroom, we believe that core content should likewise have an important status in instructional materials.

The second category of content is content that provides grounding context for the core content, thereby enriching its understanding. These are ideas that relate the abstract domain concept to the real world. Examples of these kinds of content include instances of the concept, the history of the concept, and ways in which the concept can be usefully applied. We identify three categories of enriching content: *antecedents*, *postcedents*, and *instances*.

Antecedents (Inputs). While each student encounters a domain concept at a particular instant in time, a concept is something that stretches across time, and its past can tell us something about its present. Antecedents are the category of concepts that come prior to (chronologically or causally) the core concept. Examples of antecedent content in scientific disciplines include descriptions of key research, and paradigmatic assumptions.

Postcedents (Outputs). The second category of enriching content involves the ways in which the concept can be usefully applied in the real world. Since applying the concept comes after mastering it, from the reader's point of view this category of concepts mirror antecedents; we therefore call these postcedents. If a concept's use is an important element of its meaning (if not meaning itself), this category of concepts will be of great interest to learners. And if the primary goal of education is to foster the development of skills that are socially useful—which we hold—then this category of concepts is essential.

Instances (Real-World Examples). The concepts students are asked to learn are all abstractions of instances. There is evidence that abstract concepts are easier to understand when they are linked to a grounding situation. An example of an instance of the abstract concept truth is a legal verdict. The three types of enriching content provide three different types of grounding for each abstract core concept. We think that linking abstract ideas with ideas relating this knowledge to the real world will help readers develop better situation models than they might without this information.

We consider the proposition that these three types of enriching concepts are important for learning to be uncontroversial as they already feature prominently in textbooks. For example, in psychology textbooks, a domain concept is often accompanied by real-world scenarios instantiating the concept, key studies providing empirical substantiation for the concept are often summarized, and information regarding how the concept can be applied in one's life. Our proposed design gives these enriching concepts an elevated status in the text's structure. For each core concept, students will be able to quickly see a number of different ways in which it relates back to the material world.

Non-linear Organization/Navigation. According to our literature review, concepts have a non-linear structure. That is, they are hierarchical and multidimensional. However, learning materials are typically presented linearly. In linear texts, hierarchy is signalled (a) linguistically through sentences such as "x is a kind of y", and (b) typographically through headers (e.g. chapter, section, subsection). The dimensions of a concept, when they are provided, are presented in-line with the core domain content.

We think a linear ordering of material that is inherently non-linear is problematic for a number of reasons. First, strict linearity forces a single ordering of learning material. This is a problem because it seems to us that there is no single optimal way to arrange learning material: what will be optimal for one student will be sub-optimal for others, and what will be optimal for one student at one time under one set of circumstances may for that same student be sub-optimal at some other time under other circumstances. A non-linear organization of content will allow students the flexibility of choosing the order that suits them at the time of reading. A linear arrangement of non-linear material also introduces a number of sources of extraneous workload [34]. This problem is especially severe in the deep approach to learning. We discuss this in more detail in Sect. 4.1.

We think that, rather than present concepts in a linear order and signal their underlying non-linear features with language and typography, it is better to simply present the material non-linearly.

We think we avoid the pitfalls of non-linear texts covered in the review by DeStefano and LeFevre [12] for three reasons. 1. We structure the material according to the domain hierarchy; 2. we take care to limit navigational freedom so that working memory capacity is not exceeded; and 3. we provide a hierarchical visual overview of the content.

3.2   The Model

We propose the following model for an e-textbook interface, incorporating the key design concepts just discussed.

There are many different ways of positioning core and peripheral elements with respect to each other. We elect the arrangement depicted in Fig. 1. Core concepts are given a central position reflective of their preeminent status in education, and they are flanked by enriching concepts to the right, bottom, and left. We place antecedents to the left, and postcedents to the right of the core because these three elements comprise a timeline of past, present, and future, and in the English-speaking world we think of time as flowing from left to right [37]. We place instances beneath the core because an instance is a taxonomical concept, and taxonomies are intuitively vertical [25], with instances being the lowest element. For each domain concept, students will quickly and easily be able to see up to three kinds of grounding information.

Core-peripheral clusters (the objects depicted in Fig. 1) are organized into a hierarchy. Students navigate through the text by moving up and down this hierarchy. A visual representation of the hierarchy—that is, a tree graph—should be provided to give students an overview of the concepts they will be asked to learn, and to allow quick and easy navigation to various locations in the tree.

3.3   Early Prototypes

The sketch in Fig. 2 shows our earliest attempt at an interface that is consistent with the model just described. At this stage, we intended on providing both a partonomy, which would be descended by clicking buttons in the middle of the sketch, and taxonomy, which would be descended by clicking nodes on the extreme bottom of the page. Making a sharp distinction between partonomy and taxonomy made the interface crowded and confusing, while not offering a clear educational advantage, so this distinction was dropped in later iterations.

A high fidelity prototype featuring a simpler design is shown in Fig. 3. We conducted a cognitive walkthrough [32] with two human-computer interaction experts, who made a number of recommendations, the most important of which was to include a visual overview of the text structure to prevent overwhelming the working memory resources of readers. The experts also recommended the inclusion of text search, and slide-in/out animations for showing peripheral content, to reinforce the impression that this content is positioned either to the left, right, or beneath the core content.

3.4   High Fidelity Functional Prototype

We implemented the functional prototype of the interface, shown in Figs. 4, 5 and 6 using JavaScript, HTML, and CSS. Text corresponding to the currently selected domain concept is shown in the middle of the screen. Clicking on buttons on the periphery triggers an animation where a panel "slides-in" from the side of the window the button is on. The panel features either peripheral content (left, right, bottom), or the "treemap" (top).

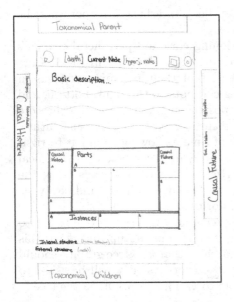

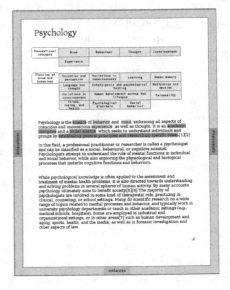

Fig. 2. Paper prototype: early design iteration

Fig. 3. High fidelity prototype: a refinement of the sketch in Fig. 2

Figure 5 shows the result of clicking on a peripheral button. Content pertaining to the peripheral concept, in this case an important prior study, is shown in the middle of this pane. Multiple peripheral concepts can be included on a single pane. When this happens, buttons are placed above the text area. When clicked, the displayed text underneath changes accordingly.

What we call the "treemap" is a visual representation of the the hierarchy linking together core concepts, which we implemented using d3.js [21]. Figure 6

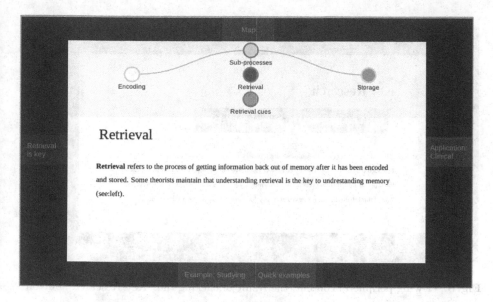

Fig. 4. Our functional, high fidelity, prototype for a non-linear e-textbook.

shows the full treemap, which is made visible after clicking the "Map" button at the top of the screen. The currently selected node is shown in red, and visited nodes are greyed-out. Clicking a node allows users to navigate to its corresponding concept. In the top-left of the treemap pane is a text box which allows users to perform a text search of the e-textbook.

A miniaturized version of the treemap is shown at the top of the main page (Fig. 4), showing the parent, sibling, and child nodes of the currently selected node. The mini-treemap shows users their local environment at a glance, and lets them easily move through the tree in single steps.

3.5 Answering Research Question 1

Our first research question was: Can we create a non-linear e-textbook that accords with the cognitive science literature? At this stage, we felt we were able to answer "yes". Our design has a hierarchical and multidimensional structure, and it provides several types of grounding for abstract concepts.

3.6 Linear Interface

To examine the effects of non-linearity on support for learning in our study (described later in Sect. 5, we created a second interface (Fig. 7 with the same look-and-feel as the non-linear interface, except with linear organization and navigation. The mini-treemap and the treemap were removed. In place of the treemap was a numbered list of concepts which, when clicked, brought the user to that part of the text. We replaced the basic functionality of the mini-treemap (i.e.

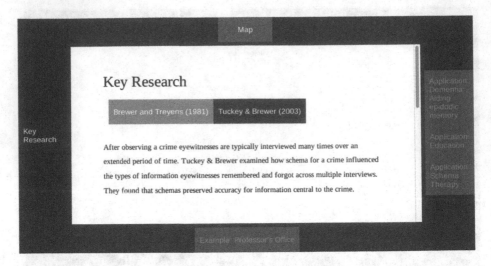

Fig. 5. Viewing peripheral content: the result of clicking the "Key Research" button

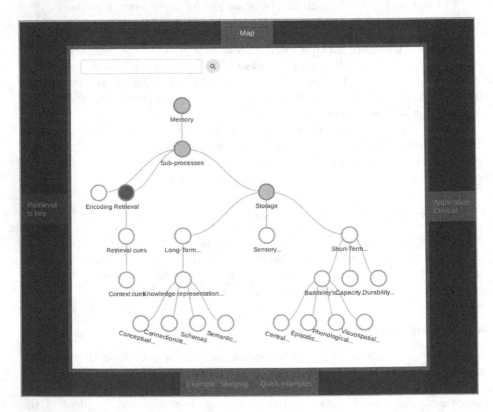

Fig. 6. The "treemap": a navigable, hierarchical table of contents (Color figure online)

incremental movements through the text) with forward and backward buttons on the left and right periphery.

4   Challenge to the Design

The model just presented is a text of higher *coherence* than the standard linear text format: The present model more explicitly shows the structural relations between entities than standard linear texts. Since the goal of education is to foster learning, and learning involves making connections between ideas, one would assume that a more coherent text would offer an educational advantage over less coherent texts.

However, research by McNamara et al. [18] suggests that high coherence texts might not always be better. In their study, they found that high coherence texts helped all learners for more superficial forms of learning (essentially text memorization). When it came to deep learning (i.e. developing a "situation model" [40] of the text), low knowledge learners benefited from the high coherence text, but high knowledge learners learned more with a low coherence text.

McNamara et al. argue that high knowledge participants were harmed because they did less active processing when using the high coherence texts. Low knowledge participants, this argument goes, are helped by the high coherence texts because it provides key knowledge that they do not already have.

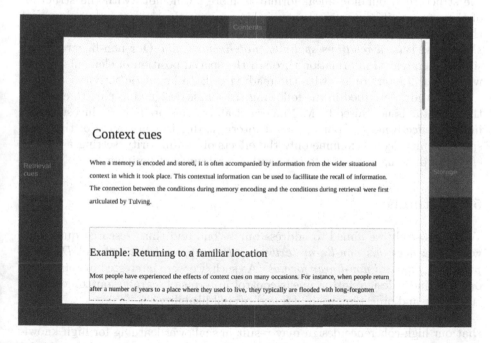

Fig. 7. The linear control interface. The mini-treemap is removed, and peripheral content is placed beneath the core content inside grey boxes.

The high knowledge learners learn more from low coherence texts because they are already in possession of the required background knowledge to form a rich situation model, and a low coherence text forces them to pay attention to the relations between the concepts presented in the text.

4.1   Examining the Challenge

Sweller, Van Merrienboer, and Paas [34] offer an alternative explanation for the results shown by McNamara et al. [18]. They say that high knowledge learners demonstrate shallower learning when using high coherence texts because, for them, these texts introduce *extraneous workload*. The information conveying the relations between concepts is redundant for high knowledge learners, and reading this information is therefore a waste of cognitive resources.

If this explanation is accurate, we believe our high coherence text can avoid the pitfalls observed in McNamara et al. because we reduce extraneous workload compared to a standard linear text in three ways.

The first is by *reducing opportunities for thinking about the structure of text that is not also thought about the structure of content*. When navigating a textbook, the students must frequently think about the text's structure. For example, when searching for a particular concept, the student thinks about chapters, sections, and pages. Whenever the structure of the text does not match the structure of the concepts it contains, this is extraneous workload—wasted thought. Since the structure of our non-linear format is more harmonious with the structure of the concepts it contains, whenever this happens the student is learning, and the opportunities for this kind of wasted thought are reduced. The second is by *showing structural relations spatially, not linguistically*. Our non-linear format signals hierarchical information through the spatial position of elements, which we think will interfere less with the reading task—a linguistic activity.

Our study, described in the following section, is designed in-part to examine the potential issues raised by McNamera et al. For this preliminary investigation into the effectiveness of our proposed interface, due to constraints of time and space, we decided to examine only the effects of non-linearity, setting aside the effects of dividing content into core and several kinds of periphery.

5   Methods

With this study we aimed to address our second and third research questions, which are: *does this non-linear textbook better support learning?* and *Do users prefer the proposed non-linear format?* As such, we were interested in comparing our non-linear design with a linear control in terms of learning outcomes, both subjective and objective, usability, and overall likability.

The results of a study by McNamara et al. (see: Sect. 4) raise the possibility that our high-coherence design may result in shallower learning for high knowledge learners compared to the standard linear format. To address this potential problem, we (a) sorted participants into high- and low-knowledge groups according to the results of a test of general knowledge of psychology, and (b) asked questions designed to target both deep and shallow forms of learning in our objective learning outcome measures.

Including two rounds of pilot testing, we tested our design with over 40 participants. Only the main study (after pilot testing) is described here. This study was approved by the Carleton University Research Ethics Board.

5.1 Participants

Twenty-six participants (13 female, 13 male) volunteered to participate in this study. Twelve had backgrounds in cognitive science, and the other half had an assortment of backgrounds. Participants were alternately assigned to either the non-linear ($n = 13$) or linear ($n = 13$) condition.

5.2 Materials

Participants read content using either the non-linear format, or the linearized control. The e-textbooks were presented using Mozilla Firefox featuring add-ons to eliminate all GUI elements except for the main display frame. The System Usability Scale (SUS) [7] was used to gauge participants' perceptions regarding the interface's usability.

Participants completed two multiple choice tests designed by us. The first was taken before the reading session and assessed background knowledge in psychology. The other was taken after the reading session, and assessed knowledge of the material they had just read. Both tests consisted of multiple choice questions (16 and 19 items, respectively). We decided against having overlapping questions between the two tests (i.e. no questions that were asked in the background assessment test were asked again in the post-reading test) to avoid priming participants.

5.3 Procedure

Participants completed a 16-item questionnaire assessing background knowledge in psychology. We later used the results of this test to sort participants into high- and low-knowledge groups.

Next, participants were presented with a demo interface, which was the interface they would be using in the main task except featuring placeholder text. Participants were given a brief verbal description of the interface and how to navigate it, while participants practiced using the interface. Once participants were comfortable with the demo interface, they were presented with the 'real' interface featuring content from an introductory psychology textbook [38]. Participants were asked to read all of the content contained in the interface, which took about 20 min. We observed the participant's interactions with the interface indirectly through the laptop's main screen.

After the reading session, participants were given a post-test on the material they read, which featured questions targeting deep and shallow learning. Participants then completed the SUS scale.

Following the completion of the post-task questionnaires, we conducted a semi-structured interview with participants about their experience using the interface, their attitudes towards reading and textbooks, and about their approaches to learning.

Finally, we showed participants the interface they *did not* use in the main task. After giving a quick demonstration, we invited participants to try the interface themselves. We then asked which interface they preferred.

6 Results

The purpose of this study was to address our second and third research questions. We address the findings for each below.

6.1 Answering Research Question 2

To answer the second research question, we asked participants to complete a 19-item multiple choice test of the material they read during the reading session. The test featured three kinds of questions: 11 text based questions, four bridging inference questions, and four problem solving questions. Text-based questions assess the reader's representation of the text (shallow learning). The latter two question types assess the reader's representation of the situation described by the text (deep learning). We are mostly interested in the deep learning questions.

A summary of the results of the post-reading scores is shown in Table 1. We divide participants into two groups, low and high knowledge, based on their performance in the pre-test assessing background knowledge in psychology. Participants who scored greater than the median score ($Mdn = 0.5/1$) were placed in the high knowledge group ($n = 13$), and participants who scored less than the median score were placed in low knowledge group ($n = 13$). We compare test scores by question type for low knowledge and high knowledge learners, for both interface conditions. For sake of completeness, we include the combined scores of low and high knowledge participants (under "Combined"), and the overall test scores (i.e. regardless of question type) (in the rows labelled "Overall").

A number of one-tailed independent samples t-tests were conducted to compare the performance of high and low knowledge participants in the two conditions for each type of question (text-based, bridging inference, and problem solving), where "performance" means the proportion[1] of correct scores on the post-reading test. For all combinations of question types and knowledge levels, *there were no significant differences between the linear condition and the non-linear condition.*

Finally, we examined the learning effects for the two conditions, where 'learning effects' means the post-reading test score minus the psychology background

---

[1] We treat the scores as continuous data.

Table 1. Proportion of correct responses in the postreading test for the two conditions by knowledge and question type

	Linear	Non-linear
High knowledge	$n = 7$	$n = 6$
Text based	.68	.62
Bridging inference	.61	.62
Problem solving	.50	.42
Overall	.62	.58
Low knowledge	$n = 6$	$n = 7$
Text based	.56	.56
Bridging inference	.33	.61
Problem solving	.42	.39
Overall	.48	.53
Combined	$n = 13$	$n = 13$
Text based	.62	.59
Bridging inference	.48	.62
Problem solving	.46	.40
Overall	.56	.55

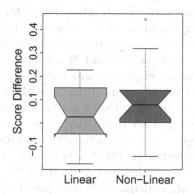

Fig. 8. Learning effects by condition

knowledge test score. Boxplots of the learning effects by condition are shown in Fig. 8. Learning effects were greater in the non-linear condition than in the linear condition. However, the notches indicating the 95% confidence interval around the median overlap, suggesting that these results are not significant.

6.2 Answering Research Question 3

System Usability Scale Scores. To see if there was any difference in perceived usability between the two conditions, we asked all participants to complete the

SUS questionnaire, and then compared the results for each condition. The SUS is generated from Likert-scale questions, which means we look for differences between the scores for the two conditions using the non-parametric Wilcoxon rank-sum test. The Wilcoxon rank-sum test indicated that there was no significant difference between the SUS scores for the linear condition ($Mdn = 50.5$) and the non-linear condition ($Mdn = 50$), $U = 71.5$, $p = 0.5$.

Interface Preference. During debriefing, at the end of the study session, participants were shown and given a description of the interface they did not use, and were asked which they preferred. 18/25 (72%) of participants said that they preferred the non-linear interface to the linear interface. A chi-square test of independence showed that the difference between the total number of participants who preferred the non-linear interface ($n = 7$) was significant, χ^2 (1, N = 25) = 8, $p = .005$.

6.3   Post-experiment Interview: Key Themes

Participants who preferred the non-linear interface tended to appreciate its organization, with several noting that it helped show how the various ideas "fit together". Many participants appreciated that the text was categorized into smaller units than one would typically find in a standard textbook. Many participants noted difficulties with the standard prose format, where content is provided in big, relatively undifferentiated blocks of text. Some felt that this format was "intimidating", and others felt going through many pages of these big blocks of text to be "monotonous" and "boring", and that these texts seem to "go on and on". A number of participants noted that the ideas presented in standard texts tended to get mixed up in their heads, and that they felt that the larger organizing structure provided by the treatment condition would help prevent this from happening. They found that organizing the content in a hierarchical tree made it appear more manageable. A few of the participants who preferred the treatment interface said that they did not enjoy reading in general, and that this interface made reading less difficult for them.

We asked a number of participants if they preferred text in textbooks to appear in smaller or larger chunks, and all said that they preferred smaller chunks of text. We thought this result was favorable to our non-linear design, which breaks up text into smaller chunks than standard linear texts as a consequence of the division of content into *core* and three kinds of *peripheral*, and keeping this content in separate locations in the UI.

Participants who preferred the linear interface tended to like its straightforwardness, and found the non-linear interface "confusing". They generally seemed to find the freedom of choice in terms of navigation overwhelming.

7 Discussion

We observed no significant differences between the two conditions in terms of objective or self-reported learning outcomes. Yet, a significantly greater number of participants preferred the non-linear interface to the linear interface.

Contrary to our expectations, we did not find that the non-linear interface offered a learning advantage. In this section, we discuss what we feel are the most likely reasons for this. Overall, we suspect that the reading session was too short and the amount of text participants read was too little for the advantages of the non-linear interface to become apparent.

Not Enough Time for Reflection. The treemap allows readers to see how all of the ideas in a domain "fit together", which should be good for deep learning. We think that participants were too busy reading to take advantage of this benefit. Each reading session was relatively short: approximately 20 min, and the amount of content contained in the interfaces meant that participants had to read at a relatively quick pace. In all except one case they did not have enough time to revisit content, let alone to reflect on how things "fit together".

The Costs of Learning a New Interface Outweighs the Benefits. Our non-linear interface is a new way of viewing and interacting with text, whereas the linear text was modeled on pre-existing e-textbooks, which in turn are modeled on physical print media. Learning something new, whether it is text or how to use a new interface, requires the deployment of working memory resources. Our text required more learning, which means there are fewer resources available for learning the content. It is possible that the benefits offered by the non-linear organization of content was overshadowed by the costs associated with learning the new interface.

Affective Advantages Negated. We think that some features of our non-linear interface would offer an affective advantage. For example, the non-linear interface does not enforce any particular path through the text: students must decide for themselves which path to take. This may give students an increased sense of agency, which could imbue their traversal through the material with more personal meaning. Our interface also breaks up text into smaller pieces than standard linear texts, which seemed to be a relief for a number of our participants who felt overwhelmed by large blocks of text. Learning outcome effects of affective advantages like these would develop over longer periods of time, and in any case would likely be too subtle to be detected by the data gathering methods we employed.

Small Sample Size. Our main study had 26 participants, which meant there were only six or seven participants in each knowledge level-interface condition group. The study by McNamara et al. [18], which we modeled our study after, had 56 participants—more than twice the amount. Perhaps increasing the total number of participants would have yielded significant results.

8   Conclusion

In this paper, we presented the design, implementation, and subsequent study and analysis of a novel non-linear e-textbook format. Our design was guided by the cognitive science literature on concepts. Out e-textbook format differs from standard textbooks by organizing content non-linearly, and by making a strict distinction between core and peripheral content. We conducted a user study where we compared our non-linear design with the standard format in terms of learning outcomes, usability, and overall likeability. We found no significant differences between the two interfaces for learning outcomes and usability, and found that our interface was better-liked by participants. We feel that many of the advantages of our non-linear format will only become apparent after long periods of use.

We were able to design and implement a functional prototype concording with the cognitive science literature on the structures of concepts. We are encouraged by the fact that participants preferred this novel non-linear design, and that the two interfaces seemed to provide similar support for learning in spite of the fact that the non-linear design was unfamiliar. For many participants, this design seemed to fulfill a need that linear texts were not providing: many students are looking for a non-linear alternative to the standard format. Future work should examine the effects of this non-linear format over longer periods of use.

References

1. Abbott, V., Black, J.B., Smith, E.E.: The representation of scripts in memory. J. Mem. Lang. **24**(2), 179–199 (1985)
2. American Association for the Advancement of Science: AAAS's Project 2061 report: big biology books fail to convey big ideas, June 2000. https://www.eurekalert.org/pub_releases/2000-06/AAft-AP2r-2606100.php
3. Atkinson, R.K., Derry, S.J., Renkl, A., Wortham, D.: Learning from examples: Instructional principles from the worked examples research. Rev. Educ. Res. **70**(2), 181–214 (2000)
4. Barsalou, L.W., Simmons, W.K., Barbey, A.K., Wilson, C.D.: Grounding conceptual knowledge in modality-specific systems. Trends Cogn. Sci. **7**(2), 84–91 (2003)
5. Barsalou, L.W., Wiemer-Hastings, K.: Situating abstract concepts. In: Grounding Cognition: The Role of Perception and Action in Memory, Language, and Thought, pp. 129–163 (2005)
6. Bleazby, J.: Overcoming relativism and absolutism: Dewey's ideals of truth and meaning in philosophy for children. Educ. Philos. Theory **43**(5), 453–466 (2011)
7. Brooke, J., et al.: SUS - a quick and dirty usability scale. Usab. Eval. Ind. **189**(194), 4–7 (1996)
8. Budiansky, S.: The trouble with textbooks. ASEE Prism **10**(6), 24 (2001)
9. Daniel, D.B., Woody, W.D.: E-textbooks at what cost? Performance and use of electronic v. print texts. Comput. Educ. **62**, 18–23 (2013)
10. Deese, J.: On the structure of associative meaning. Psychol. Rev. **69**(3), 161 (1962)
11. Desilver, D.: Pew Research: U.S. students' academic achievement still lags that of their peers in many other countries (2017). http://www.pewresearch.org/fact-tank/2017/02/15/u-s-students-internationally-math-science/

12. DeStefano, D., LeFevre, J.A.: Cognitive load in hypertext reading: a review. Comput. Hum. Behav. **23**(3), 1616–1641 (2007)
13. Edgcomb, A., Vahid, F., Lysecky, R., Lysecky, S.: Getting students to earnestly do reading, studying, and homework in an introductory programming class. In: Proceedings of the 2017 ACM SIGCSE Technical Symposium on Computer Science Education, pp. 171–176. ACM (2017)
14. Gibson, J.J.: The Ecological Approach to Visual Perception, classic edn. Psychology Press, New York (2014)
15. Johnson-Laird, P.: Mental Models. Toward a Cognitive Science of Language, Inference and Language. Harvard University Press, Cambridge (1983)
16. Jonassen, D.H.: On the role of concepts in learning and instructional design. Educ. Technol. Res. Dev. **54**(2), 177 (2006)
17. Keil, F.C.: Explanation, association, and the acquisition of word meaning. Lingua **92**, 169–196 (1994)
18. McNamara, D.S., Kintsch, E., Songer, N.B., Kintsch, W.: Are good texts always better? Interactions of text coherence, background knowledge, and levels of understanding in learning from text. Cogn. Instr. **14**(1), 1–43 (1996)
19. Miller, B.N., Ranum, D.L.: Beyond PDF and ePub: toward an interactive textbook. In: Proceedings of the 17th ACM Annual Conference on Innovation and Technology in Computer Science Education, pp. 150–155. ACM (2012)
20. National Research Council, et al.: A Framework for K-12 Science Education: Practices, Crosscutting Concepts, and Core Ideas. National Academies Press, Washington, DC (2012)
21. Ogievetsky, V., Heer, J., Bostock, M.: D^3 data-driven documents. IEEE Trans. Vis. Comput. Graph. **17**, 2301–2309 (2011). https://doi.org/10.1109/TVCG.2011.185
22. Project 2061: Benchmarks on-line: about benchmarks (2009). http://www.project2061.org/publications/bsl/online/index.php?intro=true
23. Ranzijn, F.J.: The effect of the superordinate concept and presentation form of examples on concept learning. Comput. Hum. Behav. **5**(2), 95–105 (1989)
24. Rockinson-Szapkiw, A.J., Courduff, J., Carter, K., Bennett, D.: Electronic versus traditional print textbooks: a comparison study on the influence of university students' learning. Comput. Educ. **63**, 259–266 (2013)
25. Rosch, E.: Principles of categorization. In: Concepts: Core Readings, p. 189 (1999)
26. Rosch, E., Mervis, C.B., Gray, W.D., Johnson, D.M., Boyes-Braem, P.: Basic objects in natural categories. Cogn. Psychol. **8**(3), 382–439 (1976)
27. Roseman, J.E., Herrmann-Abell, C.F., Koppal, M.: Designing for the next generation science standards: educative curriculum materials and measures of teacher knowledge. J. Sci. Teach. Educ. **28**(1), 111–141 (2017)
28. Schwanenflugel, P.J., Shoben, E.J.: Differential context effects in the comprehension of abstract and concrete verbal materials. J. Exp. Psychol.: Learn. Mem. Cogn. **9**(1), 82 (1983)
29. Shepperd, J.A., Grace, J.L., Koch, E.J.: Evaluating the electronic textbook: is it time to dispense with the paper text? Teach. Psychol. **35**(1), 2–5 (2008)
30. Shield, M., Dole, S.: Assessing the potential of mathematics textbooks to promote deep learning. Educ. Stud. Math. **82**(2), 183–199 (2013)
31. Sloman, S.A., Rips, L.J.: Similarity as an explanatory construct. Cognition **65**(2–3), 87–101 (1998)
32. Spero, E., Stojmenović, M., Arya, A., Biddle, R.: Creating a non-linear textbook format to facilitate deep learning. In: INTED2019 Proceedings of 13th International Technology, Education and Development Conference, IATED (2019, forthcoming)

33. Stern, L., Roseman, J.E.: Can middle-school science textbooks help students learn important ideas? Findings from project 2061's curriculum evaluation study: life science. J. Res. Sci. Teach.: Off. J. Nat. Assoc. Res. Sci. Teach. **41**(6), 538–568 (2004)
34. Sweller, J., Van Merrienboer, J.J., Paas, F.G.: Cognitive architecture and instructional design. Educ. Psychol. Rev. **10**(3), 251–296 (1998)
35. Toukonen, K.: The dynamic electronic textbook: enhancing the student's learning experience. Ph.D. thesis, Kent State University (2011)
36. Tversky, B.: Parts, partonomies, and taxonomies. Dev. Psychol. **25**(6), 983 (1989)
37. Tversky, B., Kugelmass, S., Winter, A.: Cross-cultural and developmental trends in graphic productions. Cogn. Psychol. **23**(4), 515–557 (1991)
38. Weiten, W., McCann, D.: Psychology: Themes and Variations, 4th Canadian edn. Nelson Education Limited (2015). https://books.google.ca/books?id=Z6vEjwEACAAJ
39. Zacks, J.M., Tversky, B.: Event structure in perception and conception. Psychol. Bull. **127**(1), 3 (2001)
40. Zwaan, R.A., Radvansky, G.A.: Situation models in language comprehension and memory. Psychol. Bull. **123**(2), 162 (1998)
41. zyBooks: zyBooks: About Us (2018). http://www.zybooks.com/about-us/

Technology-Enhanced Learning: Correlates of Acceptance of Assistive Technology in Collaborative Working Setting

Wiktoria Wilkowska[1]($\boxtimes$), Thiemo Leonhardt[2], Matthias Ehlenz[3], and Martina Ziefle[1]

[1] Chair of Communication Science, RWTH Aachen University,
Campus Boulevard 57, 52074 Aachen, Germany
wilkowska@comm.rwth-aachen.de
[2] Didactics of Computer Science, TU Dresden, Nöthnitzer Str. 46,
01187 Dresden, Germany
[3] Learning Technologies, RWTH Aachen University,
Ahornstrasse 55, 52074 Aachen, Germany

Abstract. Considering stagnant interest in science, technology, engineering and math (STEM), on the one side, and an increasing dropout rates in computer science at different levels of the university education due to difficult and complex learning contents, on the other side, appropriate technology solutions which support learners are very promising. In this study we examine a digital learning assistant in the form of tangible objects interacting with a multi-touch tabletop. This learning tool is meant to support students in the way they learn complex material. In an experimental setting, participants working in groups had the task to acquire novel learning content (i.e., regular expressions) and, using the assistive technology, to assign the correct expressions to their predefined terms. Results revealed that the users' psychological factors and performance factors which result from the interaction with the learning tool are significantly connected with the correlates of acceptance and affect, therefore, the later adoption of such technology. The positive overall assessments show a high attachment for, and willingness to, use such technology. However, user diversity has to be considered in the design and further development. Knowledge gained discloses expedient hints for technology-enhanced learning that can support and accompany the education at different levels, i.e., in schools, vocational training, and university education.

Keywords: Tangible user interfaces · Learning assisting technology · Technology acceptance · User diversity

1 Introduction

In recent years, due to the ongoing digitalization, learning and working environments have decisively changed [1]. The majority of knowledge-based, professional fields increasingly use digital tools and processes, requiring more and more basic computer science skills. This represents a high demand for professional computer scientists. In

© Springer Nature Switzerland AG 2019
P. Zaphiris and A. Ioannou (Eds.): HCII 2019, LNCS 11590, pp. 423–439, 2019.
https://doi.org/10.1007/978-3-030-21814-0_32

addition, education in the fields of science, technology, engineering and mathematics (STEM) are facing crucial challenges resulting from a ubiquitous use of, and need for, different kinds of technology.

Instead, reality unfortunately does not look very promising in this respect. Especially among the undergraduate computer science students, the university education is tremendously afflicted with high dropout rates [2]. But also, high numbers of graduates who are willing to enter STEM courses of study leave these fields or changes to non-STEM fields, leading to high attrition rates as well [3]. The complex and frequently very abstract subject matter of these study programs is difficult for learners to grasp. Accordingly, students often perceive the study programs as being too complicated to comprehend [4].

In this study we present a digital learning assistant – a learning tool that is meant to support students in the way they learn complex material – and examine its acceptance in association with different user factors.

1.1   Related Work

The Role of Technology in Education. Since the beginning of the 20th century, the introduction of technological assistance for teaching has been promoted and propagated but has also been discussed intensively. The desire to use new technologies to compensate for the weaknesses of the education system has not yet been fulfilled by any technology alone. The weaknesses of the education system worldwide are the average from teacher to pupil, the lack of promotion of individual learning speed, and the low influence on the motivation and attention of the pupils. The most important goal is the associated increase in general learning success.

Edison formulated his wish and belief in the success of new technologies back in 1922: "*I believe that the motion picture is destined to revolutionize our educational system, and that in a few years it will supplant largely, if not entirely, the use of textbooks in our schools*" [5] (p. 9). Nowadays books are just as much material in class as they were 100 years ago. Even the approach of electronic textbooks has not yet been able to replace this. Thus, this quote also reflects the central criticism of the use of technology in teaching: The use of technology alone does not improve learning success – regardless of the use of tablets, smartphones, laptops, interactive whiteboards, multi touch tables and augmented (AR) or virtual reality (VR) devices.

Many meta-studies show a positive influence on learning success when using technologies with medium or small effect size, country and culture independent (e.g., [6–11]. However, a purely technology-based comparison and evaluation is not permissible, since didactic design is at least as important a separating variable. General statements about learning success using a technology are at best dubious and at worst wrong without considering the entire didactic design.

We aim to integrate technology into the learning process, where conventional methods have weaknesses that can be compensated by technology. One example is the individual fostering of learners in group learning scenarios. Our research direction is therefore based on the one hand on the pedagogical principles [12, 13] and on the other hand on the theories and models of how multimedia content can be used with technologies in a target-group oriented way [14, 15]. The learning evaluation is based on the work of Bloom's taxonomy [16] and Krathwohl modifications [17].

User-Centered Technology Acceptance. The pace of technological advances coupled with a growing shortage of skilled workers, especially in STEM disciplines, cause a need for action and enables, at the same time, to reshape the education systems. Indeed, introducing new technologies is not an easy task: Not only that the intended device or system has to operate technically flawlessly, but also the product design must be optimally adapted to the requirements of the end user, who has to accept the technology accordingly, so that it can be implemented in the corresponding areas of life. Thus, in the end technology acceptance is the key criterion for a successful adoption in the long run.

Technology acceptance has been discussed in the literature intensively in different application fields. Originally, this topic revolved around job-related information and communication technologies that were used to increase productivity and work effectiveness. On the other side, lack of acceptance has been identified as a significant impediment to the successful implementation and adoption of new information systems [18, 19].

In the first place, this research has been strongly influenced by the theory of diffusion of innovation proposed by Rogers [20] that was focusing on the process of adoption of novel technology devices or products among the users. Ever since, several empirical models have been developed to understand key factors of technology acceptance. One of the most prominent, empirically repeatedly validated models in different fields of application is the Technology Acceptance Model (TAM) [21] and its further development the Unified Theory of Acceptance and Use of Technology (UTAUT) [22, 23], which constitute the theoretical framework for this study. According to TAM, perceived ease of use and perceived usefulness are the key components of the technology acceptance. In this model, attitude of the user serves as a key mediating aspect between beliefs and usage intentions [24]. However, since diversity of the users and performance expectancy have been proven to play an important role in the intention to use and the actual behavior, we additionally refer to the comprehensive UTAUT-model when examining these aspects in the present study.

1.2 Assistive Technology for Learning: Tangibles on Multi-touch Tabletops

For the purposes of the study, a digital learning assistant was used which was meant to assist students in learning new subject matter. The learning tool consists of a multi-touch tabletop – a large display mounted as a table – which allows its users to stand around it and collaboratively interact with presented digital items. The information displayed on the tabletop can be manipulated, using tangible user interfaces (TUI). Figure 1 depicts the learning tool as it was used in the study.

A learning application was developed to teach the students pattern recognition with regular expressions (regex) in a collaborative setup on such multi-touch display, supporting meaningful interaction with and without tangibles. The application based on an

a) A multi-touch tabletop for collabora-   b) Tangible as a user interface
tive working

Fig. 1. Assistive technology for learning as used in the study: (a) a multi-touch tabletop for displaying the digital information, (b) tangible object as an input and feedback device.

instructional approach and consisted of three modes, which are described in more detail in Sect. 3.1.

1.3 Objectives of the Research

In an experimental study, participants worked in groups of four persons and their task was to assign correct expressions to their predefined terms and, therefore, collect as many points as possible. The participants worked yet individually in the learning mode, but then collaboratively in the actual experimental trial. Prior to the interaction with the tangibles on multi-touch tabletop, participants filled in the first part of a quantitative survey, which collected demographic data and information about different user factors (e.g., attitudes toward technology use). Directly after the interaction, a second part of the survey was pursued, which evaluated the learning and the teamwork success, and the correlates of acceptance of the given technology (e.g., ease of use, intention to use). Finally, participants discussed within their groups ethical, legal and social implications (ELSI) of the learning tool for the university education.

Three main objectives were addressed in this study: First, we examine the correlative relations between the user factors, like cognitive, attitudinal, and performance factors, and factors associated with technology acceptance, such as perceived ease of use, intention to use the assistive technology and (collaboratively achieved) learning success. Second, we investigate how user diversity, which referred to participants' gender and their level of education, affects the learning success and the acceptance of the learning tool. And third, we reveal the most powerful predictors for the acceptance of the technology among the considered research variables.

2 Method

In order to examine whether collaboratively working students can learn new subject matter (i.e., regular expressions), and to understand how they evaluate and accept the learning assistant device in the context of this purpose, an experimental user study was conducted. Focus of the study was to let participants use the assisting tool for a learning task and, thereby, assess their performance and acceptance in terms of the technology.

The experiment was conducted at the InfoSphere – Student Laboratory for Computer Science at the RWTH Aachen University – in a laboratory environment. Participants were recruited partly directly from the university, and partly from the immediate social network of the authors.

In this section, firstly, used materials are described, followed by the presentation of the experimental procedure and the research approach. Description of the sample closes the method section.

2.1 Materials

Hardware Design. The learning application, which was especially conceived for our experimental purposes, was installed on an 84″ Microsoft Surface Hub. This multi-touch display is able to detect up to 100 touch points on a 220 × 117 cm display with a resolution of 3840 × 2160 pixels. The display was brought in a horizontal position on a metal frame with wheels, bringing the surface to a height of 87 cm, suitable for most adult learners. Figure 1 depicts the hardware.

Another aspect researched in this setting is the learning effect of tangibles. One strength of tangibles is to reduce the distance between the data and the way they are manipulated. Thus, tasks with a spatial representation can be solved more quickly [25]. Furthermore, the manual manipulation of toys while reading a story helps children to understand the content of the story. This approach also helps in Number Board Games to understand orders of magnitude. In addition, learners achieve better learning success when they work with haptic, visual and auditory content and feedback than with just one of these types [26].

In our setting, we use tangibles as haptic devices that are recognized by the capacitive touch screen. The tangibles offer bidirectional communication, opening another personal feedback channel by lighting up, buzzing and vibrating on interaction.

Software Design. As the task was to learn basics of regular expressions, the learning application was primary conceived for testing of the learning assistive tool in an experimental setting.

Regular expressions can be didactically reduced due to a differently complex representation. The length of the words and the iterative introduction of the different operators make it easy to design tasks of increasing degrees of difficulty.

The application consisted of three modes: one demo-mode, one learning mode and a collaborative mode. Participants were provided with direct feedback after each interaction (i.e., moving a matching word to a predefined regular expression): A green background of the regular expression and a slow 360° rotation of the word were chosen for a correct assignment, and a red background and a short twitch of the word in case of a wrong assignment of the regular expression.

During the interaction with the learning tool, in each user's personal zone appears a regular expression (e.g., a|b, c|cd*), which has to be matched with correct expressions presented in the middle of the tabletop display. There, different distractors and character sequences pop up next to the target items which have to be matched to the correct regular expressions. Each participant has a different target expression and the task is to find and match as many correct items as possible. A correct match (confirmed with green) brings two additional points, which are added up for the whole group. In case of a wrong matching, the expression returns to the central part of the tabletop, for feedback the upper bar of the personal area flushes in red, and the user – and so the group – loses one point.

2.2 Experimental Procedure

Participants were tested in groups of four persons and the experimental setting was divided in several steps:

First, participants were introduced into the general topic and motivation of the research, and they were informed about the general aim as well as the course of the study. At this point, formal framework conditions were also clarified, i.e., that their data was being recorded in order to measure performance and, therefore, the learning success. Moreover, participants were informed that their interaction with the assistive technology would be recorded on video, not exposing their faces in frame, but only their hands.

Second, previous to interaction with the learning tool, participants completed a first part of an online survey (pre-survey), filling in information about their demographic characteristics (i.e., age, gender, level of education), attitudes towards technology, as well as prior knowledge of regular expressions. After finishing this part, number connection test [27], which provided information about participants' perceptional speed was pursued.

In the third part of the experiment participants interacted with the digital learning assistant. The task was to assign the correct expressions to their predefined terms, collecting as many points as possible in the designated time (90–120 s). The task difficulty increased thereby from one experimental trial to another. Before the actual interaction started, learners got an introduction to regular expressions and a manual, where the experimenter explained the basic regex-operations with examples. Once the theoretical part was done and the emerging questions answered, the experimenter demonstrated the way the digital learning tool works, showing how to place the recognized regular expression to the individual target space. After this, participants started a learning session, where they could test the technology by themselves in order to better understand the application and the idea of regular expressions. Participants interacted with the learning application in two rounds, each 90 s; afterwards, they still had time and possibility to ask questions, when required. In the final, experimental trial, participants absolved two collaborative gaming sessions, each 120 s.

After the interaction with the multi-touch display, a post-experimental questionnaire followed. This part of the questionnaire allowed evaluation of the system usage and feedback modalities, and enabled to gather information about perceived learning success and acceptance.

Finally, participants discussed ethical, legal and social aspects connected to such a collaborative technology-enhanced learning. The time for the completion of the whole operational sequence never exceeded 90 min and averaged around 70 min.

2.3   Research Approach

The research variables used in this study focus on different user factors related to acceptance criteria, which are considered factors leading to a long-term adoption of assistive learning technologies – as such presented above – in the education. Figure 2 summarizes the research design used for the purposes of this study.

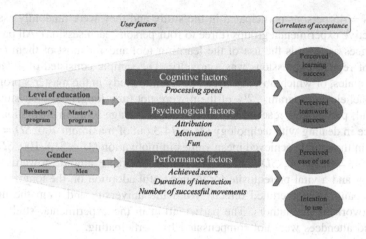

Fig. 2. Research design used in the present study.

Based on the concept of the user-centered design (e.g., [28, 29]), we included gender (females vs. males) and level of education (students of bachelor's program vs. master's program) as variables referring to the user diversity among the potential users of learning assisting technologies. Using these as *independent variables*, we examine if criteria of acceptance significantly differ between the particular user groups. Moreover, factors referring to cognitive (i.e., processing speed, according to Oswald and Roth [27]) and psychological aspects of participants (i.e., attribution in dealing with technology, according to Beier [30], motivation and fun[1]) as well as their resulting interaction performance (i.e., achieved score, duration of interaction and the number of successful movements) were considered in the subsequent analyses to get an overview of the correlative relationships and find out which of these are the best predictors for acceptance.

Finally, as *dependent research variables* acceptance criteria were used:

- Perceived learning and teamwork success: self-evaluations to be assessed on 6-point scales reaching form 1 (= 'not successful at all') to 6 (= 'absolutely successful');
- Perceived ease of use (PEoU): a score of 7 items (e.g., "It was easy for me to perform the necessary actions.") to be assessed on a 6-point Likert scale reaching

---

[1] Self-developed items for motivation (e.g., "I was inspired to do the job as best I could") and fun (e.g., "Interacting with the game was fun.") to be assessed on 6-point (dis)agreement scales.

form 1 (= 'I do not agree at all') to 6 (= 'I absolutely agree'); Cronbach's alpha = .84;

- Intention to use (ItU; "I would like to use such game environment more often for education purposes") to be assessed on a 6-point agreement scale.

2.4 Sample Description

In total N = 45 persons participated in the study and they were randomly assigned to the respective experimental groups (three to four persons each session). All participants were novices as regards the use of the learning tool and for most of them (89%) the concept of regular expressions was a novelty. The sample consisted of 49% females and 51% males, of which 56% reported to currently study in the master's program and 22% in bachelor's program; 22% of them were not (any longer) in their studies.

Overall, participants reached a relatively high average score in attributions of self-confidence in dealing with technology ($M = 74.3$ out of maximum 100, $SD = 19.7$). In addition, in the sample achieved mean values in motivation ($M = 81.8/100$, $SD = 14.5$) and fun ($M = 82.5/100$, $SD = 13.5$) indicate a favorable attitude towards the used technology and a vital prerequisite for a successful adoption on the long run.

Participants were recruited directly from the university and from the immediate social network of the authors. The participation in the experimental study was voluntary and attendees were not compensated for participating.

3   Results

Results presented in this section were analyzed, using bivariate correlations, t-tests and multiple linear regression analyses. Pearson's product-moment correlation coefficients (ρ) were calculated for continuous variables and for dichotomous variables Spearman's rank correlation coefficients (r_s) were used. For descriptive analyses, means (M) and standard deviations (SD) are reported. The level of statistical significance was set to 5% and two-tailed tests were used for the statistical analyses.

In this section we, firstly, provide an analysis of correlative relationships between the user factors and acceptance criteria for the learning tool. Secondly, we examine the influence of gender and education level on the evaluations of interaction with the assistive technology and the perceived learning success. And thirdly, we determine the best predictors for the acceptance of the used technology.

3.1   Interrelations Between User Factors and Acceptance Factors

To provide an overview of the associations between the research variables, in the first step we perform a correlation analysis for the previously described user factors and aspects referring to acceptance of the assistive technology. Figure 3 summarizes the resulting coefficients between these factors.

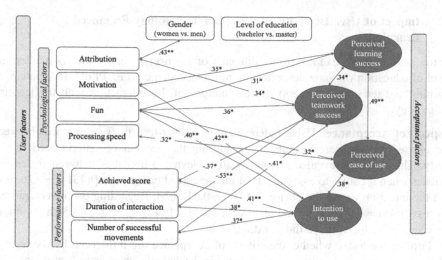

Fig. 3. Correlative relationships between user factors and acceptance factors (N = 45; gender coding: men = 1, women = 2; **$p \leq .01$, *$p \leq .05$).

The results of the bivariate correlation analysis show that user factors are moderately related to the factors of acceptance. Especially psychological factors are significantly correlated with aspects that promote accepted use of digital learning assistant. Fun, for example, seems to be a key user factor which is positively linked with all acceptance variables: It correlates significantly with the learning success ($\rho = .31$, $p = .038$) and teamwork success ($\rho = .36$, $p = .030$), and it is associated with the perceived ease of ($\rho = .32$, $p = .018$) and the intention to use the learning tool ($\rho = .40$, $p = .006$). The latter acceptance factor is also positively linked to the user's motivation ($\rho = .42$, $p = .004$), which is also positively related to the individual learning success ($\rho = .35$, $p = .019$). High processing speed makes user perceive the technology as easier to use ($\rho = .32$, $p = .030$) and higher means in attributed self-confidence in dealing with technology are moderately correlated with better teamwork success ($\rho = .34$, $p = .023$).

Moreover, performance aspects are positively connected with acceptance, indicating that a higher intention to use the assistive learning technology in the future goes along with reaching high scores ($\rho = .41$, $p = .010$), longer durations of interaction ($\rho = .38$, $p = .017$), and higher number of successful movements ($\rho = .37$, $p = .019$). On the contrary, higher average results in the performance factors correlate negatively with the teamwork success, which indicates that subjectively perceived high performance is not necessarily interpreted as a team success.

The bivariate correlation analysis shows that psychological and performance-related user factors are significantly related to the acceptance criteria.

3.2 Impact of User Diversity on Accepted Technology-Enhanced Learning

In the next step, we examined the influence of the user diversity factors gender and level of education on variables, referring to the acceptance (i.e., PEoU, ItU, perceived learning and teamwork success) and evaluations of the interaction with the learning technology.

Aspects of Acceptance. Using independent-samples t-test, firstly differences between the *gender groups* were examined, considering the acceptance criteria used in this study. The analyses revealed no statistically relevant differences between males and females when it comes to assessments of the perceived ease of use [$t(43) = -0.26$, n.s.] and the intention to use the device [$t(43) = -0.51$, n.s.]. Regarding perceived learning success [$t(43) = -0.27$, n.s.] and teamwork success [$t(42) = -1.74$, n.s.], the opinions between the gender groups did not differ either.

Further, we tested whether the criteria of acceptance are influenced by the *level of education*, comparing opinions of students in bachelor's vs. master's program. The analyses disclosed statistically significant differences for the perceived ease of use of the technology [$t(33) = 2.08$, $p < 0.05$] with bachelor students ($M = 77.9$, $SD = 8.2$) reaching considerably lower means than master students ($M = 85.4$, $SD = 12.6$). The main effect of the level of education on the PEoU is depicted in Fig. 4.

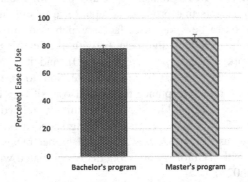

Fig. 4. Main effect of the level of education on the acceptance criterium perceived ease of use (PEoU; n = 35).

On the contrary, differences in the education groups are absent for the intention to use the tool [$t(33) = -1.91$, n.s.] as well as with regard to the perceptions of learning [$t(33) = 0.14$, n.s.] and teamwork success [$t(32) = 0.25$, n.s.]. Overall, the reached means consistently show a quite high acceptance of the technology.

Evaluation of the Interaction. In addition to the acceptance-related criteria, after the interaction with the learning tool participants assessed it by means of semantic differential – a method according to Osgood [31]. To derive the attitude towards the technology participants assessed series of bipolar pairs of adjectives, defined by verbal opposites (e.g., useful – useless) on a seven-steps scale. We examined whether there are meaningful differences between the gender- and education-related groups.

The resulting means for males and females are depicted in Fig. 5. Overall, the evaluations indicate a high attachment for learning with tangibles on multi-touch tabletops, as the average values distinctly lie on the positive side of the scale. *T*-Tests, which were run for examination of statistically relevant differences between men's and women's opinions, revealed significant difference solely referring to perceptions of the technology being exciting vs. boring [$t(43) = 2.01$, $p < 0.05$]. Thereby, male participants assessed the digital assistive technology as considerably more exciting than their female counterparts.

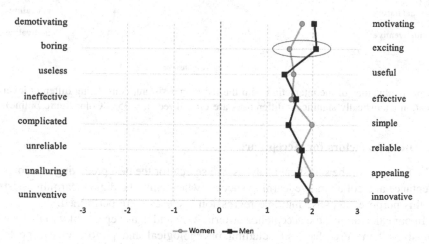

Fig. 5. Evaluations of the interaction with the learning assistant, considering gender groups (statistically significant difference is circled red; n = 45). (Color figure online)

In addition, assessments of interaction with the learning technology were examined for both education groups: The opinions of bachelor's vs. master's program students were compared and tested for differences. Statistical analysis revealed significant differences between the groups in terms of the perceived (in-)effectivity [$t(33) = -2.45$, $p < 0.05$] and enthusiasm vs. boredom [$t(33) = -2.92$, $p < 0.01$]. As can be seen from Fig. 6, students in bachelor's program reached basically lower means than students in master's program.

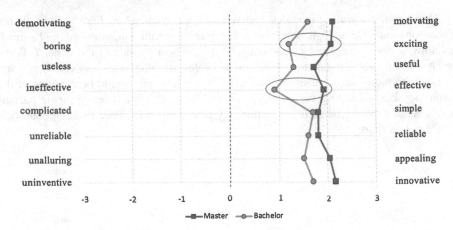

Fig. 6. Evaluations of the interaction with the learning assistant, considering different levels of education (statistically significant differences are circled red; n = 35). (Color figure online)

3.3 Best Predictors for Acceptance

In the final step of the statistical analyses, we search for the best predicting variables for acceptance and collaborative learning success when using the digital learning assistant. For this purpose, stepwise multiple regression analyses were performed.

In our calculations, the acceptance criteria were added as dependent variables in the analysis and the user factors, including psychological and performance aspects, as independent variables. From the regression analyses resulted statistical models as summarized in Table 1.

Table 1. Statistical models resulting from multiple regression analyses for acceptance and collaborative learning success when using assistive learning technology (N = 45; **$p \leq .01$, **$p \leq .05$; VIF = variance inflation factor)

Acceptance correlates	Predictors	R^2	β	t	VIF	ANOVA
Perceived learning success	Motivation	30.2%	.50	3.44**	1.1	$F(2, 38) = 7.8$, $p = .002$
	Duration of interaction		−.42	−2.89**	1.1	
Perceived teamwork success	Fun	49.5%	.48	3.90**	1.05	$F(2, 37) = 17.1$, $p \leq .001$
	Duration of interaction		−.63	−5.14**	1.05	
Intention to use	Motivation	29.5%	.37	2.56*	1.09	$F(2, 38) = 7.5$, $p = .002$
	Achieved score		.30	2.05*	1.09	
Perceived ease of use	Processing speed	11.2%	.33	2.16*	1.0	$F(1, 38) = 4.7$, $p = .037$

Perceived Learning Success. From the upper part of Table 1 it is evident that the prediction model for perceived learning success [$F(2, 38) = 7.8, p = .002$] entered two out of nine possible predictors and accounted for over 30 percent of the variance. The user factor motivation received the strongest weight in the model ($\beta = .50$), followed by the performance factors referring to the duration of interaction with the assistive technology ($\beta = -.42$). For this model, thus, motivation [$t(36) = 3.44, p = 0.002$] and duration of interaction [$t(36) = -2.89, p = 0.007$] are the significant predictors for the perceived learning success.

Perceived Teamwork Success. The regression model for perceived teamwork success is statistically significant [$F(2, 37) = 17.1, p \leq .001$] and explains almost 50% ($R^2 = .495$) of the variance. Among the predictors entered in the model, the duration of interaction with the tool reaches the largest beta coefficient of $-$, making the strongest unique contribution to explain the perceptions of teamwork success, which is followed by the also strong contribution of fun ($\beta = .48$).

Intention to Use. For the intention to use the examined assistive technology, again, two variables were included into the regression model [$F(2, 38) = 7.5, p = .002$] which accounted for almost 30% ($R^2 = .295$) of the variance. Motivation ($\beta = .37$) and the achieved score ($\beta = .30$) reached the strongest contributions to explain the intended use of tangibles on multi-touch tabletops in the future.

Perceived Ease of Use. Finally, for the perceived ease of use the regression model contained only one out of nine possible predictors. The model reaches statistical significance [$F(1, 38) = 4.7, p = .037$] and explains overall only 11.2% of the variance ($R^2 = .112$). Processing speed was the only predictor (beta coefficient = .33; $t(37) = 2.16$, p = .037) that was included into the model, making the unique contribution to explain PEoU.

For all presented regression models, VIF values are all well below the value of 10 and the tolerance statistics lie all well above 0.2. These results allow to conclude that there is no collinearity within the present data.

4   Discussion

In the presented study we experimentally examined how students manage to acquire novel study matter (i.e., regular expressions), using a learning assisting technology in the form of tangibles on multi-touch tabletop. The aim was to take a closer look at the associations between factors brought by the potential users in dependence on their perceptions of accepted and successful technology-enhanced collaboration for learning purposes. In the discussion section, we firstly focus on the most relevant findings of our study and bring them in the broader context of education. Secondly, we consider the limitations of the study and discuss further research directions.

4.1   Acceptance of Assistive Technology in Collaborative Learning

Results presented in this study are insightful and indicate that the users' psychological and factors resulting from the interaction with the learning tool – we called these performance factors – are significantly connected with the correlates of acceptance. The moderate correlations show that especially fun and motivation play an important role for an accepted use of the assisting technology. Moreover, better performance positively affects the user's intention to use the technology, which is an acknowledged criterium for acceptance and successful adoption in the future. Based on this knowledge, assisting technologies that use serious games, which already have been repeatedly showed to be useful in different areas of application (for overview see e.g., [32, 33]), should be considered a meaningful learning support for learners and teachers, and be increasingly integrated into educative settings.

The overall assessments after interaction with the learning assistant were (very) positive, showing a high attachment for, and willingness to, use such a technology. The opinions were quite consistent among the queried persons. However, the resulting differences in the particular gender and education groups for enthusiasm/excitement and boredom, on the one hand, and for (in-)effectivity of the technology, on the other hand, suggest that one part of the potential users either not yet perceives the added value of the assistive technology or represents potential user profiles among the learners, who simply decline the use. This valuable result shows that there are clear limits of this technology in education. This finding is additionally underpinned by the negative correlations resulting between performance and perceptions of teamwork success, which indicate that higher performance not necessarily leads to a perception of teamwork success but rather suggests in that case that a well-performed task does not necessarily require a collaboration.

Moreover, the performed regression analyses showed that the examined user factors solely partly contribute to explanation of the variance of acceptance. From the psychological user characteristics, especially motivation and fun to use the assistive learning tool seem to play a relevant role for the long-term adoption of the technology in education. Among the performance data, the duration of interaction turns out to be a reliable indicator for perceptions of learning and teamwork success. The negative orientation of the resulting beta coefficients suggests thereby that perceptions of success are associated with a short duration of interaction. In other words: the shorter the interaction time, the greater the perceived learning success. This outcome can be either explained by the fact that the today's students expect, or are used to, fast and efficient technology solutions. On the other side, interpreting the outcomes some caution is required, because the results can be artifact-related and only refer to the content examined in the presented experiment.

Summarizing, the technology as described here is promising. Creating and ongoing development of a well-functioning, accepted, and didactically meaningful learning technology that serves learners as an assistant can lead to a significant change of learning motivation and learning success also for the difficult subject matters, like these required in the STEM study programs. This study demonstrates that students exhibit positive mind-sets towards such a technology-enhanced learning and show overall welcoming reactions in interacting with it. These are optimal conditions for long-term adoption of such learning aids in education. Thus, even though the learning tool cannot serve for all potential learners, for example these who are in wheelchair or are somehow disabled in their movements, or those who simply do not want to work with it, it represents an option for the clear majority, who is willing to be supported by this technology in their learning process.

4.2 Limitations and Future Research

Despite providing relevant insights, it is also important to note limitations of the study, which should be addressed in future research.

The first limitation relates to necessary caution in the interpretation of the results. The outcomes are based on an examination of a first prototype of the assistive learning technology, which in many respects might not yet be mature, especially in the didactical sense. Further research is needed in parallel with a further development of the learning tool in order to validate the findings.

Another limitation refers to the methodological approach: One shortcoming is a relatively small sample size and a not perfectly distributed proportions of bachelor and master students in the educative groups. Strictly speaking, the number of persons considered in the statistical analyses in this regard, reaches the threshold of possible proportion of comparable group sizes. The unequal group sizes can increase the risk of type II error. Thus, this issue should be better considered in future research.

Further, in the current study we examined the learning success for all participants and did not include a control group nor consider other learning methods for comparison of the effectivity. Next studies should conceive such competitive settings in order to validate a didactically useful learning assistance.

Future research and the subsequent in-depth developmental activities of the assistive technology should ensure that the present requirements of the potential users are accordingly considered without compromising the didactically necessary principles. This means a further integration of the stakeholders in the design and optimization processes.

5 Conclusion

Assistive technology for learning affords a great potential for the learners of today. Sophisticated learning assistants, which optimally convey contents for the learners through various feedback modalities, and are didactically sound and well-elaborated, can offer great advantages, especially for complex learning material that is difficult to grasp.

The present study makes its contribution to the development of such cleverly designed technology. Results evidence that individual characteristics considerably influence the users' perceptions of the learning tool and, therefore, affect the interaction, perceived success and acceptance. In addition, this study provides insightful information about the existing willingness to use assistive technology for learning purposes.

Acknowledgements. We would like to thank Christian Cherek and the company Elector for providing the tangible prototypes, which were used in the study. Furthermore, we thank all participants for their engagement and interest in contributing their ideas and thoughts to novel developments in digitally assisted education. The work was funded by the German Federal Ministry of Research and Education [Project TABULA, reference number 16SV7574K].

References

1. Harasim, L.: Shift happens: online education as a new paradigm in learning. Internet High. Educ. **3**(1), 41–61 (2000)
2. Vergel, J., Quintero, G.A., Isaza-Restrepo, A., Ortiz-Fonseca, M., Latorre-Santos, C., Pardo-Oviedo, J.M.: The influence of different curriculum designs on students' dropout rate: a case study. Med. Educ. Online **23**(1) (2018). https://doi.org/10.1080/10872981.2018.1432963
3. Chen, X.: STEM attrition: college students' paths into and out of STEM fields. Statistical Analysis Report, National Center for Education Statistics, Washington (2013)
4. Schäfer, A., Holz, J., Leonhardt, T., Schroeder, U., Brauner, P., Ziefle, M.: From boring to scoring–a collaborative serious game for learning and practicing mathematical logic for computer science education. Comput. Sci. Educ. **23**(2), 87–111 (2013)
5. Cuban, L.: Teachers and Machines: The Classroom Use of Technology Since 1920. Teachers College Press, New York (1986)
6. Saito, T., Kim, S.: A meta-analysis on e-learning effectiveness in higher education. Jpn. J. Educ. Technol. **32**(4), 339–350 (2009). https://doi.org/10.15077/jjet.kj00005353782
7. Shakibaei, Z., Khalkhali, A., Andesh, M.: Meta-analysis of studies on educational technology in Iran. Procedia – Soc. Behav. Sci. **28**, 923–927 (2011). https://doi.org/10.1016/j.sbspro.2011.11.170
8. Karich, A.C., Burns, M.K., Maki, K.E.: Updated meta-analysis of learner control within educational technology. Rev. Educ. Res. **84**(3), 392–410 (2014). https://doi.org/10.3102/0034654314526064
9. Fan, Z., Cheng, W., Chen, G., Huang, R.: Meta-analysis in educational technology research: a content analysis. In: 16th International Conference on Advanced Learning Technologies (ICALT), Austin, TX, USA, pp. 460–62 (2016). https://doi.org/10.1109/icalt.2016.94
10. Chauhan, S.: A meta-analysis of the impact of technology on learning effectiveness of elementary students. Comput. Educ. **105**, 14–30 (2017). https://doi.org/10.1016/j.compedu.2016.11.005
11. Rahman, M.N.A., Zamri, S.N.A.S., Eu, L.K.: A meta-analysis study of satisfaction and continuance intention to use educational technology. Int. J. Acad. Res. Bus. Soc. Sci. **7**(4), 1059–1072 (2017). https://doi.org/10.6007/ijarbss/v7-i4/2915
12. Bruner, J.S.: The Process of Education. Harvard University Press, Cambridge (1977)
13. Meyer, H.: Leitfaden Unterrichtsvorbereitung, 9th edn. Cornelsen, Berlin (2018)
14. McCombs, B.L., Whisler, J.S.: The Learner-Centered Classroom and School: Strategies for Increasing Student Motivation and Achievement, 1st edn. Jossey-Bass, San Francisco (1997)
15. Mayer, R.E.: Multimedia Learning, 2nd edn. Cambridge University Press, Cambridge (2001)
16. Bloom, B.S.: Taxonomy of Educational Objectives: The Classification of Educational Goals Handbook I. Longmans, Green and Company, New York (1956)
17. Krathwohl, D.R.: A revision of Bloom's taxonomy: an overview. Theory Pract. **41**(4), 212–218 (2002). https://doi.org/10.1207/s15430421tip4104_2
18. Gould, J.D., Boies, S.J., Lewis, C.: Making usable, useful, productivity-enhancing computer applications. Commun. ACM **34**(1), 74–85 (1991)
19. Davis, F.D.: User acceptance of information technology: system characteristics, user perceptions and behavioral impacts. Int. J. Man Mach. Stud. **38**(3), 475–487 (1993)
20. Rogers, E.M.: Diffusion of innovations, 3rd edn. The Free Press, New York (1983)
21. Davis, F.D.: Perceived usefulness, perceived ease of use, and user acceptance of information technology. MIS Q. **13**(3), 319–340 (1989)
22. Venkatesh, V., Davis, F.D.: A theoretical extension of the technology acceptance model: four longitudinal field studies. Manag. Sci. **46**(2), 186–204 (2000)

23. Venkatesh, V., Morris, M.G., Davis, G.B., Davis, F.D.: User acceptance of information technology: toward a unified view. MIS Q. **27**(3), 425–478 (2003)
24. Agarwal, R., Prasad, J.: A conceptual and operational definition of personal innovativeness in the domain of information technology. Inf. Syst. Res. **9**(2), 204–215 (1998)
25. Carroll, J.M., Thomas, J.C., Malhotra, A.: Presentation and representation in design problem-solving. Br. J. Psychol. **71**(1), 143–153 (1980). https://doi.org/10.1111/j.2044-8295.1980.tb02740.x
26. Han, I., Black, J.B.: Incorporating haptic feedback in simulation for learning physics. Comput. Educ. **57**(4), 2281–2290 (2011). https://doi.org/10.1016/j.compedu.2011.06.012
27. Oswald, W.D., Roth, E.: Der Zahlen-Verbindungs-Test (ZVT) [The Number Connection Test (NCT)]. Hogrefe, Göttingen (1987)
28. Abras, C., Maloney-Krichmar, D., Preece, J.: User-centered design. In: Bainbridge, W. (ed.) Encyclopedia of Human-Computer Interaction, vol. 37, no. 4, pp. 445–456. Sage Publications, Thousand Oaks (2004)
29. Mao, J.Y., Vredenburg, K., Smith, P.W., Carey, T.: The state of user-centered design practice. Commun. ACM **48**(3), 105–109 (2005)
30. Beier, G.: Kontrollüberzeugungen im Umgang mit Technik [Locus of control while interacting with technology]. Rep. Psychol. **24**(9), 684–693 (1999)
31. Osgood, C.E.: Semantic differential technique in the comparative study of cultures. Am. Anthropol. **66**(3), 171–200 (1964)
32. Connolly, T.M., Boyle, E.A., MacArthur, E., Hainey, T., Boyle, J.M.: A systematic literature review of empirical evidence on computer games and serious games. Comput. Educ. **59**(2), 661–686 (2012)
33. Wouters, P., Van Nimwegen, C., Van Oostendorp, H., Van Der Spek, E.D.: A meta-analysis of the cognitive and motivational effects of serious games. J. Educ. Psychol. **105**(2), 249–265 (2013)

Author Index

Printed in the United States
By Bookmasters